## ArtScroll History Series®

Rabbi Nosson Scherman / Rabbi Meir Zlotowitz

*General Editors*

Published by

Mesorah Publications, ltd

# A Tale of Two Worlds

Devora Gliksman

**RABBI DOVID AND REBBETZIN BASYA BENDER**

the bridge between the Yeshivah–Bais Yaakov worlds
of pre-War Europe and post-War America

FIRST EDITION
*First Impression … February 2009*

Published and Distributed by
**MESORAH PUBLICATIONS, LTD.**
4401 Second Avenue / Brooklyn, N.Y 11232

*Distributed in Europe by*
**LEHMANNS**
Unit E, Viking Business Park
Rolling Mill Road
Jarow, Tyne & Wear, NE32 3DP
England

*Distributed in Australia and New Zealand*
*by* **GOLDS WORLDS OF JUDAICA**
3-13 William Street
Balaclava, Melbourne 3183
Victoria, Australia

*Distributed in Israel by*
**SIFRIATI / A. GITLER — BOOKS**
6 Hayarkon Street
Bnei Brak 51127

*Distributed in South Africa by*
**KOLLEL BOOKSHOP**
Ivy Common
105 William Road
Norwood 2192, Johannesburg, South Africa

Typography by CompuScribe at ArtScroll Studios, Ltd.
Printed in Canada
Bound by Sefercraft, Quality Bookbinders, Ltd., Brooklyn N.Y. 11232

# Table of Contents

# Book II

# Book III

*Foreword*

HE BOOK YOU ARE ABOUT TO READ, THE STORY OF OUR ILLUS-
trious parents, Rav Dovid and Rebbetzin Basya Bender, *zichronam
livracha*, is in a sense the culmination of a journey. This journey
began as an intensely personal one with our father's untimely passing
over forty years ago. Throughout those years, and particularly recently
during the preparation of this book, I sought to gain a fuller appreciation
of who my parents were and the lives they led. Today my siblings and I
are privileged to share this journey with the Jewish people.

I was a boy of fifteen when my father passed away suddenly at the age
of 53. My world was shattered. I was called home from the out-of-town
yeshivah where I was studying, to live with my grieving mother, a widow
in the fullest sense of the word, who nonetheless valiantly succeeded in
raising my four unmarried siblings and myself in a positive and loving
manner. (My oldest sister was married.)

In my grief, I wrote. I authored my own home-made "biography" of my
father, a sort of scrapbook that incorporated photos, newspaper clippings
and my own emotions. I arranged it according to the chapters of the classic
*Mussar* works, demonstrating how my father excelled in each area. I wrote
and researched, not only to channel my grief, but also because I felt that I
never got to really know my father. I knew that despite our close relationship, there was a great deal about my father that I had never known, and,
being a teenager, even more that I never fully understood. My search for

understanding who my father was began with that scrapbook and continued well into adulthood.

Our mother lived for another thirty-one years. I often lamented my lack of a dormitory yeshivah experience and the camaraderie and friendships that I could have made, instead riding the train home each night from yeshivah. It was only later that I began to realize how fortunate I was to have spent so much time in the proximity of someone endowed with such a brilliant mind and noble heart.

After our mother's *petirah* in 1996, my siblings and I began to seriously consider producing a biography about our parents. I accepted the task of shepherding the project, the culmination of which you are holding in your hands today.

Throughout this journey, my siblings and I became aware of stories of our parents and aspects of their lives of which we were heretofore unaware. My parents were not secretive people, but we children had seen only a limited view of who they were and their lives' achievements. Working on this book has given us a fuller picture.

On the most basic level, then, this is a family portrait, the result of a personal quest.

But it is a picture that we feel compelled to share.

Because there is so much that *Klal Yisrael* can learn from it.

❧

Our parents were selfless people, lifelong *mechanchim* who gave their all to develop a new generation of American Jewish youngsters. Our father taught boys, primarily in Yeshivah Torah Vodaath, while our mother was one of the pioneer Bais Yaakov educators on American shores and remained one of the most prominent for half a century.

Our father was raised in pre-war America and he abandoned it all to pursue his dream of learning in the European Torah bastion of Mir. Our mother was born and raised in Europe, yet she completely related to and understood her American *talmidos*. Both parents entered the nascent field of American *chinuch* and remained there for the rest of their lives. They both loved their pupils and were completely devoted to them, making an indelible imprint on generations of students who in turn went on to build Torah homes and communities throughout the United States.

But Rav Dovid and Rebbetzin Basya Bender were, first and foremost, parents. Together they built a home steeped in Torah ideals, inculcating their children with the full gamut of mitzvos, *middos* and *hashkafos* of our heritage. With very little in the way of material possessions, they succeeded in building a family whose wealth and aspirations were of the spiritual kind. The fact that my two sisters, three brothers and I are all, *Baruch Hashem*, involved in Jewish education and transmitting the same values to our own progeny, is testimony to our parents' success.

The primary lesson that we hope will come out of this book is how to simultaneously be exemplary parents and devoted public servants. Our parents' story is proof that it is possible to raise normal children and build a healthy household and still be busy day and night helping others. The two are not contradictory goals. They are, in fact, inalienable, complementary facets of every Jew's mission in this world: to be *mekadesh shem Shamayim*.

The second principle that emerges from this book is the importance of knowing from where we come. Every Jew has his or her own family story, whose arc usually parallels ours: we descend from great people who overcame exile, poverty, war and personal tragedy to fulfill the Torah and realize their lives' purposes. The potential for greatness is in our genes. With a little research, and a new attitude to what we already know, we can better address the question: "When will my deeds reach my forefathers' deeds?" (*Tanna Devei Eliyahu* 25). It is a challenge whose answer is up to us.

It is our hope that this book will both inform and inspire a new generation of readers who never had the privilege of knowing our parents and can now learn from their ways.

⌒⌒⌒

This journey and the resulting book would not have made the transformation from dream to reality without the dedication of many individuals. Foremost among them is the author, Mrs. Devora Gliksman. When our family set out to write this book ten years ago we could not have imagined where it would take us. The information we did have was disorganized and amorphous. The sheer volume of interviews Mrs. Gliksman conducted, the documents and photos she unearthed and her painstaking research is beyond description. The fruits of her efforts is this remarkable volume. Mrs. Gliksman has truly made our family come alive — to us, and now to the wider public. We owe her a debt of gratitude that is impossible to adequately repay. May Hashem reward her and her family with כל משאלות לבם לטובה.

We are also very grateful to my dear friends, Rabbis Meir Zlotowitz and Nosson Scherman. From the very first moment that I came to them with the beginnings of the early draft, they were extremely supportive and encouraging. The beautifully finished work you are holding is testimony to their incredible genius.

May we see the coming of *Mashiach Tzidkeinu b'karov*, so that all of us may be reunited with those close to us speedily and quickly.

Rabbi Yaakov Bender

Shevat 5769 / February 2009

We would be delighted to receive additional anecdotes, photos and information about our parents. Please address all correspondence to The Bender Family, 312 Hicksville Road, Far Rockaway, New York, 11691.

# Acknowledgments

THE BRISKER RAV CALLED HER "AN ELASTIC DIAMOND." A DIA-
mond: rare and valuable, multifaceted, hard when the situation
called for strength. Elastic: soft and pliable, able to bend and
stretch, ready to adapt to each situation as needed. An uncannily accurate
description of Rebbetzin Basya Bender.

This book began as a tribute to Rebbetzin Basya Bender, a woman who
touched the lives of thousands of people. Yet she was first and foremost a
wife and mother and her story would only be complete in conjunction with
that of her illustrious husband, Rabbi Dovid Bender. What emerged was
not only the story of an extraordinary couple, but a picture of the changing
times in which they lived.

In the course of researching this book, well over 100 people were contacted for information. The response was heart warming. Almost every
person we contacted responded with enthusiasm, happy to be part of a
book that had to do with the Benders. Almost everyone had something to
contribute – a memory, an anecdote, an impression. They are too numerous to mention, but to all these wonderful people, we thank you.

There were some people who contributed more than just snippets of
information here and there. They expended time and patience to paint a
picture of the era and their contributions were invaluable. Though they
did not live to see the book printed, they still deserve our thanks: Rabbis
Avrohom Pincus, Avrohom Barnetsky, Nesanel Quinn, Alex Weissfogel,
and Dr. David Kranzler.

Rebbetzin Zlata Ginsburg was full of enthusiasm for this book. She
admired Rebbetzin Bender and maintained that she was unique even in

her generation. Rebbetzin Ginsburg sat for hours going through telegrams, reminiscing about the people mentioned, sharing her impressions and her memories. At one point she asked, "Nu, will I live to see the book?" Sadly, she did not. But her input made many parts of this manuscript come alive.

Other helpful people who generously gave of their time were Rabbi Yonason Shapiro , Rabbi Henoch Cohen, Rabbi Yisroel Belsky, Rebbetzin Devorah (Applegrad) Cohn, Rebbetzin Tybel (Shereshevsky – Fishman) Wernick, and Mrs. Sudy Rosengarten. Thank you for your interest and patience.

As a friend of Rebbetzin Bender commented, "Who had a heart as large as hers?" Her expansive heart, her genuine warmth and concern for others, her love toward family, friends, and students came through in interview after interview. Perhaps this was why she accumulated so many letters and documents. Scraps of paper with her parents' handwriting were priceless. Yellowed letters from her brother were precious. Wartime telegrams just could not be thrown away. Her collection of memorabilia included letters in English, Hebrew, Yiddish, Polish, and German. Most documents were handwritten and had faded with age. Many thanks to Mrs. Chanah Frihan, Mrs. Rochel Landsberg, Mrs. Toby Weiss, Mrs. Malky Feurst, and Mrs. Atara Weiss for translating and organizing these documents. Thank you to Rabbi Yehuda Horovitz of Har Nof for helping decipher some of the difficult handwriting.

We had many tapes of *hespedim*, interviews, and speeches which had information that greatly enhanced the book. Thank you to Mrs. Toby Weiss and Mrs. Malky Feurst for transcribing these tapes in a clear and readable manner.

Being that Rebbetzin Bender's forte was history, and since her story could only be appreciated against the backdrop of the times, we felt that simple name-dropping — without an understanding of who is being mentioned — would not do justice to the subject. Therefore, we included biographical information about almost everyone mentioned in the book. Special thanks to Mrs. Toby Weiss for her work in this area. Many thanks to Rabbi Avrohom Birnbaum, who has generously shared his articles about *gedolei Yisroel*. May you have continued success in your wonderful work. Kudos to Rabbi Avrohom Kober and Messers. Jeff and Robert Katz for always being extraordinarily helpful.

Thank you to Dr. Brenda Idstein for reviewing the manuscript with a professional eye. Your perceptive comments and wise advice was invaluable. To Mrs. Varda Branfman, a superb editor whose enthusiasm for this project came at the perfect time, thank you for your warmth and encouragement.

Many families took time to unearth appropriate photographs to contribute to this book. We truly appreciate their efforts. A special thank you to Rebbetzin Devorah (Applegrad) Cohn who sifted through her archives and graciously contributed rare and original photographs. Thank you to Rabbi Moshe Kolodny of the Archives of the Agudath Israel of America. Your loyalty and reliability are truly admirable. In addition, thank you to Rabbi Dovid Kaminetsky and Rabbi Noson Schechter for generously allowing us use of their photo libraries and to Rabbis Asher Tzvi Bergman, Aharon Chaim Nishri, Chaim Shlomo Rosenthal, Shimon Meller, Leibel Karmel, Tsemach Glenn, and Mr. Chaim Freedman for their photo contributions. Many thanks to Rabbi Berish Schechter for all his help.

Most importantly, we owe thanks to the *Ribbono shel Olam* for the tremendous *siyata d'Shmaya* we have seen throughout the years. Sometimes, finding contacts and information seemed like searching for a needle in a haystack, and then suddenly, we saw a breakthrough. Like the time we tracked down two students that Rebbetzin Bender taught almost eighty years ago through a passing reference in a letter. Or the time a student of Rabbi Dovid Bender "happened" to answer the phone in the Torah Vodaath office. The 10 years of work on this book have been 10 years of *siyata d'Shmaya*.

Perhaps the greatest thanks that we owe the Almighty is that He, in His infinite kindness, granted us a close association with the Bender family. As Rabbi Yud'l Gordon wrote in a letter "… The Bender family is a family whose name means goodness." We have experienced that "goodness" and are immensely grateful for their kindness and friendship. May *Hakadosh Baruch Hu* bless them with all that is good.

D.G.

Shevat 5769 / February 2009

---

**A Note to the Reader:**

Many people are mentioned in this book. In order that the reader not get lost in a sea of names, biographical information has been included about almost everyone mentioned in the text (not in footnotes and captions). If the person plays a significant role in the text, the biographical information is on the page with the text, either in a photo caption or a footnote. Otherwise the information appears in the biography section or perhaps in another place in the book. Biographical information is usually given the first time that the person appears or the reader is informed where to find the information later in the book. The next time the name appears, no reference is included. People quoted by name are also in the biographical section. Only people who are no longer living are in the biography section.

# Book I

# Part I:
# Rabbi Avrohom Bender
### 5655-5693 / 1895-1933

### *Chapter One:*
## A European Childhood

### *Chapter Two:*
## In the Halls of the Slonimer Yeshivah

### *Chapter Three:*
## America

This section is primarily based on interviews with the Bender Family. Other main contributors to this section include Rabbis Avrohom Pincus, Avrohom Barnetsky, Nesanel Quinn, and *ybdl"ch* Rabbis Yonason Shapiro, Avrohom Gassner, and Yitzchok Karpf. Information about Williamsburg was based on *The Jewish Community of Williamsburg* by Gershon Kranzler. Additional sources include *A Fire in His Soul: The Story of Irving Bunim* by Amos Bunim, *Reb Yaakov* and *Reb Shraga Feivel* by R' Yonason Rosenblum. Other sources are quoted.

### Chapter One

# A European Childhood

**Radin: 5656 (1896)**[1]

VROHOM WALKED BRISKLY THROUGH THE DARK DIRT paths of tiny Radin. It was late and he was anxious to be home already, just up the hill and around the bend. He fingered the papers in his pocket. Good, they were still there, safe and sound. And why shouldn't they be? He glanced over his shoulder as he slipped inside. *Ridiculous*, he chastised himself silently, *to think that anyone would care to follow little me. Besides, I am doing something hundreds of others have done before.*

The house was quiet as he slid into bed, his precious papers snugly under his pillow. His heartbeat slowed to normal as he tried to relax. *Too bad it is so late*, he thought. *I will have to wait till tomorrow. When will I find a break in the day to memorize all the information?* The prospect was daunting, but fatigue overtook the young boy and sleep pushed his concerns out of his mind.

Rays of sunshine filtered into his room a few hours later. Last night's fears faded with the darkness, and Avrohom was able to face the task at hand with optimism. The situation was not as bad as he had thought; the papers were better than expected. He would keep his first name, and the change from Berman to Bender was easy to remember. With a little memorization, his new identity would be firmly imbedded in his mind.

---

1. Rabbi Avrohom Bender was born in 1878. In 1896 he would have been 18, the formal age for the draft.

"Let's see: Avrohom Bender. I come from Pinsk. Father: Shmuel; mother: Rochel; paternal grandfather: Moshe; paternal grandmother: Yenta …"

Over and over he repeated the information until it felt right. He was actually convinced that he was Avrohom Bender. Avrohom Berman: Who was *he*? A poor unfortunate soul being drafted into the czar's army. A poor unfortunate missing soul who would never again resurface. Quietly, Avrohom spread the word among his friends and acquaintances. He was Avrohom Bender, a young yeshivah *bochur* who was exempted from army service. Avrohom Berman had disappeared.

This ploy was not new. Since the mid-1800's czarist Russia had periodically passed laws drafting young Jewish boys into the army. For many Jewish youths, service in the Russian army was akin to a death sentence. Most boys from religious homes were not cut out for the grueling regimen of a soldier in a gentile army. Their gentile "comrades" had no love for their Jewish brothers, and their feelings were obvious. In addition, remaining a religious Jew in the army was difficult, if not impossible. Shabbos, Yom Tov, kashrus: everything fell by the wayside. By the time a Jewish boy returned to his people after 25 years of service, his *Yiddishkeit* was in shambles. And it goes without saying that the lost years of learning could never be retrieved.

Avrohom was determined to escape the draft. There were various ways of doing this. Some boys failed the physical exam. Poor eyesight and flat feet were common exemptions. Other young boys, hale and hearty, made themselves sick in order to fail the examination. Some hid, hoping the government would forget about them. And some did as Avrohom did; they purchased false papers and created new identities for themselves.

Usually these papers were not completely false. They were authentic identities of people whom the government had for some reason deleted from their records. For example, the law stated that an only son was not to be drafted. If a young couple with one son immigrated to another country, Russia had no record of that family ever having more children. Therefore that boy was considered an only son who was then exempt from the draft.[2] It was relatively easy to take over his identity by copying his papers. Black marketers were kept quite busy churning out false papers for desperate yeshivah students.

Once papers were purchased, the young boy would slip into his new identity. Suddenly he had a new name, new parents, new siblings, new aunts, uncles, and cousins. All these names had to be memorized well for if at any given moment his papers were inspected and the young boy was questioned, it would be quite suspicious if he could not remember his grandmother's name! But after the initial `newness wore off, the new identity stuck, as

---

2. Reb Avrohom's papers were from such an "only child" (Rabbi Shmuel Sholom Bender).

in the case of Avrohom Bender. Avrohom Berman simply ceased to exist.

Avrohom's yeshivah years began in 1890 when his father, Rabbi Yitzchok Isaac Berman, sent him off to learn in nearby Minsk. In those pre-Communist times, Torah learning in Russia was not illegal and the large city of Minsk hosted many scholars and yeshivos. Establishing a yeshivah then was not contingent on having a building, a dormitory, or a kitchen. Groups of boys, organized according to age and level, assembled in the various shuls in town. There was *Blumka's Kloisz*, the Water Carriers' Shul, the Butchers' Shul, and other shuls as well.

The Bermans were very poor, as were most Jewish families in Russia at the time. Avrohom's father sent him off with train fare and perhaps a few *kopecks* but, other than that, the 12-year-old boy would have to fend for himself. He arrived in Minsk and found a place for himself in a shul/

*Rabbi Yitzchok Isaac Berman was the father of Rabbi Avrohom Bender. Among his descendants are the illustrious Berman family of B'nei Brak.*

yeshivah. There he learned, slept, and ate for three years, rarely even venturing outside. Kindly women of the city brought food to the shul, sustenance to the children. The ages of the boys ranged from 11 to 14. Many a bar mitzvah was celebrated in the hallowed building, as most of the boys from outlying villages were too poor to go home.

Avrohom made friends with his classmates, among them a boy his age, Uri Meir Kahanow. Uri Meir came from a nearby village called Petrowitz and, like Avrohom, his family did not have money to waste on visits home or even simple room and board. He, too, learned, ate, and slept in the shul. Without family nearby, they became like family to each other.

Living and learning in the Minsker shul was not easy for these young boys. Many had left their homes at a young age, when children still yearn for the security of home. The Russian winters were frigid and the large oven in the middle of the shul did not heat the room thoroughly; the boys in the back were always cold. Seats were allotted based on seniority; the longer you had been there, the closer you sat to the oven. Uri Meir had a brother learning in the same shul who had preceded him. When his brother was ready to move on to a more advanced yeshivah, Uri Meir had one consolation: He inherited his brother's seat closer to the oven.[3]

---

3. Rabbi Elya Kanarek.

Though their time in Minsk was bereft of creature comforts, the boys were not resentful or restless. The Torah they learned there, in poverty and hardship, whetted their appetite for more. When they outgrew the Minsker shul, they parted ways. Avrohom headed for Novarodok to learn under the famed Alter of Novarodok, Rabbi Yosef Yozel Hurwitz.[4] Uri Meir continued on to a different yeshivah. The two would meet again in very different circumstances, many years later, and renew their childhood friendship.

AVROHOM SPENT A NUMBER OF YEARS IN NOVARODOK AFTER WHICH he went to Radin to study under the illustrious Chofetz Chaim, Rabbi Yisroel Meir HaKohen Kagan. From this time on, he considered himself a product of the yeshivah in Radin and a student of the Chofetz Chaim. His years there would mold his way of learning, his character, and his outlook on life.

*"Ich bin arine gegangen tzu Reb Yisroel Meir'l …"* he would reminisce fondly. *"Reb Yisroel Meir'l hut azoi gezugt …"* he quoted with love and reverence.[5] He spoke of his rebbi's exceptional love for Torah and how removed he was from the temptations of this world. And yet the Chofetz Chaim was eminently approachable. When Avrohom turned to his rebbi for advice he found wisdom, concern, sympathy, and encouragement.

Avrohom had taken medication for stomach problems and found a problematic side effect: He could not concentrate. The Chofetz Chaim's words of empathy soothed the distraught boy as he related a similar experience, adding that the doctors had told him not to learn from any sefer for two years. Just as he had gotten better, he assured Avrohom, so too would Avrohom get better.[6]

The Chofetz Chaim concluded, "Also, you must remember, even when you cannot learn, do not distance yourself from learning. *Shtitz Torah*, support those who can learn. Support Torah by collecting money for yeshivos."

The suggestion startled the youth. He had never tried to collect money before and he was not certain that he was suited for such a mission. Actu-

---

4. Rabbi Yosef Yozel Hurwitz (1849-1919), known as the Alter of Novarodok, was a disciple of Rabbi Yisroel Salanter. In 1896 the Alter founded Yeshivas Beis Yosef of Novarodok. a yeshivah characterized by intense Torah study combined with the practice of *mussar*. Over time, the yeshivah expanded into a chain of yeshivos. Amid barbarous riots and deadly epidemics *der Alter* tended his *talmidim* devotedly, physically as well as spiritually, until he too succumbed to the typhoid epidemic.

5. "My grandfather was in Radin in the late 1800's when Rabbi Yisroel Meir HaKohen Kagan was not yet known by the name of his sefer *Chofetz Chaim*. In his day, they called him 'Reb Yisroel Meir'l,' and that was how Zaidy continued to call his rebbi" (Rabbi Paltiel Bender).

6. This story, related by the family, is consistent with a similar story written in the multivolume biography of the Chofetz Chaim, *Meir Einei Yisrael*, Vol. II, pp. 168-169.

ally, he was decidedly unsuited for the job. People often commented that he spoke too quickly and that it was difficult to understand him — certainly not the qualities of a smooth-talking fundraiser. Besides, he was only 21. The role of *meshulach* traditionally belonged to one much older than he.

Stranger still was a chance meeting he had with his former Rosh Yeshivah, the Alter of Novarodok, a short time later. After asking about his student's well being, the Alter made an astonishing proposal. "You know, the *yeshivos hakedoshos* are in great need of money. The situation is so difficult; I might have to close down some of our institutions. I think that you would be successful at raising money for the yeshivos. Perhaps you would go to America to raise funds?"[7]

Avrohom was too surprised to respond. Could the Chofetz Chaim's suggestion to "*shtitz Torah*" be brought to fruition so quickly? It certainly seemed so.

And that was how the 21-year-old *bochur* found himself on a ship bound for the bright shores of America.

*Rabbi Yisroel Meir HaKohen Kagan (1839-1933), popularly known as the Chofetz Chaim, which is the name of his first major work on the laws of shemiras halashon. He was Rosh Yeshivah in Radin and the recognized leader of his generation. His acknowledged masterpiece and expression of his Torah genius is the six-volume Mishnah Berurah, rendering universally accepted decisions in halachah.*

෨෪෨

Avrohom walked briskly down the street. Suddenly he stopped short. *This is it?* he thought in surprise. The building before him was small and plain, hardly what he pictured a U.S. post office would look like. Gray stucco that might once have been white, framed brown wooden windows, and a large heavy door. Above the door was a large white sign with bold black block letters: Post Office. *This must be it*, he thought, bemused. With his usual springy step, he climbed the stairs and entered the building.

---

7. Written in a letter from Rabbi Chaim Berman of B'nei Brak. Rabbi Avrohom Bender was Rabbi Chaim Berman's uncle. When Reb Avrohom lived in Tel Aviv, Reb Chaim often came to visit and they were quite close.

*The Woodridge post office in the early 1900's*

The main room was short and narrow. Metal post office boxes set in light brown woodwork lined the walls. In the center of the room, there was a worn wooden table. It stood chest high to provide comfortable writing facilities for those who still wanted to fill in forgotten names and addresses. To one side of the table a line had formed, and Avrohom took his place at its end. The atmosphere in the room was one of cheerful camaraderie. Most of the people knew one another, and they used their time on line to catch up with the local news.

Avrohom quickly realized that life in Woodridge, New York, was slow paced and easygoing. Though the post office was not all that crowded, the chances were that he still had quite a wait ahead of him. This did not really bother him. Young as he was, Avrohom was a patient man. Something about him gave one the impression that he had all the time in the world. He was not one to rush a conversation or cut short a visit. The moving madness that was New York would never overtake him. Long after his "greenness" would wear off, he would still exude tranquility, simplicity, patience.

As the line moved forward, Avrohom noticed the man in front of him. Funny, he had not noticed him before. He hastened to tap the man on the shoulder.

"*Shalom aleichem, Reb Yid.*" Avrohom held out his hand in greeting. "What brings you here?"

"*Aleichem shalom,*" the man answered, smiling shyly. It was impossible not to respond to Avrohom's warmth and obvious happiness. "I am here to register."

"Oh, so you are new in America. So am I," Avrohom answered amiably. "What is your name?"

"Avrohom Bender."

Avrohom was taken aback. What a coincidence!

"What town are you from?"

"I am from Pinsk. And you?"

"I am also from Pinsk." The man looked puzzled. "Funny, I wonder why we have never met before ..."

"Is your father Shmuel?" Avrohom interrupted him.

"Yes ..."

"... and your mother is Rochel?"

"Yes, but how ..."

By now, Avrohom knew exactly what had happened. If they continued exchanging information, he had no doubt that they would find that they had the same grandparents, aunts, uncles, and cousins. Here he was, waiting to register as Avrohom Bender and the real Avrohom Bender was standing right in front of him!

Normally the calmest of men, Avrohom panicked. If they would register, one after the other, as Avrohom Bender, son of Shmuel and Rochel Bender from Pinsk, the postmaster would immediately realize that one set of papers was forged! Would they be arrested? Deported? *I have to get out of here*, he thought wildly.

"*Oy!*" He slapped his forehead. "Why am I here? I came to mail a package, but I see that I have left it at home. I am sorry to leave so abruptly, my friend, but I must run." With a hurried handshake, Avrohom bid good-bye to his new acquaintance and ran out of the building all the way to the train station. Only when he was aboard a Brooklyn-bound train was he finally able to relax.

As the train whizzed passed the wide green pastures of upstate New York, Avrohom thanked Hashem for saving him from disaster. That he could take partial credit for what had happened never occurred to him. He was just overwhelmed with gratitude to his Maker for having extricated him from the situation. But those who heard the story nodded their heads knowingly. How like Avrohom who, overcome with love and excitement upon seeing a fellow Jew, set out to befriend him. And had he not, who knows what the outcome might have been. There was a lot to be learned about the power of a friendly hello.[8]

Once in America, Avrohom set out to fulfill his commitment to "*shtitz Torah*." He knocked on hundreds of doors, appealed to stranger after stranger. In polished Yiddish and broken English, his sincerity and genuine good-heartedness won him friends and supporters.

His single-minded dedication set him apart from the hundreds of other young Jewish immigrants arriving daily, rushing to claim their share of the

---

8. A few days later, Rabbi Avrohom Bender returned to Woodridge where he registered uneventfully. In the 60-plus years that followed, over the three continents on which he lived, he never again met this Avrohom Bender (Rebbetzin Esther [Bender] Epstein).

American dream. Like them, Avrohom had grown up in extreme poverty. There were never a few extra *kopecks* for even basic necessities when one was the youngest of 14[9] children. And yet, Avrohom was never blinded by the promise of material wealth that lured millions of immigrants to the shores of America. His years in Radin cast him in a different mold. He could hear the voice of his rebbi, the Chofetz Chaim, echoing in his ears: *"Vos iz oilam hazeh? Di ikkar iz Torah, ahavas haTorah* — What is this world? The important thing is Torah, love of Torah." Those were the themes of his rebbi's *shmuessen.* Torah is all-important. Wealth, possessions, the bounties of *olam hazeh* are nothing. We must devote our lives to Torah.[10]

Though the poverty of his youth was something he would never forget, climbing the ladder of financial success was never a goal. When his fund-raising stint was over, he was eager to return to Europe, to the hallowed halls of a yeshivah.

---

9. There were actually 16 children born to Reb Avrohom's parents, but two of the children died in infancy. Reb Avrohom therefore considered himself to be one of 14 (Rebbetzin Blumie [Bender] Shapiro).

10. "My grandfather often mentioned that these were the themes of the Chofetz Chaim's *shmuessen"* (Rabbi Michoel Bender).

*Chapter Two*

# In the Halls of the
# Slonimer Yeshivah

**Slonim: 5663 (1903)**

*U*PON RETURNING TO EUROPE, RABBI AVROHOM BENDER
married Pelta Sbarconi of Slonim. The young couple settled
in Slonim, home to the illustrious Slonimer Yeshivah.

Like Yeshivas Ohel Torah of Baranovich, the Slonimer Yeshivah was a
*yeshivah ketanah,* geared to younger boys between the ages of 14 and 18.
From there the boys would go on to Grodno, Kaminetz, Mir, Radin, or other
yeshivos geared to older boys. Rabbi Avrohom Bender enjoyed learning in
the *beis medrash* of the Slonimer Yeshivah.

In 1905, Rabbi Shabsi Yogel became the Rosh Yeshivah of the Slonimer
Yeshivah. Under his tenure, the yeshivah grew greatly and became one of
the elite *yeshivos ketanos* of the time. One of Reb Shabsi's early decisions as
Rosh Yeshivah involved Rabbi Avrohom Bender.

The *Mashgiach* of the Slonimer Yeshivah was a well-respected Torah
scholar who gave regular *shmuessen* in the yeshivah. His duties included
the spiritual development of the *bochurim*, encouraging their learning, and
if necessary, chastising them when appropriate. The job was a challenge.
To inspire young boys to disregard the distractions of this world and focus
on their learning was difficult. At times, a strong rebuke, a targeted action,
or a talking-to was necessary. The *Mashgiach* was aging and the burden of
his position weighed heavily on his shoulders.

*Rabbi Shabsi Yogel (1874-1957) learned in Volozhin under the tutelage of the Netziv and Rabbi Chaim Brisker. After his marriage he joined a kollel founded by the Alter of Novarodok. Reb Shabsi became famous as the Rosh Yeshivah of Slonim and was active in Agudas Yisroel. At the onset of World War II, he escaped to Eretz Yisroel. He opened a yeshivah in Ramat Gan and built a Bais Yaakov, cheder, and kollel as well.*

The Rosh Yeshivah, Rabbi Shabsi Yogel, was faced with a difficult dilemma. He did not want to dismiss his distinguished *Mashgiach*, a Torah scholar of note. The students of the yeshivah had gained and would gain from his mere presence in their midst. Yet, the elderly *Mashgiach* could not attend to all the responsibilities of his position. Rabbi Shabsi Yogel was aware of the respect the *bochurim* had for Rabbi Avrohom Bender, an unassuming *kollelnik* who learned in the *beis medrash*. He appointed Reb Avrohom to the position of *menahel*, a new position devised as a solution for this unique situation. Thus, Reb Shabsi could assign Reb Avrohom to attend to acute issues requiring immediate attention without slighting the *Mashgiach*.

As *menahel*, Reb Avrohom had several duties, some specific and others less so. He was now responsible for monitoring the boys' spiritual development: Were they learning? Were they growing in spirituality and fear of Heaven? Who should be asked to return for the next *z'man*? Who should be asked or encouraged to leave? Reb Avrohom was also the *bochen*, the one who tested applicants to the yeshivah and decided if they were worthy of being admitted into the Slonimer Yeshivah.

Reb Avrohom approached his new job with zeal. For Reb Avrohom the ideal *bochur* would be a *shaleim*, a complete person, one who was not only growing in his learning, but also in his fear of Heaven.

Handling difficult situations with wisdom and tact made Reb Avrohom an invaluable *menahel*. As time went on, Rabbi Shabsi Yogel recognized Reb Avrohom's strengths and decided that he needed him in other capacities as well. The Slonimer Yeshivah was facing a severe financial crisis and, at Rabbi Shabsi Yogel's request, Reb Avrohom went to collect money for the yeshivah. In search of funds, Reb Avrohom traveled to some of Russia's biggest cities: Moscow, St. Petersburg, and others.

As was his practice after returning from a fund-raising trip, Reb Avrohom stopped to visit Reb Shabsi. During these visits, Reb Avrohom and the Rosh Yeshivah would review what had happened during his absence. Reb

Avrohom was no orator and the Russian language did not easily flow from his lips, but his unusual charming personality was enchanting. He would regale Reb Shabsi with tales of his trips to the homes of multimillionaires: Pollavkov and Pietrisky in Moscow, Ginsburg in St. Petersburg. Somehow, Reb Avrohom managed to receive audiences with them all. Reb Avrohom walked through the main doors of many a magnificent estate, an almost unheard-of phenomenon for a *meshulach* in those days.

Reb Shabsi's young son Peretz would listen in the background, spell-bound, as Reb Avrohom matter-of-factly told of his adventures. The young *menahel* found nothing special or unusual about succeeding where many others had failed. He had a special charm. Despite his mediocre verbal skills in a situation where verbal skills were essential, Reb Avrohom won the hearts of all who met him. People felt privileged to donate for whatever cause Reb Avrohom was collecting.[11]

Reb Avrohom never chose to be a fund-raiser, nor did he feel that collecting money was his main role in the Slonimer Yeshivah. He agreed to fill a need, and when he saw an extension of that need, even if he was not specifically approached, he stepped in. For example, Reb Avrohom once noticed a leak in the Slonimer Yeshivah building. Upon examination, he saw that the entire ceiling was damp. The only way to solve the problem was to reconstruct the entire ceiling. While no one asked Reb Avrohom to raise money to cover such a large expense, Reb Avrohom could not sit idly by while Torah scholars were learning under a leaky roof. So, Reb Avrohom went traveling and came back with the needed funds.[12]

REB AVROHOM HAD A DEEP LOVE FOR TORAH SCHOLARS. HIS MANY fund-raising trips were conducive to providing opportunities to observe the *gedolim* of Europe. Once, when visiting Rabbi Yosef Rosen, the famed Rogatchover Gaon of Dvinsk, he observed the Gaon writing Torah thoughts with an old-fashioned pen that had to be dipped into ink repeatedly. Every few minutes the Gaon would pause, dip the pen back into the inkwell, and continue writing.

*What a pity*, Reb Avrohom thought. *Every time he dips his pen in ink, he is wasting precious time. If only he had a fountain pen …* A fountain pen was one of America's newest inventions.[13] He had bought a few when he was in America, but unfortunately, he did not have one with him.

*Bli neder*, Reb Avrohom promised himself, *when I pass through this area again, I will bring one for the Gaon.* The image of the Rogatchover bent over

---

11. Retold by Rabbi Peretz Yogel at the *sheloshim* for Rabbi Avrohom Bender.

12. Rabbi Chaim Shereshevsky in his eulogy for Rabbi Avrohom Bender.

13. Louis Waterman invented the fountain pen in 1884. The first one had to be filled manually but the ink inside lasted far longer than the quill (World Book Encyclopedia p. 209).

*Rabbi Yosef Rosen (1858-1936) was born in the Latvian city of Rogatchov and became known as the Rogatchover Gaon. He developed into a unique Torah luminary, through his tremendous diligence and rare genius. He studied in Slutzk under the guidance of the famed Bais HaLevi and later served as Rav in Dvinsk, Latvia for many years. His seforim, Tzofnas Paneiach on the Rambam, are studied throughout the world today.*

his paper writing and dipping, writing and dipping, concentrating intently on his work, became firmly embedded in his mind. Avrohom looked forward to the day when he could return with the precious pen as a present.

The day finally arrived. Reb Avrohom found himself in Dvinsk standing opposite the Rogatchover Gaon. Once again, the Gaon was bent over his work, writing and dipping, writing and dipping. Reb Avrohom was itching to give the Gaon the pen from his pocket, but he was suddenly uncomfortable. He cleared his throat. "Rebbi …" The Rogatchover looked up impatiently. "I have a pen that does not have to be dipped into ink when you write." Reb Avrohom showed the Rogatchover the fountain pen and how it worked. The Rogatchover marveled at the invention. A pen with ink inside — how wonderful! The Gaon tried the pen several times and commented on how much time he could save with such a pen. More time for learning!

"Please," Reb Avrohom offered, "take the pen as a gift from me."

"A present?" the Rogatchover echoed, horrified. "Oh, no! In my entire life I have never accepted a present.[14] Let me pay for it. How much does it cost?"

---

14. In fulfillment of the verse in *Mishlei* 15:27: "*Sonei matanos yichyeh* — One who hates gifts will live."

*Rabbi Avrohom Bender —*
*Menahel of the Slonimer Yeshivah*

Reb Avrohom was in a quandary. The fountain pen cost $1, a distinct luxury. If he told the Gaon the price, it would be much too much for the Gaon to pay. But the Rogatchover would never take the pen as a present, no matter how time saving and useful.

*Think of all the Torah that could be gained*, Reb Avrohom pondered. "It is rather expensive," he finally said. "Would the Gaon be able to pay 20 cents?"

"Twenty cents," the Rogatchover wondered aloud. "So much money, so much money ..." He swayed back and forth in thought. "Ah," he declared as he pounded his desk with his fist, "*Ah sach gelt, ober s'vert de gelt* — it is a lot of money, but well worth it." The Gaon then began to search his house until he gathered the 20 cents to pay for the pen.

HAPPINESS WAS IN THE AIR. A SON WAS BORN to Reb Avrohom, the *menahel* of Slonim, and Rebbetzin Pelta Bender. The birth of a Jewish child is naturally a cause for celebration but in this case, the joy was even greater. Reb Avrohom and Rebbetzin Pelta had been married 11 years before this child was born. The birth of a daughter had preceded this birth, but the daughter had not survived infancy. This little boy held much hope and promise for his grateful parents. "*Ahn oisgebetteneh kind* — a fervently prayed-for child," Reb Avrohom proclaimed, as he fondly gazed at his newborn child.

*Rebbetzin Pelta*
*(Sbarconi) Bender*

The town was abuzz with excitement. The bris was scheduled for *bein hasedarim* so as not to disturb the regular learning schedule in the yeshivah.[15] Many of the townspeople wanted to share in Reb Avrohom's joy for he commanded both their love and respect.

At the *seudas mitzvah*, in addition to various *talmidei chachamim* who

---

15. Usually, the Rav of the town, in this case Rabbi Yehuda Leib Fein, served as *sandak*. Rabbi Fein had a custom that when he was *sandak*, he would fast until after the bris. Reb Avrohom's unusual scheduling made it difficult for Rabbi Fein to accept the honor, since it would have been difficult for him to fast until *bein hasedarim*. Thus, he declined the honor of *sandak* and the honor went to Rabbi Shabsi Yogel, the Rosh Yeshivah (Rabbi Paltiel Bender).

spoke, one of the city's wealthiest citizens wanted to say a few words. Reb Avrohom granted him that honor. He began with words of Torah and proceeded to bless the baby with wealth and riches and all the bounties this world has to offer …

Interrupting the flow of blessings, Reb Avrohom jumped up and shouted, *"Mir hart nit az er vet oiszen an oni v'evyon; ober er zol oisvaksen grois in Torah —* It makes no difference to me if he turns out to be poor and destitute; I only want him to grow in Torah."

Since Reb Avrohom loved both Torah and his son, he had no greater wish for his son than that he become great in Torah. Wealth, riches, the bounties of this world meant little to Reb Avrohom. He only hoped that his son succeed in his learning and grow to be a *talmid chacham.*

IN 1917, REB AVROHOM DECIDED TO RETURN TO AMERICA. HIS MOTIvations may have included the constant latent layer of anti-Semitism throughout Russia, Poland, and Lithuania with "Jewish-looking Jews" as its prime targets. Furthermore, with the onset of the Communist Revolution, chaos was sure to follow.

Since he had already been there, Reb Avrohom realized the advantages of living in America — safety, financial opportunities, a better standard of living — and the disadvantages—the lack of quality yeshivos, the basic ignorance of Torah and mitzvos even among the *frum Jews*, assimilation, and intermarriage. He was aware of the disadvantages and intended to fight them, in his own way.

*Chapter Three*

# America

## Spring Valley: 5677 (1917)[16]

he Benders settled in Spring Valley, New York. Pelta Bender
worried about her Dovid'l ever since he survived a case of
rheumatic fever. She and her husband felt that the healthy
mountain air would be good for the little boy. But there was a serious
problem: Spring Valley had no Jewish school for Dovid. Compulsory education was the law, and few dared — or cared — to challenge it. After all,
most Jewish parents in America of the early 1900's were eager to provide
their children with a quality education. They saw education as the key to
success, the guarantee that their children would not waste away in sweat-
shops earning poverty-level salaries. Besides, the many Jewish parents in
the region found nothing wrong in sending their children to the local public school. As for Jewish studies, a few after-school sessions would have to
suffice.

Years of this dangerous policy exacted its toll on American Jewry. Pious
parents, who suffered poverty and indignity to avoid desecrating the Shabbos, watched their children abandon those values for which their parents
had sacrificed so much. A major cause was their public school education.
Public school succeeded in replacing Yiddish with English so that parents
and children now spoke different languages. Public school succeeded in

---

16. Documents at Ellis Island record their arrival to America on January 3, 1917. They are listed
as having been residents of Slonim, Russia, and that they arrived via Holland. Dovid is listed as
being 3 years old at the time, which coincides with family records.

*Rabbi Avrohom Bender
with his son Dovid*

forging a common cultural bond between the Jewish children and their gentile classmates so that their differences seemed non-existent. Public school showed Jewish children how easy it was to assimilate, and many did.

The after-school Jewish lessons did little to alleviate the situation. The children were preoccupied with their public school lives, the stimulating secular lessons, the extracurricular sports and activities, and their newly formed friendships. In contrast, Jewish classes were held after a long day of school with elderly male teachers to whom the children did not relate. These were a boring ordeal the children attended only to satisfy their parents.

Rabbi Avrohom Bender was determined to raise his only son differently. He wanted his son to realize that Torah is the focus of life, not a mere afterthought. He wanted his son to realize that *Yidden* are different, and not just "Jewish gentiles" who can spend the entire day absorbed in gentile culture with an hour or two after school to be informed about Jewish traditions.

His child would know *aleph-beis* before the ABCs, the *parshiyos* before the presidents, and *Bava Kamma* before baseball. Yet, where in Spring Valley would he find a school with such a curriculum? Nowhere; not enough Jewish parents in Spring Valley shared his vision.

This did not deter Reb Avrohom. When Dovid turned 6, the age at which he was legally required to attend school, Reb Avrohom simply did not register him. Instead, he hired private tutors who came to the house to teach his son. The home schooling consisted of lessons on a broad range of Jewish subjects as well as basic math and English. Truant officers patrolled the streets of America. Although the Benders felt that they were providing their son with an excellent education at considerable personal expense, it was most unlikely that a judge would agree. It was much safer to avoid the arm of the law altogether. So for the next seven years, during school hours, Dovid Bender never left his house.

UNTIL DOVID REACHED BAR MITZVAH AGE, REB AVROHOM FELT HE had been fairly successful in keeping American culture and foreign influences out of his home. But, how far would tutoring take his son toward becoming a *talmid chacham*? With Reb Avrohom constantly on the road, the time he could spend learning with his son was limited. Dovid needed qualified teachers, challenging study partners, and a stimulating learning environment, none of which existed in Spring Valley. In fact, such an institution did not exist anywhere in America. Dovid needed a yeshivah, but where?

For one who trusts in Hashem, His help is never far away. The same year Dovid became bar mitzvah, Torah Vodaath opened its Mesivta. The Benders moved to Williamsburg, and Dovid's life was changed forever.

WILLIAMSBURG OF THE 1920'S WAS A NEIGHBORHOOD IN TRANSITION. Formerly an upper-class, gentile, and genteel area, with large impressive churches attracting residents from all across Brooklyn, and well-kept lawns and stately mansions lining its wide boulevards, Williamsburg was a desirable neighborhood.

In the early 1900's, a few brave, wealthy Jewish families dared to move into the elite Williamsburg. They wanted to escape the lower-class, densely populated, predominately Jewish neighborhoods where they had lived since their arrival on American shores. The Williamsburg apartments were generally larger and airier than those on the Lower East Side, and the neighborhood was not nearly as overcrowded. These Jews were willing to risk the scorn and vilification of their non-Jewish neighbors to provide their families with a higher quality of life.

Beginnings are never easy; gentile Williamsburg did not take kindly to the new immigrants. A Jew with a beard and sideburns, who dared to tread on these non-Jewish streets, was sure to be bullied. For many of the newcomers, beards and *peiyos* were easily snipped away as they tried to blend in with their neighbors.

The neighborhood slowly changed and as more Jews moved in, more gentiles moved out. Ornate, elaborate churches became impressive synagogues. Storefronts on Lee Avenue now advertised kosher meat. Williamsburg became a neighborhood of contrasts: a community of ethnic Jews whose commitment to Judaism was often weak. Although they built synagogues and patronized "kosher" butchers, the Jews of Williamsburg were no different than most American Jews from Chicago to Tennessee. They were proud of their cultural heritage, but their aspiration was that their children would become American.

Although Torah Vodaath had opened its elementary school in 1917 and its Mesivta in 1926, Williamsburg Jews were not banging down its doors to gain admission. On the contrary, even families with a high level of religious life were reluctant to send their children. They gave varied reasons for this. Some cynically dismissed the possibility of children becoming Torah scholars or even simple G-d-fearing Jews in America. They felt that the effort was a waste of time and energy. However, for many the issue was financial. Public school was free, while tuition at Torah Vodaath was several dollars a month. When an average salary ranged between $15 to $25 dollars a week,[17] setting aside a few dollars per child in the form of tuition was no small matter.

As Rabbi Avrohom Bender and his family settled happily in Williamsburg, the dichotomy that existed was disturbing. On the one hand, Williamsburg was teeming with Jews. It was common for one to walk down the street, meet a *landsman*, and strike up a conversation in *"de mamme lashon."* The Jewish flavor was definitely there, yet something was missing.

One day as Reb Avrohom was walking down the street, he met to his delight a *landsman*.

*"Shalom aleichem,"* he joyfully greeted R' Shimon Rosen.[18]

*"Aleichem shalom,"* R' Shimon answered, equally pleased. R' Shimon came from Slonim and remembered Reb Avrohom with fond respect.

*"Nu*, how are you?" Reb Avrohom inquired. "How is your family?"

*"Baruch Hashem,"* he answered. "I have two little boys."

"Where are you sending them to yeshivah?"

The man looked sheepish. "Well, Reb Avrohom, you see, I am sending them to public school." Reb Avrohom responded with stony silence. "You have to understand, Reb Avrohom, I just can't. Torah Vodaath wants $2 a month per child for tuition. In times like these, it is just impossible."

Reb Avrohom did understand. Even when they could hold down a job, new immigrants drew paltry salaries. Yet Reb Avrohom could not accept the possibility that another family, a precious family he knew from back home, might be lost in the abyss of assimilation.

"Listen, R' Shimon, let me pay the tuition for you, just for now. When you can afford it, you will pay it back."

R' Shimon could not thank Reb Avrohom enough. Most happily, he withdrew his sons from public school and enrolled them in Torah Vodaath.[19]

Reb Avrohom left the conversation in wistful contemplation. *Baruch Hashem*, another two Jewish children were saved from the perils of public school education. However, this was by no means a guarantee that they would turn out to be *ehrlicher Yidden*. Unfortunately, many who came from good homes and attended religious schools nonetheless became irreligious. The lure of the street was overwhelming, especially since everyone had contact with Jewish friends, neighbors, and relatives who were not religious. Would his family emerge unscathed?

---

17. Rabbi Henoch Cohen reports that in the 30's his father earned about $25 a week and that was average. In the Depression years and before, salaries were markedly lower.

18. Name has been changed.

19. These two little boys grew up to be *ehrlicher Yidden*, prominent members of the communities they lived in, and parents of generations of beautiful *Yiddishe* families.

One calculated step Reb Avrohom took when he moved to Williamsburg was to share a house with his brother, R' Archik Berman. Reb Avrohom was frequently on the road and he felt it would be more pleasant and less lonely for his wife and child if they lived with his brother's family.

The Benders and the Bermans began their new lives together at 189 Rodney Street. Archik was a partner in a men's suit business called *Berman and Feinerman's* — the only suit store in America at the time that sold suits guaranteed to be free of *shatnez*. In contrast to Reb Avrohom's profession as a *meshulach*, Archik's business kept him home most of the time. The Bermans had five children: Hannah, Mary, Mike, Abe, and Bluma. The house was full of laughter and noise, and the Berman children and Dovid Bender became very close, almost like siblings. Dovid felt part of a warm and happy family; there was no need to look outside his family structure for love and fulfillment.[20]

*Rabbi Uri Meir Kahanow (1883- 1960) journeyed to Eretz Yisroel where he learned under Rabbi Yitzchok Yeruchem Diskind and Rabbi Yosef Chaim Sonnenfeld. A malaria outbreak sent Reb Uri Meir back to Europe, where he married and became a Rav. Later, the Kahanow family immigrated to America. Reb Uri Meir became a maggid shiur in Mesivta Torah Vodaath, rosh beis din of the Williamsburg Beis Din, and author of two seforim, Mishmeres Kohanim and Imrei Kohein.*

Enrolling his son in the newly formed Mesivta of Torah Vodaath was the next step Reb Avrohom took in guiding his son toward becoming a *ben Torah*. Although most of his classmates had been together since elementary school, Dovid adjusted quickly and fit right in at the Mesivta of Torah Vodaath. There he forged lifelong friendships with Avrohom Pincus, Feivel (Phil) Ritholtz, and others. They formed a close-knit group, a barrier against the pitfalls of the times.

DOVID OFTEN REMINISCED ABOUT HIS YEARS AT THE MESIVTA. EACH year opened new vistas of learning for the Torah Vodaath boys. Each rebbi was a serious *talmid chacham*, educated in the sacred yeshivos of Europe. Each rebbi was different; each added his unique contribution to his students' growth in Torah.

Rabbi Uri Meir Kahanow was the rebbi for the first level. Reb Avrohom was delighted that his son would be learning Torah from his childhood friend. Their days of learning together in Minsk were deeply engraved in

---

20. Generally, youth who came from extended families who were also happily religious found safety and camaraderie in their own surroundings and were more likely to remain religious than others from dissimilar situations (inferred from various interviews ).

his memory. Reb Avrohom remembered how, even as a young child, his friend Uri Meir exhibited a tremendous love of Torah and self-sacrifice for learning. How fortunate that his Dovid would now have him as his rebbi.[21]

During that first year, Dovid became very close with Rabbi Kahanow. It was easy to recognize Rabbi Kahanow's extraordinary personal qualities. His fine and humble character and his love for his fellow man endeared him to his students and all who met him. Rabbi Kahanow was both devoted to his students and dedicated to the community. He was rarely seen without a sefer, and his Torah knowledge was wide ranging.[22]

206 Wilson Street was home to the yeshivah, the Mesivta, and the Torah Vodaath *minyan*. Rabbi Kahanow was the rabbi to whom the women would come with their chickens and their halachic questions. In those pre- and post-Depression years, chickens were extremely expensive, and women coming with a questionable chicken were anxious for the Rav's ruling. Rabbi Kahanow would come to the Mesivta, his knife in his bag, and, if a worried woman was awaiting his answer, he would interrupt his lesson. With patience and concern, Rabbi Kahanow would cut and examine the chicken and deliver a ruling. He was always happy when he could declare the chicken kosher and save a poor family additional expense.[23] The boys in his class observed firsthand the patience of a *tzaddik*, the authority of a *posek*, and the concern of a Rav for the gravity of rendering halachic decisions.

Rabbi Shmuel Kushelevitz was the rebbi for the second level.[24] Could boys of their age growing up in America fully appreciate the Torah giant they had for a rebbi?[25] Rabbi Kushelevitz was an authority in both *Talmud Bavli* and *Yerushalmi* and could quote from all of *Shas* including the most difficult tractates. When Rabbi Kushelevitz gave a Torah lecture, he stood

---

21. Rabbi Avrohom Bender and Rabbi Uri Meir Kahanow lost contact after that period in Minsk. Reb Avrohom once knocked on a random door on Bedford Avenue to ask the resident if he knew where a particular person lived. Lo and behold, the man who opened the door was Reb Uri Meir. They stared at each other and then embraced. Thereafter, they remained in close contact (Rabbi Paltiel Bender).

22. "Except for the few minutes he would spend eating, I do not recall ever seeing my grandfather without a Gemara in his hands. Fittingly, he passed away holding a Gemara" (Rabbi Elya Kanarek).

23. Rabbi Eliyahu Kahanow.

24. It is possible that Rabbi Dovid Bender did not have Rabbi Kushelevitz as a rebbi. Rabbi Avrohom Pincus did not list him as one of their rebbeim, and some of the advanced students would skip some of the *shiurim* (ed.).

25. Rabbi Kushelevitz was a cousin through marriage to Rav Shach. Upon receiving a copy of Rabbi Kushelevitz's sefer, *Nesivos Shmuel*, Rav Shach addressed his cousin in a letter: "To the great genius who possesses broad Torah knowledge, who uproots mountains with his complex reasoning, who is a treasury of Torah and fear of Heaven." This letter, complete with comments on his cousin's sefer, appears at the end of Rav Shach's sefer *Avi Ezri* (*Chelek Kedushah*).

in front of the class, his *rabbanishe koppel* standing tall on his head, his thick black eyebrows knitted in concentration, fiercely focused on the *shiur*. Woe to the boy who was caught dozing off or who was not learning during *chazarah*. The rebbi's face would become most serious, and his penetrating eyes would bore holes straight through the guilty party. The rebbi would holler like thunder, yet because he was genuinely goodhearted and could not remain upset, immediately after the harangue, he resumed laughing and smiling. Actually, he had not really been upset at all. The whole scene was performed for the benefit of a beloved student who needed the *mussar*. His Torah lectures were so stimulating that his students were reluctant to leave when the year ended.

*Rabbi Shmuel Kushelevitz (1887-1963) was a student of Slabodka and Radin. As a young man, he immigrated to America and became a maggid shiur in Mesivta Torah Vodaath. He later held the position of masmech (one who tests the students and grants semichah). He wrote the sefer Nesivos Shmuel on sugyos in Gemara.*

The *maggid shiur* for the third level was Rabbi Avrohom Chinitz. Rabbi Chinitz used his powerful oratory skills to maintain his students' attention. Synthesizing his roles as Rav and *maggid shiur*, both his lectures in Torah Vodaath and his discourses in shul were meticulously prepared and masterfully delivered.

Rabbi Chinitz's *shiur* was no place for fooling around.[26] His eyes perused the entire room during the lecture and during review with study partners, as well. And when he spotted a student lax in his learning, he had an apt quip ready to roll off his tongue. Once, he came up behind a group of boys during the review period and caught them idling. The boys sheepishly looked at their rebbi and waited for his rebuke. He smiled benevolently at them. *"Bochurim, battel ah bissel! Battel ah bissel!"*[27] he said. The boys looked at one another in surprise; rebbi is telling them to *"battel"*? Rabbi Chinitz answered their questioning looks. "Our Sages say, '*Battel retzoncha m'pnei retzono* — Nullify your will in favor of His will' — so *battel ah bissel!"*

---

26. Rabbi Yitzchok Karpf remembers those years: "I came from the Rabbi Shlomo Kluger *cheder* on the Lower East Side. It was a *chassidishe cheder* and my Yiddish was *Galitzianish*. I managed to get by in Rabbi Kahanow's *shiur* with my Galician pronunciation, and I skipped Rabbi Kushelevitz's class. But, when I came to Rabbi Chinitz, his Yiddish was so heavily Lithuanian, he did not understand a word I said. I had to adapt."

27. "*Battel*" means to nullify or waste. "*Battel ah bissel*" can mean to waste a little bit of time.

*Rabbi Avrohom Chinitz (1896-1986) learned in the famed yeshivah of Mir for a number of years and in 1924 left for America. He was a rebbi in Mesivta Torah Vodaath from 1924 until 1946 and was also Rav of the famous Logan Street Shul (Ahavas Achim B'nei Avrohom) and later Rav of the Nusach Ashkenaz minyan in the famous Elton Street Shul.*

*Rabbi Yosef Adler (1875-1938) was a talmid of Slabodka. He taught in Mesivta Torah Vodaath for a number of years, eventually leaving to found the High School and Beis Medrash Division of Mesivta Tiferes Yerushalayim. In 1937 he invited Rabbi Moshe Feinstein, a cousin through marriage, to join the yeshivah. Reb Yosef was niftar in a drowning accident in 1938, and Rabbi Moshe Feinstein succeeded him as Rosh Yeshivah.*

Rabbi Chinitz's uncle, Rabbi Yosef Adler, was the fourth-level rebbi. Rabbi Adler was a Torah Vodaath old-timer. In 1923, he had been hired as the eighth-grade rebbi and for the next three years, he advanced with his class. His "class" was a group of boys who wanted to continue learning in Torah Vodaath after they completed eighth grade, even though the Mesivta had not officially opened. Rabbi Yosef Adler taught this group in the morning, and at 2:30 p.m., they would go to the high school division of Yeshivas Rabbeinu Yitzchok Elchonon for secular subjects. When the Mesivta opened, Rabbi Yosef Adler's original class of eighth graders became the oldest class in the Mesivta, with Reb Yosef as their *maggid shiur*.

During Dovid's fourth year in Torah Vodaath, Rabbi Shraga Feivel Mendelowitz, founder and principal of the Mesivta of Torah Vodaath,[28] stepped down from his position and appointed Rabbi Moshe Dov Ber Rivkin as the new *menahel*. Rabbi Rivkin was known as an exceptional rebbi and a capable principal. His duties in Torah Vodaath were to gauge the boys' progress in learning, to test them, and in general to keep tabs on their spiritual growth. The boys greatly benefited from his presence.[29]

---

28. Torah Vodaath elementary school was founded by R' Binyamin Wilhelm (1878-1972).

29. In 1931, Reb Shraga Feivel returned to his former position as *menahel* and Rabbi Rivkin stepped down. Rabbi Rivkin was given the fifth *shiur* — the class right below that of the Rosh Yeshivah (Rabbi Avrohom Barnetsky).

*Rabbi Moshe Dov Ber Rivkin (1891-1976) learned in Yeshivas Lubavitch in Russia. Reb Moshe served as menahel in the Lubavitcher Yeshivah in Yerushalayim. He left for America in 1927 and served both as a menahel and then rebbi in Mesivta Torah Vodaath. He was an exceptional educator who was remembered by his talmidim decades later.*

The Mesivta rebbeim were all graduates of the most illustrious Lithuanian yeshivos, and they brought the Lithuanian method of learning to their classrooms. For these *Litvishe rabbanim*, teaching regular all-American youth could not have been easy. Although most of the Mesivta boys had attended Torah Vodaath elementary school, their level of learning was far below their European counterparts. Furthermore, there were many out-of-towners who knew even less than the Torah Vodaath graduates. Another obstacle was the cultural barrier. Although most of the boys were from European homes, the lure of being "all-American" was enticing. Avrohom Chaim became Abe, Feivel became Philip, and Shloima became Sol. Their "Americanism" was obvious not only by their names, but by their language and culture marked by their accented Yiddish, their thoughts and mannerisms, and their goals and aspirations.

Rabbi Chinitz once remarked to his class, "During the week, when we take out the sefer Torah to read, we say, '*Yehai ra'ava kadamach d'sorich lan*

*Rabbi Shraga Feivel Mendelowitz (1886-1948) studied under the Arugas Habosem (Rabbi Moshe Grunwald), Rabbi Shmuel Rosenberg, and Rabbi Simcha Bunim Sofer. He immigrated to the United States where he became principal of Torah Vodaath elementary school and founder of the Mesivta, the Beis Medrash, and Beis Medrash Elyon. In 1944 he founded Torah Umesorah, an organization that establishes Jewish Day Schools. With ahavas Hashem and ahavas Yisroel Reb Shraga championed the growth of Torah in America.*

*chayin b'tivusa v'lehevei ana f'kida b'goy tzadikaya* — may it be Your will that You extend our lives with goodness and that I be numbered among the righteous.' Now, what does having a long life have to do with becoming righteous? One can live a long life and only accumulate sins, Heaven forbid! What is the connection between a long life and righteousness?

"I realized the answer here, in America. In this country, everything is low and sinking even lower. How can a place like this produce *gedolim*? I was raised in Europe. I learned in European yeshivos. I saw European Torah giants. I witnessed true Torah greatness! But how can America, a place sinking in impurity, produce greatness in Torah? Then it came to me: If I live long enough — a person like me who is not really great, but has witnessed greatness — I will be revered as a *tzaddik*, just for sharing my experiences with greatness! Now I understand this prayer: Master of the Universe, grant me life! The longer I live, the more likely that I will be numbered among the righteous. Simply by having witnessed the greatness of the previous generation, I will be considered a *tzaddik*!" He ended on a rueful note, poking fun at himself while lamenting the state of *Yiddishkeit* in America.

Improving *Yiddishkeit* in America was the single-minded goal of Rabbi Shraga Feivel Mendelowitz. Well aware of the prevailing attitudes in America, Reb Shraga Feivel used a pun on the words "*Lechtech acharai bamidbar b'eretz lo zeruah* — Walk with Me into the desert, a land where nothing grows."[30] America, he used to say, is "*eretz* **lo** *zeruah*" — it is a land where "*lo!* — **no!**" is implanted. When it comes to *Yiddishkeit*, everyone says, "No! It can't be done!" In this country, negativity grows in abundance. Reb Shraga Feivel urged, "We must fight this negativity!"

Undaunted by the naysayers, Reb Shraga Feivel founded the Mesivta of Torah Vodaath. He now had students with solid foundations in learn-

---

30. *Yirmiyah* 2:2.

ing, molded by the rebbeim and administration of the Mesivta. His optimism about the future was infectious. Through warmth, song, Torah, and authentic Jewish philosophy he would reach these boys, and with each student, the face of American Jewry would change.

From the very beginning, Reb Shraga Feivel sought to crown his Mesivta with greatness. He searched for ideal roshei yeshivah, illustrious Torah scholars whose very presence would mold and inspire his boys. In Dovid Bender's time, the crown of Torah Vodaath was its Rosh Yeshivah, Rabbi Dovid Leibowitz.

FOR DOVID, THE YEARS WITH RABBI Dovid Leibowitz had a critical impact on his future. Under the tutelage of his rebbi, Dovid sharpened his analytical skills and learned how to learn. Reb Dovid's learning style followed that of Reb Chaim Brisker.

*Rabbi Dovid Leibowitz (1889-1941) was a great-nephew and student of the Chofetz Chaim. Reb Dovid also studied under the Alter of Slabodka, Rabbi Nosson Tzvi Finkel. In 1926, on a fund-raising trip to America, he was invited to join the staff of Yeshivah Torah Vodaath and became its Rosh Yeshivah in 1929. In 1933 Reb Dovid founded Yeshivas Chofetz Chaim in New York which he led until his passing.*

Reb Dovid did not focus on many commentaries, but rather concentrated on the text itself, forcing his students to examine, reexamine, and analyze what they thought they knew. He pushed them to question, to answer, to think deeply. He showed them how to consider the text from different angles and imparted his original perspectives toward the understanding of the Gemara.

Reb Dovid encouraged his students to think for themselves, to challenge his words, and to be dynamic in their learning. His classroom was afire with *milchamta shel Torah*.[31] Through Reb Dovid's *shiur*, his students saw how vast the sea of Talmud is, how much they still had to learn, and how exhilarating learning could be.

The *beis medrash* students loved their Rosh Yeshivah and Reb Dovid loved his students. His enthusiasm was contagious; his search for truth in learning was inspiring. He influenced his students in many ways, particularly

---

31. I.e., the battle of Torah study, as students debated what they were learning. "I'll never forget my years in Reb Dovid's *shiur*. His son, Reb Henoch, sat directly opposite him and they would argue it out! It was fire! Reb Dovid brought his proofs and Reb Henoch would not budge when he defended his position. There was such excitement; we all became caught up in it. That was Reb Dovid's *shiur*" (Rabbi Avrohom Barnetsky).

through *mussar*. The boys eagerly awaited his weekly *mussar shmuessen*, one of the highlights of the week. Younger *bochurim* were allowed to attend these *shmuessen* to give them a taste of the future.

Dovid's seven years in Torah Vodaath were years of growth. In the challenging years ahead he would fondly reminisce about the many aspects that made Torah Vodaath precious to him: the beloved *menahel*, Rabbi Shraga Feivel Mendelowitz; the Rosh Yeshivah, Rabbi Dovid Leibowitz, with whom he shared a special relationship; and the rebbeim who, each in his own way, gave him the foundations to build upon. Nonetheless, eventually, the time came for Dovid to move on.[32]

Rosh Hashanah, 1932. After *Ma'ariv,* Dovid Bender turned to his father and said, "Papa, when I was *davening*, it suddenly occurred to me that I would like to go to Europe to learn."

Reb Avrohom nodded. "I had the same thought, my son. This year, G-d willing, you will go to learn in one of the great European yeshivos."

FROM THE INITIAL IDEA TO THE ACTUAL TRIP, THERE WERE MANY stages. Mir was the popular choice among American *bochurim* studying in Europe and the Benders' choice as well. Since Reb Avrohom was a *meshulach*, his job forced him to be on the road for weeks at a time. It seemed ridiculous for all three of the Benders to be alone: Reb Avrohom alone on the road, Rebbetzin Bender alone at home, Dovid alone in Mir. Thus, in Elul of 1933, it was decided that Rebbetzin Pelta Bender, Dovid's mother, would accompany her son to Mir.

The following years were lonely years of sacrifice for Reb Avrohom. His only wish was for his beloved son and his beloved Torah to become one. The knowledge that his son was growing in Torah and fear of Heaven in ways that would have been difficult, if not impossible to achieve in America, was consolation in itself.

With his wife and son overseas, Reb Avrohom spent even more time on the road collecting money for Yeshivas Rabbeinu Yitzchok Elchonon. From the time he arrived on American shores in 1917, Reb Avrohom had been collecting for the yeshivah — then, the only yeshivah of higher learning in America. Illustrious *talmidei chachamim*[33] served on their staff, and their alumni[34] went on to take prestigious positions throughout the country.

---

32. "Attending a European yeshivah was still a goal to strive for. Torah Vodaath had accomplished a lot but the level of learning was still not the same as the yeshivos in Europe. In my time Rabbi Hershel Genauer went to Kelm, Rabbi Simcha Weissman went to Mir, and his brother Reb Avrohom went to Kaminetz. I went to Otvock" (Rabbi Avrohom Barnetsky).

33. Such as Rabbi Shlomo Poliachek, the Meicheter Illuy.

34. Actually, the goal of Yeshivas Rabbeinu Yitzchok Elchonon was to train rabbis. Opened in 1917, the yeshivah was compatible with American Orthodoxy because becoming a pulpit rabbi was a respectable career (*Reb Shraga Feivel*, p. 76).

Some of the guiding lights of American Jewry learned there.[35] Although very different than the yeshivos in which Reb Avrohom had been privileged to learn, Yeshivas Rabbeinu Yitzchak Elchonon disseminated Torah, and Reb Avrohom was pleased with his share in their learning.[36]

His love of Torah impressed all those who met him and he was a very successful fund-raiser. Yet, that was not enough for Reb Avrohom. For him, collecting money for yeshivos was important; collecting *Yiddishe neshamos* was even more important. Traveling from town to town, from city to city, as he traversed the East Coast and Midwest, Reb Avrohom met many Jewish families, all different types with different levels of *frumkeit*. Nonetheless, there was one common denominator: They all sent their children to public school.

Time and experience polished Reb Avrohom's oratory skills, and he became a very popular *darshan*. Local *ba'alei battim* looked forward to his yearly visit to their town, eager to see his warm smile, hear his powerful *mussar*, and benefit from his sagacious advice.[37] They would ask him to speak in the shul on Shabbos — night, morning, and afternoon — whenever he could. *Shalosh Seudos*, when the *ba'alei battim* would gather at the end of the day for a bit of herring and schnapps, was the meal at which Reb Avrohom most often spoke. Reb Avrohom expounded on the weekly Torah portion, expertly employing *d'rush* to explain textual difficulties and arouse the interest of the audience.[38] After he spoke, the men would gather around to discuss what was said or to ask Reb Avrohom for advice. They knew that his opinions were rooted in Torah and fear of Heaven.[39]

---

35. Some students of Yeshivas Rabbeinu Yitzchok Elchonon became Torah giants of the generation. Examples include: Rabbi Avigdor Miller (1908-2001), Rabbi Mordechai Gifter (1915-2001), and *ybdl"ch* Rabbi Chaim Pinchos Scheinberg. It must be pointed out, though, that these three went on to study in the European yeshivos of Slabodka, Telshe, and Mir, respectively. All have maintained that it was their years abroad that defined them.

36. The yeshivah was originally just that — a yeshivah. In 1928, the yeshivah became a department of Yeshivah University.

37. "He was a *gevaldige* speaker, like a traveling *maggid*. People remembered him years later. When we opened a yeshivah in St. Louis and Rabbi Bender's grandson, Paltiel, was one of our students, the old-timers favored him because they so fondly remembered his grandfather" (Rabbi Osher Green).

38. Told by Rabbi Yaakov Kurland to Rabbi Yaakov Bender.

39. "When I was a kid in St. Louis in the 40's, my father was trying to decide where to send me to yeshivah. He approached Rabbi Bender who advised my father to send me to Torah Vodaath where his son, Reb Dovid, was teaching. My good friend, Rabbi Yaakov Moshe Kulefsky (1925-2000), later a leading *maggid shiur* in Yeshivas Ner Israel of Baltimore, was attending a different yeshivah. His father also approached Rabbi Bender to discuss with him whether his son should stay there or make a change. Rabbi Bender recommended that he send him to Torah Vodaath as well. It was interesting that Rabbi Bender made these recommendations even as he was collecting funds for Yeshivas Rabbeinu Yitzchok Elchonon. It was clear to everyone that his recommendations were based on what he felt was good for the individual. People appreciated his wisdom, clear-headedness, and honesty" (Rabbi Osher Green).

**From Avoka, Pennsylvania to St. Louis, Missouri, Rabbi Avrohom Bender's influence was far reaching. Rabbi Shlomo Gruskin was among the many boys who Rabbi Avrohom Bender sent to yeshivah.**

*Rabbi Shlomo Gruskin (1917-2004) studied in Yeshivas Rabbeinu Yitzchok Elchonon for a year, and then went on to Torah Vodaath and then Yeshivas Chofetz Chaim. He moved to Detroit in 1947 when he was hired as a fundraiser for the Beth Yehudah Day School. One year later he became the rabbi of the Bnai Zion Congregation. He served his community faithfully until three years before his passing.*

During the week, he would make the rounds to houses soliciting donations for Yeshivas Rabbeinu Yitzchok Elchonon. At each house, he would talk about Torah: our love for Torah, our need for Torah, and our need for yeshivos to teach Torah. At some point in each conversation, he turned personal.

"And where do your children go to school?"

"Reb Avrohom, where do you expect them to go to school? They go to public school like everyone else!"

"*Reb Yid*, why don't you send your son to a yeshivah?"

Reactions to this question ranged from outright scorn to regret and despair.

Moshe Gruskin shrugged his shoulders with sad but rueful acceptance. "What can we do? There are no yeshivos here. My children have to go to public school."

"*Vos*?!" Reb Avrohom roared. "*Du vilst az er zol arine brengin a shikse in shtub* — What?! Do you want him to bring home a gentile girl?!"

Mr. Gruskin was taken aback. "What can I do? Besides, my son is only 6 years old!" he protested.

"R' Moshe, if you do not send your son to a *cheder*, Talmud Torah, yeshivah, *something*, even at this young age, in time he will bring home a gentile girl."[40]

---

40. Moshe Gruskin was so taken aback at Reb Avrohom's vehement assertion that without some form of formal Jewish learning his son was destined to marry a gentile, that he acted immediately. They lived in Avoka, Pennsylvania, a tiny little town with barely 800 residents. There were only 16 other Jews living in Avoka and the Gruskins were the only Shabbos-observant family. Opening any type of school was impossible. Yet, R' Moshe was determined that his child would stay *frum*. Every day, after public school, he closed his tailor shop early and took his children to nearby Wilkes-Barre, a relatively large city with a significant Jewish population and a Talmud Torah. R' Moshe escorted his children to the Talmud Torah, waited as they learned there, and then took them home. This continued for many years, until his son was old enough to attend a proper yeshivah in New York. The Gruskins always remembered Rabbi Avrohom Bender with gratitude.

Reb Avrohom's strong words made an equally strong impression. The Gruskins heeded Reb Avrohom's call, as did many others. Reb Avrohom traveled from upstate New York — Hunter, Rochester, Syracuse, Woodridge — across the Midwest to Pittsburgh, Detroit, and Cleveland. Wherever he went he spoke, exhorting his brethren to send their children to yeshivos. In some places, he was successful; in others, less so. Despite many negative responses, Reb Avrohom was not deterred. He tried again and again and again, fired by the experience that every once in a while he met with success. All the derision was worthwhile when he succeeded in sending even one child to yeshivah.

PITTSBURGH OF THE 1920'S AND 30'S WAS A TYPICAL EXAMPLE. THE CITY had many Jewish families, most of whom were newly arrived immigrants with a poor command of English and certainly no formal higher education. The Pittsburgh Jewish community was primarily middle- to low-income families for whom life was a struggle. Fitting into this strange new country was a struggle. *Yiddishkeit* was a struggle. Making a living was a struggle. Most parents dreamed of a better future for their children. They were happy to see their children adjusting to their lives in America and were not interested in an alternative to public school. Besides, the ticket to that brighter future seemed to be a quality secular education followed by college. What purpose was there in sending their children to yeshivah?

*In 2007, Rabbi Yitzchok Scheiner spoke before an audience of over one thousand students and teachers of Yeshivah Darchei Torah and Mesivta Chaim Shlomo. There he declared, "I am Rosh Yeshivah of Yeshivas Kaminetz today, thanks to your Rosh Yeshivah Rabbi Yaakov Bender's grandfather. I had graduated Peabody High School and had already begun studies at Pittsburgh University. Rabbi Avrohom Bender convinced my parents to send me to a yeshivah in New York. If he had not succeeded, I would probably be a professor of mathematics today."*

Mr. Berel Scheiner was a well-meaning Pittsburgh baker[41] with an only son, Yitzchok. Although Mr. Scheiner would have wanted Yitzchok to have a better Jewish education, it never occurred to him to do anything other than what all his friends and neighbors were doing with their children. While at the Scheiner house, Reb Avrohom saw Yitzchok, a pure Jewish boy, attending public school. Genuinely pained, Reb Avrohom turned to Mr. Scheiner and asked, "Why not send your son to yeshivah?"

With a shrug of his shoulders, Mr. Scheiner answered, "Reb Avrohom, there is no yeshivah in our town." He meant well; he struggled to keep Shabbos, he wanted his son to grow up to be a G-d-fearing Jew, but what was he supposed to do?

"I know that," Reb Avrohom replied. "I meant, send the child to New York. There he can attend a yeshivah."

Mr. Scheiner was taken aback. "Reb Avrohom, he is my only son! How can you ask me to send away my only son?"

"I sent away my only child. Do you know where I sent him? To Europe! Why? So that he should grow in Torah and fear of Heaven. I can send my only son to Europe, and you cannot send yours to New York?"

Sometimes the argument worked; often it did not.[42] But when Reb Avrohom convinced a parent to send his son to yeshivah, he felt both satisfied and proud. Such successes made the sacrifice of sending his beloved son overseas a bit more bearable.

---

41. Rabbi Avrohom Bender often stayed in the Scheiner home when he passed through Pittsburgh for they were one of the few reliably kosher homes in the city.

42. "Rabbi Avrohom Bender felt that it was his job not only to collect money for yeshivos but also to collect boys for yeshivos. In the 1930's, sending a boy to yeshivah was radical. Sending a boy from Pittsburgh to New York was almost unheard of. But, Rabbi Bender kept on trying" (Rabbi Yitzchok Scheiner).

# Part II:
# **Dovid Bender**
## 5693-5698 / 1933-1938

### *Chapter Four:*
## From America to Mir

### *Chapter Five:*
## Becoming "Ah Mirrer"

### *Chapter Six:*
## Letters from Mir

### *Chapter Seven:*
## Living in Mir

This section is based primarily on information from Rabbi Avrohom Pincus, R' Elchonon (Heiry) Ehrlanger, Rabbi Alex Weisfogel, and the Bender Family. Other primary sources include *My Father's Legacy* by Noam Gordon, an unpublished collection of letters written by R' Yehudah Leib (Yud'l) Gordon to his family (heretofore referred to as Gordon), and a collection of letters written by Rabbis Dovid Bender and Avrohom Pincus to their friend Rabbi Feivel Ritholtz. Additional sources are quoted.

*Chapter Four*

# From America to Mir

### The Aquitania: 5693 (1933)

*T*ODAY WAS A MOST BEAUTIFUL DAY. AS I SIT HERE IN THE *library and reminisce about the scene I have just left, the setting sun sinking into the ocean, and the ship surrounded by water, as Coleridge wrote, 'Water, water, everywhere ...' Captains, engineers, and stewards carefully directing hundreds of people entrusted to their care and delivering them to their destination in six days ... While this scene is flitting across my mind, I compare this scene with my life. Is there any analogy between the ocean and the yam haTalmud?[1] Can I not compare myself to the ocean liner? Does not my will somehow resemble the captains'? I ponder these thoughts and draw the comparisons. The sun is the home I am leaving behind. My parents and sisters who provided my life with light are now sinking into the boiling sea of my New York life only to arise again on the morrow and again shed light on my path. I find myself surrounded by the yam haTalmud. I wonder, counting yom leshanah, yom leshanah,[2] if I will be able in six years to traverse that other yam? I try to console myself. If Hashem Yisbarach blesses me with six years of a calm ocean, a clear and bright horizon, a shining sun at home, and He places no obstacle in the way of my will, just as He has not placed any today in the path of the captains, I will reach my destination."[3]*

---

1. "Ocean of Talmud" is a common reference to the vastness of the Talmud.

2. *Bamidbar* 14:34. "One year for each day" — for each day that the spies spent on their journey, *Klal Yisroel* had to then spend a year in the desert. Yud'l Gordon's prayer was that, for every day on the ship, he should be worthy of a year of learning in Mir, Poland. Indeed, he spent six days on the ship and merited to learn seven years in the Mir.

3. Adapted from *My Father's Legacy* by Noam Gordon, an unpublished collection of letters written by Rabbi Yehudah Leib (Yud'l) Gordon to his family. He is heretofore referred to as Gordon.

*Top left to right clockwise: Harry Horowitz, Avrohom Pincus, and Dovid Bender*

YUD'L GORDON'S POIGNANT words home tell the story of a unique generation. He and his friends — Dovid Bender, Avrohom Pincus, and Harry Horowitz — were pioneers. They left America, the continent of comfort and convenience, to journey to a less progressive, poor continent for the sole purpose of learning Torah from Lithuanian *gedolim*.[4]

Most of these boys were young; Dovid Bender was 20 and Yud'l Gordon was 18, but other boys were as young as 13½.[5] Not only were these youngsters leaving their family and friends, they were entering a life and culture completely foreign to typical apple-pie Americans. Their optimism and idealism would be constantly challenged. Yet, those who weathered the challenges achieved satisfaction. After one or more years of studying in a yeshivah abroad, no one returned to America quite the same as he had left.

IN THE NEW JERSEY HARBOR, THE *R.M.L MAJESTIC AQUITANIA* AWAITED its passengers. Among the passengers were Rebbetzin Pelta Bender and Dovid and two of Dovid's good friends, Avrohom Pincus and Harry Horowitz. The four travelers had purchased their tickets through the White Star Line, a reputable shipping company.

For the next six days, the *R.M.L Majestic Aquitania* would be home: a home without the comforts of home. The berths were small and cramped, with hard beds. The ship claimed to have a kosher kitchen with a *mashgiach*, but the Benders and friends were skeptical about the level of kashrus. So they ate bread and sardines, potatoes cooked in their own separate pot, hard-boiled eggs, tea, and fruit. However, as one *bochur* ruefully commented, the same menu three times a day, six times a week, does not taste as good as it reads.[6]

On Friday, Erev Shabbos, the ship docked in Cherbourg, France, a short train ride from Paris where the shipping company had made hotel arrange-

---

4. Dovid was different than the other American boys since he came with his mother and thus would not have to fend for himself.

5. Rabbi Shmuel Scheinberg, the brother of Rabbi Chaim Scheinberg, was only 13½ when he went to Mir (*All for the Boss*, p. 289).

6. Gordon, p. 3. Reiterated by Rabbi Avrohom Pincus.

*This is a postcard from the ocean liner that the Benders and their friends traveled on from America to Europe*

ments. After Shabbos in the hotel, they would continue their journey.

The hotel was a typical gentile establishment; kosher food was not on the menu. There were still a few hours until Shabbos and despite being tired from the journey, the foursome — Rebbetzin Bender, Dovid, Avrohom, and Harry — headed to town to find food for Shabbos. After filling their bags with long rolls of kosher French bread, sardines, eggs, and a wide array of fruits and vegetables, they happily headed back to the hotel. Although buying food seemed simple enough, getting back to the hotel was a different matter. After turning one corner, and then another, and finally a third, the consensus was that they were lost.

"Don't worry," Avrohom Pincus reassured his friends. "I took French in high school. Let me try and get directions."

Armed with two years of high-school French, Avrohom confidently approached a stranger on the street. With a friendly smile, he struck up a conversation, carefully enunciating the words he had learned in French class. The Frenchman stared blankly with no sign of comprehending what was being said. He seemed to think that whatever language Avrohom was speaking, it could not possibly be French. The *bochur* tried again, punctuating his words with grand motions. The Frenchman merely waved him aside and walked away.[7] The forlorn group had made no progress.

---

7. Many years later, when Rabbi Dovid Bender's daughter Esther entered high school, Rebbetzin (Basya) Bender wanted her to study on the academic track; Esther preferred the clerical track. They turned to Reb Dovid for his opinion. "Academic? What will you learn in academic —

Although they did not know the exact time of sunset and the onset of Shabbos, the purplish-gray sky signaled its imminent arrival. The unanimous decision was to leave their bags of food behind a tree rather than to continue carrying and possibly desecrate the Shabbos. They planned to return on Shabbos and eat right there.

Still searching for their hotel, they continued walking, when suddenly, there it was. The hotel was directly across the street from the tree. Had they not been so anxious about sunset they would have laughed out loud. However, just then, they were focused only on one thought: Shabbos. Deciding that it was too late to carry their purchases, they left their food behind the tree and proceeded to the hotel.

They dressed for Shabbos and davened in their rooms. After davening, Rebbetzin Bender, Dovid, Avrohom, and Harry made a beeline for the tree, joking about their picnic under the stars. They found the site immediately, but where was their food? They looked miserably at one another. A long, hungry Shabbos loomed ahead.

Early the next morning, the group started out again. This time they were in search of a shul. Perhaps if they found a shul, someone would notice four lonely strangers and invite them for a meal. They went down one street and then another. Then one of the boys noticed a man with a long beard … and just beyond him was a shul.

Happily, they made their way inside. While the boys took their places alongside the men, Rebbetzin Bender headed for the women's section. After davening, there was a shul-sponsored *kiddush* which the Benders and their friends eagerly and hungrily enjoyed. After eating enough to satisfy some of their hunger, but not too much to appear gluttonous, they stood at the side, waiting expectantly. Surely, someone would notice a lonely group of strangers. As the room slowly emptied, the boys tried not to look too anxious. Maybe that person over there would invite them, or him, or …. Rebbetzin Bender, Dovid, Avrohom, and Harry were dismayed to find that they were the only ones left in the room.

"Let's try to find the Rav of the city. I heard his name is Rabbi Herzog and he lives in the *Pletzel*."

"In the what?"

"The *Pletzel* is what they call the Jewish Quarter. Hopefully, the Rav will be able to help us."

The group cautiously but optimistically left the shul. They approached

---

French? You want her to know French? What for? When my friends and I were lost in France, we tried using our high-school French; it was useless. They did not understand one word. For that she needs French?" To Rebbetzin Bender's chagrin, Esther enrolled in the clerical track (Rebbetzin E. Epstein).

strangers in the street. *"Pletzel?"* they asked, and then walked in the direction of the pointed finger. They continued walking and asking, *"Pletzel? Pletzel?"* With each wave of a hand, they found themselves down another street or alley. Finally, they found the Jewish Quarter and the Rav's house.

They were warmly welcomed by the Rav, Rabbi Yoel Leib Herzog, and his son, Rabbi Isaac Herzog, then Rav of Dublin,[8] who was in France visiting his parents. The elder Rabbi Herzog sat them around his table and asked them what brought them to France. As they told their exciting saga, the Rebbetzin realized that the group had not eaten a decent meal in quite some time. She excused herself and immediately returned with a complete Shabbos meal. The famished Americans gratefully eyed the food and, with minimal urgings, accepted the generous portions: their first real meal in days.

Years later, more than the memory of the food remained; it was the warmth of the Rav and Rebbetzin, the feeling that they were being welcomed as long-lost cherished relatives, and the relief of not being abandoned that they would always remember. The ordeal of the previous 24 hours taught them how truly alone and forlorn one could feel, even when surrounded by people. Only among family — and all Torah *Yidden* are family — can one feel at home.

AFTER SHABBOS, THE FOURSOME BOARDED A TRAIN TO POLAND. DURing the three-day trip, they traveled through four countries: France, Belgium, Germany, and Poland. The train made various stops and others boarded and disembarked, but the American travelers stayed put.

Wealthy patrons who paid to travel Pullman class reserved beds and meals. Everyone else slept and ate in their seats. However, when the Benders and company bought their tickets from White Star, they requested and paid extra for meals on the train. Therefore, they were able to enjoy fruits and vegetables, sardines, and other kosher food in the train's dining car.

As the train sped through Poland, the American passengers peered curiously through the window. Poland's wide flat plains were speckled with numerous tiny towns and insignificant hamlets. Each town and hamlet looked similar: fifty or sixty small bungalowlike houses clumped together, a church somewhere in the middle, and forests. On the outskirts of the town, there were usually some grazing cows, goats, and sheep, and sometimes pigs. Here and there, there was an ancient castle in the background, a reminder that Poland would always be a great deal older than youthful America.

---

8. See Biography Section.

*Rabbi Elchonon Wasserman (1875- 1941) was the prime disciple of the Chofetz Chaim. He was also a close disciple of Rabbi Shimon Shkop of Telshe and had spent two years studying under Rabbi Chaim Soloveitchik. By 1929 he was distinguished not only as the head of the yeshivah in Baranovich, but as a teacher of the generation and an illustrious leader of the Jewish world.*

HARRY HOROWITZ DISEMBARKED at an earlier stop. He was en route to Baranovich to study under the famed Rabbi Elchonon Wasserman. Harry was from Pittsburgh, Pennsylvania and had never formally attended yeshivah before. He would make up lost ground in Baranovich where the *bochurim* were young, before going on to Mir, a yeshivah with older *bochurim* and a more advanced learning level.

The others continued on to Horodzei, the train station closest to Mir. They arrived there in the evening and spent the night in a hotel. The next day they rode by *fuhr* — horse and buggy — into the famed city of Mir.

Mir was larger than a village, but much smaller than a city. Mir could best be described as a small town. Unlike the typical tiny Polish village, Mir boasted of two-story buildings, two windmills, and even electricity. Including the gentiles who lived on the outskirts of the town, Mir certainly had a few thousand residents, among them several hundred Jewish families.

Yet, coming from any major American city, Mir was tiny. The entire city could fit into a few New York city blocks. To walk from one end of the city to the other took 10 minutes or less. The smallness made the town seem quaint. Mir was a novelty. For the young, eager *bochurim* everything was different from what they were used to: the houses, the beds, the stoves, the heating system, the (lack of) plumbing, etc. Fresh from the States, where running water and indoor plumbing were considered necessities, the American *bochurim* had to make many adjustments. For example, electricity was only available between 8:30 p.m. and 1 a.m. The houses had neither running water nor modern bathroom facilities. Boys observed, discussed, *kvetched*, laughed, and adjusted.

The Mirrer Yeshivah was renowned for having the largest and most varied group of international *bochurim*. There were boys from Belgium, France, Germany, Switzerland, Sweden, England, Ireland, and America. The boys

**… Unlike the typical tiny Polish village, Mir boasted of two-story buildings, two windmills, and even electricity …**

*The town of Mir: note the two-story building in the foreground and the one-story residential houses in the back.*

*A different view of Mir: note the castle of the poritz looming high in the background.*

who came from afar were very different from their Eastern European counterparts. They were also very different from one another. Learning in the Mir involved making adjustments, and not just to the lack of physical amenities. The international *bochurim* knew they were coming to a place where the level of learning was way beyond what they had known in their home countries. They would have to struggle to keep up and, concurrently, they would have to get used to living with *Yidden* who were culturally very different. The cultural differences and the need to broaden their mentality could best be described by one boy's initial reception upon arriving in the Mir. This *bochur* was introduced to a Polish boy who was given instructions to show him around.

*A typical home in Mir. As Yud'l Gordon described in a letter home, "… the buildings are no larger than bungalows. A cellar, a ground floor, and a bit of an attic is the general rule. These wooden structures of unformed logs bring reminiscences of Lincoln's log cabin …"*

*The Mirrer
Yeshivah
in Poland*

*Mir had a large
international contin-
gency. Pictured here
are students of the
Mir Yeshivah, at the
stanza of Etka Miranka.
(Miranka was not her
last name, but the name
of the street where she
lived.)
Seated from left to
right: Avrohom Pincus
(American), Alex Weis-
fogel (English), Theodore
Lewis (Irish), and Avro-
hom Orlan (Polish)*

"Where will I sleep?" the newcomer asked innocently.

"Did you come here to sleep?" was the obscure answer.

"Where will I eat?" he pressed on.

"Did you come here to eat?" was the response.

Mystified, the American *bochur* allowed himself to be shown around, to the house where he was given a bed, to the *stanza*[9] where he was given a meal, and finally to the yeshivah, where he was given life.

As he allowed himself to be led from place to place, understanding dawned. No, he had not come to the Mir to eat or sleep. He had come for one purpose: to merit a taste of the sweet words of Torah as taught in a European yeshivah.

---

9. *Stanza* referred to the eating stations where *bochurim* took their meals.

*Chapter Five*

# Becoming "Ah Mirrer"

**Mir: 5693 (1933)**

OVID BENDER ALWAYS LOOKED BACK AT HIS YEARS IN MIR AS the years that molded him into the person he became. His connection to his rebbi, Rabbi Dovid Leibowitz of Torah Vodaath, remained strong, so much so that the first piece of *Torah* that he wrote in the Mir[10] he sent to Reb Dovid. Nonetheless, he absorbed so much Torah and *mussar* in Mir that he would forever consider himself *"ah Mirrer."*

THEY ARRIVED IN ELUL, THE BEGINNING OF A NEW *Z'MAN*. GONE WAS the easygoing vacation atmosphere, the normal lingering of summer, that they had left in America. *Bochurim* walked briskly between the yeshivah and the homes where they boarded, their brows furrowed, their faces earnest, as if something ominous was impending.

---

10. The letter that Rabbi Dovid Bender sent to Rabbi Dovid Leibowitz began, "I promised you, Rebbi, that the first *shtickel Torah* I create, I will send to you. Here are the fruits of my labor ..." This might have remained unknown if not for a fortuitous incident: Rabbi Avrohom Pernikoff (1916-1986) had been a *maggid shiur* for many years in Yeshivas Chofetz Chaim of Queens. After his heart attack, he could no longer give *shiur*. The yeshivah asked him to go through Rabbi Dovid Leibowitz's correspondence. Among the piles of letters and *divrei Torah*, he found the piece of *Torah* that Rabbi Dovid Bender wrote to his rebbi. Rabbi Pernikoff insisted on personally delivering the letter to his nephew, then learning in *kollel*, so that his nephew would not have to waste time from learning to get it (Rabbi Yaakov Bender).

*Rabbi Yeruchem Levovitz (1875-1936), reverently referred to as "Reb Yeruchem," was the legendary Mashgiach of Mir. He was a close talmid of the Alter of Slabodka and also learned in the yeshivos of Kelm and Radin. He served as Mashgiach in Radin and Mir and was renowned as an outstanding Mashgiach in the yeshivah world of Lithuania.*

Two days later, Dovid and his friend Avrohom already felt at home in the big Mirrer *beis medrash*. They were prepared for, and looked forward to, the subdued solemnity that permeated the room. There was no talking, no joking, and no easy banter. Everyone was focused on their davening: *Bircas HaShachar, Korbanos, Pesukei d'Zimrah, Shema* … Each *tefillah* thrust them higher and higher. By the time they reached *Shemoneh Esrei*, even the newcomers were completely immersed in conversation with the Master of the Universe. *Chazaras HaShatz* ended, and the crowd waited for the *chazzan* to continue. Moments passed. No one moved. Everyone seemed to be waiting for something. Silence reigned.

Suddenly, all those present surged forward. *Bochurim* pushed themselves past chairs and *shtenders*. By now, Dovid and Avrohom found themselves facing a wall of backs, their vision totally obscured. They looked at each other, utterly bewildered. Cautiously following the crowd, they moved in closer until they could peek over the heads of those in front of them.

Somehow, in a matter of minutes, the crowd in the study hall had organized itself into a semicircle. In its center stood the *Mashgiach*, Rabbi Yeruchem Levovitz. His expression was intense, his thoughts unreadable. The study hall grew silent. There was no shuffling of feet, no scraping of *shtenders*, no furtive whispering. Everyone stood absolutely still and silent as each man strained to listen to the words of the saintly *Mashgiach*.

Reb Yeruchem began in a low voice. Even those near him found it difficult to hear. Slowly, his voice rose higher and higher until it thundered throughout the *beis medrash*. His rousing words seared the hearts of his listeners. Who could hear such exhortations and not be moved to become closer to his Maker? Who could walk away from such a talk unaffected? The *shmuess* did not last long, but the impression it made lasted a lifetime.

THE AMERICANS LEFT THE STUDY HALL IN A DAZE. THE *SHMUESS* WAS different than any other they had ever heard. It was penetrating and profound, fervent and fiery. When would the *Mashgiach* speak again? He had not spoken the day before and they did not hear of any announcement that he would be speaking that morning. Had anyone known he was scheduled to speak? Upon inquiring, the *bochurim* discovered that it was clear to everyone — except the "green" Americans — that he was going to speak.

The answer lay in the very persona of the *Mashgiach*. Throughout davening, Reb Yeruchem sat facing east. Only when he spoke to those in the study hall did he turn to face the crowd. When Reb Yeruchem davened, he was completely focused on his dialogue with the Master of the Universe. He never made even the slightest motion to see what was happening behind him. As soon as Reb Yeruchem made the slightest, almost imperceptible movement away from *mizrach* to face the yeshivah, all the students realized he would be speaking, and they clamored to get as close as possible to the *Mashgiach*. The result was a burst of controlled chaos.

Although it would be impossible to stage such an event, it happened spontaneously over and over again,[11] each time because of the unique self-control of the *Mashgiach*. Watching Reb Yeruchem — in the *beis medrash*, in learning, in davening, in everyday life — was a lesson in self–discipline: No action was impulsive, no word was uttered without contemplation, no limb moved without reason. He taught that the true *eved Hashem* is a person whose every step is calculated; nothing is done on a whim, nothing is done randomly without forethought or, Heaven forbid, at the behest of the evil inclination. A person can, if he works hard, totally dedicate himself to the Master of the world. Yet to do so, he must become master of himself, his thoughts, and actions.

MONDAY, THE 16TH OF ELUL, 5693. JUST AFTER *SHACHARIS*, THE *MASH-giach* made his almost-imperceptible move toward the crowd in the study hall. By now, even the raw Americans could sense what was about to occur. They joined the forward rush, the clamor for seats, and the few minutes of controlled chaos. Desperate not to miss one word of the *shmuess*, they craned forward eagerly. The *Mashgiach* spoke about the

---

11. "The first time I experienced this, I did not know what hit me! It was as if, for one minute, the *beis medrash* erupted" (Rabbi Avrohom Pincus).

subject of judges, their role and function, and their importance to *Klal Yis-roel*. His voice rose as he correlated the role of a judge to the role of each person in this world:

> *A judge should always see himself as if there were a sword between his legs and Gehinnom were open beneath him.*[12] *Rabbi Yisroel Salanter*[13] *explained that every person has to be his own judge; that is the role of man, to be his own judge. He is obligated to be careful about every action that he takes. He must weigh every action on a scale; he must measure it as closely as a hairsbreadth. (While judging himself,) he must realize that a sword is poised between his legs and, if he deviates even a hairsbreadth, Gehinnom is open beneath him ready to catch him as he falls.*[14]

Reb Yeruchem minced no words. There is Gan Eden and Gehinnom. Make no mistake; a person must constantly be aware that Gehinnom awaits those who sin. The newcomers to the Mir were taken aback by the strong words, and the lack of sugarcoating that accompanied them. The casual mention of Gehinnom and how it awaits those who sin shocked them out of their complacency. The evil inclination, they learned, surrounds the individual, tricking him, enticing him to follow, leading him away from serving his Creator and into endless darkness. These words, so different and so new, seeped in slowly. In time, they also learned to think this way. They learned to make *mussar* an integral part of their lives.

Rabbi Yeruchem Levovitz was brought to the Mir to introduce *mussar* in a yeshivah whose strength was its *lomdus*. He was handpicked by his rebbi, Rabbi Nosson Tzvi Finkel, the Alter of Slabodka, for this unique role. As the Alter had hoped, Reb Yeruchem transformed the Mirrer Yeshivah into a bastion of *mussar*.

Throughout the year, Reb Yeruchem gave *chaburos* — rousing talks exhorting his students to work on their relationships between themselves and their Creator, between man and his fellowman. These *chaburos* were given twice a week, on Shabbos evening between *Kabbolas Shabbos* and *Ma'ariv*, and *Motza'ei Shabbos* right before *Ma'ariv*. These *shmuessen* lasted about an hour and a half. The *Mashgiach* would discuss one subject for several weeks; at each *shmuess* he discussed different sources and inter-pretations on the topic. During Elul, Reb Yeruchem wanted to inject more

---

12. *Sanhedrin* 7.

13. Rabbi Yisroel Lipkin (1810-1883), known as Rabbi Yisroel Salanter, revolutionized *Klal Yisroel* with the *mussar* movement. He led a yeshivah in Kovno and lectured in Salant and Vilna. His teachings encouraged learning of *mussar*, working on one's character traits, and coming closer to the Almighty through perfecting oneself. Reb Yeruchem's teachings were heavily based on those of Reb Yisroel Salanter.

14. *Parashas Ki Savo — Tes Zayin* Elul, 5693/1933 (*Da'as Torah* ).

*Rabbi Nosson Tzvi Finkel (1849 –1927), known as the Alter of Slabodka, was a close talmid of the Alter of Kelm, Rabbi Simcha Zissel Ziv. Reb Nosson Tzvi founded the Slabodka Yeshivah in 1884, serving as its Rosh Yeshivah. He later traveled to Eretz Yisroel and established a branch of his yeshivah there. His talmidim developed into great rabbanim and roshei yeshivah who perpetuated his teachings.*

*mussar* into the daily lives of the *bochurim*. Several times a week right after *Shacharis*, at the start of their day, he would give short spontaneous *shmuessen*. No one was told in advance whether there would be a *shmuess* or not. The fervor generated by these spontaneous *shmuessen* was part of the unique Elul atmosphere in Mir.

ELUL IN MIR WAS LEGENDARY. FORMER STUDENTS, WORTHY ROSHEI yeshivos and rabbanim, returned to the Mir for Elul.[15] *Bochurim* who had never learned in the Mir, but merely heard about the experience,[16] came to

---

15. "Everyone knew that Elul in Mir was special. My uncle, Rabbi Meir Epstein, had been a *talmid* in Radin when Rabbi Yeruchem Levovitz was *Mashgiach*. Later, when Reb Meir became a Rav in Bakst, he would leave his town for Elul to return to join Reb Yeruchem in Mir. He was one of many" (Rabbi Henoch Cohen).

16. "My brother-in-law was learning in Kaminetz. He came to Mir from Elul until after Yom Kippur. Many *bochurim* did the same" (R' Elchonon [Heiry] Ehrlanger).

spend Elul in the Mir. There were those who could not come for such an extended period, and came only for the *Yamim Nora'im*. They all wanted to be in the Mir for as many of the Days of Judgment as possible.

During Elul, the *Mashgiach* spoke four or five times a week: the usual two and an additional two or three times immediately after *Shacharis*. The entire month of Elul, from the very first moment, was a preparation for the Day of Judgment. The Day of Judgment itself was something that words cannot describe.[17]

The first *Borchu* of Rosh Hashanah was thunderous. In unison, the assemblage affirmed its commitment to the Holy One, Blessed is He. In unison, they declared Him blessed forever and ever. In unison, they accepted His yoke upon them.

Contrary to the custom all year, every prayer, every *Shemoneh Esrei*, was said aloud. With intense concentration, enunciated with tears of anguish, agonized calls for mercy and kindness echoed through the study hall. The voices of the crowd drowned out that of the *chazzan*.

Rosh Hashanah davening took many hours. After *Shacharis* and *Mussaf*, the *bochurim* ran home for a quick meal. Then they would rush back to the yeshivah to daven *Minchah*. The day was short and there was so much to be done.

The *Yamim Nora'im* were the culmination of weeks of prayer, *mussar*, and introspection. By *Ne'ilah* of Yom Kippur, the supplicants were physically and emotionally exhausted, but on a spiritual summit, nonetheless. Although they were tired and hungry, they did not want their ascent to end. As the sun set and the sky darkened, the *ba'alei battim* of the city finished *Ne'ilah*, left their shuls, and hastened home to break their fasts, but the *bochurim* stayed rooted to their posts, still crying, davening, and begging *HaKadosh Baruch Hu* for a new year of opportunity to serve Him. They were soon joined by the *ba'alei battim* of the city, who came to watch them after breaking their fast, in awe of the spiritual level these young men had attained.

Through the cramped rows of young men, a solitary figure wove his way, walking carefully and purposefully, from seat to seat, scrutinizing each *bochur*. He motioned to Chaimke, a young *bochur* who looked frail and weak, to leave the *beis medrash* and proceed to his house where his rebbetzin would give him food. He continued down the rows, oblivious to the unusually charged atmosphere, observing and assessing each *bochur*, to determine if the *bochur*, by continuing his fast, was pushing himself too far.

Who was this unobtrusive individual who, at this moment of spiri-

---

17. Most of the description of Elul in Mir is based on the 2001 interview with Rabbi Avrohom Pincus. Even as he described his experience, he repeated a number of times that Elul in Mir was beyond description.

*Rabbi Eliezer Yehudah Finkel (1878-1965), fondly called Reb Leizer Yud'l, was the son of the Alter of Slabodka. He learned under his father and then studied under the roshei yeshivah of Telshe, Brisk, and Kamenitz. Reb Lezer Yud'l came to Mir upon his marriage to the daughter of the Mirrer Rav, Rabbi Eliyahu Boruch Kammai. By 1907 he was recognized as his heir. During World War II, Rabbi Finkel escaped to Eretz Yisroel, where he founded the Mirrer Yeshivah in Jerusalem.*

tual peak, was so concerned with the physical health of his *bochurim*? It was their revered Rosh Yeshivah, Rabbi Leizer Yud'l Finkel. Twenty-four hours of fasting, crying, and davening were both physically and emotionally taxing. Nonetheless, Reb Leizer Yud'l did not want to break the spell, the electricity in the air, by speeding up the very last prayer of the holy day. After all, *Ne'ilah*, when the gates of Heaven close, is our last chance to beseech our Creator. Yet, this final salvo must not be at the expense of the frail and weak. Thus, Reb Leizer Yud'l disregarded his personal needs, his desire to concentrate solely on his davening, his connection to *HaKadosh Baruch Hu*. Instead he continued through the rows of *bochurim* and *yungeleit*, scrutinizing face after face, ensuring that no one was fasting beyond his limits.[18]

In his letter to his good friend Barney Belsky,[19] Dovid Bender relates the invaluable spiritual experience of the *Yamim Nora'im* in the Mir.

*Dear Barney,*
*... With much sorrow, I read that G-d willing at the end of the summer, you expect to go back to the States. Naturally, I do not know what made you decide on leaving so early, but it was somewhat of a surprise to me. Still greater was my sur-*

18. Remembering this practice of Reb Leizer Yud'l, Rabbi Avrohom Pincus commented that the *bochur* sent to break his fast would find it embarrassing and would often protest. Perhaps, the reason Reb Leizer Yud'l personally surveyed the *beis medrash* was because if he, the Rosh Yeshivah, insisted that the *bochur* break his fast, the boy would obey. No messenger would have been as effective. Rabbi Avrohom Pincus also mentioned that Reb Leizer Yud'l's father, the Alter of Slabodka, had the same practice.

19. Rabbi Berel "Barney" Belsky was learning in Radin at the time. See Biography Section.

prise that you expect to leave before Elul. After experiencing the Yamim Nora'im here in the Mir, I am positive that if I were in the States and I had enough money, I would come to the Mir for the Yamim Nora'im. How much more so, if I were in Europe; I would not leave the Mir before the High Holy Days … During the month of Elul until after Yom Kippur, I gained tremendously in ruchniyus … Rabbanim and lamdanim from all parts of Poland come here for the Yamim Nora'im. Besides the 450 yeshivah bochurim (of the Mirrer Yeshivah), you have over 100 guests: former yeshivah bochurim and lamdanim of this generation. Imagine! The davening of Rosh Hashanah lasts from 6:30 a.m. until after 3:30 p.m. — with no piyutim, and no chazzanus. The "shtille" Shemoneh Esrei lasts over a full hour. Fellows from Kaminetz, Grodno, and other yeshivos come to the Mir for Yamim Nora'im, and they all say it is "gevaldig." I can't see how (you can) leave Europe before Elul and not come here to the Mir and spend the holidays. Think it over. You will never regret it.

From your friend, Dovid, waiting to see you, G-d willing, with us here in the Mir.

The Days of Judgment in the Mir were on a different plane. It was understood that the efforts expended working on oneself during Elul had to continue. The heights reached at *Ne'ilah* were not a peak to jump down from, but rather signaled the potential to go higher, on to Succos, Chol HaMoed, and Simchas Torah. The intense spiritual atmosphere continued through Succos, where the spiritual heights were transformed into profound joy and happiness, not a light-headed joy, but a happiness at the core of which is closeness to the *Ribbono shel Olam*.

Many of the *bochurim* in the Mir were very poor. Few, if any — even those who lived in the vicinity — went home for Succos, or for any of the other holidays. There were two sets of *arba'ah minim* for the entire yeshivah: one for the Rosh Yeshivah and one for the *Mashgiach*. The *bochurim* stood on a very long line, and one by one were given a chance to hold the *arba'ah minim*, make the *berachah*, and make one movement. Although this was very time consuming, there were no complaints, only anticipation for the opportunity to fulfill this mitzvah with love.

The Simchas Torah dancing was otherworldly, a reflection of the bond the students had formed with their Maker throughout Elul and Tishrei. Finally, it was time to return the *sifrei Torah* to the *aron kodesh*:

Uplifting words said with tremendous fervor and joyous song accompanied the sifrei Torah to the aron kodesh. Each Torah thought was followed by a round of "Ashreichem Yisroel." Reb Yeruchem was on the bimah, his hands outstretched to the sky. The students were crowded below, dancing in front of him. When he finished speaking, Reb Yeruchem came down from the bimah dancing. The tremendous feelings of holiness brought tears to the eyes of all those present. How

*wondrous the sight! Hundreds of students, among them Gedolei Olam, were danc-*
*ing with tears and song … Reb Yeruchem himself once said, "Ich veis nisht vos iz*
*hecher baym Borei Oilam, der Yom Kippur unzereh, tzu der Simchas Toirah — I*
*don't know what is holier to the Creator of the World, our Yom Kippur or our*
*Simchas Torah!"*[20]

DURING SUMMER *BEIN HAZ'MANIM,* SOME OF THE MIRRER *BOCHURIM*
went on *dacha* — vacation. There were several popular vacation spots: Maitzek, Nowohjelna, and Druzgenyk.[21] Dovid and his mother usually went
on *dacha*, sometimes to Nowohjelna and other times to Druzgenyk. Dovid
looked forward to these weeks because aside from the rest and relaxation
they afforded, they presented him with opportunities to meet some of the
greatest contemporary Torah personalities. Dovid always looked for opportunities to meet *gedolim* personally, to observe them, to hear their words of
Torah, and to learn from their actions. He looked forward to *bein haz'manim*
for he knew that although he would not be in yeshivah, he would still be
growing spiritually. One thing *"ah Mirrer"* absorbed in the Mir was the
idea that spiritual growth is not confined to a specific time or place. One
must spend one's entire life attuned to *HaKadosh Baruch Hu.*

Some of the roshei yeshivah of the Mirrer Yeshivah also went on *dacha*. On
the day that Reb Leizer Yud'l left, all the *bochurim* escorted him out of their
city, with love, awe, and respect obvious in their actions and on their faces.

The first time Dovid Bender went on *dacha*, he saw Rabbi Boruch Ber
Leibowitz, the Rosh Yeshivah of Yeshivas Kenesess Bais Yitzchok of
Kaminetz, lying in a hammock. Dovid was agape; here was Reb Boruch
Ber — *the* Reb Boruch Ber — on *dacha*! In a hammock! What was even more
astounding was that no one considered the sight unusual. Dovid spotted
a photographer, a common figure at these resorts since many vacationers
wanted mementos of their vacation. Dovid approached him and asked,
"Do you see that man over there? I will pay you five American dollars to
take his picture." Money was exchanged, and the picture was taken. Dovid
repeated this transaction several times, eagerly collecting pictures of the
*gedolim* of Europe. He finished his vacation with little money left, but he
felt very rich.

Dovid looked back on his vacations in Mir with nostalgia and reminisced about the *gedolim* he saw, and how their actions on vacation showed
him how a *ben Torah* should live.

---

20. Rabbi Shlomo Wolbe — *Kuntrus HaAdam Bikor*, p. 27.

21. Druzgenyk was a health spa with therapeutic baths and treatments and was far more expensive than Maitzek and Nowohjelna. In addition, the train fare was also more costly. Roshei
yeshivos and rabbanim (some of whom were older people with health problems) often went
to Druzgenyk while most of the Mirrer boys opted for Maitzek or Nowohjelna (Rebbetzin Z.
Ginsburg).

**Two of the pictures Dovid Bender collected while on vacation. In photo at right, Rabbi Boruch Ber Leibowitz is surrounded by *talmidim*. Dovid Bender is standing to the left.**

*Rabbi Boruch Ber Leibowitz (1863-1939) entered Yeshivas Volozhin when only 16, and became the foremost disciple of Reb Chaim Brisker. In 1903 he became Rav in Halusk and later succeeded his father-in-law in Karmentzug. He headed Yeshivas Kenesess Bais Yitzchok of Kaminetz until World War I and reestablished it after the war. At the onset of World War II, he and the yeshivah escaped to Vilna. Reb Boruch Ber passed away shortly thereafter.*

THE MIRRER ROSH YESHIVAH WAS BOTH REVERED AND BELOVED BY THE *bochurim*. Their reverence stemmed from the realization that, under his tenure, Reb Leizer Yud'l had raised the standard of learning in the Mir to surpass that of almost any other yeshivah in Europe at the time. This was a direct result of Reb Leizer Yud'l's intense love for Torah and legendary diligence in learning. Reb Leizer Yud'l encouraged his students to approach him at any hour of the day, even at home, to tell him a *chiddush* in their learning, something they had worked on, that would meet his exacting standards and critical mind. He created a spirit within the yeshivah that fostered a healthy competition, a drive among the *bochurim* to master as much knowledge as possible.

Reb Leizer Yud'l was beloved because of his love for others, his warmth, and self-effacing humility. For example, he never took an *aliyah* to the Torah on the *Yamim Nora'im*, a privilege most people would not refuse. He refused because Rosh Hashanah is the awesome Day of Judgment. A person should hide his head in shame when coming to be judged, and not be called up with honorific titles — *Moreinu, Rabbeinu* … The Rosh Yeshivah refused. "I want to remain in hiding," he would say. "I am afraid of the Judgment! When they call out *"Moreinu, Rabbeinu,"* the *Ribbono shel Olam* will look at me: '*Moreinu? Rabbeinu?* You?' I would rather stay in hiding!"[22]

The relationship between the Mirrer Rosh Yeshivah, Reb Leizer Yud'l, and the Mirrer *Mashgiach*, Reb Yeruchem, was extraordinary. Although Reb Leizer Yud'l was a formidable *talmid chacham* and *ba'al mussar* and although he was the Rosh Yeshivah, Reb Leizer Yud'l respectfully deferred to the *Mashgiach* and allowed him to lead. Indeed, the *Mashgiach* led; he led with his mind, with his heart, and with his whole being.

"*… His was the heart that beat in the Mirrer Yeshivah. Not only was he the power that led, that commanded, that advised. No, he was not an outsider who was interested, a friend who cared. The yeshivah became so much a part of him that it was rather as one who is devoted to himself, who is interested in himself… Any sickness in its smallest form was immediately felt by him — for the entire yeshivah was merely shessah giddin[23] — which were contained in his person …*"[24]

The *Mashgiach* forged the personality of the Mir. It was his rousing *shmuessen*, his private exhortations, his constant encouragement that pushed the students to examine themselves continuously and work on their own levels of *avodas Hashem*. Dovid concentrated on his message and allowed it to penetrate his being.[25]

REB YERUCHEM WAS LIKE A FATHER TO HIS STUDENTS — AN EXACTING father, a demanding father, a loving father. As such, on the one hand, his students feared his rebuke and strove to become what he expected of them; on the other hand, they were confident in his love and approached him regarding mundane matters as well.

When Dovid had a question about his mother's passport, he went to discuss it with Reb Yeruchem. Reb Yeruchem was in his usual place in the *beis medrash* right next to the *bimah*. Dovid went over to him with the passport. Reb Yeruchem listened intently and examined the document. "Presumably this only applies to your mother's passport, not yours …"

"Why?" asked Dovid.

"… because you were born in America."

"No, I was born in Europe."

---

22. This was also the practice of his father, the Alter of Slabodka (Rabbi Avrohom Pincus).

23. *Shessah giddin* refers to the 365 sinews and blood vessels that, together with 248 organs and limbs, make up a person.

24. Gordon, p. 47.

25. From two of Reb Dovid's *talmidim* in Torah Vodaath: "Reb Yeruchem was Reb Dovid's idol," recalled Rabbi Hershel Mashinsky. "Reb Dovid was always quoting his rebbi, Reb Yeruchem," Rabbi Yonason Shapiro commented.

> "... His was the heart that beat in the Mirrer yeshivah ... Any sickness in its smallest form was immediately felt by him — for the entire yeshivah was merely *shessah giddin* [sinews and blood vessels] which were contained in his person ..."

*Reb Yeruchem walking with talmidim. From left to right: Rabbi Peretz Yogel, Reb Yeruchem, Moshe Leib Levovitz (son of Reb Yeruchem), and Rabbi Yaakov Sender (Rav of Maitsch)*

"*Takeh!*" Reb Yeruchem's face lit up with excitement. He clasped hold of Dovid's hand and rose to his feet. "*Horaso v'leidaso b'kedushah*,"[26] the *Mashgiach* exclaimed joyfully. Dovid was amazed at the *Mashgiach's* reaction, which reminded Dovid of a father's reaction upon hearing good news about his child. The warmth of that moment would always remain with Dovid.

The relationships Reb Yeruchem developed with his students began from their very first encounter. Every *bochur* who entered the yeshivah had to meet with Reb Yeruchem. He would use the opportunity to understand the *bochur*, size him up, assess his specific needs, and determine how he would most benefit from the Mir. The Mir's large international contingency meant that it had a variety of ingrained mentalities and personalities. Only Reb Yeruchem, with his unusually perceptive understanding of human nature, could relate to all the *bochurim*, despite their differences in culture and background.

One day, Max Segal, an Irish boy, brought two new British arrivals, Alex Weisfogel and Yankel Goldman, to see Reb Yeruchem. Although they both hailed from London, they were very different from each other. Reb Yeruchem welcomed them warmly and inquired about their trip to Poland.

---

26. Based on *Bava Basra* 149a. Literally, "conceived and born in purity." Reb Yeruchem and many of the other Torah personalities of their day considered America a "*treifene medinah*," a country where Jews had abandoned Torah and mitzvos, a country that, despite the millions of Jews who had been living there for decades, failed to produce European-caliber *gedolim*. Poland/ Lithuania, on the other hand, was a bastion of learning, home to some of the greatest *gedolim* for several centuries, truly a place of *kedushah*. To Reb Yeruchem, hearing that his beloved student merited to have been born in Lithuania was an occasion to rejoice.

The *Mashgiach* wanted them to compare the journey through Germany to the journey through Poland: what their impressions were and what they had seen along the way. After they had spoken for half an hour, Reb Yeruchem set them up with *chavrusos*. Only later did the boys understand what had actually occurred. Reb Yeruchem knew the differences between Germany and Poland and the sites along the way. He used this conversation to understand the two *bochurim*. Based on what each noticed and how they processed what they saw, he was able to gain insight about their personalities. After a half-hour conversation, he understood them well enough to arrange *chavrusos* that suited each *bochur* perfectly. That was Reb Yeruchem.

Isolated incidents fail to transmit the exceptional bond between Reb Yeruchem and his students and how, in turn, they revered the *Mashgiach*. They were in awe of his giant personality, afraid of his penetrating *mussar*, and warmed by the knowledge that he truly cared for them. Even one *shmuess* was enough to permanently affect a person's life. Throughout his years in the Mir, Dovid heard hundreds of *shmuessen* and indeed became a different person. For the rest of his life, he would quote his beloved *Mashgiach* and repeat the *mussar* he had learned from him.

Dovid was merely one of the hundreds of *talmidim* who was profoundly affected by the *Mashgiach*. Reb Yeruchem was the yeshivah and the yeshivah was Reb Yeruchem. And when Reb Yeruchem became ill, the entire yeshivah was distraught.

The doctors recommended that the *Mashgiach* travel to Vilna for treatments. Reb Yeruchem did not stay long in Vilna. The treatments seemed not to be helping, and the *Mashgiach* felt he was wasting his time. "Why should I stay? My health is not improving. It would be better for me to be near the yeshivah and say *inyanim*."[27] So Reb Yeruchem returned to the Mir, as was his wish, and he continued to speak to the *bochurim*. However, the illness continued to drain his strength. One Shabbos he told those around him, "The doctors say that it is nothing, but I feel that I am not well. Soon I will no longer be able to lead the yeshivah. I believe the older students, who have heard the *inyanim,* will be influenced by them for another three years. I will ask them to influence the younger students who have not yet heard them. This way they should be able to continue the spirit of the yeshivah."

Doctors were consulted; the prognosis was grim. Yud'l Gordon, then learning in the Mir, wrote to his brother about those difficult days:[28]

*The Mashgiach started to show signs of recovery. Bochurim took shifts of half a day sitting at his bedside. He was under doctor's orders to lie in bed and not to move for three weeks. On Thursday, bochurim reported that his heart was*

---

27. Literally, "topics." This was how Reb Yeruchem referred to his *shmuessen*.
28. Gordon, pp. 43-46.

*very weak. A professor from Vilna was brought in and another important doctor arrived by airplane from Leipzig on Friday morning. Telegrams were sent to all the yeshivos, and the Mir waged war. Day and night, two shifts said Tehillim continuously.*

*The doctor from Leipzig wore a yarmulke and prayed three times a day. With unbelievable dedication, the doctor put up a strong fight and did not leave Reb Yeruchem's bedside. The doctor slept in the house and commanded the bochurim that the morning shift should wake him. He trusted no one. He himself cooked food for and fed Reb Yeruchem.*

*They tell of a mofes, a wonder. On Sunday, the Mashgiach was unconscious of his surroundings. The doctor from Leipzig boiled a chicken, which was ritually slaughtered, but the doctor did not permit it to be salted.[29] The doctor cooked soup from the chicken and brought it to Reb Yeruchem's bedside. The Mashgiach pushed it aside saying, "Give it to the goya." The Rosh Yeshivah [sic] relates a similar story about Reb Yosha Ber.[30] Once when Reb Yosha Ber was traveling with someone, the fellow traveler opened his valise and took out a chicken. Reb Yosha Ber pushed it aside and did not allow him to eat it. A little while later, a telegram arrived stating that, by mistake, the chicken in his valise was treif. When Reb Yosha Ber was asked to explain why he had not allowed the person to eat the chicken, he answered, "It is not ruach hakodesh; it is zakus hanefesh — purity of the soul."[31]*

*Dovid Bender told me that a week or so before the catastrophe the Mashgiach told his rebbetzin, "Before I got sick, I often dreamt of a sickness; however, on the morrow, I would dream I would be well. Lately, I had the terrible sickness dream, but the second dream did not follow."*

*Monday was bad. The administration of the yeshivah declared a fast with more and louder Tehillim. The boys mustered their strength and demanded of the Yeshivah Shel Ma'alah that the Mashgiach be left there with them.*

*The doctor took drastic action: A 500-gram blood transfusion taken from two boys[32] was administered. At 2 p.m. on Monday afternoon, in the midst of the blood transfusion, the Mirrer Yeshivah let out a cry that was heard from one end of*

---

29. A ritually slaughtered chicken is not considered kosher unless properly salted.

30. Referring to Rabbi Yosef Dov Soloveitchik (1820-1892), known by the title of his famous sefer, *Sha'aylos U'Teshuvos Bais HaLevi*. When he was only 10 years old, young Yoshe Ber came to Volozhin Yeshivah to learn by his great-uncle, Reb Itzeleh Volozhiner, and in 1853 was appointed Rosh Yeshivah. In 1864, upon the recommendation of Rabbi Yitzchok Elchonon Spector, he was appointed Rav of Slutzk, one of the most prominent Rabbinical positions of the time. In 1879 he replaced Rabbi Yehoshua Leib Diskin (1816-1898) as Rav of Brisk, a position he held for the rest of his life.

31. Meaning, he did not stop the other person from eating because he had a prophetic vision. Rather, in his purity he sensed that something was wrong with the chicken.

32. Reb Yeruchem had the rarest blood type: type O. Theodore Lewis, a new arrival at the yeshivah at the time, also had type O blood. Seventy years later, Rabbi Theodore Lewis recalled with pride how privileged he felt when his blood was used for one of these transfusions.

the world to the other. The Yeshivah Shel Ma'alah had demanded Reb Yeruchem.

In the Mir, you see desolation. The boys walk the streets as if in a dream. They stop, look around as if they are searching for something or someone, and resume their slow, painstaking walk. Everyone's eyes are swollen, cheeks sunken in, and it seems as if their minds are elsewhere. They keep asking, "What will be?" To everyone in the Mir it seems that the earth has disappeared from underfoot, and they are left in midair.

There was a din Torah between the yeshivah people and the chevra kaddisha about who should have the honor of doing the taharah. Of course, the yeshivah people

Reb Yeruchem is leaving for Marienbad, a famous health spa, in 1935, a year before he passed away. He is surrounded by students who have come to wish him good-bye. Dovid Bender is in the foreground toward the right of the Mashgiach. Rabbi Chaim Lechowitz can be seen in the middle.

did not permit outsiders to participate. Each of the participants immersed himself in the mikveh before participating in the taharah. The taharah started later than scheduled because the Rosh Yeshivah felt weak and had to rest up a bit.

The levayah started at about 3 o'clock. The bier was carried through the marketplace to the yeshivah. Among the maspidim were the Rav, Rabbi Avrohom Tzvi Kamai, Rabbi Shabsi Yogel, Rabbi Meir Karelitz (who began but after but a few minutes could not continue), the Lomza Mashgiach, and Rabbi Yosef Leib Nendik.

Then, Peretz Drevner[33] cried his way through a hesped that each of the 500 students present could have delivered, if they could have gathered up the courage. In the midst of the next eulogy it started to rain. The eulogy continued and when it was completed, we started toward the cemetery. The heavens continued to shed tears in a steady downpour, but nobody seemed to notice that he was drenched through and through.

The next day there were more eulogies, this time in the big shul. Reb Reuvain was the first maspid followed by Rabbi Dovid Lifshitz — the Suvalker Rav — and finally the Vilna Maggid.[34]

---

33. "Peretz Drevner was one of Reb Yeruchem's 'Cossaken,' " stated Rabbi Shimshon Brodsky. An elite group of Reb Yeruchem's close talmidim were referred to as his "Cossacks," his soldiers.

34. Of those who were maspid the next day, "Reb Reuvain" remains unidentified.

Rabbi Dovid Lifshitz (1906-1993) learned in Grodno and Mir. Upon marrying the daughter of Rabbi Yosef Yoselevitch of Suvalk, Poland, he became its Rav and succeeded his father-in-law as Chief Rabbi of the 27 congregations there. During World War II he traveled through the Soviet Union to Japan until he reached America in 1941. He served as Rosh Yeshivah in Chicago until 1944 when he was invited by Yeshivas Rabbeinu Yitzchok Elchonon to take on a position as Rosh Yeshivah there.

## The *levayah* of Rabbi Yeruchem Levovitz, Mirrer *Mashgiach*

*One of the Rabbanim speaking at the levayah*

*Rebbetzin Rivka Levovitz with her daughter,*
*Rebbetzin Chasia Kaplan, and her grandson,*
*Hershel Kaplan, at the levayah*

... We met the Lomza Mashgiach who said, "Klal Yisroel has gaonim, gedolim, ba'alei mussar, and tzaddikim; yes, we still have some. But, if you search
from one end of the world to the other, you will not find the kind of wise man that
was Reb Yeruchem. His wisdom! When he was still young in Kelm, you could
see wisdom and more wisdom in everything he did. Every action was weighed
and measured. The kind of wise man that Reb Yeruchem was does not exist anymore."

... So many eulogies were delivered, so many words were written, so much ink
was used. Nevertheless, we received only a hint of who the Mashgiach, ztz"l, really
was ... Years back, when he was still young, a few minutes after he was told the
dreadful news of a pogrom against the Jews of a certain small town, when they took

---

Rabbi Chaim Moshe Zuchovitz (d. 1943) was known as the Vilna Maggid, though he was
originally the Baranovicher Maggid. An exceptional *talmid chacham* and an effective *maggid*,
the Vilna Maggid spoke at gatherings in Remmailes Yeshivah and was a sought-after *darshan*.
People spoke in awe of his *hadras panim;* just observing him inspired them to heed his words of
*mussar*. He was one of the *maspidim* at the *levayah* of Rabbi Chaim Ozer Grodzenski where he
"dared" speak of "changes taking place" and was forcibly removed by Russian militiamen.

## Maspidim at the levayah of Rabbi Yeruchem Levovitz:

| | | | |
|---|---|---|---|
| *Rabbi Avrohom Tzvi Kamai* | *Rabbi Meir Karelitz* | *Rabbi Moshe Rosenstein* | *Rabbi Yosef Leib Nendik* |

*Rabbi Avrohom Tzvi Kamai* *(1859-1941) learned under the guidance of his father, the Mirrer Rav, and succeeded him as Rav and Rosh Yeshivah in Mir. After the passing of the Chofetz Chaim, Rabbi Chaim Ozer Grodzenski advised people to discuss halachic issues and public affairs with Rabbi Kamai. As a faithful leader, he refused to leave his flock during World War II and subsequently perished with the remaining 1500 Jews of Mir.*

*Rabbi Meir Karelitz* *(1876-1955) learned under his father, Rabbi Shmaryahu Yosef, and with his younger brother, the Chazon Ish. He was ordained with semichah by Rabbi Chaim Susnitzer, the Ba'al Shaarei Deah. He married the daughter of the Ba'al Cheshek Shlomo, Rabbi Shlomo HaKohen, dayan of Vilna. In Vilna, he founded a yeshivah, succeeded his father-in-law as a dayan, and became a beloved and effective leader of Klal Yisroel. He immigrated to Eretz Yisroel in 1937 and he continued to lead his people.*

*Rabbi Moshe Rosenstein* *(d. 1943), known as the Lomza Mashgiach, was a talmid of the Alter of Kelm, Rabbi Tzvi Hirsch Broide, and Rabbi Shimon Shkop. Reb Moshe was appointed Lomza Mashgiach in 1912, and remained with the yeshivah and its Rosh Yeshivah, Rabbi Yechiel Michel Gordon, throughout World War I. He stayed with the yeshivah during World War II as well, and passed away during their travels.*

*Rabbi Yosef Leib Nendik* *(d. 1943) was one of the most illustrious talmidim of the Kelemer Talmud Torah, a close disciple of the Alter of Kelm and Rabbi Hirsch Broide. Reb Yosef Leib learned in Telshe when Rabbi Shimon Shkop was a Rosh Yeshivah there, and he considered himself a talmid of Reb Shimon as well. He served as Mashgiach in many illustrious Lithuanian yeshivos, including Radin, Ponevezh, Kobrin, and Kletzk.*

*his temperature, they were surprised to see that it had gone to 103 degrees. Can we imagine such ahavas Yisroel? Can we understand, even slightly, the warmth of the heart that was beating in his chest? …*

*… As the Vilna Maggid pointed out, how many Heavenly decrees did he prevent*

*with the tears he shed as he stood Shemoneh Esrei for hours on Yom Kippur …?*

*… When one of us has something on his mind … it is only with the utmost difficulty that he can keep his mind on the Gemara for even 15 minutes, without thinking of his problems … Who under the sun had more worries on his head than the Mashgiach? Who had as many boys so near his heart and on his mind as much as our Mashgiach who worried for all the yeshivos? In spite of everything he had on his mind, you would see him in the yeshivah for three hours every day learning with extraordinary diligence …"*

THE VACUUM LEFT BY REB YERUCHEM'S PASSING FORCED HIS STU-
dents to realize the magnitude of their loss. The *Mashgiach's* students did not want to forget his teachings; they did not want to fall from the heights they had reached. On Tuesday of *Parashas Vayechi,* 1937, about half a year after the passing of the *Mashgiach,* Dovid put pen to paper and transcribed some of the ideas he had learned. As the minutes went by, the list grew. When he at last set down his pen, he had outlined 52 different ideas and practices. The greatest tribute he could give to his rebbi would be to internalize his lessons.

ALTHOUGH REB YERUCHEM WAS GONE, THE MARK HE LEFT ON HIS
students was eternal. Through Reb Yeruchem's fiery *mussar,* Dovid had become a different person. Although he eventually left the Mir, he would forever remain "*Ah Mirrer.*"[35]

---

35. Being in the Mir, especially under the influence of the *Mashgichim,* Rabbi Yeruchem Levovitz and later Rabbi Yecheskel Levenstein, made an indelible impression. The "Mirrers" wore — and still wear — the title with pride. "I was only in the Mir a few years, but it gave me lifelong direc-
tion. The *mussar* in the Mir was so strong; I have never forgotten it. We learned that the *yetzer hara* is on the right and the left, in front and behind, tricking you, enticing you to follow his lead away from *avodas Hashem.* But because of my years in the Mir, I never lost direction — not me, nor 99 percent of those who came out of the Mir. People today *mach vertlach* — they play with Torah and *divrei Chazal.* We were afraid to do this. We were infused with a strong sense of "this is *da'as Torah*" and "this is not *da'as Torah*" (R' Elchonon [Heiry] Ehrlanger).

*Chapter Six*

# Letters from Mir[36]

HILIP (FEIVEL) RITHOLTZ SLIT THE ENVELOPE OPEN WITH A sharp movement. Two folded sheets of ship stationery fluttered out. He laid them flat on his desk, smoothing out the creases to better decipher his friends' handwriting. "White Star Lines" was emblazoned on the top of each page. Had they been written while still aboard ship? If so, why had it taken so long to arrive? He read on with interest.

*19th of Cheshvan 5694*
*November 8, 1933*
*Wednesday, Parashas Chayei Sarah*

*Dear Phil,*
*You will have to excuse me for not writing sooner. Out here we do not have a minute of spare time: Eight o'clock in the morning is davening, which lasts over an hour. After davening, I learn Mishnah Berurah with Pincus until 10 o'clock. At 10:30, we are back in yeshivah for the first seder which lasts until 3 o'clock. After 3 o'clock, we daven Minchah and go home to eat dinner, which is usually at 3:30. After dinner, I have a seder in Tanach for 15 to 20 minutes. This leaves half an hour to take a walk and grab some fresh air. Then from 5 o'clock until 9:30 is the second seder. From 9:30 until 10 o'clock, we learn mussar, daven Ma'ariv, and go home for supper. Immediately afterward, we come back to the yeshivah*

---

36. These letters were found in 2003 by the Honorable Martin E. Ritholtz. They have been adapted and condensed.

*and learn for another hour or two. In addition to these sedarim, we have shiurim from the Rosh Yeshivah[37] on Sunday and Thursday and from the Rav[38] on Tuesday. Reb Yeruchem gives us three shmuessen a week: one on Friday night before Ma'ariv, the second one on Shabbos after davening, and the third after shalosh seudos. Sometimes, he gives us a shmuess during the week.*

*I am learning with Chaim Avrohom (Pincus). We learn with such diligence that before we realize it, the seder is over. You know Pincus from the States, but I know Chaim Avrohom from Mir. He is not the same fellow. He does not waste a minute and is growing in Torah from day to day. When we take a walk, we talk in learning. When we eat, we talk in learning. Between each bite, a question is asked and an answer is given. We spend all our time with Gittin and this is still not enough.*

*But not a day goes by that Pincus and I don't mention Mr. Feivel and "why isn't he out here?" This is the place for you. You are out of place in New York. This is your real home, where you should strive to be. True, a person is supposed to learn a trade to make a living and at the stage you have reached it is really hard to quit. But, you must not forget that the Torah way expects all Jews to learn Torah and become lamdanim. "Yafeh Talmud Torah im derech eretz"[39] is true when you learn Torah.[40] However, when you grab the second half and leave the first, the way you are doing, "dos heist nit gelernt — this is not considered learning." College? You can continue when you come back. I am not saying you should quit if you have only another half-year to finish (although in some ways, it might pay) but you must keep in mind that after you finish this course, you will definitely come here. Every day that you put off coming will make it harder for you to eventually come. As a good pal of yours, I would advise you to join our ranks out here immediately. You will get a different perspective on life.*

*Now, let me hear about you. How are you doing in the States? Most likely, you are one of the fellows who joined Rebbi[41] in starting the new yeshivah. How is it managing, financially and spiritually? I hope it is successful. You ought to hear the reputation Rebbi has in Europe. Any yeshivah here would be honored to have him as their Rosh Yeshivah. You should thank Hashem that you merit having him. America does not know how to appreciate Rebbi and get all it can from him, for*

37. Rabbi Leizer Yud'l Finkel (see previous chapter).

38. Rabbi Avrohom Tzvi Kamai (see previous chapter).

39. *Pirkei Avos* 2:2. Literally, "How good is learning Torah together with the ways of the world." Rabbi Shimshon Raphael Hirsch explained that "*Torah im derech eretz*" is "the realization of the Torah in harmonious unity with all the conditions under which its laws will have to be observed amidst the developments of changing times" (*Rabbi Samson Raphael Hirsch,* p. 201). An extension of this principle encourages a Jew to take on a profession while still learning Torah.

40. Meaning, when Torah is the more important part.

41. "Rebbi" in this letter refers to Rabbi Dovid Leibowitz. In 1933, Reb Dovid left Torah Vodaath to establish his own yeshivah, Yeshivas Chofetz Chaim. As a result, Torah Vodaath students were forced to choose between staying in Torah Vodaath with Reb Shraga Feivel or joining "Rebbi" in his new yeshivah. Rabbi Dovid Bender was always grateful that Divine Providence had ordained his departure for Mir before this split.

there is much to gain. Give my best regards to Rebbi, all of the boys, and to Mr. Mendelowitz,[42] and the bunch left in the Mesivta.

Expecting to see you here one of these days,

*Your friend,*
*Dovid*

PHIL SMILED, AMUSED. HOW LIKE HIS FRIEND DOVID BENDER TO GET caught up with something new and become set on convincing others to follow. Had Abe Pincus also become so enamored of his new home? Phil read on curiously.

*To my dear friend Feivel,*

*I deeply apologize for not writing sooner, but you are well aware of how lazy I am. Another reason for my not writing is that there really has not been any time. My sedarim are all encompassing and in normal learning times, one hardly finds time for even dropping a card to the folks at home. But this is not normal learning time as I am laid up — ill, nothing serious, of course.*

*I really do not know where to start. I have so many things to tell you that I don't know what to say first. But, you should know, the underlying motive for my writing is to acquaint you with the marvels (not at all exaggerated) of a great yeshivah like "Mir." Rittie, you ought to be here for Yamim Nora'im! It pays for one to spend a few hundred dollars to witness one thing: the Yamim Nora'im davening. I have never davened with so much hislahavus as I did here these High Holy Days. My vocabulary is entirely too meager to even attempt to describe what took place.*

*Ma'ariv, Rosh Hashanah, the atmosphere was tense and solemn. Suddenly, a clap was heard and the chazzan said, "Borchu es Hashem haMevorach." In one harmonious voice the congregation responded, "Baruch Hashem haMevorach ..." Can you picture 400 young men who were imbued with a love for Judaism from early childhood, raised in an atmosphere of Torah and yiras Shamayim, all who realize the meaning and seriousness of Rosh Hashanah and Yom Kippur, crying, "Baruch Hashem haMevorach l'Olam Va'ed"? Oh, how much meaning their cries bear! The love, devotion, and fear were almost palpable. Need I write anymore? Can you not feel what I am trying to share? Oh, Rittie, how can I even describe what the Avinu Malkeinu of Ne'ilah was like? Ten more minutes to the p'sak!! Another yell, another tear, another cry — maybe they can help, and they did help! We are confident of that, aren't we?*

*Now, about the learning: The first seder I learn b'chavrusah with a Polish fellow and the second seder I learn with Bender.*

*You know, not a day passes without one of us, Bender or myself, remarking, "Boy, wish Ritholtz were here; he'd gain a lot." I mean it — that's what we say*

---

42. Rabbi Shraga Feivel Mendelowitz, who insisted on being called "Mister."

*every time we mention your name. You really can't imagine what a European yeshivah does for a guy. I never realized it either, until I came here. I don't know what it is, but learning here is different than in the States. Every batlan — every "nobody" — can come to the Mir and become, I won't say a masmid, but he'll surely learn 10 hours a day. No one knows why, but that's how it is. We go through the Gemara very thoroughly and we talk in learning with almost anyone. The Polish fellows are very friendly and willing to devote time to talk in learning with the Americans. There isn't a day that Bender or I aren't in one of the "cliques" arguing in learning. Well, this way of learning can turn you into a lamdan in a just a few years. You know you can't do that in the States. My advice, Rittie, is pack your things and be one of us. Here, you will have no worries of school and the other crazy things that distract you from real learning. Here, when you finish a mesechta, you know it with Rishonim and Acharonim and a couple Ketzoses mixed in. You know "vertlach azoi"[43] and yeshivishe Torah. You know well that in the States you have not got that. Think it over and maybe soon we'll get word that Philip Ritholtz is aboard a liner, bound for the great Mirrer Yeshivah.*

*Yours,*
*Abe Pincus*

PHIL THOUGHTFULLY FOLDED BOTH LETTERS AND PUT THEM BACK in the envelope. He would not deny that his friends' letters piqued his interest. These were levelheaded fellows, not easily swayed by emotions. Could the Mir really be all they made it out to be? They seemed to think that no other yeshivah could compare. What about the famed Slabodka Yeshivah of Eretz Yisroel? If one were already traveling so far, embracing a Spartan way of life in an unfamiliar country, then why not go to Eretz Yisroel? Besides, who says one has to travel so far? Was it so bad to stay in the good ole U.S.A.?

***8th of Sivan, 5694***
***May 22, 1934***
***Tuesday, Parashas Nasso (Isru Chag)***

*Dear Phil,*
*I received your letter last night, Motza'ei Yom Tov. To my surprise, only while reading the letter did I find out that you had written a 14-page letter full of news of yourself and the yeshivah. The reason I did not receive your letter is quite obvious. At the Polish border, exceptionally thick envelopes are opened, in search of money, and then re-mailed. We have good reason to believe that sometimes the border police rip them up.*

---

43. Literally, "such words," referring to a variety of interpretations.

As for your going to Eretz Yisroel to study: If you intend to settle in Eretz Yisroel, or if your parents also want you to go to Eretz Yisroel, that is a separate issue. But if you are going for the learning, there is no question: The yeshivos in Palestine cannot compare to the European yeshivos. You can come here to learn, and later settle in Eretz Yisroel.

As for learning in the States: I repeat, learning in the States doesn't come anywhere near the learning here. Here, when you're finished learning the blatt, you know that you really have that blatt of Gemara. The yeshivah way of attacking a Gemara teaches you to become a piece of Gemara and enables you to become a lamdan. In the States, you learn a piece of Gemara simply. You have other things on your mind and you don't spend as much time on any one blatt. Furthermore, the actual time spent learning is only about seven hours of the day and some days not even that much. What if you would quit school and learn full-time? What you learn after the yeshivah sedarim, which in the States is about 4 o'clock, doesn't have any ta'am. At that time of day, there are only a few boys learning and it is hard to get a chaver. One day you come late, another day you leave early, and another day you don't come at all. I know, from experience, because I tried it. I remember I thought I would learn for three or four hours after Ma'ariv, and in the end I only learned for about two hours and even those two hours were "gefunfett."[44] I can't say that I didn't learn at all, because even learning for an hour or two is something. But it is nothing compared to what I could have done.

Dovid Bender with friends in Mir.

Here we have two long sedarim — one for four and a half hours and the other for five hours — altogether nine and a half hours of compulsory learning. Then each and every fellow makes his own additional sedarim. Fellows make sedarim for the hour after davening: some learn Shulchan Aruch, others learn a differ-

---

44. Played with.

ent mesechta, others learn the Ketzos on other shaylos u'teshuvos. Other talmidim go straight to breakfast and start their first seder earlier. Many bochurim have a two-hour seder after Ma'ariv. During the winter nights, you can find a crowd of about a hundred boys learning after Ma'ariv. Others get up earlier in the morning. At all hours, you have a crowd learning in yeshivah.

While I am at this point, you can't compare the geshmak of learning with 400 fellows to that of learning in a little beis medrash with about 50. It is so inspiring to learn with a big crowd. When you see everybody around you learning, you don't even feel like "batteling."

You also have to remember, "Hevei goleh l'makom Torah."[45] To succeed in learning, a person must leave home and go to a yeshivah. Even if he has a yeshivah where he lives, he should leave for somewhere else, especially when the other yeshivah is better. Even here in Europe, fellows from Mir go to other yeshivos, and those from Grodno come here, etc.

Leaving home is a great yoke with many responsibilities, especially when you are coming from America. Parents assume a great burden when they send their children here. Bochurim leave so many conveniences, family and friends, and they know that everybody, at home and yeshivah, is expecting great things from them. Such responsibility forces them to make every second count, and not to waste any time.

There are other benefits of the yeshivah — davening the likes of which do not exist in the States. The yeshivah teaches you how to daven like a Jew. Shacharis takes a full hour. The kavanah that you have — that you cannot help having — when you hear the "Amen" of nearly 400 voices puts shivers through you. However much you try to visualize this, you would not even come close to the real thing.

As for expenses, because of the falling dollar, they are naturally higher than they used to be. $15 to $17 (per  month) should be enough for you. You could live on much less. If you want to take an older chavrusah to learn with you the full seder of four and a half hours, it would cost you $5. The hanhalah holds that you should take someone as a chavrusah who walks with you through the Gemara, and not as a rebbi. The chavrusah knows where to stop, where to look into seforim, and through him you gain a lot of knowledge. There are about 50 young Polish boys who the hanhalah pairs up or they pair themselves up to learn with others.[46]

I would like to hear about you all over again, since I did not receive what you wrote. How is the old Mesivta? How is Mr. Mendelowitz feeling? How are the

---

45. *Avos* 4:18: "One should exile oneself to a place of Torah."

46. "Foreign *bochurim* — those from America, England, France, Switzerland, and Germany — were usually on a far lower learning level than that of the rest of the yeshivah. They were often paired up with a rebbi/*chavrusah* from Poland/Lithuania. The '*shidduch*' was often arranged by the *hanhalah* and the Polish/Lithuanian *bochurim* were paid to learn with these *bochurim*" (Rebbetzin Z. Ginsburg).

*older boys getting along — Quinn, Karp, the newcomers, etc. ...? Did they get semichah yet? How is Rebbi feeling? How is the new yeshivah getting along, spiritually and financially? Give everyone my heartiest regards.*

*Dovid* [47]

AFTER HE HAD FINISHED WRITING HIS LETTER, DOVID FELT DEPLETED and somewhat defeated. Mere words could never capture the magic of Mir. Could a budding lawyer comprehend a community where a youth was considered wealthy, even as his clothing was in tatters, but he owned his own copy of the *Ketzos HaChoshen*? Could his friend even fathom the eagerness of other *bochur*im just to use that same *Ketzos*, so much so that a lending system was arranged granting two-hour time slots for those *bochur*im who signed up? The desire to learn from the *Ketzos* was so fervent that *bochur*im felt privileged to use it even from 2 to 4 o'clock in the morning. How could anyone who had never seen such excitement for learning imagine it from a verbal description alone? Dovid placed the sealed letter on his desk and made a mental note to remember to mail it the following day. This time again, Avrohom Pincus included his letter in Dovid's envelope.

***11th of Sivan, 5694***
***May 25, 1934***
***Friday, Parashas Nasso***

*Dear Philip,*
*... This letter I shall devote solely to writing about the advantages of studying in a European yeshivah. Words fail me in adequately describing everything I am trying to convey. My heart is simply bursting with hispa'alus about everything I behold here and I am very much afraid I won't be able to describe everything I feel. All I can say is that in the yeshivah there is a "certain something" that transforms batlanim into masmidim and am ha'aratzim into talmidei chachamim.*

*I have to cite a few examples simply to prove my point: Gordon is now learning between 11 to 12 hours a day (and I am not exaggerating). Levenberg is learning b'hasmadah rabbah in Grodno. When I was in America, my concept of lamdanim was so limited that, to me, the older fellows in the Mesivta were the gedolei hador. I don't deny that they are quite good for their age, but their knowledge is certainly not the "last word" in Torah. When I came here, I was stunned when I beheld how the fellows so nonchalantly quoted the Ohr Somayach, Machane Ephraim, Ketzos,*

---

47. Those referred to in this letter whom we can identify: "Rebbi" – Rabbi Dovid Leibowitz, Rabbi Shraga Feivel Mendelowitz, Rabbi Nesanel Quinn, R' Yud'l Gordon and *ybdl"ch* Rabbi Elias Karp (see Biography Section).

As a young boy, Rabbi Shmuel Berenbaum arrived in Mir with his own *Ketzos HaChoshen.* The news spread quickly that a "rich boy" came to Mir. Considering that the yeshivah had only two copies of the *Ketzos,* a boy who had the money to purchase his own must surely be rich. When Reb Shmuel heard how he had earned the reputation of being rich, he responded in frustration, "My mother sold her Shabbos dress and her good shoes to buy me this *Ketzos!"* Nonetheless, he magnanimously lent out his sefer for two-hour shifts. Rabbi Aharon Kreiser, a notable *masmid,* gratefully took the 2-4 a.m. slot.

Below is a picture taken in America at the wedding of Rabbi Yankel Finkelstein. Among those present are Rabbi Shmuel Berenbaum and Rabbi Aharon Kreiser.

*Standing left to right: Shmuel Berenbaum, Nachman Nacham, Reuvain Fein, Abba Carmel, Aharon Kreiser, Yoel Rosen, Moshe Bunim Pirutinsky, Dovid Kostrovitzky, Moshe Maruch, Yaakov Kupkowitz, Nachum Partzovitz, Boruch Rosenberg*
*Sitting left to right: Yaakov Moshe Leizerson, Asher Lichtshein, Yaakov Shlomo Mordechai Finkelstein, Chaim Pruzansky, Yaakov Maggid*

*Ramban, Rashba, Ra'avad, Rambam, etc.*[48] *In the course of their conversations, they would refute some of Reb Shimon's or Reb Chaim's Torah and were mechadesh many chiddushim on their own. I felt so very envious and at the same time very sad that I not only didn't know what they said, I had never even heard of the gedolim they were quoting. Little by little, David and I became acquainted with the sources, looked into their chiddushim and found that we, too, could even comment on them. Not a day passes when David and I are not amid circles arguing about the machlokes between the Ran and the Rashba, the Rambam and the Ra'avad, and*

---

48. Meaning, they were able to quote from many different commentaries.

**"… They would refute some of Reb Shimon's or Reb Chaim's Torah, and were *mechadesh* many *chiddushim* on their own …"**
**Both Rabbi Shimon Shkop and Reb Chaim Brisker were known for their innovative ways of learning. Expertise in understanding and the ability to even refute their opinions were the hallmarks of a real *lamdan*.**

*Rabbi Shimon Shkop (1860-1939) was a student of Volozhin. He became a maggid shiur in Telshe Yeshivah under Rabbi Eliezer Gordon, his uncle by marriage. In 1903 Reb Shimon opened his own yeshivah in Maltch. He later became Rav of Breinsk. During World War I, he wrote his classic analytical work on the Talmud, Shaarei Yosher. In 1920 he became Rosh Yeshivah of Yeshivas Shaar HaTorah, in Grodno, Poland. Under his leadership, it became one of the prominent Lithuanian yeshivos of the time.*

*Rabbi Chaim HaLevi Soloveitchik (1853 –1918), also known as Reb Chaim Brisker, was a child prodigy who married the granddaughter of the Netziv of Volozhin. In 1880 his father-in-law, Rabbi Raphael Shapiro, abdicated his position in the yeshivah in his favor, and Reb Chaim became associate head of Yeshivas Volozhin. His derech in learning — analytical and clear thinking — became the hallmark of the Lithuanian yeshivos. He succeeded his father, the "Beis HaLevi," as Rav of Brisk.*

*difficult sections in Tosafos. Believe me, you become a lamdan here! Why, we even formed a chaburah to say chiddushei Torah and we don't let anyone get away with shtus — stupidity.*

*My advice to you is to pack your things and come out here as soon as possible. You remember what I was in New York — a batlan, a gornisht — a loafer, a nothing. Why, I bless the day that I set foot onto the boat bound for Europe. I can never properly repay my dear parents for all they have done for me. New York yeshivos are all right for the preliminary steps, but the "finals" are here. Out here you learn! When you eat, you "talk in learning," when you walk, you "talk in learning." Why, even when you sleep, pages of Gemara race through your mind. This is no exaggeration. Many instances when I would awaken, I discovered that I had learned a few pages of Gemara in my sleep.*

*I will close now with the hope that Hashem help you in seeing this matter properly and lead you in the path of Torah and yiras Shamayim.*

*Your friend,*
*Abe*

TIME PASSED, BUT THE DISCUSSION REMAINED THE SAME: TO GO OR not to go. Letter after letter, year after year, Phil wrote his reservations and his friends refuted them. Through these arguments of the merits of learning in the Mir, we get a small, but significant glimmer of the glory that was the Mir and an appreciation of those who merited learning there.

*3rd of Kislev, 5697*
*November 17, 1936*
*Tuesday, Parashas Toldos*

*Greetings, blessings, and success to my dear friend, Shraga Feivel,*

*A pretty long time has past since I received your last letter ... I haven't much news to write. This week I started to learn Yoreh De'ah and I am getting along quite nicely. The reason I started now is that I am uncertain as to whether I will be able to stay here another year.[49] Last year, I had plenty of trouble obtaining a passport for my mother. As for Pincus, he was here with us in Mir for the holidays, at present is back in Kaminetz, and is learning very well. I sent him your letter immediately, and I presume he has answered by now. About your letter, Rittie, to tell you the truth, I couldn't make heads or tails of it. Let me write you a little observation I thought of while learning mussar:*

*The Ramchal writes about harmful friendships. The simple explanation given for keeping a distance from bad people is that one will invariably learn from their ways. Yet, if I feel grounded in my beliefs, then what do have I to fear? The Ramchal tells us, "Often, although one is steadfast and scrupulous in carrying out what he believes (to be right), he may weaken his resolve or (even) omit things (he would otherwise be doing) so that his friends do not mock him ..." Reading this led me to think: True, one must keep a distance from bad friends not to learn from their conduct, but this is not the main point. While a person is learning, he is*

---

49. Learning *Yoreh De'ah* is a requisite for receiving *semichah* — rabbinical ordination. Many *bochur*im studied for *semichah* before they married so that they would be eligible for a rabbinical position if necessary. In an unpublished letter, Dovid comments that he hopes to "return and learn some Gemara." This might refer to the fact that in Mir one was not allowed to learn *semichah* topics in the *beis medrash*. Dovid Bender and his friend Yisroel Freedman had a *seder* in *Yoreh De'ah* outside the *beis medrash*. The *beis medrash* was only for Gemara learning and the policy was strictly adhered to (R' Yehudah Freedman).

*growing and shteiging — slowly, step by step; he is taking baby steps that are barely noticeable. One can be learning for a year and seem to be the same, for it takes a long time for change to be noticeable. Conversely, one does not learn from the foolish deeds of bad friends immediately, but if he keeps contact with them, he falls, step by barely noticeable baby step. The concept is all inclusive. While in yeshivah, one grows slowly. He keeps acquiring minute amounts until, after learning a nice few years, he becomes a ben Torah. The opposite holds true for a boy who leaves the yeshivah. Rabbi Yisroel Salanter, ztz"l, says a yeshivah bochur becomes a different person as soon as he "zet zich nur ofen fuhr — gets onto the wagon." Slowly, he reneges on level after level … he thinks he's the same person, but unfortunately he is not. Soon enough the yeshivah velt will conclude, "He is already becoming a balabos." The lamdan, ba'al middos, and ba'al mussar that he was, is no longer. It is not possible to leave the confines of the yeshivah for a new environment without becoming a different person.*

*Rabbi Shraga Feivel Nachum HaKohen Ritholtz (1912- 2003) attended Yeshivah Torah Vodaath and then Yeshivas Chofetz Chaim. He married and moved to Alexandria, Virginia where he served as a rabbi and a chaplain. Later, he was a rabbi in Salem and Highland Park, New Jersey. He used his law expertise to assist yeshivos and Bais Yaakov schools and the gedolim of the generation.
He was known for his generous spirit and desire to help his people.*

*Rittie, this concept is amitah shel Torah [i.e., the absolute truth]. I know from experience, when I leave the yeshivah for even a short time, I feel the change in me. I am sure the same applies to you, and yet it is almost three years since you left the yeshivah.*

*You have your plans, but you do expect to go back to yeshivah. The longer you stay away, the harder it becomes to go back. You cannot feel it; you feel like you're the same lamdan, etc. But, try going back and you will see how hard it is for you. Rittie, think well, don't hesitate, come back to the yeshivah life, if possible here in Europe, or at least in the States.*

*Best regards to all. Write all the news that would interest me.*

*Wishing you all the best,*
*Your friend, Dovid*

Dovid's words of *mussar* impressed Phil. He saw that his letters were not just expressions of allegiance of loyalty to the institution he had chosen; rather, they bespoke a complete change in perspective and personality. Even from afar, Phil could sense that change and he had the wisdom to realize the sincerity and accurate description of what being at the Mir was all about.

Eventually, the years of letters flying back and forth produced the desired results. Feivel Ritholtz was convinced that Mir was the place for him. He sent off a letter to his friends informing them of his decision and asking their advice. His friends in Mir were overjoyed.

*10th of Nissan 5698*
*April 11, 1938*
*Monday, Parashas Acharei Mos*

*Greetings, blessings and success upon my dear friend, Shraga Feivel,*

*A few hours have elapsed since I received your letter with its surprising news. Philip is coming to D'Mir! Isn't that great! Pincus was in the house when the letter arrived and we both danced from joy.*

*Well now, down to the facts. Traveling is simple. Buy a ticket to Bialystok — it is advisable to travel on the Cunard White Star Line as their boats are big and more convenient — they will take care of you the whole way to Warsaw. Stay on the train all the way to Horodzei, where a bus to D'Mir will await you.*

*Bring:*
*At least a dozen shirts*
*about 9 pairs of summer underwear*
*4-6 pairs of winter underwear*
*between 1½ – 2-dozen high socks*
*a few suits (the old ones are good enough)*
*2 or 3 hats (even old ones)*
*ties (not very loud ones)*
*a dozen Turkish towels*
*a dozen bars of soap*
*2 washcloths*
*a big pillow and a heavy quilt*
*2-3 pillowcases*
*1-2 quilt covers*
*3-4 sheets*
*any other small articles you think might come in handy.*

*These are the necessary quantities for staying for about two years or more. Even if you plan to stay for less time, it can't hurt to take the above quantities.*

*The z'man starts on Rosh Chodesh Iyar and it is always good to come at the begin-ning of the z'man; the earlier the better. Don't think long; just leave immediately.*

*Yesterday was Shachne Zohn's[50] wedding in D'Mir. It was a nice affair. We rejoiced until dawn... We are anxiously awaiting your arrival. Regards from my mother, Pincus, Gordon, Horowitz, etc. Wishing you all the best.*

*Your friend,*
*Dovid*

*Don't fool us this time! Come! The earlier the better![51]*

---

50. Rabbi Shachne Zohn, later a *maggid shiur* in Torah Vodaath.

51. Feivel Ritholtz ultimately did not travel to Mir, perhaps due to the war's imminence.

*Chapter Seven*

# Living in Mir

**Mir: 5697 (1937)**

*Dear Mother,*

*I* WOULD LIKE TO LET YOU KNOW THAT I AM VERY SATISFIED *that I remained in the Mir. You will agree with me when you will read the Torah discourse that I will, iy"H, write to Father. I am not trying to imply that I would not have been able to prepare one like it if I were in Kaminetz. It is possible that if I had made the appropriate effort I would have succeeded. The reality is that there I did not do it, and here I did … This is not the main point I want to write about.*

*There is something outstanding in the Mir that cannot be found anywhere else. I refer to the home of Mrs. Bender. The Bender family is a family whose name means goodness. The Bender home is where we, the students at the yeshivah, can refresh ourselves. Their home is always wide open and everyone is a welcome guest. Even if one comes several times a week, he is welcome and treated with the same goodness. Friday night, after learning in the yeshivah for four hours, one gets thirsty. He does not think for a very long time but goes directly to the Benders for a glass of tea and cake. If he doesn't come, he will eventually hear from Mrs. Bender, "We waited for you; why didn't you come?" For the young men in our circle, where to eat melaveh malkah is never a problem. Even when one comes late on Motza'ei Shabbos and can't find his friends, he eventually finds them at the Benders having a bite. Where does one find such generosity? Both Mrs. Bender and her son Dovid make us feel at home. This is a great advantage for us which cannot be found at any other yeshivah ....*

*Yehudah Leib*[52]

YES, THE BENDER HOME WAS OPEN TO ALL. THE AMERICAN *BOCHURIM* enjoyed stopping at the Bender home where they knew they could count on a warm meal, a listening ear, and friendly advice. Mrs. Bender was able to speak to them in their own language; she reminded them of their own mothers so far away. A warm and friendly atmosphere, unusual kindness, and respect characterized the Bender home. Their visitors left satiated both physically and spiritually.

Although the American *bochurim* were the primary beneficiaries of this kindness, Dovid brought home boys from other countries as well. His

---

**Reb Dovid fondly remembered his *chavrusah*, Rabbi Moshe Shmuel Shapiro, who later became a cousin through marriage. Below is a picture of Reb Moshe Shmuel together with other illustrious *talmidim* of the Lomza Yeshivah. Rabbi Shmuel Rozovsky, later Rosh Yeshivah of Ponevezh, and Rabbi Zalman Rotberg, later Rosh Yeshivah of Bais Meir, are part of the group.**

*Sitting from left to right: Shmuel Kivalewitz, Aharon Ben Zion Shurin, Shmuel Rozovsky.*
*Standing from left to right: Zalman Rotberg, Moshe Shmuel Shapiro, Yaakov Rotbard, Yechiel Villensky, Shlomo Shilowitzky*
*Rabbi Moshe Shmuel Shapiro (1917-2006) learned in Baranovich and Mir. He immigrated to Eretz Yisroel in 1937, and was thus rescued from the Holocaust. He continued his studies in Yeshivas Lomza in Petach Tikvah and later became a prized student of the Brisker Rav. He also learned in Kollel Chazon Ish and Slabodka. With the encouragement of the Chazon Ish, he established a yeshivah in Be'er Yaakov, where he inspired talmidim for many decades.*

---

52. Gordon, p. 139.

**The Bender home became a home away from for many of the international *bochurim* in Mir. Here is Dovid Bender on *dacha* with his friends, most of whom were American or English *bochurim*.**

*Mirrer bochurim on vacation pose for a picture. Sitting from left to right: Akiva Chill, Shlomo Chill, Avrohom Pincus, unidentified. Standing from left to right: Shaya Lebor, Leibel Baron, Dovid Bender, Yankel Goldman, and unidentified*

*Simcha Weissman playing chess with a friend*

**Friends gather together to make Shepsel Broide a good-bye party before he leaves for America. The guest of honor is the one wearing a suit.**

*Kneeling from left to right: Harry Horowitz, Dovid Bender, Shmuel Scheinberg, and Shmuel Shain. Standing from left to right: unidentified, unidentified, Moshe Shain, Shmuel Shain, Shepsel Broide, unidentified, Yud'l Broide, unidentified, Pinchas Berliner, Simcha Weissman, Ber Elya Gordon, and Yud'l Gordon*

*From left to right: Joshua Chinn, Moshe Shain, Harry Horowitz, Dovid Bender, Shepsel Broide, unidentified, unidentified, Shmuel Shain, Simcha Weissman (behind), Pinchas Berliner, unidentified, and Mordechai Yoffe*

*chavrusah*, Moshe Shmuel Shapiro, was a regular *shalosh seudos* guest. Uri Hellman,[53] one of the *Deutsche* boys, often frequented their home. Rebbetzin Bender welcomed her guests with joy and pride: joy in the mitzvah of *hachnosas orchim*, and pride in her son and his generous heart.

When Rebbetzin Bender was asked to host a boy from the *Mirrer cheder* on a regular basis, she made an unusual request. Rather than have one boy every day for the main meal as was customary, she asked that the administration send her five *bochur*im on one day. She felt that one additional *bochur* would not prompt her to go out of her way to make anything special. She wanted five *bochurim* at once. On that day, when she would have to feed six hungry boys (her own Dovid included), she cooked and baked as if for a Yom Tov — soup, *kugelach*, cakes. She wanted the boys to feel as if they had been invited to a royal feast.

REBBETZIN BENDER HUMMED TUNELESSLY AS SHE CHEERFULLY PUTtered about her small apartment. The years passed so swiftly, it was difficult to believe that they had already been in Mir for five years. She softly chuckled at the memory of their early years. She, having being born and raised in Europe, had been certain that returning to her birthplace would be like returning home. Little had she realized the effects of her years in America. She missed the physical amenities, the middle-class existence, the general standard of living she had grown accustomed to in America. Nonetheless, these were things she had been prepared for. She remembered what life in Europe had been like, and she came to the Mir knowing that little had changed since she left.

Rebbetzin Bender had found the cultural gap between her and her former *landsleit* even more shocking. She had not realized how American she had become. Even her Yiddish was more English than Yiddish, and she was often puzzled and frustrated when no one understood her "perfect" Yiddish. "*Vu iz de* butcher?" she asked; her neighbor looked back at her blankly. She tried again: "*Ich darf* chicken and meat." Again, she was awarded a blank stare. She would plead, "*Bitte, nem mir tzum* butcher store," completely confused as to why these people did not understand a word of Yiddish.

Thankfully, she met wonderful friends who stepped in with warm advice, helpful (and tactful) hints. She became very close with the other

---

53. "In general, the German boys did not have much to do with the American boys. We were from different worlds and we tended to stick with our own kind. It was only with Reb Dovid's sweetness and genuine love for others that he succeeded in forming relationships with some of our crowd (German *bochurim*). He truly found favor *b'einei habriyos*. Reb Dovid was a part of the *chevra kaddisha* in Mir. Usually participation in the *chevra kaddisha* was an exclusively European domain. That Reb Dovid was a part of it was another indication of how accepted he was by everyone" (Rabbi Uri Hellman).

American women in Mir: Bessie Scheinberg[54] and Ruchoma Shain.[55] Both women were very young, young enough to be her daughters. Yet they found comfort in each other's company. Together they reminisced about America, commiserated about the difficulties in Mir, and shared in the vicissitudes of life.

When Ruchoma experienced a medical crisis after the birth of her first child and became temporarily paralyzed due to blood poisoning, Pelta was eager to help out. She was told that what was most needed was a *bochur* who could come to the house at night and care for the baby so that his father could get some much-needed rest. This was not an easy job. There were nights when the newborn baby was up most of the night. Despite the difficulties, Pelta urged her Dovid to volunteer and, as the weeks passed, Dovid became one of the night shift regulars. Even after Ruchoma recovered from her illness, the special relationship between the two families endured.[56]

Pelta peered out the window of her small apartment. *Dovid should be home any minute,* she thought to herself. His food was waiting on the stove, freshly made, ready to be served, so that he could eat quickly and return to yeshivah.

She glanced nervously at the clock. It was not even late. Nonetheless, Rebbetzin Bender was anxious for her son to be home. Although she tried not to let him notice, she worried about him. Dovid had suffered from rheumatic fever as a baby,[57] and his survival was a miracle for which his parents were forever grateful. Ever since then, she kept a close eye on him. It was a tough balancing act. On the one hand, her maternal desire to care for and protect her son was that much stronger because of the unique circumstances. On the other hand, she wanted to give him enough space to grow up normally, to be just one of the boys. Dovid, in turn, never took advantage of being an only child. The respect he showed his mother was extraordinary. He was an only child, but he treated his mother as if *she* were the only child; he was particularly solicitous and attentive to her needs.

She had tremendous satisfaction whenever she heard, from friends and

---

54. "We lived across the street from the Benders. Pelta Bender was a very warm, friendly, smart woman. She often invited *bochurim* for meals and was particularly friendly with us neighbors" (Rebbetzin Scheinberg).

55. "When Dovid Bender arrived to the Mir with his mother, they were the talk of the town. Whoever heard of a *bochur* coming with his mother? It was highly unusual" (Rebbetzin Shain).

56. When speaking about Rabbi Dovid Bender, Rebbetzin Shain added, "His *kibbud eim* was extraordinary. He was devoted to his mother. It was clear that his constant volunteering to help was because she encouraged him to do so."

57. This was well known in Mir. Some thought that this was the main reason that Mrs. Bender came to Mir: to keep an eye on her son because he had been sick as a child (Rebbetzin Z. Ginsburg).

relatives, how her Dovid was not a typical, pampered only child. Dovid loved taking care of others and looked for such opportunities. Once, he spotted a new *bochur* looking lonely and forlorn. A warm and friendly greeting elicited pertinent information: Yisroel had just come to the yeshivah and had no idea with whom he was supposed to speak or where he could stay for the night. How typical of Dovid to take him by the arm and bring him home.[58]

*He is a real mentsch*, Pelta mused fondly.

She heard him before she saw him. He was walking with a group of American boys who sometimes ate at their house.

*Dovid Bender with his parents on one of his father's visits to Poland*

From the distance, she made out the tall figure of Avrohom Pincus, flanked by Harry Horowitz and Yud'l Gordon. Shlomo and Akiva Chill were right behind them.[59] Today she was a bit more eager than usual to see everyone. She had just received a letter from her husband. The *Yamim Nora'im* were approaching. He would be arriving for his annual trip to Europe in a few weeks. Her son would be thrilled and the other boys would be happy too: happy for their friend and eager to receive the news and warm regards from their families that he would surely bring.

RABBI AVROHOM BENDER ARRIVED IN POLAND IN ELUL OF 1937 WITH more than one purpose in mind. Of course, he was eager to see his wife and son. All year, he looked forward to those precious few weeks together. But Reb Avrohom had other things to see to, as well. Dovid was already 25, and although in Mir the *bochurim* traditionally married late, Reb Avrohom felt the time had come to look for a *shidduch* for Dovid.

RABBI AVROHOM BENDER PAUSED; HE WAS NERVOUS. HE HAD researched the girl thoroughly. She was a respected graduate of Bais Yaakov in Crakow and her years of teaching in Otvock had earned her much praise and admiration from the townspeople. Attractive, articulate, a

---

58. Rabbi Yisroel Post arrived in Mir after Reb Yeruchem was *niftar* but before Rabbi Yecheskel Levenstein stepped in as *Mashgiach*. With no *Mashgiach* at the helm, Reb Yisroel was lost and bewildered until Rabbi Dovid Bender took him home to sleep (heard from Rabbi Eli Post, son of Rabbi Yisroel Post).

59. See Biography Section.

*ba'alas middos* from a good home — what more could he want for his son?[60] He wanted to meet her and observe her parents' home. A girl's home is important and often indicative of the kind of home she would strive to create. He had heard many wonderful things about the Epsteins of Otvock; but, as *Chazal* say: *Lo tehei sh'miah gedolah mi'riyah.*[61] What he heard was fine and good; now he came to see for himself.

He glanced at his watch; it was almost Shabbos. He had better move. Reb Avrohom raised his hand and rapped briskly on the door. A chair scraped the floor, a soft shuffle of feet, and the door opened.

"Yes?"

Reb Avrohom looked at the man in front of him with curiosity and interest. He was about average height, nothing unusual. Yet, he was undeniably distinguished looking. Perhaps it was the trimmed goatee that created this aura of distinction. The warm, friendly eyes welcomed him, beckoning Reb Avrohom into his home.

"I have a bit of a problem," Reb Avrohom began. "It is very close to Shabbos, and I have nowhere to stay."

"Then, you will stay with us," was the prompt reply.

Reb Avrohom was already feeling at ease. If the girl is as pleasant as her father is, she would surely be a welcome daughter-in-law. What was her name again? Oh, yes — Basya. Basya Epstein.

---

60. "… She is one of the most important teachers in Bais Yaakov … a girl with all the finest qualities … there is great excitement in the yeshivah …" (Gordon letters, p. 139). This was written in reference to Rabbi Dovid Bender's engagement. Evidently, his bride's sterling reputation was well known.

61. *Rosh Hashanah* 26b: "There can be no comparison between hearing and seeing."

# Part III:
# Basya Epstein
## 5677-5697 / 1917-1937

### *Chapter Eight:*
### Under Russian Rule

### *Chapter Nine:*
### Otvock — A Healthy Haven

### *Chapter Ten:*
### Bnos

### *Chapter Eleven:*
### Bais Yaakov of Crakow

### *Chapter Twelve:*
### A Bais Yaakov Teacher

---

The primary source of information in this section is an interview with Rebbetzin Basya Bender conducted in 1990. Much of the information about Bais Yaakov has been culled from *Rebbetzin Grunfeld*, *Daughters of Destiny*, and *Carry Me in Your Heart*. Rebbetzin Devorah (Applegrad) Cohn filled in many more details about Bais Yaakov of Crakow and Sara Schenirer. Snippets specifically regarding Rebbetzin Bender in Bais Yaakov were provided by the Bender Family. Other sources of information are documented. Rabbi Avrohom Barnetzky and *ybdl"ch* Rebbetzin Chaya (Kalisch) Milikovsky and Mrs. Sarah (Taub) Rosen contributed their memories of Otvock and the Epsteins.

---

*Chapter Eight*

# Under Russian Rule

*"… He lived in Minsk before World War I, a wealthy man with an open hand. Although he was in business, he was a learned man and his love and submission to Torah leaders knew no bounds. He surrendered his home for a 'beis vaad lachachamim — a gathering place for the wise,' a home of 'Hevei shoseh batzama es divreihem — where the words of the rabbanim were imbibed thirstily.'[1] This training (that she received in) her home, she transmitted to thousands and thousands of students. (It was through this training that) she had the capacity to influence …"[2]*

**Minsk: 5677 (1917)[3]**

BASHA[4] WALKED RESOLUTELY DOWN THE SNOW-LINED sidewalks of Minsk. She was just a child; 4 years old, maybe — certainly not a day older than 5. Her sweet round cheeks were shiny red from the bitter cold. Soft brown baby curls peeked out from her trendy hat tied securely at her chin. She stuffed her hands in her new muff, which matched her hat and coat, and thought how smart she must look.

---

1. *Pirkei Avos* 1:4.

2. Told by Rabbi Shraga Moshe Kalmanowitz, when speaking about R' Yankev Epstein, Rebbetzin Bender's father, in his eulogy for Rebbetzin Bender.

3. The date is approximate.

4. Rebbetzin Bender's full name was Basya Chaya. "Basha" was the *Litvishe* nickname for Basya. Virtually all her family and friends referred to her as Basha or Bashke. For the remainder of the book, we will do the same, except in situations where she would have been called Basya (e.g., when signing correspondence).

**Lifsha Epstein was a great-granddaughter of Rabbi Chaim Leib Shachor, a son-in-law of Rabbi Yaakov Berlin, the father of the Netziv. As such, the Netziv was a great-uncle of Lifsha Epstein and Reb Raphael Volozhiner was a cousin.**

*Rabbi Naftoli Tzvi Yehuda Berlin (1817-1893) was commonly known as the Netziv, an acronym for his name, as well as the Hebrew word for "prince." The Netziv was born into a well-known rabbinical family and spent his boyhood years devoted solely to diligent Torah study. He married the daughter of Reb Itzeleh Volozhiner, son of the famed Rabbi Chaim of Volozhin. He was appointed Rav of Volozhin and head of the yeshivah which he led until its closing in 1892.*

*Rabbi Raphael Shapiro (1837-1921), known as Reb Raphael Volozhiner, was the son of Rabbi Leibele Shapiro, the Kovno Rav. He married the daughter of the Netziv and spent many years learning in Volozhin. He became Rav in Babroisk and then in Novo-Alexanderovsk. In 1892 the Netziv refused to allow secular studies to be taught in the Volozhiner Yeshivah and, in response, the Russian government closed the yeshivah. The Netziv passed away the following year. Later Reb Raphael reopened the yeshivah.*

She rounded the corner and then stopped. Yes, this was the house. She knocked softly on the door. It opened just a bit, just enough to let the little girl in. Basha smiled shyly at the elderly man who greeted her, and pulled her hands out of her muff. In one hand, she held a cup with a precious pat of butter.

*"A dank eich, a dank! Der Ribbono shel Oilam zol dir bentchen mit alles gut …*
— Thank you! Thank you! G-d should bless you with everything good …" The whispered good wishes of Reb Raphael Volozhiner followed her out of the house and Basha headed swiftly home. She did not want to be late, because she did not want her parents to worry. In the newly Communist Russia, possession of black-market contraband was a criminal offense. She

knew that her parents were anxiously awaiting her safe return home.

The scheme had been her mother's idea. Reb Raphael Volozhiner, the illustrious son-in-law of the Netziv, was a distant relative. The Epsteins had maintained a special connection with their Volozhiner family, and when they heard that the elderly *talmid chacham* was residing in Minsk, they were eager to be of service. Reb Raphael was not well. The doctors felt that to give him strength and improve his health, it was imperative that he have some fat in his diet. Yet in war-torn Russia, this was illegal. Foods like butter, chocolate, and sugar were considered luxury items and unavailable to the masses. They could only be bought on the black market and even then, only on an erratic basis.

Black-market transactions were conducted in a nondescript house on a small side street in Minsk. There, a large man stood in front of a vat full of butter. His customers lined up with their own little cups and bowls, and he dispensed small pieces of butter. Those who did not bring a cup or bowl had him place the butter directly into their hands. They then stole home, quickly and quietly, so as not to attract attention.

At first, Basha's father, R' Yaakov (Yankev) Epstein, used to buy and bring the butter to the ailing scholar. The local Communists were suspicious of his activities. They knew he was a Jew still living a Jewish life. Visiting the same Jewish house daily would arouse suspicion. Sooner or later, he would surely be caught. But for Reb Raphael, the butter was life-sustaining nourishment. So what choice did he have?

That was when his wife thought of little Bashke. She was so young; who would suspect such a young child of smuggling? Lifsha Epstein had sewed many of her daughter's clothing, including her warm winter coat. She decided to sew a muff to match her coat. The effect was an adorable ensemble and a wonderful disguise. Who would think that this angelic-looking little girl carried contraband in her muff? Although Lifsha was certainly concerned for her daughter's safety, she knew that if, G-d forbid, the child was caught, the police would not arrest a 5-year-old girl; they would arrest her husband, R' Yankev, the father of the child. Although the person in danger was the same, the risk seemed smaller.

Basha was young enough to consider the mission an adventure. Day after day, for many weeks, she brought Reb Raphael his precious butter. Reb Raphael always greeted her with a warm smile and a shower of blessings. Long after Reb Raphael left Minsk, and long after she herself left, the *"kos shel berachah* — the cup of blessing,"* as they called it, the little cup she had used for the butter, remained with the Epsteins. Wherever they lived, the cup rested proudly on a kitchen shelf and every so often, Lifsha would notice it and turn to Basha. *"G'deinkst?* Do you remember?"* she would ask. And Basha certainly remembered.

THIS WAS BUT ONE OF MANY SUCH CHAPTERS OF *CHESSED* IN THE Epstein home, founded on Torah, mitzvos, and good deeds. Although R' Yankev was an unassuming person, whose good deeds were done quietly, often secretly, his reputation as one who loved Torah and mitzvos was well known. The Epstein home was the address for many Lithuanian Torah leaders who found themselves in Minsk in need of a place to stay, particularly during the difficult years of World War I.

Throughout those years of war, the yeshivah population of Europe fled deeper into Russia, away from the battlefront, the draft, and the local gentiles who might recognize them and hand them over to the conquering armies. Minsk was a choice destination because it was both far from the front lines and big and busy enough to get lost in. Furthermore, Minsk had the reputation of a city of scholars, The long list of scholars who lived in Minsk extends from the early 1700's, when Rabbi Aryeh Leib Ginsburg, the *Shaagas Aryeh*,[5] was the *dayan* of Minsk, to the early 1900's when some of Slabodka's brightest lights hailed from Minsk.[6] Minsk, although not immune to the secular winds sweeping through Eastern Europe, kept most of its children on the right path, earning for itself a name as a place of Torah.[7]

As a result, many of the Torah leaders of Europe were constantly coming and going, staying for a day or two, a week, and longer. Among the illustrious visitors who frequented the Epstein home was the Chofetz Chaim. In the early years of World War I, the Chofetz Chaim, some family members, and his *talmid muvhak*, Rabbi Elchonon Wasserman, fled from Radin to Minsk. Little Bashke gave up her bed, something she did often and willingly, for the *gadol hador*. Although too young to remember the visit, the Epsteins always reminded her of her great privilege. Basya Epstein merited to give up her bed — she slept on the floor for six weeks — for the Chofetz Chaim.

Ultimately, the transient influx of rabbanim, roshei yeshivos, and yeshivah students only temporarily enriched the city. The presence of the majority of the yeshivah students was for a temporary stay of a few days, a week, a few months … Minsk was merely a way station for these fleeing refugees.

---

5. Rabbi Aryeh Leib Ginsburg (1695-1785) is widely known for his acclaimed *teshuvos* sefer, *Shaagas Aryeh*. At the young age of 28, he was appointed Rosh Yeshivah and *maggid* of Minsk, Lithuania, famed for its *lamdanim*. Beginning in 1742 he suffered many years of humiliation and was ousted from Minsk twice. Finally, he was invited to Mitz, where he served peacefully as Rav for the latter 20 years of his life. He was the acknowledged *posek* and saintly Torah giant of the generation.

6. Rabbi Reuvain Grozovsky, Rabbi Aharon Kotler, and Rabbi Yaakov Kamenetsky were among the most famous.

7. Religious observance in the small cities, towns, and villages was far more stable than in the big cities. The typical tiny Polish *shtetl* had no more than 50 or 60 observant Jewish families, who were usually a homogeneous group. In the big cities, with large populations of gentiles and Jews numbering in the tens of thousands (for example Lvov or Warsaw), Jewish parents encountered greater challenges in maintaining their children's level of observance.

Then came the Communist Revolution. Suddenly, the Jews of Russia found themselves in a new and terrifying situation. The civil war raging between the Reds (the Bolsheviks) and the Whites (the Counterrevolutionary Army) was ripping the country asunder. The chaos caused by more than three years of World War I and four more years of civil war made recovery difficult. Minsk, situated in White Russia, remained relatively calm during this period. Yet, when the dust cleared and the fighting ended, its future seemed bleaker than ever.[8]

By 1922, with the Communist regime well established, their agenda to stamp out religion, particularly Judaism, was being implemented. Shuls and *chadarim* were closed. To encourage their resignation, rabbanim were slapped with high taxes. Religious objects were taxed. Learning and teaching Torah was forbidden. People were afraid to assemble in public since large gatherings were considered "revolutionary." The atmosphere was tense.

R' Yankev Epstein was in a quandary. He, an ordained student of the Slabodka Yeshivah, knew that the life of a *Yid* is a life of Torah. He also knew that to learn Torah properly, he had to learn in a group. He needed other Jews and together they would sound the voice of Torah. He wanted to hear the *shiurim* of the Minsker Maggid, Rabbi Binyomin HaKohen Shakovitzky, and the Minsker Rav, Rabbi Eliezer Rabinowitz, two outstanding Torah scholars who illuminated the words of the Gemara. He knew that together, he and the other religious residents of Minsk would be able to reinforce one another's determination to defy the Communists and learn Torah. Although he was no longer a yeshivah *bochur* in Slabodka, R' Yankev revered the time he had spent there. Slabodka represented Torah, and a true *talmid* of Slabodka remained a true *ben Torah*. The Communist Revolution stripped him of his business[9] but could never strip him of his Torah.

R' Yankev joined the community leaders in Minsk, a group of *ehrliche*

---

8. *Reb Moshe* pp. 37-38.

9. Rebbetzin Bender used to tell over the following story: When her father, R' Yankev Epstein, went traveling on business, he used to keep cash in his breast pocket. His wife had sewn a special pocket on his jacket to keep the money secure, yet discreet. On one of his train trips, a man approached R' Yankev and said, "Oh look, you have a spot right over here." The man began scratching at the pocket, ostensibly to rub off the dirt. "There," the man said, "it is off." Before R' Yankev realized what was happening, the man was gone and there was a gaping hole where the pocket had been. The crook "rubbed off the stain" with a pocketknife, and slipped the cash out. How could the crook have known about the valuables in R' Yankev's pocket? R' Yankev felt that even though the money was well concealed and he knew he had to appear nonchalant, he must have subconsciously kept checking his pocket to make sure that the money was in place. This is what is written in the Gemara: "*Adam asui l'mashmeish b'kiso b'chol sha'ah v'sha'ah* — A person usually feels his pocket from time to time" (*Bava Metzia* 21b). Over half a century later, Rabbi Yaakov Bender used this story about his grandfather to teach this concept to his students.

**… He wanted to hear the *shiurim* of the Minsker Maggid … and the Minsker Rav, two outstanding Torah scholars who illuminated the words of the Gemara …**

*Rabbi Binyomin HaKohen Shakovitzky (1873-1938), better known as the Minsker Maggid, was an illustrious talmid chacham who was famous for his powerful mussar shmuessen and Talmudic discourses. The Steipler Gaon was quoted as having said that he grew in yiras Shamayim from listening to his speeches. The Minsker Maggid immigrated to Eretz Yisroel in 1930.*

*Rabbi Eliezer Rabinowitz (1859-1924) was known as the Minsker Rav. He came from Slutzk where he learned with the Bais HaLevi for many years. He married the daughter of the Minsker Gadol, Rabbi Yeruchem Yehudah Leib Perelman (the Ohr Gadol), and moved to Minsk where he remained at his father-in-law's side, assisting him by learning with bochurim. Reb Eliezer assumed the position of Rav after his father-in-law was niftar in 1896.*

*bnei Torah*, and they set up a schedule for regular *shiurim* and learning. R' Yankev would leave his apartment at 1 a.m. and would walk quickly to the meeting place: sometimes the home of the Minsker Maggid and other times the home of the Minsker Rav. He was among 24 men assembled in the basements of these homes, eager to learn. The four hours spent together immersed in learning passed quickly. These precious hours provided respite from the fears and dangers that constantly haunted their lives.

A LONG RING PIERCED THE SILENCE OF THE NIGHT. OVER AND OVER IT resounded, like the wailing of a baby, insistent that its cries be heard.

*"Obysk! Obysk!"* Shouts, accompanied by pounding on the door, finally woke the sleeping family.

Lifsha Epstein glanced at the clock. It was 2 a.m. Her heart thumped as she threw on her dressing gown and ran to the front room. The children, Bashke and Yosef, were already there, their eyes wide with fright. Next to the doorway, lying on the bed, was Lifsha Epstein's close friend and guest, Guttel Gillomovsky. Now she too was wide awake.

This was not the first time the NKVD had come. They were on R' Yankev's trail, in search of a reason to implicate him. What did they think they would find — "revolutionary literature" such as a siddur, a Chumash, or a Gemara? Perhaps, they thought they might catch him learning. Last time, they ransacked the apartment. Riffling through the rooms, they emptied drawers and closets, and even searched under the beds. Nevertheless, they left empty-handed. Who knew what would happen this time?

The shouts and pounding grew louder, and louder still. Crash! The door flew off its hinges and landed on frightened Guttel, who was sitting up in bed. The officers framed in the doorway were startled. They had not intended to break the door down and even seemed embarrassed when it landed on the young woman. Suddenly, they made an about-face and left the apartment in unison.

Lifsha slumped into a nearby chair. She never knew if they would find anything "incriminating." Even worse, they might demand to know her husband's whereabouts, particularly at these late night hours. She had her story prepared. She would say that her husband was away collecting bread for poor people — but would they believe her?

As she led the children back to bed and bid her friend good night, her mind was elsewhere. Certainly, she most sincerely thanked the *Ribbono shel Olam*, but as long as she lived in Russia, her prayers of thanks would always be accompanied by a desperate plea: *Please, Hashem, send those officers to their homes. Please, do not let them enter any other Jewish home tonight. Protect my husband and the other holy Yidden who are risking their lives to learn your holy Torah. Please, Hashem, save us!*

DURING THOSE DIFFICULT TIMES, PERHAPS BECAUSE TIMES WERE DIFficult, the Epstein home was always open for visitors. Despite the experience of having a door crash down upon her, Guttel Gillomovsky remained a frequent guest. Since she could not find work as a pharmacist in her hometown, she traveled to Minsk where she rented a room in a nearby town. This town was too far from where her family lived to go home, even for Shabbos. Whenever Guttel wanted company or a Shabbos among friends, she went to the Epsteins, her home-away-from-home.

For Basha, Guttel was her adopted aunt. True, Basha had real aunts, yet none of them were frequent houseguests. There was Tante Raizel, Tante Mushke, and Tante Basya. Tante Raizel was elderly, and they almost never saw her. Tante Mushke had moved to Eretz Yisroel. Tante Basya also rarely visited. Guttel was a wonderful substitute. She was kind and helpful, pretty and poised, and she was both a role model and a friend. Basha looked up to her and wanted to emulate her. On one of her visits, Tante Guttel gave Basha a small elephant-shaped pin. Basha treasured the pin for two reasons: because she liked the pin, and because Tante Guttel gave it to her.

Guttel's mother was a sister of the illustrious Rabbi Isser Zalman Meltzer, the Rosh Yeshivah in Slutsk. He chose one of his most prized students, Rabbi Elazar Menachem Man Shach, as a husband for his smart and talented niece. Guttel Gillomovsky became the wife of Rav Shach, prince of Torah, the future Rosh Yeshivah of Ponevezh, whose name would resound in the yeshivah world for decades. After Guttel's marriage, her visits to the Epstein home stopped. Basha missed her role model and mentor, yet she and her mother followed with pride news of the young couple and the course they were charting for themselves in the Torah world.

*Rabbi Isser Zalman Meltzer*

**… Guttel's mother was a sister of the illustrious Rabbi Isser Zalman Meltzer, the Rosh Yeshivah in Slutsk. He chose one of his most prized students, Rabbi Elazar Menachem Man Shach, as a husband for his smart and talented niece …**

*Rabbi Isser Zalman Meltzer* (1870-1953) *was a student of Volozhin and Slabodka. In 1897 he was one of 14 students sent by Rabbi Nosson Tzvi Finkel to Slutzk to build Yeshivas Eitz Chaim. He became the Rosh Yeshivah and Rav of the city. During World War I, the yeshivah reestablished itself in Kletzk under the leadership of his son-in-law, Rabbi Aharon Kotler. Reb Isser Zalman later immigrated to Eretz Yisroel where he served as Rosh Yeshivah of Yeshivas Eitz Chaim until his petirah.*

*Rabbi Elazar Menachem Man Shach*

*Rabbi Elazar Menachem Man Shach* (circa 1894-2001) *was a talmid of Reb Itzele Ponevezher, Slabodka Yeshivah, Rabbi Isser Zalman Meltzer, and the Brisker Rav. He taught in various European yeshivos, including Kletzk, Novarodok, and Karlin. Rav Shach escaped to Eretz Yisroel in 1941. He continued to disseminate Torah and, in 1951, he became Rosh Yeshivah of Ponevezh. Rav Shach led the yeshivah for 50 years and became renown as an idealistic Torah leader, who fought valiantly for Torah values.*

Although Tante Raizel was not a regular guest, she was an important personality in Basha's childhood. She had given Basha her first clock, a present Basha always treasured. Yet Basha cherished her more for what she represented: a slowly fading era.

Tante Raizel was actually Basha's great-aunt on her mother's side. She was very old, well into her 90's.[10] Basha loved to hear her mother tell the secret of her aunt's longevity. She, and all who knew her, attributed it to a *berachah* she received from the *posek hador*, Rabbi Yitzchok Elchonon Spector.

IT HAPPENED DURING THE ERA OF THE CANTONIST DECREES.[11] ONE Friday night, the czar's soldiers stormed the streets of Tante Raizel's hometown, Staiptz. On that Shabbos, about 300 Jewish children were kidnapped. Crazed with shock and grief, a group of fathers walked to the home of the Kovno Rav, Rabbi Yitzchok Elchonon Spector. After considering the options, Reb Yitzchok Elchonon sent a messenger to summon Tante Raizel.

Tante Raizel's father had been the wealthiest man in their small town of Staiptz. She had received a large inheritance, which she used to help her oppressed brethren. The Kovno Rav chose her as the representative of the town, an emissary to bribe the district governor.

Tante Raizel listened to the Rav's instructions with trepidation. There were so many reasons to be afraid: She would be going alone, a woman among gentile men; she would have to desecrate Shabbos; she would be risking her life. Reb Yitzchok Elchonon sensed her fear and encouraged her. "Go! In the merit of your carrying out this mission, the *Ribbono shel Olam* should grant you a long life."

She left immediately in her nicest clothing and rode in her best and most beautiful wagon. She waited nervously in the governor's office, her mouth moving ever so subtly as she whispered words of *Tehillim*. Time elapsed. She realized that the guards had no intention of allowing her to meet with the governor. Suddenly propelled by determination, Tante Raizel pushed herself past the guards and straight into the governor's chamber. Even with the Rav's blessing, her rash actions could cost her life.

"I come with my life …" she blurted, the figure before her blurred by her tears.

---

10. Tante Raizel lived to be 97 (Rebbetzin E. [Bender] Epstein).

11. During this time, it was common for the czar's soldiers to snatch children away from their families and ship them off to the Russian army. Since the army had no use for little children, these boys were first sent to camps and monasteries to forget their *Yiddishkeit*. There they remained until they were old enough to serve in the army. By the time their years of army service were over, their *Yiddishkeit* was a vague memory. How many Jews were lost to their people during this terrible time? The full scope of this tragedy will never be known.

> … Tante Raizel was very old, well into her 90's … She, and all who knew her, attributed it to a *berachah* she received from the *Posek HaDor*, Rabbi Yitzchok Elchonon Spector …

*Rabbi Yitzchok Elchonon Spector (1817-1896) was a child prodigy whose main teacher was his father, Reb Yisroel Isser, Rav of Resh, Russia. Reb Yitzchok Elchonon served as Rav in various communities, eventually succeeding Rabbi Yehoshua Leib Diskin as Rav of Kovno. He was the foremost rabbinical authority of his time and was active in communal affairs, bravely fighting the harsh decrees of the Russian government.*

"Madame, do you not recognize me?"

The man facing her stood up. Tante Raizel stepped back fearfully.

"I am not standing up against you, but rather for you."

Tante Raizel stared back, immobile.

"You do not recognize me? Perhaps if I remind you …"

As he unfolded the forgotten tale, it all came back …

As a 12-year-old girl, Raizel had happened upon a crying youth, a strapping lad of 15, the son of their gentile neighbor. She gently asked the reason for his tears and slowly the story emerged. The peasant boy worked with his father on the family farm despite his desire for education and knowledge. He begged his father to allow him to attend university, but his father adamantly refused. "A peasant you were born, and a peasant you shall remain!" They argued and argued until finally, the father threw his son out of the house. Now the boy had another reason to cry. He had no place to go, no money, and no real plans.

Raizel urged the boy to accompany her home. Then she ran to her father. "Tatte," she cried, "I found this gentile boy crying and I could not bear the sound of his tears. Please, Tatte, can't we help him?"

Bemused, Raizel's father questioned his daughter. He listened quietly, pondering her words. "*Nu*, Raizeleh," he said, "when you have an urge to help another, even a gentile child, do it. '*Shalach lachmecha al p'nei hamayim* — Cast your bread upon the waters';[12] one never knows how

---

12. *Koheles* 11:1.

one day it will return to nourish he who threw it." Then he handed her some money. "Here, go with him to town, buy him some books and clothing and give him money for a train ride to a big city where he can attend university."

This seemingly trivial episode of Raizel's childhood elicited no further thought, attention, or follow-up. Meanwhile, the lad did exactly what he had intended. He found his way to a large city and enrolled in the university. He excelled in his studies and rose through the political ranks until he became the district governor.

"I have never forgotten the kindness that you and your father showed me. Keep your gift, ask for whatever you want, and I will try my best to help you."

Raizel told him the story of the children of Staiptz who were being conscripted into the Russian army. The district governor immediately composed a proclamation freeing the children permanently and instructed her to rush back to the town, for if the children had already been taken away, the proclamation would be worthless.

Raizel raced back to Staiptz, arriving there by nightfall. She heard the cries of the children, assembled in the town square, as they were being loaded onto wagons and the heartbreaking goodbyes of their mothers as the army officers pulled the children out of their arms.

"Wait!" Raizel called out, holding the proclamation high in her hand. "You cannot take them! They are free! They are free!"

The commanding officer looked at her in annoyance, snatching the paper from her hand. He read the proclamation in disbelief. Yet he recognized the signature and had no choice but to honor it. That night, all the children returned home, to their profound happiness and relief.

Raizel returned home, dazed and awestruck by the intricate design of the Master of the World. And to think that it was all a result of a kindness she did 35 years earlier! She was overflowing with love and gratitude to *HaKadosh Baruch Hu.*

BASHA WAS ENCHANTED BY TANTE RAIZEL'S SAGA. THE TALE CONtained all the values her parents held dear: reverence for Torah leaders and a deep *emunas chachamim,* compassion for others, selflessness for the community, and recognition of G-d's munificence for His people, even in situations that seem hopeless. The story was a rich resource that she would be able to draw upon on many occasions in the years to come.

ANOTHER FREQUENT VISITOR TO THE EPSTEIN HOME WAS RABBI BORUCH Epstein,[13] the author of the renowned *Torah Temimah.* The years Reb Boruch

---

13. Rabbi Boruch HaLevi Epstein (1860-1941) was the son of the renowned *Aruch HaShulchan,*

frequented the Epstein home were some of the most difficult years of his life. World War I had changed his life forever: he lost his wife, his children fled Europe, and his bank collapsed. Widowed, alone, and poverty stricken, Reb Boruch tried not to succumb to depression. Children — all children, but especially the Epstein children — brought him tremendous joy. Visiting the Epsteins worked wonders on his moods. Reciprocally, the Epstein children always spoke of Reb Boruch with affection. They never forgot the attention he showered upon them. Although he lived in poverty, Reb Boruch never came to the Epstein home empty-handed; there would always be something for the children. His eyes shone with love, as he presented them with the newest treat or trinket. On one of these visits, he called little Bashke over.

"*Mammale,* look what I have for you." Reb Boruch smiled warmly as he pulled out a small package.

Basha stretched out her hand and shyly accepted the gift. She could barely contain her excitement when she opened the package. Colored pencils! For Basha, regular pencils were still a treat and colored pencils — why, she did not know anyone who had colored pencils. For days, she walked around elated. She was certain that she was the luckiest girl in the world.

VISITORS USUALLY CAME DURING THE DAY. THE EVENING HOURS WERE quiet and peaceful. The children were sent to bed, and the adults had time for a bit of conversation or comfortable silence.

Ten o'clock. A short, sharp ring of the doorbell broke the silence. R' Yankev raised his eyebrows and looked at his wife. It was late, long after most people had already retired for the night, who could it be? They waited. It rang again, short and sharp, as if embarrassed to disturb. It was too early for the NKVD — they usually made their rounds in the wee hours of morning. It was also too polite.

R' Yankev walked to the door and peered through the peephole. On the other side of the door stood the building's watchman, flanked by a distinguished-looking official. R' Yankev opened the door. "Yes?" he inquired.

"Good evening, Mr. Epstein. This gentleman requested to speak with your wife. I thought you, too, might be interested in speaking with him."

"Certainly," R' Yankev answered, as he gestured to the gentleman to enter. The watchman lingered, hoping for an invitation. He was more than a little curious at to why a prestigious member of the Communist Party would want to speak with Lifsha Epstein. Thanking the watchman for

---

Rabbi Yechiel Michel Epstein. At the age of 13 Reb Boruch became the youngest student of his uncle, the *Netziv,* at the Volozhiner Yeshivah. When his dire financial situation forced him to leave the yeshivah world, the *Netziv* made him promise to continue, among other works, his famous sefer *Torah Temimah.* He was *niftar* in the ghetto in Pinsk, Russia.

doing his job so well, R' Yankev politely steered him out and softly closed the door behind him. The stranger then turned to Mrs. Epstein.

"You are Lifsha Epstein?"

She nodded.

"My name is Y. from Volozhin." He looked at her intently, expecting her to recognize his name.

"Yes," Lifsha answered softly, "I believe we are related."

The stranger nodded. "We are cousins, many times removed …" As he spoke, Y. unwrapped the package he was holding. To the astonishment of his hosts, Y. revealed a peacefully sleeping baby, an infant less than a month old. Lifsha gave a startled gasp and reached out to embrace the sleeping child. "He, too, is your cousin. He is my son, a Jew, born of a Jewish mother."

Lifsha stared at the newborn baby sleeping in her arms. So young and innocent, and already trapped in a web of secrecy, intrigue, and fear.

Y. stared at his son, his gaze never wavering from the baby's face. "Since he was born, I have not been able to sleep. At night, I toss and turn, but sleep never comes. I feel the reason for my sleeplessness is that I have not circumcised my son."

A heavy silence hung accusingly in the air.

"YOU CANNOT UNDERSTAND," HE EXPLAINED ALMOST APOLOGETI-cally. "I hold a very high position in the Communist Party. If anyone were to find out that I circumcised my son, my life, my wife's life, and my son's life would all be endangered."

No one moved. The moment was tense, electric. This high-ranking Communist official, who evoked fear in the hearts of many, was afraid. He was afraid to do what he knew was right. He was afraid that his so-called friends would kill him.

"You are embarrassed by me, embarrassed that I am a member of your family. I will have you know that there are other people just like me in the best of families." He paced the room, his words defensive. "Your eyes accuse me. You feel that I should run away, leave my position, and return to my people. Well, I cannot. I cannot give up what I have worked so hard for all these years. I have finally achieved a position of wealth and power. I have attained a high standard of living that very few Russians can even dream of. I just cannot …"

What good was all his wealth and power when he was denied the free-dom to follow his conscience?

"Yet, I cannot go on," his voice dropped to a whisper. Pain, fear, and uncertainty echoed from his barely murmured words. "I cannot sleep. I am tormented by the need to circumcise my son. So, I turn to you. Can you help me? Please?"

Asking for a favor was especially difficult for someone used to giving orders. Moreover, he knew he was not asking for an ordinary favor. His request of these virtual strangers would jeopardize their lives.

He did not wait for their answer. "Look," he said as he scribbled on a piece of paper, "I cannot pay you for this. But what I am giving you now is more valuable than money. This is my private phone number. If you are ever in trouble and need help, call me, and I will do my best. But I am warning you; my name must never be mentioned. If you mention my name, everything is over — your life, my life — everything. When you call this number, only say your name, and I will understand."

Suddenly, he was gone. The encounter had been swift, but dramatic. Were it not for the "package" he left, the entire incident might have been a fleeting dream. The Epstein apartment became a bevy of activity. Blankets, towels, sheets, pillowcases, rags, and old clothes were stuffed into all the cracks and crevices of the walls of the apartment. The spaces around the windows and doors, holes in the floorboards, and even the keyholes were filled with fabric in an effort to soundproof the apartment as effectively as possible. The baby slept, but soon enough he would wake up; when he did, his cries could endanger them all. Although Lifsha Epstein was still of childbearing age, babies do not appear overnight. Lifsha could not pass him off as her own, so where did he come from? She shooed her children, Bashke and Yosef, off to bed and sat with her husband to work out the details of the arrangements.

Basha lay in bed, too excited to sleep. Imagine — a newborn baby right here in her home! She strained to eavesdrop on her parents' conversation. "… Formula … Maybe we could wash the diapers at night? … We must keep him quiet … Where? Maybe the forest …" Their muffled words continued well into the night. Basha's eyelids drooped with fatigue and soon she was asleep.

For the next six weeks, Lifsha put the rest of her life aside and devoted herself to caring for the baby. She fed, held, rocked, and played with him. She may have given him more attention than she would have given her own child. She wanted to compensate him for the absence of his mother and above all, she wanted to make sure that he did not cry. Somehow, they managed. R' Yankev arranged for a *mohel* to perform the *milah* and despite the danger, and accompanying fear, the *milah* was performed. Even in the days after the *bris*, when the baby was certainly in pain, Lifsha kept him quiet. Weeks passed.

One dark night, the doorbell rang. Even before she reached the door, Lifsha knew who it was. The baby's father had arrived to reclaim his child. Lifsha bundled the child in blankets and handed him back to his father. Y. thanked the Epsteins and seemed relieved that the ordeal was over. He reached for the doorknob to leave. Suddenly he turned around.

"You have my number?" he asked. Lifsha nodded and he disappeared into the night.

LIFE WENT ON. THE SITUATION IN RUSSIA WORSENED AND R' YANKEV sought ways to return to Poland, his country of birth. The Epsteins' ties to post-World War I Russia were weak. It was only during World War I, when Russia still controlled vast amounts of territory including Poland, that the Epsteins moved to Minsk. Their citizenship papers listed them as residents of Warsaw, which was within the borders of newly independent Poland. This meant that legally the Epsteins were Polish citizens residing in Russia. The problem was that Russia did not allow such residents to leave.

Their only option was to leave Russia illegally, a dangerous course of action that R' Yankev was not prepared to take. In the meantime, R' Yankev continued to attend his nightly *shiurim,* and Lifsha continued her prayers for her husband's safe return.

One morning, R' Yankev did not return home. Frantic inquiries revealed the dreaded facts. The basement learning group had been discovered. All 24 participants were arrested and sent to Siberia. They were meant to stay there until their trial and sentencing.

Lifsha Epstein trembled when she heard the news. Siberia! Trial! Sentencing! The worst had happened. Then she composed herself. As *Chazal* say, "*Afilu cherev chadah….*"[14] — there is always hope. Her eye caught a glimpse of a slip of paper peeking out of a kitchen drawer. Her heart pounded. It was the paper with the phone number. With shaking hands, she dialed the number a few times before anyone answered. It took supreme effort to remain calm. Lifsha tried once more.

"Hello?" the voice on the other end was curt, impatient.

"My name is Lifsha Epstein."

"Call back later." Click, the line went dead.

Lifsha was undeterred. She recognized the voice, and she knew that he recognized her name. A few hours passed. She dialed again.

"Hello?"

"It is Lifsha Epstein."

"Yes, I can talk now."

Surprisingly calm, Lifsha reviewed the events of the past night. The man at the other end was silent. Finally, he spoke. "Do not do anything. Just wait." The line went dead.

Lifsha hung up, relieved. She had not placed her trust in this man and his possible efforts on her behalf. For that matter, she did not rely on any

---

14. "Even when a sharp knife is held at one's neck, one should not despair of Hashem's compassion" (*Berachos* 10a).

mortal. Her hope lay exclusively in the benevolence of the *Ribbono shel Olam*. Yet, she knew that such reliance had to be accompanied by *hishtadlus*, reasonable human effort. Now she could appeal to Him saying, "Master of the Universe, I have done mine; now You do Yours."

Weeks passed and so did many hours of prayer. Rosh Hashanah arrived. Lifsha wanted some quiet time to pour out her soul in prayer. She sent the children out to play and they were happy to go. Perhaps they sensed that this Rosh Hashanah was different than those of the past.

Basha and Yosef sat on the steps outside their apartment building. They talked lazily about nothing very important, and thought about which games to play to pass the time. The faraway sound of horses aroused their faint curiosity. They took turns guessing where the noise was coming from.

Clip … clop. Clip … clop. Clip … clop. Basha and Yosef watched with interest as a very old horse plodded slowly down the street. Clip … clop. Clip … clop. Clip … clop. Would the old mare ever reach its destination? The dilapidated wagon was too heavy for her. As it came closer, the children saw that the wagon carried three passengers. In the front, holding the reigns, sat the driver. He looked ordinary enough, although he seemed rather bored, as if driving such a pathetic horse and wagon was a tedious chore for him.

The passengers in the back piqued the children's interest. They had never seen such strange-looking people! Their curiosity was further aroused when the wagon pulled up right in front of their building. The children watched in astonishment as the two strange-looking men slowly climbed out. They were so tall, or maybe they just seemed so tall because they were so thin. The skin on their faces was stretched tightly over their cheekbones, as if the artist who fashioned them could not spare an extra inch. Their head and faces were shaven. The two skeletal men passed right by the children and entered the Epsteins' building. Quietly, the children followed, eager to see what this was all about. They watched in surprise as the men headed straight for the Epstein home. One of them knocked softly on the door.

Lifsha Epstein had been davening and crying all morning. Her eyes were red and she felt completely drained. Who would be disturbing her at this time of morning, on Rosh Hashanah, no less? The knocking continued, so she dragged herself over to the door and opened it.

Lifsha let out a shocked scream. Her hand moved involuntarily up and she covered her mouth as if to prevent herself from uttering another sound. The men quickly slipped into the apartment, with the children close at their heels. Lifsha pulled out chairs and drinks and urged them to sit down.

ALL AT ONCE, BASHA KNEW WHAT HAD HAPPENED. THE FUNNY-looking man, smiling in relief, was Papa! *It cannot be,* she thought. *It must be a mistake. This man looks nothing like Papa. Where are his beard and peiyos? This man is not even wearing a hat or a yarmulke! Why would Papa wear such strange clothes?*

As Lifsha plied the men with cake and drinks, R' Yankev recounted the miracle of his survival. Several weeks earlier on that fateful night, he and his friend Rabinowitz and the other members of the *shiur* were "arrested." They were immediately shipped off to Siberia. There, the prison officers shaved off their beards and *peiyos,* shaved their heads, and handed each prisoner a prison uniform. They were assigned to the barracks until their trial. The trial was held and all the men from the *shiur* were accused of conspiracy to revolt against the government. At the farce of a trial no evidence was produced and no defense was presented, but they were found guilty. The sentence: death by firing squad.

Days passed. Maybe a miracle would occur and the death sentences would not be carried out. One day, the prison officers ordered the men to march out into the field. They lined them up and assigned each man a number. R' Yankev was near the end of the line and was given the number 23; Rabinowitz was last in line with number 24. They faced a group of soldiers whose guns were poised to shoot. The soldiers began with number one. R' Yankev closed his eyes and softly whispered words of *Tehillim.* A shot rang out followed by the thud of a body falling to the ground. R' Yankev lost track of the shots as he tried to block out the pain. He was aware of only two things: that each shot brought him closer to his death and that he yearned to die with prayers to Hashem on his lips. The shots continued with an eerie rhythm and R' Yankev continued murmuring *Tehillim.* He knew that his turn was near.

"Halt!" A desperate shout was heard through the shots.

R' Yankev opened his eyes. On one side of him stood Rabinowitz, as white and scared as he was. On the other side of him lay the bodies of their 22 friends. In front of them, a heated discussion between a high-ranking officer and the officer overseeing the executions was taking place. R' Yankev's heart pounded. Dare he hope …?

"You two — Epstein, Rabinowitz — you are free to go." The high-ranking officer motioned them to come closer. He proceeded to give them and an officer in charge instructions for their transport. That afternoon, they were sent home.

Nobody spoke. The realization of the miracle that had occurred made its full impact. The Epsteins never found out exactly what had transpired, but they were fairly certain that Y. had somehow engineered the rescue. This was only the first time that Hashem sent this messenger to save them. [15]

AN IMPORTANT ANNOUNCEMENT PEALED OUT THROUGH THE STREETS of Minsk: All Polish citizens with proper citizenship papers should report to a government office where they might receive permission to return to Poland. The Epsteins were excited. Finally, after all these years of suffering, they might be allowed to leave Russia. They yearned to live openly as *Yidden*, without fear. Moreover, they still had the deed to a two-story apartment building in Warsaw. If they could claim this valuable piece of property, they would have a means of income and their financial situation, which had been precarious ever since the rise of the Communists, would be greatly improved.

A quick trip to the local government office confirmed the news. Within a few days, the Epsteins sold their furniture, packed their belongings, and notified the superintendent of their building that they were giving up their apartment. They left Minsk on the next train.

Basha took a window seat so she could watch the Russian plains roll by. Outwardly, she appeared calm, but inside, her heart was singing. Finally, finally, they were leaving Russia.

A few hours later, the train arrived at Baranovich. From there, they were supposed to catch a connecting train to Warsaw.

"Attention, all passengers. We have just been notified that Warsaw is overcrowded. All those traveling to other locations in Poland may continue to their destinations. Those with tickets to Warsaw must return to Russia. I repeat: At this time, Warsaw is not accepting any new arrivals. Anyone whose papers allow them entrance to Warsaw must return to Russia."

Basha wanted to scream. No, no, no! They cannot do this to us! She looked at her parents, frozen in their seats, and realized that they too found this disappointment almost too difficult to bear. In less than a minute, their moods had changed from bright to bleak. They seemed too paralyzed to cope. Yet the train had just pulled into the station and passengers were filing out; they would have to follow.

Moments later, they stood, dejected, bewildered, and tired, on the station platform surrounded by their valises. They had no food and no idea where to go or what to do next. If they would return to Minsk, they would have nowhere to stay. Yet their entry permit to Poland was specifically for Warsaw. They had no permission to settle anywhere else. What should they do?

---

15. Rebbetzin Bender repeated this story annually at the Pesach Seder when they reached "*Vehi she'amdah lavoseinu v'lanu*," which reminds us of how, in every generation, the gentiles try to destroy the Jewish people, and yet *HaKadosh Baruch Hu* continues to saves His nation.

They looked around at their fellow passengers. Parents looked help-less and bewildered while their babies wailed for food. Children sat on the floor, shivering in the cold. Families huddled together, abandoned, alone, and waiting for someone to tell them what to do. Since no one knew what to say, there was little interaction or mutual comforting.[16]

"Wait," Lifsha exclaimed. "Let us call Y. Hashem sent him to help us before; perhaps he will be His messenger once again." She left her husband and children in charge of the packages and ran to find a phone.

With trembling fingers, Lifsha dialed the familiar number. This time, Y. answered on the first ring. All her pent-up emotions of the last half-hour burst forth as she poured out her heart in a rare show of emotion. She described their plight: how she, her husband, and two little children were stranded at the Baranovich train station and had nowhere to go and no one to turn to. They were exhausted from the journey and had not eaten for hours. If only someone would give them some advice, some indication as to what to do.

Y. listened silently. For a fleeting moment, Lifsha wondered if they had been disconnected. She clutched at the phone willing it to produce some sound.

"Well," the voice on the other end said softly, slowly, as if considering each word, "you definitely cannot enter Warsaw at the moment. Stay where you are. I will try to send someone to help you make other arrangements."

Click. The line went dead. As usual, his words were clipped and brusque. Lifsha was not quite certain if the conversation had taken place at all. She trudged back to her family, waiting on the platform, and spoke with her husband. They decided that they might as well heed Y.'s instructions and wait there for a while; after all, they did not have many options.

A short while later, the Epsteins noticed a dapper young man enter the station. His eyes scanned the faces of the thin crowd until they came to rest on the bewildered family huddled on the train platform. He hurried toward them with a welcoming smile. Nonchalantly, without formal intro-ductions, he rattled off the familiar phone number and that was enough. Names were superfluous.

While distributing kosher food to the family and milk for the children, he started a casual conversation with R' Yankev. The young man energeti-cally heaved the valises out of the way and motioned for the Epsteins to join him.

---

16. In recalling this incident, Rebbetzin Bender reflected, "It was such a difficult time. We felt lost and abandoned, truly homeless. There were many much larger families in the same situa-tion. Yet, these stories have been largely forgotten. The events of the Holocaust eclipsed these experiences — in their horror and in the scope of the tragedy — so that everything else became minor."

"Listen, I suggest that you find somewhere else to stay in Poland for the time being. Right now, Warsaw is truly overcrowded, and no amount of *protectzia* will grant you permission to enter. Yet, Warsaw will not be closed forever. Stay somewhere small and quiet where you will not be noticed, and when Warsaw opens you will be able to enter. Do you know anyone who lives nearby?"

R' YANKEV WAS SILENT. HE HAD A BROTHER WHO LIVED IN NEARBY Stolptza, but he was afraid to mention it. Stolptza was near the Russian border. R' Yankev was not sure that his brother was on good terms with the Communists there. Perhaps his brother would be afraid to take them in. Perhaps their presence would disrupt some secret illegal activities. So R' Yankev kept quiet out of fear: fear of telling the truth and fear of lying; fear of saying too much and fear of saying too little; and ultimately, fear of confiding in someone, even someone sent to help.

"Maybe we should go to Mir," R' Yankev suggested with hesitation.

Lifsha considered the idea. At least Mir was familiar territory. Many years earlier, one of her grandfathers had been the Rav of Mir, and she had many relatives there. She looked toward the stranger who had come to help, wondering what he was thinking

The stranger shrugged his shoulders. Mir seemed fine to him. Anywhere in the area would be fine for the time being. He proceeded to help them buy tickets and make arrangements. When they bade the stranger good-bye, the Epsteins were effusive in their thanks. They parted ways, never to see each other again.

For several months, the Epsteins wandered from *shtetl* to *shtetl*. They stayed with relatives for two weeks, friends for three weeks … Legal entry and the possibility of legal permanent residence in Warsaw seemed close to impossible. For a family accustomed to hosting others, the ordeal was exceptionally painful.

One day, unannounced, the Epsteins received a letter with the long-awaited entry permit for Warsaw. It was clear enough that Y. had sent the papers from Russia. How he had located them was a mystery that would always puzzle Basha, but when remembering the ordeal, her parents focused on Y. being a Divine messenger sent to save and help them. They had no doubt that it was in the merit of the mitzvah of *milah* that they were worthy of this Divine assistance.

*Chapter Nine*

# Otvock — A Healthy Haven

**Warsaw: 5682 (1922)[17]**

S THEIR TRAIN APPROACHED WARSAW, THE EPSTEINS allowed themselves a modicum of excitement. Could it be true that after months of wandering they would finally be able to settle down? Considering that they were entering Warsaw, what could possibly go wrong now? The train pulled into the station. The passengers claimed their baggage and waited for their papers to be examined. The Epsteins waited their turn and thankfully, nothing went amiss. They emerged from the station buoyant. Finally, they were considered legal Polish citizens, residents of Warsaw and its environs.

They proceeded toward the neighborhood where their apartment was located. Lifsha was tired and could not wait to settle down in familiar territory. Alas, another disappointment. The newly formed Polish government had appropriated the building for their own use and refused to acknowledge R' Yankev's deed. Once again, the Epsteins were out on the street.

R' Yankev and his wife took the disappointment in stride. One thing was certain: they had to find an apartment, at least for the night. With his family trailing behind him, R' Yankev proceeded to knock on doors and ask if anyone knew of an available apartment. Quite quickly they discov-

_____
17. Approximate date.

*Chapter Nine: Otvock — A Healthy Haven* / 123

ered that what they had heard was true; Warsaw was overcrowded. There were no available apartments in Warsaw.

One Warsaw resident suggested that they seek accommodations in one of the suburbs. Otvock, close to Warsaw with excellent transportation to the city, sounded like the most attractive alternative. Besides, in Otvock, R' Yankev had a friend who he hoped would help them get settled.

Once again, the Epsteins boarded a train. Basha sat quietly and pensively. She would try to emulate her parents' patience. They barely uttered a complaint and neither would she. Surely *HaKadosh Baruch Hu* would soon resolve their continuous wandering.

A very subdued Epstein family disembarked in Otvock. They quietly made their way to the home of R' Yankev's friend. He welcomed them warmly. They had not seen each other for many years and much had changed in the interim. Lifsha was relieved to realize that at least they would have a place to stay for the night. But as the conversation continued, and R' Yankev hesitantly asked about the availability of apartments in Otvock, Lifsha felt her spirits plummet. Otvock was just as overcrowded as Warsaw. Their chance of finding permanent housing in Otvock was dubious.

"Wait a minute — just today, someone told me that the H. family decided to move. I do not know if this is true, but it is certainly worth checking out." R' Yankev's friend jotted down the address and handed it to him. "Leave the children with us, and you and your rebbetzin immediately run over there. *Hatzlachah rabbah* — be successful!"

R' Yankev and Lifsha hastened to the address. When they got there, they saw a large villa with six apartments. From one of the apartments, the flurry of activity could be heard even on the street. The Epsteins knocked cautiously. The sight they beheld was astounding. The father, mother, and their three children were all running around the apartment and packing. Not only had they decided to move that very day, but they were leaving immediately! There was no time for too many questions. The Epsteins asked if they could take over the apartment, and the exiting tenants happily agreed. For them, the Epsteins were an answer to an important unresolved issue. In their haste, they had had no time to make arrangements for all their furniture. If reliable Jewish people were taking over the apartment, they would certainly be careful with the property of another Jew. Lifsha offered to pay for the furniture, but they refused, saying they hoped they would eventually send for it. In the meantime, the Epsteins were welcome to use everything that was left behind.

Lifsha stayed in the apartment and her husband ran to his friend's home to bring the children and their belongings. She was afraid to leave lest someone, in her absence, come and stake claim to the apartment. That evening, the two families slept in the same apartment; bright and early the next morning, the previous occupants left. The Epsteins found themselves standing at the threshold of their new apartment waving a relieved good-bye to their briefly met acquaintances. R' Yankev and Lifsha stood staring at each other, barely believing their good fortune. Not only had they found an apartment in overcrowded Otvock, but their apartment was larger than most. In contrast to the standard one-bedroom apartments, theirs had two bedrooms.

To the Epsteins, the reason why the previous tenants had made such a hasty departure was irrelevant; it was clearly an act of Divine intervention. The scarcity of apartments was well known; nevertheless, the very day they arrived in Otvock, a family who was not even planning to move suddenly decided to leave, and the Epsteins got their apartment. Hashem had decreed that Otvock was an ideal place for the Epsteins to continue their lives of Torah, *chessed*, and *hachnosas orchim*.

OTVOCK WAS VERY DIFFERENT FROM MINSK. ONE SECTION OF OTVOCK was citylike; it had residential houses, offices, and stores. On the other side of town was a section set higher into the mountainous forest area. There lay quaint villas surrounded by majestic pine trees and glorious green grass. People came from all over Poland to breathe in the healthy mountain air. Others came to recuperate from illnesses. Still others came to Otvock

*Otvock was famous for its invigorating mountain air. People came to recuperate from illnesses, to vaca-tion, or just to enjoy the fresh, clean, healthy environment for which Otvock was known.*

to vacation. All enjoyed the fresh, clean, healthy environment for which Otvock was known.

The Epsteins were delighted with their new home. They had a tremendous appreciation for the beauty of Hashem's world spread out before them in all its glory. Basha could not dream of a more beautiful, enchanting place to live.

R' YANKEV HAD HOPED THAT NOW THAT HE WAS IN POLAND, FAR AWAY from Communist Russia, he would be able to devote more time to learning. R' Yankev desperately wanted to remain in the Torah world, and so he decided to accept an administrative position in a yeshivah. He was happy to have some connection with Torah scholars. He traveled daily to Warsaw where he collected funds for the yeshivah and managed their finances. In the afternoon, he worked for a wealthy aunt in town.

The Jews of Otvock were meticulously observant Chassidim. Although R' Yankev was a *Litvak* through and through, he soon earned the respect of his *Chassidishe* neighbors. They appreciated his level of religious observance, integrity, and erudition. While always warm and friendly, his actions were calculated, and he eschewed small talk and unnecessary chatter. What happened to be going on here and there did not interest him; a *vort* on the *parashah*, a *p'shat* in a Mishnah, a *s'vorah* in Gemara[18] — these were constantly on his lips.[19] He gave a Mishnayos *shiur* in the local shul every day between *Minchah* and *Ma'ariv* and was considered a prominent member of the community.

The children also settled into life in Otvock. Every day they traveled to Warsaw where Basha attended gymnasium and Yosef attended *cheder*. They went by electric train — one of the few that existed in Poland at the time — so the trip took only half an hour.

Lifsha stayed at home, but housework was not her only preoccupation. Lifsha was an extremely talented woman. Although she had never taken any formal sewing classes, she was able to look at clothing she liked and replicate them. At that time, it was fashionable to wear bed-jackets — lightweight jackets worn over a nightgown. Bed-jackets were a dressier alternative to a robe. She sewed one for herself and one for a friend. Soon other neighborhood women besieged her with requests for bed-jackets. That was how she and her friend began a business, sewing and selling bed-jackets, robes, and other such garments.

Although Lifsha grew up before the Bais Yaakov era, before Jewish education for girls was common, she was well versed in all areas of Jewish

---

18. A lesson from that week's Torah portion, an insight into understanding a Mishnah, a logical argument on a topic in Gemara.

19. Repeated at the *shivah* for Rebbetzin Bender.

knowledge, a credit to her illustrious home. Lifsha was the daughter of Rabbi Shmuel Tzvi Shachor. The Shachor family was renown for their piety and scholarship. Reb Shmuel Tzvi was one of five brothers all of whom were rabbanim. Many of the women in the family were distinguishable by their vast Jewish knowledge,[20] a rarity among women at the time.

Even as a married woman — with children to care for, a house to run, and her responsibilities to contribute to the family coffers — Lifsha was constantly reading, learning, and teaching.

As Torah education for girls was becoming more and more accepted,

*Rabbi Shmuel Tzvi Shachor*
*— father of Lifsha Epstein*

people wanted their daughters to receive some form of religious instruction. Some women approached Lifsha Epstein and asked her if she would be willing to teach their daughters. Lifsha was overjoyed. To merit transmitting Torah while contributing to the family's livelihood was an ideal situation. She taught her young charges *Chumash*, *Nach*, *Lashon Kodesh*, and how to read and write Yiddish. It was a beneficial arrangement for everyone.

YET, THE DOMINANT FEATURE OF THE EPSTEIN FAMILY WAS THEIR HOME of *chessed*. Otvock was a city that beckoned to guests and the Epstein door was always open. Even those who did not actually stay at the Epstein home would drop by to find out where to rent a room or who was the best doctor to see.

---

20. *Zechor Mordechai*, p. 3: Rebbetzin Tzartyl Shachor, Lifsha's aunt, is described as "the wondrously learned," and her daughter, Rebbetzin Shaindel Feinstein, Lifsha's cousin, is described as "outstandingly wise." Shaindel was married to Rabbi Mordechai Feinstein (d. 1938), *Av Beis Din* of Shklov, and the brother of Rabbi Moshe Feinstein. The high esteem that Reb Moshe granted his brother is recorded in the salutation of a letter that Reb Moshe addressed to Reb Mordechai: "... My beloved brother the *gaon*, the sharp one ..." (*Igros Moshe, Even HaEzer* 128). This was not his standard salutation. With the Communists' rise to power, Rabbi Mordechai Feinstein gave up his opportunity to leave Russia, refusing to forsake his mother-in-law who could not leave the country. He was arrested by the Communists, together with other famous rabbanim, and died in prison. Few of his manuscripts were rescued. Reb Moshe never forgot his illustrious brother and requested that his name and that of his family members who were killed in the war be inscribed on his headstone. Reb Moshe always told Rebbetzin Bender, "*Mir zenen mishpachah* — we are family."

*Rabbi Chaim Ozer Grodzenski (1863- 1940) became
Rav of Vilna at the age of 23. He headed the Vilna beis
din for 56 years and was revered for his wide-ranging
Torah knowledge and dedication to Klal Yisroel. Reb
Chaim Ozer was the undisputed gadol hador. He
helped found Agudath Yisroel and established the
Vaad HaYeshivos and the Vaad Hatzalah. His halachic
responsa are printed in the sefer Achiezer.*

Rabbi Chaim Ozer Grodzenski, the illustrious Rav of Vilna, rarely left
his town. The long lines of people waiting to meet with the *gadol hador*
spilled over onto the streets. His dedication to *Klal Yisroel* knew no bounds.
Rebbetzin Leah (Grodnensky) Grodzenski, though, at times found herself in need of a vacation. She would come to Otvock and stay with the
Epsteins. The Epstein children were always glad to vacate their room for
their guests. One child slept in the kitchen while the other slept in the wide
hallway that led from the kitchen to the bedrooms.[21]

Lifsha Epstein was a great-granddaughter of Rabbi Chaim Leib Shachor
who was a son-in-law of Reb Itzele Volozhiner, the son of Reb Chaim Volozhiner.[22] As such, she was a descendant of royalty and related to some of
the most illustrious families in Poland and Lithuania.[23] Members of the

---

21. Looking back fondly at these years, Rebbetzin Bender was wont to comment how she never
thought much about these arrangements. Giving one's bed up for guests, even for weeks at a
time, was the natural thing to do and she never thought otherwise.

22. Rabbi Chaim Itzkowitz (1749-1881) is known as Reb Chaim Volozhiner, the "Father of
Yeshivos." He learned under the guidance of Rabbi Rafael HaKohen Hamburger and the *Shaagas
Aryeh*. Reb Chaim married the daughter of Rabbi Aryeh Leib Ginsburg of Vilna, moved to Vilna,
and became the premier student of the Vilna Gaon. Later, Reb Chaim returned to his hometown,
Volozhin, where he served as Rav for 45 years. He founded the great Yeshivah of Volozhin in
1803, changing the face of the yeshivah world.

Rabbi Yitzchok Itzkowitz (1780-1849) was known as Reb Itzele Volozhiner. He was the son of
Reb Chaim of Volozhin, and was one of his closest disciples in Torah and *Kabbalah*. He was the
illustrious successor of his father in the position as Rosh Yeshivah in Volozhin and named the
yeshivah Eitz Chaim, after his father's passing.

23. Lithuania/Poland refers to an area that, at one time, belonged to Lithuania but, between
the wars, belonged to Poland. People who resided there considered themselves "*Litvish*" —
Lithuanian.

Soloveitchik family of Brisk were cousins, as was the Shachor-Kossovsky family. No matter how distantly related the Volozhiner descendants were, they considered one another family and remained close.

The Brisker Rav, Rabbi Yitzchok Zev "Velvele" Soloveitchik, often came to Otvock. While the Rebbetzin and the younger children would stay by the Epsteins, the Rav slept in an apartment next door. This would allow the Brisker Rav to get his much needed rest, and the children would benefit from the fresh mountain air.

Occasionally, Rebbetzin Soloveitchik came to Otvock without her husband, usually with a few of the children — active little boys who kept the young Rebbetzin on her toes. During one of their stays, a man from Brisk happened to pass through the Epstein home. Before he began his return trip to Brisk, he asked the Rebbetzin if she had any messages for the Rav.

She thought for a moment. "Tell him that the children are being very difficult. They are not listening to what I say, and they are not eating properly."

The man nodded, thanked Lifsha Epstein for her hospitality, and left the house. As he was walking, he heard a noise behind him. He turned around and found himself facing the Brisker Rav's 5-year-old son. The little boy was panting from running to catch up. He caught his breath and looked up at the man with a bright innocent smile. "*Reb Yid,*" he said, "would you really say *lashon hara* about another Jew?"

For a moment, the man did not know what the child meant. Suddenly, he recalled the Rebbetzin's parting message, and he began to laugh. The 5-year-old child had outsmarted his mother! The man went back inside to share the child's "*chochmah*" with his mother. The women laughed heartily and for days, they repeated the tale of the boy's quick wit.[24]

RABBI HERSHEL GLICKSON,[25] THE BRISKER RAV'S BROTHER-IN-LAW, WAS another frequent visitor. He lived in Warsaw and came to Otvock regularly. He and R' Yankev Epstein became friends. One day, when Basha was reading a book, Reb Hershel walked in. He asked to see the book and quickly skimmed its pages. He then took out a red pen and began to mark different lines and paragraphs. When he handed the book back to the young girl, he commented that he was surprised she was reading "such a book." Basha shrunk back in embarrassment. Surely, she — a good *frum* girl — would

---

24. Rebbetzin Bender loved to repeat this story. She always enjoyed the sharp wit of children.

25. Rabbi Tzvi Hershel Glickson (d. 1943) was a close *talmid* of Rabbi Chaim Soloveitchik of Brisk. Reb Hersh later married the Rav's daughter, Sarah Rasha. After their marriage, they lived in Warsaw where he served as Rosh Yeshivah of Yeshivas Toras Chaim. He and his family perished during the Holocaust.

have noticed any improper ideas.

Just then, R' Yankev walked in. Basha ran to her father and blurted out what had happened. "Look at it yourself," she said, thrusting the book at her father. "What is wrong with it?"

R' Yankev took the book from his daughter and found the pages marked in red. After a cursory glance, he understood exactly what Reb Hershel had found disturbing. Immediately, he ripped the book into tiny little pieces and threw it into the garbage. Basha learned a profound lesson. Although she prided herself in being a good student and a *frum* girl, she had read the entire book and had not seen anything wrong with it, while a *talmid chacham* skimmed only a few pages and saw the evil ideas that the author had cleverly incorporated into an innocent story. This is because our Torah leaders are *"einei ha'eidah* — the eyes of the congregation"; they see things that ordinary people cannot. Basha was grateful to Reb Hershel for his intervention.

Many young yeshivah *bochurim* found their way to the Epstein door. In their zeal to avoid being drafted into the Polish army, these boys would starve themselves sick. After they failed the physical exam and were deemed too weak for army service, they went to Otvock to recuperate. R' Yankev Epstein took the young scholars into his home. They ate, slept, and convalesced there — sometimes for extended periods.[26] Many of the boys were from very poor homes and could not afford to pay for the treatments they needed. R' Yankev made an arrangement with a local nurse who agreed to treat the *bochurim* at a greatly reduced price. This solved the problem for some, but not for all. One boy, Moshe Yehudah Blau,[27] needed a series of injections and he did not want a female nurse to administer the treatment. R' Yankev expended extra effort to find a male nurse qualified to treat the *bochur*.

The Epstein family performed *chessed* with a style that was uniquely their own. Not only did they care for the sick *bochurim*, they worried about their caretakers: family or friends who came along to help care for the invalid. Notka Volozhiner was a penniless Mirrer student stricken with tuberculosis. He came to Otvock accompanied by Moshe Cohn,[28] a German *bochur* who had undertaken to raise money for his care. After seeing that Notka had a place to stay and was beginning treatments, Moshe returned to Mir. He visited Otvock periodically to see how his friend was faring. Each time he came, the Epsteins greeted him with warmth and love, as if a member of

---

26. The gentile armies of Eastern Europe were rife with anti-Semitism, especially toward religious Jews. While a gentile who entered the army might or might not be killed in action, for a young yeshivah *bochur*, army service was a death sentence, either physically or spiritually. Many boys were left with lifelong health issues from the drastic steps they took to avoid the draft.

27. See Biography Section.

28. See Biography Section.

### Rabbi Avrohom Kalmanowitz on a fund-raising visit to America:

*Bottom row, from left to right: Rabbi Reuvain Levovitz (brother of Rabbi Yeruchem Levovitz), Rabbi Avrohom Kalmanowitz, Rabbi Leizer Yud'l Finkel, Rabbi Isaac Sher (Rosh Yeshivah of Slabodka), and Rabbi Zalman Permut (Menahel of Kovno Kollel)*
*Top row, from left to right: Rabbi Kotzultzki (Menahel Misrad of Slabodka), Rav of Vilna, R' Moshe Yitzchok Mendelowitz, Rabbi Nissan Wachsman, Rabbi Yosef Adler, and Rabbi Avrohom Chinitz*

*Rabbi Avrohom Kalmanowitz (1891-1964) was a talmid of Slabodka. He served as Rav of Rakov and later in Tiktin, Poland, a town of great lamdanim. In 1926 Rabbi Kalmanowitz was appointed president of Mirrer Yeshivah, a responsibility he carried for the rest of his life. He reached America at the start of World War II and assumed full responsibility for the yeshivah's support during its exile in Shanghai. He founded Yeshivas Mir in Brooklyn, N.Y. and served as its Rosh Yeshivah.*

the family had come home.

As the years went by, the Epstein home acquired a reputation for selfless hospitality and *chessed*. Many Lithuanian Torah leaders passed through their doors. The Brisker Rav's family and Rabbi Boruch Ber Leibowitz were frequent visitors. Rabbi Avrohom Kalmanowitz, the Rakower Rav, remembered R' Yankev from Minsk. When Reb Avrohom moved to Otvock and established his own kollel there, he became a frequent visitor to the Epstein home as well. Often, he brought along his young son, Shraga Moshe, to share a Shabbos meal and sometimes even to stay for a few days when

*Rabbi Shraga Moshe Kalmanowitz (1918-1998) learned in Mir and Kaminetz. Upon arriving in America at the onset of World War II, he learned in Torah Vodaath and Bais Medrash Elyon. Reb Shraga Moshe served as a maggid shiur in the Mirrer Yeshivah in America and then became Rosh Yeshivah. He was a beloved father figure to the many Syrian, Moroccan, and Egyptian bochurim whom his father brought to the United States.*

yeshivah was not in session. Reb Avrohom was often away from home on *Klal* matters and was grateful that his son always had somewhere to be in his absence. He and his son, Shraga Moshe, always remembered the Epstein home fondly.

---

### A young Shraga Moshe Kalmanowitz with his friends from Mir

*Left to right: Shmuel Berenbaum, Hersh Feldman, Shraga Moshe Kalmanowitz, and Yosef Kaplan Years later, Rabbi Shraga Moshe Kalmanowitz and Rabbi Shmuel Berenbaum would be brothers-in-law and joint Roshei Yeshivah in the Mirrer yeshivah of Brooklyn. Rabbi Hersh Feldman would serve as Mashgiach.*

*Top to bottom: Shmuel Berenbaum, Yosef Kaplan, unidentified, and Shraga Moshe Kalmanowitz*

*Chapter Ten*

# Bnos

### Otvock: Tishrei 5691 (September 1930)

*L*IFSHA EPSTEIN WAS A TALENTED, EDUCATED, AND LEARNED woman. For years, she taught her daughter *limudei kodesh* and Basha was well ahead of most girls her age. Nonetheless, Lifsha had even higher expectations for her daughter. She wanted Basha to receive the best Jewish education available. She wanted Basha's exceptional abilities to be honed and challenged. She wanted Basha to attend the illustrious Bais Yaakov of Crakow.

Founded after the 1923 Knessiah Gedolah of Agudas Yisroel, the Bais Yaakov movement had 49 Bais Yaakov schools[29] with 6,585 students by the year 1925. When the younger girls — those about 14 and 15 years old — were ready to graduate, Frau Sara Schenirer worried that these teenagers might become ensnared by the many temptations of the time. While at school, the young Bais Yaakov girls had their own safe social network and the lure of secular family, friends, and neighbors was less compelling and persuasive. These girls, too old for Bais Yaakov but old enough to enter the working world, were still young and vulnerable. They felt the need to feel accepted within a peer group and, craving a social life, could easily be lured into joining the popular secular youth movements which were

---

29. The term "Bais Yaakov School" refers to elementary-level girls' schools set up through the Bais Yaakov movement. Bais Yaakov of Crakow refers to the seminary. Many Bais Yaakov schools were eventually established throughout Poland; however, there was only one seminary.

already heavily populated by Jews. The peer pressure was intense enough that even girls from strong religious families succumbed.

In 1926, Sara Schenirer launched Bnos, a branch of Bais Yaakov. Bnos was created as an alternative youth group geared to girls who were too old for the local Bais Yaakov, yet still sought a Bais Yaakov atmosphere where they could grow and flourish. Bnos would serve as a positive social network, reinforcing the values and ideals of Bais Yaakov and mitigating the allure of the secular organizations.

When Basha was growing up in Otvock, there was no Bais Yaakov school, but Basha was a member of the local Bnos chapter. Sara Schenirer was actively involved in Bnos. She kept in touch with her Bnos leaders and was kept well informed of their lessons and activities. She sent letters to the various Bnos chapters — warm, precious letters that showed her love and concern. Basha kept and always treasured the letter her Bnos chapter received.

*To My Dear "Bnos" Daughters of Otvock,[30]*

*I am sorry it has taken so long to reply to your letter, my dear girls. But, what can I do? "Lady Time" rules over me with an iron hand, and it is almost impossible for me to overcome her grasp. I must write briefly, for my time is precious.*

*I was delighted to receive the letter and hope that you have accomplished even more since then in your organization …*

*Listen, my dear daughters! The Torah is a Code of Laws. Unlike laws composed by human authors, Torah is an "Aish Dos — a Fiery Law," from the Omnipotent Creator, conceived especially for us, Yidden. This Torah, this "Aish Dos — the Fiery Law," with its special flame — can kindle and rouse the soul of a Jew and imbue him with everlasting joy …*

*Torah is (like) refreshing water, an illuminating fire, milk that satiates, and wine that gladdens. Torah is the hammer that splits rocks, the sword that governs worlds, the crown that crowns his life, the jewel that adorns his neck, the cane that supports his steps, and the candle that lights his way. Torah accompanies him in joyous times, is his adviser in times of need, his song at night, his torch on a journey, his guardian when asleep, and his first greeting in the World to Come! Torah is to a Yid an inestimable pearl, a treasure that cannot be duplicated. Torah is a wellspring of life and joy. The Torah is intrinsically good and in addition is a tree of life. One who plants and tends to this "tree" seriously will merit a taste of Gan Eden in this world.[31]*

*On the other hand, the Torah, our joy and treasure, obligates every Jew, both individually and collectively. It obligates the Kohen and the Yisroel, the learned and the ignorant, the judge, laborer, prophet, and villager all the same. The mitz-*

---

30. This letter has been translated and condensed.

31. All these images are from the *Midrash, Tehillim, Mishlei*, etc.

*vos of the Torah must be fulfilled at home and in the field, in private as in public, in shul as in the street, in business as in trivial activities. The Torah teaches us that we are children of a nation, unlike other nations, whose existence is not based on territory, or national sovereignty. Our existence is supported by the "Aish Dos," the code of fiery laws, which bind us as a nation, even when we are dispersed throughout the world …*

*As you already know, Bnos Agudas Yisroel was established for this holy cause, and is bringing Torah to the world of women, its youth, so that the Torah's flame can warm the hearts of those who have become indifferent. Do you, dear children, know what youth means?*

### *YOUTH MEANS JOY, COURAGE, OPTIMISM, AND A FIRM BELIEF IN ONE'S IDEALS!*

*Every youth organization requires such attributes, for doubt and sadness are the opposite of youth! Torah is a wellspring of joy and cheerfulness, as Dovid Hamelech says in Tehillim, "Pekudei Hashem yesharim <u>mesamchei lev</u> — the commands of Hashem are upright and gladden the heart." How much joy and gladness must accompany a youth organization, such as yours! How much optimism and trust in the Almighty must be part of your youth movement!*

*So, let us get to work, to the work of our holy Torah ideal! We cannot allow ourselves to rest until the "Aish Dos — the Fiery Laws" — pulsate in the hearts of all our sisters! So, get to work, sisters; proudly raise the banner of Torah! Never be embarrassed to wash, bentch, make berachos before or after eating, to keep Shabbos properly, not to comb or braid your hair, not to carry without an eiruv, not to wear loud clothing, short sleeves, sheer socks, etc. Remember that:*

*"Toras Hashem temimah meshivas nafesh — Hashem's Torah is perfect; it restores the soul!"*

*"Pekudei Hashem yesharim mesamchei lev — The commandnents of Hashem are upright, gladdening the heart!"*

*I know, though, that it is relatively easy to be inspired. At first, when you read my letter you may be inspired, but (you must) hold on to the inspiration for many years, decades, and your whole life! As long as Hashem gives us strength, we must use it exclusively to serve Him! That feeling is all that is missing, especially for us women! So get down to serious business, my sisters! Here are my first principles:*

*"Ivdu es Hashem b'simchah — Serve Hashem with joy!"*

*"Shivisi Hashem lenegdi samid — I will always consider that Hashem is before me!"*

*"Limnos yameinu kein hoda — Teach us to make our days count!"*

*Then our prayer shall be fulfilled!*[32]

*And we will surely merit that the nations proclaim:*

---

32. *Tehillim* 19:8; 19:9; 100:2; 16:8; 90:12. Sara Schenirer made these verses the foundation of Bais Yaakov. "*Reishis Chochmah Yiras Hashem*" was another one of her mantras. These verses were woven into classes and conversations and were constantly reinforced.

*"Bais Yaakov lechu v'neilchah b'ohr Hashem — Bais Yaakov, go and we will follow you by the light of G-d!"*[33]

*Sara Schenirer*

BASHA HAD NOT YET MET FRAU SCHENIRER, BUT THROUGH HER POW-erful words, Basha already considered Frau Schenirer her teacher.[34]

Perhaps Basha's role in Bnos and the connection she felt to Sara Schenirer was part of what drew her to Crakow. For Basha to go to the seminary in Crakow was certainly not an easy decision, neither for Basha nor for her parents. The journey was 10 hours long and very expensive. When family finances permitted such a trip, girls came home only twice a year, for Pesach and Succos. Their stay at home was short, only for the duration of the Yom Tov. Communications between the girls and their homes would be limited to letters. Lifsha and her daughter were exceptionally close. Both knew that the prolonged separation would be painful and yet they sent off her application in hopeful anticipation; they both hoped Basha would be accepted.

The Bais Yaakov Committee made thorough inquiries about each appli-cant. They checked their family background and scholastic ability. Each girl had to proffer her transcripts from gymnasium (secular high school), a

*Basha Epstein – Fourth from the right, seated with her fellow Bnos members in Otvock*

---

33. *Yeshayah* 2:5.

34. For more than 60 years, Rebbetzin Bender kept this letter among her treasured possessions. The papers are yellowed and difficult to read, but nonetheless have obviously been read many times. When Frau Schenirer's signature began to fade, Rebbetzin Bender traced it lightly with a pencil to enhance its legibility.

letter of recommendation from the town Rav, and other letters of approbation from rabbanim and community leaders. Concurrently, the purpose of the Bais Yaakov Seminary in Crakow was to produce teachers. They had limited space and could not afford to devote their limited resources on a girl who might not be suited to become a teacher. As a last precautionary measure, they inserted a clause into the acceptance letter that the administration has the right to send any girl home if, for any reason, it felt that she did not belong there.

Finally, the Epsteins received word that Basha would be welcome at Bais Yaakov Crakow Seminary. They were very proud of their daughter, and Basha was eager to prove herself worthy of that honor.

### Chapter Eleven

# Bais Yaakov of Crakow

**Poland: 5691 (1931)**

ASHA WAS FIDGETING. THIS WAS STRANGE BECAUSE SHE WAS not normally a fidgety person. She looked at her watch again and then back at her ticket. The train was not due in for another 10 minutes. She sighed. She wanted to be there already, to face the unknown, rather than wonder what lay ahead …

"Excuse me, may I sit here?"

Basha looked up.

A young girl stood before her, her light brown hair parted at the side, cut to the cheek, framing a sweetly serious face. Her eyes — intelligent, frank, mature — met Basha's inquisitive gaze.

"Oh, of course." Basha began rearranging her packages on the bench. "Are you on your way to —"

"Crakow?" Her seatmate smiled.

Basha nodded.

"Yes. I gather so are you. My name is Vichna Eisen."

"Basya Epstein," Basha responded.

The two smiled. A lifelong friendship had begun.[35]

---

35. *Yated Ne'eman*, Nov. 25, 2002. Vichna Eisen would later become the renowned Rebbetzin Vichna Kaplan, founder of Bais Yaakov in America.

IN ELUL OF 1931, 157 NERVOUS YET EXCITED TEENAGE GIRLS assembled at 10 Stanislawa Street, the Bais Yaakov Seminary in Crakow. There to welcome her newly arrived daughters was Frau Sara Schenirer.

She stood at the steps of the school building, smiling her sweet, loving smile, gazing benevolently at her new charges who were slowly assembling before her, pulling their battered suitcases behind them. The young girls were shy, tired, and overwhelmed. They looked toward Frau Schenirer, hoping for some sign that life here in Crakow would be good, that their homesickness would dissipate as quickly as the puffs of smoke that billowed from the Crakow chimneys in the cold winter.

And so it was. From that very first meeting, any tinge of uncertainty or nervousness Basha might have felt, disappeared. Frau Schenirer, in her nondescript clothing, in her unfashionable brown wig pulled back in a conservative bun, in her sensible shoes and thick stockings, seemed an unlikely savior, especially in a generation that turned to youth and modernity for answers to their unsolved burning questions. Yet, these girls were inexorably drawn toward her. With her innate modesty and infectious warmth, Frau Schenirer exuded stability, truth, and purity of purpose. Her sole motivation was fear of Heaven,[36] and the girls sensed this immediately. Basha and her friends stood in awe and yet they felt warmed by her presence. There was an immediate feeling of belonging between her and her girls.

"*Zee iz azei vi ah gutte Mamme* — She is like a wonderful mother," one girl whispered to her friend. Indeed, Frau Sara Schenirer, tragically childless, was the epitome of motherhood. Serenely selfless, she turned to the daughters of *Klal Yisroel* in warmth and love and welcomed them into her heart. That first encounter lasted a few fleeting minutes, just enough time to capture a glimpse into a unique soul that cleaved to its Creator and embraced His children.

The girls were assigned classes and living quarters. The Polish (*Galicianer/Chassidishe*) girls were by far the majority. The second largest group was the Lithuanian girls, and finally there were girls from other European countries. The administration felt that it was best to split up the girls by their area of origin. The Polish girls had a different dialect of Yiddish and

---

36. "… Sara Schenirer told me that she was indeed a dressmaker. She had many customers, but when they came to her for fittings, she found herself philosophizing with them … They were very particular as to every little detail of fashion or workmanship. *But*, the little dressmaker mused, *after the fittings were over and the ladies had departed, did they really know what they needed?* She envisioned them beautifully dressed but spiritually in rags and tatters …" (Rebbetzin J. Grunfeld in an article printed in *Jewish Leaders*). "Sara Schenirer said that she lost many customers due to these discussions" (Rebbetzin D. Cohn).

## Sara Schenirer: a modest, unassuming Crakow seamstress

*Sara Schenirer (1883 -1935) was born into a Chassidic home. While secular movements ensnared many Jewish girls of her era, Sara Schenirer undertook the awesome task of reversing that trend through education. With the backing of gedolim, she created Bais Yaakov, a network of schools that included the famous Crakow Seminary. The Bais Yaakov movement has educated generations of women who have created Torah-true homes.*

were culturally very different than the Lithuanian girls. Similar differences applied to the girls from France and Germany. Dividing the girls by their country of origin made their acclimatization process easier.[37]

Subtle attention to the girls' needs was a hallmark of Bais Yaakov. Although these girls were bright, intelligent, and highly motivated, ultimately, this was not enough. All of that enthusiasm could dissipate quickly if the girls felt lost, alone, and uncared for. Rabbi Dr. Shmuel "Leo" Deutschlander, one of the first to assist Sara Schenirer, decided that the primitive conditions of the fledgling Bais Yaakov — a two-room apartment that served as classrooms by day and a dormitory by night — was unsatisfactory and that a true home for this burgeoning movement was a necessity.

When Basha arrived in 1931, she moved into a beautiful, modern, new building, in its beginning stages. On the ground floor was the kitchen and dining room. The meals prepared there were simple but tasty, and no one went to bed hungry. Across the hall was a small apartment for the caretaker and his family. The second floor had the dormitory and classrooms.

Great effort was exerted so that the building would be warm and welcoming. The rooms and hallways were brightly painted and immaculate. Cheerful curtains framed generous windows and light brown wooden parquet floors. Each girl was assigned a bed, closet space, and next to her bed, a private night table.

For many girls, the dormitory was more luxurious than their homes. In some poor Polish cities, people lived without running water and even without enough beds for each of the family members. At home, many of these girls did not have a drawer to call their own, let alone an entire night

---

37. Eulogy delivered by Rebbetzin Chava (Shlomowitz) Wachtfogel for Rebbetzin Bender.

table. The accommodations in Bais Yaakov were homey and inviting, comfortable and comforting.[38]

THE GIRLS WHO ATTENDED BAIS YAAKOV WERE EXCEPTIONALLY MOTIvated. They had come with a singular goal: to learn and absorb as much as they could so that they could then go on and teach others. During Basha's time there, the primary goal of Bais Yaakov Seminary was to produce teachers. The attitude of both the girls and the administration was that there was an all-consuming fire burning pure Jewish souls by the minute, and the only antidote was a Torah-true education. The girls were incredibly eager to learn, learn, learn … so that they could go back to the small towns in Poland and teach.[39]

This unusual motivation created a natural bond between the girls. Language was another unifying factor. Although almost all of the girls had attended gymnasium and were proficient in Polish, Yiddish was the language most commonly spoken in Bais Yaakov. Classes were taught in Yiddish,[40] texts were translated into Yiddish, and notes were taken in Yiddish. Sara Schenirer's letters, skits, and plays were all in Yiddish. While among the more modern Jewish youth, speaking Polish was considered sophisticated and speaking Yiddish was deemed old fashioned,[41] the trademark of a Bnos/Bais Yaakov girl was her affinity with the Yiddish language.[42]

In 10 Stanislawa, among friends who shared common goals, who "spoke the same language," the girls turned to their teachers in excitement and eagerness. They wanted to hear, to learn, to absorb, to grow, and to change.

---

38. "I was touched by the little details; for example, the personal night table next to each bed. It was clear that the administration cared about us" (Rebbetzin D. Cohn). At the groundbreaking ceremony for the construction of the new building, Sara Schenirer stood among the girls, moving her lips in prayer. Now that her dream was coming to fruition, would comfort breed complacency? Bais Yaakov had been founded on idealism and nurtured by self-sacrifice; would it grow and flourish in a palace of plenty? Sara Schenirer was only interested in what would be best for her daughters (*Rebbetzin Grunfeld*, p. 99).

39. R' Yonason Rosenblum in an interview with Rebbetzin Chana (Zehnwirth) Rottenberg.

40. Classes were given in Yiddish with the exception of those given in German by some of the German-born teachers who were more comfortable in their mother tongue.

41. "Speaking Polish is not a sin, but speaking Polish because you are ashamed to speak Yiddish is a great sin" (*Bais Yaakov Journal*, 1930, as quoted in *Agudath Israel in Poland, 1916–1939: An Orthodox Response to the Challenge of Modernity*, an unpublished thesis by Gershon C. Bacon).

42. The early graduates of Bais Yaakov in America also identified Yiddish with Bais Yaakov. Upon hearing Rebbetzin Wachtfogel's eulogy for Rebbetzin Bender, Rebbetzin Leah Kreisworth commented: "When I hear Rebbetzin Wachtfogel's voice, I hear the voice of every student of Sara Schenirer, *a"h*. That beautiful *Litvishe* Yiddish, without my realizing it, has become such a part of me, a part of the *mesorah*, a part of the Torah we learnt in Bais Yaakov." It is interesting to note that in Crakow, *Galicianer* Yiddish characterized Bais Yaakov of Crakow, but since the faculty of Bais Yaakov of Williamsburg was mostly of Lithuanian lineage, there a *Litvishe* Yiddish was more common.

FRAU SCHENIRER TAUGHT *PEIRUSH HATEFILLAH*, *PIRKEI AVOS*, AND *Hashkafah*. Her lessons were brought to life through stories and relevant examples. For example, when she was teaching *Tefillah*, she mentioned as an aside, "It is lovely to see so many girls going to shul on Shabbos. I am honored to join you. Yet, sometimes I notice that girls enter the shul, take off their coats, and proceed to daven while still wearing their gloves. It is almost as if they could not be bothered to take them off …" her voice trailed off wistfully. There was no need for her to belabor the point. While sleek leather gloves were very fashionable and women were wont to keep them on indoors as well as out, Frau Schenirer was implanting a gentle reminder that style and service of G-d do not always converge.

In the classroom and out, Frau Schenirer was the undisputed mother of Bais Yaakov. Yet, Bais Yaakov also had two strong father figures: Rabbi Dr. Shmuel Deutschlander[43] and Rabbi Yehuda Leib Orlean.[44]

DR. DEUTSCHLANDER STEPPED IN WHEN BAIS YAAKOV WAS VERY YOUNG and gave structure and direction to facilitate its growth. Basha, merely a student then, saw nothing of his behind-the-scenes work: the hours he spent on the road fund-raising, the letters he sent to the administration guiding Frau Schenirer and her staff even in minute details, the selfless devotion he had for Bais Yaakov in a myriad of ways. To Basha and her seminary friends, Dr. Deutschlander was a larger-than-life personality who appeared from time to time — sometimes expectedly and other times by surprise — to teach, to inspire, and to rejuvenate their souls just when seminary became a tad monotonous.

He was a regular lecturer when they went up for their summer mountain retreats. There he stood, behind a makeshift lectern, *Tehillim* in hand, facing eager students, his eyes focused somewhere above and beyond them. It was as if he spoke to the world at large, its majestic mountains and bright blue sky illuminated by the sun smiling down at this eager group.

"*Nachste damme*,"[45] he intoned in his rich German, motioning to the next girl to read. Dr. Deutschlander did not know the girls' names. He used this very fine mode of address to instruct his pupils with honor and deference.

RABBI YEHUDA LEIB ORLEAN WAS A REGULAR, STEADY PRESENCE IN the seminary. He was acutely aware that the purpose of his lessons was

---

43. Rebbetzin Dr. J. Grunfeld refers to Dr. Deutschlander as the "Father of the Bais Yaakov Movement" (*Rebbetzin Grunfeld*, p. 153).

44. Rebbetzin Tzila [Neugerscholl – Orlean] Sorotzkin referred to Rabbi Yehuda Leib Orlean as the "Father of the Bais Yaakov Movement" in a eulogy at the opening of the dormitory of the Bais Yaakov High School in Be'er Sheva, dedicated in his memory.

45. "*Nachste damme*" means "next young woman."

**Dr. Shmuel Deutschlander was a German-educated Rabbi who chose to use his exceptional talents to mold the Bais Yaakov Movement. Rabbi Yehuda Leib Orlean was a Gerrer Chassid, who, at the behest of his Rebbe, left a promising career in service to Agudas Yisroel of Europe to do the same. Their backgrounds and personalities were very different, but their contributions to Bais Yaakov were both invaluable.**

*Rabbi Dr. Shmuel Deutschlander (Leo) (1888-1935) was a magnetic teacher, who abandoned a prestigious position as a professor in Germany, and dedicated his efforts to Torah institutions instead. Dr. Deutschlander organized the Yavneh school system in Lithuania and, as an Agudah emissary, led Keren HaTorah which established religious schools throughout Europe.*

*Rabbi Yehuda Leib Orlean (1900-1943) was a self-taught intellectual who, upon the urging of the Imrei Emes of Gur, Rabbi Avrohom Morde-chai Alter, joined Sarah Schenirer in building the Bais Yaakov movement. "Herr Orlean," as he preferred to be called, built a network of over 250 schools within 12 years, thereby saving thousands of young Jewish girls and, in essence, preserving the Jewish nation. He perished in Bergen-Belsen during World War II.*

to inculcate in the minds of his pupils the image of a true *bas Yisroel*. They should think like *Bnos Yisroel*, eat like *Bnos Yisroel*, walk like *Bnos Yisroel*, and breathe like *Bnos Yisroel*. With this goal in mind, rather than teaching *Chumash, parashah* by *parashah,* or *Navi*, sefer by sefer, he chose to create a unique course of his own. He created an entire curriculum called *Yahadus*.[46] He divided the school year into topics, such as holidays and seasons. He taught *Navi* in the order of the *Haftarah* so that its lessons would be

46. This was the blueprint for all *Yahadus* courses taught in the Bais Yaakov system today (Rebbetzin Tz. Sorotzkin).

immediately relevant. His goal was to cover an array of topics essential to a proper Jewish mind-set, month by month.

*"Let us try to understand the negative commandment of 'Lifnei iver lo sitein michshol[47] (Do not place a stumbling block before a blind person)', in a broader fashion. Let us take the child who routinely sticks his foot out in the aisle to trip his friend, unaware. He has certainly transgressed the prohibition of 'Lifnei iver…' and we all agree that this kind of behavior is reprehensible. How do we teach a child not to behave in this way?*

*"We must understand the reason for this behavior. The child wants to have a good time, and he enjoys watching the other person's surprised reaction. In a way, the child is also 'a blind person with a stumbling block' — his youth causes him to be blind, and his need for the surprise and the fun that he gets out of it is his stumbling block which causes him to sin. Scolding him might be necessary, but this will not cure the problem because his desire to create a surprised reaction and then laugh at it still exists. We must find a way for him to have his fun in a constructive fashion. Encourage the child to treat his friend warmly and surprise him by bringing a sandwich or snack to school and placing it on his friend's desk when he is not looking. The child will not get any less pleasure from this than he did from pulling out someone's chair. By channeling his nature in a different direction, you are removing his self-set stumbling block."[48]*

IN AN ERA WHEN THE WORLD WAS CONVINCED THAT TORAH WAS about mixing milk and meat, and not about understanding people and human nature, Rabbi Yehuda Leib Orlean was a pioneer. Not only did he show them the beauty of Torah, he taught them that Torah guides us in all areas at all times.

PERHAPS THE TEACHER WHO LEFT THE MOST INDELIBLE IMPRESSION on the heart and mind of young Basha Epstein was the legendary Dr. Judith Rosenbaum.[49] "Fraulein Doctor," as she was affectionately called, was the personification of Western sophistication, elegance, and education

---

47. *Vayikra* 19:4.

48. Rebbetzin Sorotzkin recalled this lesson many decades after it had been delivered.

49. Dr. Rosenbaum (1902-1998) was a granddaughter of generations of Hungarian rabbanim. Her family moved to Frankfurt, Germany where she was educated in the Hirsch School. After receiving her diploma from the prestigious Frankfurt Teachers' Seminary and upon the advice of Moreinu Yaakov Rosenheim (1870-1965), and due to the unrelenting persuasion of Dr. Leo Deutschlander, she joined the staff of Bais Yaakov of Crakow. She later married Rabbi Isadore Grunfeld, a prominent Hirchian scholar who was a dayan on the London Beis Din. During World War II, as a married woman living in London, she moved to Shefford where she guided over 500 Jewish children who were evacuated to the countryside for five years.

while embracing Eastern eagerness and emotion. The young teacher captivated Basha and her classmates. They were spellbound by her carefully constructed lessons. They were taken by her charisma. They marveled at how such a natural aristocrat could be so warm and caring. Fraulein Doctor truly loved her students. She loved their fierce determination, their unswerving search for truth, and their insatiable appetite for learning. She loved their youthful spirit, their joyous laughter, and their lack of affectation. She loved them for themselves: priceless Jewish daughters, yearning to grow.

Every seminary class had a homeroom teacher: one teacher who was directly responsible for that specific class. The homeroom teacher usually taught many lessons and took an especially focused interest in the girls in her class. Basha was forever grateful that her homeroom teacher was Dr. Judith Rosenbaum.[50] She taught Basha's class *Chumash*, *Navi*, *Hashkafah*, and the Torah perspective of psychology. Her lessons were captivating; her presence was awe inspiring. Long after they left school, Dr. Rosenbaum's students spoke most reverently of their beloved teacher.

Aside from her teaching, Dr. Rosenbaum had other responsibilities. She was the assistant to both Frau Schenirer and Dr. Deutschlander in developing the seminary into a formal institution with high pedagogical and academic standards. At her side was Fraulein Dr. Esther Hamburger,[51] another Western-bred and educated woman devoted to the seminary.

Frau Leah Wasciarz, a native of Crakow, was another very active staff member. As a married woman with a young family, she gave a certain balance to the school. She served as a warm and nurturing presence, a fine *Yiddishe Mamme*. She never invited girls to her home nor did she bring her children to school. Yet, they saw in her manner, in her interaction with them, and in what she taught, the synthesis between a knowledgeable, thinking Jewish woman and her role as a wife and mother. She taught prac-

---

50. Rebbetzin Grunfeld was equally fond of Rebbetzin Bender. In a message delivered by her daughter, Naomi, at the Bais Yaakov Spring Tea, she described Rebbetzin Bender as "a wonderful pupil: understanding, intelligent, highly responsive, a light which remains strong and undiminished, loyal, warm, a pillar of integrity, and an example to everybody." Naomi Grunfeld went on to compare Bais Yaakov to a chandelier with many lights. Without a switch, the chandelier remains dark. Rebbetzin Bender, with Rebbetzins Kaplan, Wachtfogel, Yudasin, and others were the switch. They enabled the light of Bais Yaakov to shine brightly.

51. Mrs. Esther Simcha Gross (1911-1970) was famous as Fraulein Esther Hamburger, even after her marriage. A descendant of the Chasam Sofer, young Esther was raised in Germany and attended the teachers' seminary there. She went to Crakow to teach with her long-time family friend, Dr. Judith Rosenbaum. She also taught in the seminaries of Vienna and Chernowitz. Fraulein Hamburger spent the war years in the Ukraine with her husband and daughter and after liberation opened a school for teenagers in Bucharest. She and her family arrived to Eretz Yisroel in 1949 and the Chazon Ish immediately asked her to lead the Sarah Schenirer School for Refugees in Bnei Brak. She dedicated her life to the education of Jewish girls despite physical ailments.

*Frau Leah (Lacia Szaransky)*

*N'shei of Slonim*

*Frau Leah Wasciarz (Lacia Szaransky) was a much beloved teacher who taught dinim in Bais Yaakov of Crakow. She served as an assistant to Sarah Schenirer and Fraulein Dr. Judith Rosenbaum. Her duties included organizing the kitchen and dormitory, and seeing to the girls who became ill during the school year. Leah was married with a number of children before World War II, and she perished with her family during the war.*

*Frau Leah Wasciarz was active in the N'shei of Crakow. N'shei was an important force in Jewish community life in cities throughout Poland. The women who were active in N'shei were as idealistic as the girls who attended Bais Yaakov of Crakow. In this picture of the N'shei of Slonim, second from the right in the middle row is Mrs. Miriam Shereshevsky, wife of Rabbi Yitzchok Elchonon Shereshevsky who literally created Bais Yaakov of Slonim as a school for his daughters. Second from the left in the bottom row is Gruna Weinstein (later Kivalewitz), the first teacher of Bais Yaakov of Slonim, and later a popular teacher in Eretz Yisroel.*

tical halachos that every conscientious Jewish mother should know. She showed them how to salt meat, a task that for generations, Jewish mothers taught their daughters. The girls knew of her involvement in Crakow community life — Bnos and N'shei in particular — but when she was in school, she was completely theirs.

Some early Bais Yaakov Seminary graduates became teachers in their alma mater. Among the first were Gittel Teitelbaum and Hanka Grossfeld. Gittel's teaching debut became something of a Bais Yaakov legend. For her first job, when she was barely 15 and her diminutive height and childlike features made her appear even younger, Frau Schenirer had her dress in a long skirt and arrange her hair in an adult fashion, thereby adding a few years to her age. A few years later, Frau Schenirer called Gittel back to Crakow, this time not as a student, but as a teacher. Knowledgeable, disciplined, well organized, and devoted, soon Gittel became a beloved and invaluable staff member.

Hanka Grossfeld was another graduate-cum-teacher. She came to the Crakow seminary in its early years. She was a brilliant, would-be rebel searching for answers. She found those answers in Bais Yaakov. From Cra-

*Basha Epstein and her friends surrounding their teacher Fraulein Hanka (Chana) Grossfeld. Basha is seated at the far left. Fraulein Grossfeld is in the center of the girls who are sitting.*

*Hanka Grossfeld (Frau Biegun) was a spirited and independent Bais Yaakov student who went on to become a teacher. Her primary teachers were Sara Schenirer and Dr. Judith Rosenbaum (Rebbetzin Grunfeld). Hanka became Sarah Schenirer's first assistant in the seminary and the central figure of Bais Yaakov after her death. She and her husband, Rabbi Joseph Biegun, were killed during World War II.*

*Gittel Teitelbaum (Frau Pass) (d. 1942) was one of the first students of Sara Schenirer. Gittel was a mainstay of the Bais Yaakov movement after Sara Schenirer and Dr. Shmuel Deutschlander's passing. Gittel was a brilliant teacher with a beautiful speaking voice and the ability to bring her lessons to life. She perished with her four children when they liquidated the Crakow Ghetto in 1942.*

kow she went on to Vienna to train further under Dr. Deutschlander. She later returned "home" to her beloved Bais Yaakov of Crakow, as a teacher.

BASHA FONDLY REMEMBERED HER TEACHERS AND WAS FOREVER grateful for their knowledge and devotion. She kept in contact with some of her teachers long after she left school, a testimony to her loyalty and appreciation.

The students of Bais Yaakov Seminary began their day at 6 a.m. and continued with a full schedule until 10 p.m. when lights went out. The schedule allowed much time to review and process the information learned in their classes. The girls wanted to master what they learned, to review their notes and allow the lessons to seep in, to integrate and internalize their new knowledge. There were tests, but their purpose was not to reinforce the importance of paying attention or to encourage the girls to be responsible. Tests were given as a challenge. *You think you know the material; let us see!* The girls wanted to rise to that challenge.

As important as the classes and the tests were the lessons absorbed simply by being in Bais Yaakov. Just as a child subconsciously patterns herself after her mother, Sara Schenirer's pupils emulated her. They began to speak like her and think like her because by being in her proximity, they absorbed her values. They saw a woman free of a desire to do anything bad; they wondered why they would want to go astray. They saw a woman free of vanity and self-indulgence; they wondered why they would want to expend too much energy on externalities. They saw a woman allied with her Creator and His wishes and yet so utterly free; they yearned for that freedom.

Wherever Sara Schenirer went, she carried her big black handbag — her archive of *chessed* — stuffed with ledgers listing those she was helping and with what amounts of money. *Klal Yisroel* — its poor families, orphans, indigent brides, sickly Torah scholars — were her concern. She collected and distributed money discreetly and modestly. She drafted her students in these efforts, sending them to various addresses to collect money that had been pledged. She did this purely for the sake of the mitzvah, and not for the educational value, yet this was one of the most valuable lessons learnt in Bais Yaakov of Crakow: A Jewish life is a life of giving, and the boundaries of giving are expandable. Frau Schenirer — their revered teacher and principal, busy beyond reason, without pomp or fanfare, characteristically modest — was always stretching herself a little further, giving a little more, not only to her beloved students, but to any Jew in need.

A large part of their seminary experience was centered on Shabbos. Friday night, after candle lighting, a group of girls would go to Frau Schenirer's home to escort her to the seminary. The remaining girls assembled in the dining room, awaiting her arrival. Although technically the building was the same, the girls were the same, and the dining room was the same, somehow everything felt different.

Frau Schenirer was dressed in a white apron and a white headscarf covering her Shabbos *sheitel*;[52] her lively, shining eyes exuded warmth and nobility. As she moved to the front of the room, her students scrambled for seats along benches arranged in the form of the Hebrew letter *ches*. Then she led them, slowly, word by word, through the sublime verses of *Shir HaShirim*. One hundred twenty voices in unison praised their Creator. Who could forget the sincere love in her voice as she intoned, *"Mayim rabbim lo yuchlu lechabos es ha'ahavah,"* for indeed, no one could extinguish the fire of love for Torah that Sara Schenirer had lit.[53]

Shabbos transformed the seminary. Amid joyous singing, the festively clad girls passed around fluffy white challah, generous portions of sweet gefilte fish — prepared in the traditional Polish way — rich chicken soup with hearty lima beans — another novelty for the Lithuanian girls — plat-

---

52. During the week she wore a *sheitel* that was similar to hair, but on Shabbos, as a special *hiddur*, she wore a *sheitel* that was less hairlike (Rebbetzin D. Cohn).

53. *Shir HaShirim* 8:7: "Many waters cannot extinguish the love …"
   "Frau Schenirer's voice, saying these words, still rings in my ears" (Rebbetzin D. Cohn — 70 years later).

Sarah Rokach                     Devorah Applegrad

**"When I was in Bais Yaakov of Crakow, Frau Schenirer sent us collecting on Purim. I was paired up with my friend, Sarah Rokach. We had never collected money before and we were shy. 'Listen,' I told Sarah, 'I have five zlotys and you have five zlotys. Let us pool our money and give it to Frau Schenirer. Then we will not have to collect.' In the end, we summoned up the courage and raised much more money for *tzedakah* by collecting" (Rebbetzin Devorah [Applegrad] Cohn).**

**This is how Rebbetzin Cohn's career in collecting *tzedakah* began, a holy mission that she continues to this day. Sara Rokach perished in the Holocaust.**

ters of roasted chicken, and spicy potato kugel. The menu rarely varied, but the food was tasty and plentiful. Rounds of *zemiros* contributed to the special Shabbos atmosphere. A lively harmony of dialects competed in song, all in good fun and high spirits. Occasionally, Herr Orlean would appear to offer a few words of inspiration during *Shalosh Seudos*.

On long winter evenings or during long summer afternoons, the girls would assemble after the meal in the *reutesalle*, the classroom-cum-auditorium, where a fellow classmate delivered a *d'var Torah*. As part of the public speaking course, each girl had to speak in front of all the other girls twice during her stay in the seminary. She was informed weeks in advance and she would spend many hours preparing a lesson that would be both enlightening and inspiring. At the front of the *reutesalle*, there was a raised platform referred to as the *cattedra* where normally the teacher stood. On Shabbos there was a role reversal. Poised at the *cattedra*, a student spoke to her teachers. Following the speech there was always singing, dancing, and a general atmosphere of warmth and happiness.

When the weather was nice, Shabbos also allowed time for a refreshing walk down *Ulica Ditlowska*, a wide two-way street with a scenic promenade down the middle. The promenade, or the *planty* as it was known, was a grassy center median lined on either side with bushes. On the inner side of each line of bushes was a row of benches separated by a walkway. The girls could stroll down the center walkway or lounge on the benches. There, amid the blooming trees and grassy islands, Basha and her friends reviewed what they had learned, discussed where they had come from and where they were headed, exchanged goals and aspirations, and expressed their gratitude for their time in Bais Yaakov.

Frau Schenirer was cognizant of the need to give her students opportunities for inspiration. A yearly event that the school took part in and that remained an inspiration for Basha was the Rema's *yahrtzeit* on Lag B'Omer. Thousands of Jews, from all over Poland, poured into Crakow to visit the burial site of the Rema. On Lag B'Omer, there were so many Jewish travelers traveling to Crakow that proprietors of the gentile train offered a discount. Crakow became black with frock coats and black hats as more and more religious Jews crowded its streets. Basha watched the crowded yet orderly procession with pride. *Who is like you, Klal Yisroel? Almost 400 years have passed since the passing of the Rema, and Your children still honor his memory because he honored You.*

IN THE SUMMER, THE SCHOOL ORGANIZED CLASSES IN THE CARPATHIAN Mountains. The simple combination of learning and pleasure brought home the most profound lesson of all: *Yiddishkeit* is *geshmak*! Learning is *geshmak*! The girls found themselves looking forward to the lessons on the verdant lawns as much as to the outings and physical activities. The weeks in the mountains blurred the line between learning and pleasure. Pleasure was learning and learning was a pleasure.

On the last night of their stay in the mountains, the seminary organized a campfire with songs and a skit. For Sara Schenirer, this was not an extra; this was a significant part of the Bais Yaakov experience. Just as joy and happiness were intrinsically characteristic of Sara Schenirer, they became intrinsically characteristic of seminary life. "*Ivdu es Hashem b'simchah* — Serve Hashem with joy,"[54] she exhorted her students. Motivation to learn should not dampen one's excitement for life. Frau Schenirer loved and appreciated youth; she had no intention of squelching their youthful energies for the sake of teaching. She wanted them to use their natural enthusiasm and high spirits in service of *HaKadosh Baruch Hu*. Laugh, sing, dance, be animated, but all in a Jewish way. She searched for ways to show the girls how one

---

54. *Tehillim* 100:2.

*The burial site of the Rema*

*Rabbi Moshe Isserles (1520-1572) was universally known as the Rema, an acronym for his name. After his bar mitzvah, the Rema left for Lublin, to the yeshivah of Rabbi Shalom Shachna, and was subsequently chosen as a match for his daughter. In 1550 he was elected Chief Rabbi of Crakow, where he gained acclaim as a great posek and a worthy leader of his people. His work on the Shulchan Aruch of Rabbi Yosef Karo remains one of the foundations of the edifice of halachah.*

must serve Hashem with joy and how joy helps one serve Hashem.

Basha's class put on a skit, a parody based on one of the more humorous features of their vacation. Every day when her class assembled outside for their lessons, a goat loitered around them. As soon as class was over, the goat disappeared. All summer long, the girls joked that the goat was undoubtedly a reincarnation receiving his rectification by listening to the class. They decided to call their skit "In the Eyes of the Goat," a comedy of the classes and girls as perceived by the goat. They needed a student to play the part of the goat. Who would volunteer to jump around and bleat like a goat in front of the entire seminary? Who would make a joke of herself to bring tears of laughter to the eyes of her friends and mentors? The volunteer was none other than Vichna Eisen! Vichna was a studious, serious girl and one of Sara Schenirer's prize students. She was a legend in the seminary, someone everyone admired. The girls shook with laughter as they watched the school's most illustrious student entertain them and their teachers.

The camaraderie, joy, and cheer felt that night was not one of wild lack of restraint, but rather a result of the overwhelming happiness in having together completed several weeks of pleasure and growth. They had learned together, lived together, and laughed together. Moreover, they had learned that serving Hashem with joy was a goal they could attain.

THE GIRLS IN BAIS YAAKOV GREW TOGETHER AND EMBRACED A LIFEstyle. As the years passed, their differences melted away and all that remained were their common goals: to build Jewish homes where the light of Torah would burn eternally, to rise constantly in their service of the Almighty, and to strive to provide every Jewish girl with a Bais Yaakov education.

*The graduating class of Bais Yaakov of Crakow - 1934.*
*Teachers seated in the middle row, from left to right:*
*Frau Leah Wasciarz, Frau Gittel Pass, Fraulein Yehudis Bamberger, Fraulein Hanka Grossfeld, Fraulein*
*Esther Goldstyn, and Frau Bella (Gross) Fastag.*
*Of the girls present, only Tzirel [Sapir] Feigenbloom (bottom row, fourth from the left) and Devorah*
*[Applegrad] Cohn (bottom row, seventh from the left) survived the war.*

### Chapter Twelve

# A Bais Yaakov Teacher

### Radomsk: Chanukah 5693 (1932)

Introduction to School Opening: Bais Yaakov
— Its Essence and Objectives

*B*EFORE I BEGIN THE MOMENTOUS JOB FOR WHICH I WAS CHO-
*sen (i.e., teaching) [in this Bais Yaakov School], I would like to speak
about the essence of Bais Yaakov ...*

*Girls' education is different (from boys'); they are our future mothers ... Bais
Yaakov was founded to raise girls in the spirit of Torah and to implant within them
knowledge of Hashem. Did our parents need Bais Yaakov? No! The home was their
"Bais Yaakov"; proper performance of mitzvos and the highest ideals were part of
their daily life.*

*Our patriarchs and matriarchs were devoted to Hashem with their whole heart
and soul; they were replete with fear and love of Him. Our first mother, Sarah,
transmitted this spirit and attitude to her son Yitzchok, who was willing to be led
to the Akeidah. He was raised to be an independent and mature child, yet he was
united in ideology with his father: "Vayeilchu shneihem yachdov — The twosome
went together."[55] Yaakov, too, was trained (by his parents) to surrender his will*

---

55. *Bereishis* 22:6. Rebbetzin Bender explained that Sarah Imeinu successfully educated her
son Yitzchok so that when *HaKadosh Baruch Hu* tested Avrohom Avinu with the *Akeidah* by
commanding him to sacrifice his beloved son, not only did Avrohom pass the test, but so did
Yitzchok. They went together, united in their service of Hashem. This was the ideal: that a
mother could raise her child to be completely united with the ideals of his home.

*under all circumstances to that of Hashem. Many such men and women have been raised in our nation. They are our role models and we should strive to conduct ourselves as they did.*

*Unfortunately, fierce winds have made their way into our midst, and as of late, they have been gaining more and more intensity and are uprooting entire plants. Due to our many misfortunes — the Great War or maybe prior — the rationalization has become that suffering exempts one from the performance of mitzvos. Parents eventually became so involved in making a living, the pursuit of a piece of bread, that the spirit has been forgotten and they have neglected their most important role, i.e., the education of their children ...*[56]

BASHA RESTED HER PEN. FROM THERE SHE WOULD CONTINUE TO SPEAK about Bais Yaakov and how a Bais Yaakov education augments the *chinuch* from the girls' homes and inculcates Jewish children with Torah-true *hashkafos*. She would stress how Bais Yaakov was a complement to the Torah-true homes these mothers had created. Together, the Jewish home and Bais Yaakov would mold these girls into noble servants of their Creator.

Basha yawned. The trip from Crakow to Radomsk had been draining. It was winter[57] and the harsh Polish weather made traveling difficult. Basha rubbed her frozen toes hoping that eventually she would feel warmth. Waves of loneliness washed over her. Just yesterday, cherished friends, cheerful banter, and bubbly laughter had surrounded her. Now she was alone, in the small, plain, bare apartment with only her thoughts for company. To make matters worse, tomorrow she would have to present herself to the parents of the student body. *Baruch Hashem*, both the seminary and the demand for teachers had grown. It was no longer possible for every girl to enter her new job with a staff member at her side. Basha was on her own.

Frau Schenirer's parting words rang in her ears: "When you succeed, do not be proud; if you do not succeed, do not be discouraged." Which would be her test: pride or discouragement?

Despite her initial nervousness, Basha's first half-year in Radomsk went very well. The children, all ages, attended public school in the morning and Bais Yaakov in the afternoon. Preparing lessons that would keep everyone's attention was a challenge. In the evenings, Basha met with sweet Bnos girls, who were grateful for her guidance.

---

56. Translated and condensed from Rebbetzin Bender's notes.

57. The duration of the seminary program was usually two years. It began in Elul, and the newly trained teachers took their positions two years from then. When Basha was in seminary, the need for teachers was so great that they decided to cut the second year in half and send the young teachers to their positions that year. This was why Rebbetzin Bender began her teaching in Radomsk on Chanukah 1932 (*Daughters of Destiny*, p. 182).

*Sixth grade in Bais Yaakov of Slonim. Rebbetzin Bender probably taught in a similar classroom in Radomsk and then Otvock. Note the brick heater next to which Devorah Applegrad, the teacher, is standing.*

At the end of the school year, the Bais Yaakov and Bnos girls presented their teacher with an autograph book.[58] The book opened with a greeting from the Bnos girls:

*To my beloved teacher,*
*I give over to you my wishes,*
*And those of my group*

Each page that followed had an autograph. Many of the Bnos girls added a short missive, a thought or wish they wanted to share with their teacher, a memory for her to keep:

*In everlasting remembrance,*
*Long life in this world among children who love and appreciate you*
*Your little pupil,*
*Shprintza Fireman*

---

58. Autograph book from Radomsk. This was one of the few pieces of nostalgia that accompanied Rebbetzin Bender from Europe to America.

*In everlasting memory,*
*We live a little, but we love a lot*
*Your pupil,*
*Chaya Leiberman*

*Life is a dream*
*It should always be sweet*
*To my teacher whom I love,*
  *signed, Sarah Eibeschitz*[59]

THE BAIS YAAKOV GIRLS WERE YOUNGER. THEY NEATLY PENNED, IN childish scrawl, their names written in Hebrew, no doubt taught to them by their beloved teacher. Basha would have many occasions to flip through these pages and remember her first pupils.[60]

A teacher's first pupils often earn a special place in her heart. Basha had been in Radomsk from Chanukah until the end of the school year. In those few months, she captured their hearts and they captured hers. Basha kept the sweet book of autographs and took it back to Otvock, where she accepted a different teaching position. It remained with her throughout her life. It was an auspicious beginning to what would be an auspicious teaching career.

Basha returned to Otvock in September 1933. Otvock had opened a new, modern school where the girls would learn secular studies — as required by Polish law — and Jewish subjects, all under one roof. The administration of the school wanted Basha to teach there. The central office of the Bais Yaakov network, known as the Mercaz, was responsible for sending teachers to Bais Yaakov schools throughout Poland. Any town or city that needed a teacher applied to the Mercaz, which would select a suitable candidate. The Mercaz had a rule: They did not send teachers to teach in their hometowns. They were afraid that the girls would get distracted by family and home life and would neglect their obligations to their students.

---

59. Other Bnos girls included: Tzina Eibeschitz, Toibe Weiss, Zisel Fireman, Rivka Biberman, Frimet Frank, Rivka Sklartchik, Chaya Rochel Shimkowitz, Dobra Wertheim, Chaya Rosenfeld, and Tzivia Leah Kalisch.

60. As listed in the autograph book: Chaya Shertzelovska, Gnendel Weitzenblatt, Leah Fireman, Shaindel Fireman, Leah Shabiash, Shprintza Gelbardt, Leah Zilbershtatz, Fradl Kolko, Leeba Rozenfeld, Esther Lieberman, Mindel Bontch, Esther Grossman, Chana Bachman, Yehudis Frank, Roizel Groshka, Fradl Golcener, Rochel Troskolaska, Chava Zambeck, Necha Leiberman, Nena Gliksman, Miriam Barzakovska, Sarah Gaslovoska, Freida Mirovka, Tzivia Schmulewitz, Necha Wolkowitz, Esther Yakobowitz, Baila Biberman, Feigel Starovinska, Rivka Sobel, Rochel Grossman, Chana Barzikoviska, Ita Miriam Goldberg, Vitel Goldberg, Chaya Eizen, Rada Shteinitz, Choma Reichman, and Bella Groshka. Many of the girls also included the date and place, Radomsk 1933, which corresponds with the dates mentioned by Rebbetzin Bender. Most of these girls perished in the war, their names recorded here their only monument.

*Basha Epstein and her Bnos group in Radomsk*

*Bais Yaakov of Radomsk. Basha is sitting in the third row from the bottom, fifth from the left.*

That is why, at first, Basha had been sent to Radomsk, quite a distance from Otvock. But when the city of Otvock specifically requested that Basya Epstein be sent to be their teacher, for some reason, the Mercaz agreed to bend its policy and allow Basha to return home.

Basha was thrilled with the transfer. She had not been home for two years and she was very excited to move back home to her family. The school in Otvock was much more advanced than the makeshift school arrangement in Radomsk. The Otvock school was situated in the poorer section of Otvock and the building was not new, but it was a proper building with proper classrooms, definitely a step up from Radomsk. She threw herself into her job with joy and enthusiasm.

The school in Otvock had seven classes, each one with eight to fifteen pupils. Basha was the only teacher of *limudei kodesh*. She rotated among the classes and taught all the students of the school. As in Radomsk, Basha won the hearts of her young students. They adored their teacher and were eager to please her.

Basha had her work cut out for her. Although she taught all the standard *limudei kodesh* courses — *Chumash, Navi, Dinim* — each course had to be designed for each of the seven different grade levels she taught. She worked diligently to make her lessons interesting and exciting. Her students saw her warmth and dedication; each student felt special in her eyes and returned her love.[61]

The school day was typical. The girls arrived in the morning, bright eyed and eager to learn. Basha floated in and out of the classrooms as her schedule dictated. Midday, the classes would crowd together in the large main room, which had a huge wood-burning stove. The children took out their lunches, lovingly prepared by their mothers, and the teachers prepared hot tea for the children, a balm against the frigid Polish winters. Then it was back to class.

At the end of each day, the children headed home, but Basha did not leave her job at the school door. She was very involved in the lives and the needs of her students. She knew everything about them — what was going on in their homes, which children were going through a difficult time and why, and when a *simchah* was about to take place. When the Modzhitzer Rebbetzin, Rebbetzin Nechama Taub,[62] was ill, Basha visited her and lavished extra attention on her two little girls, Tziporah and Sarah. After five years of ill health, the young rebbetzin passed away. Basha's heart went out to the young orphans, and she tried her best to ease the pain of their loss. In school, she acted as if she were personally responsible for them, seeing to their needs and making sure that they were cared for. Warmed by Basha's kindness, understanding, and exceptional care, the young girls blossomed.

Basha sought unusual ways to make her students feel special. The Shabbos morning before Rosh Chodesh, she would meet a group of her students and bring them to the Modzhitzer Beis Medrash for Rosh Chodesh *bentching*. Although she was of solid *Litvishe* stock, she was open minded enough to appreciate other streams in *Yiddishkeit* as well. She found the Modzhitzer melodies uplifting and she knew that the Rebbe's emotional davening would inspire her students. However, those were not the only reasons she came. She knew that her arrival with a group of students would be a treat

---

61. The fondness of her students endures 70 years after she taught them! "We loved her," recalled Rebbetzin C. Milikovsky in 2004. "There was no one like her; she was absolutely the kindest teacher," reminisced Mrs. S. Rosen that same year.

62. Rebbetzin Nechama Taub (1889-1935) was the third wife of the Modzhitzer Rebbe, Rabbi Shaul Yedidya Elazar Taub, and the daughter of Rabbi Asher Halberstam, Bochnia Rav. Rebbetzin Nechama was known for her sweet and gentle nature. She passed away after five years of ill health, leaving over several young orphan children.

*Bais Yaakov Otvock – 1935. Basha is standing on the left holding a school-bag.*

for Tziporah and Sarah, the Rebbe's daughters. They would glow with pride when their teacher and classmates came to daven in their father's shul. Basha understood that although the two girls were sweet, cheerful, and friendly, they carried the burden of having had a mother who had been sick for most of their childhood and was now gone forever. She knew that her small gesture would be meaningful to them.

Basha's feelings for her students were genuine and deep. She enjoyed their company and conversation; she did not seek to escape from them after the school day ended. In fact, she often walked home with her students, sometimes taking them home with her. Tzivia Leah Kalisch, a student from Radomsk, married the son of the Otvocker Rebbe, Rabbi Yitzchok Kalisch. Tzivia Leah moved to Otvock and lived with her in-laws in a small house near the school building. From time to time, Basha would drop by to visit her former pupil and see how she was faring. She would often take along her student, Chaya Nechama Kalisch, the daughter of the Amshinover Rebbe, Rabbi Shimon Shalom Kalisch[63], and a cousin of Tzivia Leah. Then there were times when Tzivia Leah and Chaya came to Basha's house to visit. Although Basha was their teacher, they considered her a true friend and mentor. They also understood, through Basha's actions and demeanor, that she enjoyed their company as well.

IN AN ERA OF POWERFUL AND PERSUASIVE SOCIAL MOVEMENTS, BAIS Yaakov gave women and girls a social movement of their own. Basha and

---

63. See Biography Section..

her peers were zealous in perpetuating its message. They wanted to give every Jewish girl a Bais Yaakov education; they wanted to instill in every Jewish girl pride in her heritage and a sense of belonging to something larger and more significant; they wanted to provide the ammunition for every Jewish girl to fight the secular threats of the times.

The Bais Yaakov graduates and teachers were the backbone of the Bais Yaakov movement and even as they went on in life, they never really left Bais Yaakov. They kept in touch with their friends from school through letters; they kept up on the growth of their movement through the *Bais Yaakov Journal*. The *Bais Yaakov Journal*, first published in 1923, provided an alternative to the poisonous secular literature of the day. It was a medium through which Sara Schenirer and her colleagues could transmit their messages in education and *hashkafah*. The *Bais Yaakov Journal* kept its readers abreast of all the happenings within the Bais Yaakov movement, thereby also serving as a vehicle of unity.

Sara Schenirer passed away in 1935, but her able heirs carried on her vision. In 1937, Bnos held its first annual convention at the prestigious Philharmonic Music Hall in Lodz. The convention excited Bais Yaakov students and Bnos members worldwide. Two thousand delegates attended. The convention was a fulfillment of Sara Schenirer's vision of a strong, vibrant, uniting movement — one that would fill Jewish girls with joy and pride.

In advance of the impending occasion, Basha wrote an article in the *Bais Yaakov Journal* outlining the purpose of the convention, how the girls should be preparing, and what they hoped to accomplish. Basha's article demonstrated her strong connection to Bais Yaakov. Not only did she teach in a Bais Yaakov school, but she also clearly identified with its goals and aspirations and was still eager to be a part of the movement.

NONETHELESS, BAIS YAAKOV WAS ONLY A PART OF BASHA'S LIFE. BASHA'S return to Otvock was a return to her home, and life at home was multi-faceted. She was a devoted daughter to her parents and she shared their rock-solid Jewish values. Her family had devoted their lives to acts of *tzedakah* and *chessed*, and she eagerly joined their efforts.

As usual, the Epstein home was a magnet for guests and a bastion of *chessed*. One of their periodic guests was Rabbi Boruch Ber Leibowitz, Rosh Yeshivah of Kaminetz. That year, Reb Boruch Ber recommended to his daughter and son-in-law that they send their 12-year-old daughter to Otvock. The child was ill and no medicine or cure seemed to be helping. Reb Boruch Ber was convinced that the healthy robust air in Otvock would do wonders for his grandchild. The child arrived at the Epstein home, sickly and sad. The child was reluctant to stay in Otvock, in the home of strangers, so far away from her family. She missed her parents and siblings and wanted to go home. Basha set out to befriend the girl and the girl took an instant liking to Basha. The child begged Basha to allow her to share her bed with her at night. She was used to sleeping in one bed with several siblings and found it difficult to sleep alone.

Basha's heart went out to the girl, so forlorn and alone, and she agreed to share her bed. This was only Basha's second year teaching and her first in Otvock. Basha had worked very hard, late into the previous night, to prepare interesting lessons. By the time she turned in for the night, she was very tired and assumed that she would drop off to sleep easily. But the new child in her bed made that impossible. That first night, Basha twisted and turned. She was not used to sharing her bed and found it very uncomfortable. When morning came and she prepared to go to school, Basha stifled her yawns. She now faced a full day at school on very little sleep. She tried to teach with her usual vigor and enthusiasm but she was very, very tired.

After school, she returned home and after her usual activities and preparation, she went to sleep, hoping for a rejuvenating night. However, the second night was no better than the first. Once again, Basha found herself yawning in school, and she considered her lessons to be only second rate.

Lifsha saw what was going on and realized that something would have to change. Lifsha convinced the child to join her in her bed rather then Basha's, and after some persuasion, the child agreed. For several months, until the child returned to her youthful strength and was able to go home to her family, Lifsha slept with the girl in her bed.

Basha continued to seek opportunities of *chessed*, while never neglecting her responsibilities to her students. She heard that Yocheved Levenstein, daughter of the renowned Rabbi Yecheskel Levenstein, the *Mashgiach* in Mir, had arrived in Falinice, a neighborhood near Otvock. Like Otvock, Falinice was known for its healthy air and therapeutic facilities. When Basha heard that Yocheved, sick with tuberculosis, had come to her grandmother's home in Falinice to recover, she went to visit her. Despite Basha's busy schedule, she continued to visit Yocheved regularly for the duration of her stay.[64]

Basha's days were full: teaching, preparing, doing *chessed*, and helping at home. She was never bored, never had time to idle away, and was content with her lot. Yet, as all young girls do, Basha thought about marriage. She yearned to marry a *talmid chacham*. Although she was going against the trend, Basha wanted someone who would learn for as long as possible. Even her Bais Yaakov classmates viewed her goals with skepticism. Most

---

64. Yocheved Levenstein (1917-1996) married Rabbi Reuvain Ginsburg (see Biography Section). They accompanied the *Mashgiach*, Rabbi Yecheskel Levenstein, on all his travels, eventually settling in B'nei Brak. Rebbetzin Ginsburg was known for her devotion to her parents, her piety, and her wisdom.

girls wanted to marry someone who knew how he would support a wife and family. They scorned the stereotypical yeshivah *bochur* as naïve and unworldly. "A girl wants to marry a man, not a Gemara," they would say.

For Basha, the entire discussion drew her back to her days in Bais Yaakov, when their teachers tried with gentle encouragement to make girls realize what a privilege it was to marry a *"yeshivah man."* The words of Rabbi Yehuda Leib Orlean, spoken so softly yet so forcefully, rang in her ears: *"Du zolst vissen, unter a kapote klapt oich a hartz* — You should know, under a *kapota* there also beats a heart."[65] And Basha knew intuitively that this was true. A man who was learning would make a fine husband, a wonderful husband, an ideal husband.

Names of potential suitors were suggested and rejected. Then one day another name came up. He was an American boy learning in Mir. Dovid Bender was a true *ba'al middos*, a genuine *lamdan*, and wanted to continue learning for many years. R' Yankev inquired further and was satisfied with all the information he received. He arranged with the *shadchan* for his daughter to meet this young yeshivah man in a few days' time. They would get to know each other, discuss views and goals, and see if they wanted to continue their lives together.

---

65. Rebbetzin Bender repeated this often, specifically when she taught brides. One woman recalled this phrase many years later: "These few words carry volumes," this woman recalled, "and they are as meaningful today as they were when I first heard them from Rebbetzin Bender decades ago."

# Part IV:
# **New Beginnings**
## 5698-5699 / 1937-1939

## *Chapter Thirteen:*
### Engagement

## *Chapter Fourteen:*
### Marriage

## *Chapter Fifteen:*
### On to the Mir

## *Chapter Sixteen:*
### Leaving Europe

---

The information in this section was culled from an interview with Rebbetzin Bender in 1990 and a collection of letters. The letters have been translated and condensed. The Bender family filled in many details. Other sources are documented.

---

# Engagement

### Vilna: Cheshvan 5698 (October 1937)

*T*HE COUPLE OFFICIALLY CELEBRATED THEIR ENGAGEMENT IN Vilna, the city of Rabbi Chaim Ozer Grodzenski, so that they could receive the first *berachah* on their marriage from the *gadol hador*. The *tena'im* took place in the home of Rabbi Aharon Berek, Reb Chaim Ozer's personal secretary. Reb Aharon had stayed with the Epsteins for many weeks when he was sick with pneumonia. After that stay, he returned to Otvock periodically and stayed by the Epsteins. Hosting the Epsteins on this momentous occasion gave Reb Aharon much satisfaction, since it provided him with an opportunity to express some of the gratitude he felt toward them.[1]

The terms of the engagement specified that the young couple would remain in Mir for 10 years and thereafter, they and Basha's parents would move to Eretz Yisroel. Since they knew that the process could be tediously long, the Epsteins had already applied for immigration papers. In the interim, the couple looked forward to spending many years in Mir.

Following the engagement in Vilna, Dovid and his mother returned to Mir while Basha and her parents returned to Otvock and Rabbi Avrohom Bender went back to America. They would all meet again a year later at the wedding.

For the new bride and groom, the yearlong engagement was not merely a waiting period, but a time of growth. They met only a few times dur-

---

1. Rebbetzin Rashel (Berek) Kravitz.

> ... Hosting the Epsteins on the occasion of their children's engagement gave Reb Aharon much satisfaction, since it provided him with an opportunity to express some of the gratitude he felt towards them ...

*Rabbi Aharon Berek (1900-1941) was a close student of Rabbi Shimon Shkop. He was instrumental in establishing Reb Shimon's yeshivah in Grodno. Reb Aharon then moved to Vilna where he became head secretary and administrator of the Vaad HaYeshivos under the auspices of Rabbi Chaim Ozer Grodzenski. Reb Aharon was killed in the Vilna Ghetto during World War II.*

ing that year. Their mode of communication was biweekly letters through which they shared ideas and aspirations.

During the engagement period, a bride and groom — focused as they are on their plans, their dreams, and their goals — could easily become self-absorbed. They are often in their "own world" and their parents and acquaintances accommodate this indulgence. Basha's engagement, however, was just the opposite. She understood that as a preparatory step toward marriage, engagement should be a time to broaden, not narrow, her circle of relationships. She used that precious time to develop relationships with her future mother-in-law and father-in-law, not because it was a "nice" thing to do, but because she truly wanted a close relationship with them. She viewed them as a second set of parents. She insisted that they give their opinion, for "who, if not parents, knows what is good for us?" She shared her thoughts and feelings as easily as the words of Torah that were so much a part of her. She used the year of engagement to build a relationship that would remain forever strong.

Since her visits to Mir were infrequent, and visits to America unheard of, Basha's primary means of communication with both her fiancé and her in-laws was letter writing. She wrote regularly but few letters remain.[2] Those that do remain tell the story of a unique *kallah*.

---

2. The letters that Basha wrote to her future husband and mother-in-law, and the letters they wrote back, were lost with their luggage on the way to America. The letters that survived were those sent to her father-in-law in America.

*Dear Father!*

*Being as this is the first time I am addressing you, dear Father, I take the courage to honor you with the title "Father." Generally, children hold their parents, sheyichyu, in such high esteem that they can not easily call others Mother or Father. With you, dear Father, it is different, you are now taking the same role as my parents, shlita, and it gladdens me that, b"H, I have acquired such relatives. I feel as close to you as a child would. I believe you see in me not only Dovid's future wife, but also a daughter of your own ...*

*We (Dovid and I) have had the opportunity to spend some time together and get to know each other. It gave us much courage and joy to think about our future when we noticed that we think along the same lines and have many similarities. We are filled with the same expectations, the same direction, the same aspirations, and desires. We want to build our home, our future, in the same spirit and approach to Yiddishkeit. We are full of hope that the harmony between us will be accompanied by the blessings of our parents, shlita, iy"H.*

*Dovid and I are keeping in contact through letters. As per your request, we will be writing only once every two weeks. Had I been asked to decide this issue on my own, I am sure I would have decided likewise. I too, do not want Dovid to have the slightest disturbance in his learning. My constant wish for Dovid is that he should continue growing in Torah. He should only shteig more and more and draw from the deepest waters of eternal wisdom.*

*This realm is not strange to me. I also draw warmth from the same source, the fire of Hashem. Of course, my scope in this area is minute compared to his. Nevertheless, I feel we share a strong connection in this area.*

*I am already involved in my work, perhaps even more diligently than before, because I know — only for good reason — I will be giving my job to someone else soon. I wish I could put a "piece of myself" into the young neshamalach and tender hearts of "my children." These youngsters would want me to work it out with the council that the Bais Yaakov of Otvock be allowed to travel with me to America.[3] The world of Bais Yaakov is so close to my heart. I am so fond of the "field" I work in.*

*How are you feeling, dear Father? How is it going in America? Do you miss Poland? We were very excited to receive your gift for which we thank you very much. Now, we curiously await the honor of your letter. We will gladly write back, iy"H.*

---

3. There are several references in Rebbetzin Bender's letters to Reb Avrohom's request that the young couple visit America sometime after their wedding. There was no intention for this visit to become permanent. Rebbetzin Bender stated numerous times that she and her husband were planning to be in Mir for 10 years.

> "... I wish I could put a piece of myself into the young *neshamalach* and tender hearts of 'my children' ... The world of Bais Yaakov is so close to my heart ..."

*Basha Epstein with her students in Otvock, 1938*

*I write to you in Yiddish. Yiddish has always been close to my heart; it unites all our brethren in galus. During this galus, all of our nation's tribulations have been expressed through Yiddish. Now, more than ever, Yiddish has become close to me since it is also the language that connects me to Dovid, n"y.*

*Be well,*
*Fondly, Basya*

Chanukah passed pleasantly. It was almost two months since Dovid and Basha's engagement and both sides were preparing for the wedding. Together, R' Yankev and Reb Avrohom purchased a *Shas* and a *Tur* for Dovid. The foundation of the couple's new home was being established.

**Erev Shabbos, Parashas Beshalach,**
**5698 (1938)**

*To our very esteemed and beloved Father, shlita*
*Honestly, it is difficult for me to express in writing my impressions upon receiving your letter. I felt pure joy. I reread the letter a few times wanting to enjoy the feeling of tremendous devotion and connection that you, dear Father, have to me. Yes, I have also pondered the question that you, dear Father, have put to me. Namely, is it possible for a person to care and connect to several people at the same time?*

*Logically, I came to the same conclusion. The greater a person is, the more he can love others. A person should not live only within the narrow confines of his own family. Of course, he must aim to be a most faithful family member. Yet, concurrently, one must be able to accept others into one's inner circle within his heart, placing them all within the chain of people connected to him.*

*A person should not be narrow-minded; he should be able to expand. Thus, as* one reaches higher levels, he can remember and befriend more and more people, even ones not related to him …

I was, simply put, a bit offended, dear Father, that when we will be independent iy"H, you intend to refrain from giving us advice. Who then knows so well [what is good for us] and wishes only the best for us, if not our parents? Parents are always richer in experience than their children. Parents are surely their children's best friends, and only they can best advise the children. Just as it is with my parents, sheyichyu, so too it is with you. Dear parents, I am always ready to hear and accept your sound advice. As is known, "Tiferes banim avosam[4] — Parents are their children's glory." I am sure that Dovid thinks along the same lines.

I am keeping up my contact with Dovid through writing. Although it is not the same as a personal conversation, it is our way of discussing things. Nevertheless, I would like him to be able to get away for a few days, so we can meet at least once before Pesach. With my request, I do not, Heaven forbid, mean to plan against your wishes. However, since you, dear Father, asked me, I am answering honestly, what I would really like.

I believe this will not take too much of Dovid's time. We will not keep him at our house long. "Talmud Torah keneged kulam[5] — Learning Torah is equal to all else." Yet, there is also a time for this [visit] now. I assume that this request does not contradict my understanding of Torah learning.

I feel I have the strength, b"H, to bring others closer to Torah, not to weaken them. I consider myself qualified to be included among the "Serach bas Ashers."[6] Serach bas Asher represents the Jewish woman, who plays the strings of her instrument, symbolizing her individual talents. With her specific gentleness and emotions, simultaneously giving her influential power, she guarantees the existence of the next generation. Thus, every Jewish woman should be the bearer of the tidings, "Yosef b'ni chai" — the young generation is alive.

Is it possible that I am being too proud when I want to include myself in the chain of Serachs? However, just as one may not be too haughty, one may also not lose one's self-respect. If one does not believe in his own potential, he cannot attain anything. One should not overestimate oneself, but one should honestly evaluate oneself. That gives us courage and endows us with energy. Through believing in one's self-worth, the initial nourishing sets in and allows accomplishment …

Now, dear Father, how are you? Are you still on the go or are you settled in New York? I hope my next comment will not offend you: "Just take care of yourself!"

I send my heartiest wishes and regards.

*Yours, Basya*

---

4. *Mishlei* 17:6.

5. *Shabbos* 127b.

6. *Bereishis* 45:28.

Dovid Bender as a chosson          The young couple in an early photo

*P.S. I forgot to express my highest regard for your support of Reb Noach.[7] It was unbelievably appropriate. Understandably, if you, dear Father, can manage to help, it would be greatly appreciated.*

It was understandable that Basha wanted to see her *chosson* sometime before Pesach, especially since they hadn't seen each other since Cheshvan, and the year the Benders were engaged was a leap year with a very long winter. The family agreed that Dovid would visit Otvock toward the end of the first month of Adar.

***Tuesday, Parashas Tazria,***
***5698 (1938)***

*To our very esteemed and dear Father, shlita*
*We received your letter more than three weeks ago. I cannot give you a specific reason why I have not written until now. I know it is not right, but it is not from*

---

7. Rabbi Noach Osher Velkovitch, known as Reb Noach Minsker, was a distinguished *talmid chacham* from Mir. He contracted tuberculosis and spent much time in Otvock at the Epsteins (Rebbetzin Z. Ginsburg). The Epsteins may have known him from Minsk. Dovid Bender had been acquainted with Reb Noach even before his engagement. In an unpublished letter to his friend, Feivel Ritholtz, he requests help in raising money for Reb Noach's treatments.

bad intentions, it just happened. However, "Hamodeh b'emes patur miknas[8] — One who admits the truth is exempt from a fine." I hope you will excuse me, dear Father.

I read your letter with great interest. On the one hand, it put me into a very serious mood. It set me thinking. We are beginning to build our permanent home very soon. The responsibility, the mission, and the obligation we are taking upon ourselves struck me like a bolt of lightning.

On the other hand, the letter made me consider another direction as well. It filled me with courage, willpower, and hope for a good and bright future iy"H. I calm myself with the thought that luckily, b'siyata d'Shmaya, we will also have our closest and most devoted friends nearby and they will help us settle in.

A few weeks ago, Dovid, n"y, was our honored guest. He spent a week in our home. We spoke, schmoozed comfortably, and spent our time well. Now I look forward to Pesach when we hope to meet again happily. This time, I will probably give in to your request and accept your invitation to Mir. I will be traveling to acquaintances and hope, iy"H, to feel comfortable there.

I would love to schmooze in writing some more now, but I will leave it for another time. I wish you a happy, kosher, and cheerful Pesach!

Stay well,
Your Basya
Please honor us with your reply.

My mother sends best regards and wishes you a happy and kosher Pesach.

AS BASHA WALKED TOWARD SCHOOL TO BEGIN HER DAY OF TEACH-ing, she took in the sights around her. The mounds of snow were melting, the air no longer nipped her cheeks, the sun shone in benevolent splendor. Spring was arriving and that meant that Pesach was just around the corner. Soon, she would visit Mir and spend time with her *chosson*. She continued on, a small smile on her lips.

### Sunday, Parashas Emor, 5698 (1938)

To our very dear and esteemed Father, shlita

Had I the literary talent, I could now fill many pages giving an accurate report of my visit to Mir. Yet, what can a paper tell? It is but cold and silent. The truth is, for people who have no real connection, the page is truly cold. To those who feel close to each other and only distance separates them, for them the written word is a convenient means of communication, which only serves to bring them closer.

---

8. *Bava Kamma* 14b.

*I traveled to Mir on Chol HaMoed Pesach. Dovid met me at the train station in Horodzei. After spending a few hours in Horodzei, we eagerly went to meet our dear Mother, Mrs. Bender, shetichyeh.*

*Truthfully, I did not imagine that I would enjoy this week so much. B"H, from the beginning, I was very happy. Dovid and his mother, shetichyeh, tried to please their guest 100 percent and they were successful, b"H. The whole week we had visitors. In addition to members of the yeshivah community, many other acquaintances came. Everybody danced, sang, ate, and drank to our health as well as to yours, dear Father. The atmosphere was merry and joyous; we sensed the oneg Yom Tov. Let us hope that we will always be able to spend our time happily and together. We constantly expressed our dismay that you have to rejoice with us from afar.*

*As a pleasurable conclusion, on Motza'ei Yom Tov I received your letter, dear Father. I was extremely happy. I was proud that Dovid did not receive a personal letter and I did. I was right to feel so proud, wasn't I?*

*…(Regarding your letter) For us Yidden, there is a wonderful connection between earthly pleasures and spiritual needs. "Linto'a shamayim velisod aretz[9] — To be planted in heaven and to be established on earth" has always been our motto. [Among the nations of the world] some accept the concept of "linto'a shamayim" — the ideology of only the spirit, embracing asceticism. Others are governed by "lisod aretz" — materialism. They crave only pleasure and do not recognize the spiritual world.*

*We, Yidden, combine G-dliness with worldliness. We wrap every mundane pleasure in holiness. We eat bread, but our bread is earned honestly, following the dictates of Torah law. In the Beis HaMikdash, the Menorah, which symbolized the spirit, stood opposite the Shulchan, which symbolized material pleasures.*

*There are many other examples in the Torah that prove that the purpose of the Jew is to combine reaching for the heavens while being established here on earth. Let us hope we will, iy"H, successfully accomplish this, in our world, as a prelude to fathers rejoicing with their children and children rejoicing with their fathers.*

*Stay well,*
*Yours, Basya*

*P.S. Even before I send my letter, I already await your reply, which will bring me great pleasure.*

BASHA EXEMPLIFIED HER NOBLE WORDS. HER THOUGHTS AND ASPI-rations were lofty, yet her feet were on the ground. She was practical and down to earth, yet she was never weighed down by materialism. Life experiences provided her with constant reminders of *HaKadosh Baruch Hu*'s will

---

9. *Yeshayah* 51:16.

in this world. She concentrated on those experiences and sought to learn from them.

*Thursday, Parashas Balak,*
*5698 (1938)*

*Dear and Esteemed Father, shlita*

    *I believe you do not suspect me of keeping silent so long. I sent you a long letter, but not by registered mail. Maybe, as I write these lines, you have already received that previous letter. In any case, I will not experiment anymore. From now on, I will only use registered mail.*

    *Writing this letter makes me think. What would have happened if I really had not written? Would that have upset you? But I believe one does not judge a person by only one incident. [Let me elaborate...]*

    *Leafing through today's parashah, we find Balak advising Bilaam, "Efes kotzeihu sir'eh v'chulo lo sir'eh*[10] *— A minor part you shall see and the whole of it you shall not see." Had Bilaam looked at the full picture — chulo — he would not have accomplished anything. Only when he concentrated on a weak point — efes kotzeihu — could he possibly achieve his goal. Although every community, as well as every individual, has weaknesses and makes mistakes, the most important factor is the overall image, negative or positive.*

    *Balak knew that, despite their faults, the Jews represent a positive whole. He therefore told Bilaam to concentrate only on the weaknesses, and not to look at the total positive picture (since the individual faults would give him the power to curse).*

    *Dear Father! How are you? Here, life is predictable. Otvock is a summer home in every sense of the word. I am already on vacation, but I am doing some volunteer work.*

    *I regularly receive letters from Dovid with warm regards from Mother, shetichyeh. Of course, I am not lazy and reply promptly. I heard that they are going on vacation to Nowohjelna. I wish them a pleasant and happy summer.*

    *I received a letter from the wife of the Rav of Riga. The letter was written in lashon kodesh, with beautiful language and rich in content. I was very happy to receive the letter and understandably will respond, iy"H.*

    *Best regards from my parents, sheyichyu.*

    *Well before my letter is on its way, I would like to experience the pleasure of reading your reply.*

*Stay well,*
*Yours, Basya*

---

10. *Bamidbar* 23:13.

AS THE WEEKS OF SUMMER PASSED SERENELY, DOVID AND BASHA wanted to meet once more before their marriage. As with all the other arrangements made throughout their engagement, this too was discussed by their parents. The written word is sometimes a difficult medium of communication, which elicits no immediate response, no facial expressions, nor any personal nuances to interpret. Therefore, both the Benders and the Epsteins were exceptionally careful with what they wrote and how their words were phrased. This unusual sensitivity on the parts of both parties ensured pleasant relationships and a smooth engagement period.

*Erev Shabbos, Va'eschanan,*
*5698 (1938)*

*Dear and esteemed Father, shlita*
*We read the (first) letter with much interest and respect …*
*Yes! I often think about this. In spite of the all-too-often strife in our nation's past, within every ehrliche Yid's psyche lies the strongest will to keep and spread peace. Shalom is a foundation of Yiddishkeit. Shalom is peace; it also means completion: shaleim. When complete harmony reigns, completion sets in. The Torah speaks about shalom, for shalom is G-dliness. The Creator is known as "Melech she'hashalom shelo*[11] *— The King of Peace." In Shir HaShirim, the greatest of great, this concept is also expressed by the word Shlomo — shleimus, perfection. Peace is the foundation of our lives. At the birth of our nation, Hashem gives us Aharon HaKohen as an example of the greatest pursuer of peace. Our prayers are replete with requests for peace. When we ask for life, we concurrently ask for peace: Lechaim u'leshalom — for life and peace. The Altar, which symbolizes everything holy, may not be built with metal for metal is used in war as a tool of bloodshed (the opposite of peace). The holy blessing — Bircas Kohanim — includes shalom. Greetings exemplify national character. For Jews, there is no greeting other than shalom aleichem.*
*As much as one expands on this topic, it is still not sufficient.*
*I have allowed myself to speak too much, but never mind; women sort of have a patent on the "Tish'ah kavin devarim*[12] *— the nine measures of speech."*
*Everything is, b"H, fine with us. I will now allow myself to travel to Nowohjelna for a short time to visit our dear Mother, shetichyeh and Dovid. I hope to spend the time together pleasurably and tell you all about everyone, personally.*
*Keep well,*
*Yours, Basya*
*My parents, sheyichyu, send warm regards.*

---

11. *Midrash Rabbah, Bamidbar* 12:4.
12. *Kiddushin* 49b.

INDEED, THAT SUMMER OF 1938, BASHA JOINED DOVID AND HIS MOTHER in Nowohjelna,[13] a vacation spot frequented by students of the Mir. They also traveled around Poland, visiting friends and relatives of the Epstein and Bender families. They visited various European *gedolim* and received their blessings in honor of their forthcoming marriage. One of the stops they made was in Vilna, at the home of Rabbi Chaim Ozer Grodzenski.

The *chosson* and *kallah* were brought into Reb Chaim Ozer's room. Three *dayanim*, his secretaries, were standing near him. Their hands were full of letters that had come by mail with halachic questions for the *posek hador*. One *dayan* read a query. Reb Chaim Ozer answered with a list of sources and a halachic decision. Then the next *dayan* read a query and Reb Chaim Ozer once again responded with a list of sources. And so it continued, question after question, each letter related to a completely different portion of Gemara. Different sources and different decisions were rendered. Reb Chaim Ozer, in his greatness, would continue, seemingly automatically, to fire answers and sources, one after another, with assembly-line efficiency.

In the midst of all this, Reb Chaim Ozer paused to greet the young couple. First, he made Dovid feel at home by discussing family connections.[14] Reb Chaim Ozer then went on to speak to Dovid in learning; their discussion continued for almost an hour. Then, Reb Chaim Ozer stood up to walk the couple out. He was elderly and it was not easy for him to get around. Nonetheless, he walked the couple downstairs and outside, speaking softly with Dovid the entire time. Basha walked shyly behind as they went down one block and then another. Then Reb Chaim Ozer stopped, wished the couple well, and walked back home.

When Reb Chaim Ozer was out of earshot, Basha turned to her *chosson* and asked, "What were you speaking about?"

Dovid smiled. "The entire time, the *gadol hador* was telling me about the bride that I have merited."[15]

---

13. "My mother used to reminisce about that summer they spent in Nowohjelna. On a walk there, they passed a bungalowlike cottage with a front porch. Lying on a chair with his feet up was a young boy of no more than 16 or 17. My father remarked to my mother, 'You see that *bochur*? One day we are going to hear great things from him.' Years later he became the world-renowned Rosh Yeshivah of Mir, Rabbi Shmuel Brudny" (Rabbi Yaakov Bender).

14. The Epsteins were distantly related to Reb Chaim Ozer.

15. Rebbetzin Bender often told of the greatness of Reb Chaim Ozer that she had witnessed personally. She usually stopped the story in amazement over the humility of Reb Chaim Ozer in accompanying a young couple so far. Her son, Reb Yaakov, once prodded her, "But Ma, what was he talking about with Daddy so long?" At that point, she looked sheepish and tried to avoid answering the question. She never wanted to talk about herself or the special things people said about her. It was only when she was cornered that the truth came out (Rabbi Yaakov Bender).

### Chapter Fourteen

# Marriage

Otvock: Cheshvan 5699 (November 1938)

ASHA HAD STOPPED TEACHING WHEN SCHOOL LET OUT IN the summer. In the fall, when she became engaged, she shared her joy with her pupils; they sang and danced the day away. Rucha'la Donska and Brocha Edelman[16] wrote poems describing their joy and happiness upon their beloved teacher's engagement. However, when the young girls learned that Basha's marriage would take her far away from them, their joy turned to sorrow. On Basha's last day of school, her students cried bitter tears. Now, as her wedding day drew near, Basha went to the school to invite her former students, to let them know that she still remembered them, and that she still cared for them. The wedding was to take place in Warsaw and not all the children would be able to attend, but the warmth with which she invited them would remain a fond memory.[17]

While the *kallah* was busy with her preparations, the *chosson* was busy with his. It was accepted that before marriage, a *bochur* would obtain *semichos* attesting to his proficiency in learning. This way, if at any time it would become necessary to take a rabbinical position, his *semichos* would ensure that his application would be taken seriously. He first went to Slonim, his birthplace.

---

16. "Rucha'la was a lovely girl, about two years older than me. Her younger sister was in my class. Brocha Edelman was a neighbor of ours in Otvock. I remember her well. She was also about two years older than me, and an exceptional writer. Sadly, neither girl survived World War II" (Rebbetzin Milikovsky).

17. "We all went," Mrs. Sarah Rosen recalls nostalgically, referring to her family and friends. Some students found attending too difficult, as the wedding was held in Warsaw.

*Wedding invitation of Dovid and Basya Bender*

Over the years, Dovid had been back in Slonim numerous times to visit family and friends. Whenever he returned, he stayed with his uncle, a candy manufacturer who was also a well-respected member of the community. During these family visits, he would also visit with Rabbi Shabsi Yogel and other dear friends.

This time, Dovid came to speak in learning with one of the great *gaonim* of the generation, Rabbi Yehudah Leib Fein,[18] the Slonimer Dayan. The next day, he traveled to Novarodok where he met with the illustrious Rabbi Meir Abowitz.[19] From there, he went to Warsaw, to Rabbi Shlomo Dovid Kahana, the Warsawer Rav,[20] and the next day he traveled to Grodno to

18. Rabbi Yehuda Leib Fein (1871-1943) studied under Rabbi Yitzchok Rabinowitz, known as Reb Itzele Ponevezher, in Slabodka. He was also a close *talmid* of the Alter of Slabodka. After his marriage he learned by the Minsker Gadol, Rabbi Yeruchem Yehuda Leib Perelman. Rabbi Fein served as Rav in Slonim, one of the most prestigious rabbinical positions in Lithuania. He was also head of Agudas HaRabbanim of Poland.

19. Rabbi Meir Abowitz (1875-1941) learned in the yeshivos of Radin and Kovno. Before World War I he served as Rav in Delatycze, White Russia. After the war, he assumed the post of Rav in Novarodok, heading the city's *beis din*. Reb Meir authored the *Pnei Meir* on Talmud *Yerushalmi*, and two others titles, *Kochvei Ohr* and *Zichron Yeshayah*. He was the father–in–law of Rabbi Simcha Wasserman, the surviving son of Rabbi Elchonon Wasserman.

20. Rabbi Shlomo Dovid Kahana (1866-1954) studied in Volozhin and Kovno, where he was ordained with *semichah* by Rabbi Yitzchok Elchonon Spector. His rulings were widely accepted during his leadership in Warsaw. He survived the Holocaust and devoted much of his time to freeing *agunos*. He made his way to Eretz Yisroel where he served as Rav of the Old City until his retirement in 1948.

**"My father and Rabbi Avrohom Bender were *yedidim ahuvim* (beloved friends). Reb Avrohom came with his wife and son to visit in Slonim from time to time. We were like family" (Rebbetzin Rivka [Yogel] Markowitz).**

*Left to right: Rabbi Peretz Yogel, Rebbetzin Baila Yogel, Rabbi Shabsi Yogel, Rabbi Avrohom Bender, Rebbetzin Pelta Bender, Dovid Bender*

Rabbi Shimon Shkop.[21] All these *geonim* wrote glowing approbations about Rabbi Dovid Bender.

The year of engagement finally came to a close. On the 9th of Cheshvan, the date of the wedding, telegrams from all over Poland were received in Otvock, wishing the couple mazel tov. The Epstein family had close relationships with many Torah leaders, both Polish and Lithuanian, who joyfully participated in the event with words of blessing. The young couple received so many telegrams that they bound them into a small book.

Lifsha was putting the final touches on the exquisite trousseau she had painstakingly prepared over the years for her beloved only daughter. Delicate embroidery graced fine linen tablecloths and napkins. Hand-sewn sheets, pillowcases, and decorative shams, all with matching designs, were fit for royalty. Throughout her childhood, Basha had watched as the collection grew. Each piece was a labor of love. As her mother patiently stitched, she envisioned Basha's wedding day, That day, she would present her daughter with the lovely trousseau, a reminder of a mother's love, devotion, and confidence in her daughter's future.

---

21. These visits actually occurred a year earlier, at around the time of Rabbi Dovid Bender's engagement.

Since I have been introduced and have become acquainted with the outstanding genius HaRav Moreinu Reb Dovid the son of HaRav Reb Avrohom Bender, of New York, who learns in Yeshivas Mir, I have recognized his excellence in Torah wisdom and his knowledge of Gemara and Tosafos and its commentaries. He is extremely adept at pilpul and the depths of halachah (and he has the ability) to commentate and develop upright and correct ideas. He is praised for his Torah ways (and for following) the mesorah complemented by his pure and lofty middos. He has already been presented with semichus for hora'ah by distinguished rabbanim, I therefore also endorse it and bequeath him with semichus chachamim, yorah yorah, yudin yudin, his future p'sakim are supported by our semichah. The community that will elect him as Rav will find in him all the virtues that chachamim have enumerated. May "notzer teineh yochal piryah" (reaping the fruits of his labor) be fulfilled by him, and may he rise and advance continuously so that he join the ranks of distinguished Torah rabbanim and be a pride to Klal Yisroel. May Hashem be with him.

Signed in honor of the Torah,
l'seder V'heyei Berachah
11th of Cheshvan, Parashas Lech Lecha, 5698
Shimon Yehuda HaKohen Shkop

Guests began arriving in Otvock. Among them were the Brisker Rav and his sons. The Rav sent his son Reb Berel[22] to the Epstein house on the day of the wedding to caution the *kallah* not to fast. Basha was in a quandary; it was a family custom to fast, and she desired to do so. Besides, she was nervous and did not have an appetite. Furthermore, she wanted the merits that fasting brings. Yet, how could she disobey the Brisker Rav? The Rav realized that she might be hesitant to break her fast and sent his son several times throughout the day to remind her of his words. Basha appealed for a compromise. She would fast until sunset and she would eat something light to have strength for the wedding. Late that afternoon, Basha went to the hairdresser to have her *sheitel* fitted. The Jewish community of Otvock

---

22. Rabbi Yosef Dov (Berel) Soloveitchik was the Brisker Rav's oldest son.

*The Brisker Rav and his son Reb Yosef Dov. Rabbi Yitzchok Zev Soloveitchik (1886-1959), known as Reb Velvel, and later as the Brisker Rav, spent the greater part of his youth learning with his illustrious father, Rabbi Chaim Soloveitchik. He became Rav of Brisk after his father's passing and many young scholars came to learn under his tutelage. In 1941 the Brisker Rav immigrated to Eretz Yisroel where elite bochurim and talmidei chachamim came to hear his shiurim in Seder Kodshim. He was one of the gedolei hador whose daas Torah was eagerly sought.*

was by and large a *Chassidishe* town. A *Chassidishe kallah* customarily wore a *sheitel* to her *chuppah*. Although she was Lithuanian and did not have this custom, Basha did not want to be different. At the hairdresser's at sunset, she broke her fast. The Brisker Rav's behest was followed.

The wedding was joyous and well attended by family and friends. The Brisker Rav was not feeling well, so he sent his son Reb Berel in his stead. Rabbi Shabsi Yogel and Rabbi Avrohom Kalmanowitz were among those who had traveled from afar to participate in the happy event.

Rabbi Shabsi Yogel was very close to the Bender family from the time Reb Avrohom had served in his yeshivah in Slonim. He had been Dovid Bender's *sandak* and, on this momentous occasion, his *mesader kiddushin*. The Slonimer Rosh Yeshivah brought beautiful gifts for the new couple: a set of Rambam for Dovid and a set of silver *Kiddush* cups for his new rebbetzin. The set of Rambam had gold stamping on the front and was inscribed as a gift to the new young couple from HaRav Yogel. The set of *Kiddush* cups consisted of one large cup and six small ones, each engraved with the initials of the young couple.[23]

Rabbi Avrohom Kalmanowitz felt a tremendous sense of gratitude to the Epsteins for all the times they had hosted him and his son, Shraga Moshe. He found true *nachas* at the wedding, for at last he had found a way to repay this special family. He had been the *shadchan* for the new couple and took pride in the beautiful *simchah*.

For Shabbos *sheva berachos*, the Epsteins rented part of a hotel. They hosted many guests, among them the Brisker Rav and his sons. The meals passed pleasantly. Words of Torah flowed freely and were intertwined with praise of the *chosson* and *kallah*.

The Brisker Rav's son, Rabbi Yosef Dov (Berel) Soloveitchik, spoke at the *sheva berachos* in his father's name. He described Basha as an *"elastishe*

---

23. Rebbetzin Bender commented in wonder how such a great man took the time to give them such a thoughtful gift (Rabbi Yaakov Bender).

*Left to right, sitting: Rabbi Shabsi Yogel, Rabbi Avrohom Bender, Dovid Bender, R' Yankev Epstein, Rabbi Avrohom Kalmanowitz Standing in the background are friends of the chosson.*

*At the wedding of Dovid and Basha Bender - Left to right sitting: Rebbetzin Pelta Bender, Dovid Bender, Basha (Epstein) Bender, Lifsha Epstein Left to right, standing: Rabbi Avrohom Bender and R' Yankev Epstein*

diamond." A diamond is strong and unyielding, valuable and multifaceted. In contrast, the value of elastic is in its flexibility, its ability to stretch and change. The reference was clear. The *kallah* is a diamond: rare and valuable, multi-faceted, with a beauty that is deep and enduring. She could be hard, when the situation called for strength. Yet, she was also elastic, soft and pliable, able to bend and stretch, ready to adapt to each situation as needed.

Spirits were high as one meal led to another. At one point, the *chosson* and *kallah* and the Brisker Rav found themselves at the entrance to the dining room at the same time. The young couple stopped and waited for the Rav to pass. The Brisker Rav motioned to Dovid to go first. When the Rav saw Dovid hesitate, he insisted, "Reb Dovid, you must go first. Look, you are carrying a sefer."

Dovid looked at the sefer in his hand and back at the Rav. With a twinkle in his eye, he passed the sefer to the Rav. "I think the Rav must go first since now he has the sefer."

The Rav handed the sefer right back. *"Vos? Ich bin a shamash bie dir?* — What? Am I your attendant?" he answered in mock indignation. Everyone had a good laugh as the *chosson* and *kallah* obeyed and entered.

The meals were served in a large room with tall potted plants as a par-

*Dovid Bender with his good friends Yud'l Gordon and Avrohom Pincus*

tition. After the morning meal, the waiters and waitresses, Jewish youths, wanted to arrange the room a little differently. One girl hoisted a heavy plant and began carrying it from one place to another. The Brisker Rav was passing by at that moment.

"Shabbos!" he called out and signaled her to stop.

She continued on her way, ignoring his cry.

"*Chatzufah!*,"[24] he responded angrily.

She still did not heed.

"*Chatzufah, tu dos nisht!* — Brazen one, do not do that!" With this last warning, the Brisker Rav turned his back and walked out.

Minutes later, the girl started screaming from a pain in her side. She collapsed on the floor. A doctor was called and he diagnosed her problem as a ruptured hernia, and she was carried away.

Later, word of what happened reached the Brisker Rav. "*Ah moifes, ah moifes!* — A wonder, a wonder," people were saying.

"*Ah moifes?*" The Rav dismissed the comment. "If a laborer had tried to lift such a heavy plant, he, too, would have had an attack." The Brisker Rav's reaction was expected but most of the guests present felt *middah kineged middah*[25] was a more accurate explanation for what had occurred.

ON THE LAST DAY OF *SHEVA BERACHOS*, RABBI AVROHOM BENDER WAS walking the streets of Warsaw, when he met a *landsman*.

"*Shalom aleichem!*" he joyfully greeted the *bochur*.

"*Aleichem shalom!*" Chaim Shereshevsky[26] grinned as he shook the older man's hand.

"Tell me, what brings you to Warsaw?"

Chaim shook his head ruefully. "A dream," he answered. "I am considering making a trip to America. Things are not very good here and I thought that it would be wise to explore other possibilities. I thought that I had everything worked out, but the consul gave me a difficult time. For no real reason, he refused to issue the visa and he would not even grant me another appointment."

"So, what are your plans now?" Reb Avrohom inquired.

Chaim shrugged his shoulders. "I guess I will just go back to the Mir. What a pity for all that time wasted …"

"You came so far and you are giving up now? Let me go with you to the consul and see what I can do."

"Would you?" Chaim asked hopefully. Then he stopped. "But, wait — where are the *sheva berachos* tonight? Will you make it back on time?"

---

24. One who acts with chutzpah.

25. Literally "measure for measure."

26. See Biography Section.

Reb Avrohom had already taken the young man by the hand and was steering him in the direction of the United States Consulate. "Tonight's *sheva berachos* are in Otvock at the home of Dr. Poupko and his family. They are distant relatives and close friends of the Epsteins. I hope to make it back to Otvock on time. In the meanwhile, let us see what we can do about arranging a visa for you."

Chaim gratefully allowed himself to be led. As they waited in the office, he began counting in his head the days that had elapsed since Dovid's wedding.

"Reb Avrohom, I think that tonight is the last night of *sheva berachos*," Chaim whispered in alarm.

"*Nu, nu …*" Reb Avrohom commented.

"I am afraid that if you stay with me, you will be very late or perhaps even miss the *sheva berachos*. I cannot let you do that."

"Look." Reb Avrohom rose from his seat, ignoring the protests of the *bochur*. "The consul is motioning for us to come forward. Come."

"But, Reb Avrohom, the last *sheva berachos*! My visa is not so important. Perhaps, I can come back a different time …"

Reb Avrohom purposefully strode into the consul's office with Chaim at his heels. He smiled warmly at the stern official. Although his English was accented and his vocabulary was poor, Reb Avrohom charmed him with his irresistible sincerity. With a bit of negotiation, the problem was resolved.

"So, now we can go." Reb Avrohom smiled at Chaim, and they quickly walked out of the consulate. "Perhaps we can still manage to be at the *sheva berachos*."

To Chaim's relief, they did make part of that last *sheva berachos*. Yet, he saw that the highlight of Reb Avrohom's day was the joy he experienced in helping a fellow Jew. The last *sheva berachos* for his only child was a precious time, but not any more precious than time spent helping another Jew.[27]

THE NEXT DAY, RABBI AVROHOM AND PELTA BENDER LEFT EUROPE FOR America. Although Pelta was very close with her son and the two had spent most of the last five years together, she had no need to stay even one extra day. "You do not need your mother-in-law around," she told her daughter-in-law, good-naturedly. Reb Avrohom had to get back to his rounds of collecting, and Pelta was happy to return to the role of wife, waiting at home for her husband to return from weeks on the road.

---

27. Rabbi Chaim Shereshevsky in his eulogy at the *sheloshim* for Rabbi Avrohom Bender.

*Chapter Fifteen*

# On to the Mir

*"In my mind's eye, I picture a little house in the vicinity of the home of the Rosh Yeshivah, z"l, in the City of Torah (Mir) — a small town by physical dimensions, but in Torah learning it extended from one corner of the world to the other ... The foundation of their home (in Mir) was mesiras nefesh ... It was a home known for the greatness and mesiras nefesh that emanated from within."*[28]

**Mir: Winter 5699 (1939)**

REB DOVID AND HIS REBBETZIN SETTLED INTO THEIR LIFE IN Mir. For Reb Dovid, not much had changed. He had been living in Mir the past five years and was used to life in the little Polish town. For Basha, it was a completely different story.

Basha had grown up in Otvock, a city far more developed than Mir. She was accustomed to indoor plumbing, electricity, electric trains, and sidewalks. Agreeing to live in Mir, knowing she would have none of these

---

28. "Everybody knows that our friend, the *gaon v'tzaddik v'gibor*, Reb Dovid, was an only child and he traveled to drink of the *mekor mayim chaim*. He came to the Mir in the years of sunset for the *heilige Mashgiach*. His mother, the older Rebbetzin Bender, traveled with him to keep an eye on her only child. His father, the *gaon v'gadol b'Torah*, Reb Avrohom, stayed behind in America, alone" (Rabbi Binyamin Zeilberger in his eulogy for Rebbetzin B. Bender). Being that Reb Dovid and his rebbetzin settled into the same house that Reb Dovid shared with his mother when he was a *bochur*, Rabbi Binyomin Zeilberger referred to it as a home where its foundation was *mesiras nefesh*.

*Going to a wedding in Mir. Note the horse-drawn carriages making their way through unpaved streets, a far cry from Basha's wedding held in sophisticated Warsaw. Rebbetzin Bender often reminisced about the difficulty she had in moving to Mir, a city much more backward than Otvock.*

amenities, was admirable. Agreeing to live there for 10 years was truly valiant.

Basha found it hard to get used to the primitive mentality of the simple Mirrer townspeople.[29] She had attended gymnasium and Bais Yaakov where she had always excelled in her studies. She found it difficult to understand that there were people growing up ignorant and backward.

The couple moved into the apartment Reb Dovid had shared with his mother before he was married. Basha had always been friendly and beloved to all those who met her. Characteristically, she befriended her landlady and they spoke regularly. One day, the landlady's child was sick and Basha wanted to take his temperature. As she prepared to do so, the woman stopped her and took the thermometer from her hand. Basha watched in confusion as the woman dunked the thermometer into hot water!

"Excuse me … but, what are you doing?" she sputtered.

The landlady touched the thermometer to her wrist. "I am heating it up," she answered confidently. "How can you put a cold thermometer into a little baby?"

"But …" Basha did not know where to begin; the idea was so ludicrous. "But it will not give an accurate reading."

"Why not? It is the same thermometer and the same baby. What could possibly be wrong?"

---

29. The extent to which Mir was backward was obvious to anyone coming from the Western world and even more sophisticated parts of Poland. When Rabbi Yeruchem Levovitz was sick, two local Polish-Jewish doctors were attending him and they recommended that an expert be brought in from Germany. As the Polish doctors briefed the specialist about the case, they told him, "His blood is not Type A and not Type B; it is Type C." The German doctor rolled his eyes in exasperation. "There is no Type C! You must mean Type O!" He was amazed and frustrated at the level of ignorance (Rabbi Theodore Lewis).

The baby's mother was beyond convincing. Finally, Basha just gave up.

The terrible poverty in Mir also took Basha by surprise. She had grown up in a comfortable middle-class environment and had rarely seen such drastically poor conditions.[30] Reb Dovid had told her about some of the poor people he had encountered in Mir and how he and his friends from America raised money for the most needy cases. One of his friends was throwing away a suit jacket that he considered beyond repair. A Mirrer businessman took it to wear on Shabbos![31]

Yet, there was so little that they could do to ameliorate this poverty. Sometimes, creativity served as a useful band-aid. For example, many *bochurim* did not have a presentable winter coat. Rabbi Avrohom Bender had a warm, top-quality winter coat that he would use when he came to Mir for the *Yamim Nora'im*. The rest of the year, the coat was loaned out to *bochurim* when they needed to "look good and make a good appearance." To make sure things ran smoothly, Reb Dovid had *bochurim* "reserve" the coat in advance. Yet, this borrowing arrangement also created some comical situations. One afternoon, two *bochurim* showed up for the coat. One *bochur* had reserved the coat for a first date. The other *bochur* had not reserved it, but he insisted that he had rights to the coat. His claim was that he had already met with a particular *shidduch* wearing this coat; how could he show up for a second date in a different coat!

Although, with time, Basha got used to the small-town mentality, the lack of sophistication, and yes, even to the dearth of physical amenities, the poverty would always tug at her heart.

THERE WERE A NUMBER OF AMERICAN COUPLES IN MIR. RABBI MORDE-chai and Hannah Yoffe,[32] cousins of Reb Dovid, planned to join the American-Mirrer contingency. The Benders were thrilled. To have first cousins in Mir would be exhilarating. The Benders arranged an apartment adjacent to their own for the Yoffes.

Understandably, Hannah was nervous about her trip. She had heard so much about Mir; some of which was uplifting, some amusing, and some preposterous. Shortly before leaving for Europe, she came across a newspaper article comparing the standard of living in America with that of several European cities. The reporter discussed the various European cities he had toured and commented about each, "... and the worst level of poverty was in Mir, Poland."

---

30. R' Yud'l Gordon discusses this poverty in a letter home (Gordon Letters, pp. 10-11) as does Rebbetzin Shain (*All for the Boss*).

31. Recounted by a visitor at the *shivah* for Rebbetzin B. Bender.

32. Rabbi Mordechai Yoffe was R' Archik Berman's son-in-law.

Hannah's heart sank. *Oh, no! Is this where I am going? How will I manage?* Immediately, she knew what she had to do. Since she was not going to be able to get the American products she was used to in Mir, she would just have to bring them along. As if she was journeying into the wilderness, Hannah packed as much of America as could fit into her suitcases. Toilet paper, powdered detergent, salami, and more were all packed tightly into Hannah's overstuffed luggage. She finished her packing and looked at her handiwork with satisfaction. *There,* she thought to herself, *Mir might be the poorest place in Europe, but I think I will survive it.*

When the Yoffes arrived in Mir, the Benders, who had been waiting in anticipation for their arrival, greeted them joyfully. The newcomers were tired but happy. Such a warm welcome helped banish any traces of homesickness.

"Here," Basha offered Hannah, "let me help you unpack." Eager to help, Basha energetically opened a suitcase. Suddenly, as she unzipped the zipper, there was a gust of soap-powder fumes and Basha began to cough. "What in the world —?" More white powder sprayed into the air and now everyone was coughing. The huge box of powdered detergent had burst! Basha grabbed a rag and began dispersing the pungent odor in different directions. Everyone else waved their hands vigorously, trying to keep the powder away from their faces. Between coughs, Hannah tried to explain why she had *shlepped* laundry detergent all the way from America, but none of the explanations made much sense when they were all coughing so hard. When the air cleared somewhat and the coughing subsided, the story became clear and everyone had a good laugh. For the next week, every conversation was punctuated by coughing, with a few giggles for good measure.

Mir became as beloved to Basha as it was to her husband. In a letter to friends living in America, she wrote of it fondly.

### Sunday, Parashas Tetzaveh, 5699 (1939)

*... Although our shtetl is physically very small, it is mighty in spirit. The yeshivah, popular around the globe, is in fact mighty. The yeshivah is housed in a big beautiful building, always full of those learning Torah, a crowd of 400 men from all corners of the globe, may their numbers increase. Many European languages are heard in the streets here. It is noteworthy that such a crowd of people with different character traits, homes, and upbringings get along so well and all find their purpose here.*

*It is also amazing that the economic and political situation does not diminish the radiance of the yeshivah. Everyone is learning diligently and delving into mussar and shiurim as if the situation in the world were ideal. Yes, such is the eternal power of Torah ...*

*Pictured here are illustrious Mirrer bochurim, shortly before the war. Many went on to become leading Torah disseminators, such as Rabbi Levi Krupenia (Rosh Yeshivah of Kaminetz), Rabbi Reuvain Ginsburg (Mashgiach of Ponevezh), and Rabbi Henoch Fishman (Rosh Yeshivas Rabbeinu Yitzchok Elchonon).*
*Back row – Right to Left: Boruch Milikowsky, Feivel Zuchovicki, Chaim Milikowsky, unidentified, Levi Krupenia, Shlomo Shmulevitz*
*Front row – Right to Left (beginning third from right): Henoch Fishman, Berel Freidin, Leib Baron, Reuvain Ginsburg, next three unidentified, Meir Getzel Kagan, unidentified, Shmuel Fajveshewitz, Velvele Turtzin*

SPRING, THE SEASON BASHA LOVED BEST, FINALLY ARRIVED. WATCH-ing the melting snow, her heart sang. Spring heralded Pesach, and Pesach meant going to Otvock. Pesach in Otvock was idyllic as many guests flocked to enjoy the lush greenery and country air. Otvock boasted of special hotels for Pesach with the best *hechsherim*. The Benders looked forward to meeting friends and other American couples[33] who would also be there for the Yom Tov.

Yet, for Basha, Otvock's main attraction was her parents. Basha was exceptionally close with her parents. This was not only because she was an only daughter, although that certainly was a factor. Basha always had an enormous capacity to care for others, a trait undoubtedly nurtured in her parents' home.

The legendary Epstein *hachnosas orchim* was an extension of the tremendous love, respect, and concern they had for others. Their hospitality encompassed a wide circle of acquaintances, but was even more effusive with family.

After Pesach passed and the young couple returned to Mir, the Epsteins were eager to share the details of their children's visit with their *mechutanim*. The warmth and respect they expressed when they wrote to Reb Dovid's parents was unusual. Every letter was full of appreciation for them,[34] praise for their son, a yearning to be together, and concern for everybody's well-being.

> *Dear Mechutanim, shlita*
> *We thank you very, very much for your lovely letters. They were very meaning-ful to us. They imbued us with courage and brought us joy and satisfaction; we read much more than the written words. We see within each word faithfulness and devotion.*
> *Yes! "Without praising one in his presence ..."[35] I must speak the truth. We recognize the greatness inherent in you, b"H, honored Mechutanim. You are the type of people we were looking for. We strongly believe that your son Dovid'l also has ingrained within him these good traits, for which we are doubly happy ...*
> *How are you, dear and esteemed Mechutanim? How are you feeling, dear*

---

33. "I was learning in Otvock and spent Pesach there. I met Rabbi Gedalya Schorr (later Rosh Yeshivah of Torah Vodaas [1910-1979]) , Rabbi Binyamin Bernstein, and Rabbi Dovid Bender — young newlyweds who came to Otvock for Yom Tov. Pesach in Otvock was beautiful" (Rabbi Avrohom Barnetsky).

34. The typical salutation with which R' Yaakov Epstein began every letter to his *mechuten* went as follows:

"Your highness, honored, and very dear *Mechuten*, HaRav HaGaon, a treasury of Torah, fear of Heaven, and wisdom, favored and precious, HaRav Avrohom, *shlita*, along with his esteemed and remarkable wife, Mrs. Pelta. (May you be blessed) with all the best forever.

Following my greetings with fondness and high regard ..."

35. *Eruvin* 18b.

*Mechuteinista? How did you settle in? Where do you plan to spend the summer? How are things in general? I am sure you received many regards from the children and (hopefully) you do not miss them as much anymore. Please write us. The Mechuten has a talent for writing … Should we not also enjoy your talent?*

*Pesach with the children here in Otvock was pleasant and joyous. We remembered you, our dear Mechutanim, many a time. We wished to have spent the Yom Tov together. We are so happy with your son, Dovid'l, in every respect … We can now declare "Ashrei yoladito! — Lucky is the one who bore him!"[36]*

*They are a very suitable couple, may they live long and share good years brimming with mazel, iy"H. May our dear Father in Heaven bless our beloved children with health, happiness, and satisfaction — spiritually as well as materialistically — for many good years. Amen! Amen!*

SIMILARLY, BASHA WROTE TO HER IN-LAWS. SHE KNEW THAT RELATIONships are built on shared confidences and on opening one's life to others. Events important to her must certainly be important to them, especially an event as meaningful and uplifting as the gathering held in Mir in honor of the *yahrtzeit* of Rabbi Yeruchem Levovitz. When writing to her in-laws, she vividly tried to make them feel as if they were there.

### Erev Shabbos, Parashas Shelach, 5699 (1939)

*Dear and beloved Parents,*

*… On Sunday and Monday evenings, we commemorated the yahrtzeit of the Mashgiach, z"l … People came from every end of Poland to honor the memory of the Mashgiach, z"l, together and to strengthen the ideals that the Mashgiach, z"l, worked and lived for.*

*People started coming to Mir for Shabbos Parashas Beha'aloscha — "gutte Yidden,"[37] with black, blond, and gray beards. Roshei yeshivos, mashgichim, rabbanim, and other Torah leaders came. The shtetl was brewing. The joyful expressions and greetings observed while watching people meet each other warmed even the coldest observer. Most of the guests are old friends, former students of the Mashgiach, z"l. Now, they hold prestigious positions and are pillars of Klal Yisroel. On Sunday evening everybody gathered in the yeshivah, some rabbanim spoke, and Mishnayos were learnt.*

*On Monday, all the students and guests went to the cemetery and, according to what was told, it was a very moving experience. The Mashgiach, z"l, should indeed be an effective intercessor for all of Klal Yisroel.*

---

36. *Avos* 2:8.

37. An expression used to denote special people.

**"… Our home is, b"H, always open to all, and is a *'bais vaad lachachamim* — a meeting place for the wise …"** Note the illustrious personalities who stayed with the Benders in the Mir:

*Rabbi Yosef Rozovsky, as a bochur in Mir*

*Rabbi Peretz Yogel*

*Rabbi Yosef Berkowitz*

*Rabbi Michoel Barenbaum*

**Rabbi Yosef Rozovsky** *(1910-1976) learned in Mir for over 11 years until his brother, Reb Shmuel, sent a visa for him to immigrate to Eretz Yisroel. There he learned in Yeshivas Lomza of Petach Tikva. He helped establish the Yeshivah Ketanah Ohr Yisroel of Petach Tikva and said the highest shiur. He was devoted to his many students, helping them to grow in learning and avodas Hashem.*

**Rabbi Peretz Yogel** *(1894-1986) learned under his father, Rabbi Shabsi Yogel, followed by many years in Yeshivas Mir, Poland. Reb Peretz then served under his father in the Slonimer Yeshivah. He immigrated to the United States during World War II and became a maggid shiur and boichen in Yeshivas Rabbeinu Yitzchok Elchonon High School. Reb Peretz excelled in his love for his students and his wide-ranging Torah knowledge.*

**Rabbi Yosef Berkowitz** *(1900-1941) was known as Reb Yosef Kossover. He studied in Yeshivas Mir in Poland and became one of Reb Yeruchem's closest talmidim. He was at the Mashgiach's bedside during the last days of his illness. Reb Yosef served as Rosh Yeshivah of Karlin, a position later held by Rav Shach. He went on to become Rav in Ostrow, where he led Yeshivas Maharsha. Reb Yosef perished during the Holocaust. His writings were published in a sefer called Chelkas Yosef (Tiferes L'Moshe).*

**Rabbi Michoel Barenbaum** *(1906-2003) was also known as Reb Michoel (Michel) Kossover. When the Kossover Rav, Rabbi Shmaryahu Yosef Karelitz, was away, Rabbi Ephraim Barenbaum, father of Reb Michoel, was the acting Rav. Reb Michel learned in the Mirrer Yeshivah in Poland for many years, traveled with the yeshivah during the war, and immigrated to the United States. For over 50 years, he served as the revered Mashgiach in Mesivta Tifereth Jerusalem where he guided hundreds of talmidim.*

*Michel Barenbaum as a bochur, standing second from the left, together with friends from Mir. (Yud'l Breskin is in the back, wearing a hat. Henoch Fishman is to the far left. Shlomo Shmulevitz is seated in the middle.)*

*Walking to the cemetery on the yahrtzeit of the
Mirrer Mashgiach, Rabbi Yeruchem Levovitz*

*A closer view of the gathering. Among those identi-
fied are Rabbi Mordechai Karpenshprung, Rabbi
Pinchos Pinchuk, and Rabbi Mottel Ginsburg.*

*A view of the crowd at the cemetery*

At home, the whole week was very hectic. Our home is, b"H, always open to
all, and is a "bais vaad lachachamim"³⁸ — a meeting place for the wise. This week
we had the honor of having many distinguished rabbanim visit us: Rabbi Yosef
Rozovsky, Rabbi Yosef Kossover, Rabbi Michoel Kossover,³⁹ his brother (from Tel

---

38. *Pirkei Avos* 1:4.

39. Rabbi Yosef Kossover and Rabbi Michoel Kossover were both from the town of Kossov, the
hometown of the Chazon Ish, but they were not related.

*Aviv), and other rabbanim. Many other Jews, among them Rabbi Peretz Yogel and Rabbi Aharon Berek from Vilna, were also with us this week. Most of the guests were former acquaintances and very good friends. We were thrilled with these visits. They affected the air in such a pure and Torah'dik way; the atmosphere felt so warm and noble. This is how the week flew by, full of inspiration. Let us hope it will leave an indelible impression, in favor of the strengthening of Yiddishkeit, in the hearts of all Jews who experienced and were present at the commemoration of the Mashgiach, z"l ...*

*I would write some more now since I still owe you a reply to the letter we received on Erev Shabbos, Parashas Beha'aloscha. However, because it is Friday and I am a bit of a balabusta, you will excuse me for dividing the letter into parts.*

*Be well and strong,*
*Your Basya*

*My parents and Yosef send best regards with every letter. Regards from Hannah and Mordechai (Yoffe).*

THE THIRD *YAHRTZEIT* OF REB YERUCHEM WAS A MOMENTOUS EVENT. Students came from all over Poland to participate. Meetings were held to discuss how, despite his absence, they could hold on to the teachings of the *Mashgiach*. A list of resolutions was drawn up and the members involved in the decision-making affixed their signatures. A formal letter was circulated to all the participants of the gathering.

Among the signatories to this document was Rabbi Dovid Bender. Throughout that week, the Bender home was a hub of activity as Reb Dovid participated in the flurry of meetings while still hosting the guests that flocked to their door. Basha was thrilled with the activity. She had grown up in a *bais vaad lachachamim* and endeavored to create one of her own. With supreme joy, she opened the doors of her home to friends and relatives who had frequented her parents' house, as well as her husband's American friends who had been *bnei bayis* by her mother-in-law when she had lived in Mir.

She shared her happiness with her parents and in-laws. They read her letters with pride, happy that their young couple was creating the type of home they had envisioned for them.

### Chapter Sixteen

# Leaving Europe

**Summer 5699 (1939)**

RABBI AVROHOM BENDER WAS NERVOUS. EVER SINCE HE HAD been in Europe for the wedding months earlier, he had a feeling that something was not right. Maybe it had to do with his experience on the way to Poland. He had taken the usual route: a ship to France and then a train from France to Poland. While the train passed through Germany, a gentile man boarded and sat down next to him.

"Hello. Have you been traveling long?" the man asked.

Reb Avrohom was uncomfortable. Although he could converse in German, it was very strange for a German gentile to strike up a conversation with a Jew, especially such a Jewish-looking Jew. The man continued to make conversation. Reb Avrohom reluctantly complied and just wished that the trip would end quickly. Reb Avrohom had to change trains midroute and he disembarked with great relief.

As he boarded the next train, Reb Avrohom noticed a gentile man snap a picture of him. By then, he was really nervous. What was happening? What did they want? He could not solve the mystery of these strange incidents, and he resolved to take a different route after the wedding, when he and his wife would return to America.

On the way back to America, the Benders took a train from Poland to England and another from England to France, thereby avoiding Germany.

They could not know it, but they may have saved their own lives by doing so. Had they taken the train from Poland to Germany, they would have been in Germany on November 10, 1938 — *Kristallnacht*.[40]

Reb Avrohom followed the news from Europe with growing alarm. The situation did not seem to be improving. He really wanted Dovid and Basha to come to America, at least until things calmed down. His *mechutanim*, the Epsteins, agreed. They urged the young couple to obtain all the necessary papers so that if, Heaven forbid, a war broke out, they would be able to flee on a moment's notice.[41]

### Thursday, Parashas Devarim, 5699 (1939)

*Dear Parents,*

*I am in Warsaw now for Basya's papers. Three of them are ready now and I hope to get the fourth at 2 o'clock this afternoon. Once I get the document, I will go to the consul to get permission for an immigration pass for Basya. I will also book an appointment, in approximately three weeks, for her to get a visa. In the meantime, because it does not pay to travel with all our belongings to Nowohjelna, we will be on vacation in Druzgenyk. Basya is already there.*

*Now, in reference to the tefillin: Last time, I wrote that I need a pair for myself. Chill also took a pair of tefillin and a shel yad. Now, Pincus did the same, and Gordon[42] took a pair without retzuos. As far as ordering a pair of tefillin from your friend in Tel Aviv, his address is: Chaim Rozovski, Tel Aviv, Neveh Sha'anan Tzrif 397. The tefillin should be from one piece of leather[43] and written in a nice ksav yad. Pincus will tell you about the price and all the other issues. He is leaving with the Aquitania on July 26. I am sending along some of my seforim and the leichter we bought for Mike.[44]*

---

40. *Kristallnacht* (the Night of Broken Glass) was a preview of Nazi intentions toward the Jews in World War II. On November 7, 1938 Hershel Grynspan, a 17-year-old Polish Jewish student, shot Ernest vom Rath, a German diplomat. When vom Rath died of his wounds on the evening of November 9, the Nazis formally sanctioned "spontaneous" protests against the Jews, using the occasion to give the Jews in Germany a glimpse of their future intentions. The riots intensified on the night of November 10, as fires blazed throughout Germany (*The War Against The Jews* by Lucy Davidowicz, pp. 134–137). The Bender wedding took place on the tenth of Cheshvan — November 4, 1938. The Benders left Poland on November 10, the day after the last night of *sheva berachos*.

41. In the 1990 interview with Rebbetzin Bender, she credits her parents for the foresight to insist that they procure immigration documents, just in case war would break out.

42. Shlomo Chill, Avrohom Pincus, and Yud'l Gordon were American boys and close friends in Mir at the same time.

43. There is a stringency that the *bayis* of the *tefillin* should be made of one piece of leather.

44. Mike Tress (see Biography Section).

*I spoke to my father-in-law about the money for Rabbi Noach Minsker. He will write a letter today to the Brisker Rav, shlita, with all the details. The letter the Brisker Rav sent to you was not intended to place the responsibility upon you, but rather to make it easier for you to collect. I will take care of the money that you asked me to send, iy"H.*

*I am rushing, so I will end for now. I will write again from Druzgenyk.*
*Stay well,*
*Your Dovid*

REB AVROHOM READ THE LETTER. HE SAT BACK IN HIS CHAIR, PENSIVE. The letter was typical of Dovid: down to earth, not focused on himself, and full of his latest projects. However, this time, the calmness of the tone bothered him. True, Dovid was not a worrier. His attitude toward life was usually upbeat and optimistic. Yet, there was a time for everything and right now, with the ominous forecasts broadcast daily, a little concern was in order. Did he realize that a war might break out imminently? Perhaps the European newspapers were not as ominous as the American newspapers.

Suddenly, Reb Avrohom was very nervous. He knew that his Dovid dearly loved Elul in Mir and wanted to stay there as long as possible. Nevertheless, what if he did not leave in time? Reb Avrohom had vivid memories of the Great War and the hardships he had suffered. He did not want his son and daughter-in-law to be in Europe during a war. At present, they were in Druzgenyk, and even the most worrisome reports did not forecast anything happening immediately. Reb Avrohom would allow them to enjoy their vacation for the next few weeks until they returned to Mir. Then he would insist that they expedite their travel plans. For now, he would just wait.

THE YOUNG COUPLE, OBLIVIOUS TO THE OMINOUS NEWS BROADCASTS across America, spent an idyllic vacation in the popular vacation spot of Druzgenyk. People from all across Poland came to bathe in its healing waters. Many European *gedolim* regularly spent the intersession in Druzgenyk. The summer of 1939 was no exception. Reb Dovid was thrilled to meet Rabbi Shimon Shkop, Rabbi Boruch Ber Leibowitz, Rabbi Shraga Feivel Hindis, Rabbi Aharon Kotler, Rabbi Moshe Shatzkes, Rabbi Avrohom Kalmanowitz, and Rabbi Henoch Eigish, among others. He had met many of these *gedolim* before and viewed his time there as an excellent opportunity to renew their acquaintance.

He could think of no better way to enjoy his vacation than to bask in their presence. He would do whatever he could to be near them, to serve

*Left to right:
Rabbi Boruch Ber
Leibowitz and Rabbi
Henoch Eigish with Rabbi
Moshe Shatzkes on dacha*

**Rabbi Henoch Eigish** *(1864-1940) was commonly known by the title of his sefer, the Marcheshes. His main teachers were his father, Rabbi Simcha Reuven Aidelman-Eigish, the Beis HaLevi, and Rabbi Yitzchok Elchonon Spector. In 1898 he succeeded his wife's grandfather, Rabbi Shmuel Lyubetzer, as Rav in Vilna. In 1906, with the passing of the famed Vilna Dayan (Rabbi Shlomo HaCohen), Reb Henoch took over the leadership of the Vilna community, in partnership with Rabbi Chaim Ozer Grodzenski.*

**Rabbi Moshe Shatzkes** *(1882-1958) was raised and guided by his stepfather, Rabbi Itzele (Petterberger) Blazer, one of the primary disciples of Rabbi Yisroel Salanter. Reb Moshe studied in the yeshivos of Telshe and Slabodka and was eventually appointed Rav of Lomza. In 1940 he left for Vilna where he was appointed Rosh Yeshivah of Grodno after the passing of Rabbi Shimon Shkop. He arrived in the United States in 1941 and took on the position of Rosh Yeshivah in Yeshivas Rabbeinu Yitzchok Elchonon.*

**Rabbi Shraga Feivel Hindis** *(1881-1937) was called the "Slutzker Illuy." He was a talmid of Slabodka and taught in Yeshivas Shaar HaTorah in Grodno until his marriage. After his marriage to the only daughter of Rabbi Shimon Shkop, Reb Shraga Feivel served as a rebbi in Yeshivas Toras Chessed of Lodz. In 1912, his father-in-law, Reb Shimon, requested that he rejoin the yeshivah as assistant Rosh Yeshivah, a position he held for the rest of his life.*

*Left to right: Rabbi Shraga Feivel Hindis and Rabbi Shimon Shkop,
with Rabbi Boruch Ber Leibowitz on dacha*

them, and to speak with them in learning. Every night, Reb Dovid accompanied Rabbi Shimon Shkop while he returned from learning to the house where he slept. Reb Dovid treasured those walks. Later, he would recall those walks with awe and the wonderful opportunity he had been granted to speak with this Torah giant on a regular basis.

Basha's reverence for *gedolim* was no less than her husband's. She shared his joy and was proud that her husband could enjoy this unique opportunity. She, too, was excited to be in a place surrounded by the giants of the Torah world, even though her exposure to them was from a distance.[45]

One Shabbos, Reb Dovid came home with a surprise he knew would please his wife. All the guests at the inn were eating in a communal hall. Tables were set up so that families and friends could sit together, if they so chose. Reb Dovid had arranged that he and Basha would be eating with Rabbi Aharon Kotler and his rebbetzin. Basha was very happy with the news.

The hall was divided in two, with some people eating inside and others eating on the large porch. The two families chose a table off to the side of the hall, not in the middle of the "tumult." Their meal began quite pleasantly. However, during the meal, a bee began to dance over their heads. Basha instinctively raised her hand to swat at it.

"No, no, no!" Reb Aharon admonished. "We do not do it like that." He explained that she had swatted at the bee in the direction of the interior of the hall. "We do it like this," he said, and he waved his hand in the opposite direction, toward the empty part of the porch. "One must be careful when swatting at a bee not to swat in the direction of people." Basha marveled at how the *tzaddik* was teaching her that even instinctive actions should be given attention and done correctly.

In the course of their vacation, Reb Dovid decided to approach Rabbi Boruch Ber Leibowitz and request that he write up a *semichah* for him. Though Reb Dovid already had quite a few impressive approbations, he recalled the words of his Rosh Yeshivah, Rabbi Leizer Yud'l Finkel, who encouraged his American students to seek rabbinic ordination from the illustrious European Torah greats. Reb Leizer Yud'l understood that American congregations would be impressed by *bochurim* with ordination from world-renowned personalities. In addition, Reb Dovid realized that a letter from Reb Boruch Ber would be a document he would always treasure.

Reb Boruch Ber had been a guest in Otvock eight years earlier. At that time, R' Yankev Epstein was having trouble with his eyes and was scheduled to see a specialist. As soon as Reb Dovid and Basha were introduced to Reb Boruch Ber, he asked Basha, "But how does your father feel? What

---

45. Rebbetzin Bender would later recall that summer and wistfully declare it the best summer of her entire life (*Der Tzeitung*, Friday, September 18, 1998).

Rabbi Aharon Kotler in America. Walking behind him is his son Reb Shneur, behind him is Rabbi Nosson Wachtfogel, and in the back to the right is Rabbi Yaakov Schiff.

Rabbi Aharon Kotler (1891-1962) was a student of the Alter of Slabodka and the son-in-law of Rabbi Isser Zalman Meltzer, Rosh Yeshivah of Slutzk/Kletzk. Reb Aharon became Rosh Yeshivah of Kletzk when Reb Isser Zalman immigrated to Eretz Yisroel. In 1941 Reb Aharon escaped to America and founded Beth Medrash Govoha of Lakewood, pioneering the concept of kollel in the United States. He was one of the gedolei hador and the driving force behind Agudah Yisroel, Vaad Hatzalah, Chinuch Atzmai, and Torah Umesorah.

is with his eyes?" Basha was astounded. It had been years since the Rosh Yeshivah was in their house. It seemed impossible that anyone so busy, whose mind was constantly immersed in learning, and had many students and visitors coming with their problems, should remember about her father whom he had not seen for several years! Obviously, Reb Boruch Ber's concern for his fellow Jew was beyond that of a regular person. As she had written to her father-in-law the previous year, the greater the person is, the greater his capacity to care about others.[46]

When the weeks of *bein haz'manim* drew to a close, the young couple headed back to Mir. Reb Dovid was looking forward to spending an uplifting Elul *z'man* in his beloved Mir before heading to America for a visit with his parents. The trip to America promised to be expensive and tiring; therefore, they planned to stay for a while. Most of their papers were prepared and they had already sent most of their belongings overseas. There was little left to do and that was how Reb Dovid wanted it. Elul was a time to focus on preparing for the *Yamim Nora'im*. Nothing should distract him from that purpose.

However, shortly after their arrival in Mir, the telegrams began:

URGENT! RETURN HOME IMMEDIATELY![47]

Reb Dovid was puzzled. It was the beginning of Elul, and his father knew he wanted to stay for the *z'man*. What was going on? Why the urgent summons? Reb Dovid did not know that in America the State Department

---

46. Reb Dovid received a beautiful *semichah* from Rabbi Boruch Ber Leibowitz.
47. The original telegrams no longer exist. This was the general message.

*Rabbi Yecheskel Levenstein (1885- 1974) learned in Kelm under Rabbi Tzvi Hirsch Broide and became renown as a true student of Kelm. "Reb Chatzkel" was an influential figure in the yeshivah world, beginning as Mashgiach in Mir, followed by his years in Kletzk, then as Mashgiach in Lomza Yeshivah in Petach Tikva, and then back to Mir. Under his leadership, the Mirrer Yeshivah continued to function throughout the war years, even as they fled to safety. In his latter years Reb Chatzkel was famous as the revered Mashgiach of Ponevezh in Eretz Yisroel.*

had issued recommendations for all American citizens in Europe to return home. Newspapers were predicting war any day. Living in the protected cocoon of Mir, Reb Dovid did not understand the fuss his parents were making. Yet, the telegrams continued to come daily, and their message was the same every time.

Reb Dovid decided to consult the revered *Mashgiach* of the yeshivah, Rabbi Yecheskel (Chatzkel) Levenstein. Reb Chatzkel was a living legend in the Mir. He had been *Mashgiach* from 1921 until 1924 when Reb Yeruchem decided not to return after the Great War. Under his leadership, the yeshivah had grown tremendously. After Reb Yeruchem returned to Mir in 1924, Reb Chatzkel decided to leave. He served as *Mashgiach* in Kletzk for a number of years.

In 1931, Reb Chatzkel returned to the Mir. He did so knowing that no position and no salary awaited him. He, who had held prestigious positions, was content to join the ranks of the *bochurim*, learning side by side with those much younger and less learned than he. Who could forget the sight of Reb Chatzkel sitting shoulder to shoulder with the *bochurim* — many of whom had been his own students — drinking in every word of Reb Yeruchem's *shmuessen*? Who was not moved by the sight of his face, creased in intense concentration, listening intently to every word? Reb Chatzkel, who himself had once delivered *shmuessen* from the same spot as Reb Yeruchem, never missed a *shmuess*.

Throughout those years, Reb Chatzkel was regarded with awe and reverence. Stories of his *mesiras nefesh* for learning abound. Without a salary, he often did not know if he would have money for bread the next day. In the winter, the house was bitterly cold for he had no money for wood to feed the stove. The students realized that Reb Chatzkel was on a level above and beyond them, and his presence inspired them to strive higher.

Reb Chatzkel would give regular *shmuessen* in his house during the winter. During the summer, when Reb Yeruchem went on *dacha*, he gave *shmuessen* in the yeshivah. When Reb Yeruchem was *niftar*, Reb Chatzkel was the natural choice for successor. Students approached him for guidance and direction in all areas. Reb Dovid now had to make a major decision — to leave yeshivah during Elul *z'man* was no small matter — and he, too, turned to Reb Chatzkel for advice.

Reb Dovid prepared his case well. He loved Elul in the Mir and did not want to leave. Yet, what should he do? His father was urging him to come home immediately. However, Reb Dovid was certain that he could never properly prepare for the *Yamim Nora'im* anywhere else. How many times had he told others that it was worth paying the ship's fare just to come to Mir for Elul? How could he leave now? To Reb Dovid's relief, Reb Chatzkel reassured him that it was not necessary to leave the yeshivah just yet. With rejuvenated energy, Reb Dovid went back to his learning. However, the telegrams kept coming. The days passed quickly, one flying on the heels of the other. Reb Dovid went to the *giminy*[48] to fill out an identification form and continued learning.

By the second week in Elul, the telegrams were being phrased differently:

YOU MY SON ARE AN ONLY CHILD STOP MOTHER IS VERY ILL STOP COME IMMEDIATELY!

Was she really so ill? Was she becoming ill from worry? It could not be! It just could not be. What was his father trying to tell him?

The next morning, another telegram arrived.

PLEASE COME MOTHER VERY VERY ILL

A few hours later, another telegram came.

MOTHER GETTING WORSE STOP COME HOME

On Wednesday, August 30, 1939, seven telegrams arrived. Reb Dovid was determined not to let the telegrams faze him. He wanted to finish the Elul *z'man* in the Mir, as he had planned.

That evening, Reb Dovid received a phone call from Tomlin Bailey, the American consul in Warsaw. Reb Dovid had an unusual relationship with the consul. Since there were over 25 American students in Mir at any given time, Reb Dovid would arrange for the consul to come to Mir periodically to process any paperwork that needed to be seen to. This helped the boys avoid the long trip to Warsaw. Whenever Tomlin Bailey came to

---

48. In every Polish town there was a *giminy* — a combination miniconsulate and police station. There, one received passports, birth certificates, and other official documents (Rebbetzin Z. Ginsburg). On August 25, 1939, Reb Dovid received an identification paper from the *giminy* of Mir. This undoubtedly was related to his upcoming travel plans.

Mir, he stayed at Reb Dovid's house. This relationship began when Reb Dovid was a *bochur* and continued after his marriage. Reb Dovid invited him to his wedding in Warsaw and the consul happily attended. Now this friendship, begun purely out of the desire to help others, was to bear interesting fruit.

"Dovid," the consul began, "we have just been informed that America is advising all their citizens to leave Poland immediately. At any moment, Germany might invade Poland and turn this country into a battlefield. The American government takes no responsibility for its citizens who choose to remain. We are packing out tonight, and I advise you and all our fellow Americans to do the same."

Reb Dovid thanked the consul for relaying the news and headed straight to Rabbi Leizer Yud'l Finkel to apprise him of the situation. Just the day before, he had been to the Rosh Yeshivah to pick up his *semichah,* and they had discussed the possibility of war breaking out. How strange that their fears were to be realized so soon.

The Rosh Yeshivah pondered the situation. "I do not know what to say. There have been so many rumors, so many stories — who knows what to believe? But, if the consul says that you should go, then I think you should inform all foreign citizens that they should heed his words."

Immediately, Reb Dovid summoned all the foreign students of the yeshivah and reported the latest developments. The only country bordering Poland that would allow them easy entry was Latvia. The train from Horodzei to Latvia ran in the evening. Thus, they decided that the following evening they would begin their journey.[49]

Reb Dovid and Basha could not wait for the next evening. They realized that before they could embark on their trip to Latvia, they had one more thing to take care of. They were missing one paper that Basha desperately needed and that paper could only be obtained in Warsaw. So, that night they fled to Warsaw in pursuit of that precious paper, without which Basha could not travel. Time was ticking away …

IT WAS MORNING WHEN REB DOVID AND BASHA UNEXPECTEDLY arrived in the Epstein house with their packages piled up beside them. With a cry of joy — it was always a thrill to see her daughter and son-in-law — Lifsha ushered them into the house. R' Yankev quickly joined them as they gathered around the table. Reb Dovid told them about the previous night's phone call and the consul's urgent message.

R' Yankev was pensive. It was not as if this was unexpected; he had urged Dovid and Basha to have their papers ready, just in case something

49. The details of Tomlin Bailey's phone call, Rabbi Dovid Bender's conversation with Rabbi Leizer Yud'l Finkel, and the decision to travel to Latvia were supplied by Rabbi Alex Weisfogel.

like this would occur. Nonetheless, now that the moment had arrived, it was so difficult. Basha was their only daughter, and they loved Dovid as a son. "You will have to go." R' Yankev spoke quietly, but decisively. "It is clear that war is imminent. The Polish Army is mobilizing and there have been reports that the Germans are preparing to attack Poland from the Polish-Czech border. Once war breaks out, travel will be very difficult. You must go now."

Basha was taken aback by her father's words and the urgency that accompanied them. When she had left Mir, she knew that she would be leaving Europe — hadn't they been planning this trip to America for weeks? But suddenly, everything was different. They were no longer taking a trip to America; they were fleeing Europe, parting from her beloved parents just as a war was about to break out! How could she leave them like this? Her parents would be all alone!

"Bashke," her mother said softly, almost reading her thoughts, "you have all the necessary papers, and we do not. You will go, and *b'ezras Hashem*, the danger will pass and we will be reunited very soon."

"But that is the problem," Reb Dovid interjected. "We do not have all the papers. As the wife of an American citizen, Basha is automatically welcomed into the United States. Processing the necessary paperwork was easy. However, the law in Poland states that when a Polish citizen leaves Poland for immigration purposes,[50] he must go through Danzig, otherwise his immigration visa is invalid. However, I am very wary about heading toward Danzig just now ..."

R' Yankev nodded in agreement. This was a real problem. Danzig was one of the leading port cities of Eastern Europe. At times, Danzig belonged to Germany, and at times it belonged to Poland. After the Great War, Danzig was declared a Free City belonging neither to Germany nor to Poland. Poland had control of its railroads and customs duties, but other than that, Danzig was autonomous. This was still a point of contention between Poland and Germany. Germany never accepted its loss of Danzig, and it was a matter of pride that they reestablish themselves there. Early in 1939, Germany had demanded that it be reunited with Danzig, but Poland had refused. It seemed logical that as one of its first acts of war against Poland, Germany would try to seize Danzig. This would cut off Poland's access to the outside world, give Germany a major port city, and salvage Germany's wounded pride.[51]

R' Yankev sat in quiet contemplation. He looked at his watch; time refused to stand still. "I do not know what to tell you. You will have to

---

50. Though the Benders had not planned to stay in America, it was sensible for Basha to apply for American citizenship.

51. The World Book Encyclopedia, Vol. 5, p. 28.

exit Poland through Latvia like all the other foreign citizens are doing. The question is how can you do this without a visa …?"

As R' Yankev felt around in his pocket for a pen, his wife brought a piece of paper. Hastily, he scribbled the name and address of a friend. "Go quickly to this address," he instructed. "It is the home of a good friend of mine. He is a lawyer and a very clever man. Perhaps he has an idea that will help you. Take everything with you; hopefully, you will have your visa shortly. Then, take the next train back to Horodzei and join the other foreign citizens leaving Mir. Hurry! You have no time to lose!"

Lifsha Epstein had been quietly listening and observing in the background. Her heart was heavy with sadness and fear, but now was not the time to allow those emotions to show. She had to be strong, for the sake of her children. As Reb Dovid and Basha stood up to leave, she approached them. "Basha," she said, as she thrust a wad of bills into her daughter's hands, "take this and save yourselves."

Basha stared at the pile she now held. She knew exactly what it was: her mother's savings, carefully hoarded under her mattress for a rainy day, all 1500 *zlotys*.

"Mamma, no! It is yours. You might need it. We will manage …"

"*Nein, nein, mein kind.* Take it." She held her daughter's hands in her own, the money pressed tightly inside. "Your journey should be with *hatzlachah* …"

Basha stared at the money in her hands. How could she take this money? She knew that it was the only money they had in the house. Any money they had in the bank would probably be locked up at the start of a war. How could she take this? Even worse, how could she leave her parents at a time like this? They needed her; she needed them. For those few endless moments, Basha felt as if her feet were glued to the floor. If they could only have some more time together! She had so much she wanted to ask, to discuss, to reminisce. She wanted just a bit more time — time to bask in their loving presence, time to hear their wise words of advice, time to laugh and cry together. Just a bit more time …

But, the clock kept ticking. Lifsha Epstein took her daughter by the hand. "Go, Bashale, and write to us often. We want to hear all about your trip and about life in America. The important thing is that you should be happy and healthy. Do not worry about us. *B'ezras Hashem*, we will be reunited soon." With that, she practically pushed her daughter out the door. "Go! It should be with *hatzlachah*!"

"Come," Reb Dovid urged, "it is late; we must go!" Basha had no time to think. She obediently followed her husband as they ran to the lawyer to hear his advice.

THE LAWYER LISTENED INTENTLY TO THEIR PREDICAMENT. "HERE IS what I recommend," he said. "There is something called a transit visa. A transit visa is a visa that allows you into another country temporarily, while you are in transit. Unlike the American visa you have now, a transit visa will be accepted at any of the Polish borders, not just through Danzig. You have to apply to a consulate of another country for a transit visa to their country. Unfortunately, just this morning, the radio announced that of Warsaw's six consulates, only the Estonian Consulate is still functioning. You have to pray that they will issue this transit visa."

"May I ask a question?" Basha interjected. "Do I have to actually go to Estonia?"

The lawyer shook his head dismissively. "No, no! You may cross the Polish border into Latvia using this transit visa as if you are on your way to Estonia. Once you are out of Poland, use your regular American visa and board a ship out of Eastern Europe. I suggest that you sail to Sweden. From there you will surely be able to book passage to America.

"The tricky part is dealing with the Estonian Consulate. They really have no reason to issue a transit visa on the spot. A visa usually takes time to process and they will probably insist on dragging their feet. You will have to make a proposition that will be attractive to them." He looked at the young couple meaningfully. They were puzzled; what was he suggesting? The lawyer shook his head impatiently. "Do you have any extra money?"

Reb Dovid looked at Basha and suddenly they both understood. "We have 1500 *zlotys*," Basha answered softly.

The lawyer nodded. "That should be sufficient. You," he looked point-edly at Basha, "will go in alone. They should not even catch a glimpse of your husband. Dress nicely and try to appear confident and upper class. Tell them how much you love Poland but, unfortunately, you must leave because your mother-in-law is dying. Show them all the telegrams from America and explain that this is the only reason you are seeking to leave Poland. If the consular official guesses that you are a Jewish couple flee-ing Poland, it is highly unlikely he will issue the transit visa. You must make a very convincing act. I have no idea what will happen and there-fore I cannot tell you exactly what to say or do. You understand what must be accomplished, and you will have to use your own wits to see this through."

Reb Dovid and Basha sat quietly, digesting the information. They were both wary of this plan and their fears must have been obvious. "Look," the lawyer stood up in dismissal, "this is the situation. You can choose to take my advice or …"

His guests took the hint and Reb Dovid and Basha thanked the lawyer and excused themselves. On the way to the consulate, Basha tried to organize her thoughts. She, a young woman, would have to enter alone and bribe a government official. The idea terrified her. What if the government worker was a stickler for legalities and had her arrested? What if he took the money and did not give her the visa? What if …? She did not want to think of all the frightful possibilities.

*Please, HaKadosh Baruch Hu*, she prayed desperately, *put the right words in my mouth!*

AT 9 A.M. ON THURSDAY, AUGUST 31, 1939, JANUSH HAD JUST ARRIVED at his office. He was in a bit of a temper. Most of the staff had been laid off, and he was certain that this would be his last day on the job, as well. There was not much to motivate him to take his duties seriously, and therefore he planned to spend his time doing as little as possible. He settled himself comfortably in his office chair, his head leaning back against the upholstery, his feet resting upon the desktop. Perhaps he would even get a bit of a nap.

The door opened. Janush quickly put down his legs and assumed a suitably stern demeanor. He busied himself with the papers on the desk, shoving them from one place to another lest his visitor think he was not sufficiently busy. Keeping his eyes averted he ignored the stranger's arrival.

The visitor cleared his throat. Janush slowly raised his head. *Now, this is rich*, he thought. *It's a she, not a he. And a fancy uptown lady at that.*

"Yes?" he said impatiently. Although his curiosity was piqued, he would not let it show.

Basha trembled inwardly. "Sir, I am so sorry to trouble you." She took a deep breath and plunged ahead. "You see, I have lived in Poland all my life. It is my *Mutterland*, and I love it so. I was born here. I have been educated here. My family and friends live here. I have deep ties to my beloved Poland." She paused nervously. "But, I married an American, an only son to his parents. His dear mother is deathly ill and she is desperate to see him one more time. We must leave immediately for we have no idea how much longer she will live."

"Madam, I sympathize," the consular official interjected most unsympathetically. "But what do you want from me?"

Basha took another deep breath and continued. "You see, I have all the necessary papers, except my visa. If only I had a transit visa to Estonia …" She left the suggestion hanging, as she plunged ahead with the rest of her speech. "I do feel terrible abandoning my country at a time like this. *Der Mutterland* is so dear to me! My heart is still here! I hope there will not be a war. However, just in case war does break out, I want to help my country in her hour of need. I have brought along a donation for the Polish Air Force. I am certain that you will make sure it gets to the proper department.

"Please have sympathy on my dear mother-in-law, lying on her death-bed. Read these telegrams and you'll understand."

Basha placed a pile of telegrams on the desk. On top, she placed several bills.

Janush stared in disbelief. It would not do to greedily count the money, but he could tell at a glance that several hundred *zlotys* lay in waiting on his desk. He picked up the pile and began reading through the telegrams, fingering the bills at the same time. It certainly seemed like this woman's mother-in-law was dying, and if his estimate was correct, he was holding about 1500 *zlotys*. Fifteen hundred *zlotys*! More than a half-year's salary! Of course, the Polish Air Force would not see a penny of it …

"Just a minute." He got up abruptly and left the room.

Basha stood alone, terrified. What if he had gone to call the authorities?

REB DOVID WAS OUTSIDE THE CONSULATE, PACING NERVOUSLY UP and down the street. He glanced at his watch. She had gone up there almost an hour ago. What could be taking so long? Maybe he should go in to see what was happening. The lawyer had given him strict instructions not to show his face, and yet …

Suddenly, the door flew open and out she came. "I got it!" Basha triumphantly waved her visa. "We have to get it stamped. Quick, let's go!"

"What took so long?" Reb Dovid panted as they ran down the block.

"I think the first man was too nervous to take the bribe. He went to get his superior. I guess he figured that he would rather split the money than risk having his superior find out what he did. Anyway, it's done. Come, the office is right here!"

After they got Basha's visa stamped, they headed straight for the train station where they boarded a train for Horodzei. They wearily sank down in their seats, exhausted from all that had transpired in the past few hours.

Basha closed her eyes and her thoughts wandered back to her beloved parents. As usual, their thoughts that day had been only about her. Their concern was that she leave, that she have the money to do so, and that she be safe. Why, oh, why did she allow herself to take the last few zlotys they had in their house? Perhaps they would need those funds in the uncertain weeks ahead. The wheels of the train, turning over and over, were taking her far away from her beloved parents. She would never return.

# Part V:
# **The War Years**
## 5699-5703 / 1939-1943

---

The information in this section has been culled from interviews, published works, and many letters, telegrams, and documents that Rebbetzin Bender saved. Many of the documents have been translated and abridged but are otherwise authentic. Primary contributors to this section include Rabbi Alex Weisfogel, Dr. David Kranzler, R' Elchonon [Heiry] Ehrlanger, and Rebbetzin Zlata (Levenstein) Ginsburg. Other contributors include Rebbetzin Rashel (Berek) Kravitz and *ybdl"ch* R' Aryeh (Bert) Lehman, Rabbi Moshe Pivovitz, Rebbetzin Devorah (Applegrad) Cohn, Rebbetzin Rochel (Leschinsky) Brudny, Rebbetzin Tybel (Shereshevsky-Fishman) Wernick, Rebbetzin Chaya Nechama (Kalisch) Milikovsky, Mrs. Sara (Taub) Rosen, Rebbetzin Rivka (Grodzinsky)Wolbe.

---

*Chapter Seventeen*

# The Journey
### Horodzei: 16th of Elul, 5699 (August 31, 1939)

HE BENDERS RETURNED TO HORODZEI THAT EVENING JUST as a busload of Mirrer *bochurim* pulled into the station. Most of the international *bochurim* were there:[1] Chuney Scheinerman, Yisroel Spinner, and some of their American friends; Swiss-born Elchonon and Sholom Ehrlanger; two boys from Belgium, and the English and the Irish boys: Alex Weisfogel, Yehoshua Chinn, Shmuel Bloch, Shaya Lebor, Pinchas Berliner, and Mannis Moore. The Benders' cousins Rabbi Mordechai and Hannah Yoffe were there, as were Rabbi Binyamin Bernstein and his young rebbetzin, another American couple who had been living in Mir.

Just a few weeks earlier, most of these *bochurim* and even the young couples had been carefree vacationers in the resort areas of Poland. Once again they were traveling together, only now they were soberly heading in a very different direction.

They boarded a train to Latvia together. If Germany was invading Poland, as the consul had warned them, it was unlikely that the Baltic States would be affected so quickly. Either it would be safe to stay in Latvia or they would try to travel from there.

The *bochurim* were not fleeing in mindless desperation. The English boys carefully weighed their options. They could return to England, but if the

---

1. See Biography Section for information on many of the people listed here.

**... Just a few weeks earlier, most of these *bochurim* and even the young couples had been carefree vacationers in the resort areas of Poland ....**

*Shaya Lebor and Pinchas Berliner in a hammock*

*Summer 1939 — Mirrer bochurim in the summer resort of Nowohjelna, Poland Left to right: Moshe Friedman, Simcha Weissman, Shaya Lebor, Elchonon Ehrlanger, Yehuda Klein, and Pinchas Berliner*

*Left to right, around the table: Rabbi Mordechai Yoffe (the summer after his marriage), Mordechai Benzinger, Shlomo Chill, Pesach Cohen, Shaya Lebor (standing — owner of the cottage), Yehoshua Chinn, Shmuel Scheinberg, Yosef Schroit, and ybdl"ch Yisroel Spinner*

rumors were true and England joined the war,[2] they would be drafted into the English army. None of them wanted to jeopardize the spiritual heights

---

2. On April 6, 1939, England and France signed a treaty with Poland pledging their support if any action was taken threatening Poland's independence (*The War Against the Jews* by Lucy S. Davidowiez, p. 144).

they had reached in the Mir with a stint in a gentile army. Perhaps there was an alternative.

The American, Belgian, and Swiss boys wanted to return home. Some of them had all their papers in order and only needed to purchase ship tickets. Others had problems with their documents, and still others were short of money. Their predicament was one of indecision as to what to do and how to go about it, rather than despair that they might be caught in Nazi hands. Having been sheltered in Mir, the *bochurim* had not been exposed to Hitler's periodic raving radio broadcasts. They understood the need to leave Poland and many wanted to join their families out of respect for their parents, yet few were overly concerned about being trapped in Europe.[3] Mannis Moore and Shmuel Bloch were busy debating where in Europe they could continue their learning.

ON FRIDAY MORNING, SEPTEMBER 1, THE MIRRER GROUP ARRIVED IN Riga, Latvia. To their dismay, they discovered that the war — with all its implications — had begun. The lines in front of the American Consulate extended around the block. *Bochurim* who went to banks to pick up money to pay for their ship tickets were disappointed; all cabled funds were being detained.

Shabbos was approaching. The tired refugees turned their attention toward finding food and lodging for the next 24 hours. The yeshivah in Riga warmly welcomed their unexpected guests. Community activists found lodgings for them in the neighborhood and arranged their Shabbos meals in a local kosher restaurant. The *bochurim* were invited to join the yeshivah and soon the *beis medrash* reverberated with sounds of learning louder and stronger than Riga had heard in a long time.

SHABBOS ENDED. THE REFUGEES HAD TO CONFRONT THEIR PREDICAment once again. Reb Dovid was settled; his papers were in order, his tickets were paid for, and his ship was due to leave for Sweden on Tuesday. True to his generous and giving nature, he could concern himself with his friends and their problems. The Ehrlanger brothers, Swiss natives, were short of funds for their passage home and Reb Dovid wanted to help.

The most influential Jew in Riga was Rabbi Mordechai Dubin, a respected scholar and an extraordinarily generous person. Reb Mordechai was a senator in the Latvian parliament, despite the beard and *peiyos* he sported proudly. His name was synonymous with charity, kindness, wis-

3. The frenzied panic of the Benders had nothing to do with doomsday premonitions. They were simply afraid they would not make it to America as Reb Dovid's parents were demanding. At this stage, no one imagined the horrors that were to take place (ed.).

## ... A Jew to whom any Jew in need could turn ...

*Rabbi Mordechai Dubin (d. 1957) was head of the Agudath Yisroel in Latvia from 1922 until 1934 and its chief delegate in the parliament. At one period of his life he held two high positions in the Latvian government, but his talents made him a target of the Communists and he had several close encounters with death. He engineered the release of the Lubavitcher Rebbe from Russia in 1927. He survived the Holocaust but remained in Russia. After years of persecution, he perished at the hands of the Russians.*

dom, and *Yiddishe shtoltz*. He was renowned as a Jew to whom any Jew in need could turn.

Reb Mordechai was a Lubavitcher Chassid. As such, he often journeyed to Otvock where the Lubavitcher Rebbe, Rabbi Yosef Yitzchok Schneersohn,[4] lived. He combined his pilgrimage to the Rebbe with a visit to his son who studied in the large yeshivah that the Rebbe had established.

Basha was a good friend of Reb Mordechai's daughter-in-law Aidel, a classmate of hers from Bais Yaakov of Crakow. The Benders heard that Reb Mordechai was staying in a *dacha* near Riga. Reb Dovid went to speak with him about the plight of the *bochurim* who were short of funds. Reb Mordechai immediately gave him 2,000 *lotte*[5] to lend the Ehrlanger brothers.[6]

Word traveled that Rabbi Mordechai Dubin was a man who could help with most problems: documents, legalities, border crossings, money, etc. Many turned to this special man and he, in turn, did whatever he could to help his fellow Jews.[7]

Reb Dovid and Basha did not remain in Latvia for long. On Tuesday, September 5, 1939, the Benders boarded the *S.S. Aeolus*,[8] bound for Stockholm, Sweden. They were of the first of their group to leave Eastern Europe.

---

4. See Biography Section.

5. Latvian currency.

6. Sixty years later, R' Elchonon remembered this *chessed* that Reb Dovid had done for him.

7. "I was also a recipient of his help. My father gave money to Moreinu HaRav Yaakov Rosenheim who telegraphed it to Rabbi Mordechai Dubin. This money was enough to cover the expenses of all the English *bochurim*. This unique individual was constantly trying to help others. In the end, he himself did not get out in time and died *al Kiddush Hashem* at the hands of the Russians" (Rabbi Alex Weisfogel). "Rabbi Mordechai Dubin had an idea to conduct legal marriage ceremonies between all the American *bochurim* in the Lubavitcher Yeshivah in Otvock with the local Lubavitcher girls. This way the girls would be able to immigrate to America. However, since these marriages would be only 'paper marriages' and the girls would ultimately be on their own in a foreign land, their mothers were reluctant to agree. Subsequently, the girls and their families perished" (Rabbi Avrohom Barnetsky).

8. Swedish National Archives.

THE LINE OF PASSENGERS BOARDING THE *S.S. AEOLUS* MOVED SLOWLY but steadily. The waiting passengers were anxious and the atmosphere on the pier was tense.

"Come on! Come on!" the stevedores shouted. "Let's go! Let's go!"

While Reb Dovid and Basha were swept up with the crowd, most of their luggage patiently waited to be loaded. The Benders stood on deck, watching the frenzied shipyard workers run back and forth. There were still many pieces of luggage to load and time was swiftly passing. Suddenly, the ship began to move. Reb Dovid and Basha stared in disbelief; their luggage remained on the pier as the boat sailed away! Aside from their hand luggage and the few items sent ahead in crates with friends, everything they owned remained on the wharf. Basha's exquisite trousseau — the linens, tablecloths, and handkerchiefs all painstakingly hand-embroidered by her mother — was gone.

Basha was devastated. Still reeling from the emotional parting with her parents, still exhausted from the makeshift Shabbos in Riga, seeing her belongings left on the pier was a crushing blow. She thought about all the years of labor and love invested by her mother in her trousseau, of the exquisite beauty of each item. She recalled her mother, sitting by dim lamplight, sewing stitch after stitch with a serene smile on her face and her eyes full of love, and the loss was all the more painful. She now also recalled that the album of mazel tov letters from many of the *gedolim* of Europe was also packed in the luggage left on the pier. This album, a memento of her profound reverence for *gedolim* and so precious to her, was now lost forever.[9]

Her husband tried to console her that perhaps the luggage would be sent on a later ship and might eventually reach them. Basha listened to his

9. When Rebbetzin Bender recounted the miraculous chain of events that led to their safe arrival in America, she always focused on the constant *hashgachah pratis*: She reached the last open consulate on the last day before the war broke out and, with uncharacteristic courage that she attributed only to the *Ribbono shel Olam*, managed to get a visa just in the nick of time. If not for the insistence of her father-in-law, the many telegrams he sent, the fact that they had almost all the necessary papers in advance, the money from her parents, etc. who knows what would have been?

Nonetheless, Rebbetzin Bender often spoke wistfully of the loss of her precious trousseau (Rebbetzin E. Epstein; Mrs. H. Mandelbaum). On her journey, she had no idea what kind of war it would turn out to be. She was concerned for her parents because her father was elderly and they were alone, but she had no inkling that she would never see them again. At the time, she could not comprehend the full extent of her own miraculous survival. No one knew that in one day the border would be sealed tight. No one imagined that eventually, even people with valid immigration papers would be unable to leave. No one realized then that the situation for most Jews left in Europe was hopeless.

Later on, when she learned how lucky she was to have escaped Europe, the loss of her belongings retreated into the background. She was grateful to be alive! But she never forgot that moment when her beautiful trousseau was left abandoned on the pier, igniting in her a sense of despair. Her trousseau was a tangible testimony of her mother's boundless love and devotion.

soothing words, but she remained unconvinced. She masked her despair, so as not to concern him. Although the rest of the trip proceeded with relative calm, Basha found it difficult to relax. Her heart was in turmoil. How she wished she could turn back the clock and return to her parents' home in Otvock. There, war was only a topic studied in history lessons and far removed from real life …

THE TRIP FROM RIGA TO STOCKHOLM TOOK ABOUT AN HOUR AND A half. The Benders disembarked in Sweden and went to visit Rabbi Shlomo Wolbe,[10] an acquaintance of Reb Dovid's from the Mir, who was living in Stockholm. There they discussed how to proceed.

There were two ways to travel from Sweden to America. Large ocean liners sailed directly, with no stops, from Sweden to America. The less convenient route was with smaller simpler ships that stopped in England.[11] The Benders were still unsure of which route to take. Then, just as Reb Dovid and Basha were feeling lost and bewildered, a letter arrived from Poland. As Basha read her mother's familiar handwriting, she felt her mother's arm around her shoulders and her warm reassuring presence right at her side.

*Dearest children,*

*… We received a very friendly letter from your parents yesterday, with one phrase stating that we are impeding your trip a bit. When you get there, please defend us, and tell them the truth.*

*If there is unrest in London, it is wise to stay off the streets … Bashale, you have some acquaintances in London: Baruch Abrahamson and Rabbi Gedaliah Schneider. In case you forgot, we made their acquaintance in Otvock. Again, dear daughter, I want to warn you: If there is unrest, do not go out in the streets!*

*The Brisker Rav, shlita, came to visit with Harav Berel, shlita. They are feeling quite well, b"H.[12] Harav Noach, sheyichyeh, sends his many, many blessings.*

*We are expecting letters, dear children, describing your joyful trip, may you feel well. Bashale dear, be careful with the food on the ship; the conserves may not be so fresh. May it all be to your good health … We have not yet heard about any new people leaving Mir for the far-off countries. No one from around here is leaving either.*

*There is no special news to share, only our blessings to you, dear children.*

---

10. See Biography Section.

11. Swedish National Archives.

12. The Brisker Rav was in Warsaw for approximately one month, from just before Rosh Hashanah until after Succos. Perhaps he stopped in Otvock en route to Warsaw or when travel between Warsaw and its nearby suburb was still possible (*The Life and Times of Reb Rephoel Soloveitchik*, p. 30).

"When my father (Rabbi Gedaliah Schneider – see Biography Section) learned in Poland as a *bochur*, he frequently went to Otvock for health reasons and stayed by the Epsteins. My father described R' Yankev Epstein as an exceptionally sincere *Yid*. My father knew Reb Dovid from Mir, held him in high regard, and marveled at the wondrous ways of the Almighty in arranging such an appropriate *shidduch*" (Rabbi Chaim Zev Schneider).

*"Beruchim atem b'tzeischem, beruchim atem b'vo'achem*[13] — *May you be blessed upon your departure and may you be blessed upon your arrival." May you meet your dear parents in health and joy, gladness and good luck.*

Your devoted mother,
Lifsha

*One more thing: Basha Chaya'la, don't get homesick, enjoy yourself wholeheartedly, b'ezras Hashem, and keep up your good mood, Amen, Amen, Amen.*[14]

BASHA FELT HER MOTHER'S LOVING CARE AND CONCERN IN EVERY LINE. She was happy to hear about the guests staying with her parents as this indicated that life was still proceeding normally. She suddenly felt more lighthearted and optimistic. Her life continued to fall into place as the Benders secured passage on the *S.S. Drottingholm*, one of the large luxury liners of the Swedish-American Line. They would not be stopping in England after all.

The ship was scheduled to leave on September 12, and the emergency visas they had received were valid until then. For the meantime, they found lodgings in the Jewish section and prepared to remain in Sweden for the week. They took their main meals at the home of Frau Zeidel, an *ehrliche* widow who ran a soup kitchen for the infrequent religious Jewish guests.

On September 12, the Benders traveled to Gothenburg, Sweden, where they boarded the *S.S. Drottingholm*, bound for America.[15]

THE CRUISE SHIPS ON THE SWEDISH-AMERICAN LINE WERE RENOWNED for their beauty, luxurious comfort, and the highest-quality service provided by their Swedish crew. Wealthy patrons, members from families

---

13. Paraphrase of *"Baruch atah b'vo'echa, baruch atah b'tzeisecha"* in *Devarim* 28:6.

14. Those identified in this letter include: Rabbi Gedaliah Schneider, the Brisker Rav, and Rabbi Yosef Dov (Berel) Soloveitchik, and Rabbi Noach Velkovitch (Minsker).

15. Swedish National Archives.

with names like Rockefeller and Rothschild, appeared on the passenger list more than once.

This luxury liner was equipped with everything a carefree vacationer could ask for: saloons and smoking rooms, a music room and library, a steam room and bathhouse. Professional barbers and hairdressers were on call. There were doctors and nurses and a complete staff waiting to be of service.[16] Indeed, most of the passengers were vacationers enjoying the delights of an ocean cruise.

Reb Dovid and Basha were strangers afloat in foreign territory. They had little in common with Rudolf, Marlene, Mary, or Hans.[17] Even their fellow Jewish passengers were of an alien ideology, mentality, and nationality. Consequently, the Benders kept mainly to themselves. Their time aboard ship was merely a means to an end. The purpose of their journey was to reach America, not the journey itself.

One day, as Reb Dovid and Basha strolled leisurely on deck, they saw a young man addressing a crowd of people. Reb Dovid became incensed. Centuries had passed since a young upstart had tried to lure Jews away from the holy Torah and here on board was one of his modern-day followers. Reb Dovid sidled up to the crowd.

Basha stood by nervously. She was reared in the typical European Jewish mentality. Lie low. Make yourself unobtrusive. Avoid confrontation. Police were to be feared, not to be trusted for protection. Basha watched the unfolding scene with alarm.

"Your presentation was very impressive," Reb Dovid commented as the speaker paused. "May I see your literature?" The man readily agreed. What could be better than a Jew requesting his pamphlets? He handed Reb Dovid the modest pile. In front of the entire crowd, Reb Dovid took the pamphlets and ripped the pages into little pieces. Then he spit on the confetti and threw it into the sea. The missionary and his audience were dumbfounded.

Basha was so terrified she could hardly breathe. The missionary was purple with rage. He looked as if he were planning to throw Reb Dovid overboard to join the shredded papers.

Reb Dovid motioned to his wife to follow him as he walked toward their room without a backward glance. Basha waited for crowds to come pounding at their door, for the police to cart them off to jail, or for some other repercussion. Reb Dovid tried to calm her down. He explained to her that they were on their way to America, a free country. Even if the police did come, their job was to help, not to hurt. No one would arrest a Jew on minor charges, just because he was a Jew. Basha was skeptical. A

---

16. Passenger list of the *S.S. Drottingholm*, Swedish National Archives.

17. These are actual names that appear on the passenger list. Most were American citizens and a few other nationalities were represented, but only one passenger was from Poland.

"free country" was a lovely idea, but she could not imagine that its benefits extended to Jews. Surely, in due time, she would find out what this strange new country was all about.

THE SHIP WAS SCHEDULED TO DOCK ON EREV YOM KIPPUR. THE DOCK-ing time would give the Benders little time to disembark, get through customs, and arrive home before sundown. Rabbi Avrohom Bender went to the police station and explained the situation. He asked if he could request a police escort to pick them up from the Port Authority station and speed through traffic to get them to Williamsburg before candle lighting. The police were very understanding and said they would try to arrange the escort.

As the ship docked, a squad car pulled up and an officer alighted. He entered the Port Authority building and asked that the authorities locate Mr. and Mrs. David Bender who were to come with him immediately. The officer paced back and forth impatiently.

BASHA WAS EXHAUSTED. SHE GLANCED AT HER WATCH ANXIOUSLY. IT was so late. Would they get to her in-laws' house before the Yom Tov?

"Dovid," she murmured softly. Then she stopped short. A police officer and a customs official were walking toward them, talking animatedly together. Her heart began to pound. *What do they want from us?* she thought wildly. *Perhaps that missionary sent them to arrest us. Have I journeyed all this way just to be carted off to jail?* Her pounding heart was making so much noise, she was certain that everyone in the room could hear it.

"Are you David and Basya Bender?" the officer inquired.

"Yes," Reb Dovid answered serenely. "Pleased to meet you."

*Pleased to meet who?* Basha's thoughts screamed. *How can he be so calm?*

"Your father asked that we escort you home so that you arrive before sundown, but I was told that not all the paperwork has been taken care of …"

Reb Dovid looked at his watch. It was very late.

"Thank you so much for coming for us, officer. Perhaps my wife can go with you to Williamsburg while I remain here to finish the paperwork. At least she will arrive home before sundown."

Basha tried to follow the conversation, but her English was still rudimentary and the officer's presence was so unnerving she found it difficult to concentrate. How she wished she were home already!

Reb Dovid picked up their hand luggage and motioned to Basha to follow him out the building. "Listen, Bashale, I have to stay here to finish off the paperwork. You will go with this policeman …"

"I will what?" she exclaimed in horror. However, Reb Dovid had already opened the squad-car door and was heaving their luggage inside.

"You will go with this nice policeman to my parents' house. I will finish here and then I will find a place nearby to spend Yom Kippur."

"But, Dovid, police —"

Reb Dovid guided her into the car, a faint smile on his lips.

"Don't worry," he reassured her, closing the door as he spoke, "this is America." Did she detect a twinkle of amusement in his eyes? "Relax; everything will be fine." He waved to her as the car drove off.

Basha leaned back in her seat with her eyes closed. She was barely aware of how fast they were speeding through the streets of New York. She could not believe what was happening. She, of all people, alone in a police car and in New York, of all places — all because "this is America"! Would this trip ever end?

REB DOVID FINISHED FILLING OUT THEIR PAPERS SHORTLY BEFORE SUN-down and then set out to find a shul where he could spend Yom Kippur. He entered a shul at the beginning of *Kol Nidrei*. Relieved that he could begin the Yom Tov properly, he focused his full attention on the *chazzan*. He was barely aware of the congregation around him. After *Kol Nidrei*, a man arose and made a heartfelt appeal for *tzedakah*. Reb Dovid observed in shock as men began to take out their checkbooks and write checks. On Yom Kippur! At that moment, he felt far, far away from Mir.

Reb Dovid stalked out of the shul and walked back to the pier. It was late at night and too dangerous to risk walking from the West Side of Manhattan to Williamsburg. He spent the remainder of the night on the couch in the Swedish-American lounge. At 5 a.m. he arose and began his trek home. He walked for two hours until, at approximately 7 a.m., he arrived at 168 Hooper Street.

He was finally home.

*Chapter Eighteen*

# Settling In

**Williamsburg: Tishrei 5700 (September 1939)**

ASHA HAD ARRIVED AT HER IN-LAWS HOME ON EREV YOM Kippur just minutes before candle lighting. She was exhausted from the preceding whirlwind weeks.[18] That Yom Kippur, Basha fasted for two days: the last day on the ship they had not had anything to eat and the following day was Yom Kippur. She felt exhausted, overwhelmed, and lost. America was not the land of her dreams. Quite the contrary, the entire yeshivah world of Europe knew that America was a spiritual desert. She had never had the slightest desire to settle here. Yet, as she had watched the waves pull her further and further away from European shores, she intuitively knew that her "visit" to America would last much longer than planned.

At the end of a most difficult Yom Kippur, she sat down with her husband and in-laws to break her two-day fast and the telephone rang.

"Basha, it's for you," her mother-in-law said and handed her the telephone.

A host of thoughts ran through her mind as she took the receiver. *Me? The telephone? Who in this strange place knows that I am here? Who could possibly be contacting me?* She held the telephone to her ear.

"Basha?" How sweet! How pleasant! What a friendly voice!

"Vichna?" Basha was overcome with emotion. It was her good friend from Bais Yaakov, Vichna Kaplan. Just a few minutes earlier, she had felt so alone; how many people did she know in America? To hear the voice of

---

18. The Benders left Mir on August 31 (the 14th of Elul) and arrived in America on September 22 (Erev Yom Kippur).

someone so dear so soon after her arrival was a balm for her soul.[19] They exchanged pleasantries and caught up on old times. Then, Vichna came to the point.

"We have started a wonderful Bais Yaakov. There are two classes of precious girls waiting impatiently to learn. They thirst for knowledge. We need you immediately. Any day now, I will have to be out because, *besha'ah tovah*, we are expecting a *simchah*. I would like you, Basha, to take over and teach for me right after Succos."

"How can I?" Basha protested. "I do not know any English." Basha knew Latin, German, French, Spanish, Polish, Yiddish, and *Lashon Kodesh*, but she had never had any desire or need to learn English. She was so happy conversing with her friend in Yiddish; she did not even want to think of learning English.

"Sure, *du kenst gayin tzu schule* (you can go to school), O.K.?"

"*Ober* (But) …"

"*Du vest lernen English* (you will learn English), all right?"

Basha hung up the telephone, bewildered. *Sure, O.K., all right — what do these words mean?* Her closest friend's "perfect" Yiddish was already mixed with English. *Oy*, how was she supposed to master this strange new language in just a few days? It was *Motza'ei Yom Kippur*; Succos was in just a few days, and then she would be going to school. How in the world would she manage?

SUCCOS CAME AND WENT. SUDDENLY, IT WAS HER FIRST DAY OF SCHOOL. She rehearsed her lesson at home with Reb Dovid and hoped that all would go well. Reb Dovid accompanied her through the neighborhood, showing her how to get to school and pointing out landmarks along the way.

She stopped walking abruptly, perplexed.

"What is wrong?" Reb Dovid gently inquired.

Basha was staring at the street sign. Her training in Latin had come to good use and she had already mastered the rudiments of spelling. "I do not understand. How will I know where to go? All the streets have the same name."

"The same name?" Reb Dovid was perplexed.

Basha pointed to the bold sign beneath the street sign. "All the streets are called 'One Way'!"

Reb Dovid laughed and then attempted to explain away her confusion.

---

19. Rebbetzin Bender recounted this entire story at the Bais Yaakov Spring Tea in 1990, when Bais Yaakov honored her for 50 years of teaching. In recalling this phone call she said, "I still get a chill in my heart when I think of how I felt. I felt the heartfelt concern of a very close person. I felt her warmth."

They reached the corner building at Marcy Avenue and Keap Street. There they came to a stop.

"This is it," Reb Dovid cheerfully exclaimed.

*This is it?* Basha was too shocked to enunciate her thoughts. *This cannot be it!*

While Poland was not a very wealthy country, its schools looked like schools. The buildings were modest, but official looking and immaculate. This looked like … well, not like a school.

Basha cautiously climbed the rickety steps. The "school" was really two rooms above a shul. The rooms were old, dilapidated, and neglected. Plaster hung from the ceilings and the paint on the wall was peeling. Yet, sitting around on a conglomeration of mismatched furniture was the most beautiful sight Basha could have wished to see. Seventeen bright and eager faces were beckoning her to begin.[20]

Rebbetzin Kaplan was already out, so Basha introduced herself. The girls immediately began to ask questions. They wanted to know about Sara Schenirer and the Bais Yaakov movement. Basha was captivated by their interest, by their thirst for knowledge, and by their open eyes and ears. She knew that despite the language barrier,[21] her words, spoken from her heart, would enter theirs. She walked home with a light stride and a song in her heart; she had found herself a place on this soil that just yesterday had seemed so foreign.[22]

THE BENDERS WERE SETTLING INTO LIFE IN AMERICA. REB DOVID WAS learning in Torah Vodaath and Basha was teaching in the fledgling Bais Yaakov. They allowed their lives to move forward, but their family and friends remained on their minds, in their hearts, and in their lives.

When Reb Dovid and Basha had left Europe, people were nervous, but they were not overly concerned. Some remembered the Great War, a most difficult period, but nonetheless survivable. The Polish newspapers, with their unrealistically optimistic headlines, may have given their populace a false sense of security. Now, in America, Reb Dovid and Basha began to see things differently. Their family and friends in Europe were helplessly caught in the web of war. Clearly, they would be better off in America.

If only they could help …

---

20. There were already two classes then; one with 17 students and one with 14 students.

21. Many of the girls knew Yiddish and within a short time, Rebbetzin Bender mastered English. The language barrier she feared was quickly conquered.

22. Rebbetzin Bender at Bais Yaakov Spring Tea in 1990.

### Chapter Nineteen

# Rescue Efforts Begin

### Riga: Tishrei 5700 (September 1939)

ALEX WEISFOGEL SAT IN THE YESHIVAH IN RIGA, LATVIA, wondering what he was doing there. Weeks earlier, he had telegrammed friends in America, begging them for a visa. By now he was itching with impatience. Most of his friends had either found their way home or moved on to a different yeshivah where they felt they could progress in their learning. Only a handful of *bochurim* from the original Mirrer group remained in Riga.

The mark of *"ah Mirrer"* was unmistakable: even while concerned over how and when to leave Europe, Alex and his friend Shaya Lebor were frustrated that they were not progressing in their learning. They decided to go to Shavel to discuss the situation with Rabbi Archik Bakst. Reb Archik, a renowned Torah scholar and *ba'al mussar,* had lived in England for a number of years and could understand the boys and their considerations. Alex and Shaya stayed in Shavel overnight to speak with Reb Archik. The next morning, Alex headed for Kelm while Shaya went to Telshe.

In Kelm, Alex met other friends from the Mir, including his good friend Yankel Goldman, a fellow Englishman. Yankel had been reluctant to leave his beloved Mir, so even when all the other international boys left, he had stayed. He clung to the hope that the German invasion of Poland would be squelched quickly and that the panic was for nought. When it became clear that this was not the case, he left the Mir and headed for Kelm, where Alex now joined him.

There were other foreigners who stayed in Europe because they wanted to continue their learning. Shmuel Bloch, a fellow Englander, was learning in Kelm and so was Nosson Wachtfogel, a Canadian *bochur*. Rabbi Chaim Dov Silver, an English native who had married a girl from Kelm and already had a family, also remained. Mannis Moore had gone to Telshe.[23] The war had not yet reached Lithuania and these *b'nei Torah* clung to the hope that it never would. Yeshivos were functioning with regular *sedarim* and tremendous diligence in learning.[24]

Nonetheless, Alex was concerned. He was not convinced that staying in Europe was safe. He knew that British citizens requesting an American visa were not subject to the same quota regulations as Polish citizens. Thus, he was hopeful.

In February of 1940 both Alex Weisfogel and Shaya Lebor received student visas from Torah Vodaath. The hopeful telegram that Alex sent Rabbi Dovid Bender finally bore fruit.

*Rabbi Aharon Yosef Bakst (1869-1941), fondly known as Reb Archik, learned in Volozhin where Rabbi Yitzchok Blazer introduced him to mussar. He served as a rav in 13 cities, establishing yeshivos and other Torah institutions, disseminating the mussar philosophy beyond the yeshivah system to the greater Jewish public. He perished al Kiddush Hashem. Some of his manuscripts were miraculously smuggled out of Russia.*

THE SITUATION WAS NOT AS ROSY FOR citizens of Eastern Europe, especially those trapped in German-occupied Poland. R' Yankev and Lifsha Epstein were resigned to remaining in Otvock. In those early months of war, they were not allowed to send or receive mail. Thus, they were effectively cut off from the rest of the world. Although Basha was settling into life in America, her mind and her heart were with her parents, trapped in Poland.

She wrote letters and telegrams, but received no response. She felt so helpless. In her family, writing was a powerful means of communication. Basha was very worried.

She wrote letters to family and friends from different parts of Europe begging them to find out how her parents were faring. She wrote to HIAS and the Red Cross asking them for information. She wrote and waited, wrote and waited. She wasn't hearing terrible stories; she just heard nothing, and that was bad enough. How she longed to know what was happening in her hometown of Otvock!

---

23. See Biography Section for some of the people mentioned here.
24. Rabbi Dovid Moore.

Many of these British nationals (such as Rabbi Nosson Wachtfogel, Rabbi Chaim Dov Silver, Mannis Moore, Shmuel Bloch, Yehoshua Chinn, Pinchas Berliner, and others) escaped from Europe to Australia where they helped build up the Jewish community there before traveling on to permanent destinations.

*Rabbi Pinchas Berliner learning in Australia*

*Rabbi Chaim Dov Silver learning with a chavrusah in Kelm*

*Alex Weisfogel*

**Alex Weisfogel and Shaya Lebor came to America on visas supplied by Rabbi Dovid Bender and Rabbi Avrohom Pincus. (See Biography Section.)**

*Shaya Lebor*

*Yankel Goldman, hy"d*

"… My good friend, Yankel Goldman, was so happy learning in Kelm. He hoped the war would end so he would never have to abandon his beloved yeshivah. In the end, he remained and was killed *al Kiddush Hashem* with the rest of the *kehilla* … " (Rabbi Alex Weisfogel).

### Chapter Twenty

# Back Home

**Otvock: Tishrei 5700 (September 1939)**

*T*HE NEWS OF THE GERMAN INVASION OF POLAND DID NOT come as a surprise to R' Yankev and Lifsha Epstein. They observed their neighbors' reactions with apprehension.

Otvock had always been a popular vacation area for illustrious Jewish personalities and some even made it their home. Now, they too had to make a decision. The Lubavitcher Rebbe had already fled the city. The Amshinover Rebbe and his family were packing to leave Otvock. The Modzhitzer Rebbe was hesitant to leave the Modzhitzer *hoif*, where he had succeeded his father 11 years earlier. It was only when his son-in-law, R' Avrohom Wiskowsky, arrived with a rented car that the Rebbe reluctantly agreed. The Rebbe took along his two sons, 26-year-old Chatzkel and 20-year-old Yitzchok, and they fled the city.[25]

However, R' Yankev Epstein was almost 70 years old and not well. He could not realistically consider racing away from the Germans. The trains were packed full, the schedules erratic, and the journey was fraught with unpredictable dangers. For now he and his wife would stay in Otvock and face the consequences.

The Germans marched through Poland, conquering city after city, and the Polish troops fell like dominoes, one after another. Only Warsaw was stubbornly holding out against the German siege. By September 17 (the 4th of Tishrei), the Western half of Poland, with the exception of Warsaw, was in German hands. Then Germany intensified their offense against the beleaguered city.

---

25. See Biography Section.

*Rabbi Shimon Shalom Kalisch (1863-1954), the Amshinover Rebbe, established his beis medrash in the resort city of Otvock where it became a center of Torah and Chassidus. With the outbreak of World War II, he escaped to Vilna where he joined the Mirrer Yeshivah in their travels. After the war, he immigrated to America where he set up his beis medrash on the East Side of New York.*

*The Amshinover Rebbe was renown for his exceptional piety, wisdom, and ahavas Yisroel.*

*Rabbi Shaul Yedidya Elazar Taub (1887-1948), the Modzhitzer Rebbe, had been Rav in Rakow before he succeeded his father as Rebbe in 1928. He moved to Otvock, close to his Chassidim who lived mainly in Warsaw. He was involved in many communal matters and was an active member of the Moetzes Gedolei HaTorah and Agudath Yisroel. In 1941, the Rebbe escaped the Nazis, temporarily settling in America. In 1947 he was finally able to realize his lifelong dream and settled in Eretz Yisroel.*

On route to their targets, German bombers flew low over Otvock. Each time a bomber passed, the air-raid siren would go off, sending the frightened people scuttling for shelter. Almost as if by accident, a stray bomb or two landed in the quaint suburb. The *Wehrmacht* surrounded Warsaw, plunging the city into a mini-siege. By crossing the Parga Bridge with food and words of encouragement, residents of Otvock tried to help their brethren in Warsaw. The city was in ruins; dead and wounded victims of the bombings lay helpless in the streets. On Erev Succos, September 27, the bombings ceased and the Germans rolled into a humbled Warsaw. On that same day, the Germans arrived in Otvock.[26]

LIFSHA EPSTEIN STARED OUT HER WINDOW. THE STREETS OF OTVOCK were eerily quiet, quite unlike the previous chaotic weeks. She thought about the letter she had written to her daughter in Sweden. Had it arrived? Was it nonchalant enough? Did it convey the tumult they had been suffering? She hoped not. Every word she had written was true. The Brisker Rav

---

26. *The War Against the Jews*, pp. 149, 533.

and Reb Berel had come for a visit, but only because they were trapped in Warsaw and unable to return to Brisk. As for the other visitors, they too were passing through because of war-related circumstances. No one was stopping in Otvock simply to take in its air; such visits were long past. Had Bashale picked up that things had changed? The last thing she wanted was for her Bashale to worry. She was doing enough worrying for both of them.

At first, the German arrival had little effect. Lifsha and her fellow Jewish friends and neighbors were careful to step off the sidewalk when a German soldier passed. They abided whatever foolish laws the Nazis instituted. They joked halfheartedly about the irrational Nazi whims; their humor was a shield to hide their fears. Lifsha would not show her worries and plunge herself or others into despair and depression.

As time went on, whispered words recounted stories of Nazi whims turning into Nazi cruelty. No major incident occurred in their sleepy suburb, but the rumors from afar were enough to arouse fear.

The situation grew progressively worse. It was very cold and there was no food. Relatives and friends running from other places often ended up in Otvock. They came knocking at the door with outlandish and frightening stories. Still, Lifsha knew that she and her husband would have to stay. How would they leave? Where would they go? The youth were more adventurous. They embarked on journeys into the unknown, hoping and praying for success.

*B"H Vilna: Motza'ei Shabbos,*
*Parashas Vayechi, Dec. 16, 1939*

*Dear friend, Mrs. Basya Bender, tichyeh,*
*We received your postcard, but it took some time to look for someone from Otvock. Today my wife, tichyeh, found the right people (i.e., the daughters of the Modzhitzer Rebbe) who are here now. They know that no calamity has befallen your parents, and they are, b"H, well. In general, Otvock is fine.*

*According to what we have heard, it is possible to arrange it[27] through America. You have to contact the Joint or other institutions for the information on how to go about getting the assistance you need.*

*Thank G-d that at least you got out in time, at the last minute — a real miracle from Heaven. We have suffered much already, continue to suffer, and only Hashem knows what still lies ahead. But, we are from the lucky ones in our family, on both sides. Best wishes and regards to your husband and his parents.*

*Wishing you well,*
*Yisroel Lipshitz*

---

27. The reference is unclear — probably to immigration possibilities.

*One of the postcards that Basha received from her parents in 1940*

My dear and beloved Basya!

I was very happy to receive your letter, and even more so to be able to give you regards from your dear parents, sheyichyu. The daughters of the Modzhitzer Rebbe, Sarah and Tziporah, asked that I send warm regards. They say that everything is in order in your parents' home.

Regards to your husband and his parents.[28]

BASHA READ AND REREAD THE LETter. Her parents were alive and well! Her dear pupils, Tziporah and Sarah Taub, sent regards from them! If they had successfully made the trip from Otvock to Vilna, perhaps her parents would soon follow. She was certain that from Vilna she would be able to help them.

She knew little of the painful trials these two young girls had undergone in their dangerous journey from Otvock to Vilna. The trip, which under normal circumstances took 24 hours, took them six weeks! It was fantasy to hope that her parents could endure what had been so very difficult for two young energetic teenagers. But Basha did not know this and the letter gave her hope and comfort.

Later, in the winter, she received notification from HIAS that all was well, but it was only during the summer of 1940 that letters and postcards finally began coming. Basha held the first postcard with trembling hands. Her father's familiar handwriting brought tears of pain and relief.

*Otvock: April 15, 1940*

Dear and beloved children, Basya and Dovid,

We have received your postcard from the seventh of January and we are most grateful. Please write us more often telling us of your well-being. We are quite well. Please give our regards to all our friends. Yosef — why doesn't he write?

Jacob and Lifsha

---

28. Mrs. Yisroel Lipshitz added her own greetings.

THIS LETTER, DATED APRIL 15, 1940, WAS IN RESPONSE TO HER LETTER OF January 7. That meant that her parents had not received her correspondence for three months! Basha's heart ached for them. She could only imagine how lonely and helpless they felt.

She turned over the postcard and studied the other side. From the left side, the Nazi insignia stared at her menacingly. Clearly, a censor had read the card, which was probably why her father had written in German. A letter written in German was more likely to pass the censor than one written in Yiddish. The card had been sent to her cousin Rabbi Yosef Dovid Epstein who had fled to Keidan. Perhaps her parents had realized that letters to America were not getting through, so they decided to send this one via Lithuania, hoping it would reach her from there.

Basha thought of a plan. She and Reb Dovid had already discussed sending packages from America through various channels, such as the Agudah, HIAS, European Parcel Service, or Overseas Distributors. Yet, none of these channels was foolproof. Although certainly less direct, maybe if she would wire money to friends in Latvia and Lithuania, they could arrange to have packages sent to her parents in German-occupied Poland.

Basha continued to write letters, investigate new possibilities, daven, and hope for the best. The letters and postcards from her parents continued to arrive erratically, anytime from a week to six weeks after they were sent. There was something almost regular about their irregular arrival.

*Otvock: May 21, 1940*

*Dear and beloved children,*

*Always be happy! We've received your letter from the 14th of April for which we are grateful. Why do you not write about your health? We are well and everything is fine. Please let us know about your health and how it is there [in America]. We thank you for your regards from Yosef. Please send regards to your parents and to Yosef.*

*Regards and kisses,*
*Jacob and Lifsha*

HOW TYPICAL OF HER DEAR PARENTS! IN ALMOST EVERY LETTER, THEY let her know that their greatest wish was that she be happy and healthy. While trapped in Europe where the conditions were certainly difficult, they thought about their children, her and her brother Yosef.

Yosef. Basha sighed. What would become of her brother Yosef? She so wished that he would come join her in America. Eretz Yisroel was a volatile place. She worried for both his physical and spiritual welfare. Yosef had immigrated to Eretz Yisroel and hoped that their parents would soon follow. Had her parents been there with him, she would be much less concerned about everyone. Her parents were trapped in Poland, and her brother was charting his own course in Eretz Yisroel. Here she was with pen in hand, her only weapon in this confusing war.

*Otvock: May 28, 1940*

*Dear and beloved children,*

*Be happy and satisfied! Since your letter of the 14th of April, we have not heard from you. We are asking you today to write us about your general well-being and especially about your health. We have heard that Basya is working in the semi-nary. Is this true? We are well. Please send our best regards to your parents and to Yosef.*

*Regards and kisses. We are homesick for our children.*

*Jacob and Lifsha*

BASHA REREAD THE POSTCARD OVER AND OVER. SHE WAS AS HOMESICK for them as they were for her! She knew her mother would be happy to hear that she was teaching; her mother knew how important teaching was for Basha. Yes, her hours in Bais Yaakov were some of the most pleasant hours of the day, but teaching in America was not the same as teaching in Otvock. She yearned for her mother's sage advice and practical wisdom. When would they next be together?

*Otvock: August 26, 1940*

*Dear and beloved children,*

*We have received your two letters of the 16th and 21st of August and we thank you for them. Your letter of the 21st of August made us very, very, homesick, but please continue to write to us often. We are well and everything is normal. Please give our best regards to your parents and to Yosef.*

*Regards, Jacob*

*Regards, dearest children.*

*Basya, I would like to know about everything.*

*Mama Lifsha*

BASHA LONGED TO TELL HER MOTHER EVERYTHING IN PERSON. SHE was still a newlywed; which young bride does not need her mother? She had so much she wanted to share. Seasonal visits would have sufficed, but the few short lines they exchanged could hardly be considered real communication. Issues arose and she felt she had to share them. However, within the few cryptic sentences she allowed herself, she would only make them concerned and worried, which was the last thing she wanted.

Time passed slowly and brought little change. There was no real information. Basha tried different ways to send her parents money and food packages. She continued to write and they continued to reply. Basha was certain that her parents wrote with caution for fear that their letter would not get through the censor or cause terrible consequences, Heaven forbid. With each letter, she felt more helpless and frustrated.

*Otvock: October 14th, 1940*

*Dearest Children,*

*Be happy! We've received your kind letters of September 24th and 27th. We thank you for your kindness. We cannot describe our joy when we receive news from you. Please write us often. We are well and everything is fine. I think that you would also like to know the dates of birth of our parents, which I cannot give you. I was born in Drigcol on March 18, 1870 and your mother was born in the same town on March 11, 1883. Give my best regards to your dear parents and to Yosef. I wish you happy years.*

*Jacob*

*Dear children,*

*Be well. I wish you all the best.*

*Mama Lifsha*

BASHA READ THE POSTCARD WITH INTEREST. HER PARENTS WERE 13 years apart in age. She knew there was an age difference between them, but she never realized how great. Truthfully, she never thought of asking. Her parents never focused on themselves; their lives were always about doing for others. It was only now, when she was trying to arrange immigration papers, that the topic arose. *Father is no youngster,* she silently mused, *could he manage the journey?* She shoved all her skeptical thoughts aside. For now, she had the information she needed.

AS TIME WENT ON, BASHA LEARNED MORE AND MORE ABOUT THE immigration process. The terms affidavits, visas, and sponsors became part of her daily lexicon. Letters and telegrams — appeals for help — poured in from friends and relatives in Eastern Europe. Many of those appeals came from friends in Mir. The Mirrer Yeshivah had just embarked on a daring journey in search of safety and the Benders wondered how they might help.

### Chapter Twenty-One

# Friends in Flight

Mir: Tishrei 5700 (September 1939)

ONE DECEPTIVELY PLEASANT FALL MORNING, THE TOWNSPEOPLE of Mir awoke to a day of sunshine and tranquil blue skies.

"*Oy vey, oy vey*, the Russians are here! The Russians are here! A war! A war!"[29] Shmeryl,[30] an eccentric acquaintance, walked into the home of the Mirrer *Mashgiach*, holding his head in his hands and bearing a doomsday expression on his face. He sunk morosely into a chair and stared glumly into space.

Zlata Ginsburg,[31] the *Mashgiach's* daughter, ran out into the street. Rows of tanks were advancing, crowding the dirt roads. Her thoughts flashed back to the events of the past few days. The town had been alive with frenzied shopping as the older people passed along rumors of an imminent Russian invasion, and hastened to prepare. They, who still remembered the Great War, when the Russians looted each town they conquered, ran to stock up on food. People grabbed loaves of bread, bags of rice, sacks of flour, and pounds of potatoes. They hoarded their precious wares in their pantries hoping to outsmart the boastful Russians.

---

29. The war had actually begun a few days earlier with the German invasion of Western Poland. Concurrently, Russia began invading Poland from the East, a result of the Molotov-Ribbentrop pact between Germany and Russia, which divided Poland between the two countries. For the residents of Mir, the arrival of the Russians was their first exposure to World War II.

30. Not his real name.

31. Rebbetzin Zlata Malka Ginsburg (1914-2004) was married to Rabbi Ephraim Mordechai Ginsburg. Her illustrious husband passed away at 54 years of age, leaving behind five unmarried orphans. With tremendous *emunah* and *bitachon*, the legacy of her upbringing, Rebbetzin Ginsburg raised her children single-handedly, guiding them toward becoming *talmidei chachamim* and *b'nei Torah*. Rebbetzin Ginsburg was also known for her clarity and wisdom.

"*Unas vso yest*! (By us we have everything!)" The Russians used to say.

"*Vso yest*? (They have everything?) *Spicki yest*! (Matches they have)," the Jews answered scornfully. Russia looted other countries because they had nothing in their own country. Maybe matches, a basic necessity, they had, but not much else.

Zlata had not stocked up on food in the assumption that the old people were concerned over nothing. Now she was not so sure. She ran to the general food store but found the shelves empty. Her fear mounted as she realized that she had very little in the house to feed her baby daughter and no money to buy anything substantial. She approached her *balabusta* (landlady) and asked if perhaps she could have a little milk for the child on credit.

The old woman sighed. "If there will be a world, you will pay me back. If there will not be a world, we will not need the money!" With that she went to fill up a little container of milk for the child.

As Zlata took the milk over to her apartment, she thought about those fatalistic words: if there would be a world, if there would not be a world … truly, could it be as bad as she made it seem?

THE RED ARMY ARRIVED IN MIR DURING THE *ASERES YEMEI TESHUVAH* of 1939. Within hours, they emptied the stores, took whatever buildings they wanted, and demanded that the residents put up their soldiers for the night.

Bewildered and afraid, the Mirrers unhappily complied. By morning, most of the soldiers were gone, but the havoc they wreaked remained. Stores and homes were looted and ruined; the streets were eerily silent. And, so no one would dare forget who the true rulers of Mir were, a token group of Russian soldiers were left in the city.

Russia was notorious for its brutal reign and intolerance of religious Jews. Some people, especially those of the previous generation who remembered the gallant Germans of World War I, were disappointed that their area in Poland did not come under German jurisdiction. Anything, they felt, would be better than the Russians. Would they close the yeshivos? Would they send the *bachurim* to Siberia?

Their despair was palpable.

ON CHOL HAMOED SUCCOS, NEWS ARRIVED THAT VILNA, NOW PART OF Russian-occupied Poland, would soon be handed over to Lithuania. The *yeshivaleit* discussed this development. Since Vilna was now a part of Poland, they should have no trouble getting there. In a few weeks, when Vilna would become part of Lithuania, they would automatically be in Lithuania, and not Russia. Brilliant!

## Rabbi Mottel Ginsburg, the son-in-law of the *Mashgiach*, felt it was imperative to leave.

*Rabbi Ephraim Mordechai Ginsburg (1906-1960), "Reb Mottel Lipnischker," went to learn in Yeshivas Mir at age 16. Ten years later, he went to Brisk to study under the Brisker Rav with whom he developed a close relationship. He carefully recorded his rebbi's chiddushim, which were later published in the Chiddushei HaGriz on Shas. Reb Mottel reached the shores of America in 1947 and served as Rosh Yeshivah of the Mirrer Yeshivah in Brooklyn. His analytical shiurim introduced his talmidim to the Brisker way of learning.*

Rabbi Leizer Yud'l Finkel, the revered Rosh Yeshivah of the Mir, spread the news that, immediately after Succos, the yeshivah would travel to Vilna. The initial excitement was tempered by reality. For over 100 years, Mir had produced thousands of Torah scholars who were imbued with the fear of Heaven and the desire to serve Hashem. How could one rejoice when the Mirrer Yeshivah was going into exile?

Succos was uncharacteristically somber. Would this be the last Succos in Mir? The last Simchas Torah? Perhaps by some miracle, Succos would never end …

ON *MOTZA'EI SUCCOS* THE FIRST EXODUS BEGAN. WITH ACHING HEARTS, the *yeshivaleit* packed and readied themselves for the journey. The inky darkness suited their solemn mood. Slowly and silently, wagon after wagon of Torah scholars stole away into the black night. By morning, a large portion of the yeshivah was missing.

Rabbi Mottel Ginsburg, the son-in-law of the *Mashgiach*, felt compelled to leave despite the difficulties of traveling with a baby. He was also reluctant to leave his elderly in-laws behind. He approached his father-in-law to discuss the situation.

The *Mashgiach* listened carefully. "You should go," he agreed. "You are young, who knows what they plan to do with young Torah students? However, for me, there is no reason to leave. They have no use for an old couple. Your mother-in-law and I will stay; your sister-in-law, Yocheved, will go with you." The *Mashgiach* maintained that as long as *bochurim* remained in Mir, he would not leave.

Reb Mottel tried to convince his nephew, a student in the Mirrer *yeshivah ketanah*, to join them. Yankele lived by the Ginsburgs and was treated as a son in their home and yet the boy insisted on going home to his parents and no amount of convincing could change his mind.

Reb Mottel appealed to their landlady, a widow with one son, to let him take her son; perhaps the child would be saved. But the widow would not part with her child.

Exasperated, Reb Mottel turned to his wife. Was there no one to speak to?[32]

The next morning, Rabbi Mottel and Zlata Ginsburg exchanged hasty goodbyes with the *Mashgiach* and his rebbetzin. They had barely enough money for their journey and barely enough food for one day. They took a change of clothing for each adult and several diapers for the baby — the sum total of their possessions.

With a knapsack on her shoulders and her baby in her arms, Zlata followed her husband out to the waiting horse and buggy. As they rode out of Mir toward Horodzei, they could hardly have known that they were saying their final goodbye to Mir.

> *A golden era ended, its door slamming shut with finality. Mir, a town that had echoed with the sounds of Torah learning for over 120 years, was empty — empty of the black-frocked scholars etching pathways from their houses to the yeshivah in their haste to be on time for their day's schedule, empty of the eager young men whose voices rose enthusiastically as they argued emphatically in their learning, empty of the sanctity and the spirit, the sincerity and the soul that had made Mir what it had been.*
>
> *The Mirrer Yeshivah would survive, but the town of Mir would never be the same.*[33]

---

32. To appreciate these events, it is imperative to realize that no one imagined that World War II was a war against the Jews. People thought that this war, like World War I, would be hard but survivable. They assumed that the men were in danger, but not the women and children. A prominent *talmid chacham* fleeing to Vilna wanted his wife and child to accompany him. "What!" she exclaimed. "How will I take the coats?" She pointed to the expensive fur coats she and her husband had for the winter. She was neither materialistic nor petty; rather she honestly felt that the danger would pass. If she left her possessions, they would be looted and she would return from Vilna a pauper.

33. Paraphrased from the unpublished memoirs of Rebbetzin Itka (Starobin) Epstein.

### Chapter Twenty-Two

# Haven of Hope

### Vilna: Cheshvan 5700 (October 1939)

HEN THE MIRRER YESHIVAH FLED FROM POLAND TO Vilna, they hoped for one thing: to escape from atheistic Russia. Though their initial concern was strictly spiritual, in the few short weeks of Russian rule, they saw that their economic situation was also precarious. Even matches were in short supply.[34] So the yeshivah fled to Vilna, along with *bochurim* from Kletzk, Kaminetz, Grodno, and other yeshivos.[35] After initial settlement arrangements were made, the yeshivah students resumed their regular learning schedules.

Meanwhile, people spoke of leaving volatile Europe altogether. There were many reasons why leaving Europe seemed impossible. Most of the refugees were Polish citizens with Polish passports. Now that Poland had been carved up between Russia and Germany, there was no such country as Poland, and their passports were invalid. They were stateless. As such, they had no legal way to travel. Even if they had had passports, they had

---

34. One *bochur* in the Mir knew how to split one match into four. During these few weeks, he would regularly go to the *Mashgiach's* house to split his matches. He later became one of the prominent Roshei Yeshivah in America, Rabbi Leib Bakst (Rebbetzin Z. Ginsburg).

35. Some of the *bochurim* from these other yeshivos joined the Mir. For example, Rabbi Yisroel Garber and Rabbi Berel Klor were Kaminetzer *bochurim* who joined the Mir. The Mirrer Yeshivah delegation was the largest and most organized group. The Roshei Yeshivah felt that the presence of so many *yeshivaleit* in one place was potentially dangerous. They moved to Keidan, and then later they split up between four small towns. The miraculous escape of the Mirrer Yeshivah has been documented in many books.

no visas, no places to go, and no money to get there. Leaving Europe was but an abstract notion.

Yankel Ederman,[36] a *bochur* learning in the Mir, discovered a way for the refugees to procure identification papers, which could serve as passports. The Polish government-in-exile was in Britain and therefore, the British legation of Russia allowed a Polish diplomat to function there. This man happened to be a kindhearted soul. He agreed to issue identity papers — for a price — that would give Polish citizens legal status and enable travel.

The Mirrer Yeshivah kept a regular schedule of learning. The *Mashgiach* Rabbi Chatzkel Levenstein[37] had been exhorting his students to concentrate on their learning; if they would be saved, it would be in the merit of their learning. Therefore, Ederman would go to the consulate alone and request papers for everyone. Ederman went from house to house, asking the Mirrer refugees if they were interested in purchasing identification papers. On his rounds, he also came to the house of Rabbi Mottel Ginsburg.

Reb Mottel was sitting and learning diligently. With him was Rabbi Yona Karpilov, a brilliant *talmid chacham*[38] and one of Rabbi Mottel Ginsburg's best friends. Yankel Ederman explained his mission.

Reb Mottel was excited. "Do whatever you can to get these passports for myself and my family. We will pay whatever it costs."

Reb Yona was skeptical — with good reason. Who could say that these pseudo-Polish passports would be recognized? Russia was notorious for not allowing their people to leave. They might even arrest such passport possessors, since such passports acknowledged the existence of Poland. Was it appropriate to squander the little money they had on this wild chance that might even be a dangerous risk? Besides, where would they go? America was not issuing visas and it was virtually impossible for a non-Zionist Jew to receive a certificate of immigration to Eretz Yisroel.[39]

---

36 See Biography Section.

37. As Vilna filled with *yeshivaleit* from all over, and especially from Mir, Reb Mottel Ginsburg's daily telegrams to his in-laws became more potent. The yeshivah was in Vilna; what purpose was there in remaining in Mir? Finally, the *Mashgiach* and his rebbetzin joined their children in Vilna. The *Mashgiach*'s presence with the yeshivah enabled the *yeshivaleit* to learn with unparalleled diligence.

38. When the Brisker Rav arrived in Eretz Yisroel during World War II, Rabbbi Isser Zalman Meltzer asked him, "Nu, so who is left in Europe (meaning, since the Brisker Rav left, which *choshuv bachurim* in the *olam hayeshivos* are still there)?" To which the Brisker Rav answered simply, "Just one, Reb Yona Minsker" (as told by Rabbi Zev Willensky to Rabbi Aryeh Fishel).

39. Reb Leizer Yud'l himself tried very hard to get certificates for the entire yeshivah to immigrate to Eretz Yisroel. He appealed to Rabbi Yitzchok Isaac HaLevi Herzog and Rabbi Moshe Blau (1885-1946), then leader of Agudath Yisroel, for help. Despite intensive efforts, they were unsuccessful (*Hazricha Mipa'asei Kedem*, Vol. I, p. 223). Among the very few non-Zionist Jews in Vilna to receive immigration certificates to Eretz Yisroel was the Brisker Rav and his family.

*Rabbi Yona Karpilov (1909-1941) was known as Reb Yona Minsker. He studied under Rabbi Elchonon Wasserman, Rabbi Boruch Ber Leibowitz, and the Brisker Rav. He spent many years in Mir as well. Reb Yona was recognized both for his lomdus and his diligence. With no means of escaping Europe, he was killed in the summer of 1941. After World War II, his brother, Rabbi Zev Willensky, printed some of his chiddushei Torah in a sefer called Yonas Ilaim.*

Even if, by some miracle, a Polish national managed to acquire a visa to Eretz Yisroel or America, he then had to apply to the Russian government for an exit visa – a move that could mean a one-way ticket to Siberia.

Reb Yona mulled silently for a few minutes. "Only up to seven *lits*."[40]

The passports cost nine *lits*. Ederman did not buy one for Reb Yona.[41]

NOSSON GUTWIRTH[42] WAS PORING OVER a map, his brow creased in thought. *Where should I go, where should I go, where should I go …?* Something niggled in the back of his mind. At his side was Dutch Ambassador I.P.J. de Dekker with whom Gutwirth, a Dutch national learning in Telshe, had come to consult. Together, they hit on a plan.

Gutwirth wanted to go to America but he had no American visa. He was optimistic that, if he could somehow leave Europe, he would eventually get that precious paper. Meanwhile, he needed to go somewhere.

The logical but now impossible way to leave Europe for America was to head west through and past Western Europe. A highly illogical but remotely feasible alternative was to take the Trans-Siberian Railroad across Russia to the easternmost coast of Russia — Vladivostok. From there, he could take a boat to Japan. The ambassador mused about the papers required for such a trip: he would need to get a transit visa to Japan — the only type of visa the Japanese consul was issuing. But the Japanese would only issue a transit visa if he had an end visa. If he had no ultimate destination, the Japanese would not issue the transit visa.

"Where can I go?" Gutwirth appealed to de Dekker.

The ambassador thought of Curacao, the Dutch-owned island in the

---

40. A *lit* was the Lithuanian currency.

41. Reb Yona was part of the illustrious group of Torah scholars learning with Rabbi Elchonon Wasserman when the Nazis, *yimach shemam*, killed them all *al Kiddush Hashem*. Upon hearing of the slaughter of the Jews of Mir and their deaths *al Kiddush Hashem*, the *Mashgiach*, Rabbi Chatzkel Levenstein, began to cry bitterly: "My neighbor merited to die *al Kiddush Hashem*, and this neighbor also, and this one … and this beloved friend — they merited to sanctify Hashem's Name, but I did not have that merit" (*Reb Chatzkel*, p. 132).

42. See Biography Section.

Caribbean. In an effort to populate the island, the Dutch allowed people to stay there without a visa. The ambassador agreed to give him a signed paper stating that no visa was required for residence in Curacao. With this "non-visa visa," Nosson Gutwirth went to the Japanese consul in Kovno, Senpo Sugihara, and procured a transit visa for Kobe, Japan. All that he now needed was to apply for an exit visa from the Russians and he could be on his way.

Word of Gutwirth's intended coup spread. The yeshivah students began a full-scale operation arranging for Curacao end visas and Japanese transit visas. Then they sat back and tensely waited for the Russian response to their applications for exit visas. Would the Russians consider this a rebellion and ship them all off to Siberia? Had they foolishly placed themselves in danger? Why should the Russians grant them permission to leave?

They prayed for a miracle.[43]

AT THE END OF NOVEMBER 1940, THE UNBELIEVABLE HAPPENED: THE Russians began releasing the names of those allowed to leave. As the lists went up, the exodus proceeded, and panic set in. All those who had not gotten "passports" — the Curacao visas and Japanese visas[44] — were now clamoring to join their friends. Some had all the right papers, but lacked the money to buy ship tickets. Intourist, the Russian Agency of Tourism, had recently raised the price of tickets on the Trans-Siberian Railroad from $20 to the astronomical sum of $170. Desperate refugees appealed to friends in America for help.

168 Hooper Street, the home of Rabbi Dovid and Basha Bender, was the address to which many turned.

---

43. "… And the greatest wonder, beyond understanding, was that the Russians gave us permission to travel as we wished. This was totally opposite to their natures and their laws" (the *Mashgiach*, Rabbi Chatzkel Levenstein, in a letter to *ybdl"ch* Rabbi Elchonon Yosef Hertzman printed in his book *Nes Hatzolah*). One of the most comprehensive and authoritative works on the topic of the escape of the Mirrer Yeshivah is *Japanese, Nazis, and Jews: The Jewish Refugee Community of Shanghai 1938–1945* by Dr. David Kranzler.

44. "At every stage of the plans, there were skeptics. A family friend, one of the illustrious *talmidei chachamim* of Kelm, came to visit us in Vilna. 'Come to Kelm,' he said. 'The Yellow People (the Japanese) will kill you!' My husband answered strongly, 'Here, we will be killed! You can stay here, but we are leaving' " (Rebbetzin Z. Ginsburg).

*Chapter Twenty-Three*

# Escape!

**Vilna: Cheshvan 5701 (November 1940)**

VISA EXPIRES FEW DAYS DESPERATE SITUATION ENDEAVOR AT AUNT MARCUS 1310 UNION AVE BRONX AND GOTTHOLD AND CABLE TICKET MON
    MEJER JANKIEL GRYNGRAS

DESPERATE SITUATION VISA EXPIRES COMMUNICATE BROCHE GSEBRIEL 352 AVENUE 19 STREET NEW YORK MORIC GORDON 286 MONTGOMERY STREET BROOKLYN NEW YORK CABLE 150 DOLLARS
    ELLA SOLTAN

ELEGRAMS POURED INTO 168 HOOPER STREET.[45] THEY CAME from Vilna, Kovno, Vladivostok, and Moscow.[46] In bold black letters, they screamed for help. Their Russian exit visas, valid for only three months, were expiring.[47] The Mirrer *bochurim* needed to buy ship tickets to leave Europe, but they did not have the money. "The quota of Poles allowed to leave Russia is open," they wrote in their telegrams. Who knew how long this would remain so? As he searched for his friends'

---

45. The people mentioned in the telegrams above are: Rabbi Chaim Gryngras and R' Ella Soltan. See Biography Section.

46. With the exception of Vilna, where some Mirrers were still staying, all these cities had American consulates. When people were working on getting documents, they often stayed in the cities with a consulate (Epstein Memoirs).

47. "The *bochurim* had student visas which expired after three months" (Rebbetzin Z. Ginsburg).

*Rabbi Elya Chazzan, one of the many people who appealed to the Benders for help, signed his name "Elya Brainsker" for he was from the town of Brainsk.*

*Rabbi Dovid Kronglass: Rabbi Dovid Bender's liaison in rescue.*

**Rabbi Eliyahu Chazzan** *(1906-1982) studied in Telshe, Kaminetz, and Mir. Rabbi Boruch Ber Leibowitz was his primary Rebbe and Reb Elya adopted his way of learning. He escaped Europe in 1941 and was appointed Rav in Montreal in 1942. There he served as maggid shiur in Yeshivas Merkaz HaTorah. In 1946 he became a maggid shiur and later Rosh Yeshivah in Torah Vodaath.*

**Rabbi Dovid Kronglass** *(1910-1973) was a talmid of the Mirrer Yeshivah. He journeyed with the Mir to Shanghai, arriving in Baltimore on immigration papers arranged by Rabbi Naftali Neuberger. Reb Dovid had a tremendous influence on his talmidim in Yeshivas Ner Yisroel as a European Mashgiach who nevertheless understood the needs of the American yeshivah bochur. His mussar shmuessen moved and molded many a talmid.*

relatives, Rabbi Dovid Bender traveled uptown and downtown, becoming intimately acquainted with the New York subway system. He went to strange homes with his prepared speech and hoped that they would open their hearts and their pockets.

> I BEG COMMUNICATION WITH ABE MARGOLIN IN DAN-
> VILLE ILLINOIS PACKING CO ABOUT GETTING 300 BOOKS FOR
> HIS SISTER HINDE CABLE ELYA BRAINSKER

Reb Dovid understood immediately which "books" his friend Rabbi Elya Chazzan was referring to. He needed American money, but since it was illegal to possess foreign currency in Russia he did not write more explicitly. Other telegrams asked for the transfer of "Gemaras" or "mezuzas." The word "money" rarely appeared. To be extra safe, Reb Elya disguised his name as well.

Reb Dovid received telegrams from many people in Europe, but his main contact was his good friend, Rabbi Dovid Kronglass. Rabbi Dovid Kronglass signed his telegrams in one of four ways: David, Kronglass, Ben Ezra (his father's name was Ezra), or Kobryner (he was from Kobryn). Because they were never sure what the Russians had up their sleeves, they tried to disguise their names, or only include half a name, so as not to conclusively incriminate any particular person.

Rabbi Dovid Kronglass appealed to Rabbi Dovid Bender numerous times. One of his goals was to help *bochurim* obtain the money needed for ship tickets. Each *bochur* had different financial circumstances and thus different needs. Rabbi Dovid Kronglass telegraphed Rabbi Dovid Bender with the amount of money that each *bochur* needed.

> PASSAGE COST KANAREK 250 STEINFELD ROKOWSKY 120
> WELWELE COHN 100 HOLLANDER BLAU 50 BORENSTEIN 80
> EIDELMAN[48] 130 FOR ALL PAY SAKS[49]
> BENEZRA

Although it was illegal for people in Russia to possess American currency, the Russian Intourist Agency, through which they had to purchase ship tickets, insisted on payment in American dollars! Thus, the codes were created. When Reb Dovid collected the money and transferred one lump sum, he would then send a telegram explaining how to divide the money. He made up a code to indicate what should be done, without being too specific. For example, if he sent $40 for Steinfeld, he would write MSTEINFELD. The "M" in the front corresponded to the Hebrew letter "Mem" which has a numerical value of 40. Although Rabbi Dovid Bender and Rabbi Dovid Kronglass never discussed this code, they understood each other perfectly.[50] The money was transferred directly to Intourist through the Russian Consulate in America under the name of the appropriate individual.

---

48. Those listed in this telegram are: one or all three Kanarek brothers (Rabbi Yisroel and *ybdl"ch*, Rabbi Avrohom, and R' Yosef Kanarek), Rabbi Binyamin Steinfeld, Rabbi Chaim Grozovsky, R' Velvele Cohen, *ybdl"ch* Rabbi Feivel Hollander, Rabbi Moshe Yehudah Blau, Rabbi Noach Borenstein, and Rabbi Lipa Eidelman. See Biography Section.

Note: Exactly what role Reb Dovid played in the ultimate survival of each person listed in the many telegrams is unclear. Since Reb Dovid did not speak much about his activities during or even after the war, much has been inferred from the large volume of telegrams and documents he kept and the bits and pieces that he and others told his children. The telegrams listed here are a sample of the many that he received. In the eulogies about Reb Dovid, his efforts to help people during the war was mentioned repeatedly.

49. Saks was a lawyer with whom they worked.

50. Not always were coded messages understood. That Rabbi Dovid Kronglass and Rabbi Dovid Bender constantly communicated in code and always understood each other (as they verified after the war) was a minor miracle (ed.).

Rabbi Avrohom Kalmanowitz, as *nasi* of the Mirrer Yeshiva, took personal responsibility for every member of the Mirrer Yeshivah and worked tirelessly on their behalf, but the reality was grim. For example, there were 435 persons listed as members of the Mirrer Yeshivah stranded in Europe and each person needed approximately $280 for his exit visa and ship ticket. The total was a huge sum. Those who had contacts and acquaintances in America were told to appeal to them for help and many appealed to Rabbi Dovid Bender.

Reb Dovid had lists of people for whom he was collecting money and how much money he collected for each person. The sums ran into the thousands of dollars. Sometimes, he was given the names and addresses of relatives who could also sponsor some of the costs. Other times, Reb Dovid was told of a soul in need and he had to try to find a way to help.

> IN LIST OF FORMER LODSER NAME NUCHIM LESMAN[51] IS MISSING PLEASE CABLE FOR HIM QUICKLY 170 DOLLARS VISA EXPIRES PITY
> FINKEL

> RABBI SHLOMA JOSEF GURWICZ[52] FROM MIRRER SMALL YESHIVAH HAS STARTVISA HAS NOT STARTCOSTS TIME SHORT PLEASE UNDERSTAND WITH JOINT AND RABBI HEIMAN[53] CABLE

Money was only one obstacle. Reb Dovid had been active in helping people get affidavits and visas almost from the very outset of the war. His in-laws, the Epsteins, were first on his list but they were still in German-occupied Poland. He turned his attention to his friends in Vilna, among them Rabbi Shabsi Yogel.[54]

The most direct way for a European to immigrate to America was for someone in America to fill out an affidavit and send it to the potential immigrant in Europe. That potential immigrant had to take the affidavit to the American consul in Russia and ask the consul to issue an American visa. During the war years, there was a strict quota system in force and the

---

51. Rabbi Leizer Yud'l Finkel sent this telegram on behalf of his student, Nochum Lesman, one of the stellar students of the Mirrer Yeshivah. See Biography Section.

52. Rabbi Yosef Shlomo Horowitz (though the telegram reads Gurwitz) was a rebbi in the Mirrer Yeshivah Ketanah (hence, "Mirrer Small Yeshivah") and a man of unusual caliber. See Biography Section.

53. Rabbi Shlomo Heiman.

54. Rabbi Shabsi Yogel received the proper papers for himself and his family to immigrate to Eretz Yisroel in 1940. Rabbi Peretz Yogel mentioned in his eulogy for Rabbi Avrohom Bender the many kindnesses the Bender family did for the Yogels, including sending documents.

consul was not issuing visas. Nonetheless, an affidavit would eventually be useful and so Reb Dovid worked hard to procure American affidavits for his friends and relatives.[55]

There were inherent difficulties in obtaining affidavits. An affidavit was issued by a sponsor who agreed to assume full financial responsibility for the immigrant. The sponsor had to produce income tax returns and bank records to confirm his claim that he could support these refugees. Some people were reluctant to assume this responsibility. Eager applicants might be rejected due to insufficient proof of income.

Even when an affidavit was procured, there could be difficulties. For some people, the timing was crucial and therefore, although the usual process was to mail affidavits, some people requested that their affidavits be telegraphed. Even when a telegraphic affidavit was received, the American consul in Russia could still cause trouble by demanding additional proof of income or assets. Sometimes even when the affidavit was perfect, the consul would still refuse to issue the visa. In such cases, only intervention from Washington could help.

Every setback required another round of efforts. Even when he thought that all the arrangements were taken care of, another hitch could still arise. For the Benders, this period was one of frenzied activity and much anguish. They took each appeal for help to heart and every day brought a new appeal.

*Basya,*

*Although I am here about one and a half weeks, I delayed writing until today due to my illness. Please forgive me. I cannot, at this time, express on paper all that is in my heart …*

*I was forced to sell my most necessary possessions to gentiles and I was left bereft of everything I owned. Then I was warned, in the name of the authorities, to leave the country immediately … All the great expenses I have incurred and everything that is happening are only because I received absolutely no help from anyone. … Mrs. Leschinsky[56] knows that I arrived here without anyone's help.*

*Now, you should know that I do not have anyone on whom to rely. I am hanging between the sky and the earth and if you want to save me, you can. I have seen that your Reb Dovid and you already have saved many people and I do not believe that you will forget about me since I am your relative.*

*I am making this short. Please read between the lines.*

---

55. Eventually, these affidavits came to good use. When the war ended, the consuls granted visas to those who had American affidavits. For example, R' Ber Elya Gordon sent affidavits to Rabbi Mottel Ginsburg. After the war, the Ginsburgs received visas based on these affidavits (Rebbetzin Z. Ginsburg).

56. This refers to Mrs. Batsheva Leschinsky, wife of Rabbi Dovid Leschinsky, a remarkable *ba'alas chessed*, devoted to helping others.

*Rabbi Yosef Dovid Epstein was always grateful to the Benders for their role in helping him and others to escape Europe. Here he is pictured with his rebbetzin (Itka Starobin/Epstein) and two children, Chaim and Esther.*

*Rabbi Yosef Dovid Epstein (1911-2002) learned under Rabbi Elchonon Wasserman in Baranovich and then in Mir. Later, he served as secretary to Rabbi Leizer Yud'l Finkel. During World War II he befriended government officials and worked with them, even risking his life many times, in order to help with the yeshivah's miraculous escape through Shanghai. As a trusted confidant of the Mirrer Rosh Yeshivah, he developed close relationships with gedolim of the times and published many seforim on mussar topics.*

*The important thing is that you dedicate all your strength to bring my family and me to America. I promise you that I will not be a burden to you there. Please remember that every person has, in his life, a "sealed" amount of time from Hashem. It is possible that the time will come when I will not be dependent on a "basar vadam." I hope that you will do everything you can, not merely out of pity, but rather from a feeling of love, closeness, and purity of heart.*

*Before I sign off, I must apologize to Reb Dovid that I am addressing the letter to you, though he is the actual "doer." I am writing quickly and at length and I can not be careful with my wording and when I write to you I feel a little less obligated in carefulness.*

*Waiting to hear from you,*

*Yours,*
*Yosef Dovid*

Rabbi Yosef Dovid Epstein, who was Reb Leizer Yud'l's personal secretary and Basha's first cousin, had a problem with his papers. When most of the *yeshivaleit* were receiving exit visas, he and his family did not. Reb Yosef Dovid went to the Bureau of Immigration every day and was repeatedly told that their papers were lost. They had submitted all their documents to apply for exit visas. Now they were in a difficult position; they had neither exit visas nor any other valid documents. Reb Yosef Dovid was desperate to replace what had been lost and he appealed to the Benders for help.[57]

DURING THOSE FRANTIC MONTHS, REB DOVID AND HIS REBBETZIN expended great effort to help everyone who appealed to them. In many cases they were successful. In some cases, they were not. One of the saddest sagas of futile attempts to save lives was the story of the Internat.

---

57. Reb Yosef Epstein ultimately credited the Benders for sending him the documentation that allowed his family to immigrate to America.

# Chapter Twenty-Four

# The Internat

### Eishishok: 5700 (1940)

"I THINK WE ARE ALMOST THERE."

"Really, how do you know?"

Shrug. "A feeling."

"It's about time, don't you think?"

"Sh ..."

The girls fell silent as they plodded on. Devorah Applegrad, Tybel Shere-shevsky, and Batsheva Ziv[58] had been on the road for a full week. They had traveled from their hometown of Slonim to Lida and from Lida to Eishishok. They had braved border crossings and bitter weather, bribing their way past Russians guards, and stoically marched along lonely deserted roads, with only the moonlight to guide them through the icy snow.

"There," Devorah whispered triumphantly, "see the sign? I was right! We are almost there!"

The girls followed her pointed finger. *Vilnius* — the word looked so welcoming. Could it be? Had they finally reached Vilna?

WORD HAD SPREAD THAT VILNA HAD BECOME A HAVEN FOR FLEEING *yeshivaleit*. Girls heard from their brothers, neighbors, and cousins that in Vilna, Torah was alive and well. Entire yeshivos had relocated and continued functioning while exploring escape plans. Stuck in Russian-occupied

---

58. Devorah Applegrad would marry Rabbi Moshe Cohn (See page 130). Tybel Shereshevsky would marry Rabbi Henoch Fishman and, after his passing, Rabbi Moshe Wernick. Batsheva Ziv would marry Rabbi Yehoshua Hutner. All these Bais Yaakov graduates remained active in educating Jewish children and young women.

Slonim, Devora and her friends, Tybel and Batsheva, feared a grim future. How could *Yiddishkeit* flourish under a government intent on destroying it? For weeks they had discussed the possibility of fleeing to Vilna. But for three girls to venture out on their own was daring and by the time they decided to go, the border between Russia/Poland and Lithuania was closed and the journey was dangerous. The threesome was undeterred. Their infectious optimism was what had motivated them to leave home to learn in Bais Yaakov of Crakow and the training and idealism they absorbed there propelled them further.

"THIS IS IT," BATSHEVA WHISPERED, "THE INTERNAT — 2 KIJOWSKA Street."

A man came to the door.

"Yes?"

"We have fled from home and we need help ..."

The man's eyes narrowed in suspicion and he took his time answering. "Come," he finally said, "the girls will give you some tea and tell you what being here in Vilna is all about. But tomorrow you must make sure that your papers are in order or else you will have to leave." He showed them where the other girls had apartments and then disappeared.

The three new refugees were tired and unnerved. They had come to the Internat because they had heard that it was for girls like themselves, *frum* girls fleeing Russia. Why was this man being so cold to them? The reception the new refugees received from the other girls was much warmer. Most of the girls in the Internat were Bais Yaakov of Crakow graduates. There was a natural kinship, even with students from other years, because they shared similar experiences, values, and a vision. Whereas Tybel and Batsheva were disheartened by the initial cold reception and found other places to stay, Devorah moved into the Internat.

The Agudah rented the building and the girls were allowed to stay there free of charge. Rabbi Chaim Ozer Grodzenski, the acknowledged *gadol hador* for his supremacy in learning, as well as for his role in carrying the burdens of *Klal Yisroel*, was very concerned about the plight of these young girls. At the outset of the war, he established the *Vaad Hatzalah*, an organization that would provide financial assistance for the refugees fleeing Europe. He had the *Vaad Hatzalah* provide a stipend for the girls of the Internat as well.

Nonetheless, the stipend the girls received was insufficient for their day-to-day expenses. Basha Bender learned of the Internat through Aidel Dubin, Rabbi Mordechai Dubin's daughter-in-law. Basha had contacted Aidel as a friend and someone who might be able to help send parcels to her parents. When Aidel responded to Basha's letter, she told her about the Bais Yaakov girls in Vilna and the difficulties they were having. Never one

**Rabbi Chaim Ozer Grodzenski, the *gadol hador*, was very concerned about the plight of these young girls ...**

*Reb Chaim Ozer, surrounded by talmidim.*

to procrastinate, Basha hastened to find out who was there and how she could help. She sent food parcels and money. She packed boxes of clothing and shipped them overseas. She notified Rabbi Dr. Leo Jung[59] of the American Beth Jacob Committee of their situation and appealed for funds.

Like the *bochurim* stationed in Vilna, the girls of the Internat quickly realized that they had better start looking for ways to leave Europe. Unfortunately, no one was officially in charge of them. They had to seek their own means of escape and the funds to finance it.[60] Some of these girls turned to the Benders, begging for affidavits and visas and the money to pay for them.

WE ALL HAVE EXIT VISAS DIFFICULT OBTAIN JAPANESE TRANSIT DESPERATE ONLY WAY SEND US TELEGRAPHIC AMERICAN VISAS HELPLESS REGARDING EXPENSES TILL

---

59. See Biography Section.

60 The sad fact is that no single individual was working on behalf of these girls. Left to fend for themselves, most of them did not know about the Curacao visas or the Japanese transit visas until they were impossible to get. Although some girls were more energetic than others, the ways and means available to girls were very limited. In the end, most of them perished (Rebbetzin Z. Ginsburg).

JAPAN COUNT DAYS DO UTMOST BEFORE TO LATE REJZLA
BODNER MUST LEAVE NEXT WEEK WIRE
SCHENIRERS

THESE GIRLS OFTEN SIGNED THEIR TELEGRAMS "SCHENIRERS" SINCE
Bais Yaakov was the thread that bound them together. They were all "Schenirers" — Sara Schenirer's children. They were sisters of the same family.

THESE BAIS YAAKOV GRADUATES WERE KNOWN IN THEIR COMMUNITIES
for their intelligence, energy, and most significantly, their idealism. They
dreamed of marrying *b'nei Torah* and establishing homes upon a foundation of fear of Heaven. Until they married, they would not sit idly by and
allow time to pass. *"Limnos yomeinu kein hoda* — Teach us to make our days
count" was one of the principles Sara Schenirer had constantly taught.
Laziness and inactivity were the antithesis of Bais Yaakov. A true Bais Yaakov girl yearned to achieve and accomplish.

Thus, as they waited in Vilna for a way out of Europe, these intrepid
Bais Yaakov girls kept busy. Although jobs were scarce and worries about
the future dominated their days, these motivated young women searched
for jobs and, just in case their stay in Vilna would be extended long term,
they organized courses to study Lithuanian.

Chava Shlomowitz[61] and Fryda Kaplan, two outstanding Bais Yaakov
graduates, became the unofficial leaders of the group. They prodded their
peers to learn and grow in Torah and *yiras Shamayim*. They organized classes,
often giving lessons themselves and at times asking other girls to speak.
They tried to maintain a calm and optimistic atmosphere rooted in belief
and faith in Hashem. Mrs. Sara Friedman,[62] her two little girls quietly at her
side, would come to encourage and strengthen the Bais Yaakov girls.

On Shavuos, Rabbi Shlomo Harkavi, *Mashgiach* of Grodno, and his student Rabbi Zeidel Epstein appeared at the Internat. Reb Shlomo came from
time to time to give *shmuessen* to the girls, to encourage them and to give
them the spiritual stimulation these Bais Yaakov girls craved. Now Reb
Shlomo delivered a powerful *shmuess*, leaving the girls excited and uplifted.
The *shmuess* had been long and involved and since it was given on Yom Tov,
no one took notes. One girl turned to Chava Shlomowitz and commented,
"You were listening with such rapt attention; I am sure that you can repeat
the entire *shiur* by heart. Would you mind reviewing it for us?"

---

61. Chava Shlomowitz and her sister Basya did not actually live in the Internat, but they spent
a lot of time there. A number of girls initially came to the Internat but moved out when they
earned enough money to pay for better accommodations.

62. The Friedmans had lived in Memel. When Hitler's popularity rose, they left Memel which
was on the German border, and moved to Telshe. Mrs. Friedman's daughter later married Rabbi
Shneur Kotler, the son of Rabbi Aharon Kotler.

Rabbi Shlomo Harkavi (1890-1943) learned in Radin when Rabbi Yeruchem Levovitz served as Mashgiach there. Subsequently, he followed Reb Yeruchem to Yeshivas Mir, and from there his rebbi sent him to study in Kelm. Reb Shlomo became Mashgiach in Grodno where he was beloved and respected by the talmidim for his Torah, his mussar, and his wisdom. When the Russians captured Grodno, he escaped to Vilna where he continued to learn with refugees. He died in the war, al Kiddush Hashem.

Rabbi Avrohom Yaakov Epstein (1908-2007) was known as Reb Zeidel. He grew up in Grodno where he learned under Rabbi Shimon Shkop and Rabbi Shlomo Harkavi. He survived the war and made his way to America. After a short stint as a maggid shiur in Yeshivas Torah Vodaath, Rabbi Shraga Feivel Mendelowitz sent Reb Zeidel to fortify Yeshivas Rabbeinu Yaakov Yosef. Later, Reb Zeidel moved to Eretz Yisroel where he served as Mashgiach of Yeshivas Torah Ohr for the rest of his life.

Rabbi Shlomo Harkavi with his student Rabbi Zeidel Epstein

By now, quite a crowd had formed around Chava. She eyed their eager faces in warm amusement and proceeded to speak. On the spot, she repeated the entire *shiur* verbatim! The girls were impressed.

TIME PASSED SLOWLY. THERE WAS LITTLE PROGRESS, LITTLE NEWS, AND escape from Europe seemed a distant dream. Nonetheless, the girls worked hard not to succumb to depression or despair. On Lag B'Omer, the girls organized a trip to the woods, just as they had done in their Crakow days. Everyone appreciated the break and the sensitivity of the trip organizers to recognize this need.

A TELLTALE MARK OF A BAIS YAAKOV OF CRAKOW GRADUATE WAS THE desire to teach. These graduates considered it their duty and mission to perpetuate the legacy of Sara Schenirer by infusing every Jewish girl with Jewish knowledge. The Internat girls were such girls.

They gathered younger girls from the neighborhood in Vilna — refugees like themselves, there with their families — and organized Bnos groups. Chaya Nechama Kalisch, Sarah and Tziporah Taub, Ruchka Harkavi, Leah Reiss, Rochke Hindis, Raizel Maggid, Aidel Berkowitz, Tybel Vernikovsky, Rochel Levinson, and Rochel Leschinsky[63] were among the girls

63. Most of the girls in this group were from illustrious homes: Chaya Nechama Kalisch was the Amshinover Rebbe's daughter, the Taubs were the Modzhitzer Rebbe's daughters, Ruchka Harkavi was Rabbi Shlomo Harkavi's daughter, Rochke Hindis was the daughter of Rabbi Shraga Feivel Hindis, Rochel Levinson was a granddaughter of the Chofetz Chaim, and ybdl"ch Rochel Leschinsky (later Rebbetzin Rochel Brudny) was the daughter of Rabbi Dovid and Batsheva Leschinsky.

who attended these classes. Devorah Applegrad and Fruma Nachamczyk[64] were two of the girls who taught.

Even when they were not technically learning, the Bnos girls hung around the Internat to be in close proximity to the special girls who were there. Although not a resident of the Internat, Batsheva Ziv was there often. Younger Bnos girls enjoyed just being around her, learning from her everyday conversation, emulating her regal bearing, and hoping that one day they would be as accomplished and intelligent.

On Shabbos afternoons, Bnos girls came to the Internat to visit and have a good time. They admired the older girls and enjoyed their company. *Shalosh Seudos* was a highlight. The girls assembled in the darkened dining room, where they softly escorted Shabbos out with melodies sung in unison. As young Tziporah Taub led the group in soulful song, the timeless tunes of her worthy ancestors lived on in that darkened room in Vilna.

Mrs. Batsheva Leschinsky took a great interest in the Internat girls. She was a warm, caring, and outgoing woman who became a mother figure to them. To these refugees, bereft of family, she became family. The girls knew they could count on Mrs. Leschinsky for their day-to-day problems. She visited them often, listened to their concerns and helped plan their futures. The girls were grateful for her warm attention and wise advice. When a new girl arrived in Vilna with nowhere to go because the Internat would not accept her until her papers were in order, Mrs. Leschinsky would send her own daughter, Rochel, to sleep in the Internat to make room for the lost soul. The girls of the Internat welcomed her warmly and vied for the privilege of sharing their bed with her. Rochel basked in their loving attention.

Considering the complexity of the situation, Mrs. Leschinsky realized that the best way to help these girls was to find them *shidduchim*. On a personal level, they would not feel so alone and on a practical level, men could pursue escape opportunities much more aggressively than these young single girls.

When the engagement of one of their own was finally celebrated, sounds of joy and laughter shook the walls of the Internat. On Chol HaMoed Succos, the Internat shook with cries of excitement. Chava Shlomowitz had disappeared the day before and the girls just found out that she had traveled to Kovno where she became engaged to Rabbi Nosson Wachtfogel, a Canadian *bochur* who had been learning in Kelm. The *shadchan* was Mrs. Leschinsky. They rejoiced with her from afar, knowing that from Kovno she would be traveling out of Europe on her fiance's passport.

---

64. Fruma Nachamczyk was the sister of Rabbi Nachum Nachamczyk (later changed to Nacham), a prominent Mirrer student who later was a *maggid shiur* in the Mirrer Yeshivah in America.

The lists of names of refugees granted exit visas were posted daily. Suddenly, people realized that for some of these Bais Yaakov girls, their only hope of escape from Europe was through marriage to a boy who already had all the necessary papers.[65] Rabbi Leizer Yud'l Finkel advised *bochurim* to arrange bogus marriages. A *bochur* with a Curacao visa would agree, on paper, to "marry" a Bais Yaakov girl. The girl would then be listed on the Curacao visa as a spouse and be allowed to leave Europe for Japan. Some of these fake marriages eventually became real marriages. However, most of these Bais Yaakov girls were not able to take advantage of this innovative idea. The Mirrer *bochurim* were no longer in Vilna; they were in outlying cities. Besides, a girl usually needed someone to make these arrangements for her and most of them did not have those connections.

DESPITE THE ENORMOUS DIFFICULTIES, THESE BAIS YAAKOV GIRLS PERsevered. They tried to get their own papers and raise their own funds. Some of them appealed to the Benders. Reb Dovid and Basha tried to help whomever they could, but the layers of bureaucracy were difficult to penetrate. Basha kept lists of each girl's specific situation and what she could do to help. On one page, in her neat European handwriting, were their names:

Basia Shlomowitz — poised, pretty, and sweet — had been teaching in Bais Yaakov of Slonim and was as smart and accomplished as her sister Chava. Calm and capable Fryda Kaplan was the engine behind anything going on in the Internat. Redheaded Rachela Peker, with spunk and spirit that matched her hair color, dazzled the girls with her excellent memory and clear presentation of classes. Fruma Nachamczyk and Rysa Machlis,[66] sisters of fine Mirrer *bochurim*, were in the Internat as were Chaya and Esther Mallin,[67] cousins of the illustrious Reb Leib Mallin. Shulamis and Golda Starobin,[68] daughters of a prominent Mirrer family, and Chana Rud-

---

65. A similar idea was proposed by Rabbi Mordechai Dubin regarding the *bochurim* in the Lubavitcher Yeshivah in Otvock. See earlier in this section.

66. She was the sister of Rabbi Yankel Machlis, later head of Tashbar in America, a prominent personality who was also the longtime *ba'al tefillah* in the Mirrer Yeshivah in Flatbush.

67. See Biography Section.

68. When it seemed clear that they had no way to leave Lithuania, many of these girls went back home. The Starobin girls returned to Mir. Golda Starobin was an exceptional girl, elegant, caring, and wise. She and her sisters could not bear to see their mother struggle under the Germans and they begged to work in her stead. For this terrible act of protecting their mother, they were brutally beaten. They perished *al Kiddush Hashem* with the rest of the Jews of Mir (Rebbetzin Z. Ginsburg).

nicka[69] were on the list as well. [70] And there were so many others.

How Basha wished she could help them!

She looked at her notes at the bottom of the page: Rivka Eidelman[71] is in Japan, but she needs a recommendation as soon as possible or else they will deport her to Shanghai. Reizel (Orlanska) Bodner is in Moscow. Her situation there is very precarious; without a recommendation, they might send her to Siberia. Nechama Steinberg[72] is in Moscow in need of papers. Devorah Cohn,[73] Rashel Berek,[74] Basia Malinzewitz,[75] and Tziporah Taub[76] are all in Kobe, Japan.

The papers burned her fingers. So many dear people were trapped, and it was so difficult to help them! These were not just faceless names; these were family and friends, people she knew and loved. She could never imagine what they were going through.

THE BAIS YAAKOV GIRLS WATCHED HELPLESSLY AS THE *BOCHURIM* OF Mir, Kletzk, Kaminetz, and Radin streamed out of Lithuania headed toward Japan. By April 1941, Vilna and its surrounding cities were emptied of the majority of their male refugees. These Bais Yaakov girls stayed behind in Europe. They were doomed to remain.[77]

---

69. Chana Rudnicka did receive the proper papers and fled to Japan and then Shanghai. She married Rabbi Berel Freidin (see Biography Section) and was a very active teacher in the Bais Yaakov in Shanghai and later in Eretz Yisroel.

70. This is only a partial list because some of the writing on the papers has faded. Even counting the names to figure out how many girls Rebbetzin Bender felt responsible for is impossible because some of the names were written twice. Nonetheless it remains as a poignant chronicle of someone who cared.

71. Sister of Rabbi Lipa Eidelman. Rivka Eidelman married Rabbi Mottel Springer. (See page 443.)

72. Nechama Zuchovicki was engaged to Rabbi Yosef Steinberg, a *bochur* from Mir. Even when marriages were arranged, there were no guarantees that the papers were in order and that the girls would be allowed to leave.

73. Devorah Applegrad became engaged to Rabbi Moshe Cohn in Vilna and consequently escaped.

74. Rashel Berek was the daughter of Rabbi Aharon Berek, secretary of the Vaad HaYeshivos in Vilna. She was an energetic and capable young woman who helped out her friends in the Internat whenever she could. She became engaged to Rabbi Mendel Kravitz (see Biography Section) in Vilna and thereby escaped Europe.

75. Basia Malinzewitz later married Rabbi Yitzchok Shafran in Shanghai.

76. Tziporah Taub was too old to be included on her father's papers. Her father had traveled ahead with her younger siblings while she traveled with her brothers. Perhaps that is why she is listed here without her family.

77. The Benders continued to try to help these girls, but were largely unsuccessful. In June of 1941, the Germans invaded Lithuania. Mrs. Sarah (Taub) Rosen commented that most of the names on the Internat list were Lithuanian. Rebbetzin Z. Ginsburg mentioned that the Russians were not granting exit visas to Lithuanian citizens, only to Polish citizens. This might be an additional reason why the girls in the Internat had such a difficult time escaping.

### Chapter Twenty-Five

# Japan: A Short Stopover

### Sea of Japan: 5701 (1941)

IXTY COLD, WET, BEDRAGGLED *BOCHURIM* HUDDLED together in dank misery. Night and day merged, as voluminous dark clouds covered the sun. Japan was so near, and yet they could not seem to reach it. Wind and rain conspired, and violently pushed the poor, overcrowded cargo boat from side to side. One day passed and then another. Would they ever reach safe shores?

"Hmmm, hmmm, hmmm," a rich baritone hummed softly, a familiar tune emanating from closed lips. Then he began to chant:

*"Fun darten triebt min arois* — From there they threw us out
*Dah lost min nit arein* — Here they will not let us in
*Zog di Tattenu, vi lang vet dos zein?* — Tell us Father, how long will this be?
*Zog di Tatte, Tatte Tatte* — Tell us Father, Father, Father
*Mosai Yibaneh?* — When will we rebuild?
*Yibaneh Hamikdash?* — Rebuild the *Beis HaMikdash*?
*Mosai, mosai, mosai, mosai* — When, oh when, oh when, oh when
*Mosai Yibaneh?* — When will we rebuild?
*Yibaneh HaMikdash?* — Rebuild the *Beis HaMikdash*?"

SWAYING BACK AND FORTH WITH HIS EYES CLOSED, RABBI SHMUEL Charkover continued singing. Slowly, the *bochurim* joined in, the poignant words encouraging them in their pathos. *True, right now nobody wants us; yet we still turn in faith to our Father. We know with certainty that He will rebuild the Beis HaMikdash. The only question is ... when?*[78]

---

78. Rabbi Moshe Pivovitz.

*Rabbi Shmuel Villensky was known as Reb Shmuel Charkover. He was one of the prize talmidim of the Yeshivah of Grodno before he went to Yeshivas Mir. Rabbi Naftoli Wasserman (the son of Reb Elchonon) was known to have said, "Grodno bochurim in general have an important presence in the yeshivah, with the exception of Shmuel Charkover whose name goes from one end of the yeshivah to the other." In America Reb Shmuel held the position of Rosh Yeshivah in Bais HaTalmud.*

BY MARCH 1941, MOST OF THE MIRRER YESHIVAH PEOPLE WERE already in Kobe, Japan. The telegrams sent from Japan were not much different than those sent from Vilna.

> APPLIED YOKOHAMA CONSUL REFUSED OUR AFFIDAVIT SEND IMMEDIATELY GOOD AFFIDAVITS FROM SEPARATE SPONSORS TENENBAUM CALKO LEIB KAPLAN MOWSA FAJWUSZOWITZ SZMUEL ROTTENBERG TUVIA[79]

> CABLE IF SENT AFFIDAVITS FOR LISS SZACHER FREIDIN GOTTLEIB[80]

The yeshivah in Japan was on borrowed time. The transit visas of its *yungerleit* would soon expire and they had nowhere to go. The American consul in Japan was resisting granting visas, but that did not deter Reb Dovid. One never knew when America would ease its quota restrictions.

In Japan, the financial situation of the yeshivah was becoming more difficult. In Vilna, the Vaad Hatzalah had been well organized and effective. The JEWCOM (pronounced Yovcom by the Europeans), the National Council of Jews in East Asia, was less organized. With Pesach a few weeks away, the yeshivah needed immediate funds and, just as important, they needed matzah for hundreds of people.

> PROVIDE WITH SHMURAH SIXTY KILOGRAM URGENTLY SUPPORT FOR YESHIVAH ESPECIALLY PASSOVER ADVISE OUR REQUEST VAAD HATALMIDIM SZMUELEWITZ[81]

---

79. Those listed in this telegram are: Rabbi Bezalel Tennenbaum, R' Leib Calko, Rabbi Moshe Kaplan, Rabbi Shmuel Fajveshewitz, and *ybdl"ch* Rabbi Tuvia Rottenberg. See Biography Section.

80. Those listed in this telegram are: Rabbi Feivel Zuchovicki (Zakkai), Rabbi Yosef Liss, Rabbi Berel Freidin, and *ybdl"ch* Rabbi Shalom Menashe Gottleib. See Biography Section.

81. Rabbi Chaim Shmulevitz.

**Rabbi Chaim Shmulevitz accompanied the Mirrer Yeshivah throughout their travels, serving as Rosh Yeshivah in his father-in-law's absence. In this picture, he is walking with a *talmid*, Yud'l Broide, on vacation back in Poland.**

*Rabbi Chaim Shmulevitz (1902-1979) joined Yeshivas Grodno as a youth and within three years he was lecturing at the yeshivah. Reb Chaim continued on in Mir where Rabbi Leizer Yud'l Finkel chose him as a match for his daughter. Reb Chaim stayed with the yeshivah in the exile to Shanghai, and then after a short period in America, he immigrated to Eretz Yisroel. With the passing of his father-in-law, he served as Rosh Yeshivah of the Mirrer Yeshivah. His mussar discourses were published as Sichos Mussar.*

REB DOVID COLLECTED MONEY, RESPONDED TO APPEALS, PROCURED affidavits, and helped friends and family. As time went on, his familiarity with the New York subway system was so extensive he could tell someone exactly which car to board so that when the train would stop at the next station, the person would be close to the stairs.

The name Bender appeared on so many telegrams, the Japanese police wanted to know, "Who is this Bender?" They put his name on a blacklist and were on the lookout for people who received telegrams with his name.[82]

THE REFUGEES IN VILNA AND JAPAN WERE NOT THE BENDERS' ONLY concern. They had lists of friends and relatives trapped in German-occupied Poland to whom they were sending food packages, including R' Gershon Friedenson, Rabbi Yehuda Leib Orlean, Rabbi Yosef and Chana Biegun,[83] and Fraulein Esther Goldstuff, all pillars of the Bais Yaakov movement. Next to each name, Basha recorded how large a package would be sent, usually between one and two and a half pounds. Some of the money for these packages came out of her pocket; Ezras Torah[84] subsidized other

---

82. Rabbi Peretz Yogel in his eulogy for Rabbi Avrohom Bender, and *ybdl"ch* Rabbi Zelig Epstein in his eulogy for Rabbi Dovid Bender.

83. See Book I, Part III, Ch. 4. Chana (Hanka Grossfeld) Biegun took over leadership of the seminary in Crakow when Sara Schenirer passed away.

84. At the behest of the Chofetz Chaim and Rabbi Chaim Ozer Grodzenski, Ezras Torah was founded during World War I (1915) by the Agudas HaRabbanim (Union of Orthodox Rabbis of the United States and Canada) to aid newly destitute rabbis, including some foremost roshei yeshivos in war-torn Europe (Rabbi Avrohom Birnbaum).

packages, and some of the money had to be raised. Every step required thought, effort, organization, and often diplomacy. Sometimes, after all was done, the arrangements fell through anyway.

Of course, the people who weighed most heavily on Basha's mind and heart were her parents. She thought of them constantly. They were trapped in Poland; she had no way of bringing them to America. She hoped to at least lighten their load by sending them food packages. Reb Dovid contacted Elchonon Ehrlanger, one of the Swiss boys from the Mir they had met in Riga, hoping that perhaps he would be able to send packages from Switzerland.

Even before the outbreak of World War II, Elchonon and his brother Sholom had sent food packages to Jewish boys serving in the Polish army. These parcels made their lives a bit easier and showed them that someone cared. When the war broke out, the Ehrlangers continued sending packages, this time to friends trapped in German-occupied Poland or exiled to Siberia. The Ehrlanger brothers graciously agreed to add the Epsteins to their list.

A short while into the war, Switzerland stopped allowing the export of food and goods. Food was scarce and expensive and the government wanted to save what they had for their own citizens. The Ehrlangers discovered Mrs. Dizendruk of Lisbon, Portugal who agreed to purchase food and ship it to Nazi-occupied Poland. The Ehrlangers sent her money and addresses and she took care of the rest.[85]

For a while, this system worked well. In the letters and postcards that Basha received from her parents, they thanked her for the packages from Lisbon and even wrote exactly what they had received. Coffee, cocoa, tea, and soap were standard items on the list.[86] Occasionally noodles, margarine, honey, marmalade, and sardines[87] also graced the packages. Basha was exceedingly grateful to, at least in this small way, be able to help her parents.

The Benders and the Ehrlangers corresponded about other rescue activities as well. Just as boys from the Mir were sending telegrams to the Benders in New York, others were sending telegrams to the Ehrlangers in Switzerland. The Benders and Ehrlangers exchanged information and requests.

---

85. R' Elchonon [Heiry] Ehrlanger could not remember this woman's first name and only recalled sending food packages in this fashion to the Mirrer *bochurim* in Shanghai. Letters and telegrams show that this system was already in place in March 1941, before the Mirrer Yeshivah arrived in Shanghai. The packages the Epsteins received were sent this way.

86. In the later telegrams, the Epsteins report that the packages they were receiving from Lisbon were useless. It is unclear whether this was actually so or if they were trying to hide their gratitude from the Nazis so that the packages would not be confiscated.

87. These items were sent through Bulgaria; how they were sent remains unclear.

*To our dear and honored friend, Mr. Ehrlanger,*

*... I have no words to thank you for the tremendous favors you do for my par-ents. You are fulfilling the mitzvah of saving lives, in every sense of the word. You can well imagine what a food parcel means to them. Hashem will certainly reward you, but on our part, we would like to express our genuine appreciation ...*

*We contacted the office today about Mordechai Shreibman.[88] There are no rec-ommendations, nor is there an affidavit. We can no longer get recommendations; Washington has not been issuing them for a long time already. Of the 250 Mirrer Yeshivah bochurim,[89] 100 have no recommendations. We can only arrange an affi-davit; the office promised it to us. We will certainly do whatever we can for him. In general, the whole idea of sitting in Japan, waiting for visas, is very complicated and many of the difficulties are unforeseen ...*

AWAITING AFFIDAVITS AND VISAS IN JAPAN WAS NO SIMPLE MATTER. The transit visas that the Mirrer Yeshivah *bochurim* had received in Russia were only valid for a few days.[90] By some miracle, the Japanese extended the visas for six months, but even that grace period was ending. Japan was a German ally, and as relations between Germany and America grew increasingly frosty, a distinctly anti-American attitude also existed in Japan. Although the Americans were no whiter than the Germans, in Japan, anti-American meant anti-white. The Japanese were suspicious of the Mirrer refugees and eager to get rid of them.

Only 10 percent of the requests filed with the United States Embassy in Japan resulted in visas; most people who received them had either influen-tial friends or positions waiting for them in America.[91]

The situation became even more complicated. In August 1941, the Mir-rer Yeshivah was deported to Shanghai.[92]

---

88. Rabbi Mordechai Shreibman (see Biography Section) had been R' Elchonon [Heiry] Ehrlanger's "older *bochur*" in Mir. After R' Elchonon fled back home to Switzerland at the beginning of the war, he still kept in contact with his friends. He often sent money with which Reb Mordechai would buy coats, shoes, and other basic necessities for needy Mirrer *bochurim* (R' Chaim Shreibman).

89. There were over 400 people on Rabbi Avrohom Kalmanowitz's list. Perhaps she is only refer-ring to *bochurim* of whom she knows when she writes 250.

90. Even though no end visa was required for Curacao, only the governor of Curacao could authorize a landing visa. Therefore, actually landing in Curacao was almost impossible (*A Fire in His Soul*, p. 84).

91. Among those who received visas in Japan were Rabbi Avrohom Yaffen, Rabbi Aharon Kotler, Rabbi Yisroel Chaim Kaplan, Rabbi Moshe Shatzkes, Rabbi Reuvain Grozovsky, Rabbi Elya Chazzan, Rabbi Michel Feinstein, and the Modzhitzer Rebbe. These giants of Jewry laid the groundwork for the future growth of Torah in America.

92. This ended up being a tremendous *chessed* from Hashem. A few months later, Pearl Harbor was bombed and all foreign nationals residing in Japan were interred in camps. By then, the Mirrer Yeshivah was safely in Shanghai.

### Chapter Twenty-Six

# In the Land of the Yellow People

### Shanghai: Tishrei 5702 (October 1941)

*H*ONORED MRS. BASYA BENDER, SHETICHYEH
*... Let me write to you about life in Shanghai. There was a big fight here last week ... This happens often here in Shanghai. There is also a lot of crime here — thievery and shootings in the street. In general, this is the worst corner of the world.*

*I must tell you that I have become very, very weak here in Shanghai. The climate here is very difficult and the heat is bad. I have no energy to be outside for more than a few minutes. I hardly go out here. I also cannot sleep at night due to the heat. Worst of all, I have no money to buy fruit, or anything else. Since I have come to Shanghai I have not tasted any dairy: no butter, no milk, no cheese, or eggs. Here, they give margarine because butter is too expensive and so is milk. Whoever has money buys. I do not have money for other necessities, either. They also took away the $10 in Kobe and I heard that it is hard to send money from America now. If it is still possible, it would be best to send (money) by telegraph. Since I am here in Shanghai, I have not had any (money). I am terribly weakened ...* [93]

IN SHANGHAI, THE SITUATION OF THE MIRRER YESHIVAH COMMUNITY became life threatening. Elchonon Ehrlanger received a desperate plea from his cousin, Rabbi Mordechai Schwab: "Save us from starvation!" The

---

93. The signature on this letter, addressed to the Benders, is very difficult to decipher.

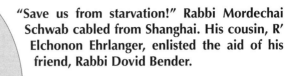

**"Save us from starvation!" Rabbi Mordechai Schwab cabled from Shanghai. His cousin, R' Elchonon Ehrlanger, enlisted the aid of his friend, Rabbi Dovid Bender.**

*Rabbi Mordechai Schwab (1911–1994) was brought up on the German model of Torah im derech eretz. As a young man, he learned at the Mir for three years, after which he went to Kaminetz to study under Rabbi Boruch Ber Leibowitz. Reb Mordechai escaped to Shanghai and then to America with the Mirrer Yeshivah. He was widely revered as Mashgiach of Yeshivas Bais Shraga in Monsey.*

Ehrlangers acted. R' Yaakov Ehrlanger, Elchonon's father, sent 1,000 francs, an enormous sum of money; a family could live for a month or two on 1,000 francs. Yet it was far from enough. They began to collect money from others.

R' Elchonon Ehrlanger sent letters to his friends in America begging them to help the Mirrer Yeshivah in Shanghai. Rabbi Dovid Bender responded repeatedly.[94]

The oppressive heat and humidity in Shanghai, the lack of money and nutritious food, and the cramped living conditions combined to create a fertile climate for disease, and many of the refugees became ill.[95] Despite — or perhaps because of — the incredibly difficult living conditions in Shanghai, the diligence of the yeshivah students soared. Elul *z'man* opened with a *shmuess* from the *Mashgiach*, Reb Chatzkel.[96] In his *shmuess*, he established the principle that would carry the yeshivah through its difficult years in Shanghai:

---

94. R' Elchonon [Heiry] Ehrlanger rattled off "168 Hooper Street" as the Bender address. Over 60 years later, this address was ingrained in his mind because they had corresponded so frequently. R' Elchonon referred to Rabbi Dovid Bender as *"ah gutte"* because he always wanted to help others.

95. Many refugees and even the native Chinese died of respiratory illnesses. Yet throughout the five years that the Mirrer Yeshivah was in Shanghai, not one of the *bochurim* died, nor did any of them suffer any lingering aftereffects of illness (*Reb Chatzkel*, pp. 181–195).

96. Rabbis Chatzkel Levenstein and Chaim Shmulevitz were offered visas either to Eretz Yisroel or to America, but they refused to abandon their students. By staying with the yeshivah, they enabled the last surviving European yeshivah to function. The quality and caliber of learning under their leadership in Shanghai was unparalleled.

*"All of us, everyone who arrived in Shanghai, did so through tremendous chasdei Hashem. The wonders and miracles we have experienced carry obligations. We are obligated to recognize the kindness of the Ribbono shel Olam and use our experiences to raise ourselves. The world is caught in the maelstrom of war and the only thing that can save it from destruction is the power of Torah. The Hand of G-d has saved us — we who hold high the banner of Torah — so that we can support a collapsing world."*[97]

No *bochur* present remained unmoved. Each was certain that the hope for the future lay right there in that *beis medrash* in Shanghai, completely dependent on his own diligence in learning. Under the tutelage of their revered *Mashgiach*, the students of the Mirrer Yeshivah applied themselves exclusively to learning Torah.[98]

Indeed, their lives did depend on it. The *Mashgiach* exhorted his students, again and again, to strengthen their learning, for they and *Klal Yisroel* desperately needed the merits of Torah learning. Moreover, the only reason they were granted continuous Divine assistance was for the survival of Torah.

*"Who cannot see the tremendous chessed and great hashgachah that HaKadosh Baruch Hu has done for the yeshivah students! I saw a Midrash on Parashas Noach: HaKadosh Baruch Hu made a treaty with Klal Yisroel that Torah will never be forgotten. How is this possible? HaKadosh Baruch Hu established that there will always be two yeshivos that will learn Torah day and night. These two yeshivos will never experience captivity, nor destruction, nor plunder. Neither Greece nor Rome will subjugate them. Even during the days before Mashiach, they will not experience the suffering that others will endure."*[99]

Why? For the survival of Torah. The *Mashgiach* inculcated within his students a tremendous sense of purpose. The survival of Torah and their survival were one and the same. Otherwise, why had they been spared?

---

97. Paraphrased from *"Hazricha Mipa'as HaKedem"* in which students recall the gist of what was said (Book 2, Chapter 26).

98. When people asked Rabbi Pesach Stein (1918-2002), Rosh Yeshivah of Telshe, about Shanghai, he would answer, "What is there to say? *Mir haben gelernt, un gelernt, un gelernt* — We learned, and learned, and learned!"

99. *Ohr Yecheskel, Michtavim* p. 39.

## Chapter Twenty-Seven
# From Those Still Trapped

*A*S DIFFICULT AS THE CONDITIONS IN SHANGHAI WERE, the conditions in German-occupied Poland were even worse. Although postcards were infrequent and censored, Basha could sense that her parents were suffering. This was reflected in what she wrote to R' Elchonon Ehrlanger in 1941:

*The situation is so bad that my parents are totally dependent on the packages they receive. Of course, Hashem has many ways to help them. In the meantime, though, the situation has worsened and we can no longer send anything through Vilna and Japan. These routes are barred. From here, it has also become extremely difficult. The companies that usually send parcels now doubt that (it is) at all possible. The only route remaining is through Portugal, where I have neither friends nor acquaintances ...*

BASHA KNEW THAT WHEN SHE HAD LEFT POLAND, HER MOTHER HAD given her all the money in the house. She knew that the Germans did not allow Jews private professions or any other means of income. She knew that they had to be suffering.

One small consolation was that at least her parents were among friends. Otvock was a small town and good friends were like family. Rabbi Noach Minsker, whom her parents treated like a son,[100] was certainly good company for them. R' Leib Fromm and his wife were surely looking out for their health and well-being. From the cryptic words of her father's postcards, Basha gathered that, as of December 1940, her parents' house had been confiscated and they had moved into "Zolberg's Pensionat," a hotel

---

100. Just as the Epsteins treated Reb Noach as a son, Rebbetzin Bender treated him as a brother. Whenever she sent packages to her parents, she sent something for him as well. She also sent him letters and postcards.

run by the Zolberg family. Rumors abounded that the Jews of Otvock were confined to a ghetto and her parents' change of address seemed proof of this. In the ghetto, old friends became new neighbors. The Fromms now lived near the Epsteins and assisted the elderly couple. Basha included them in her correspondence; it was her way of showing them that she appreciated their help.

As for herself, Basha's main comfort came from the erratic postcards she received from her parents. She read and reread their words, drawing hope from the knowledge that as long as they were still sending her postcards and enjoying her photographs, they were still alive.

*February 24, 1941*

*Dearest children,*

*We received your letters of December 2, 6, 10, 17, 26, and of January 23 and we thank you very much. Our most sincere wish is only to receive good news from you. Please write often and inform us of your health. We are healthy and every-thing is normal. We now live in the neighborhood with Mr. Fromm and Velkovitch. We cook for ourselves in the kitchen. Please give best regards to your dear parents and regards to dear Yosef.*

*Jacob and Lifsha*

BASHA STUDIED HER FATHER'S FAMILIAR HANDWRITING. WAS IT ANY shakier than usual? Were they truly healthy? A letter her father wrote to her cousin, Rabbi Yosef Dovid Epstein, had been forwarded to her. In it her father wrote that her mother was not well and that Dr. Kushelevsky had been giv-ing her glucose injections. Was her father shielding her from the truth?

She turned the postcard over. Ever since December 1940, the postcards looked different. Until then, they had been using the postal reply cards she had been sending them. These cards were printed in the United States and stamped with American stamps. This saved them the cost of the card and postage. Either they had run out of these or the Germans were not allow-ing them to use them. The postcards she was now receiving were bought from the German government in Poland and had German stamps. Basha felt bad that they had to spend the little money they had on purchasing postcards to send to her. Even more disturbing was the Nazi insignia that defiantly appeared on the side. Perched above it was a new stamp: "*Juden-rat der Stadt Otvock.*"[101] What in the world did that mean?

*March 17, 1941*

*Dearest children,*

*Be happy! We've received your dear letters of January 27, February 9, and 14,*

---

101. The Judenrat was the Jewish ghetto authority.

*and we thank you very much. The joy that your letters bring us is indescribable. Write to us often. We were very pleased with the picture of Basya ... but the original is even better. We would love to receive new pictures of you and Dovid. We are well and everything is normal. We live together with family Fromm and Velkovitch in Shpitalna 11. Best regards to your parents and to Yosef. Wishing you all the best,*

*Papa Jacob*

BASHA SMILED WISTFULLY. SHE WOULD ALSO RATHER SEE HER MOTHER in the "original," but at least the picture brought some joy to her suffering parents. She resolved to send more pictures[102] in the future.

*October 14, 1941*

*Dearest children,*

*Be happy! We have received your letters of September 12 and 18 with the beautiful picture for which we are very grateful. Your letters bring us much, much pleasure. Please write us often and about your health. We are healthy and everything is normal. Please give our best regards to your dear parents and to Yosef. Why doesn't he write? As you requested, I have visited your friend Mr. Frankel. He is very weak, but he went with me for about a 10-minute walk.*

*Wish you all the best. Best wishes,*

*Jacob*

EVERY LETTER OR POSTCARD BASHA RECEIVED FROM HER PARENTS calmed her and gave her hope. They were still alive, still managing to take care of themselves, and still giving of themselves to others. Her father had written that it had been a while since Mr. Frankel had received a letter from his son Shabsi in America, and he was worried about him. Basha promptly informed the son of his father's concern. Shabsi asked Basha if her father could look in on him occasionally and perhaps her father would take his father out for some healthy fresh air. Basha was pleased to read that the arrangement had worked out and hoped that it was satisfying for both men.

Basha read the letter once again. They wanted to know about Yosef and why he had not written. She sighed. It was better for them not to know. The letter she received from her brother in Eretz Yisroel several weeks earlier still weighed heavily on her heart.

*August 7, 1941*

*Dear Basya and Dovid,*

*You will be surprised when you receive this letter. I think you are very well*

---

102. Once Rebbetzin Bender realized how much joy her pictures brought her parents, she sent pictures whenever she could (Bender Family Documents).

*aware of every young man's duty at this time; I joined the army half a year ago. As my close relatives, you will be very worried about me, but there are hundreds of thousands of brothers and sons in service of their nation for the defense of their freedom. I cannot be an exception. In this war, not only are the soldiers in the fight, but the whole civil population shares the same danger. I cannot write to you where I am stationed. I can only say that I am in a very good place. In our unit, there are fine fellows. One is a professor at Hebrew University.*

*I am feeling well. Do not worry and do not think too much about me. Of course, Father and Mother do not have to know any of this. Give them my best regards and tell them that I am in good health and spirits ...*

*Be well,*
*With love, Yosef*

DO NOT WORRY? DO NOT THINK TOO MUCH ABOUT ME? HOW COULD she not think about and not worry about her brother? He was her only sibling and they had always been unusually close. They almost never fought, not even as young children. From the day he set sail to Eretz Yisroel, she had worried about him for many reasons.

For the last 40 years, immigration to Eretz Yisroel had become popular among the downtrodden Jews of Poland and Russia. Yearning for Eretz Yisroel had always been an intrinsic part of *Yiddishkeit*. However, for most of the centuries of the exile, reaching Eretz Yisroel had been impossible, or nearly so. As travel became easier and life in Eastern Europe became harder, going to Eretz Yisroel was a dream that many tried to turn into reality. Granted, there were those who had been swept up with Zionism, who to some extent traded their *Yiddishkeit* for their love of Eretz Yisroel. Yet, for many Jews, their longing for Eretz Yisroel was sincere; for these *Yidden* their love for Eretz Yisroel stemmed from a profound love of *HaKadosh Baruch Hu*.

Despite the inevitable and intrinsic difficulties and dangers that were part of living there, Basha's parents dreamed of Eretz Yisroel. Some of their close family had moved there; Basha's mother's sister Tanta Musha and her husband had moved there. Her father's sister Tanta Basya and her husband had moved there as well. Basha and her parents also wanted to move to Eretz Yisroel, though they understood firsthand the dangers involved. Barely three years earlier, her beloved aunt, Tante Musha, had been killed by Arabs in Tiveria.[103] This was not an isolated instance. Ever since the

---

103. In the 20's and 30's there were Arab uprisings in Palestine. A poignant letter from Yosef Epstein to his parents in Otvock details his aunt's death at the hands of the Arabs:

*Tel Aviv – 11/10/38*

*To my dear Father,*

You will probably be surprised when you receive this letter at the post office. I do not want it to go directly to your home, since I do not want mother to read it. The newspapers probably preceded me, and you might already know the news that I write but you may not yet know

Chevron pogrom of 1929, there were periodic Arab uprisings.

Though this did not dampen her love for Eretz Yisroel, Basha was naturally concerned about her brother's welfare. She worried about his physical well-being and she worried about how he was managing in a society plagued by poverty. Above all, she worried about his spiritual progress. Now, with his enlistment in the army, her worries were compounded. She certainly was not going to share her worries with her parents. Yosef's instructions were superfluous; she would not write to her parents about her brother's current adventures.

*December 7, 1941*

*Dearest Parents,*

*We are happy and content! We've received your beautiful letters and it is our greatest wish to receive your regards. Our dear Yosef is well, B"H, in every respect. My dear Papa and Mamma, write us good news and also keep us informed about your health. My dearest Papike and Mammike, may you be well and strong for many more happy years.*

*Your children,*
*Basya and Dovid*

SHE ENDED THE POSTCARD WITH A HEAVY HEART. MANY WEEKS HAD passed since she received any communication from her parents. She hoped

---

the names. Last Monday, there was a tragedy in our family. In the "pogroms" in Tiveria, Doda Musia and her husband were killed.

It is difficult to write in a letter how this happened but we can just say that a few Arabs entered their room, shot at them, and then threw firebombs into their house. Everything in the house including their bodies was entirely burned. As soon as I heard of this, I immediately contacted Uncle and we went together to Tiveria. We could not get there the same day because of the imposed curfew and therefore we slept in Haifa. The next day, we went to Kiryat Shmuel. All we found were the walls, darkened by smoke. There was nothing inside. We were told that there wasn't even a burial. Everything that was found in the room was gathered in sacks and buried. It was a house full of gold, but, of course, this too is gone.

This terrible happening caused much sadness in the entire city and enveloped the whole family in mourning. After suffering for years in Eretz Yisrael, she (Doda Musia) just now started living. Her husband was a kind–hearted man and a wonderful giving person. He was loved and cherished. But this tragedy occurred and put an end to both of them. There is nothing left but to say *Baruch Dayan HaEmes.*

Doda Musia's husband left his will by the Rav of his neighborhood as of the 10th of Adar, 1938. According to the will, he distributed his money to various institutions, especially to yeshivos. For executors, he appointed Rabbi (Meir) Berlin and another important person in Tel Aviv. The first condition of his will is that if he passes away first, the money goes to her.

The question now arises: Who was killed first? The investigation shows that he was killed first because he was found thrown near the door. We hope that justice will rule and that Jews everywhere will have no sorrow.

*Shalom* and *kol tuv,*
*Shanah Tovah* and *Piskah Tovah,*
Yosef

that this letter would arrive safely and cheer them up. Yet, after that morning's events, she was very skeptical. Just a few hours earlier, it had been reported in the news that the Japanese had bombed Pearl Harbor. It seemed inevitable that America would soon enter the war.

*December 8, 1941*

America declared war against Japan: in effect, declaring war against Germany and Italy, formerly its allies. Now that Germany and America were enemy countries, it was unlikely that any mail would be allowed through. Basha decided to make one more attempt to communicate with her parents. She had just written to them two days earlier. Now, she wrote the Fromms as well. Perhaps, her letter would reach them and they could pass on her regards to her parents.

*December 9, 1941*

*My loving Family Fromm,*
*What is the good news with you? How is your health? How are the children? We have not received a letter from you in a long time and this worries us. We have also received nothing from our parents nor from R' Noach. It has been several months since we have had any news. We hope that you are well and that we will hear only good news from you.*

*I stopped in the middle of writing because I just received a postcard from you dated October 10. It is so nice how it happened! The postcard came just while I was writing to you. See how one heart feels the other? Thank you very much, my dear, for those few words. You cannot imagine the joy of the moment when we get news of our closest friends. May there always be good news from everyone.*

*Life passes by interestingly. How can I sit quietly and enjoy? Day and night, I think about you, our closest … Dovid has a position and I, too, give shiurim twice a week in a school. All my life, I was hoping for just such a position, where I would teach children — even for no salary. We have a very nice home and many friends. We live with my parents-in-law. They are very good people and think only of how to make things easier for their relatives.*

*Your relationship to us and my parents is very dear. They are weak and whatever you can do to help them will be appreciated. Please give regards to your parents and your children. Be well.*

*All the best, Dovid and Basya*

BASHA WAITED HOPEFULLY FOR A REPLY. A FEW WEEKS LATER, BASHA received an answer of sorts: both her letters were returned to sender.
Basha had lost contact with her beloved parents.

### Chapter Twenty-Eight

# The Situation Changes

### Erev Shabbos Kodesh, Parashas Vayeishev, 5702 (1941)

TO OUR HONORED FRIEND, FAMOUS FOR HIS VIRTUES AND *middos tovos, Harav Wolbe, shlita,*

*I feel guilty that I have not replied to your cable of a few months ago. Please judge me favorably. My head is not working properly and lately we have invested so much energy in trying to help those in Shanghai. We have been sending money and arranging affidavits. Now that they already received their visas and bought ship tickets, for many of them the situation suddenly (with the bombing of Pearl Harbor) changed so drastically. It is frightening. May Hashem have mercy on us!*

*In addition to the general worry, we all have our personal pain. I know it is not right on my part to take of your time and patience, but what can I do? For me this is a matter of life and death. Truthfully, it does concern me more than my own life. As you can well imagine, until now my only consolation was the contact I kept up with my parents. Yet now, how can I continue?*

*Please excuse my audacity, but I would like to request that you arrange for my parents to get my letters.[104] I have no one else to turn to. I write to you, not as I would to a friend, rather as a brother. Believe me, it is not easy for me to bother you. I am doing this only for my parents' health. I have no words to express my*

---

104. As enemy countries, Germany and America did not allow mail from one country to the other. She was forwarding her letters to Sweden, hoping that from Sweden, a neutral country, the letters would reach her parents.

*thanks. In any case, please let me know, honestly, if I am troubling you too much.*

*Honored friend! I have written all about my issues. Now I would really like to know how you, personally, are doing. Your name resounds everywhere as a messenger who helps anyone in need …*

*May Hashem send his salvation to all Jews, speedily; that is most significant now.*

*With deep feelings of gratitude,*
*Basya Bender*

DESPITE HER EFFORTS, EVEN THROUGH A NEUTRAL COUNTRY, BASHA was unable to communicate with her parents. Nonetheless, she never gave up hope that she would hear from them. She davened for their welfare and never stopped yearning that they might soon be together again.

WITH THE ATTACK AT PEARL HARBOR, THE BENDERS LOST CONTACT with all their family and friends in Poland and Shanghai. There were no more requests for visas or affidavits, no more telegrams begging for money. From then on, they could only communicate with their brethren in Shanghai through a neutral country such as Switzerland, which was how the Benders continued to send money.

Without the personal requests and telegrams, Reb Dovid ceased to be a one-man rescue organization. With the establishment of HIJEFS, the highly competent rescue organization of Yitzchok and Recha Sternbuch,[105] the support to the Mirrer Yeshivah became more formal. Similarly, the Vaad Hatzalah and Agudath Israel had both become very organized and efficient in dealing in rescue efforts and Reb Dovid's participation as a private individual became superfluous.

THE LONGING FOR HER PARENTS, AND THE PAIN OF NOT BEING ABLE TO help them, weighed heavily on Basha's mind and heart. Yet, the Almighty tempered her sorrow with joy. After four years of marriage, their daughter was born. They named her Esther.

Perhaps, like Esther of yore, the birth of their Esther would be the beginning of the long-awaited salvation.

---

105. See Biography Section.

# Book II

# Part I:
# **Builders**
## 5700-5708 / 1940-1948

*Chapter Twenty-Nine:*
### Building B'nei Torah

*Chapter Thirty:*
### Building on Strong Foundations

*Chapter Thirty-One:*
### Building Bais Yaakov

*Chapter Thirty-Two:*
### Building a Home

*Chapter Thirty-Three:*
### Bais Yaakov Survivors Rebuild

*Chapter Thirty-Four:*
### An Era of Rebuilding

---

The first chapter in this section is based primarily on interviews with *talmidim* of Rabbi Dovid Bender. Among the *talmidim* interviewed were Rabbi Shmeryl Shulman, Rabbi Shloime Lefkowitz, Rabbi Mordechai Eliezer Leiner, Rabbi Yonason Shapiro, Rabbi Henoch Cohen, and Rabbi Hershel Mashinsky. The rest of this section is based on letters that Rebbetzin Bender saved, the *hesped* of Rabbi Mordechai Shapiro on Rebbetzin Bender, and an interview with Rabbi Henoch Cohen. Members of the Bender family filled in many details. Other sources are documented.

# Chapter Twenty-Nine

# Building B'nei Torah

### America: 5700 (1940)

*W*HILE THE FIRES IN EUROPE WERE STILL BLAZING, A HOME for the survivors was being built. Rabbi Dovid and Rebbetzin Basha Bender were among the builders.

BALTIMORE'S YESHIVAS NER ISRAEL, FOUNDED BY RABBI YAAKOV YITZ-chok Ruderman in 1933, went through several years of slow growth. Then, between 1937 and 1939, with the deteriorating situation in Europe and its resulting influx of refugees, the yeshivah doubled its enrollment.[1]

The yeshivah had approximately 40 *bochurim*. The Rosh Yeshivah, Rabbi Ruderman, gave the highest *shiur,* and Rabbi Shimon Schwab gave the second *shiur*. Rabbi Schwab was a Rav in the city and was always very busy with his community. As such, he would say his *shiur* and leave; he did not have the time to stay around and be available to the *bochurim*. Rav Ruderman was looking for someone to give a *shiur* and be involved with the *bochurim*. He turned to Rabbi Dovid Bender in the winter of 1940.

For Rabbi Dovid and Rebbetzin Bender, the offer was tempting. Reb Dovid relished the opportunity to share with others what he had gained in his years in Mir, and Rebbetzin Bender shared his enthusiasm. But Rebbetzin Bender felt that she had committed herself to Bais Yaakov, and Reb Dovid agreed that her contribution there was invaluable.

---

1. *Hamodia* (June 27, 2007).

**Rabbi Dovid Bender joined the staff of Yeshivas Ner Israel of Baltimore, becoming a colleague of Rabbi Ruderman and Rabbi Schwab.**

*Rabbi Shimon Schwab (1909-1995) was brought up on the German model of Torah im derech eretz. He went on to learn in Telshe and then Mir. He served as assistant Rav in Darmstadt, and later district rabbi of Ichenhausen in Bavaria. In 1936 he immigrated to America, becoming Rav of the German congregation of Baltimore. In 1958 Rabbi Joseph Breuer invited him to be his assistant Rav of K'hal Adas Yeshurun of Washington Heights. Upon Rabbi Breuer's passing, Rabbi Schwab became his successor.*

*Rabbi Yaakov Yitzchok Halevi Ruderman (1899-1986) was known as the Dohlinover Illuy and his sefer, Avodas Levi, written in his youth, astounded the yeshivah world. He was a close disciple of the Alter of Slabodka. In 1929 Rabbi Ruderman went to America to join his father-in-law, Rabbi Sheftel Kramer, Rosh Yeshivah of the yeshivah in New Haven. Three years later, he founded Ner Israel in Baltimore where he served as Rosh Yeshivah for over 50 years.*

Reb Dovid went to Rabbi Shlomo Heiman, Rosh Yeshivah of Torah Vodaath, to ask his opinion. Reb Shlomo felt that, given the need for yeshivos in America, and given the need for Bais Yaakov in America, if Rebbetzin Bender would agree, they should make an experiment for one *z'man*. Reb Dovid should spend his week in Baltimore, returning home only for Shabbos, and Rebbetzin Bender would remain in Williamsburg.[2]

AFTER PESACH OF 1940, REB DOVID BEGAN SERVING AS *MASHGIACH* and giving the second *shiur* in Yeshivas Ner Israel. With the aura of the

2. "Can we begin to understand this? A woman married less than two years, or maybe just two years, separates from her husband the entire week long, with no one, her entire family trapped in Europe ... She stayed here because she had a job to do in Bais Yaakov. My father went to Baltimore because he had a job to do as *Mashgiach* in Baltimore. And for half a year, less than two years after marriage, they did not see each other from Shabbos to Shabbos. Why? Because it was in her (Rebbetzin Bender's) blood: sacrifice for Hashem, sacrifice for *Klal Yisroel*" (Rabbi Yaakov Bender at the *shloshim* for his mother).

Mir still enveloping him, he sought to transmit its lofty lessons. His *shmuessen*, delivered regularly to the entire yeshivah, were replete with Rabbi Yeruchem Levovitz's teachings.

Reb Dovid was in yeshivah all the time. He circulated among the *bochurim*, speaking with them in learning, encouraging them, and being available for them. Even boys who were not in his *shiur* became close to him by the sheer warmth of his personality. Engaging and likable, yet a figure of respect, Reb Dovid attracted a following and was able to influence his *talmidim* to grow in Torah and *yiras Shamayim*. [3]

Reb Dovid influenced his students because he embodied what he taught. When he encouraged them to be caring, they understood because they saw this trait in him. When he spoke about the importance of davening with *kavanah*, his own davening came to mind.[4] It was just the beginning of the war, and everyone was fearful for the situation in Poland. Reb Dovid led the *Tehillim* in yeshivah with his heart and soul, crying out to the *Ribbono shel Olam*, beseeching Him to annul the evil decree. His *talmidim* were entranced; most had never heard *Tehillim* said with such feeling by one so young.

He was idealistic and eager: idealistic in his pursuit to carry on the traditions of the yeshivos of Europe and eager to put those traditions immediately into practice. He even sought to introduce the European system of calling boys by the names of the towns they came from. For example, in Europe, when Mordche came from Kobrin, he was called Mordche Kobriner. So he tried: Chaim Detroiter, Shloime Pittsburgher ...

"Rebbi," one of the boys called out, "what about Shmuel? He's from Michigan. Should we call him Shmuel 'The *Mishigener* (The Crazy One)'?"

That drew a round of laughter, even from Reb Dovid, who had given up the idea for other reasons as well. After all, with a large percentage of boys hailing from New York, you could not have everyone called "New Yorker"!

Reb Dovid enjoyed his *z'man* in the yeshivah, and his *talmidim* enjoyed him. He had a talent for taking lofty concepts and explaining them at a level appropriate for his *talmidim*. His *shiur*, neatly and clearly explained,[5] was given with enthusiasm.

---

3. "Reb Dovid was considered a second Rosh Yeshivah in Ner Israel and although I was not in his *shiur*, I became very close to him. I kept up with him even after he left. I remember his father coming to the yeshivah for a visit. He made a tremendous impression: a tall, older man with a long beard and long *kapota*. This was not a common sight in Baltimore in those times" (Rabbi Shmeryl Shulman).

4. "I cannot forget Rabbi Dovid's *Ma'ariv* in the Mirrer Minyan on a *Motza'ei Shabbos*. It was a 25-minute davening, from the heart and soul" (Rabbi Yisroel Belsky).

5. "I still remember what I learned in his *shiur* 64 years ago. It was *Mesechta Shavuos, Perek Shlishi, Perek Shavuos Shtayim*. Rabbi Dovid was very well liked. We were sorry to see him go" (Rabbi Moshe Shuvalsky).

When summer ended and Elul drew near, Reb Dovid faced a new dilemma. Torah Vodaath offered him a position as a *maggid shiur* in the Mesivta, and he would now have to choose between Baltimore and Torah Vodaath. The boys in Torah Vodaath were younger than the *bochurim* in Baltimore, and therefore the potential for Reb Dovid's own growth in learning was diminished. However, neither he nor his rebbetzin wanted him to continue commuting, and they were not certain they wanted to move to Baltimore. Then there were financial considerations. In Williamsburg, they shared an apartment with his parents; in Baltimore they would have to pay the rent on their own. Making ends meet would be difficult.

Reb Dovid was confused. He once again turned to Rabbi Shlomo Heiman for advice. He explained to Reb Shlomo how, through his position in Baltimore, he had grown in his own learning and how fearful he was that he would not experience that growth in Torah Vodaath. He brought up the issue of moving to Baltimore or staying in Williamsburg, including Rebbetzin Bender's work in Bais Yaakov. Almost as an afterthought, he reluctantly mentioned the financial considerations.

Reb Shlomo listened quietly. "I understand your situation. When I was in Baranovich, I faced a similar dilemma. I had to decide between staying in Baranovich and accepting a position in the Remmailes Yeshivah in Vilna. The level of learning was higher in Baranovich, but the salary was higher in Vilna. My rebbetzin knew that we barely had enough money to buy our daily bread. Gently, but tactfully, she urged me to accept the position in Vilna. I was very disturbed that money was a factor in my decision. One day, I was traveling on a train when I met Rabbi Naftoli Trop.[6] My heart jumped. Reb Naftoli was so completely immersed in Torah, he did not even know a *tzuras hamatbei'a;*[7] money was an alien concept to him. I was certain that he would tell me to stay in Baranovich, and I knew that my rebbetzin would not question his advice. So, I went over to Reb Naftoli and explained the situation."

Reb Shlomo paused. "Reb Naftoli just made one small comment. '*Nu*,' he said, '*gelt iz oich an inyan* (money is also a consideration).' "

Like Rabbi Naftoli Trop, Reb Shlomo would not tell him what to do, but he was making him aware that, at times, money is a factor in a decision and that is just fine. Then Reb Shlomo made Reb Dovid an offer that made returning to Torah Vodaath even more attractive. He asked Reb Dovid if he would like to be his nightly *chavrusah* when Reb Shlomo prepared his

---

6. Rabbi Naftoli Trop (1870-1929) studied in the yeshivos of Kelm, Slabodka, and Telshe. He served as Rosh Yeshivah in Yeshivas Ohr HaChaim of Slabodka and in the Chofetz Chaim's yeshivah in Radin. Reb Naftoli disseminated Torah and *mussar* during and after the troubled times of World War I, until his passing.

7. Literally — "the shape of a coin."

*shiur*. To learn as a *chavrusah* with Rabbi Shlomo Heiman was a priceless opportunity. He now could face his new position in Torah Vodaath with enthusiasm and excitement because it would not be at the expense of his own growth in learning.

In September 1940, Reb Dovid began teaching in Torah Vodaath. He would later look back at those years as a *maggid shiur* as his best years in *chinuch*. He was learning daily with Rabbi Shlomo Heiman while transforming young American boys into true *b'nei Torah*.

TORAH VODAATH HAD GROWN TREMENDOUSLY SINCE REB DOVID attended. The Mesivta now had parallel grades with up to 25 students in each class. The *beis medrash* was growing, and the *kol Torah* that emerged was louder and stronger than ever. Yet the challenges facing the Torah Vodaath *talmidim* of the 1940's were eerily similar to the challenges their rebbi had endured.

Jewish America of the early 1940's was still in the throes of an identity crisis. *Ehrliche frum Yidden*, who sacrificed much by not working on Shabbos, could not make those same demands of their children. The burden of finding work, the tension of not knowing if next week they would have a job to report to, the struggle to make ends meet from the meager wages they earned, made it difficult for parents to demand that their children follow the same path. Many did not even bother trying.

"It's America," they would say, as they shrugged their shoulders and watched their children go off to work on Shabbos. Some watched with tears in their eyes.[8] Others looked on with approval and relief; their children would not suffer as they had.

The general atmosphere in Jewish communities throughout the States was a combination of nostalgia and practicality: gefilte fish and chicken soup; Yiddish humor and Yossele Rosenblatt; *The Morgen Journal* and working on Shabbos. The Jewish flavor was there, but the soul was missing.

The boys who attended Torah Vodaath were fighting the trend, which was not easy. They all had friends, neighbors, and relatives[9] who publicly

---

8. "I knew a man who was a *shomer Shabbos*. He was weak and could not work, so his boys were the breadwinners. He could not bring himself to wake his sons to work on Shabbos. Yet, if they overslept, they would be fired. If they were fired, there would be no food. So he would go into his boys' room and begin reading the week's *parashah* aloud and the boys would usually wake up on their own. When relating this to me, although many years had already passed, he had tears in his eyes" (Rabbi Yonason Shapiro).

9. "My parents once took us to visit cousins. The first thing my cousin did was take away our *yarmulkes*. 'This is America,' he said. 'We don't need these things here. The non-Jews will get angry at us.' I was young, but my older brother attacked him and they fought until he gave us back our *yarmulkes*. We refused to visit that family again, but we could not cut ourselves off completely. Another cousin once came to visit, and she spent her time trying to convince my mother that my father should work on Shabbos. It was very hard" (Rabbi Yonason Shapiro).

*Rabbi Moshe Aharon Stern (1926-1998) learned in Torah Vodaath and then Yeshivas Kaminetz in Eretz Yisroel. He was also a talmid of the Brisker Rav. He served as the Mashgiach of Yeshivas Kaminetz, where bochurim from many yeshivos attended his discourses. He traveled widely to raise funds for the yeshivah, spoke and advised in many places, and thereby affected the lives of hundreds of people.*

desecrated Shabbos. The Jewish kids they played stickball with on the street mocked the religious dedication of the Torah Vodaath crowd. Peer pressure was enormous. Yeshivah students were taunted and teased from their *yarmulkes* to their *tzitzis*. Devotion to baseball, the great American pastime, was what made them feel normal. Aspiring to *gadlus,* Torah greatness? Aspiring to be a simple *ben Torah* was hard enough.

Reb Dovid, by virtue of what he was and what he had become, showed his students that even someone born and raised in America could be different. He taught that there is a choice. Choose Torah. Once you choose to learn Torah, do not do it halfway. Become a *ben Torah*. Become a *gadol b'Torah*.

His students absorbed what he said and what he left unsaid. Yes, they could choose to become *b'nei Torah*, maybe even *gedolei Torah*, but that did not mean that the path to Torah would come easy. For Reb Dovid, it meant traveling all the way to Europe. His *talmidim* would not have that unique opportunity. Nonetheless, their road to acquiring Torah would not be any easier. They were a generation of fighters. Anyone who was not a fighter could not become a *ben Torah*.

ONE EREV SHABBOS, YANKEL, A *BOCHUR* IN REB DOVID'S *SHIUR*, ASKED A question. Reb Dovid paused for a moment and then answered, "What you are asking is not a question at all," and he proceeded to explain why. The *bochur* refuted his answer and an argument ensued, each one defending his position. The class watched excitedly as the two went at it. A real *milchamah shel Torah* — Torah battle!

Reb Dovid returned home exhilarated. This was what he wanted! His boys should learn how *geshmak* it is to learn. As he immersed himself in the Shabbos preparations, the incident slowly faded from his mind.

It was an exceptionally cold night. Although Reb Dovid's *bochurim* often joined them Friday night after the meal, it was unthinkable that anyone would venture out in such weather. Snow was falling, blanketing New York in a thick layer of white. The Benders were warm and cozy sitting around the table eating their *seudah*.

Then they heard knocking at the door. Reb Dovid arose to answer. There stood the *bochur*, Yankel Schiff, his face beaming with happiness. He found his question in *Chiddushei Rabbi Akiva Eiger* and he wanted to show Reb Dovid. Reb Dovid was amazed. Yankel lived quite far away and moreover, no one ventured out in such weather. He invited him in and they proceeded to go over the question together.[10]

THIS WAS REB DOVID'S VISION. HE WANTED HIS *TALMIDIM* TO ENJOY learning as much as he did. While he was a *maggid shiur*, a large portion of the day was allotted to his *talmidim* and many other hours were devoted to "Hatzolah" efforts to help the surviving Jews in Europe and Shanghai. Nonetheless, he always found time for his own learning. His nightly sessions with Rabbi Shlomo Heiman were precious. Reb Dovid was learning and teaching. His excitement about learning filtered down to his students.

"LET ME TELL YOU AN INTERESTING STORY THAT HAPPENED TO ME back in the Mir," Reb Dovid began. His students leaned forward in anticipation. They loved a good story and a story about the Mir was bound to be good.

"The pace of the davening in Mir was much slower, especially in Elul. Each word was enunciated clearly and with *kavanah*. I loved the davening in Elul.

"One day, I and a few *chaverim* had to go to a different town. We stopped in a shul along the way to daven *Minchah*. The pace of the davening in the shul was much faster than the Mir and we Mirrer *bochurim* tried hard to keep up."

---

10. When Rebbetzin Bender recounted this story to a grandchild, she said that this boy's overwhelming love of learning made an indelible impression on her. She was not surprised when the Brisker Rav later chose him as a son-in-law.

"I was relieved to arrive in the Mir on time for *Ma'ariv*. In Elul every *tefillah* is special and I did not want to have to daven in such a fast *minyan* again. I began that *tefillah* with a *bren*, as I appreciated how fortunate I was to be davening in the Mir once again. I finished *Shemoneh Esrei* and was waiting for the *chazzan* to begin *Kaddish*. When I glanced around, I noticed that no one else had finished except ... except for me and my *chaverim* who had been out of town that day. I was so disappointed! Imagine, we spent one *tefillah* away from the yeshivah, and it affected us. One *tefillah*!"

"Now boys, does that give you a little idea of how important it is to daven in a *choshuve minyan*?"

THIS WAS JUST ONE OF THE MANY "MIR STORIES" WITH WHICH REB DOVID peppered his classes. He spoke about the Mir often and the boys were in awe that an all-American youth, not much older than themselves, had journeyed to Europe and lived there for six years to immerse himself in Torah. They realized that there was something special about the yeshivos of Europe, particularly the Mir. Reb Dovid wanted his students to drink from the waters that he himself had, so he incorporated Mirrer practices into his classroom. His *talmidim* glowed with pride. They felt as if their classroom was a miniature Mirrer Yeshivah.

He gave *shmuessen* at least once a week, regularly quoting his beloved *Mashgiach*, Rabbi Yeruchem Levovitz. During a *Chumash* or *Navi* lesson, he would intentionally veer off the topic to bring in some thought or example from the *Mashgiach*. He repeated the *shmuess* in such a way that his *talmidim* remembered the *mussar* years later.[11]

As in the Mir, Reb Dovid's goal was to address the totality of each *talmid*. It was not enough for a rebbi to give his students knowledge; he was obligated to turn them into "*menschen.*" He used his *shmuessen* as a platform for *mussar*, attempting to rebuke in a way that the boys understood what needed improvement, without their rebbi having to single anyone out privately.

"*Nosei b'ol im chavero*" was a theme he spoke about often. "How does one help shoulder his friend's burden?" he asked. "Friendship means to help your friend. It is not just sharing the good times. A true friend looks for ways to help his friend feel better when he is down, even when he cannot make that particular problem go away. Show him that you care." Another popular theme Reb Dovid taught: "Do things *b'shleimus*, completely. See projects to their completion; don't do things halfway."

He gave concrete examples to illustrate a point. "Care about your friends. Be thoughtful. I was in the Mir with our very own Rabbi Boruch

---

11. "His *mussar* was always focused on how we could be better and not on 'look how bad you fellows are' ... a boy who was not a class star said that even if one does not remember anything from Rebbi's class, his *mussar* was impossible to forget" (Rabbi Yonasan Shapiro).

Kaplan.[12] Reb Boruch was a tremendous *masmid* who learned late into the night. When he would return to his room, his roommates were sleeping. He would take off his shoes outside the room, so as not to make any noise that would disturb his friends. G-d forbid that he should steal their sleep!"

At times, Reb Dovid used dramatic, almost shocking images, to convey his message. With one hand shoved firmly into the front pocket of his jacket, and the other poised for emphasis, he drove home his points.

"Imagine Hitler, *yimach shemo*, would be in front of you right now." Reb Dovid's gaze shifted slowly from one *talmid* to another. "Hitler, that very same wicked man who is killing and torturing *Klal Yisroel*. But now he is broken, beaten, and bloody. He is in a pitiful state. As he falls to his knees, he looks into your eyes, tears are flowing as he begs for forgiveness … what would you do? Right now, he is kneeling before you, crying in anguish, begging for mercy … who could be so stone hearted and not be moved?" Reb Dovid paused dramatically and then thundered. "*Achzarius*! Cruelty! Compassion for a wicked person is not compassion, it is cruelty!"

These *shmuessen*, delivered from the heart, remained with Reb Dovid's *talmidim* for years to come.[13] Although there would be many other rebbeim who would successfully bring the ideas of European yeshivos to American boys, Reb Dovid was one of the first.

HIS *TALMIDIM* LOVED HIM AND WANTED TO BE LIKE HIM, BOTH IN HIS *middos* and in his drive to learn. His huge smile and booming "*Vos macht min?*"[14] made his students feel warm and cared for. When he saw that a *bochur* seemed down or was not learning well, Reb Dovid would take him aside, talk to him, tell him how much he appreciated him, and remind him how much confidence he had in him. Long after his *talmidim* left his *shiur*, they still felt as if they were his *talmidim*.

Reb Dovid encouraged the *bochurim* to take charge of their personal growth. One way he did so was by arranging *vaadim*. The idea of the *vaad* was that groups of boys should get together regularly, on their own time, for a learning session. Each boy was scheduled to speak at some point during the year, and the highlight of each *vaad* was when the boys listened to the *divrei Torah* of their *chaverim* before enjoying refreshments.

Reb Dovid did not attend these *vaadim*. He wanted the boys to learn to enjoy learning together without adult supervision. Their desire to learn, to hear from one another, should create a serious environment that would make an adult presence superfluous. In addition, he wanted the atmo-

---

12. Rabbi Boruch Kaplan taught parallel to Reb Dovid and all the *talmidim* knew him.

13. Sixty-five years later, all the *talmidim* interviewed recalled specific stories from their year in his class, *limudim* they learned from him, and anecdotes he related.

14. "What is doing?"

1943 — Reb Dovid, when he was a maggid shiur in Torah Vodaath, at the wedding of ybdl"ch Rabbi Yisroel Spinner, a good friend from Mir. Rabbi Yisroel Spinner went on to hold many distinguished positions in the world of Torah and chinuch.

sphere to be relaxed and comfortable; he knew that his presence might intimidate his students.

The *vaadim* were a great success and created a unique relationship between friends, a kinship created through shared ideas and learning. Reb Dovid encouraged participation and most boys chose to attend but no one felt forced. Some of Reb Dovid's *talmidim* kept up these meetings, even after they finished his class. Long after each *talmid* went on his own way, the friendships created through these *vaadim* endured.[15]

IN ELUL, REB DOVID GAVE MORE *SHMUESSEN*. REB DOVID REALIZED that he could not bring the same atmosphere of Elul in Mir to his classroom, but he could try to teach them that they too could create an Elul mood uniquely their own. He was very successful. His *talmidim* felt a distinct difference in their classroom during Elul. Elul became a time of *mussar*, introspection, and self-improvement. "The important thing about Elul is that what we are doing now is not just for Elul!" he would encourage. "We must carry the spirit of Elul through the entire year!"

In Elul, Reb Dovid would daven for the *amud*. He davened very slowly with the inspiring Mirrer *nusach*. *Talmidim* tried to imitate his davening. Sometimes, he would call a *talmid* to the *amud* to be the *chazzan*.

"Sholom," he would call out, and Sholom Flamm,[16] the youngest in the class and the class star, would come obediently to the front of the class. Who could forget the sweet beautiful voice of little Sholom leading the class in the *hartzige Mirrer nusach*, the rousing style of the Mir, as their rebbi

---

15. "The *chaverim* of our *vaad* always remained close, even 50 and 60 years later. Some of those in our group were Rabbi Moshe Aharon Stern, Rabbi Avrohom Moseson, R' Chaim Auerbach, and ybdl"ch R' Yosef Benlevovitz [Bain]" (Rabbi Hershel Mashinsky).

16. See Biography Section.

had taught? His heartfelt lead prompted the boys to respond with unusual feeling.

Yes, in Rabbi Dovid Bender's tenth-grade classroom the davening in Elul was different, the *shmuessen* in Elul were different, the atmosphere in Elul was different. As a result, the spirit of Elul affected the entire year.

SOMETIMES, ALL A REBBI DOES IS LECTURE AND THE NEXT YEAR HIS *talmidim* forget that he was even their rebbi. Learning from Reb Dovid was quite different. The excitement with which he embraced his position, the warmth and love he showed his students, the dedication he had both in and out of the classroom made an unforgettable impression on his students.

Friday night, when his *talmidim* would come over, Reb Dovid and his rebbetzin greeted them with warmth and happiness that made the boys feel welcome. Rebbetzin Bender set up nosh, drinks, candies, and cake. Reb Dovid sang *zemiros* and his *talmidim* joined in. Between the songs, Reb Dovid told stories of the Mir, of *gedolim* he had been privileged to meet, but mainly stories about the *Mashgiach*. The boys never tired of Reb Dovid's stories. They learned to revere the *Mashgiach*, to view him as their rebbi because he was their rebbi's rebbi. As the hour got late, the boys reluctantly drifted home, looking forward to the next opportunity to visit.[17]

Some returned on Shabbos afternoon; others came less frequently. Rebbetzin Bender welcomed them as if they had just been there the past Friday night, even after they had left Reb Dovid's *shiur*. She plied them with food as they sat around the table and reminisced with their rebbi; when they left the Bender home, it was with the same warm feelings they remembered from years ago.[18]

WHEN REB DOVID RETURNED TO AMERICA AFTER HIS STAY IN EUROPE, much had changed. His rebbi, Rabbi Dovid Leibowitz, an integral part of Torah Vodaath in his student days, was no longer at Torah Vodaath. Recon-

---

17. "Shabbos, Reb Dovid would sing with us. Yom Tov he would dance with us. He danced beautifully, *leibedig* and *freilach*. On Simchas Torah, Torah Vodaath made *hakafos*. Reb Dovid would jump up on the table and drag his *talmidim* to dance there with him. To this day, I remember those *hakafos* and how he pulled me up on the table to join him" (Rabbi Hershel Mashinsky).

18. The effect he had on his *talmidim* was lasting. Rabbi Paltiel Bender once approached Rabbi Moshe Aharon Stern at a *bris* and introduced himself. "Oh! The oldest son of my teacher, Reb Dovid. How is your mother? Send her my thanks for all the favors she granted me in her house." Reb Paltiel was puzzled. Reb Moshe Aharon added, "We were American boys. We had no concept of what it meant to be a yeshivah *bochur*. We used to come to your father's house every Friday night from 8 o'clock to 12. He used to sit with us. He would tell us *vertlach* on the *parashah*, sing *zemiros* with us, and tell us stories of the European *gedolim*, and he would talk to us about what a yeshivah *bochur* is, what a *ben Torah* is. Those evenings changed us."

"*When I was in Reb Dovid's shiur, I saw a sign that Rebbetzin Bender was going to be speaking somewhere. 'Look, that's my rebbetzin!' The words were out before I realized what I was saying. My chaverim burst out laughing but I understood what had happened. I felt so close to my rebbi; if he was my rebbi, his wife was my rebbetzin! The same held true for my rebbi's father. He was part of our lives and I remember him well ... a tall and impressive personality ... a role model for us boys ...*" (Rabbi Hershel Mashinsky).

necting to his rebbi required conscious effort. He would visit his rebbi on Yom Tov, particularly Succos, and he would try to stop by Yeshivas Chofetz Chaim when he had a chance. Sadly, this renewed relationship was not meant to last long.

Rabbi Dovid Leibowitz was *niftar* Thursday night, the 15th of Kislev, 5702 (1941). When Reb Dovid heard that his rebbi was *niftar,* he rushed to the Leibowitz house to see how he could be of help. He found his rebbi's only child, Henoch, alone with his mother, bewildered and bereft. Henoch was barely 20 and weighty decisions were now leaning on his shoulders. Reb Dovid took charge. He helped make the arrangements for the chapel, the funeral, and the burial. Since his rebbi was *niftar* on Thursday evening and the next day, Friday, was too short a day, the *levayah* (burial) had to be on Sunday. From Thursday evening until Sunday, Reb Dovid was at Henoch's side, helping, advising, and comforting. He did not go home for Shabbos; he did not leave his rebbi's son.[19]

The day after the *levayah,* Reb Dovid returned to yeshivah. The boys were speaking excitedly. Just the day before, December 7, 1941, at four o'clock in the afternoon, the Japanese bombed Pearl Harbor. The newspapers reported that the United States was entering the war in Europe. The world was in an uproar and the boys were eager to hear what their rebbi had to say.

Reb Dovid began. "*M'pnei hara'ah ne'esaf hatzaddik.* The simple meaning is that if people are bad, a *tzaddik* passes away because of their sins." Reb Dovid paused. "The Midrash says, *m'pnei hara'ah* — before the bad,

---

19. "Every time I met Rabbi Henoch Leibowitz, it might have been twice in one year or not at all for two or three years, he told me again what tremendous gratitude he had to my father. Each time, he recalled the details all over again" (Rabbi Yaakov Bender). See Biography Section.

*ne'esaf hatzaddik* — the *tzaddik* is taken away. When *HaKadosh Baruch Hu* has to bring a tragedy into this world, he first removes the *tzaddik* so that the merit of the *tzaddik* will no longer protect the world. The Rosh Yeshivah was taken away and now we've lost the merit he brought with him."[20]

The message was clear. How lofty are our *tzaddikim*! How bereft we are when they are taken from us.

A more subtle message remained as well. When Reb Dovid connected his students to his rebbeim, he bound them to the past. Rabbi Dovid Leibowitz was his rebbi and therefore theirs; Reb Yeruchem was his *Mashgiach* and therefore theirs; the Chofetz Chaim was his father's rebbi and therefore theirs. They were not American boys who happened to be Jewish. They were links in the glorious chain of *Mesorah*.

*Rabbi Dovid Bender with Rabbi Aharon Kotler at Rabbi Shmuel Kamenetsky's chasunah. Reb Shmuel had learned in Ner Yisroel when Reb Dovid was there. Later, he and Rabbi Elya Svei became Roshei Yeshivah of the Talmudical Yeshivah of Philadelphia and leaders of their generation. Left to Right: Shaul Goldman, Nachum Goldberg, Berel Peker, Rabbi Aharon Kotler, Chatzkel Horowitz, Rabbi Paul Z. Levovitz, Shmuel Kamenetsky, Elya Svei, Rabbi Dovid Bender. All went on to hold positions in the world of Torah and chinuch.*

---

20. "This was how Rabbi Elya Svei was *maspid* Rabbi Avrohom Pam (1913-2001), Rosh Yeshivah of Torah Vodaath, on his *shloshim*, shortly after 9/11. At that moment, I remembered my rebbi's *hesped* on his rebbi" (Rabbi Yonasan Shapiro).

### Chapter Thirty

# Building on Strong Foundations

*"I was a little child when my parents sent me from Pittsburgh to learn in Torah Vodaath. At 9, 10, 11, 12, and bar mitzvah, I was in the dormitory — when business class was not in fashion and plane tickets were not used to fly home. So I saw my parents Succos and Pesach and once in between, if my mother traveled 13 hours by train to visit me in Williamsburg.*

*"I was lonely, very lonely."*[21]

**Williamsburg, 5701 (1941)**

ORDECHAI SHAPIRO WAS PART OF AN ELITE GROUP OF children, many of whom were younger than bar mitzvah, who traveled far to learn in yeshivah. Although leaving the comforts of home to learn Torah has always been part of Jewish tradition,[22] each generation has its own heroes. These young children were growing up in middle-class America, where many adults surrendered to the glamour of American culture and where sacrificing for *Yiddishkeit* was considered passé. They went against the currents of the times, forfeiting the warmth and love of their parents' homes, to learn in a yeshivah.

---

21. Rabbi Mordechai Shapiro in his *hesped* for Rebbetzin Bender.

22. *Pirkei Avos* 4:18: *"Hevei golah limkom Torah* — one should exile oneself to a place of learning."

**... Rabbi Yosef Shapiro, a close *talmid* of the Meicheter Illuy, was a *talmid chacham* and a visionary ... When his oldest son, Mordechai, was 6½ years old, Reb Yosef sent Mordechai to New York ...**

*Rabbi Yosef Shapiro (1904-1995) went from Montreal to New York to learn under the Meicheter Illuy at Yeshivas Rabbeinu Yitzchok Elchonon. Reb Yosef became very close to the Meicheter Illuy, practically living in his home. Reb Yosef was Rav of Congregation Poalei Tzedek in Pittsburgh for many years, introducing many innovations including the first Jewish day school in Pittsburgh. Rabbi Aaron Kotler was known to have said about him "he is the masmid of America."*

*Rabbi Shlomo Poliacheck (1878-1928), known as the Meicheter Illuy, was famous for his Torah scholarship. Rabbi Elchonon Wasserman quoted Rabbi Chaim Soloveitchik as having said that he had never come across such an extraordinary genius as the Meicheter Illuy. After his arrival in the United States he assumed the position of Rosh Yeshivah in Yeshivas Rabbeinu Yitzchak Elchonon. He passed away suddenly at the age of 50.*

The Shapiros lived in Pittsburgh, Pennsylvania where Rabbi Yosef Shapiro, a close *talmid* of the Meicheter Illuy, was Rav of the Congregation Poalei Tzedek. Rabbi Yosef Shapiro was a *talmid chacham* and a visionary. Pittsburgh was like many other all-American towns from the East to the West Coast. The Pittsburgh community boasted of several shuls with healthy memberships, but the average shul member was only minimally Shabbos observant, if at all. Reb Yosef was undeterred. He hoped that with perseverance, the level of religious observance in Pittsburgh would rise. Maybe one day there would even be a yeshivah.

Yet Reb Yosef was also a realist. Plans for the future were important, but they would not change the present. At present, he had little children and these children needed a Jewish education. So when his oldest son, Mordechai, was 6½ old, Reb Yosef sent Mordechai to New York to his grandparents, R' Archik and Sara Leah Berman.[23]

> *"I was lonely, very lonely. The Bender house, 168 Hooper Street, was my 'stant-zia,' it was my home away from home. Reb Dovid was mikarev me, not only on Shabbosos and Yamim Tovim, but during the week. His great rebbetzin, with her kiruv, in her way, did her hachnosas orchim. If a person eats gefilte fish or chulent, it may be a d'var gashmi, unless one is a baal madreigah; but when you feed a lonely young child gefilte fish or chulent, it is a pair of tefillin, it is hachnosas orchim."*[24]

THE BENDER HOME WAS A HOME AWAY FROM HOME TO MORDECHAI Shapiro and many other young children who had come to Williamsburg to attend Torah Vodaath.

"Come with me to my cousins, the Benders," Mordechai invited his new-found friend Henoch Cohen. This was Henoch's first Shabbos away from home. He had left his comfortable cocoon — parents and siblings, aunts, uncles, and cousins, grandparents and great-grandparents[25] — to come to New York, where everything was so big, busy, and distinctly unfamiliar.

Back in Ottawa, the Cohen clan stuck together. Henoch never went to public school. His father, R' Meyer Cohen, had organized a *cheder* of eight boys from three families: the Cohens, the Rudmans, and the Drazins. For a child who had never attended a school of more than eight pupils, entering an institution with a student enrollment in the hundreds was daunting.

"Come," Mordechai urged, "you will have a nice time. You will see." Henoch hesitated only a bit; he hoped that spending time with a friend would make the long Shabbos afternoon more bearable.

Henoch was not disappointed. 168 Hooper Street was alive with laugh-

---

23. Within a year, he contracted pneumonia and was hospitalized. His mother came from Pittsburgh and spent several weeks nursing him back to health. She then took him back to Pittsburgh and did not send him back to Torah Vodaath until he was 9 years old (Rabbi Meir Shapiro).

24. Rabbi Mordechai Shapiro in his *hesped* of Rebbetzin Bender. Note: Rabbi Mordechai Shapiro was more fortunate than most. He was staying with his grandparents and he had family in the neighborhood yet he still remembered his loneliness decades later.

25. The Cohens were unusual; they remained religious through several generations. Rabbi Henoch Cohen's great-grandfather, R' Binyomin Silver, fled from White Russia to Ottawa, Canada where he opened a general store and still clung to his traditions. The rabbanim and *meshulachim* who came to Ottawa stayed in his kosher home. When it came time to marry off his only daughter, Liba, he looked for values unheard of in Ottawa at that time: a boy who wanted a girl who would cover her hair. Liba married R' Aryeh Leib Cohen, a gentleman who shared her family's ideals. Liba's home, like her parents' home, became the address for rabbanim and *meshulachim*. Reb Henoch grew up in a large, warm, extended family that was also religious.

ter and warmth. The table was laden with nosh and drinks. Reb Dovid was singing with the boys. At the door, his rebbetzin welcomed everyone with her motherly smile and friendly greeting. The atmosphere was easygoing and happy, pleasant and congenial. It did not matter if one was *Litvish*, *Chassidish*, Hungarian, or just plain all American. It was irrelevant if, back at home, Shabbos was kept less stringently by one and more stringently by another. At the Bender home, they were the out-of-towners: unified in their shared experiences, bolstered by each other's courage, and nurtured by the special *oneg* Shabbos. Reb Dovid told over *divrei Torah* and stories; the boys listened most attentively. They all felt less homesick when the afternoon ended.

TORAH VODAATH HAD ANYWHERE FROM 100 TO 400 OUT-OF-TOWN boys, depending on the year. Most were 12 and older but some were very young. Chaim Werner came to Torah Vodaath when he was 8 and Mordechai Shapiro was 6½.

In the 1930's, when there was no dormitory, boys boarded either by family or by Mrs. Doppelt, a childless widow who took in boarders. With tremendous self-sacrifice, mothers willingly sent away their little boys who, chins stoically up, grew up on their own.

Mrs. Doppelt's "minidorm" was not much of a dorm. This one slept on a couch, that one slept on a rug; few had a bed of their own. "Carefree childhood" was an oxymoron. These children had to fend for themselves, budget their allowances, and see to their laundry and meals. Under such conditions, they grew up very quickly.

Even those boys who came at age 12 and 13 faced challenges. Henoch and his brother Shmuel Elya Cohen, 13 and 14 respectively, returned home only once a year, for Pesach. At a dollar a phone call, they were left to imagine their mother's comforting voice.

Rabbi Shraga Feivel Mendelowitz realized that while the out-of-town boys were troopers, they deserved a more organized framework. In 1941, Torah Vodaath opened its dormitory.[26]

The dormitory was the fourth and fifth floors of the Mesivta building on South Third Street and the two private houses next door. As soon as the dormitory opened, it was filled to capacity. To accommodate the demand, most of the rooms had bunk beds.

The boys were assigned tables in the Mesivta dining room, and the dorm supervisor made sure that there was a *beis medrash bochur* who ate with the children to oversee that they behave, that someone say a *vort*, and to be an adult presence. During the week, the dining room offered breakfast, lunch,

---

26. At this time, Ner Israel of Baltimore also had a dormitory, but only for *beis medrash bochurim*. Torah Vodaath was the first dormitory for elementary and high-school boys.

and supper for the dormers (the elementary-school children who dormed ate lunch in the elementary school). A caring, semiformal atmosphere made the out-of-towners feel taken care of, but not overly restricted.

Another Torah Vodaath innovation was the establishment of the "Out-of-Towners Club," a means to create big brother/little brother relationships between the older and younger dormers. The dormitory staff wanted to foster a warm family atmosphere in the dorm. Occasionally, they held an "Out-of-Towners Club" *melaveh malkah*, a festive event that engendered happiness and unity in the dormitory.

Rabbi Dovid Bender was warm to all his *talmidim* and all the boys who frequented his home, but he had a special soft spot for the out-of-towners and gave them extra attention. He was very active in the "Out-of-Towners Club," giving advice, encouragement, and support when needed. The warmth of Rabbi Dovid and Rebbetzin Basya Bender so deeply touched the hearts of those boys, that many years later, they still recalled, with love, their experiences at the Bender home.

*"... And Reb Dovid was mikarev me, not only on Shabbosos and Yamim Tovim, but during the week ... I felt and still feel endless hakoras hatov ... (to Rebbetzin Bender) with her warmth and devotion and her mammalichkeit (her mothering) she taught me what hachnosas orchim is."*[27]

_____

27. Rabbi Mordechai Shapiro in his *hesped for* Rebbetzin Bender.

*Chapter Thirty-One*

# Building Bais Yaakov

*A*LL MY LIFE I WAS HOPING FOR JUST SUCH A POSITION, *that I would be able to teach children — not even for a salary."*[28]

THIS WAS REBBETZIN BASYA BENDER. BAIS YAAKOV INSTILLED HER WITH a desire and dedication to teach *Yiddishe kinder*. Although money was never easy, she never taught for the money. She taught because she felt a mission in her life to inculcate Jewish daughters with Torah *hashkafos*.

In providing a Torah education for its daughters, Europe was far more advanced, but America was catching up. Shulamith School for Girls was the first all-girls Orthodox elementary school in North America. Some of the parents of the girls in the first graduating class wanted their daughters to continue their religious education. They turned to Rebbetzin Vichna Kaplan, newly arrived from Europe, and asked her to pioneer this venture.

In 1937, Rebbetzin Kaplan began giving classes around the dining-room table in Mrs. Necha Rivkin's home. Mrs. Rivkin, wife of Rabbi Dov Ber Rivkin of Torah Vodaath,[29] was one of the foremost teachers in Shulamith. The language of instruction in Shulamith was Hebrew, and the graduates were fluent in Hebrew. Rebbetzin Kaplan accommodated her students and taught in Hebrew.

The following year, Rebbetzin Kaplan moved the classes to her home in Williamsburg. The girls learned *Chumash*, *Navi*, *Tehillim*, and other *sifrei kodesh* around Rebbetzin Kaplan's dining-room table at night. Occasion-

---

28. See letter on p.?
29. See Book I, Part I, Chapter 3.

ally, the young rebbetzin, with a smile of apology, excused herself to take care of her baby.[30]

With time, the fledgling Bais Yaakov moved out of the Kaplan home and into a shul on top of the A&P, the local supermarket. Their next location was a small, dilapidated apartment on Keap Street. In the winter, the girls sat with umbrellas to protect themselves from the rain that seeped down through the ceiling.

Slowly, Bais Yaakov grew from a group of girls assembled around a dining-room table to a full-fledged high school and seminary.

BAIS YAAKOV IN CRAKOW ALSO BEGAN AS A SMALL ONE-ROOM CLASS. It grew into a network of schools regulated by the "Mercaz," the Bais Yaakov Center. Every branch of Bais Yaakov was still connected to Bais Yaakov of Crakow: The teachers were graduates of the seminary; the curriculums were updated through the seminary, and letters of encouragement and educational ideas passed from the novice teachers back to their instructors in Crakow.

When Rebbetzin Kaplan left Europe for America, she requested permission from Rabbi Yehuda Leib Orlean, director of Bais Yaakov of Crakow, to open a branch of Bais Yaakov in America.[31] In time, it could replicate the European Bais Yaakov system: complete with a Bais Yaakov Center, an advanced teacher training seminary, and branches of Bais Yaakov all over America.

The Kaplans were prepared to promote Bais Yaakov in America. In the 1920's and 30's, Dr. Deutschlander sent Dr. Judith Rosenbaum, his trusted assistant, all over Europe to collect money for Bais Yaakov of Crakow. She taught about the growth of Bais Yaakov in Europe, how its growth was saving Orthodox Jewry, and how contributing to its continued growth was vital to the survival of the Jewish people.[32] The Kaplans chose Rebbetzin Bender for the parallel task in America.

AMERICA WAS NOT EUROPE. ONLY AFTER MANY FUTILE ATTEMPTS AND years of persuasive arguments could America finally boast of several full-day yeshivos for boys on the elementary, high-school, and post-high-school levels. Yet the same parents who sent their boys to yeshivos were still wary about subjecting their girls to change. Was it necessary to take their daughters out of public school and into an experimental institution? Granted, the boys needed more of a Jewish education, but girls? How would *Chumash* or *Navi* enable girls to be better Jewish wives and mothers?

---

30. Mrs. Ella (Rivkin) Shurin, a member of this first class, recalls this period.

31. *Daughters of Destiny*, p. 182, p. 216.

32. *Rebbetzin Grunfeld*, pp. 104-110.

The Kaplans had to convince American Jewry that Jewish schools for girls were as important as yeshivos for boys. Girls were just as attracted to the lures of secular society as boys and, while knowledge alone might not produce loyal Jewish mothers, the sense of pride in *Yiddishkeit* provided by Bais Yaakov was a powerful defense. To succeed, the Kaplans had to assure the parents that although Bais Yaakov would provide their girls with a warm home, it would not replace their real home, but would be a wonderful complement.

Since Rebbetzin Bender also viewed the establishment of Bais Yaakov as crucial for the survival of American Jewry, she was an eager assistant in this campaign.[33] Therefore, when members of the Detroit Jewish community contacted Rebbetzin Kaplan about the feasibility of setting up a local Bais Yaakov, she took their request most seriously and sent her loyal friend and colleague, Rebbetzin Basya Bender, to see what could be done.

In 1942, before Esther, the oldest Bender child, was born, Rebbetzin Bender embarked on the 12-hour train ride to Detroit. She understood that she was to speak about the importance of Bais Yaakov, to request financial aid for building the Bais Yaakov movement, to encourage parents to send their children to Camp Bais Yaakov in the Catskills where they would forge their connection to Bais Yaakov, and to help establish a Bais Yaakov school in Detroit.

When she arrived, she realized that all was not as she had assumed.

### Detroit, 1942

*Dear Dovid,*

*… About what is happening here: I went to Rabbi Wohlgelanter[34] and discussed the whole issue again. I insisted that I must have someone to help me aproach well-known philanthropists, and I also spoke to him about the importance of establishing a Bais Yaakov here. Consequently, he told me his position on the matter.*

*This is the story: He is convinced that I must not solicit any funds here. He wants me to make my rounds here, to teach people about Bais Yaakov, and to get acquainted with the people. This will lay the foundation for another representative to come later and use my contacts.*

*Then I left with his wife to the Shemiras Shabbos meeting.[35] Most of the mem-*

---

33. There is a flier about a meeting of potential supporters of Bais Yaakov at which Rebbetzin Bender spoke. She also made notes on the paper about whom to contact with a follow-up phone call (Bender Family Documents).

34. See Biography Section.

35. Mrs. Yetta Sperka was one of the founders of The Women's Sabbath League. Their goal was to encourage Detroit Jewry to keep Shabbos. One of their main tactics was to campaign with the storekeepers to close their stores on Shabbos, and then they encouraged their friends to patronize these stores (Rabbi Shlomo Sperka).

*bers were non-religious. Their goal is to work on Shemiras Shabbos publicly. In private, it is to each his own. They were mostly assimilated, intelligent, and wealthy people. I spoke to them and they were very appreciative. However, I was warned not to mention Bais Yaakov. It is too new to them and Rabbi Wohlgelanter does not want to combine too many topics. In any case, I got to know them.*

*I went back to Rabbi Wohlgelanter's house this afternoon. Unfortunately, the father of the Cohen brothers (who are very active in the community) is critically ill, and Mrs. Sperka's children (she is a big doer) are all sick. That is how it is. Nonetheless, I did not give up. Rabbi Wohlgelanter sat by the phone and made calls for me. It was the same thing again — speak, but do not, G-d forbid, make an appeal for money.*

*So far, I've been very disappointed. But, I haven't even been here a day yet; maybe the prospects will get better. Rabbi Wohlgelanter says that he wrote all these details in advance. He wants to bring the spirit here and then bring someone over to build on this positive attitude. I assume that you get the picture from my letters. ...*

*I hope to hear only good from you.*

*Be well,*
*Basya[36]*

IT WAS CLEAR FROM THE BEGINNING THAT THERE WAS SOME MISCOM-munication. Rebbetzins Kaplan and Bender had responded to Detroit's invitation with excitement and optimism. How wonderful! An out-of-town community recognizes the importance and beauty of Bais Yaakov and wants to be a part of it. The rebbetzins were eager to welcome them into the Bais Yaakov family. Bais Yaakov was always in difficult financial straits, and they hoped that they could create a mutually beneficial situation: the rebbetzins would help establish a Bais Yaakov school in Detroit, and Detroit would join the Bais Yaakov Committee pledging support to Bais Yaakov schools everywhere. This was how Bais Yaakov functioned in Europe, and they hoped to bring that spirit to America.

The rabbanim of Detroit had written their letter with different thoughts in mind.[37] They recognized the value of Bais Yaakov and wanted to introduce the concept to Detroit. They wanted someone to lay the groundwork

---

36. These letters have been translated and condensed.

37. Perhaps the catalyst for these letters was the growth of Beth Yehudah Day School. Beth Yehudah had been a Talmud Torah: an after-school supplementary learning program for boys that was expanding to include a program for girls. In 1942, Congregation Magen Avrohom built a new building, and Beth Yehudah was given classrooms in that facility. That year, it went from being an after-hours program to becoming a day school, a first for a community outside New York. This revolution was a product of Rabbi Wohlgelanter's tremendous drive and vision and may have been the incentive for beginning full-day classes for girls (Rabbi Shlomo Sperka).

for eventually establishing a Bais Yaakov school. Later, funds could be solicited, but that should not be part of this trip.

Rebbetzin Bender was confused. She was certain that it was understood that the trip's purpose was twofold. How could they not allow her to raise money for Bais Yaakov? The school had desperate financial problems. She and the Kaplans barely took salaries.[38] Did they not understand that founding and running schools cost money?

Despite her disappointments, Rebbetzin Bender stubbornly continued. She tried to accomplish as much as possible in her short stay. Maybe some money could still be raised and, if not, at least the other part of her mission would be successful. She wanted to meet as many people as possible and introduce them to Bais Yaakov.

*... I accomplished a lot yesterday; I reached more of my contacts and by coincidence, got invited to a meeting of the World Jewish Congress[39] for women. (You are probably laughing at the type of people I am meeting, but in our circles there is no one to deal with.) They allowed me to speak there for eight to ten minutes. I also became acquainted with two distinguished well-to-do women. They took me to their car, and I spoke to them for more than two hours. They came away feeling very positive. I asked that each of them promise to raise $500. (They are famous for their fund-raising.) They protested that they are already engaged in various local projects and war activities (and therefore they cannot really help me). Finally, they promised to send me $200, by the end of June. They are serious, understanding, and considerate women whose words carry weight; whomever I ask tells me that $200 is also money. They requested that the Bais Yaakov office send them a letter with details. We will, iy"H, take care of that. They also promised to become members of Bais Yaakov, if the school will be established here. One of them even offered to drive me around in her car, if and when I need.*

*I then went to some more places (by myself). After supper, I went to Rabbi Wohlgelanter and he sent for the Cohen and Isbee brothers. I tried to convince them of the importance of establishing a Bais Yaakov here under the leadership of Young Israel.* [40] *I sat there until 1 a.m. They are of the few truly frum families here. They*

---

38. Rebbetzin Bender worked without pay for several years. Even when she took a salary, she accepted whatever was offered: never asking for a raise, never joining a strike. In time, she earned far less than younger and less experienced teachers, but she did not complain. She viewed teaching Jewish children as a holy privilege.

39. World Jewish Congress was a secular organization that convened to deal with Jewish concerns. It is not surprising that Rebbetzin Bender was appealing to people of varied streams of Judaism for support of Bais Yaakov. At that time, the Orthodox institutions received support from all segments of Detroit Jewry. There was general goodwill throughout the community, and people were inclined to donate to anything "Jewish."

40. The role of Young Israel in the 1940's, in addressing and creating Orthodox Jewish institutions, cannot be underestimated. The older rabbanim were involved in other community issues such as kashrus regulation and *mikvaos*. Few rabbis were like Rabbi Wohlgelanter who looked

*are the elite; and yet it took so much of my energy to explain to them the impor-*
*tance of Bais Yaakov. At the end, they understood and Bais Yaakov has become a*
*very strong possibility. They are already thinking about how to organize it, and*
*they asked me if we are certain we can send a teacher. My reply was "Yes!"*

*I mentioned sending someone to make appeals in the shuls, but I was told that*
*it cannot be done now, because the Vaad Hatzalah is coming. All this shows how*
*naïve we have been. Whoever I speak to tells me that these things should have been*
*prearranged and heartwarming letters should have been sent, in advance, to all the*
*rabbanim and shul presidents.*

*The Poilisher Shteibel*[41] *promised to give something to Bais Yaakov, from the*
*Shavuos appeal. Nu, so it will be $25, not more. I would have liked Young Israel*
*to make an appeal, but they cannot do so for another couple of weeks because of the*
*Vaad Hatzalah (already being scheduled).*

*I realize that if I would stay here for six weeks, I would be able to accomplish*
*something. I have recorded the contacts that I have made in this short time. At least*
*they are not stingy on compliments and honor for me, b"H, and I am gaining my*
*experience for the future. They tell me that Father should have come initially as an*
*introduction. First, there must be publicity; then the collector can come. They laugh*
*at me. I come with a new idea that appeals only to the spiritual senses (nothing to*
*do with Europe, hunger, or deprivation), and they also claim that there are already*
*enough yeshivos and Talmudei Torah, and that people in Detroit do not go collect-*
*ing for themselves in New York. We know all this already. The main thing is that*
*we are at fault; we should have worked on better communication. HaRav Wohlge-*
*lanter is helping me out. Now that I am nearby, I see how hard it is for him …*

*Be well,*
*Basya*

BY THE END OF THE WEEK, REBBETZIN BENDER UNDERSTOOD WHAT SHE
had accomplished and what she would not accomplish. Just bringing the
concept of Bais Yaakov to second-generation American Jewry was going to
be a challenge; gathering funds for its growth was going to be even more
difficult.

*… This morning a delegation of three came for Vaad Hatzalah: HaRav Yaffen,*
*HaRav Grozovsky, and HaRav Dvorkin.*[42] *They plan to stay for a few weeks. So,*

---

at Detroit with eyes toward the future, who understood the need to educate the youth (Rabbi
Shlomo Sperka).

41. The Poilisher Shteibel was a very active place. The members were old-timers, most of them
with beards and *peiyos.* At all hours of the day and night, the sounds of men learning reverberated from its walls.

42. Rabbi Avrohom Yaffen (see Biography Section) and Rabbi Reuvain Grozovsky (See page
358.). Rabbi Dvorkin remains unidentified.

you understand, with such a delegation, what kind of status do I have now?

I would go on my own to all the shul presidents and ladies' auxiliaries. I would speak to them and get commitments for annual organizational memberships. However, for one individual to try and accomplish this, it would require two months. There is no doubt that I cannot undertake it now …

As you see, the situation is quite clear. Imagine going without any help, by myself, to speak to people privately. I went to Rabbi A.[43] yesterday. You know what he thinks of our ideology; he had no qualms about telling me so very bluntly. Still, he told me to call him at 12 p.m. Maybe he will have an answer for me. If others don't show the slightest interest, how can I expect it of him? He asked me quite frankly if our schools are built in the same spirit as Mesivta, since Mesivta produces cripples, G-d forbid. So what can I really expect of him?

I then met another woman, Mrs. Klein, the Mizrachi president here; she is decent and honest. I spoke to her until 12 o'clock last night; she developed a liking toward Bais Yaakov. I do not know how long the feelings will last. She is going to the conference of the Jewish Congress tomorrow night. She promised to raise $100 by the tenth of July.

In the meantime, I am being fed promises. Maybe, I was expecting too much. Rabbi Wohlgelanter says if seeds were sown in a place like Detroit, it is already considered a success …

Be well,
Your Basya

P.S. To add to all the great advantages, it rained all week.[44]

---

43. It seems that Rabbi A. was very active in the Conservative movement and was one of the signers on the *p'sak* permitting congregants to drive to shul on Shabbos. Ironically, he was killed on Shabbos by a deranged congregant while giving a sermon.

44. A Bais Yaakov was not established in Detroit at this time. Beth Yehudah Day School held classes for boys and girls together until third grade after which, when they had enough pupils, they spun off the girls' division one class at a time until Bais Yaakov of Detroit became a school of its own. It remains a department of Beth Yehudah until today (Rabbi Shlomo Sperka).

### Chapter Thirty-Two

# Building a Home

*"I was witness to the daily building of Reb Dovid and his rebbetzin's home — a pride to Klal Yisroel. It was a home built on Torah, ahavas Torah, middos tovos, and chessed from within and without … I saw her in all kinds of situations: everyday circumstances, difficult situations, and bitter times. She was always influencing (people in) the correct way of life, and her influence was powerful."*[45]

A S REBBETZIN BENDER WAS HELPING BUILD A MOVEMENT, she was also building her own home. Blumie was born a year after Esther. The Bender home was a lively, hectic place.

Rebbetzin Bender juggled life admirably, rarely getting nervous or flustered. She was busy with many different projects, some her own, and some as her husband's *ezer k'negdo* (assistant). In spite of the busyness, Rebbetzin Bender radiated calm equanimity, an intrinsic part of her personality.[46] Peace and tranquility were the foundation of her home.

---

45. Rabbi Zelig Epstein in his *hesped* for Rebbetzin Bender.

46. One of the few things that could shake her tranquility was concern over her children. Once, while she was giving the children supper, Rabbi Yitzchok Hutner (1906-1980), Rosh Yeshivah of Yeshivas Rabbeinu Chaim Berlin, called to speak to Reb Dovid. As Rebbetzin Bender was talking to Rav Hutner on the phone, she noticed Esther, the toddler, climbing out of the highchair. Rebbetzin Bender dropped the phone and ran to catch her. She returned to the phone, slightly out of breath. "Excuse me, Rosh Yeshivah, but I had to catch the baby. She was falling out of the highchair." "*Ya, Ya,*" the Rosh Yeshivah laughed, "*Heint darf min hittin az zei zol nisht arois fallen; shpeiter darf min hitten az zei zol nisht arein fallen* (Yes, yes, now we have to watch that they don't fall out, later we have to watch that they don't 'fall in' — meaning, that they don't 'fall into' a bad situation)."

REVERENCE FOR *GEDOLIM* WAS ANOTHER CORNERSTONE IN THE foundation of the Bender home. Whenever Reb Dovid could, he clung to greatness. During his years as a *maggid shiur* in Torah Vodaath, his guiding light was Rabbi Shlomo Heiman. Reb Dovid and Rabbi Shlomo Heiman learned together every night and on many Shabbos afternoons. They also learned all through the summers in Seagate.

In Seagate, the Heimans and the Benders shared a bungalow, a kitchen, a vacation, and much more. For those few weeks, their lives intertwined. Very early in the morning, before the beach was officially open, Reb Shlomo and Reb Dovid would go out for a swim. During the war years, the Coast Guard patrolled the beaches and was strict about swimmers keeping to the posted schedule. They made an exception for "the Rabbis."[47]

During their Shabbos-afternoon learning session, Reb Shlomo inevitably became thirsty. He never wanted to ask anyone to serve him, and yet he knew that his rebbetzin would not want him to prepare his own tea. He called out gently, "Faigele, maybe you would like a glass of tea?"

"Oh!" she exclaimed, jumping up from her seat. "Maybe you would like a glass of tea?" Every week, without fail, rather than ask his wife to serve him, Reb Shlomo gave her a gentle reminder.

Both during the year and in Seagate, Reb Shlomo was meticulous about learning without a break; he and Reb Dovid rarely paused during the three or four hours they learned together. One night there was an emergency and Reb Shlomo went out of the room to speak on the telephone. He came back and he saw Reb Dovid delving into a *Shitah Mekubetzes*, a compilation of supplementary opinions beyond what was strictly necessary for what they were concentrating on.

"You are looking in a *Shitah*?" Reb Shlomo was displeased that in the middle of their *seder*, Reb Dovid was apparently passing time looking at a sefer that was seemingly unrelated to the *sugya* they were studying.

"Yes, I am looking …" Reb Dovid paused. "But I am looking with an address." Reb Dovid explained that he wanted to see what a specific commentary had to say on the topic they were learning. He was not "just looking" in a random sefer. He was looking with an "address." Reb Shlomo's face lit up. A person can look into sefarim, but not just to pass his time reading something interesting. He needs an "address." If he knows where to look, other sefarim can be a boon to his learning.

Reb Shlomo so enjoyed this expression that he began to use it often.

FOR REB DOVID, EXPOSURE TO *GEDOLIM* WAS A VALUED PRIVILEGE, ONE that he willingly shared. "Come," he told his young cousin, Mordechai

---

47. Rabbi Meir Shapiro.

"Do you know why Reb Moshe is becoming the leader of the generation? It is because his back never touches the back of his chair as he learns!" said Rabbi Shlomo Heiman about his friend Rabbi Moshe Feinstein, while they were both spending time in Seagate.

*Rabbi Moshe Feinstein*

*Rabbi Shlomo Heiman*

*Rabbi Moshe Feinstein (1895-1986) learned with his father in his youth and then went on to Slutzk to learn under Rabbi Isser Zalman Meltzer and Rabbi Pesach Pruskin. He served as Rav of Uzda and then Luban. As Communist decrees against Yiddishkeit intensified, Reb Moshe immigrated to the United States where he became Rosh Yeshivah of Mesivta Tifereth Jerusalem. He was universally recognized as the leading Torah authority of his generation as reflected in his halachic response, Igros Moshe, and in his detailed shiurim printed in Dibros Moshe.*

*Rabbi Shlomo Heiman (circa 1894-1944) studied under Rabbi Boruch Ber Leibowitz and the Chofetz Chaim. He served as maggid shiur in Baranovich and then as maggid shiur in the Yeshivah of Remmailes. In 1935 Rabbi Chaim Ozer Grodzenski advised him to immigrate to America and assume the position of Rosh Yeshivah of Torah Vodaath. Many of his talmidim went on to take prominent positions in the Jewish world.*

Shapiro, "come with us to Seagate. There is room for you in the bungalow and you will have an unusual opportunity to be with Rabbi Shlomo Heiman on a daily basis."

Mordechai was astonished. Did they really want him? He felt very close to his cousins. He ate at their house regularly and, in general, hung around their house. But, would he not be intruding if he came along with them on vacation?

"Come," Reb Dovid urged, "you will enjoy it."

Mordechai was persuaded.

"MORDECHAI, WOULD YOU LIKE TO STAY IN THE ROOM WHEN I LEARN with the Rosh Yeshivah? Here, take a chair." Reb Dovid pulled over a chair for the boy and then turned his attention to his *chavrusah*, Rabbi Shlomo Heiman. As they learned together, Mordechai quietly observed. Suddenly, Rabbi Moshe Feinstein walked in. Mordechai's eyes widened as he watched the scene unfold. Reb Moshe took a seat at the table, and he and Reb Shlomo began to talk in learning. Time froze as Mordechai watched and listened to these two *gedolim*; he could not believe his good fortune. Then Reb Moshe left and Reb Shlomo turned to Reb Dovid. "Do you know why Reb Moshe is becoming the leader of the generation? It is because his back never touches the back of his chair while he learns!"

Not only had Mordechai sat in the same room as these *gedolim*, quietly listening to them learn, but he also merited hearing Reb Shlomo's interpretation of why Reb Moshe would achieve greatness. Those words always echoed in his ears: "Because his back never touches the back of his chair when he learns."[48]

IN THE COURSE OF THE THREE SUMMERS THAT THE BENDERS SPENT with the Heimans, they came away with many messages that, while seemingly simple, taken together painted a picture of how a *Yid* was supposed to conduct himself even in mundane matters.

Torah Vodaath paid for Reb Shlomo's Seagate vacation. Once, as the Rebbetzin was itemizing expenses, Reb Shlomo interrupted her accounting. "Add on $25 for Sholom," he said.

Rebbetzin Heiman was astounded. They had a nephew Sholom who occasionally came to visit, but he did not accrue a $25 expense. And even if he did, was that an expense that could be billed to the yeshivah?

Reb Shlomo shook his head. "I did not mean $25 for our nephew Sholom. I meant $25 for the concept of *shalom* (peace). Many times, especially when one is on vacation, things can occur that cost money — a window breaks, the door must be replaced, a bathroom needs to be fixed — and with a little bit of money, the problem can be taken care of efficiently. It pays to set aside a sum of money just for this purpose, rather than have unnecessary aggravation, which generates ill feelings later on."[49] Reb Shlomo felt that it was right and proper to set aside such a large sum of money as a valid living expense, and even to bill it to the yeshivah, for the sake of peace.

The Heimans and the Benders were together the summer after Esther, the Bender's oldest child, was born. She was a colicky baby and cried often. The crying distressed Reb Shlomo terribly. "It is nothing," Reb Dovid explained, "the baby just has gas pains. It is normal and it will pass." Reb Shlomo shook his head. "It might be nothing serious, but the child is in pain. How can I not feel for a child in pain?"

REB SHLOMO HAD TO UNDERGO A SERIOUS OPERATION, AND THE DOCtors wanted to keep visitors to a minimum. Only Rebbetzin Heiman and Rabbi Dovid Bender were allowed to come and go at will, and they kept watch that no one would disturb Reb Shlomo.

---

48. "I was there," Rabbi Mordechai Shapiro declared in his *hesped* of Rebbetzin Bender, "and I have *hakaras hatov* that I was there."

49. Rabbi Michoel Bender as heard from Rabbi Simcha Schustal.

> ... Reb Dovid had had more than just a *talmid/chaver* relationship with Rabbi Shlomo Heiman ...

*Rabbi Shlomo Heiman and Rabbi Dovid Bender at a wedding*

One day, Rabbi Moshe Feinstein arrived at the patient's door. He addressed Reb Shlomo, "I know that the doctors are not recommending visitors and therefore most visitors should definitely not come. However, there is a second part to *bikur cholim* and that is, to daven that the sick person recover. Since the *Shechinah* rests over a sick person, *tefillos* are more effective there. So I have come here to daven, the place where my *tefillos* will be most effective." With that introduction, Reb Moshe said one chapter of *Tehillim* and then left.

In those few minutes, Reb Moshe accomplished the mitzvah of *bikur cholim*. He showed the patient his concern and offered a heartfelt *tefillah* on his behalf. He lifted the patient's spirits, as was evident in the way Reb Shlomo's face lit up as he left.

In 1940, Reb Shlomo was diagnosed with cancer. He received treatments and was given a clean bill of health. In grateful joy, he made a *seudas hoda'ah* in Torah Vodaath. A year later, the cancer came back. Reb Shlomo plodded on, still learning, and still giving *shiur*. In Kislev 1944, he was readmitted to the hospital, never again to leave.[50]

Reb Shlomo's passing in Kislev 5705 (1944) was felt keenly by both Rabbi Dovid and Rebbetzin Bender. Reb Dovid had had more than just a *talmid/chaver* relationship with Reb Shlomo. They had spent much time together and Reb Dovid had learned from Reb Shlomo how a *gadol* conducts himself.

After Reb Shlomo's passing, the Benders continued to regularly visit his rebbetzin on Shabbos afternoons. They never considered their visits to the rebbetzin as a "favor" to relieve her loneliness. They were profoundly grateful for what they had gained from Reb Shlomo during his lifetime

---

50. Rabbi Moshe Samuels, a close *talmid* of Rabbi Shlomo Heiman, was at his bedside during the last few days of life, when he was in a semicoma. At one point, Reb Shlomo awoke and murmured, "Bring two chairs, Reb Akiva Eiger and Reb Chaim Ozer are here." How fitting that these were his last words since most of his *shiurim* dealt with answering the questions of Reb Akiva Eiger, and Reb Chaim Ozer had been the one who sent him to Torah Vodaath where he nurtured some of America's greatest leaders.

and wanted to keep that connection even after his death. They regarded their association with his rebbetzin as a privilege and an honor.

JUST AS REVERENCE FOR *GEDOLIM* WAS A CORNERSTONE OF THE BENDER home, another cornerstone was reverence for parents. Even though Rebbetzin Bender was separated from her parents, she never stopped thinking about them or trying to help them. Her letters to them were unusually warm, a reflection of her love and devotion. Reb Dovid was equally devoted to his parents. Those who knew him well found his *kibud av v'eim* extraordinary.[51] One of his friends commented that he treated his mother as a parent treats a child and not the other way around.[52] When she passed away on the 24th of Adar 4705 (March 9, 1945), it was a double blow to Reb Dovid. A few months earlier, he had lost his beloved rebbi, and now he was mourning his mother.

Rebbetzin Pelta Bender's passing was a shock. Although she had had a heart condition, her death was sudden. There was much sadness at the time since the estimates of the Jewish death toll in Europe were rising daily. Moreover, Rebbetzin Basha Bender was losing hope of ever seeing her own parents again. Yet, one cause for grief did not mitigate the other. Pelta Bender's *petirah* left Reb Dovid and his rebbetzin bereft.

The Bender parents and children had had an unusually harmonious relationship. From the moment the young couple arrived on American shores, Rabbi Dovid and Rebbetzin Basha Bender had lived with his parents. Renting an apartment in Williamsburg was expensive and money was tight. Rebbetzin Bender did not yet receive a salary from Bais Yaakov and what Reb Dovid brought in as a *maggid shiur* was meager. It made sound fiscal sense for the two couples to share an apartment.

The Benders were a young couple, yet they never viewed sharing an apartment with their parents as anything less than ideal. What could be better than children living alongside parents? Reb Avrohom was often away and his wife was alone. Why should she not have the benefit of her children's company? Reb Dovid had exceptional respect for his mother and boundless *hakaras hatov* for her devotion, especially for accompanying him to Europe so that he could learn in the Mir.[53] Rebbetzin Bender loved

---

51. Many *talmidim* and friends interviewed commented immediately on his exceptional *kibud av v'eim*.

52. Rabbi Avrohom Pincus.

53. When Rabbi Yeruchem Levovitz's rebbetzin came to America, she marveled at the *mesiras nefesh* of the American boys who had come to learn in Mir. The standard of living in America was so much higher than that in Mir, and they willingly gave that up. Reb Dovid's mother had lived in America, yet she still accompanied her son to the Mir so he should grow in Torah. The *bochurim* had Torah to distract them from the poor living conditions; however, Rebbetzin Pelta Bender did not even have that to compensate for her self-sacrifice (Rabbi Binyomin Zeilberger).

and admired her mother-in-law and, for the rest of her life, had only good things to say about her.

At the *levayah*, Reb Dovid spoke emotionally of his mother's devotion to him. Other speakers included Rabbi Nachum Dovid Herman, Rabbi Moshe Feinstein, and Rabbi Shachne Zohn. Many of Reb Dovid's *talmidim* attended the *levayah* and they came away overwhelmed at how movingly their rebbi eulogized his mother.

IN MARCH 1945, RABBI YAAKOV YITZCHOK RUDERMAN, ROSH YESHIVAH of Ner Israel in Baltimore, approached Reb Dovid and asked him if he would consider returning to the yeshivah. Reb Dovid was in a quandary. The offer was also coming at an opportune time. Now that his rebbi was gone, he was certain that for his own spiritual growth, Baltimore would be a better place. The *bochurim* there were older, and the position would place him second only to Rabbi Ruderman. Besides, after such an emotional year, perhaps the change would be a good thing

On the other hand, for raising children, Baltimore could not compare to Williamsburg. Williamsburg was slowly becoming the "Jerusalem of America" and Reb Dovid was reluctant to leave. Reb Dovid decided to do as he had done before: He would take the position for one *z'man*, commute weekly from Baltimore to New York, and then reassess.

The news took the Torah Vodaath community by surprise. Rabbi Dovid Bender was one of the pillars of the Mesivta. The boys in his *shiur*, and the ones slated to be in his *shiur* the coming year, were very disappointed.[54] Even boys who were not in Reb Dovid's *shiur* felt a strong connection to him and would miss his warm smile. The out-of-towners knew that they were losing a father figure.

After Pesach 1945, Reb Dovid resumed his position as *mashgiach/maggid shiur* in Ner Israel. Despite the difficulties involved, Rebbetzin Bender wholeheartedly supported her husband. She was now alone from Sunday until Friday, with two babies (Esther was not yet two and Blumie was under a year) and another on the way. Her mother-in-law had just passed away, and she missed her help and companionship.

Meanwhile, the Benders planned for the hot summer months ahead. In previous years, they had gone to Seagate with the Heimans, but that was no longer an option. They chose Bagery, a small bungalow colony in Monticello.

REBBETZIN BENDER WAS FEELING VERY WEAK THAT SUMMER. SHE cared for the children and kept the bungalow neat and tidy, but she contin-

---

54. "On each grade level, Torah Vodaath had an *aleph shiur*, a *beis shiur*, and sometimes a *gimmel shiur*. Rabbi Shachne Zohn gave the ninth grade *aleph shiur* and his class went straight to Rabbi Dovid Bender who gave the tenth grade *aleph shiur*. So everyone knew who was supposed to be in Reb Dovid's *shiur* the upcoming year, and they were disappointed. Reb Dovid was a much beloved rebbi" (Rabbi Henoch Cohen).

*Esther and Blumie*

ued to find even the simplest tasks exhausting. Although she did not feel this way before the other two births, she assumed it was her condition and pushed herself to go on until she awoke one morning with a burning fever. Something was very wrong.

Reb Dovid arranged that a neighbor take the children. Then he rushed his wife to the hospital. Premature labor had begun. Rebbetzin Bender gave birth to a baby boy two months early. The child was tiny and the doctors were worried that he would not survive. They whisked him away for medical attention and turned to the mother.

Rebbetzin Bender's fever was dangerously high. The doctors ran blood tests while Reb Dovid contacted family and friends and begged them to pray for her recovery. Finally, the doctors diagnosed her condition as an aggravated kidney infection. Rebbetzin Bender's life hung in the balance. Her family and friends were davening for her and her baby around the clock. Finally, the fever broke. Rebbetzin Bender was on her way to a slow recovery. Almost miraculously, the baby passed his crisis as well.

Her family and friends were shaken; they had come so close to losing their precious Basha. Offers of help poured in, this one wanted to make a meal and that one wanted to take the children for a few hours. Warmth and love, care and concern, abounded.

WHEN SEPTEMBER ROLLED AROUND, REB DOVID DECIDED NOT TO return to Baltimore.[55] Rebbetzin Bender was still weak from her illness, and

---

55. "In 1945, I was in Reb Dovid's *shiur* in Baltimore. He was a tremendous *ba'al masbir* and a wonderful person. I remember him being around all the time. He came on Sunday and left Friday morning after *shiur*. He was devoted to the yeshivah and the *bochurim*, and we loved him in return. When we returned from summer vacation, we were sorry to hear that he was not coming back. Even in the short time that he was there, he formed lifelong connections to the *bochurim*. I kept in touch with him and when I had an occasion to be in New York, I would either call or visit" (R' Yaakov Markowitz).

she had three little ones to care for. In addition, Reb Dovid felt that he was not capable of giving Ner Israel the devotion that it deserved. He felt that for the yeshivah to accommodate its growing population, it needed a *Mashgiach*/Rosh Yeshivah more worthy than he. Reb Dovid recommended his good friend Rabbi Dovid Kronglass as being better suited for the position.[56] Rabbi Ruderman regretfully accepted his resignation, and the two parted warmly.

Reb Dovid approached Rabbi Shraga Feivel Mendelowitz to ask if he could have his old job back. Rabbi Shraga Feivel had other plans. He wanted to turn the upper classes — the seventh and eighth and the *aleph* track of the sixth grade — into its own division with its own principal to supervise the pupils and their progress. He felt that Reb Dovid was the ideal person for this job. Although Reb Shraga Feivel allowed Reb Dovid the choice of returning as a *maggid shiur*, he strongly encouraged him to accept the position of principal.

At the time, Torah Vodaath was the largest yeshivah elementary school in America, and it was growing fast. The principal of the upper grades was considered a very prestigious position.[57] Reb Dovid hesitated, because he knew that being a principal would not give him the same type of satisfaction as being a *maggid shiur*. Ultimately, Reb Shraga Feivel prevailed, and Reb Dovid embarked on a new career.

REBBETZIN BENDER SLOWLY REGAINED HER STRENGTH. THE BENDER home continued to grow and expand, poised to embrace the needs of the time which, in 1945, included the arrival of the survivors.

---

56. Rabbi Elya Svei has repeated, in awe, on a number of occasions, how unique Reb Dovid was. Most people will hang on to a position, regardless of whether or not it suits them.

Rabbi Dovid Kronglass needed no introduction to the faculty of Ner Israel. Rabbi Naftoli Neuberger (1918-2005), *menahel* of Ner Israel and Rabbi Ruderman's brother-in-law, had been a *talmid* of Rabbi Dovid Kronglass in the Mir and was the driving force behind bringing Rabbi Dovid Kronglass to Baltimore as *Mashgiach*.

57. Rabbi Don Ungarisher.

*Chapter Thirty-Three*

# Bais Yaakov Survivors Rebuild[58]

### Poland, 5705 (1945)

*Dear Basya,*

*A*FTER THE LONG YEARS OF ENSLAVEMENT WE ARE FINALLY *free. In spite of the indescribable pain that we experienced, in spite of the deep losses that burn our open wounds and refuse to let them heal, in spite of the terrible loneliness ... we strengthened ourselves in emunah and bitachon. We went out into the world, full of conviction and belief that we will never again bang on sealed doors, that now the world will open (its doors) for us!*

*A few weeks back in the old country quickly forced us into a different reality.*

*We, therefore, feel forced and obligated to leave this country. It is a week since I have come to this camp.[59] Even on our way here, we spoke about finding a place to live — such as Czechoslovakia or Germany — an asylum, until we find a haven. For our type of Jew, however, these (options) are not feasible. These choices are for those seeking to assimilate.*

*... I received a letter from Chana Zehnwirth,[60] in which she lists all the teachers who are with her in New York, and you are among them. I am writing to you*

---

58. The letters in this chapter have been translated and condensed.

59. The word in this letter is unclear. Perhaps she is referring to some kind of sanatorium or displaced persons camp.

60. Chana Zehnwirth later married Rabbi Shlomo Rottenberg of the Mirrer Yeshivah. See Page 384.

because I know that your husband is a Mirrer yeshivaman (Avrohom[61] sometimes used to mention his name). If I believe that there are still Jews who can truly understand our plight, to the degree that it would force them to provide us with true help — not parcels or money or clothing — but help in finding for us a safe haven, where we can live the rest of our lives as Jews, then it would be Litvishe yeshivaleit!

Is Avrohom Pincus in America? What about Yud'l Gordon? Dovid Kronglass? They were good friends of my husband. Perhaps they can obtain visas for a small group (myself included) to America.

Warmest greetings to you and all the other teachers,

Tzila Neugerscholl-Orlean

REBBETZIN BENDER SIGHED HEAVILY. SHE WAS HAPPY; SHE WAS SAD. She was happy her beloved friend had survived. She was sad for the pain that poured from the simple paper lying on the table.

Tzila had always been special.[62] As a student in seminary, she stood out in intelligence and maturity. As a teacher, she became a beloved role model. Tzila married Rabbi Avrohom Orlean, a *talmid* of the Mirrer Yeshivah. They barely had time to begin their life together when the war broke out and they were separated.

Was there any way to convey the intensity of emotion that gripped her when she first read her friend's words? Would her reply do justice to the writer, validating her pain while rejoicing in her survival? Could mere words bridge the vast chasm that time and suffering created between them? Did she have any choice, but to try?

*Dear Basya!*

*With an inner thrill, I awaited a letter from you. Will it lend itself to warm feelings? Will it communicate the joy of a close one who is elated that I have survived, and the sorrow that a friend would feel for my losses? Through your letter I discovered that I (still) have kinship in the world.*

*You should be aware that as much as our lives were shattered, we have become stronger in our emunah. We do not know how. It is our greatest wonder, but it is a fact. Without any tricks or contemplation, we were strengthened in our beliefs.*

---

61. Rabbi Avrohom Orlean was Tzila Neugerscholl's husband.

62. Rebbetzin Tzila Sorotzkin/Orlean (1911-1998) was one of Sarah Schenirer's early students, a teacher in several Bais Yaakov schools, and in Bais Yaakov of Crakow. Tzila married Rabbi Avrohom Orlean, brother of Rabbi Yehuda Leib Orlean. During World War II, she became known as the White Angel in Auschwitz, saving multitudes of lives at her own risk. In Eretz Yisroel she married Rabbi Elchonon Sorotzkin, the oldest son of Rabbi Zalman Sorotzkin. Here too, her home was a magnet to all those who yearned to glean from her wisdom and counsel. Rebbetzin Sorotzkin was also involved in many aspects of the Bais Yaakov movement in Eretz Yisroel.

*Our fate is not individual and we bear it with courage and strength. We, therefore, do not need, cannot stand, and do not want pity from anyone.*

*I thought Chavi Weinberg was in Eretz Yisroel; she always was inclined toward Eretz Yisroel. Send her my best regards. Why does she not write?*

*Be well, best regards and write to me about your life.*

*Tzila*

*Tell me, Basya, do you know if the Carmels from Crakow are also in Shanghai? Is Vichna Eisen with you, maybe? And Rivka Eidelman?* [63]

BASHA REREAD THE LETTER FOR THE TENTH TIME. YES, KNOWING TZILA, Basha truly believed that Tzila emerged from her *Gehinnom* strengthened in *emunah*, unfalteringly loyal to her Creator, scornful of pity, head held high, and ready to rebuild. Tzila wrote in the plural: we have become stronger in our *emunah*, we have been strengthened in our beliefs. Who is the "we" of whom she writes? How many emerged from hell on earth with their faith intact?

A letter arrived from Rebbetzin Grunfeld. Perhaps it would shed light on Basha's questions.

*My Dear Basya,*

*Yes, it is very, very strange. Here I am, in Cyprus, spending hours and hours with our Bais Yaakov girls who are as fine and noble and strong as they have ever been. Only they are so very, very few. What these people have gone through no Yirmiyahu will be able to tell. They keep themselves wonderfully erect and strong. I have written an article. Perhaps, I shall be able to send you a print. At any rate, Frau Schenirer is alive here. She is walking through the miserable tent and mothers everyone ...*

*Yours,*

*Yehudis (Rosenbaum) Grunfeld*

BAIS YAAKOV GIRLS WERE IN CYPRUS, POLAND, PARIS, AND SHANGHAI. Light-years away from the carefree days on the grassy hills of Rabka, life-times away from the small, one-room Bais Yaakov schools that dotted the communities of Poland. These women were scattered across the globe, yet nonetheless, united as idealistic Bais Yaakov students and teachers.

At the end of the war, as weary survivors looked toward the future, they found that the title "Bais Yaakov Girl" invited warmth and opened doors.

---

63. Chava Weinberg married Rabbi Avrohom Pincus, Vichna Eisen married Rabbi Boruch Kaplan, and Rivka Eidelman married Rabbi Mordechai Springer. All were good friends of the Benders and are mentioned elsewhere in this book. The Carmel family was a prominent Crakow family whose sons had learned in Mir.

Young women who had lost their entire families found family among fellow Bais Yaakov teachers and graduates.[64]

AS FAMILY, BAIS YAAKOV WOMEN AND GIRLS GAVE EACH OTHER support and comfort. They also felt a connection and responsibility to all members of *Klal Yisroel*, regardless of one's level of religious observance. Fraulein Dr. Hamburger,[65] a former teacher of Rebbetzin Bender, wrote to her student after the war.

> *... The situations of the few who have returned from the deportations are certainly tragic; not only from the physical aspect, but also from the spiritual and emotional side. Their reactions are sad; one has not the heart to rebuke the youth who are broken and do not keep (Yiddishkeit) anymore ... Since I came here, I have been doing social work with adolescents who have returned. As for teaching, nothing was happening. Then, suddenly, a seminary came into existence; one cannot sufficiently describe the (positive) psychological effect it had ... My latest seminary group consisted of six girls. Since the last summer, they have been studying with the diligence of pioneers. Today, they are all in Eretz Yisroel. Some of them continued their studies and some of them are already teaching. The main thing is that they are living in the right circles ...*

CHARACTERISTIC OF A BAIS YAAKOV TEACHER, FRAULEIN HAMBURGER was both realistic and idealistic. She saw the situation with open eyes: people were returning, broken and disheartened, many too lethargic and weak to continue to hold onto their *Yiddishkeit*. She understood and was saddened, but never jaded. Idealistically, she took up the challenge and began teaching survivors. She was confident that with a little help, they could reclaim their heritage, they could be steered onto the correct path, and, ultimately, they would not be lost to *Klal Yisroel*.

Rabbi Boruch and Rebbetzin Kaplan were of the same mind-set. When they heard of the many survivor children who ended up in Sweden, the Kaplans acted. In Sweden, these girls were in grave spiritual danger. In their kindness, Swiss people visited the refugees in hospitals and took them into their homes, often adopting these girls who were then forever lost to *Yiddishkeit*. Rabbi Binyamin Ze'ev Yaakovson[66] and his wife opened

---

64. "In any city that I was ever in, if I knew that there was a Bais Yaakov teacher there, I would go to meet her. If I was ever stranded, anywhere, I knew that if I could find a Bais Yaakov teacher or student, even one I had never met, I would be comfortable saying that I am from Bais Yaakov, can I stay with you?" (Rebbetzin Devorah [Applegrad] Cohn). Mrs. Pearl Benisch makes a similar statement in *To Vanquish the Dragon* (p. 61).

65. See page 145.

66. See Biography Section for information about Rabbis Boruch Kaplan and Binyamin Ze'ev Yaakovson.

a school in Lidingo (Stockholm) and saved many of these girls. But Sweden was not a place conducive to creating pure Jewish homes. There were few *ehrliche* yeshivah *bochurim* for the girls to marry. Orthodoxy in Sweden was weak. The only answer was to help these girls immigrate to the larger and stronger Jewish communities of Eretz Yisroel or New York.

Rabbi Boruch Kaplan insisted that neither money nor bureaucracy be an issue. They must work to bring as many girls as possible to New York. Rebbetzin Bender traveled to Washington several times to participate in hearings that would enable more girls to immigrate.

Many of these girls did immigrate to America, becoming wards of Bais Yaakov. The staff and students of Bais Yaakov of Williamsburg welcomed the newcomers warmly. Not all of the refugees came to Bais Yaakov as students. Some were older girls, past the age for sitting in classes, and ready to move on in life. Bais Yaakov took care of these young women as well. Bais Yaakov provided them with food, clothing, and everything that they needed to settle comfortably into Williamsburg.

BAIS YAAKOV GIRLS. BAIS YAAKOV TEACHERS. BAIS YAAKOV SURVIVORS. Bais Yaakov was their bond, standing for much more than family and fraternity. A true Bais Yaakov graduate had hope for *Yiddishkeit*, love for *Klal Yisroel*, visions of a better future, and belief in her ability to rebuild.

### Chapter Thirty-Four

# An Era of Rebuilding

"I REMEMBER WHEN REB DOVID AND HIS REBBETZIN WOULD *stand by the window, in that small apartment on Hooper Street, and look down at Lee Avenue across from the Tzelemer Beis Medrash… and there were Yidden walking, and they were thinking: Maybe there is someone who needs a meal for Shabbos. Maybe there is someone who needs an achsanya, a place to stay. Yes, their place was 'hashkifah mim'on kodsh'cha, on the watch from on high.' "*[67]

THROUGHOUT THE 1940'S, EVEN BEFORE THE WAR ENDED, REFUGEES from Europe trickled into America. How well Rebbetzin Bender remembered her own arrival. [68] Even in the wonderful warm home of parents-in-laws who loved her, even with her husband at her side, America was so new, different, and strange. For the first few months, Rebbetzin Bender longed for familiarity and that only dissipated slowly over time. When she heard of a friend who just arrived or saw a stranger from her window, that ache was reawakened.

---

67. Rabbi Mordechai Shapiro in his *hesped* for Rebbetzin Bender.

68. Rebbetzin Bender had gone through her own transition period. Always one to seek solutions, she enrolled herself in English classes held in the evenings at Eastern District Public High School. Her accent never completely disappeared, but she spoke very proper, grammatically correct English. She was happy with her accomplishment. She felt that the only way for her to reach American girls was through speaking their language. Furthermore, knowledge of English made her feel more comfortable in her new home.

Below is Reb Nosson seated with Rabbi Aharon Kotler on Purim in Lakewood Yeshivah. Between Reb Aharon and Reb Nosson is the "Purim Rav."

*Rabbi Nosson Meir Wachtfogel (1910-1999) learned in Kelm, Yeshivas Rabbeinu Yitzchok Elchonon, and Mir. Reb Nosson remained in Kelm until 1940 when all British nationals were evacuated from Lithuania. Then Reb Nosson and his new bride headed for Australia and from there to New York. He joined a kollel in White Plains which led him to Beth Medrash Govoha of Lakewood. He served as the revered Mashgiach in the Lakewood Yeshivah for over 50 years, guiding thousands of talmidim, and pioneering the establishment of Lakewood kollelim across America and as far away as Australia.*

Rabbi Nosson Wachtfogel and his rebbetzin arrived in New York a few years after the war broke out, and went directly to the Bender home. Rebbetzin Bender was overjoyed to see her dear friend from seminary and was eager to make her feel welcome in her new home. Unknown to the Wachtfogels, she and Reb Dovid vacated their own bedroom so that their guests would be more comfortable. The Wachtfogels stayed with the Benders for several weeks, until they found an apartment of their own.

Nochum Velvel Dessler, the young son of Rabbi Eliyahu Eliezer Dessler, arrived alone during the war years. He entered Torah Vodaath, and Reb Dovid noticed the lonely boy in the halls of the yeshivah. Reb Dovid invited Nochum Velvel to his home for Shabbos, for supper during the week, and for a bit of family atmosphere whenever the *bochur* wanted. Nochum Velvel spent many evenings in the Bender home drinking in the warm *hachnosas orchim*.[69]

"Who can we help today?" was the Bender mantra. Their home seemed to have a revolving door. Anyone who would accept their friendliness was welcomed.

Rabbi Avrohom Kalmanowitz arrived in February 1940. He remarried and his new rebbetzin, Minna Kalmanowitz, became the instant mother to a house full of children. The family was still adjusting to the move from Europe to America with all the changes it entailed, and Rabbi Avrohom Kalmanowitz was thoroughly occupied with trying to save *Klal Yisroel* in Europe. Rebbetzin Bender intuitively understood that the new Rebbetzin Kalmanowitz might be finding it difficult to cope, and she made a point of stopping in at the Kalmanowitz home and lending a subtle hand.

---

69. Told by Rabbi Nochum Velvel Dessler to Rabbi Yaakov Bender.

*"Let me mention just one period, the time when the Mirrer Yeshivah landed on the shores of America; (in the Bender home) their doors opened wide for the talmidim who found the warmth and chizuk they needed within. How many shidduchim were arranged in that home! The Benders revived an entire group of people through the beneficence and kindness of their home — a home that radiated benevolence at all stages … Their home was a place of giving …"*[70]

*"… a home of mesiras nefesh and chessed, the address for anyone in need … 'Al sheloshah d'varim ha'olam omed. Al haTorah v'al ha'avodah v'al gemilus chassadim — The world depends on three things: on Torah study, on the service [of G-d], and on kind deeds' (Pirkei Avos 1:2). Their world, their home, included all of these attributes."*[71]

WHEN THE WAR ENDED AND REFUGEES POURED INTO WILLIAMSBURG, the Bender home was where many found a warm, welcome, listening ear, an understanding heart, a hot cup of coffee, and a thick slice of chocolate cake.[72]

Though the Benders extended themselves to any refugee, their friends from Mir were first on their minds. When Reb Dovid heard of a new group of Mirrer *talmidim* arriving from Europe, he was at the pier to greet them.[73] He brought them to his home and eagerly offered to help them get settled. He invited them for meals on Shabbos or, if they preferred to just come for a visit, after a Shabbos meal, during the week, whenever they wanted.[74] His guests accepted his wonderful hospitality with gratitude.

This era of rebuilding was an era of both hope and pain. A letter from Dr. Bloch, a family friend from Otvock, was laden with these emotions.

*… WE HAVE NOT WRITTEN TO YOU IN A LONG TIME BECAUSE WE WENT from our "loving" Poland to France … Poland is saturated with Jewish blood. We heard news about everything that was happening, but could do nothing about it. We know that everyone is anti-Semitic but it is hard to believe what really happened … Here in Paris, we are quite comfortable, but if we had the option of traveling — even though it is very difficult for us and we are very nervous — we would look*

---

70. Rabbi Zelig Epstein in his *hesped* for Rebbetzin Bender.

71. Rabbi Binyomin Zeilberger in his *hesped* for Rebbetzin Bender.

72. "The first house I came to off the boat from Europe was the Bender home" (Moe Friedman at the *shivah*).

73. "When I arrived in New York on Erev Rosh Hashanah of 1946, Rabbi Dovid Bender greeted us at the station" (Rabbi Moshe Pivovitz).

74. "I remember how Reb Dovid would go to the pier to meet the Mirrer *talmidim* so that they would immediately see a familiar face. I ate at the Bender home almost every Shabbos. The house was always full of people, many of them Mirrer *talmidim* coming for a visit. I remember one prominent *talmid chacham* who had suffered tremendously, yet in the Bender house he was warm and entertaining. The atmosphere was upbeat and happy" (Rabbi Meir Shapiro).

*for a better place where our children could be educated in the proper way, where we could become citizens, where we would have better living conditions. Is there such a country?*

REBBETZIN BENDER HAD HER OWN PAIN, TINGED WITH HOPE. SHE ANX-iously awaited every letter, scanning the envelopes for her parents' dear handwriting. Eventually, she learned of their deaths in a letter from Dr. Poupko, a relative and friend. R' Yankev Epstein passed away from a heart attack in November 1942; Rebbetzin Lifsha Epstein was last seen in the Warsaw Ghetto, before its destruction. Knowledge brought closure and despite her own pain, Rebbetzin Bender continued to reach out to survivors.

The mail became a paradoxical vehicle of both joy and sadness. As Rabbi Dovid Bender slit open the latest envelope, his heart fluttered. What would today's correspondence bring?

"Basha," Reb Dovid called out excitedly, "come here quick! You will never believe this — the letter is from my dear friend, R' Zundel,[75] informing us that he is, *baruch Hashem*, alive. He writes that during the war, just before he and his wife became separated, he told her that when the war ended, if they both survive, they should contact us and we would make sure that they find each other. Just a few minutes ago, a telegram arrived from his wife, announcing that she too survived!" The Benders exulted in the rare joy of the moment.

"OH LOOK!" REBBETZIN BENDER HAPPILY CALLED OUT ONE DAY. "IT is from my good friend, Rochel Cisner. She is in Paris with her husband and children. How wonderful! I wonder how I can help."

Never one to waste time, Rebbetzin Bender put together a package of clothing and shipped it overseas. Remembering how Rochel looked as a girl in seminary, Rebbetzin Bender sent two appropriately sized dresses. Little did she know that her friend was now expecting twins, and neither of the two dresses fit. Ever innovative, Rochel Cisner took the dresses apart and made one big dress out of the two.

Rebbetzin Bender sent the Cisners $100, enough to heat the Cisner home for an entire year. She and Rebbetzin Kaplan signed the affidavits that enabled the family to get visas. There were many letters, back and forth, discussing various arrangements. The return address was always 168 Hooper Street.

When the Cisners finally arrived in America, they moved into a hostel set up by the HIAS as temporary housing, but for their first Shabbos they went to the Benders.

---

75. Not his real name. The Bender children recalled the story but not who was involved.

"Guess what?" Rebbetzin Bender announced to the children one fine Friday morning, "We are having guests for Shabbos. A friend of mine from Crakow is coming with her family, and they will be staying right here, with us!"

A few hours later, they arrived. Seven-year-old Esther stared wide eyed as the oldest girl sidled up next to her mother. *My!* she thought to herself in awe, *How very big she is!*

Yocheved Cisner did not feel big at all. She was tired from the trip, confused by all the changes, and grateful to this wonderful warm woman who seemed so happy to see them.[76]

---

76. Mrs. Y. Linchner.

# Part II:
# **Williamsburg**
## 5690-5718 / 1930-1958

*Chapter Thirty-Five:*
## A Bit of Background

*Chapter Thirty-Six:*
## Entering a New Era

*Chapter Thirty-Seven:*
## Meet the Neighborhood

Information in this section is based on *Williamsburg: A Jewish Community in Transition* by Gershon Kranzler, and interviews with the Bender family and Mrs. Sudy Rosengarten. Other sources are documented.

# A Bit of Background

$\mathcal{A}$T THE TURN OF THE 20TH CENTURY, WILLIAMSBURG WAS distinctly gentile; a Jew in the neighborhood was a novel sight. Year by year, a slow trickle of Jewish families began settling in the neighborhood. They were looking for an upscale alternative to the Lower East Side. By the late 1930's, Williamsburg, New York was considered a Jewish neighborhood.

JEWISH WILLIAMSBURG SPANNED APPROXIMATELY TWO AVENUE blocks — from Bedford to Lee and from Lee to Marcy — in one direction, and Lynch Street to the South Streets in the other direction. While its flavor was decidedly Jewish — on Friday night there were so many young people taking an after-the-meal stroll down Bedford Avenue, it was nicknamed Lechah Dodi Boulevard[1] — the neighborhood was still, by and large, not religious. It was common for men to rise for *Shacharis* on a Shabbos morning and then head for work.

This allegiance to heritage, although not to religion, fueled the growth of the large formal shuls that dominated Williamsburg of the 30's and 40's — the Clymer Street Shul, the Hewes Street Shul, the Keap Street Shul, the South Second Street Shul, and the South Fifth Street Shul. These large impressive buildings, some of which had once been churches, commanded attention. They were the kind of shuls American Jewry gravitated to: ele-

---

1. *Reb Chaim Gelb: A Life of Chessed* by Rabbi David Fisher, p. 51.

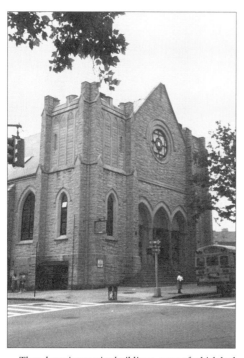

*...These large impressive buildings, some of which had once been churches, commanded attention...*
*The Hewes Street Shul*

gant exteriors, spacious interiors, equipped with a *chazzan*, a rabbi, and many congregants. On the High Holy Days, some of these shuls were filled to capacity; on a regular Shabbos, attendance was sparse. These shuls catered to the Williamsburgers: second- or third-generation Americans, many of whom had parents who, at one point, struggled to remain religious. Some were successful and some were not. Their children were more Orthodox in theory than in practice. Shul membership was often their most solid connection to *Yiddishkeit*.

The inevitable result of the "Orthodox by identity while secular in reality" trend was the gradual disenchantment of its youth. Young Jewish Americans whose parents had already compromised on many aspects of Judaism were quick to discard whatever was left. The rare young idealist became disillusioned with the large, somewhat pompous, institutionalized type of shul, where seniority was more important than religious fervor, where the honors went to the wealthy who outbid everyone else, and where excess singing was considered a waste of time.[2] Although these shuls served the valuable purpose of giving its members some religious identity and providing essential religious services, many of the young members abandoned the synagogues of their parents. Some opted for no religion at all and others found alternative places of worship.

In the early 1920's, one idealistic group of young American-born youth started davening in the Young Israel on Bedford Avenue and Ross Street. The members of the Young Israel ranged from former congregants of the big institutionalized shuls to those who had grown up davening in basement *shtiebelach*. Their common denominator was their vision for young Jewish Americans: They wanted a shul where they could be active participants, they wanted *shiurim* that they could understand, and they wanted

2. *A Fire in His Soul: The Story of Irving Bunim* by Amos Bunim, pp. 27-28.

*The first Young Israel of Williamsburg*

a place where they could grow in *Yiddishkeit*. The Young Israel Movement, begun in 1911, provided all of the above and saved generations of American Jewish youth.[3] Over the years, especially as other viable, more religious options emerged, Young Israel lost some of its momentum as a vehicle for religious progress. Nonetheless, in the 1940's, Young Israel was still a positive force in keeping young Jewish Americans religious.

Members of the famous Poilisher Shtiebel, another Williamsburg institution, met in a plain nondescript row house on Division and Marcy Avenues. As all-American as the Young Israel was, that was how European the Poilisher Shtiebel was. Many of its 300 members had beards and *peiyos*, spoke English with a Yiddish accent,[4] and waxed nostalgic about the "Old Country."

The Poilisher Shtiebel was a hub of activity. At a time when there was no unemployment insurance, welfare, social security, or health insurance, there was a serious need for internal social welfare programs. The Poilisher Shtiebel Gemilas Chessed Committee filled the gap. They raised money for the sick, needy, and elderly. Members were also active in helping their brethren keep Shabbos and encouraging families to send their boys to yeshivah. They helped people find jobs where they would not have to work on Shabbos. They enlisted the aid of wealthy people to co-sign bank loans for small businesses so that they could close on Shabbos. In addition, they raised money for yeshivos.[5]

---

3. For a comprehensive analysis of this phenomenon, see *A Fire in His Soul: The Story of Irving Bunim* by Amos Bunim.

4. One of the mainstays of the Poilisher Shtiebel was R' Shimon Shain (1880-1963) who, for many years, gave the *Mishnayos shiur* between *Minchah* and *Ma'ariv;* he was the *ba'al korei* and *ba'al tokei'a*. R' Shimon Shain was a *shochet* who immigrated to America from Mohilev, Russia. He retained his beard and *peiyos*, his European outlook and manner, and his ideals.

5. *Reb Chaim Gelb: A Life of Chessed* by Rabbi David Fisher, pp. 105-106.

**... At all hours of the day and night, the Poilisher Shtiebel was open and active, the chant of learning echoing down the street ...**

*The Poilisher Shtiebel –
A Williamsburg institution*

At all hours of the day and night, the Poilisher Shtiebel was open and active, the chant of learning echoing down the street at all hours. Scholars gravitated to its doors, certain that they would find just the sefer they were looking for on the well-stocked shelves that lined the *beis medrash*. The Poilisher Shtiebel had all kinds of seforim, from the standard *Shas* and *Mishnah Berurah* to many more esoteric seforim. The atmosphere of learning there was stimulating and contagious.

Nonetheless, the Poilisher Shtiebel would never be a means for bridging the generations. Most American Jewish youth found its members quaint and curious, but not a *minyan* they would like to join since they regarded this group as out of touch with contemporary American reality. The young and the old were too different to share the same shul experience. Then, in 1926, Mesivta Torah Vodaath opened its doors.

While still carrying an appeal to the older, more traditional generation, Mesivta Torah Vodaath created a refreshing option for young, idealistic Jewish youth. The youth naturally felt at home in their own mesivta, even while their fathers and rebbeim were naturally accorded more prestige. There was a sense that Mesivta Torah Vodaath was one big happy family where there was ample room for young and old and everything in between.

The Mesivta, as it was fondly called, had daily *minyanim* from dawn until late morning to enable anyone who wanted a *minyan* to find one at a time that suited him. Unlike the ceremonial services of the other synagogues, the Torah Vodaath *minyanim* were comfortably informal; its *beis medrash* was a lively hub of communal activity with as many as five simultaneous *minyanim* (in the main hall and the side rooms), all within earshot of one another. Concurrently, there could be someone giving a *shiur* in the back of the room as three men caught up on the news while rolling up their *tefillin* straps.

On Shabbos, many illustrious personalities graced the Torah Vodaath *minyan*. Rabbi Uri Meir Kahanow was the unofficial Rabbi of the *minyan*.

Rabbi Shlomo Heiman was in attendance, as was Rabbi Shraga Feivel Mendelowitz and other members of the Torah Vodaath staff. Rabbi Dr. David Stern, spiritual leader of the Young Israel of the Lower East Side, davened in Torah Vodaath in the morning and then trekked over the Williamsburg Bridge to the Lower East Side, to speak to his congregants. When Rabbi Avrohom Bender was in town he davened in Torah Vodaath, as did Rabbi Avrohom Kalmanowitz when he arrived from Europe in 1940.

Although the *nusach* and *minhag* of Yeshivas Torah Vodaath tended to be *Chassidish*, these Lithuanian scholars felt comfortable there. Torah Vodaath succeeded in creating a comfortable blend of Europe and America, *Litvish* and *Chassidish*, under one roof.

> ... There was a sense that Mesivta Torah Vodaath was one big happy family where there was ample room for young and old and everything in between ...

*Mesivta Torah Vodaath – 505 Bedford Avenue*

Other American-born Williamsburgers were interested in something smaller, something even more European and traditional, but a place where they, as Americans, would feel at home. They gravitated either to the Bostoner Rebbe on Bedford Avenue and Wilson Street or the Stoliner Shtiebel on Rodney Street near Lee Avenue.

Rabbi Pinchus Dovid Horowitz,[6] the first Bostoner Rebbe, introduced beautiful soul-stirring melodies from Yerushalayim to Williamsburg in 1939. Young to middle-aged American-born Jewish men were drawn by the sincerity and emotion that these melodies evoked. They were mostly working people who never really had an opportunity to learn. Some attended Rabbi Moshe Lieber's daily classes, held at 5 a.m. to enable the participants to daven and rush off to work. Others came only on Shabbos for a weekly injection of spirituality.

After the first Bostoner Rebbe passed away, his followers turned to his son, fondly known as Reb Moishele, for leadership and guidance. Reb

---

6. Rabbi Pinchus Dovid Horowitz (1876-1941) was born in the Old City of Yerushalayim, and learned in Tzfas and Tiveria as a young man. In 1914 he became Rav of the Reiyim Ahuvim shul in Brownsville, Brooklyn. In 1915 he became the leader of the Boston Chassidic community, thus becoming the Bostoner Rebbe. In 1939 he moved to Williamsburg and established his *shtiebel*, where Jews from all walks of life flocked to the elevated atmosphere.

*Rabbi Moshe Horowitz (1910-1985) was a son of the first Bostoner Rebbe, Rabbi Pinchus Dovid Horowitz. In 1941, Reb Moshe succeeded his father as Rebbe in Williamsburg, while his younger brother, Reb Levi Yitzchok, returned to Boston. Reb Moshe was instrumental in the early development of Yeshivah Torah Vodaath, was active in the leadership of Agudas Yisroel of America, and in the Vaad Hatzalah. Reb Moshe later founded the Bostoner Battei Medrash of Crown Heights and of Boro Park.*

Moishele was a Williamsburg personality who followed his father's lead, embracing young American Jews with warmth.

The marble-columned facade of the Bostoner shul was misleading. Inside, all on the same floor, there was a large but simple room for the men, a small side room for the women, a *mikveh* in the back, and living quarters for the Rebbe and his family. Since the Rebbe always had a houseful of guests — *meshulachim* from Eretz Yisroel and poor people from everywhere — the large apartment was always crowded with people, warmth, and life.

Another prayer option for the American layman or youth who yearned for an inspiring davening was the Stoliner Shtiebel at 156 Rodney Street near Lee Avenue As those inside poured out their souls in service to their Maker in loud, boisterous, heartfelt *tefillah*, their voices reverberated from the modest building all the way down the block.

The Stoliner Rebbe became mentor and host to the fledgling Zeirei Agudas Yisroel of Williamsburg. Zeirei Agudas Yisroel was founded in 1926 by a group of 25 young men from solid Orthodox families who wanted to create a youth group, in the spirit of the ideals of the Agudas Yisroel Movement founded in Europe. The Young Israel Movement allowed a certain laxity that these staunchly religious young men shunned. The Zeirei founders wanted a youth group that would reflect their ideals, allow them to grow, and accomplish what they envisioned was possible.

In the beginning, Zeirei Agudas Yisroel was more of a social organization than an agent of change. Its members assembled in the *beis medrash* of the Stoliner Rebbe to discuss ideas and plans, to learn together, and to hear encouraging words from their mentor. Eventually, they rented a basement for regular *minyanim* and meetings. Their classes became more regular,

... The Stoliner Rebbe became mentor and host to the fledgling Zeirei Agudas Yisroel of Williamsburg. Zeirei Agudas Yisroel was founded in 1926 ... in the spirit of the ideals of the Agudas Yisroel Movement founded in Europe ...

The Agudah Building at 616 Bedford Avenue

Rabbi Yaakov Chaim Perlow

*Rabbi Yaakov Chaim Perlow (1888-1946) was the third son of Rabbi Yisroel of Stolin. In 1922 Reb Yaakov Chaim immigrated to America, settling in Williamsburg, Brooklyn, where he established a shtiebel, and became a spiritual guide to many fellow Jews. Occasionally, the Rebbe traveled to visit his Chassidim and on one such visit to Detroit, he passed away there. Reb Yaakov Chaim left no descendants and his brother, Reb Yochanan, reestablished the Stoliner court in 1948.*

they established a system to take care of their own (visiting the sick and helping the poor and needy), and they established junior youth groups as a means of fostering optimism and happiness among the younger neighborhood boys.

By 1938, concurrent with an influx of young refugees, mainly from Germany and Austria who had fled Europe just before the war, Zeirei Agudas Yisroel outgrew their rented location and purchased their own building on 616 Bedford Avenue. These two events initiated an era of growth for Zeirei Agudas Yisroel. The top two floors of 616 Bedford were converted into a Refugee Home that offered temporary shelter to young refugee men who arrived in the United States alone, without family or friends to help them. Zeirei members embraced the newcomers, invited them for Shabbos meals and looked for ways to ease their adjustments. After moving out of the Refugee Home, many became permanent members of Zeirei.

Zeirei services were extended to all refugees who knocked on its doors, looking for a place to belong. Some became long-term members and others did not. Some of the refugees, mainly those from Austria-Hungary, were of a very different background and mentality; even the good-natured warmth of the Zeirei members could not bridge that gap. These refugees thanked their hosts for the warm welcome, but graciously seceded from the movement and created their own unique community. The leader of the first such group was the Tzelemer Rav, Rabbi Levi Yitzchak Greenwald, himself a European refugee, whose last rabbinic position was in Tzelem, Hungary.

The Tzelemer Rav was of Polish/*Chassidish* background, but since he had served as a Rav in Vienna, he was familiar with the background and mentality of the typical "Oberlander" Jew. "Oberlander" was a generic term used for an Austro-Hungarian Jew. The attire, breeding, and culture of the Oberlander *Yidden* were similar to their *Yekkish* (German) brethren. Both groups were polished, cultured, loyal to their Rav and community, active in social welfare programs, and supportive of any campaign their Rav advocated. They remained a close-knit group, Middle European as opposed to Eastern European, but certainly not American.

The Tzelemer shul, Cong. Arugas HaBosem, opened over the A&P supermarket on Lee Avenue, just opposite the Benders' home. Shabbos morning, when the services there ended, a small crowd of elegant and sophisticated men and women filed out. Even those who arrived penniless had an aura of aristocracy and their presence subtly added a new dimension to the neighborhood.

The Tzelemer Rav was a visionary. In Williamsburg, he created a *kehillah* structure similar to those that had existed in Europe. He opened a *cheder*, appointed a *Rosh HaKahal*, and instituted reforms that many thought could not exist in America, most notably, readily available *cholov Yisroel* (milk). He established a new standard in *shechitah*. R' Boruch Greenhut, a refugee who came at around the same time as the Rav, became the Tzelemer *shochet*. Frankel's Butcher Shop, on Lee Avenue near Hooper Street, sold Tzelemer meat. The standard of kashrus of Tzelemer *shechitah* was considered so high quality that people from as far as Chicago had Tzelemer meat sent to them.[7]

True to their nature and breeding, the Tzelemer Rav's Oberlander *kehillah* embraced his innovations and standards. While melding into the Williamsburg community, they retained their *kehillah* identity.

Since the Tzelemer Rav came from a *Chassidish* background, his Oberlander *kehillah* shared his affinity to *Chassidus*. Like their Rav, many Tzelemer *kehillah* members stemmed from Polish/*Galicianer* families who had transplanted themselves to Hungary. While they were culturally very

---

7. "My mother used to send Tzelemer meat to my cousins, the Hecht family, from Chicago" (Mrs. S. Rosengarten).

similar to the *Yekkishe* community, they davened *nusach Sefard* and had many *Chassidishe minhagim*. Over the years, the *kehillah* became progressively more *Chassidish*.

Hence the emergence of yet another group, the Ashkenazic Oberlander community. This group was also originally from Vienna, but they traced their heritage to the Chasam Sofer and were staunchly Ashkenazic. Many had been members of the illustrious Schiffschul of Vienna, the aristocracy of Viennese Orthodoxy. The Schiffschul had disaffiliated itself from the Reform elements in Hungary and created its own *kehillah*, a *kehillah* that became a model for other *kehillos*. These Viennese refugees, these Oberlander Ashkenazim, were looking to recreate their same *kehillah* in Williamsburg. They called themselves K'hal Adas Yereim, but many referred to them simply as "Vien."

Both Tzelem and Vien introduced religious practices that second-and-third-generation American Jewry considered almost fanatical. Although most Oberlander men shaved, they were not embarrassed to be seen in the street or at work unshaven during periods of mourning and Chol HaMoed. Married women covered their hair completely. They kept the genders strictly separate in all social settings. They drank only *cholov Yisroel* (milk) and were more stringent in other areas of halachah. They introduced new standards that their American counterparts would soon be scrambling to meet.

*The Chasam Sofer –*
*the mentor of Oberlander Jewry*

*Rabbi Moshe Sofer (1762/3 -1839), known as the Chasam Sofer, learned under Rabbi Nosson Adler and the Haflaah, Rabbi Pinchas Horowitz. He held several rabbinic positions. In 1806 his first wife died and he then married Rabbi Akiva Eiger's daughter. That same year he was chosen as the Rav of Pressburg, the largest Jewish community in the area. The Chasam Sofer became famous as the greatest posek of his time in Central Europe and a valiant fighter against the Reform movement.*

WILLIAMSBURG WAS CHANGING, SLOWLY. THE DOMINANT JEWISH WILLIAMSBURGERS of the 1930's and 1940's were still weak in their commitment to Judaism, but strong in their commitment to America. Typical of Williamsburg in 1939 is the story of Rabbi Dovid and Rebbetzin Bender's first Succos. Having arrived in New York on Erev Yom Kippur 1939, foremost on Reb Dovid's mind was where to build his succah. The Benders lived in an apartment building and although there was a shared courtyard in the middle, fire escapes on the side, and a spacious roof, no one even considered building his own succah. In 1939, there were very few private succahs in Williamsburg.

Most people made *Kiddush* in the shul succah and would then go home to eat the rest of their meal. For anyone living in an apartment building, making a succah was a real undertaking that included procuring the consent of the neighbors and contending with the possible legal infractions of such a venture. That first Succos, Reb Dovid and his family moved to 189 Rodney Street, where Uncle Archik Berman owned a private house and built a succah in his own backyard. Reb Dovid yearned for his own succah and was determined that the next year, he would have one.

The next year, long before Succos, Reb Dovid began his campaign. He went from neighbor to neighbor to plead his cause. With cheerful goodwill and friendly persuasion, he convinced his neighbors to allow him to build a succah; Reb Dovid even invited their participation. The result was a makeshift succah, modest in appearance, but rich in spirit. That Succos, and for many more, the Benders shared their Yom Tov with their neighbors when they all came together in their shared succah.

Year after year, as *Yiddishkeit* in Williamsburg continued to grow and change, more and more succahs were built. Most of these succahs were constructed from old doors and foraged wood. The neighborhood children ran from door to door asking for old sheets and tablecloths to hang over the mismatched walls. The old-timers scratched their heads in wonder. It was hard for them to believe that in the good ole U.S.A., succahs were going up right in their backyards.

Not all of the old-time Williamsburgers were pleased with the changes in their neighborhood. Many modern irreligious Jews still felt at home in Williamsburg and saw themselves as the ideal blend of American Jew. They were content with their lives and their position in American society. The influx of demonstrably religious Jews challenged their values and annoyed them. These new unmistakably Jewish Jews were not interested in blending into the gentile world, for they did not consider America the answer to all their problems. Worst of all, to the annoyance of the veteran Williamsburgers, these fanatically religious Jews were bent on staying in Williamsburg.

One of these old-timers lived just above the Benders on 168 Hooper Street. Mrs. A. was an old bitter woman who had grown up in a religious home, but, as many of her generation, she had forsaken the old ways. She was frustrated at the religious direction her neighborhood was taking and often vented her resentment on her neighbors.

The rocky relationship between Mrs. A. and the religious community directly affected her relationship with her neighbors, the Benders. Rebbetzin Bender washed the family laundry in her apartment, then carried the baskets of wet laundry through the hallway and up a half flight of steps to a window that overlooked their courtyard. There she hung the wash out to dry on her laundry lines.

Living in the apartment just above the Benders, Mrs. A. routinely poured dirty water over the rows of freshly washed diapers, underwear, socks, and shirts. Time and again, Rebbetzin Bender pulled in the wash to find that much of her "clean" clothing was not so clean. She barely muttered a complaint. Rebbetzin Bender just rewashed the soiled laundry and hung it again, hoping that this time the clothing would remain freshly laundered.

Succos afforded Mrs. A. many opportunities to flaunt her disapproval of her neighbors. For seven days, there were meals held outside in the Benders' humble "succaleh." In a surge of defiance and hidden by the *schach*, Mrs. A. routinely dumped dirty water during the *seudos* in the succah. This was her way of venting her frustration about the turning socioreligious tide that she was unable to stop.

## Chapter Thirty-Six

# Entering a New Era

**12th of Teves 5710 (January 1, 1950), New Year's Eve**

THE WIND WHISTLED THROUGH THE DARK NIGHT, BANGING the metal garbage cans against each other — a fitting accompaniment to intermittent drunken shouts. Occasionally, a car careened down Lee Avenue, its horn honking away, announcing the beginning of a new year.

Around the corner — past Joe's Candy Store, Weiss's Bakery, Soloff's Jewelry, Tiv Tov Hardware, the old shoemaker, and Flaum's Pickles — was the old movie house. After a loud and raucous night that announced the new year, all was quiet. The merrymakers had gone home, leaving the stench of snuffed-out cigarettes and empty beer bottles. A typical New Year's Eve.

As the wee hours of the morning chased away the previous night, one of those "snuffed-out" cigarettes still burned. Embedded in a worn velvet movie seat, the small flame slowly grew, consuming one seat after another. The flames danced up the aisles and onto the stage, filling the movie house with fire and smoke.

Suddenly, the Benders awoke to the sounds of screaming fire engines and vapors of billowing smoke. "The movie house is on fire! The movie house in on fire! Hurray! Hurray!" the children shouted to one another. Their parents disdained the movie house, and the children realized that it was a menacing presence on their block. Its Sunday matinee was a popular pastime for the neighborhood children, and the lines to the movie house snaked way down Lee Avenue. Reb Dovid discouraged his children from even walking down the block during those hours.

Firemen ordered the families in their building to wet towels and place them around the doors. They instructed the residents to go out onto the fire escapes and await further instructions. If the fire spread, they would evacuate the building.

Pajama-clad children dangled their legs over the wrought-iron fire escape, craning their necks to watch the events. Lee Avenue swarmed with the black-jacketed fire fighters hoisting their hoses and ladders and battling the flames. At long last, the fire was put out, leaving a burnt-out shell where the movie house once

*The Klausenberg Beis Medrash*

stood. Luckily, no one was hurt and no other buildings were damaged.

The Benders were thrilled that the movie house was gone. They were even happier to hear who bought the burnt-out building. The Klausenberger Beis Medrash was moving in and the Benders could not have been happier. This switch was symbolic of what was happening in the neighborhood. Mesivta Torah Vodaath outgrew its original location at 505 Bedford Avenue and moved to South Third Street. Bais Yaakov High School and Seminary were upgraded to an old public school building on South Eighth Street, and Bais Yaakov elementary school bought an old maternity hospital on 255 Division Avenue.

Yes, Williamsburg was changing and the switch from movie house to *beis medrash* was only one sign of its transformation.

*Chapter Thirty-Seven*

# Meet the Neighborhood

W ILLIAMSBURG WAS A NEIGHBORHOOD OF SUPERMARKETS and corner groceries, of shuls and *shtieblach*, of plain folks and personalities. Williamsburg was where Lithuanian scholars rubbed shoulders with Chassidic Rebbes, and all felt at home in their basement *minyanim*. Williamsburg was home to all types of *Yidden*, ranging from the strictly religious to the strictly secular and all the distinctions in between. In Williamsburg, progress and nostalgia blended as the neighborhood marched forward into an era of change. In Williamsburg, the Bender family grew and thrived as an intrinsic part of the neighborhood they called home.

168 HOOPER STREET — THE BENDER HOME — OVERLOOKED HOOPER Street on one side, Lee Avenue on the other. Lee Avenue was lined with stores: Joe's Candy Store with its boxes and boxes of sweets arranged enticingly on open shelves, Weiss's Bakery, Soloff's Jewelry Store, Tiv Tov Hardware, the old shoemaker, Flaum's "nickel a pickle" Kosher Pickles, and Louie's Grocery. On the opposite side of Lee Avenue was the A&P — the "big" neighborhood supermarket — Hirsch's Grocery, Pearl's Delicatessen, and the Fruit Store.

Further down Lee Avenue in both directions, there was more of the same. Hochberg's Dry Goods and Lamm's Butcher Shop were down near Rodney Street. Across from Lamm's was Perlstein's Shoe Store, and down on the other end of Lee Avenue was Itzkowitz's Grocery.

Every other block had another "Williamsburg landmark." The Agudah building was at 616 Bedford Avenue. A few blocks over, at 505 Bedford, was the Old Mesivta of Torah Vodaath. The New Mesivta was down on South Third Street, and the Yeshivah Chofetz Chaim was on South Ninth Street.

WITH THE END OF WORLD WAR II AND THE SURGE OF EUROPEAN refugees, *Chassidishe shtieblach* began sprouting up like mushrooms. Further down Lee Avenue, over Itzkowitz's Grocery, was the Sanzer Kloisz. Around the corner, on Hewes Street, between Lee and Bedford Avenues, was the Sigheter Beis Medrash — one of the original *"minyan* machines" where one could pick a time and find a *minyan* to fit.

Over by Hooper Street near Marcy Avenue was Stropkov. Shopron was on Hewes Street between Lee Avenue and Marcy Avenue. Stolin was on Rodney Street between Lee and Bedford Avenues. Skolya was on Bedford Avenue and Rodney Street. Vizhnitz was on Lee Avenue off Taylor Street, next door to the 90th Precinct. Skver was on Bedford Avenue and Ross Street.

In the late 1940's and early 1950's, most of these *shtieblach* were still small. Their significance was the religious spirit that they brought to Williamsburg. Perhaps greater in significance were the growing *kehillos* that had replanted themselves in Williamsburg, the most prominent of which was the Satmar *kehillah*.

The Satmar Rav, Rabbi Yoel Teitelbaum, arrived in 1947, with only a few followers. Already as a young man in Europe, the Satmar Rav was recognized for his scholarship and piety. The Williamsburg Orthodox community warmly welcomed the illustrious Rebbe, happy that a person of his stature settled in their midst. The Satmar Rav immediately began rebuilding *Yiddishkeit* on American soil. His exceptional scholarly stature drew many Chassidim. As his following grew, so did his drive to create a framework for his flourishing *kehillah*.

Satmar did not transplant itself on barren soil. The Tzelemer Rav unknowingly laid the groundwork for the arrival of Satmar. Tzelem had already introduced uncompromising standards of kashrus, education, and *Yiddishkeit*.[8] Tzelem was a vibrant *kehillah* that outgrew its Lee Avenue and Hooper Street premises and moved to Lee Avenue and Roebling Street. With the arrival of the Satmar Rav, Tzelem continued to gravitate toward *Chassidus* and away from its Oberlander roots.

In contrast, Vien tenaciously maintained its Oberlander *Mesorah*. The arrival of the venerable Rabbi Yonason Steif stimulated growth within K'hal Adas Yereim of Vien. The members welcomed him as one of their own and, when they purchased a building on Rodney and South Fifth Streets, asked him to deliver *shiurim* for them. Eventually, the Viener Dayan, as

---

8. *Williamsburg Memories*, p. 198.

**... Already as a young man in Europe, the Satmar Rav was recognized for his scholarship and piety. The Williamsburg Orthodox community warmly welcomed the Satmar Rav, happy that a person of his stature settled in their midst ...**

*The Satmar Rav greeting the king of Romania*

*The Satmar Rav in Williamsburg.*

*Rabbi Yoel Teitelbaum (1887-1979), the Satmar Rav, was widely recognized as a true giant in Torah and avodas Hashem. Following his miraculous survival from the Nazis, he made his way to Eretz Yisroel and from there to America. He settled in Williamsburg, Brooklyn, where he built a huge kehillah. The Rebbe was renowned for his strong stand against Zionism, and his leadership extended well past his community in Brooklyn. In 1953 he was appointed Rav of the Eidah HaChareidus of Yerushalayim.*

Rabbi Yonason Steif was affectionately known, became the Rav of K'hal Adas Yereim.

Equally significant was the growth of the *Litvishe/Yeshivishe* community in Williamsburg. In the early 1940's, the arrival of roshei yeshivos and *yeshivaleit* who had just escaped from Europe instilled new life into the *Litvishe kehillah*. Previously, men of Lithuanian heritage who davened Ashkenaz and studied in the yeshivos of Europe were the exception. They were not numerous enough to establish their own *minyan* with their own style of davening, and they traditionally davened at Torah Vodaath where they felt at home because many of them had been Torah Vodaath *talmidim*. Yet after spending years in the Lithuanian yeshivos of Europe, Rabbi Dovid Bender and his friends dearly missed the *hartzige yeshivishe* davening they had grown to love. To make changes in the existing *minyanim* would be

... The Tzelemer Rav unknowingly laid the groundwork for the arrival of Satmar. Tzelem had already introduced uncompromising standards of kashrus, education, and Yiddishkeit ...

*Rabbi Levi Yitzchok Greenwald (1892-1979), known as the Tzelemer Rav, was the youngest son of Rabbi Moshe Greenwald, the Arugas Habosem. In his youth he learned under his father's tutelage and later under his oldest brother, the Ungvarer Rav, whose daughter he married. He served as Rav in a number of cities including Tzelem. In 1938, he immigrated to America on an affidavit from Rabbi Shraga Feivel Mendelowitz. He settled in Williamsburg where he established the Tzelemer kehillah and yeshivah.*

... The arrival of the venerable Rabbi Yonason Steif stimulated growth within K'hal Adas Yereim of Vien ...

*Rabbi Yonason Steif (1877-1958) studied under the Shevet Sofer, Rabbi Simcha Bunim Sofer. He served as Rav in a number of cities and was elected dayan of the Budapest Rabbinical Court. He survived the war and immigrated to the United States. In 1948, K'hal Adas Yereim purchased a building in Williamsburg where Reb Yonason eventually became Rav. Thousands of people flocked to hear his derashos. He was a renowned posek and many sought his halachic decisions.*

nearly impossible. They yearned for their own *minyan*, and that was how the Mirrer Minyan of Williamsburg began.

In the early 1940's, the Agudah graciously gave one of their rooms to the Mirrer Minyan for a daily *Shacharis minyan*. Shabbos and Yom Tov, when the Mirrer Minyan had a greater attendance, they moved to the Bais Yaakov High School on South Eighth Street.

THE EMERGENCE OF STRONG *KEHILLOS* AND VIBRANT *MINYANIM* WAS an occasion to rejoice. After all that had been destroyed in the war, religious Jewry in Williamsburg applauded every new arrival and the various groups bolstered one another.

For example, the Satmar Rav barely had a *minyan* when he first arrived, while the Mirrer Minyan was already well established. When Rabbi Boruch Kaplan heard that the Satmar Rav needed a room for his *minyan*,

Reb Boruch invited the Satmar Rav to use the Bais Yaakov Seminary building, even though the Mirrer Minyan usually davened there. The Satmar Rav accepted. Despite the fact that the Mirrer Minyan was much bigger than the Satmar Rav's *minyan*, Reb Boruch gave him the large downstairs auditorium for his *minyan,* and the Mirrer Minyan moved to one of the upstairs classrooms. Reb Boruch felt that a person of the Satmar Rav's caliber required more prestigious accommodations.

The spirit among the *frum Yidden* of Williamsburg was a healthy striving for higher standards of *frumkeit* that transcended differences in heritage or *minhag*. Williamsburg was home to Torah Vodaath, with up to 2,000 students. Torah Vodaath was, by far, the largest yeshivah in America. Yet, when the *Chassidishe chadarim* opened, and they had more hours of *limudei kodesh* and a higher standard of learning, Torah Vodaath strove to measure up to the competition.

Williamsburg was also the home to the first Bais Yaakov Seminary, the first Bais Yaakov Elementary School, and the first *shatnez* laboratory. Williamsburg was the first American neighborhood to influence its main business street to close on Shabbos, truly a revolutionary accomplishment.

Closing Lee Avenue on Shabbos was no small feat. For much of Lee Avenue, Saturday was business as usual and longtime shopkeepers wanted to keep it that way. Yet Williamsburg was changing, and the zealous newcomers allied with some of the idealistic old-timers to encourage a change of attitude. They organized committees and campaigns to promote *shemiras* Shabbos. Committee members spoke to shopkeepers about the importance of Shabbos and the benefits of guarding its holiness. They rode around in the popular "Shabbos Truck" — a flatbed trailer with a little hut in the shape of a house. Inside the "house" was a table set for Shabbos. On the roof of the "house" was an open scroll, reminiscent of a *Sefer Torah*, upon which was written *"Zachor Es Yom HaShabbos L'Kadsho."* Playing Shabbos music to remind everyone of the beauty of Shabbos, volunteers drove the truck around Williamsburg.

The Shemiras Shabbos Committee organized a Shabbos Walk down Lee Avenue. One store after another closed until finally, to the happiness of most of the *Yidden* of Williamsburg, Lee Avenue became the first major street in America to close on Shabbos.

All of these "firsts" were only possible because of the extraordinary people living in Williamsburg. A quick look at the street the Benders lived on, branching out a few blocks, gives a small indication of the changing face of Williamsburg.

168 Hooper Street was a six-story apartment building. On the bottom level, there were stores. From the second floor up, there were six apartments on each floor. Rabbi Zelig Epstein and Rabbi Nosson Horowitz lived

on the second floor. Above Reb Zelig was the Bender family. Next door to the Benders was Rebbetzin Rivka Levovitz, the widow of the revered Mirrer Mashgiach Rabbi Yeruchem Levovitz, and the Goldsteins, a young Hungarian/*Chassidishe* family. Rabbi Avrohom Levovitz lived in the apartment above his mother. The Samuels and Beckers also lived there.

168 Hooper Street was attached to two other apartment buildings. The one in the middle had no religious families except R' Menashe Horowitz, Rabbi Nosson Horowitz's brother. In the next building lived the Basch, Berger, Kreiger, and Lederer families.

Directly across the street was Rabbi Yonason Steif and Rabbi Mordechai Yoffe. Two houses down was the Kashover Rav, a little further down the block was Rabbi Neuschloss of Skver, and further down was R' Moshe Zupnik. One block over, on Hooper Street between Lee and Bedford Avenues, was Rabbi Avrohom Newhouse of Bais Yaakov.[9]

The Wachtfogels lived at 110 Keap Street. Across the street, Keap Street corner Bedford Avenue, were the Tresses and the Kahanows. The Pincuses were on Penn Street between Lee and Marcy Avenues, the Kaplans on Bedford between Hooper and Hewes Streets, the Fishbeins on 199 Hewes Street, the Litmanowitzes on Bedford Avenue corner Wilson Street, the Rottenbergs on Rutledge Street between Lee and Marcy Avenues.

THE NEW GENERATION OF WILLIAMSBURGERS WORE THEIR *YIDDISHKEIT* more comfortably than their predecessors had. There were more shuls and *shtieblach*, and the louder, noisier davening replaced the sedate synagogue service that had been popular in previous generations. More men had beards, there were more boys running with their briefcases to *cheder*, and more girls skipping their way to Bais Yaakov.

Williamsburgers loved their dynamic neighborhood, its special blend of personalities and vibrant atmosphere charged by spiritual growth and hope. The Benders were proud to be part of Williamsburg and call it home.

---

9. See Biography Section for the Kashover Rabbi (Rabbi Refael Blum), Rabbi Neuschloss, and Rabbi Newhouse.

1. **Bender Home:** 168 Hooper St. — corner Hooper Street and Lee Avenue
2. **Mesivta of Torah Vodaath:** 505 Bedford — corner Taylor Street
3. **The Agudah Building:** 616 Bedford Avenue — between Hooper and Hewes Streets
4. **Marcy Avenue Mirrer Minyan:** Marcy Avenue — between Keap and Hooper Streets
5. **The Bender's new house:** 216 Hewes Street — between Lee and Marcy Avenues
6. **Bais Yaakov Elementary School:** 125 Heyward Street — between Lee and Bedford Avenues
7. **Kollel Kerem Shlomo:** Lee Avenue — between Heyward and Lynch Streets
8. **Bais Yaakov of Williamsburg:** South 8th Street — between Driggs and Bedford Avenues

Part III:

# The Bender Home

## 5705-5718 / 1945-1958

*Chapter Thirty-Eight:*
### 168 Hooper Street: "Ah Yiddishe Shtub"

*Chapter Thirty-Nine:*
### Around the Year

*Chapter Forty:*
### Founded on Chessed

*Chapter Forty-One:*
### Williamsburg Family

*Chapter Forty-Two:*
### Changes in Williamsburg: From Hooper to Hewes

The information in this section was provided primarily by the Bender family. Other sources are documented.

## Chapter Thirty-Eight

# 168 Hooper Street: "Ah Yiddishe Shtub"

**Williamsburg: Tishrei 5707 (October 1947)**

"MAMME, CAN WE GO OVER TO REBBETZIN LEVOVITZ? She loves when we visit her!" Esther smiled charmingly at her mother, and Blumie nodded eagerly.

With a tired wave of her hand, Rebbetzin Bender acquiesced, and the two little girls gaily scampered away. The young mother sunk into a chair for a few minutes of relaxation. She felt a bit guilty for allowing the girls to go visit.

It was a privilege to be the neighbor of Rebbetzin Rivka Levovitz, the widow of the revered *Mashgiach* of Mir, Reb Yeruchem. She and Rebbetzin Bender enjoyed a warm relationship and the doors between the two apartments were always being opened and closed.

"*Vos min tut, tut min far zich* (whatever someone does, he does for himself)," Rebbetzin Levovitz would comment as she did a favor. She made little of what she did for others, insisting that, in the end, she was the beneficiary. When Rebbetzin Bender would run across the hall to borrow some flour for the cake she was baking, Rebbetzin Levovitz would hand it over with a smile, pointing out how, just the day before, she had borrowed some eggs from the Benders and how wonderful it was to have neighbors with whom to share. "I am happy to lend you what you need and I know that one day you will lend me what I need."

*Rebbetzin Bender and her young family in the living room of 168 Hooper Street. She stands next to her in-laws, Rabbi Avrohom Bender and his new wife, Mrs. Ettel (Shafran) Bender. Rabbi Avrohom Bender remarried in 1948 and moved to Eretz Yisroel. They returned to America only occasionally for visits.*

Whenever possible, she would point out this phenomenon. Sometimes, she'd paraphrase it differently — *"fun a toiveh kumt ah toiveh* (one favor leads to another)." Just prior to Pesach, Rebbetzin Bender hired painters to paint the apartment. Obviously, they had to remove all the pictures, seforim, utensils, and almost everything else. It was quite a tumult. When Rebbetzin Levovitz saw what was going on, she took a stand.

"Bashale," she said, "come, bring all your things into my house. It will be so much easier for you."

"Oh, no!" Rebbetzin Bender protested. "How could I? It will make such a mess … and the Rebbetzin has already begun cooking for Pesach …"

However, Rebbetzin Levovitz insisted and she began emptying the kitchen cabinets on her own. She marched from one apartment to the other, removing dishes and silverware, pots and pans. Rebbetzin Bender stopped arguing and joined her. Before long, the kitchen was almost bare. When they got to the very end, Rebbetzin Bender reached into the recesses of the last cabinet and extracted a small package of sugar and a small package of salt from the previous Pesach. She did not know where the *minhag* came from, but her mother always had saved a bit of salt, sugar, and a piece of *afikomun* from Pesach to Pesach. Rebbetzin Levovitz saw Rebbetzin Bender with the little bags and let out a cry of excitement. "Bashale," she exclaimed, "*Kosher L'Pesach*?" Rebbetzin Bender nodded, wondering what the big excitement was. "I cannot believe it! I just began cooking for Pesach. The store I went to did not yet have *Kosher L'Pesach* salt and sugar. I was so disappointed … but look; I see you have some. May I borrow it?" Rebbetzin Bender was happy to return a favor. Rebbetzin Levovitz held the bags and smiled. "See, you thought I was helping you, but look, I was helping myself."

From time to time, Rebbetzin Levovitz urged Rebbetzin Bender to send over the kids. "You need a break, Bashale. You are tired and worn out. Send them over so you can rest a bit."

Sometimes Rebbetzin Levovitz had her grandchildren over. In those years, all her children lived in Williamsburg. Rabbi Avrohom Levovitz lived in the apartment above his mother. His brothers Reb Moshe Leib and Reb

Simcha Zissel also lived nearby, as did their sister Chashel.[1] Several grandchildren were named after Reb Yeruchem. Rebbetzin Levovitz found it difficult to use her late husband's name, and so she used to call these children "*Bebke* (bean)." There was *der greiseh Bebke, der kleiner Bebke,* and *der feteh Bebke* (the big bean, the small bean, and the chubby bean). The Bender girls loved to go over and play with all the "*Beblach.*"

*Three generations: Rabbi Dovid Bender with his father and his son*

"Tell me," Rebbetzin Bender would ask Rebbetzin Levovitz, "how is this '*vos min tut, tut min far zich?*' In this case, I am certainly the only one who is benefiting."

Rebbetzin Levovitz shook her head. "Don't worry, you will see. I am certain that there will be a time when this will be a favor for me as well."

ONE WINTER MORNING, ROSH CHODESH ADAR, 5708 (1948), AS REBBETZIN Bender was savoring a hot cup of coffee, Esther came running in. "*Mamme, Mamme,* come quick. Rebbetzin Levovitz is calling you." Rebbetzin Bender rose, startled. The children had just gone next door, and she had not expected them to return so quickly. Something must be wrong. She hurried toward Rebbetzin Levovitz's apartment.

Rebbetzin Levovitz was lying on the couch, and she looked very weak. She could barely talk. Rebbetzin Bender sized up the situation immediately. She sent her children back to their apartment and began calling the Levovitz children.

Esther knew that something was wrong. The door to their apartment was opened and she saw all the Levovitzes hurrying into the apartment. There was a tumult of activity as doors slammed open and shut, and people rushed about.

"*Mamme,* what is happening to Rebbetzin Levovitz?"

Rebbetzin Bender sighed sadly. "She is going to be near the *Eibeshter in Himmel.*"

Esther was confused. Near the *Eibeshter in Himmel*? How would she get there? Would she use a ladder? She opened the door to see if perhaps they were bringing a ladder for Rebbetzin Levovitz. Instead, she saw a long large black box being maneuvered out of the elevator. Esther's eyes wid-

---

1. Married to Rabbi Yisroel Chaim Kaplan.

ened. This was very interesting! Suddenly, she felt her mother's arm on her shoulder as her mother yanked her inside their apartment and closed the door. A few words of distraction took Esther's mind off what was going on next door and she returned to her childish play.

As Rebbetzin Bender went on quietly with her household chores, her thoughts were with her beloved friend and neighbor who had just departed from this world. What a *zechus*! Her last moments on earth were spent with all her children gathered around her. Through the kindness that Rebbetzin Levovitz did when she welcomed the Bender children into her home, she merited to have all her children around her at the time of her *petirah*.

THE BENDERS REMAINED CLOSE WITH THE LEVOVITZ FAMILY EVEN after Rebbetzin Levovitz's *petirah*. Reb Avrohom Levovitz remained their neighbor for years and the children interacted like cousins. Once, he even helped avert disaster.

"*Kinderlach*, I'm running across the street to Hirsch's Grocery. I will be back in a minute. Don't go near the Chanukah *licht*," Rebbetzin Bender admonished her children. Esther and Blumie continued playing quietly in the bedroom. They did not notice Paltiel wander toward the living room where the *licht* were burning.

Lately, there were many "fires" in Williamsburg. There was a lot of construction in the neighborhood and the companies devised an economic and efficient way to make room for their projects. They would strip the building of anything salable — doors, radiators, windows, etc.

*Rabbi Avrohom Levovitz as a bochur, with his friends from Mir, Rabbis Simcha Sheps and Henoch Fishman*
*Left to right: Simcha Sheps, Avrohom Levovitz, Henoch Fishman*

*Rabbi Avrohom Levovitz (1906-1992) learned in the yeshivos of Telshe, Grodno and Mir. Additionally he studied under the Brisker Rav for three years, longer than any other talmid at the time. His first wife and oldest child did not leave Mir in time and perished in the war. Reb Avrohom arrived in America from Japan in 1941, where he remarried and built a family. He was a maggid shiur in Mesivta Rabbeinu Chaim Berlin for a number of years. He spent his life immersed in learning and was known for his scholarship and diligence.*

— load those items onto a huge truck, and go from street to street selling their merchandise. (Doors were a great buy. With just a few doors, one had a beautiful succah.) Then they would knock down the building floor by floor, and set the pile of rubble on fire. This way they did not have to cart away any garbage. Paltiel loved to watch these fires and, since there was a lot of construction going on in Williamsburg, Paltiel had plenty of entertainment. Now with the Chanukah *licht*, he had his very own fire right at home.

"Fire!" Paltiel called suddenly. "Fire!" The girls giggled in amusement. Paltiel was forever fascinated by fire. They continued playing. "A fire! A fire!" Paltiel called out again. Did he sound a bit more anxious than usual? "A fire! A fire!" Esther decided to go take a look. As she stepped into the living room, her eyes widened. The cord of the Venetian blinds had caught fire from the menorah and the entire length of the wooden windowsill was aflame. She let out a scream and ran out of the apartment.

Rabbi Avrohom Levovitz was in the hall on his way out to *Ma'ariv*. She ran over to him. "Reb Avrohom, a fire is burning!"

Reb Avrohom was sure that the child was referring to the Chanukah *licht* and of course they were burning. "I have to go daven," he said, brushing her off.

"But there is a fire!"

Reb Avrohom was in a hurry to get to *Ma'ariv* and tried to sidestep her. Esther saw that he did not realize how serious this was. She grabbed hold of his coat and began pulling him toward the apartment. By then, the flames were climbing up the window. Reb Avrohom ran toward the flames, calling behind him, "Water, children, bring water!" He tried to smother the flames and keep them from spreading as he waited for the children to bring water.

Meanwhile Rebbetzin Bender rushed out of the grocery — she had not intended to be out for more than a few minutes — and happened to look up. Her eyes widened in horror as she realized that the window on fire was her own! She dropped her packages and ran. She entered on the ground floor and saw the elevator waiting for her. Relieved, she yanked open the door and fell inside, panting. The elevator moved up one floor … another floor … then it stopped. She was stuck in the middle of two floors and her children were alone in the apartment. She balled her hands into fists and pounded on the door. "Open up! Please!" Tears of hopelessness and fear coursed down her cheeks. Finally the elevator began to move, only it was going down, not up. When the door opened, she dashed out and ran up the two flights of stairs to her apartment.

Rabbi Avrohom Levovitz was standing by the window, pouring water over the smoldering embers. The children were huddled together in the corner, shaken but safe. Rebbetzin Bender was overcome with emotion as she sank into a chair. She had no words to thank her neighbor who had averted a tragedy. Over the years, she repeated the story to her family, stressing her appreciation to her neighbor, and her recognition that *HaKadosh Baruch Hu* had, in His infinite mercy, protected her family.

THE BENDERS AND THE LEVOVITZES WERE FITTING NEIGHBORS. RABBI Avrohom Levovitz strove to live by his father's teachings and so did the Benders. They shared the same values and understood how to appreciate one another. For example, when Rebetzin Bender sent over hot *chulent* as a warm gesture on Erev Shabbos, Reb Avrohom responded by testing the Bender children on what they had learned in school. Reb Avrohom knew that his interest in their learning would give the Benders *nachas*.

Reb Dovid was grateful for such like-minded neighbors. He wanted his home to be as pure as possible and having good neighbors was a crucial factor. Speaking Yiddish was another way of insulating his family from the American street. He and Rebbetzin Bender spoke Yiddish to each other and the children. It served as a connection to the past and a vision of the future. If they could not go back to Europe, they would bring Europe to America.

Reb Dovid was unfazed about setting standards for himself and his home that were unusual in America then. He grew a beard in the early 1940's when few young men did. Baseball cards, the rage of the 1940's and 1950's, were banned from his home. Toy guns mysteriously disappeared. The Bender girls were used to being the only children with unfashionable

*Left to right: Leib Yitzchok Tarshish, Rabbi Dovid Bender, Rabbi Shaya Tarshish, Rabbi Dovid Kronglass, Rabbi Yaakov Weinberg (later Rosh Yeshivah of Ner Yisroel), Rabbi Abba Yaakov Liff (later maggid shiur in Ner Yisroel), Rabbi Yehoshua Klavan (Rav of Washington, D.C.). Standing in back is Rabbi Yisroel Jacobson.*

sleeves to their elbows.[2] Tatty's word was law. Yet, Reb Dovid, because he was a very warm person, tempered his strictures with warmth. He pulled the children onto his lap, tickled them, and rode them up and down on his knee until they were dizzy. Even when the children were not happy with his rules, they felt his love and yearned to please him.

Rebbetzin Bender's home was her first priority. Creating a warm and relaxed atmosphere was a labor of love. When the children were little, she chose to teach in the evenings so that she could be home with them during most of their waking hours. She was concerned that they eat well and she fussed over her picky eaters. She seemed to have endless patience as she gave each child time to tell of the events of his or her day.

It was not easy. Although her first child was born four years after her marriage, the rest were close in age. Esther, Blumie, and Paltiel were each a year apart. A few years later came Yankel, a year later Michoel, and two years later Shmuel Sholom was born. She had no mother or mother-in-law to help her; she could easily have become overwhelmed and frustrated. Yet, for Rebbetzin Bender, neither fatigue nor ill health dampened her enthusiasm for the ultimate role of a woman: that of wife and mother.

Rebbetzin Bender's serene happiness radiated beyond her apartment. Many friends and neighbors affectionately called her *"Mamme* Bender"[3]

---

2. This was in the late 1940's, when the neighborhood was still overwhelmingly modern. When the Chassidim came, they brought higher standards of dress that much of the *Litvishe* crowd adopted.

3. The term *"Mamme* Bender" or "Bubby Bender" was mentioned many times in casual conversation with acquaintances of the Bender family.

as she was the quintessential mother: warm and affectionate, gracious and patient, caring and thoughtful. When the children arrived home from school, they often found a guest sitting in the kitchen enjoying a cup of coffee and a piece of cake. The attention she gave others did not detract from what she gave her own children. There was always enough love to go around.

"MA …" ESTHER HOLLERED UP FROM HOOPER STREET WHERE SHE AND Blumie were playing hopscotch.

Rebbetzin Bender peered out the window two floors above and threw something down. The girls followed the white paper with their eyes until it landed a few feet from them. They excitedly unrolled the folded paper and counted the loot. One, two, three pennies! Just enough to buy a popsicle at Joe's Candy Store. The girls jumped up and ran as fast as they could around the corner.

They slowly entered the store, savoring the sweetness of the moment. After all, they had three whole pennies and many options. Their eyes roamed slowly over the boxes and boxes of candies, neatly arranged on open shelves. The marshmallows were off limits, but oh, did they look good! They moved on to the chocolates and took box after box down to peruse the contents. They took their time, for as long as they had their three pennies, they were rich patrons with endless possibilities. There was popcorn, pretzels, Breyer's Ice Cream, and more. Never mind that they were not allowed to eat many of these products; it was fun to pretend. They finally settled on a double ice pop that they split in two, and happily left the store.

This was the pre-*hechsher* era, when people were unaware of the complications of food production and the need to have kashrus supervision from the beginning of the process to the end. Generally, products without gelatin were assumed to be kosher. Reb Dovid had his own stringencies in this area. His children were not allowed to eat tuna, pretzels, and a host of other foods.

"Educator" sandwich cookies were the first of its kind with a *hechsher*. Then Paskesz came out with pretzels, Bachman Pretzels received its kosher certification, and Dagim began producing tuna with a *mashgiach* on each boat. After Tzelem's successful campaign to make *cholov Yisroel* milk readily available, other *cholov Yisroel* products soon followed. This progress was due to the growing demand of the religious community. People like Rabbi Dovid Bender[4] were creating Jewish homes with a higher standard of kashrus. These improvements were the result.

---

4. For years, Rebbetzin Bender made her own cottage cheese from *cholov Yisroel* milk.

"LIKE PICKLES," MRS. S. COMPLAINED TO NO ONE IN PARTICULAR, "LIKE pickles and herring. All day and all night my apartment smells from pickles and herring."

Esther smothered a smile as she passed her eccentric neighbor muttering to herself, to the mailman, to the policeman, and to everyone else who had stopped to listen. Mrs. S. took her straw broom and swept some dust away from the door of her building. "It smells," she shrieked, as she leaned heavily on her broom and thrust her face close to Esther. "Don't you smell it?" Esther nodded meekly and dashed past. Of course it smelled! That was the consequences of living just above Flaum's Kosher Pickles. Esther gave a whiff. Heavenly! Maybe tomorrow her mother would give her a nickel for a pickle. For now, she was on her way to Louie's.

"AND HOW ARE YOUR AUNTS AND UNCLES?" LOUIE ASKED ESTHER AS HE rang up the few items she purchased. Louie, the genial grocer, was a typical Jewish Williamsburg native, throwing in Yiddish words for the benefit of his more traditional customers, while remaining happily complacent with his secular lifestyle. Esther smiled shyly. "You mean my cousins," she replied.

"Sure, sure," said Louie. "You know — Hannah, Mary, Mike, Abe, and Bluma? How are they all doing?"

"They are just fine," Esther answered as she swept up the change. "Bye, now!" She skipped gaily out the door. Esther loved going to Louie's. Louie's Grocery had been on the block long before she was born. He knew her whole family: her parents, grandparents, Uncle Archik, and his kids. He did not keep track of the changing generations and often mistook her cousins for her aunts and uncles. For Esther this was a special thrill. She had only one uncle and he lived in Eretz Yisroel. When all of her friends talked about their aunts and uncles, she had nothing to say. On the rare occasion that she stepped into Louie's, she basked in that warm, wonderful feeling of being a part of a large extended family. Blumie felt the same way, and she never even bothered to correct Louie when he asked her how her aunts and uncles were doing.

The Benders rarely shopped in Louie's store. Just across the street from their apartment was Hirsch's Grocery. The Hirsch brothers opened a small shop that carried almost all of the *heimishe* products available at the time. Reb Dovid tried to patronize Hirsch's for practical as well as ideological reasons. He preferred to use *heimishe* products and he tried to give his grocery business to *frum Yidden*. They only shopped at Louie's when they needed a product that Hirsch's didn't have.

The Benders shopped for their challah and bread at R' Shloima Weiss's Bakery, located on the ground floor of their apartment building on the Lee

Avenue side. Rows of fresh rye bread lined the shelves behind the counter. R' Shloima[5] was a revered and beloved figure in the Williamsburg community. He was revered for his scholarship and wisdom, and beloved for his genuine warmth and love.

On Friday afternoon, the lines for R' Shloima Weiss's fresh challos extended out the door and up Lee Avenue. Rebbetzin Bender knew that there were many poor people — *b'nei Torah*, low-income war refugee families — for whom buying challah for Shabbos was a struggle. She approached R' Shloima with a "business" proposition. She would collect money and he would sell to her challah and cake at a discount. She would then arrange that these baked goods would be delivered to families in an honorable way. This "business" arrangement lasted for many years.

One Erev Shabbos, as the clock was ticking away, Rebbetzin Bender realized that she must run down to the bakery to buy challos before they closed. That day, the lines at the bakery were particularly long. Rebbetzin Bender waited restlessly, her mind on the many things she still had to do on that short Erev Shabbos. Finally, it was her turn.

"One minute, Rebbetzin," R' Shloima said. He then proceeded to wait on the woman behind her! If that was not enough, after taking care of the other customer, he turned to the side and began to write a letter. Rebbetzin Bender looked at her watch anxiously. *How long will this take?* she thought to herself.

R' Shloima walked toward the counter, licking the lip of the envelope to seal it. "I am sending this letter to a *frum* boy who is now in the army," he explained. "His parents were killed in the war and, with no one to intercede on his behalf, he was drafted and now he is in Korea, all alone. I write him a letter every Erev Shabbos, to let him know that someone cares for him. This Erev Shabbos I had no time to write. When I saw that it was your turn on line, I seized the opportunity. I knew that if I explained the situation to you, you would understand. The woman waiting behind you is a very nervous type and she might not have had the patience to listen to my explanation so I helped her before I helped you."

Rebbetzin Bender returned home smiling. She marveled over the rare thoughtfulness of R' Shloima Weiss, and she barely noticed what the incident said about her.

"You knock on the door," she whispered.
"No, you knock on the door," her sister whispered back.
"I'm scared. He might answer."
"He's probably not home now."
"So you knock."

---

5. See Biography Section.

"No, you knock."

Finally, Esther knocked.

Mrs. G. opened the door and the two little girls breathed a sigh of relief. Blumie held out the little pushke bashfully, "We're collecting for *tzedakah*," she said.

"Oh, yes, yes," Mrs. G. nodded. "You wait right here." She scurried over to the couch and lifted up the cushion. The children were familiar with the system. Mr. G was a sour, crotchety old man, who was also a bit miserly. He rarely gave *tzedakah* and he did not want his wife giving either. Mrs. G was not very knowledgeable about *Yiddishkeit*, but she was a pious soul and always wanted to give. She would collect the pennies, nickels, and dimes that fell out of her husband's

*Reb Shloima Weiss: more than just a "simple" baker.*

pocket, or that she found in the street, and she would hide them under the cushions of the couch. When the girls came collecting, she emptied her stash into their pushkes.

As the coins clinked in the can, she would say, "*Kinderlach*, daven for a *refuah sheleimah* for Chaya Perel bas Bluma. Remember, *kinderlach*, Chaya Perel bas Bluma." The girls nodded solemnly. Chaya Perel bas Bluma was Mrs. G.'s daughter. They knew that she had some kind of illness, only they did not know exactly what. She was in and out of some kind of hospital and even when she was home, she acted strangely.

Mrs. G. reached into her pocket and took out two sticks of spearmint gum. "Here, *kinderlach*, enjoy. You are wonderful children!" The girls happily accepted the treat and went on their way. Though they were little, they already learned from their parents that even children can accomplish, provided they have the will. They shook their pushkes merrily as they scampered home.

### Chapter Thirty-Nine

# Around the Year

### Williamsburg: 5715 (1955)

C OME, *KINDERLACH*, BRING THIS PLATE OVER TO THE LEVO-vitzes, and this one to the Epsteins, and this to Mrs. M ..." It was Erev Shabbos and Rebbetzin Bender was dishing out plates of *chulent* as a tasty snack for her neighbors. In the hectic pre-Shabbos preparations, some people might forget to take the few moments to sit down and have something warm and nourishing to eat. Every week, the Bender children proudly trooped from door to door handing out portions of their mother's *chulent*. This thoughtful gesture was typical of Rebbetzin Bender, providing a small something to show others she cared about them.

Shabbos in the Bender home was a lively affair. They often had guests, relatives from out of town who were learning in Torah Vodaath or Bais Yaakov,[6] newly arrived refugees, or old acquaintances from Europe. 168 Hooper Street reverberated with lively singing and *divrei Torah*. Reb Dovid handed out copies of "*Zichru Toras Moshe*" to all the children and guests and they learned together.

---

6. "When my brothers and I were in Torah Vodaath, we ate at the Benders regularly. My sister, Rebbetzin Esther Weinberg, ate there when she attended Bais Yaakov. We were all very close" (Rabbi Meir Shapiro).

*168 Hooper Street. The Benders lived in the*
*corner apartment, two flights up.*

*Yankel, Shmuel Sholom, and Michoel Bender*
*outside 168 Hooper Street*

The Shabbos-day schedule considered everyone's needs. Reb Dovid enjoyed davening early — 7 o'clock in the morning at the Mirrer Minyan — so that he had time to learn before the meal. After davening, Reb Dovid and the boys went home for a bit of *kiddush*, cake, and *chulent*. Then he would learn, first with the children and then by himself. Meanwhile, Rebbetzin Bender went to Rabbi Nosson Horowitz's shul and davened at 9 o'clock. When she returned at 12, Reb Dovid began the *seudah*.

The *seudah* stretched well into the afternoon, as the Bender family sang and spoke, learned and laughed. Sometimes a visitor dropped by and was invited for dessert. Inevitably, friends of the children entered shyly, asking if the girls were ready to go to Bnos or the boys ready for Pirchei. Reb Dovid dismissed the children from the table and allowed them to go. Then for *Minchah*, it was back to the Mirrer Minyan.

BACK IN THE MID-1940'S, RABBI DOVID BENDER HELPED ESTABLISH THE Mirrer Minyan. Then, Rabbi Reuvain Grozovsky, Rosh Yeshivah of Torah Vodaath, was the *ba'al Mussaf* for the *Yamim Nora'im*, while Reb Dovid was the *ba'al Shacharis* and the *ba'al tokei'a*. In those years, the *minyan* was relatively small. Before any Yom Tov, Reb Dovid would recruit some of his "Cohen" *talmidim* to join the *minyan*, thereby ensuring that the *minyan*

Rabbi Reuvain Grozovsky was one of the early members of the Mirrer Minyan. When Rabbi Dovid Bender had his second daughter, Rabbi Reuvain Grozovsky commented, *"Bas techilah siman yafeh l'banim* (a daughter first is a good sign for future boys – *Bava Basra* 141a ) — so two girls are certainly *siman yafeh l'banim."* With good-natured spirit, Reb Dovid answered, "I am going to hold you to your word!" The rest of the Bender children were boys.

*Rabbi Reuvain Grozovsky (1886-1958) studied in Slabodka under Rabbi Moshe Mordechai Epstein and the Alter of Slabodka. In 1919 he became the son-in-law and life companion of Rabbi Boruch Ber Leibowitz, and served as Rosh Yeshivah in Kaminetz for close to 20 years. Reb Reuvain succeeded Rabbi Shlomo Heiman as Rosh Yeshivah of Torah Vodaath in 1944. He was chairman of Moetzes Gedolei HaTorah and a leader of Vaad Hatzalah. Reb Reuvain's published shiurim are studied around the Torah world.*

would have *Kohanim* for *Bircas Kohanim*. He saw this as a wonderful opportunity for his *bochurim* as well as a boon for the *minyan.*[7]

With the slow arrival of *Mirrer talmidim* in the late 1940's, the Mirrer Minyan continued to grow and change. In the early 1950's, the Minyan divided itself into two locations, the original location at the Bais Yaakov High School and a second location in the Boyaner Kloiz on Marcy Avenue. The origination of this split coincided with the formation of Kollel Kerem Shlomo.

Kollel Kerem Shlomo, founded by Rabbi Berel Klor, was an afternoon kollel for *melamdim.* Originally they had rented a shul from a Rav on Hewes Street, who had a *minyan* there only on Shabbos mornings at 9 o'clock. Since the kollel members were Mirrers who lived quite a distance from Bais Yaakov High School, they hit on the idea to create a branch of the Mirrer Minyan on Hewes Street for those who found it difficult to take the children all the way to South Eighth Street on winter Shabbos mornings. They scheduled davening at 7 to be out on time for the regular 9 o'clock *minyan.* They also transferred the regular weekday *minyanim* for *Shacha-*

---

7. "I have always been grateful that Reb Dovid introduced me to the Mirrer Minyan. The uplifting davening there still rings in my ears" (Rabbi Henoch Cohen).

*ris* and *Ma'ariv* to Kerem Shlomo, rather than the Agudah building where it had been until then. Meanwhile, the Mirrer Minyan on South Eighth Street kept up their *minyan* there.

Later, the Hewes Street building was sold and Kollel Kerem Shlomo had to find a new home. The kollel found a temporary location, and the Mirrer Minyan rented the basement of the Boyaner Kloiz on Marcy Avenue. The Kerem Shlomo Mirrer Minyan continued their 7 o'clock davening even when they moved to Marcy Avenue and no longer had to vacate the building by 9 o'clock. When the kollel finally bought their own building (on Lee Avenue between Heyward and Lynch Streets), some of the Mirrer Minyan moved back there

*The Marcy Avenue Mirrer Minyan assembled in the basement of the Boyaner Kloiz.*

and established an 8 o'clock schedule, while some stayed on Marcy Avenue. The Mirrer Minyan still in the Bais Yaakov High School moved over to the Old Mesivta of Torah Vodaath.[8] This gave the Mirrer Minyan of the late 1950's three separate locations: the Old Mesivta at 505 Bedford Avenue, the Boyaner Kloiz at 260 Marcy Avenue, and Kollel Kerem Shlomo at 208 Lee Avenue.

The separate locations for the Mirrer Minyan were about growth and convenience, not dissent. By the late 1950's, there were enough people davening in the Mirrer Minyan to warrant three locations. The Mirrers chose their *minyan* based on time and location, but no matter where they ended up davening, they all remained close. In fact, when a member of any of the three *minyanim* made a *simchah*, his *simchah* was announced at all three locations. If a member of the 7 o'clock *minyan* was making a *simchah* and felt that it would be difficult for his guests to daven so early in the morn-

---

8. When the Mesivta of Torah Vodaath outgrew their Bedford Avenue and Taylor Street location, they moved to 141 South Third Street. Henceforth, 505 Bedford Avenue was the "Old Mesivta" while 141 South Third Street was the "New Mesivta." Torah Vodaath elementary school was growing and the original building at 206 Wilson Street was too small for all the grades. 206 Wilson Street housed the nursery through sixth grade, while the Old Mesivta housed the seventh and eighth grades and the *aleph* track of the sixth.

*Rabbi Tuvia Kaplan as a bochur in Mir*

ing that week, he davened at the 8:30 *minyan* and made his *kiddush* there.

There were also many people who davened in one Mirrer *minyan* during the week and another Mirrer *minyan* on Shabbos. For example, Rabbi Shmuel Brudny, Rabbi Yisroel Kanarek, Rabbi Aharon Kreiser, Rabbi Pinchas Ackerman, Rabbi Ezriel Lange, Rabbi Binyamin Zeilberger, and Rabbi Elya Yurkansky[9] usually davened at Marcy Avenue during the week, but on Shabbos they went to Kerem Shlomo.[10] There was no competition and no rivalry, only a sense of practicality and unity.

Reb Dovid joined the 7 o'clock *minyan* on Marcy Avenue, for he enjoyed the early schedule. Among the regular Shabbos *mispallelim* at Marcy Avenue was Rabbi Yisroel Chaim Kaplan. Even after he became *Mashgiach* of Bais Medrash Elyon in Monsey, he remained a Williamsburg resident, commuting to Monsey during the week and remaining in Williamsburg for Shabbos, Yom Tov, and in between sessions. When Rabbi Yaakov Kamenetsky lived in the neighborhood, he often davened at Marcy Avenue and then walked over to Torah Vodaath just before *Kri'as HaTorah.*[11]

Rabbi Tuvia Kaplan was the Marcy Avenue Mirrer Minyan's faithful *gabbai* for many years. He saw his *minyan* as the carrier of the Mirrer *Mesorah* and tried to keep faithful to what he remembered from the Mir. For example, he was vigilant that there should be absolutely no talking during davening, not even by the children. If Reb Tuvia heard even the smallest whisper from a child, he was suddenly standing right next to that child, and silence once again reigned. The children were sometimes annoyed with Reb Tuvia's interference, but they soon learned that in the Mirrer Minyan there was just no talking.[12]

Reb Tuvia made sure that the davening times were kept posted. Not that the times ever varied. For years, a simply written sign dictated the weekday schedule: *Shacharis* — 7:00, *Yishtabach* — 7:15, *Shemoneh Esrei* — 7:30. No matter who was the *ba'al tefillah*, the times were adhered to, ensuring that davening would be slow, even on a weekday. *Shemoneh Esrei* was never

---

9. See Biography Section.

10. Often, one consideration was that it was difficult to have the little children dressed and ready so early in the morning.

11. Later, when Reb Yaakov moved and he was closer to the Old Mesivta, he davened there.

12. Years later, when Rabbi Tuvia Kaplan passed away, all these little children — who by then were married adults — cried openly at his *levayah*. Each one felt that Reb Tuvia's influence had instilled in them awe of a *beis k'nesess* and a reverence for davening.

before 7:30, and there was no such thing as a fast *chazzan* who rushed to finish early.

Reb Tuvia took care of the material needs of the *minyan* as well. Every Friday afternoon, he would go up two flights of stairs to bring down pails of hot water to wash the floors of the shul, because the shul did not have its own hot water source. He tidied up the shul in the evening, putting away seforim that people left around, and straightening up the tables and chairs. Erev Shabbos he set the Shabbos clocks, made sure that the *sifrei Torah* were turned to the proper place, and checked that there was food for *kiddush* after davening on Shabbos morning. Reb Tuvia's devotion ensured that the *minyan* ran smoothly.[13]

Rabbi Chaim Brandstater was the *ba'al korei* for many years. His carefully enunciated reading was memorable. He wore his *tallis* a bit lower down, and held the edge out and to the side so that it formed a barrier between his mouth and the parchment so that neither heat nor moisture would damage the ink. Reb Chaim was meticulous in everyday actions as well; when he spoke to a friend, he seemed to be counting his words, aware that nothing said is inconsequential.[14] Though he never married, never built his own family, he found family in the Mirrer Minyan where he shared a bond with all those who proudly wore the badge of *"ah Mirrer."*

R' Binyamin Zucker and Rabbi Feivel Hollander were Marcy Avenue regulars as were Rabbi Michel Unger, Rabbi Hershel Wasilski, and Rabbi Markel Greenhaus.[15] Rabbi Markel Greenhaus sat right next to the *amud* and, every once in a while, he would stand up right before *Ma'ariv* on *Motza'ei Shabbos*, and give a rousing talk.

Unofficial *shmuessen* had been a part of the Mirrer Minyan for years. For a short time during the early years of the *minyan*, Mirrer Minyan regulars gave *shiurim* based on Reb Yeruchem's *shmuessen* on a rotational basis. One week Reb Dovid gave the *shiur*, the next week Rabbi Yisroel Kanarek, the next week Rabbi Markel Greenhaus, and the next week Rabbi Chaim Gryngras. Then the cycle resumed. On "special" Shabbosos, like Shabbos Shuvah or Shabbos HaGadol, Rabbi Yisroel Chaim Kaplan delivered the *shiur*.

Most members of the Mirrer Minyan were Mirrer alumni whose coming together created a sense of what once was. No one had to establish rules or formal *shiurim* to create an atmosphere of Mir; the atmosphere was created through its participants. It was this atmosphere that even drew "non-

---

13. It seemed unusually fitting that Rabbi Tuvia Kaplan passed away in the shul that he loved while setting the Shabbos clocks after *Minchah Gedolah* one Erev Shabbos.

14. Rabbi Raphael Shain.

15. See Biography Section.

## Rabbi Yisroel Chaim Kaplan: a revered presence in the Mirrer Minyan

*Rabbi Yisroel Chaim Kaplan (1891-1970) learned in Radin under the Chofetz Chaim. He married the daughter of Rabbi Yeruchem Levovitz and later became a maggid shiur in Brisk. Upon the outbreak of World War II, Rabbi Yisroel Chaim Kaplan fled to Vilna, and from there to Japan. He arrived in America in 1941 and was chosen as a Rosh Yeshivah in Torah Vodaath and then Mashgiach of Bais Medrash Elyon in Monsey. He assumed leadership of Bais Medrash Elyon when Rabbi Reuvain Grozovsky took ill in 1951.*

Mirrers." R' Yosef Zimmerman was a rarity among the regulars because he was neither a Mirrer nor involved in learning. As one who had a real appreciation of Torah and *lomdei Torah*, he enjoyed the atmosphere of the Mirrer Minyan, where a layman was an exception and *b'nei Torah* were the rule.[16]

*"KINDERLACH."* RABBI YISROEL CHAIM KAPLAN GESTURED WITH HIS hand to the children. "Come here for a minute." Michoel Bender passed a sheepish glance at his friend. Had one of them misbehaved? In the Mirrer Minyan, children were expected to be docile participants.

Rabbi Yisroel Chaim Kaplan stood tall and straight; his shining face radiating purity was framed by a flowing white beard. Though the boys were too young to comprehend his greatness, they were awed by his presence.

*"Kinderlach,* I noticed that you went out to play during *Kri'as HaTorah."* The children were surprised. Rabbi Yisroel Chaim Kaplan concentrated deeply on his *avodah* — his *Shemoneh Esrei* lasted long after everyone had finished — how had he noticed their absence? Rabbi Yisroel Chaim Kaplan continued his gentle rebuke. "I understand that the davening is long and you feel that you need a break ... but *Kri'as HaTorah* is so important! Per-

---

16. Mr. Zimmerman's love of *talmidei chachamim* was well known. He had sent his two sons to learn in Baranovich and when Rabbi Elchonon Wasserman came to America, he stayed in the Zimmerman home. The Zimmermans merited two illustrious sons: Reb Asher, renowned *posek,* and Reb Mordechai, a prominent *mohel.*

haps you can stay in for *Kri'as HaTorah* and go out during the *Haftarah*? What do you think?"

The boys listened. They knew that Rabbi Yisroel Chaim Kaplan was making a request that came from the heart. He truly wanted them to have the *zechus* to hear *Kri'as HaTorah*, and he felt them capable of embracing such a decision. The boys solemnly agreed to try. Though they knew that going out for *Kri'as HaTorah* was acceptable for children their age in most *kehillos*, they recognized that they were different. They davened in the Mirrer Minyan; there, the standards were higher.

*For the Yamim Nora'im and Simchas Torah, all the Mirrer Minyanim assembled in the new building of Rabbi Avrohom Newhouse's Bais Yaakov on 125 Heyward Street, the new location of the growing Bais Yaakov elementary school of Williamsburg. Heartfelt tefillos replaced the gentile songs that had once reverberated from the rooms of the former public school building.*

FOR THE *YAMIM NORA'IM*, ALL THE Mirrer *minyanim* joined together. They had outgrown the Bais Yaakov High School on South Eighth Street where they used to assemble for *Yamim Nora'im* and, just in time, Rabbi Newhouse purchased an old public school building at 125 Heyward Street for his growing "little Bais Yaakov."[17] He gladly turned it over to the Mirrer Minyan for *Yamim Nora'im*. When all the Mirrer *minyanim* came together they were the largest *minyan* in Williamsburg at the time.

Reb Dovid, with his sweet voice and sincere *tefillos*, inspired the *mispallelim*.[18] Though he was not as active in the Mirrer Minyan as he had once been, Reb Dovid was no less dedicated. When Rabbi Aharon Kotler asked Reb Dovid to come to Lakewood as *ba'al Mussaf* for the *Yamim Nora'im*, Reb Dovid respectfully declined since he did not want to leave the Mirrer Minyan.[19] The davening at the Mirrer Minyan was so inspiring, there were those who, like Reb Shmuel Charkover, came to Williamsburg for the *Yamim Nora'im* just to daven in the Mirrer Minyan.

ROSH HASHANAH AFTERNOON, WILLIAMSBURG JEWRY SWARMED TO the Williamsburg Bridge for *Tashlich*. This was one *minhag* that all ele-

---

17. A nickname for Bais Yaakov elementary school.

18. A number of people mentioned how, 40 years later, they still remember Reb Dovid's poignant davening.

19. He recommended that Reb Aharon ask his good friend from Mir, Rabbi Ezriel Lange. Reb Ezriel remained the *ba'al tefillah* in Lakewood for over 40 years.

ments of Orthodoxy were eager to adopt. It was a quaint way to rid oneself of sin, and a walk along the bridge dressed in holiday finery was an exciting way to end the day. Back in the early days of Jewish Williamsburg, this very obvious show of Jewish identity, in the streets of an American city, was a beautiful testimony of Jewish faith and pride. People from other neighborhoods witnessing this phenomenon came away moved and motivated.[20]

Yet, as Williamsburg standards of religiosity kept on climbing, so did peoples' religious antennae. As Reb Dovid went to *Tashlich* one year, he noticed that the atmosphere was not as solemn as it should be. He was perturbed that this holy *minhag* was sometimes a vehicle for the unholy mingling of men and women. He was saddened that he had been a part of it and wondered what his practice should be in the future. He went to discuss the problem with Rabbi Yonason Steif.

The Rav's answer was swift and sharp. "Better to say *Tashlich* at the sink than to go to a place of *ta'aruvos* (mingling)!"

Reb Dovid spent much time with the Viener Dayan in the days between Rosh Hashanah and Succos due to his *esrog* "business." What started as a small gesture of *hakaras hatov* from brother to sister had turned into something much larger.

From the very first year they arrived in America, the Benders sent gifts and packages to Rebbetzin Bender's brother, Yosef, in Eretz Yisroel. Yosef Epstein was very appreciative of their efforts and looked for ways to reciprocate by sending things from Eretz Yisroel that could be of value to his family in America. He hit upon a novel idea. He decided to send his brother-in-law an *esrog* from Eretz Yisroel. He knew that a beautiful *esrog*, from a reputable orchard, would be much appreciated.

> ... *Today I was in Petach Tikva and bought esrogim for you from the orchard of HaRav Braverman.*[21] *He is the sole expert in esrogim in this region and his merchandise is kosher l'mehadrin. The Chofetz Chaim and Harav Chaim Ozer Grodzenski all bought esrogim from him ... From the entire orchard we found, meanwhile, only nine. They are, of course, not murkavim, and they were grown according to all the halachos that pertain to Eretz Yisroel. One of the esrogim is*

---

20. *Reb Chaim Gelb: A Life of Chessed,* p. 38.

21. Yosef Epstein was sending his brother-in-law legendary "Braverman *esrogim.*" Rabbi Zorach Braverman (d. 1938), famed *maggid* of Yerushalayim, sold *esrogim*. One day, he traveled with Rabbi Yehoshua Leib Diskin (1816-1898) to a place near Shechem where Reb Yehoshua Leib showed him a tree that he declared with certainty was guaranteed to be a non-*murkav esrog* tree. Reb Zorach cut off part of the tree and replanted it in Petach Tikva. From there he continued to replant until he had a small orchard. His son Reb Yisroel Dovid and his grandson Reb Yitzchok continued to do the same. Though the Bravermans also sold other *esrogim*, those grown in Petach Tikva were coveted as being approved by Rabbi Yehoshua Leib Diskin.

so special that it is rarely found. Near the pitem, it has dents like the impression of teeth. It is called "neshichas Chavah."[22] The Chassidim draw lots in order to get one like it. Some of the esrogim do not have pitems because the non-murkavim often grow without a pitem. It is possible that on some of them you will find very small leaves (mark caused by a leaf pressing against it as it grew). Do not worry, they were thoroughly checked …

THIS GESTURE OF *HAKARAS HATOV* BURGEONED INTO A BUSINESS. EVERY year, Yosef sent a few *esrogim* for Reb Dovid, hoping that one would meet his approval. Reb Dovid picked out one for himself and one for his father, and then he sold the rest to cover the costs of the *esrogim* and the shipping. When Rabbi Avrohom Bender remarried and moved to Eretz Yisroel, he took over the job, only with a different twist. He sent as many as 50 *esrogim*, knowing that Reb Dovid would pick out a beautiful one for himself and sell the rest at a profit. In time, the minibusiness flourished.[23]

In September, like clockwork, the boxes from Eretz Yisroel arrived. The children pounced on the boxes, eager to examine their array of exotic foreign stamps. Each stamp was carefully lifted from the cardboard and stored away in the children's stamp collections.

Reb Dovid opened the boxes and carefully examined each *esrog*, setting prices based on quality. Then he would notify his regular customers to come choose. The Klausenberger Dayan, Rabbi Fishel Hershkowitz, always bought from Reb Dovid, as did other people who wanted an *esrog* with a strong *yichus*. In a good year, Reb Dovid would sell up to 50 *esrogim*.

While dealing with *esrogim*, *shaylos* arose and that was why Reb Dovid spent so much time between Rosh Hashanah and Succos with Rabbi Yonason Steif. As the Viener Dayan grew older, he did not trust his own eyesight. Eventually, he stopped checking *esrogim* and directed Reb Dovid to the Shoproner Rav. The Shoproner Rav, Rabbi Shimon Posen, was a renowned *posek* who also served as Rosh Yeshivah in Satmar. He had a small *shtiebel* and was gradually accruing a following of loyal *talmidim*, from both Europe and America. As his reputation as an expert in halachah grew, his influence stretched far beyond the small apartment that housed his *minyan*.

---

22. Many refer to this in Yiddish as "*Chavah's bis*" or the bite of Chavah. Sometimes, in the upper third of the *esrog* there is an indentation like a "bite," alluding to the *midrash* that the fruit of the *eitz hada'as* from which Chavah ate was an *esrog*.

23. "When my grandfather began sending the *esrogim*, my father insisted in sending all the proceeds back to his father in Eretz Yisroel. As Zaida grew older and it became difficult for him to go to the orchards and pick out the *esrogim*, his nephew Rabbi Shloimke Berman would help him. This continued for many years" (Rabbi Yaakov Bender).

**Two prominent Williamsburg personalities with whom Rabbi Dovid Bender maintained relationships: The Shoproner Rav and Rabbi Nosson Horowitz**

*Rabbi Shimon Yisroel Posen (1894-1969) was known as the Shoproner Rav. He studied under Rabbi Yoel Selner in Belz and then in Uhel. In 1923 Reb Shimon was called upon to run the yeshivah in Shopron, and in 1927 was appointed Shoproner Rav. After suffering through the Holocaust, he served as Rav in Pupa. He left for America in 1947, where the Satmar Rav asked him to lead the yeshivah, with a modest beginning of two boys. He served as Rosh Yeshivah in Satmar his remaining years.*

*Rabbi Nosson HaLevi Horowitz (1913-2001) learned under the guidance of his grandfather, the Altstater Rav, Rabbi Chaim Yitzchok Yeruchem Horowitz. During World War II, the Horowitzes moved to America where Reb Nosson married the daughter of Rabbi Yissocher Ber Rubin, the Doliner Rav. He became Rav of the Sheires Yisroel Shul of Williamsburg. In 1971 he moved to Monsey where he became Rav of the Bais Yisroel kehillah, a position he filled with dedication for 30 years.*

In general, Succos was a very hectic time for Reb Dovid. In addition to the *esrogim*, he was the main "succah organizer." He took charge of building a succah in the building's courtyard and magnanimously invited his neighbors to join. The succah was of modest proportions since there was not much space in the courtyard. At night, all the men and boys in the building ate together, and the women ate in their homes. By day, the families ate in shifts: the *Litvishe* men davened earlier than the Chassidim, and they were easily able to accommodate each other.

The communal succah's warmth and camaraderie encouraged cooperation and friendship. The men sang together, a harmony of *niggunim* and dialects frequently interrupted by *divrei Torah*. The women snatched a conversation on the stairwells, pots and plates in hand, as they brought down their Yom Tov delicacies. The children ran happily up and down the steps, enjoying the departure from routine in the unusually free *seudah*.

Reb Dovid loved to spend time in his succah. Sitting at the table, decked with the special "Netziv" tablecloth[24] reserved for Yom Tov, he would sing his rebbi's[25] favorite, "*Ah Succaleh, Ah Kleine.*" In a slow, hauntingly beautiful melody, he would sing over and over of the little succah covered sparsely with *schach*, shaking roughly in the wind, yet never falling. He would enter another world as he delved into the deeper meaning behind the words. The *succaleh* was the Jewish nation in exile, always being shaken — roughly, violently — and yet who still, after 2000 years, endures. It is a song whose pathos is laced with joy. *Klal Yisroel* rejoices in the certainty that, just as they have survived through 2000 years of exile, they will survive to greet *Mashiach*.

Succos for Jewish Williamsburg was a Yom Tov of joy and confidence: joy that they had passed Yom Kippur and confidence that they had been granted a new year where they would certainly climb higher in their relationship with the One Above. For the children, Chol HaMoed Succos was a whole week when their fathers suddenly had extra time for them: time to sit together, learn together, eat together, or even go on an occasional outing.

Shemini Atzeres brought another surge of excitement. The Chassidim held *hakafos* on Shemini Atzeres at night and Reb Dovid took the children across the street to Rabbi Nosson Horowitz's shul to enjoy these *hakafos*. Rabbi Nosson Horowitz had taken over the room above the A&P supermarket that had originally housed the Tzelemer Rav's *minyan*, and opened his own *minyan* there. Rabbi Nosson Horowitz was an *Oberlander* who, like the Tzelemer Rav, had *Chassidishe* roots. The result was a shul, not a *shtiebel*, whose *minhagim* were generally *Chassidishe*, but whose *mispallelim* were a mix.

Before the Mirrer Minyan was established, Reb Dovid regularly davened at Rabbi Nosson Horowitz's shul. Rebbetzin Bender continued to daven there Shabbos morning, but Reb Dovid rarely found time to go in. As a show of warmth, friendship, and loyalty, he returned with his children, year after year, to participate in the Shemini Atzeres *hakafos* there.

ON SIMCHAS TORAH, ALL THE MIRRER MINYANIM ASSEMBLED TOGETHER in the little Bais Yaakov on Heyward Street for *hakafos*, hoping for a taste

---

24. Rebbetzin Bender's mother gave her a tablecloth that had once belonged to the Netziv. The Netziv's second wife was Lifsha Epstein's great-aunt who gave it to Rebbetzin Bender. When the Netziv's Rebbetzin passed away, the tablecloth went to her sister who passed it on to her daughter. The Netziv used this tablecloth every Succos. This was one of the rare sentimental belongings that Rebbetzin Bender had with her in her carry-on luggage when she came to America.

25. Rabbi Dovid Leibowitz. Though Reb Dovid's years in Mir eclipsed his years in Torah Vodaath, he still revered his "first" rebbi, Rabbi Dovid Leibowitz. When his son Paltiel playfully asked him, "Had I been a firstborn son, who would you have chosen as a *Kohen* at my *pidyon haben*?" Reb Dovid answered, "Rebbi's son, of course!" Although Rabbi Henoch Leibowitz was much younger than Reb Dovid, he was "Rebbi's son," and that was enough to accord him the honor.

of what they had left behind in Europe. The *hakafos* in the Mir had been so unusually joyous and uplifting that Reb Yeruchem himself once said, "I don't know what is considered greater by the Creator of the World: our Yom Kippur or our Simchas Torah!"[26]

Yet they were no longer in the Mir. They were *she'aris ha'pleitah*, survivors from the war who, after many trials, had come to America to rebuild their lives. Most of them had lost their entire families in Europe. They pulled themselves together and married, without fathers or mothers to walk them down the aisle. They accepted positions in the growing yeshivos and *chadarim* of America and were slowly redefining American Orthodoxy.

No, they would not be able to recreate the *hakafos* in the Mir but through the *hakafos* they had experienced there, they were able to create *hakafos* uniquely their own. When they began "*Utzu eitzah v'sufar, dabru davar v'lo yakum ki imanu keil,*"[27] the entire assembly exploded in song. This was the song that, back in Shanghai, the *heiliger Mashgiach* Reb Chatzkel had led them in singing with unrestrained joy. They were miles away from China, from the worry and want during the years of war, but the feelings that they felt then while singing "*Utzu eitzah ...*" were much the same as the feelings it ignited in them now.

"*Utzu eitzah v'sufar* — plan a plot and it will be annulled"; "*dabru davar v'lo yakum* — speak your piece and it will not come to pass"; "*ki imanu Keil* — because *HaKadosh Baruch Hu* is with us." True, they no longer had their beloved parents, sisters, and brothers. True, they no longer danced in the holy *beis medrash* of the Mir where, for so many years, they sat bent over their *shtenders*. True, they now lived in a world so very different from where they had come from. They were chosen by Hashem to survive when so many others had been killed. They had come to America as lonely *bochurim*, and now they were dancing with children on their shoulders. They had lost entire families, but *HaKadosh Baruch Hu*, in His infinite kindness, had allowed them to survive together so that even though they might have very few blood relations, they were family to one another.

Each *hakafah* lasted a long time, some as long as a half an hour. After *Shacharis*, the entire Mirrer Minyan went to the home of Rabbi Ezriel Lange for a beautiful *kiddush* of wine and cakes and stuffed cabbage. The Langes beamed with pleasure as their house filled with their friends from the Mirrer Minyan.

ONCE, DURING A BREAK ON SIMCHAS TORAH IN THE MIRRER MINYAN, Rabbi Dovid Bender turned to his good friend Rabbi Chaim Shereshevsky.

---

26. See page 71.

27. *Yeshayah* 8:10.

... They were *she'aris ha'pleitah*, survivors from the war who, after many trials, had come to America to rebuild their lives ... They married, without fathers or mothers to walk them down the aisle. They accepted positions in the growing yeshivos and *chadarim* of America and were slowly redefining American Orthodoxy ...

Rabbi Shmuel Brudny, Rabbi Binyomin Zeilberger, Rabbi Elya Yurkansky, Rabbi Aharon Kreiser, Rabbi Ezriel Lange, Rabbi Shlomo Rottenberg, and Rabbi Pinchas Litmanowitz are just a few examples.

*At Rabbi Pinchas Litmanowitz's wedding. Rabbi Dovid Bender and Rabbi Shlomo Rottenberg are walking him down the aisle. Rabbi Ezriel Lange is walking in the foreground.*

*At Rabbi Pinchas Litmanowitz's wedding. The chosson is dancing with the Mashgiach, Rabbi Yecheskel Levenstein (who lived in America for two years after leaving Shanghai until immigrating to Eretz Yisroel), and his father-in-law, Rabbi Moshe Yehoshua Heschel Zehnwirth.*

"Chaim," he called, "Reb Yankel Finkelstein's son is home with fever. Come, let's go over for a visit." Rabbi Chaim Shereshevsky joined Reb Dovid as he invited Rabbi Ezriel Lange and a few other friends to join them. The whole group trooped over to Rabbi Yankel Finkelstein's house, where they were welcomed in joyous surprise. They made *Kiddush* and passed around wine and schnapps. Reb Dovid drank and began singing. Everyone joined in. For 20 minutes Reb Dovid and his friends sang and danced, bringing joy and happiness to a little boy who was missing Simchas Torah.

This group of Mirrers, men in their late 30's who were already learned scholars, had paused in their own celebration to rejoice with a little boy, a son of a friend. In the Mirrer Minyan, Simchas Torah was something so special, they could not allow one of their own to miss it. If the child could not come to *hakafos*, they would bring *hakafos* to him. After all, they were all part of the Mirrer Minyan; they were family.[28]

PURIM WAS CERTAINLY REB DOVID'S YOM TOV. HE ENJOYED GIVING others pleasure, and Purim afforded him many opportunities to do so. When he sent *mishloach manos* to Rabbi Shlomo Heiman, he would include something special that he thought the rebbetzin would enjoy. After Reb Shlomo's *petirah* he was even more careful about this. He sent *mishloach manos* to his ninth-grade rebbi, Rabbi Uri Meir Kahanow, long after he had been in his *shiur*.

One Purim, he walked into the house elated. His children wanted to know why he was in such an exceptionally sunny mood. "You want to know why?" he asked. "I met Mike Tress and he told me of a family that had no money to pay their electric bill. The electric company threatened to turn off their electricity if the bill was not paid today. He told me that they needed $10. Right away, I gave him $10. Can you believe it? Because of my $10, this family will have electricity. What a *zechus*!"

---

An indication of how close the Mirrer families of Williamsburg felt toward one another: At Rabbi Binyomin Zeilberger's *chasunah*, an announcement was made that Rabbi Dovid and Rebbetzin Bender were not in attendance because Rebbetzin Bender had just given birth to a baby boy. The news was greeted with joy and happiness and very little surprise that the announcement was being made at the Zeilberger wedding.

*Rabbi Binyomin Zeilberger (1922-2006) joined Yeshivas Mir at the age of 14. After arriving in America with the Mirrer Yeshivah in 1947, he continued learning in the newly established Mirrer Yeshivah in the United States where he began to deliver regular discourses. He married the daughter of Rabbi Yisroel Chaim Kaplan. Following his marriage, Reb Binyomin joined Yeshivas Beis HaTalmud where he later served as its Rosh Yeshivah.*

---

28. Rabbi Avrohom Shereshevsky.

FOR PESACH, THE HOUSE SEEMED TO EXPAND. MANY LOST AND LONELY souls came to the Benders' Seder. For example, Mrs. M., a sweet woman in her 30's or 40's, was a Seder regular. Before the war, Mrs. M. had been young and happily married. After the war she immigrated to America, certain that her husband had died. Meanwhile, he survived the war and immigrated to America, certain that she had died. He remarried and started a new life. When they accidentally met on the streets of New York one day, it was a bittersweet reunion: sweet, because each was happy the other had survived, and bitter because they knew that they could not renew their life together. Mrs. M. resigned herself to life as a spinster.

The Benders became a surrogate family for Mrs. M. and many others. Their overflowing table on the Seder night was a symptom of their expansive heart.

### Chapter Forty

# Founded on Chessed

### Williamsburg: 5717 (1957)

THE DOOR TO THE APARTMENT OPENED EVEN BEFORE ESTHER put her hand on the knob. Her mother had heard her coming home from school and stood in the doorway to greet her. "Esther," she said in a whisper, "Mr. Gross[29] is here. Tell him he looks 50." Esther looked at her mother strangely.

She walked into the apartment and, sure enough, there was Mr. Gross sitting in the kitchen looking woebegone. "Mr. Gross," Esther declared, "you look so good, not a day older than 50!"

Mr. Gross's face lit up "Really? Oh, come on, do you mean it?"

"Yup," she said authoritatively, "50, and not a day older."

"You are such a smart girl," he beamed. "I was thinking the same thing myself. Some people are so foolish — adults, mind you. But here, in this house, even the children are smart! Well, I'm off. Everyone have a good day." He left the house in an uncharacteristically good mood.

"What was that all about?" Esther raised her eyebrows as she helped herself to a pre-supper snack.

Rebbetzin Bender smiled. "You know how it is. Mr. Gross is probably around 70, but he thinks he looks 50. Today, he was in a store when the salesman made a comment to the effect that he must be around 60. Now, most people would consider that a compliment but, because Mr. Gross is convinced that he looks 50, he was positively insulted. I wanted you to make him feel better."

---

29. Not his real name.

Esther grinned good-naturedly.

Mr. Gross was truly a character. He had learned with Rabbi Avrohom Bender back in Novarodok. Life in Europe had been very difficult and, like many others, he scraped together enough money for passage to America and left. He arrived on the shores of the *goldene medinah* with the shirt on his back and almost nothing else. He scrounged around in garbage cans looking for food until he finally landed a steady job in the subway system.

Unfortunately, the years of insecurity and deprivation had taken their toll. Mr. Gross was convinced that he was desperately poor. He found it difficult to spend money on even bare necessities and continued rummaging through the garbage for treasures. He never married but he made the Bender home his own. He ate there every Shabbos and Yom Tov and would often stop by during the week.

"READ THIS PIECE OF POETRY." MR. GROSS HANDED REBBETZIN BENDER a rumpled piece of paper. "It's beautiful! I sent it to *The Forward*. A nice, professional paper should be able to appreciate my poetry, no? They should be thanking me for sending them something so nice. How many people send them such beautiful writing? So I waited to see my poem in print. Can you believe it? They didn't print it! Where is their taste? Just my mazel; I send in beautiful poetry and the people who read it have no taste!"

Rebbetzin Bender clucked sympathetically as she went about her business in the kitchen. She placed a piece of cake in front of him and he muttered a thank-you. As he chewed his snack, he gave a start and spit something out into a napkin.

"What is it?" Rebbetzin Bender asked, anxiously.

Mr. Gross examined the napkin closely and then sighed. "It's just a peg. My mazel, the piece of cake I eat has the peg. A whole big cake, and I get the piece with a peg." He sighed with self-pity. "You know, I was in Paris once, only for a few hours. My mazel, it rained the whole time."

Paltiel walked by and Mr. Gross called him over, "Here, *yingele*, I have something for you." He took out an old, grimy ball that looked too dead to bounce. "Look, a beautiful ball. Go play! Enjoy it!" Paltiel gingerly took the ball from Mr. Gross and looked at his mother quizzically.

"That's so nice of you, Mr. Gross, so thoughtful." As Mr. Gross turned his head, Rebbetzin Bender grabbed the ball from Paltiel and motioned that he wash his hands with soap and water. She deftly snuck the offensive object where it would not be noticed until later when she would dump it into the garbage. A broken pencil, a chewed-up rubber ball, a yellowed *tallis kattan*, a half-used book of matches, and other such things made their way to the Bender home via Mr. Gross. As he scrounged around garbage dumpsters looking for valuables, he always picked out a few things for his "family," the Benders. Rebbetzin Bender was disgusted by these dirty, germy gifts — especially since she had grown up in Otvock where everyone had been attuned to guarding against germs and disease — but she would never want to hurt his feelings. He was genuinely happy that he had something to give.

"I see that you have tomatoes for the salad today. Why, when I came to America 40 years ago, tomatoes were 2 cents a pound. Now they want 4 cents a pound! *Ganavim!* Look at the pickles. They used to be a penny a pickle. Now they want a nickel. A nickel a pickle! What is it anyway? A cucumber with a little salt? Speaking about *ganavim*, the shoemakers in this country are out to take away my last penny." Mr. Gross raised up his shoe, which was in shreds. "I wanted a new sole. How much could a little piece of cardboard cost? I won't even tell you the amount of money that the *ganev* wanted from me. So, look what I'm going to do." He whipped something out of his pocket. Rebbetzin Bender looked on, amused as he triumphantly held up the sole of a shoe. "I found this on the tracks. If you give me a little glue, I think that I can fix it all by myself."

Rebbetzin Bender hastened to find him some glue and set him up at the dining-room table to do his repair job. The children crowded around to watch and Rebbetzin Bender escaped into the kitchen.

THE BENDERS NEVER CEASED TO BE AMAZED AT THEIR FRIEND'S ECCENtricity. After Mr. Gross retired, he spent a lot of his time riding the subways. He had a free lifetime pass and found it a cheap way to spend his day. One evening, at the end of a day cruising the boroughs of New York, Mr. Gross shuffled into the Benders and sat down heavily on a chair. For a while, he did not say much. Then, out of the blue, he said, "My brother just passed away."

Rebbetzin Bender looked startled. "Your brother?"

Mr. Gross nodded. "The man sitting next to me on the subway left his newspaper on the seat when he left the car. The paper was open to the obituaries. Staring back at me was a picture of my brother. He passed away a few weeks ago." Then Mr. Gross stood up abruptly. "I'm on my way," he said, and left the house.

Rebbetzin Bender and the children looked at one another in wonder. For all the time he had spent at the Benders — for years he practically lived there — Mr. Gross never breathed a word about having family in America. Then, one day, he walks in, makes this matter-of-fact proclamation, and walks out. He was definitely an interesting person.

Everyone knew that Mr. Gross was not truly poor. He had a pension from the Transit Authority for his years of work on the subway system, and he had no wife or children to support. Well-meaning friends and neighbors urged the Benders to allow Mr. Gross to help them with their expenses. Reb Dovid was horrified at the suggestion. "I would not take a broken penny from him!" Reb Dovid felt that the greatest service he could do for Mr. Gross was to be warm and hospitable toward him and to encourage him to use his money for his own comfort and merit. Reb Dovid convinced him to take a trip to Eretz Yisroel. He advised him to make a will leaving his money to various yeshivos. He guided him toward moving into an old-age home in Eretz Yisroel where he lived out his last years.

The Bender children grew up with Mr. Gross as an integral part of their lives. They accepted with equanimity that their home was his and that he had a right to take up the time, patience, and attention of their parents. The same was true for any person or project that their parents were involved in.

BLUMIE SKIPPED HAPPILY DOWN THE STREET ON HER WAY HOME FROM school. The sun was shining, the air was crisp and fresh, and she was eager to get home to her mother's warm greeting and a nice snack. From Heyward to Rutledge, from Rutledge to Penn … Wait, what day is it today? Blumie stopped skipping. She walked slowly as she tried to remember what day it was. Oh, it's Monday. Mommy is going out to teach. Blumie walked home pensively. On an evening that Mommy taught, her mother's smile of greeting was a little more hurried as she shooed the younger children to bed so that she could leave her house by 6 o'clock. Her mother would surely ask Blumie about her day, but Blumie was never sure her mother was really listening. Blumie sighed and walked even slower.

Blumie opened the door to their apartment.

"Hello, Blumale, *vos hertzach*?" Rebbetzin Bender greeted Blumie with a harried smile, as she dashed busily about. As expected, her mother was preoccupied with getting things in order before running out to teach.

"Oh, nothing special." Blumie smiled stoically, never letting her mother notice her disappointment at being barely acknowledged. "Everything is fine. What can I do to help?" Blumie asked, as she looked for ways to pitch in. Even though they never spoke about it, Blumie understood that her mother's work in Bais Yaakov was very important. She admired her mother for her position as a teacher, for the rapport she had with her students, and the respect people had for her. She understood that she was privileged to be her daughter and to have a share in her work. Only sometimes, it was difficult.[30]

---

30. "Many years later, when I told my mother how I had felt then, she felt so bad. I was sorry that I mentioned anything at all, especially since, even then, while I was disappointed, it was only because I loved having her at home so much" (Rebbetzin Blumie [Bender] Shapiro).

THE BENDER CHILDREN UNDERSTOOD THAT NOTHING WAS DONE AT their expense. They were not "entitled" to more of their parents' attention or time. Their parents showered them with love and the children realized that they were allowed to shower love on other people as well.

Rabbi Dovid and Rebbetzin Bender were exceptional doers. They saw a need and sought to fill it. One of Reb Dovid's friends from the Mir, an illustrious *talmid chacham* who had settled in Europe, passed away suddenly, leaving a home of orphans. Reb Dovid launched a campaign to raise money for the family.

He took his own letterhead and typed up a heartfelt appeal letter. Then he ran to the local print shop to make copies. Copies in hand, he gathered his children around the dining-room table and, assembly-line style, he had them stuffing envelopes, sealing them shut, and licking the stamps. In those pre-mailing-list days, he created his own mailing list, by going through the White Pages for names and addresses of friends and acquaintances.

Reb Dovid was constantly taking on new causes. He co-signed loans for Mrs. W., a young widow with a son. He raised money for the poor H. family. He did his work as discreetly as possible, often shooing the children into their rooms so that he could speak privately on the kitchen phone.

The situation did not have to be dire to prompt Reb Dovid to participate. When Esther was a little girl, Rebbetzin Malka Svei[31] fell and she was in the hospital, her foot in traction. On Rosh Hashanah Reb Dovid went to the hospital to blow shofar for her. He took along his daughter; it was a good opportunity to broaden her life experiences and allow her to feel for others.

Reb Dovid's learn-by-osmosis method bore fruit, and his children began thinking like their parents. Esther was very young when she realized that Joe, the candy-store owner whose shop was beneath their apartment, was Jewish.

"But why doesn't he close his store on Shabbos?" she asked her father, puzzled.

Characteristically, Reb Dovid decided to act. He asked Joe how much revenue the store brought in on Shabbos. Joe quoted a figure and every week, Reb Dovid collected money to pay Joe so that Joe would be comfortable closing his business on Shabbos. After a while, Joe was so appreciative of the day off that he told Reb Dovid he no longer wanted the money; he would stay closed on Shabbos regardless.

"DOVID! WHAT HAPPENED TO YOU?" REBBETZIN BENDER STARED IN alarm. It was 2:30 on a short Friday afternoon, and Reb Dovid had just come in from *Minchah*. His face was very red, as if someone had slapped him.

---

31. Married to Rabbi Shmuel Leib Svei.

"It's nothing," he muttered, and went to prepare for Shabbos.

Rebbetzin Bender was concerned. Something had happened and it was not like Reb Dovid to keep the details from her. With a little detective work, Rebbetzin Bender found out the full story. R' Y. was an older bachelor who had learned in the Mir. He was a hard-up depressed fellow, for whom life was a string of misfortunes. Reb Dovid reached out to R' Y., helping him financially and always trying to boost his spirits. R' Y. was a frequent guest at the Bender Shabbos table where he was always welcomed warmly. That day, after *Minchah*, R' Y. and Reb Dovid were talking. R' Y. became agitated and slapped Reb Dovid across the face.

Rebbetzin Bender approached her husband. "Dovid, I do not want to let this man into our house anymore! To do such a thing in public ... after all that we have done for him ..."

"Just the opposite," Reb Dovid answered. "Now that we realize how disturbed he is, it is all the more reason to invite him."[32]

THE YEARS FOLLOWING THE WAR PRODUCED MANY FORLORN AND BROken people. Some were survivors who lost their entire families in the war, and then lost their minds in its aftermath. Some were misfits who, after enduring the poverty of the Depression, never resumed leading normal lives. Some had simply gone through personal traumas and never recovered. Reb Dovid, with his good heart, felt responsible for these people.

A man once arrived in shul very unkempt and dirty. After he left, it occurred to Reb Dovid that he might not have a place to go to. He was reluctant to invite him because the man's appearance was so disturbing. He was afraid that other people at his Shabbos table might be uncomfortable, and yet, what if the man had nowhere to go? Reb Dovid sent his young son Michoel to run after him and see that he had a home. Michoel followed him and found out that people were taking an interest in him. Reb Dovid was relieved, but he was upset that he had hesitated to invite him to his home immediately. How could he have allowed the man's disheveled appearance to put him off? Nothing Rebbetzin Bender said could comfort him. A fellow *Yid* might have needed help, and he had not responded.

REBBETZIN BENDER HAD HER OWN PET PROJECTS. FINANCES BEING tight, she was happy for any hand-me-downs she received for her own children. Any extra clothing, she gave away to others. After a while, the amounts she gave away far exceeded what she kept.

Mrs. Toba Hessa (Tilly) Mehler was a kindhearted woman with girls in Bais Yaakov. Through her daughters, she became friendly with Rebbetzin

---

32. Rebbetzin Bender recounted this story at a *yahrtzeit seudah* for her husband.

Bender and began to send to her no-longer-needed clothing from her family and other families in her neighborhood of Crown Heights. Slowly, Rebbetzin Bender's used clothing distribution business grew.[33]

Rebbetzin Bender spent hours sorting through shirts and skirts, dresses and jumpers, pants and coats. An owner of a pants factory sent her cases of surplus pants. Rebbetzin Bender went through every box, discarding the ones no one would wear — the yellow, purple or orange pairs — and setting aside navys, blacks, and browns. She sorted them by size and color and then she called one friend after another, asking about the sizes of pants that their boys wore.

Rebbetzin Bender's acts of *chessed* encompassed many situations. When the Hasenfelds, a young newlywed couple, moved to Hooper Street, Rebbetzin Bender went to see how they were faring. Zissie had been her student in Bais Yaakov. She married Yissochor Hasenfeld, a survivor and refugee like herself.

Life had been hard for Yissochor and Zissie, and it seemed that their problems were not yet over. Yissochor had not found steady work and, to add to their financial difficulties, he became ill and was completely bedridden. Zissie had two little babies to care for, all alone.

Rebbetzin Bender took charge of the sorry situation. She visited with the young couple and gently probed to figure out how she could be of help. She and Mrs. Hasenfeld became fast friends. They discussed child-rearing, financial concerns, and health issues. Most importantly, Rebbetzin Bender taught Mr. Hasenfeld English so that when he had the strength to hold down a job he would be better equipped to enter the workforce.

Rebbetzin Bender came to the Hasenfeld house daily, often bringing a different book or study aid. Mr. Hasenfeld found it energizing to learn English and American history; the latter helped him to acclimate to his new land. By the time Yissochor Hasenfeld recovered, he felt more grounded in English language and American culture, and had more confidence when it was time to find a job. Eventually he became a successful businessman, a *maggid shiur* in his shul, a philanthropist, and the father of a distinguished family.

REBBETZIN BENDER WAS AN OPTIMIST. WHAT OTHERS SAW AS DIFFICULT, or even impossible, she took in stride. A woman had been killed in a bombing during the Israeli War of Independence, and the widower was coming to America with his four little children, hoping to put his life back together. The Benders immediately offered to host the entire family.

The children were little — the youngest was just a baby — and the father was collapsing under the burden of raising his young family while provid-

---

33. Miss Brocha Mehler.

ing for their needs. The Benders convinced the father to find places for the youngest two children while he looked for a job, found an apartment, and made arrangements for the older children to be cared for while he worked.

They sent the baby girl to Rebbetzin Heiman. Rebbetzin Heiman never had any children, and she was thrilled to welcome this orphan into her home. Another family took in the baby's brother. Rebbetzin Bender raised money to pay for his upkeep and kept tabs on his progress.

When summer drew near, Rebbetzin Bender wanted to send the little boy to summer camp. The child had experienced so much sadness in his life; a carefree summer with friends and fun would do him worlds of good. Yet, even with a full scholarship, camp would be expensive.

One day, Rebbetzin Bender received a phone call from one of Reb Dovid's old *talmidim*, R' Zev Wolfson. "Listen," he began, "I just heard that Henry Hirsch[34] is going to Eretz Yisroel tonight. If you catch him before he goes, I am certain that he will give you money to help send the child to camp. I'll even drive you to his house in Westchester. Just don't tell him that I sent you."

Rebbetzin Bender grew excited. "Fine," she said, "I'll be ready as soon as you are." Rebbetzin Bender ran downstairs to call her friend Rebbetzin Chaya Epstein,[35] who was more than happy to come along. As the two women went outside, they saw the car pull up. The driver, knowing that they were in a hurry, sped through the streets of Williamsburg. Suddenly, they heard sirens and R' Zev pulled over to the side. It seemed that his speeding would not get them there any faster and that they would have to deal with a ticket as well.

The cop motioned to the driver to roll down his window. "License and registration," he said in a monotone.

Rebbetzin Bender was beside herself. "Please, sir," she said, embarrassed at how desperate she must have sounded, "please, let me tell you why we were speeding …" As Rebbetzin Bender passionately spoke about her mission, she watched the officer's expression change from boredom to curiosity to thoughtful admiration. She held her breath, awaiting his response.

"Look," he said, "I'm Irish Catholic. I believe in G-d and I see that you are sincere. I'll let you go without a ticket if you promise me one thing. Promise me that I will receive a share in the World to Come."

Rebbetzin Bender was taken aback. Could she promise him a share in the World to Come? Why not? "If you continue to go in good ways and to

---

34. Mr. Henry Hirsch (1903-1987) was one of the founders of Yeshivah Torah Vodaath and was its president. He was also founder and president of the Fifth Avenue Synagogue and contributed generously to many Jewish causes.

35. Wife of Rabbi Zelig Epstein.

believe in G-d, you will surely merit a share in the World to Come." The officer wished them well and sped away without issuing the ticket.

The Bender car reached Henry Hirsch's block in record time. Providence was with them; Mr. Hirsch was just about to leave. Rebbetzin Bender made a heartfelt appeal. Mr. Hirsch wrote out a check not only for camp but for all the extras that would make the young orphan feel more comfortable. "Buy the little one new clothes. Everyone comes to camp with nice, new summer clothing; I don't want him to feel different. He should feel good about himself." With that, Mr. Hirsch excused himself and the women left.

Rebbetzin Bender was very involved with this family until Mr. W. remarried. Then he collected his children under one roof and proceeded to build a strong and stable home for them. Though Rebbetzin Heiman was happy for Mr. W., she dearly missed the little girl she had been raising as a daughter. She cried to Rebbetzin Bender, tears of hurt and pain, and Rebbetzin Bender lent a sympathetic ear, commiserating with her plight.

True *chessed* was not always easy.

PERHAPS ONE OF THE MOST TELLING EXAMPLES OF HOW CHESSED defined the Benders can be seen in a typical, everyday incident. Chana Fishbein[36] was a young woman when her mother asked her to go down to Rebbetzin Bender's house and ask her if she had any extra room in her freezer. They were making a simchah and they needed all the extra space they could find. She met Michoel Bender, all of 11 or 12 years old, outside the house. "Ask your mother if she has room in her freezer for an extra cake."

Michoel answered, "I'll ask her if you want, but I know we have room. My mother is always able to make room for others."

Yes, the Benders always made room for others: in their minds, in their hearts, and in their home.

---

36. Rebbetzin C. Lubart.

$$\mathcal{C}hapter\ \mathcal{F}orty\text{-}\mathcal{O}ne$$

# Williamsburg Family

*"For 60 years, maybe a bit more or a bit less, we were friends, best friends.*
*We were like sisters. We were together when the world went topsy-turvy. We*
*had no sisters, no close ones, they were all taken from us by those reshaim,*
*may Hashem repay them for their deeds. Thus, we were even closer, like sis-*
*ters. There was nothing we did not share, nothing that we did not tell each*
*other. After anything that happened I would say, 'We have to call Rebbetzin*
*Bender.' We lived together constantly ..."*[37]

EBBETZIN WACHTFOGEL AND REBBETZIN BENDER TRACED their relationship all the way back to Crakow. When Rebbetzin Wachtfogel joined Rebbetzin Bender in Williamsburg, the two friends rejoiced in the prospect of living near each other, teaching together, and, in general, sharing their lives with each other. Unique circumstances brought them even closer.

In the early 1940's, Rabbi Nosson Wachtfogel accepted Rabbi Aharon Kotler's invitation to join him in his new yeshivah in Lakewood. Rabbi Aharon Kotler purposely chose a location far from the center of Jewish life so that the *bochurim* would be removed from distractions and could devote themselves completely to learning.

---

37. Rebbetzin Chava (Shlomowitz) Wachtfogel at the *shloshim* for Rebbetzin Bender.

What was a boon to the *bochurim* was a drawback for families. The Wachtfogels could not see raising their children in a city without a *cheder* or a Bais Yaakov. They decided that Reb Nosson would stay in Lakewood during the week and come home only for Shabbos, while Rebbetzin Wachtfogel would remain in Williamsburg with the children.

During the week, when Rebbetzin Wachtfogel had something to share, a question to ask, an issue to discuss, she turned to Rebbetzin Bender, her friend and confidante. Their relationship was mutual. Rebbetzin Bender was as quick to dial her friend's number, to relate the latest antics of one of the children, to discuss a school issue, or to tackle a new *tzedakah* project. They happily watched their lives intertwine as one year followed another, cementing their bond with the passage of time.

Rebbetzin Bender and Rebbetzin Wachtfogel were like sisters, and their children felt like cousins. But the Wachtfogels were not the only family the Benders held dear. There were other special Williamsburg families with whom the Benders had close relationships. Certainly, it is not coincidental that the family and friends whom the Benders held near and dear were also backbones of the *Litvishe* community in Williamsburg.

*"The telephone rang. Rebbetzin Bender picked up the receiver and listened for a few minutes. Then she made a comment and the woman on the other end began to laugh. Rebbetzin Bender joined in. For several minutes there was quiet laughter, not hysterical or rowdy, but happy and sweet — happy to find what to laugh about and sweet in its unaffected joy. Such was the conversation between Rebbetzin Bender and Rebbetzin Kaplan. They communicated together with the language of the heart, a genuine warmth, love, and understanding that often made words superfluous."*[38]

THE LIVES OF THE KAPLANS AND THE BENDERS INTERSECTED IN MANY ways. They came together as members of the Mirrer Minyan, the "Mirrer Family" in Williamsburg, sharing Yom Tov together even though Shabbos they usually davened apart. The boys kibbitzed with one another in the halls of Torah Vodaath while the girls met in Bais Yaakov and Bnos.

Erev Pesach, Reb Dovid baked matzos together with Rabbi Boruch Kaplan, Rabbi Tuvia Kaplan, and Reb Tuvia's brother-in-law Rabbi Hershel Wasilski.[39] Their *chaburah* lasted for many years, another thread that joined their lives together. Reb Boruch and Reb Dovid held each other in mutual esteem, and were pleased with the connection between their families. Nonetheless, the real bond between the Benders and the Kaplans was Bais Yaakov.

Rabbi Boruch Kaplan was a tremendous *masmid*. In recognition of his *lomdus* and *hasmadah*, he was offered a position as *maggid shiur* in Torah

---

38. Paraphrasing Rabbi Avrohom Kaplan in his *hesped* for Rebbetzin Bender.

39. See Biography Section.

Vodaath. For several years he taught in Torah Vodaath and helped his rebbetzin with Bais Yaakov when necessary. As Bais Yaakov grew, Reb Boruch saw that Bais Yaakov needed more of his time and he voluntarily gave up his position in Torah Vodaath to devote his energies to Bais Yaakov. Rebbetzin Bender marveled at this self-sacrifice, and constantly attributed the success of Bais Yaakov to Reb Boruch's *mesiras nefesh*.

The Kaplans, in turn, had boundless respect for Rebbetzin Bender. They turned to her to resolve sticky issues that often came up. They trusted her to deal wisely and discreetly. They knew that Rebbetzin Bender was a loyal and devoted partner in their mission to give every Jewish girl a Torah-true education.

Rebbetzin Bender's love of Rebbetzin Kaplan was tempered by respect akin to awe. She constantly marveled at Rebbetzin Kaplan's total devotion to Bais Yaakov, devotion that commanded admiration. Even in private, Rebbetzin Bender never referred to Rebbetzin Kaplan by her first name, though she did so with other friends from the Crakow period. To Rebbetzin Bender, Rebbetzin Kaplan belonged in a category of her own.

THE WILLIAMSBURG *LITVAKS* REMAINED EUROPEAN. MOST OF THE MEN had learned in the Mir and many of the women were European; their mother tongue was Yiddish and they often spoke Yiddish at home. The Williamsburg *Litvaks* were earnest and idealistic about Torah, *yiras Shamayim*, and *chinuch*. They eschewed the conventional, realizing that many conventions were merely a result of laziness and shortsightedness rather than excitement and vision.

One Williamsburg *Litvak* innovation was the establishment of two classes for boys who did not study secular subjects. Until then, the *Litvaks* in America felt that they had found a comfortable blend of *chinuch* in the Torah Vodaath model of *limudei kodesh* in the morning and secular studies in the afternoon. Many felt that this was the only way to raise religious children in America.

The arrival of the Chassidim challenged that notion. They established school systems without secular studies and seemed very comfortable with their choice. Suddenly, some of the Williamsburg *Litvaks* wanted to try the same system with their own children. In this, Rabbi Shlomo Rottenberg was a pioneer.

Rabbi Shlomo Rottenberg organized a group of *Litvishe* boys of similar ages and levels and asked Rabbi Yosef Liss and Rabbi Chaim Pruzansky to teach the class. Rabbi Yosef Liss taught *Chumash, Navi*, general *hashkafah* and *yedios* while Rabbi Chaim Pruzansky became the Gemara rebbi. This group stayed together for many years though some boys left in the middle and some joined later on.

## Rabbi Shlomo Rottenberg and Rabbi Yosef Liss: pioneers in Jewish education in America

*Rabbi Shlomo Rottenberg*　　　　　　*Rabbi Yosef Liss*

*Rabbi Shlomo Rottenberg (1915-2001) studied in a yeshivah in Heide, Holland and then journeyed to Mir. During World War II he reached Cuba where he set up a yeshivah for refugees. In 1943, he arrived in New York where he joined the staff of Yeshivah Torah Vodaath and Bais Yaakov Seminary. Reb Shlomo served as Rav in the Agudath Israel of Williamsburg and was an Agudah activist until his passing. His life's work was his series of seforim entitled Toldos Am Olam.*

*Rabbi Yosef Liss (1912-1992) was a student of the Mirrer Yeshivah in Poland. He escaped with the Mir, while his family perished during the Holocaust. After the war, he lived in America for a number of years where he served as a rebbi for an elite group of young boys from staunchly religious homes. He moved to Eretz Yisroel where he married the daughter of Rabbi Yisroel Luria. Reb Yosef served as the menahel of Yeshivas Tashbar in B'nei Brak.*

The class was a success and, a short while later, Rabbi Dovid Bender decided that he wanted to duplicate this successful model. He and some friends put together a group of boys, hired Rabbi Avrohom Aharon Sere-browski[40] as the rebbi, arranged to use a room in the Agudah building on Bedford Avenue as a classroom, and began holding classes. This group stayed together for three and a half years, some boys leaving and some boys joining along the way. Classes were held from 9 in the morning until 3 in the afternoon. After 3 o'clock, some of the boys learned with their fathers while others returned to Torah Vodaath for secular studies. The latter group joined this private class to be part of a group more accelerated in *limudei kodesh*. Because this group was small and made up of children whose fathers learned with them regularly, they learned at a much faster pace than their grade level in Torah Vodaath.

The lack of secular studies was more than just a technical arrangement. It indicated a certain mind-set. Families who sent their boys to these spe-

---

40. See Biography Section.

cial classes were declaring that they had no interest in integrating their children into American society on any level. They had no use for polished English or higher math. If their children, born and bred in America, spoke English with a touch of a Yiddish accent, that was fine with them. Among the families to send their boys to these classes were the Litmanowitzes and the Pincuses, good friends of the Benders.

Rabbi Avrohom Pincus and Rabbi Dovid Bender were childhood friends who became colleagues as principals in Torah Vodaath. Their wives had been together in Bais Yaakov of Crakow and then became colleagues in Bais Yaakov of Williamsburg. Their decades of friendship was based on shared values.

Rabbi Pinchas Litmanowitz and Rabbi Shlomo Rottenberg were brothers-in-law. They had married sisters, Zelda and Chana Zehnwirth, of the illustrious Bobover Zehnwirth family. Rebbetzins Rottenberg and Litmanowitz both attended Bais Yaakov of Crakow, both found their way to America after the war, and both married *talmidim* of the Mirrer Yeshivah. In Williamsburg, they were part of the same circle of *Litvishe* Mirrers who remained both European and idealistic.

Rabbi Dovid Bender, Rabbi Avrohom Pincus, and Rabbi Pinchas Litmanowitz learned together regularly in the afternoons after they finished their mornings in Torah Vodaath. They became the nucleus from which Kollel Kerem Shlomo, another Williamsburg *Litvak* innovation, was founded.

Kollel Kerem Shlomo was an afternoon kollel for learned men who were rebbeim in the morning. Rabbi Berel Klor[41] founded the kollel and called it after his rebbi, Rabbi Shlomo Heiman. With the help of Rabbi Yosef Liss, Rabbi Berel Klor raised money for the rent (and later purchase) of the building and its upkeep. They also raised money to pay each participant a small stipend. Every nickel earned was hard work. Kollel was a new idea in America and an afternoon kollel for men who had morning jobs was an innovative idea that took time to catch on.

Kollel Kerem Shlomo became a hub of learning every afternoon from 3 o'clock until 7. It was a gathering place for *talmidei chachamim*, men who had already progressed in their own learning but who still learned with excitement and energy. These were men who personified "*Ki heim chayeinu v'orach yameinu*[42] — it (Torah) is our life and the length of our days." When they finished teaching in Torah Vodaath, Mir, Tiferes Yerushalayim, or elsewhere, they were eager to continue learning. Among the participants were Rabbi Avrohom Levovitz, Rabbi Aharon Kreiser, Rabbi Markel Greenhouse,

---

41. Rabbi Klor was a close *talmid* of Rabbi Shlomo Heiman from when Reb Shlomo was a *maggid shiur* in Remmailes Yeshivah in Vilna.

42. *Ma'ariv.*

*Rabbi Avrohom Pincus*　　　　　*Dovid Bender and Avrohom Pincus as bochurim in Europe*

*Rabbi Chaim Avrohom Pincus (1913-2002) learned in Torah Vodaath, Mir, and Kaminetz. Upon return-ing to America, he served as Rav in Englewood, N.J. Later, he became Rav in the South Fifth Street Shul in Williamsburg while serving as menahel of Torah Vodaath elementary school. After many years in America, he left for Eretz Yisroel, where he became menahel of the Kaminetz cheder and then of the yeshi-vah ketanah. Reb Avrohom became Rosh Kollel in Chile when he was over 70 years old.*

Rabbi Shaya Wasserman, Rabbi Ezriel Lange, and Rabbi Shmuel Brudny.[43]

They learned together, they learned with their children, they exchanged thoughts and ideas with one another. There was a fire to their learning, an exhilarating excitement. Though most of the men had set *chavrusos*, they often turned to other pairs and exchanged a question or an insight. Some-times a group discussion ensued; one *talmid chacham* quoting verbatim from anywhere in *Shas* while the other refuted his opinion. There was life and vigor to their learning.[44]

In Kollel Kerem Shlomo, its members felt at home. They were not strang-ers who had to find a corner in Mesivta Torah Vodaath or the Poilisher Shtiebel to learn with a *chavrusah*. They had their own place, their own home — a busy and vibrant home, where learning was life.

THE 1940'S AND '50'S WERE DECADES OF IDEALISM AND INNOVATION. One Williamsburg personality who seemed to have endless ideas and

43. Rabbi Berel Klor.

44. "I learned in Kollel Kerem Shlomo for a short time. It was an unusual place of learning and I found tremendous joy and satisfaction learning there" (Rabbi Elya Weintraub).

... These were men who *"Ki hem chayeinu v'orach yameinu* — it (Torah) is our life and the length of our days."* When they finished teaching in Torah Vodaath, Mir, Tiferes Yerushalayim, or elsewhere, they were eager to continue learning ... Among the members of Kollel Kerem Shlomo was Rabbi Shmuel Brudny.

*Rabbi Shmuel Brudny (1915-1981) began his studies under the guidance of Rabbi Chaim Ozer Grodzenski in Rameilles at the age of 14. He went on to learn in Mir and joined the yeshivah in its travels during the war. Rabbi Avrohom Kalmanowitz appointed Reb Shmuel as maggid shiur in the Mirrer Yeshivah of Flatbush. He was a revered Rosh Yeshivah and beloved mentor to hundreds of students.*

endless energy was Rabbi Dovid Bender's good friend and cousin, Rabbi Mordechai Yoffe.

Reb Mordechai returned from Mir in 1939, determined to establish a kollel for newlyweds like himself who wished to dedicate themselves to full-time learning. His good friend, Rabbi Hershel Genauer,[45] shared his enthusiasm. Word spread and soon a small group of pioneers were ready to begin the first kollel in America. They tried settling in Boston, Massachusetts before heading to Brownsville, Manhattan, and then White Plains, New York. They were never in any location for longer than a year. Finally, in White Plains, the group realized that they needed a better long-term plan. They wanted a leader, a *talmid chacham* who would take over both the spiritual side and the financial side of running a kollel. They turned to Rabbi Aharon Kotler.

Rabbi Aharon Kotler wanted to establish the kollel as part of a yeshivah. He chose Lakewood, New Jersey because it was outside New York, away from distractions, but close enough for him to commute and remain involved in the Vaad Hatzala. So Rabbi Mordechai Yoffe and most of the kollel moved to Lakewood.[46]

Reb Mordechai remained in Lakewood until 1949 before joining the fac-

---

45. See Biography Section.

46. Rabbi Elya Svei considered Rabbi Mordechai Yoffe's role in moving the kollel in White Plains to Lakewood Yeshivah as pivotal. At Reb Mordechai's *levayah* in Lakewood, Rabbi Elya Svei cried, "He [Rabbi Mordechai Yoffe] started Lakewood [Yeshivah]."

*Rabbi Mordechai Yoffe*

*Dovid Bender and Mordechai Yoffe as bochurim in Europe*

*Rabbi Mordechai Yoffe (1914-1993) moved from Dvinsk, Latvia to America when he was 3 years old. With the encouragement of Rabbi Yaakov Yosef Herman, Reb Mordechai journeyed to Europe where he studied in the yeshivos of Lomza, Mir, and Kaminetz. Upon returning to America in 1939, he helped found the White Plains Kollel which eventually moved to Lakewood under the guidance of Rabbi Aharon Kotler. Rabbi Mordechai Yoffe dedicated himself to harbotzas haTorah for the rest of his life.*

ulty of Yeshivas Chachmei Lublin in Detroit. A few years later, he moved to Kansas City[47] where he became the first American-born *yungerman* to found his own yeshivah.[48] In 1953, after a number of years in Kansas City,[49] the Yoffes moved to Williamsburg.

Moving to Williamsburg was returning home for Hannah Yoffe. She had been born and raised in Williamsburg, at 189 Rodney Street. Her sister

47. When Rabbi Mordechai Yoffe wanted to start his yeshivah in Kansas City, his wife Hannah was adamantly against it. She could not imagine raising religious children in Kansas City. Rabbi Mordechai Yoffe took her to Rabbi Aharon Kotler. Reb Aharon promised her that all her boys would be *b'nei Torah* and all her girls would marry *b'nei Torah.* Hannah was still unconvinced. "I want it in writing," she said. "You do not need it in writing," Reb Aharon answered. "I am telling you, all your children will be fine." And so it was.

48. Rabbi Mordechai Yoffe opened his yeshivah with Rabbi Moshe Gartner from Yeshivas Chachmei Lublin. Rabbi Elya Svei said that when he saw that Rabbi Mordechai Yoffe, American born and raised, was able to open a yeshivah, it gave him encouragement to join the fledgling Philadelphia Yeshivah that was also being established by men who had been raised and educated in America (Rabbi Yona Michel Yoffe).

49. Hannah Yoffe once told Rabbi Yaakov Bender that they were so poor in Kansas City, that she would rise early in the morning and search for empty bottles. With enough 2-cent deposit bottles, she fed her family basic food like bread, butter, and milk. She did anything she could to stretch money, including reusing the wax from used candles to make new candles.

**Rabbi Mordechai and Hannah Yoffe hosted the Skulener Rebbe in their house for several weeks.**

*Rabbi Eliezer Zusia Portugal (1898-1982) served as Rav in Skulen and Chernowitz. Following World War II, he relocated to Bucharest, Romaina. There he began his lifelong dedication to helping Holocaust survivors. In 1960 he arrived in America and established the famed Chesed L'Avrohom organization toward that objective. The Skulener Rebbe was revered for his piety and dedication to Klal Yisroel. Many of his scholarly writings were lost during the war but some have been published.*

Mary lived in Williamsburg as did her cousins, the Benders. Her niece and nephews, the Shapiros from Pittsburgh, went to school there and her sister, Bluma Shapiro, came for the summers. Returning to Williamsburg meant family and stability.

Reb Mordechai became *Mashgiach* in Stolin for a while. After that, he opened his own yeshivah in Boro Park called Mesivta d'Boro Park,[50] and established the first kollel in Boro Park. Then he opened a yeshivah in New Haven.

He seemed to never run out of ideas nor did he become discouraged when those ideas did not always turn out the way he had envisioned them. All his endeavors forced him on the road not only in routine travel, but to collect money as well. Some of his most beloved projects fell apart because of lack of money.

Reb Mordechai was also a tremendous masmid and didn't like to waste a moment. While traveling , he had to occasionally wait for a few moments. He built himself a hand made shtender that fit in the front seat of his vehicle. In that way he could learn well while waiting.

Nonetheless, Reb Mordechai refused to become jaded. He never looked at the amount of money people gave him when he collected. He thanked his benefactors and counted what he had accumulated only at the end of the day. This way he never associated the amount of money with the person who gave it to him. He was completely convinced that he would receive whatever he was meant to receive, and it did not matter from

50. Among Rabbi Mordechai Yoffe's *talmidim* from Mesivta d'Boro Park were Rabbi Eli Ber Wachtfogel (Rosh Yeshivah of Yeshivas Zichron Moshe of South Fallsburg, New York) and Rabbi Yeruchem Olshin (Rosh Yeshivah of Bais Medrash Govoha in Lakewood, New Jersey).

*199 Hewes Street – The Fishbein Home*

where it came.[51]

In Williamsburg, Hannah Yoffe reconnected with family and friends. She became the secretary of the Lakewood office in Williamsburg, a job that she filled with efficiency and devotion for over 20 years. Even when her husband founded his yeshivah in New Haven, she remained in New York during the week and commuted to New Haven for Shabbos.

Hannah was in her element in Williamsburg as she welcomed family and friends into her home. When her tenant informed her that the Skulener Rebbe, Rabbi Eliezer Zusia Portugal, was coming to America and did not have a place to stay, Hannah immediately invited him to her house. At that time, few had even heard of the Skulener Rebbe, but Hannah understood that he was a Rebbe from an illustrious background, and she wanted to host him with honor.

Reb Mordechai, Hannah, and family vacated their own apartment and moved into the attic so that the Rebbe could have privacy and comfort. The Skulener Rebbe stayed in her house for several weeks and, when he left, he thanked the Yoffes profusely, offering to reimburse them for the possible inconvenience. Hannah refused, fully convinced that the weeks of having the Rebbe as a guest had been its own reward.

THOUGH MOST OF THE BENDERS' WILLIAMSBURG FRIENDS WERE friends from before, there was one exception. Mrs. Miriam Devorah Fishbein had moved to New York from Chicago. Her husband had passed away when she was a young woman, and she was left with a houseful of orphans to raise on her own. When her oldest daughter was 13, she sent her from Chicago to New York to attend the newly formed Bais Yaakov of

51. When Rabbi Mordechai Yoffe was in his 80's and could no longer drive anymore, he would stay at Rabbi Yaakov Bender's house in Far Rockaway for a few weeks at a time. Reb Mordechai would walk around Far Rockaway and the neighboring community of Lawrence, long distances, collecting money for his various projects.

Williamsburg. A few years later, she moved her entire family to Williamsburg so that all the children could attend proper schools.

Rebbetzin Bender deeply admired Mrs. Fishbein. While raising a large family on her own, Mrs. Fishbein was also a pillar of Bais Yaakov, encouraging the formation of alumni reunions and hosting Bnos groups in her home. Rebbetzin Bender was overjoyed to see all the Fishbein girls marry illustrious *b'nei Torah*.[52]

ACROSS THE STREET, DOWN THE BLOCK, AROUND THE CORNER, AND two blocks over, the Benders were surrounded by family who were friends and friends who were family. The Wachtfogels, the Kaplans, the Rottenbergs, the Litmanowitzes, the Pincuses, the Yoffes, and many others made up the *Litvishe* community of Williamsburg in which the Benders played a significant role.

---

52. Mrs. Fishbein's sons-in-law included Rabbi Yitzchok Feigelstock (Rosh Yeshivah of the Mesivta of Long Beach), Rabbi Yaakov Finkelstein, Rabbi Mordechai Yehuda Lubart (of Yeshivas Chachmei Lublin), Rabbi Shimon Groner (*Mashgiach* of Yeshivas Rabbeinu Chaim Berlin), Rabbi Avrohom Barnetsky, and Rabbi Chaim Yankel Gryngras.

*Chapter Forty-Two*

# Changes in Williamsburg:
# From Hooper to Hewes

### Williamsburg: 5718 (1958)

AS WILLIAMSBURG GREW AND CHANGED THROUGHOUT the 1940's and the 1950's, the public learned of the construction of the Brooklyn-Queens Expressway. According to the original city hall plans, the BQE was slated to run from Boro Park through Williamsburg to Queens, along the route of the old Brooklyn Navy Yard. That route would have cut through two major factories, Domino Sugar and Schaeffer Beer, and those factories would have had to be razed to the ground. The factory owners demanded that the expressway be rerouted. City Hall agreed. They rerouted the expressway straight through the heart of Williamsburg.

When news of the plan became public, people panicked. They were certain that Williamsburg as a pleasant residential neighborhood would soon be history. As the Chassidim became more and more dominant, the irreligious gravitated to Queens and Long Island and the Modern Orthodox Jews moved out as well. Reports of the new construction plans encouraged their flight from the neighborhood.

The more religious people set their sights on Crown Heights. For a short time, Crown Heights was the neighborhood to where religious Jews gravitated before Boro Park and Flatbush.

Yet despite all the dire predictions, Jewish Williamsburg was far from over. The Chassidim wanted to be close to their Rebbes, and so they were staying put. After the Hungarian Revolution of '56, their numbers swelled further. No expressway was going to deter Chassidim from coming to Williamsburg. As such, the religious character of Williamsburg grew stronger, and therefore many of the *Litvishe* were reluctant to leave. When the Benders outgrew the Hooper Street apartment, they chose a house around the corner on Hewes Street.[53]

*216 Hewes Street – the Benders' new home.*

The Benders bought their house from irreligious Jews. Many of their new neighbors had done the same. Just across from the Benders lived Rabbi Shmuel Brudny, Rabbi Aharon Kreiser, Rabbi Ezriel Lange, and the Shoproner Rav. Rabbi Yankel Finkelstein and Rabbi Raphael Shain lived there as well. On the same side of the street was the Rosh Yeshivah of Satmar, Rabbi Nosson Yosef Meisels.[54]

The house on Hewes Street was a three-family house, very different from the large apartment building on Hooper Street. The Benders took the first floor and the basement and rented out the two upper floors. Their upstairs tenants were Reb Yaakov Koppel and Henchie Deutch, a young *Chassidishe* couple with two little children. The third-floor tenant was a newlywed young couple, Reb Eliezer Shmuel and Perri Noe, also *Chassidish*.

On Succos, the Benders invited their tenants into their succah, just as they had done on Hooper Street. The sounds of *Litvishe* and *Chassidishe niggunim* blended harmoniously as the Benders and their neighbors shared the Yom Tov. On the night of the *ushpizen* of Yaakov, Mrs. Deutch treated everyone to her special *fritlach*, sugar-coated bow-tie-shaped pastries that she made

---

53. "I was in fifth grade the year that we moved. My rebbi was Rabbi Moshe Wolfson, present-day *Mashgiach* of Torah Vodaath. I walked into class one day and made the grand announcement. Then I told my rebbi that he could change my address on the class list. Reb Moshe asked, 'To where did you move?' I told him that our new address was 216 Hewes Street. He thought for a minute and then smiled. *'Tzaddik Hu — gematria* 216.' I felt like a million dollars!" (Rabbi Yaakov Bender).

54. See Biography Section.

in honor of her husband Yaakov. The Bender children eagerly awaited the yearly delicacy and the warmth with which they were presented.

Symbolic of the unusual harmony of cultures that existed in Williamsburg, the Satmar Rosh Yeshivah stopped in for an annual Yom Tov visit. Rabbi Meisels appreciated having Reb Dovid as a neighbor, and Succos was an ideal time to enjoy each other's company.[55]

Williamsburg of the 60's remained a healthy mix of *Litvish* and *Chassidish*, united in their dedication to *Yiddishkeit* and in their commitment to recreate the type of Jewish life that had existed in pre-war Europe.

---

55. Rabbi Yitzchok Mordechai Meisels.

Part IV:

# The School of Life

5705-5725 / 1945-1965

*Chapter Forty-Three:*
The Patterns of Parents

*Chapter Forty-Four:*
Parents as Teachers

*Chapter Forty-Five:*
Rebbetzin Bender:
A Mother Who Taught

*Chapter Forty-Six:*
Rabbi Dovid Bender:
Principal and Personality

*Chapter Forty-Seven:*
Summers and Simchos:
Opportunities for Growth

---

The information in this section is based primarily on interviews with *talmidim* of Rabbi Dovid Bender, family friends, and the Bender family. Among those interviewed were Rabbi Yisroel Belsky, Rabbi Yaakov Fensterheim, R' Israel Weinstock, Rabbi Henoch Cohen, Rabbi Pinchus Brumer, Rabbi Chaim Werner, R' Reuven Rosenberg, and R' Mordechai Krieger. Other sources are documented.

---

### Chapter Forty-Three

# The Patterns of Parents

## Williamsburg, 5721 (1961)

*K*INDER, SCHNELL, SCHNELL. WE HAVE TO GO. THE PLANE is landing in just a few hours." Reb Dovid dashed from room to room, checking that everything was clean, in place, and perfect. The children — faces freshly scrubbed, dressed in their finest Shabbos clothing, shoes polished, hair brushed — watched their father hustling and bustling with fond amusement. Where was their usually unruffled, calm, and confident father? Here he was 48 years old and behaving like a kid!

"Basha," Reb Dovid called as he was straightening his tie in the mirror, "is everyone ready? I really want to go."

Rebbetzin Bender, with raised eyebrows, glanced at the clock. Did he really want to leave so early? If there were no delays, the plane was only due to land in another three hours. But, good wife that she was, she did not say a word. Reb Dovid continued making nervous comments. "Did everyone go to the bathroom? It's a long ride to the airport. Should we take food along for the way? Yankel, go check the boys' room one more time. Are you sure someone swept under the beds?"

Finally, the Benders were in the car, on their way to the airport. The weeks of anticipation were almost over. In a few hours, they would see their beloved father and grandfather, Rabbi Avrohom Bender.

Reb Dovid had spent weeks preparing. As soon as he had confirmed that his father was coming, he supervised a total overhaul of the house on Hewes Street. Everything broken was fixed and all the rooms were given a fresh coat of paint. "I don't really mind how everything is," Reb Dovid explained to his rebbetzin, "but it might just bother my father. I want him to feel comfortable in our home. He shouldn't think we do not live well or that we cannot afford to paint." With that, Reb Dovid moved all his and his wife's things out of their bedroom and organized the master bedroom for the convenience of his father and stepmother.

Today was the day, and Reb Dovid could hardly contain his excitement. He drummed his fingers along the dashboard, keeping up a running commentary with the children about how they should act in the airport, what they should expect, and memories of Zaida's other visits. They had not seen Zaida since Paltiel's bar mitzvah three years earlier, and the children could hardly wait to see him. The constant flow of letters back and forth had forged a solid connection, and they were almost as excited as their father.

They arrived at the airport and quickly made their way to the observation deck. It was only 2 o'clock in the afternoon and Zaida's KLM flight was due at 4:30. The children did not mind; after all, an outing to the airport was always welcome. As the minutes ticked away, the tension mounted. The Bender children scanned the sky. Is that a KLM jet coming in? The TWA insignia flew past with a whoosh. Yankel rubbed the back of his neck; it was sore from straining so hard. Esther stifled a yawn, and Shmuel Sholom asked, for the umpteenth time, if the plane was here yet.

Finally, KLM flight 430 slid onto the runway. The Benders watched with excitement as the passengers emerged into view, one by one. Where was Zaida? Finally, an elderly woman peeked out of the entranceway. As she descended the stairs, a tall, distinguished-looking rabbi followed.

Reb Dovid began to scream wildly, "Papa! Papa!" The turning propellers were making such a racket, it was hard to hear anything. Reb Dovid did not give up. "Papa! Papa!" he shouted. The Bender children looked at their normally controlled father and bashfully slunk away. They smiled sheepishly at the other people in the waiting area, as if to say, *Him? We don't know him. Father? Whose father? Our father?*

Reb Dovid was oblivious to them. He continued to wave his arms and call out, "Papa, Papa ..." Finally, Rabbi Avrohom Bender heard his son's voice. He looked up and their eyes met. They smiled. Then Reb Avrohom continued down the stairs.

Reb Dovid began to run. "Come, children, fast. Zaida and Tante Ettel have to go through customs. We will meet them on the other side. Come quickly." Reb Dovid was already yards ahead and the children were running to catch up with him. Down the stairs they ran until they reached a large room overlooking the customs section. A large glass partition separated the people in this balcony from the passengers below. Reb Dovid stood all his children by the wall and looked them up and down. He tucked in a shirt, straightened a tie, told a child to tie his shoes. Zaida's grandchildren should look just perfect. Then Reb Dovid turned to scan the passenger hall below. Where was his father? Had he finished with customs yet?

Then Reb Dovid caught sight of his father, still standing on line. He leaned over the partition and banged on the glass. Reb Avrohom looked up and waved. Reb Dovid waved back excitedly, like a child. They kept looking and smiling at each other, even as Reb Avrohom went through customs. Finally, the paperwork was finished. Father and son fell into each other's tight embrace.

*Rabbi Dovid Bender with his father at the airport in 1958*

Later, Reb Dovid airmail letters why he acted as he had. "I know the pleasure my father has when he sees me," he explained. "If I am here and he is here, why should he have to wait? I wanted to give him pleasure as soon as possible." This was just one example of Reb Dovid's exceptional *kibud av*. He anticipated his father's every need and desire and strove to maximize his pleasure.

THE BENDERS SPENT NUMEROUS SUMMERS AT CAMP BAIS YAAKOV when Reb Avrohom still lived in America. The staff families, including the Benders, went up to camp a few days before the official camp opening. Reb Dovid was a great handball player and once interrupted a fiercely competitive round with one of the other rebbeim. He looked at his watch and called out, "I have to go." He threw his partner the ball and sprinted off the court.

A young *bochur*, David Kranzler,[1] had witnessed the earlier handball game and was now waiting on the staff tables in the dining room. He saw that Reb Dovid was freshly showered, dressed in his finest clothing, his hat carefully brushed, and his shoes shined. He looked as if he were going to a wedding, or some other fancy affair. "Oh," David commented, "are you going somewhere?"

"No," Reb Dovid replied proudly. "My father is coming to visit."

David was dumbfounded by the preparations Reb Dovid made for his father's visit. Surely, Kranzler marveled, this must be the epitome of *kibud av*.[2]

---

1. See Biography Section.

2. Dr. David Kranzler.

FOR REB DOVID, *KIBUD AV* WAS A CONSTANT CONSIDERATION. WHEN Rabbi Avrohom Bender moved to Eretz Yisroel, Reb Dovid wrote to his father at least four times a week. His letters were about what was going on in the house, about each child, about the challenges of being a principal and about the community.

Once, Reb Dovid was bedridden with very high fever. The children tiptoed around the house, awed by this unusual occurrence. Then, in the middle of the afternoon, Yankel saw his sick father, his face flushed with fever, struggle to rise from the couch. A few minutes later, Rabbi Dovid emerged from his room, fully dressed with his boots in hand. Outside, the wind was howling and snow was falling steadily.

Yankel stared at his father incredulously. "Tatty, where are you going?"

"I have to go to the mailbox."

Yankel saw the familiar blue airmail letters on the nearby table.

"But Tatty," he protested, "let me go. It's snowing outside and you are ill."

Reb Dovid shook his head as he buttoned his coat and then slipped his hands into its pockets. "The only *kibud av* I have now, with my father in Eretz Yisroel, are these letters. I want to send my letter myself, and not through anyone else." He bundled himself up and walked into the blizzard. A few minutes later, he returned, shivering from the cold, and went right back to bed.

Reb Dovid also urged the children to write to their grandfather. "Here," he would say, taking out the long blue airmail letters he always kept in stock. "I want you to fill in the whole thing. Top to bottom. Look, you can even write along the sides and on the back."

"But Tatty," they protested, "what should we write?"

"Everything and anything," he answered. "Write exactly what you did today, from the time you woke up in the morning. Tell Zaida what you ate for breakfast, with whom you walked to school, what mark you received on your test. I want him to see you grow up. I want Zaida to feel as if he is living right here with us." They rolled their eyes, grumbled a bit more, and then they went to write to Rechov Nachmani 23, an address they would find hard to forget.

In addition to the letters, Reb Dovid sent the children's report cards, tests with good grades, and many photographs. He hired a professional photographer to come to their house and photograph the family. Mr. Fish was a popular photographer, fairly priced but not cheap. Many of the Williamsburg crowd used Mr. Fish, but few as regularly as the Benders. Reb Dovid wanted his father to receive regular photos of the children.

"Come on, kids," Mr. Fish would call, "up on the stoop."

The Bender children knew the routine. They sat patiently as old Mr. Fish arranged himself behind the big box of a camera and covered the camera with a black *shmatta*. One hand adjusted the lenses while the other motioned to the children. "One, two, three … cheese!" The children smiled on cue. A few more group shots, some individual portraits, and then they were free to go.

Often, the children would come home to find the dining-room table piled with clothing, toilet paper, and anything else that Reb Dovid thought his father would need or enjoy. Reb Dovid diligently packed these items in boxes and shipped them to Eretz Yisroel. This was just another way he felt he could bring his father pleasure.

Reb Dovid had boundless gratitude to his parents. "If I ever get to publish a sefer of my own, I would call it *Chiddushei Eifod*," he once confided in his son Yankel. "*Aleph* for Avrohom, *Pei* for Pelta, and *Daled* for Dovid. I would be nothing if not for them."

The children humored their father in his projects, but they absorbed his sense of love and devotion toward his parents. Through Reb Dovid's bond with his father, his children got a glimpse of their father as a son.

BECAUSE THEIR MATERNAL GRANDPARENTS, THE EPSTEINS, DID NOT survive the Holocaust, the Bender children had never seen Rebbetzin Bender's interaction with her parents. Nonetheless, the children saw the love and devotion she had for her only sibling, Uncle Yosef.

Rebbetzin Bender and Yosef were unusually close, even as children. When her own children would bicker, Rebbetzin Bender shook her head sadly, remembering how she and her brother had never fought. As a young child, Yosef whittled a wooden box and engraved her initial on its cover. This trinket, a token of her brother's warmth, accompanied Rebbetzin Bender to America and was kept with her other cherished treasures from Europe.

When Yosef moved to Eretz Yisroel, the siblings corresponded, and they shared each other's joy and empathized with their pain. In 1943, Yosef married Sarah Shoboska, a girl who came from a similar background. Their wedding was attended by friends and relatives, many of whom were familiar to Rabbi Dovid and Rebbetzin Bender. One of the rabbanim in attendance was Rabbi Shabsi Yogel, a close friend of Sarah's parents.

Rebbetzin Bender worried about her brother. Although he rarely complained, she assumed that money was tight and his life was difficult. When she heard that socks were expensive in Eretz Yisroel, she sent him socks. When she heard that they needed material for sewing clothes, she sent him material. She tried to help him by sending money, packages, letters, and pictures. At times, she sent so many packages that Yosef begged her to stop.

Yosef was always grateful for her efforts. They kept their sibling bond strong because, even though they had chosen different paths and lifestyles,

*Rabbi Eliyahu Shachor (1893-1973)
served as a Rav in Parostk, Poland. In
1938 he immigrated to Eretz Yisroel
where he was quietly devoted to learning Torah and serving his Maker.*

family was a value they both held dear. Again, the Bender children absorbed messages that were never expressly said: that the bond between siblings transcends differences, that to love means to give and to figure out how to give more, and that family should never be taken for granted.

REBBETZIN BENDER NOT ONLY WORKED to maintain familial relationships, she actively sought out family. Throughout the 1940's, she corresponded with aunts, uncles, and cousins who lived in Eretz Yisrael and had initiated correspondence with her. She always knew that she had more relatives there, but since her life was so busy, she had not made a move to contact them. In 1950, she decided to seek out her cousin, Rabbi Elya Shachor, an illustrious *talmid chacham* living in Eretz Yisrael. She wanted to let him know that she was alive and wished to maintain a connection.

To HaRav HaGaon HaTzaddik Reb Elya Shachor, shlita[3]
*You will probably be very puzzled as to who the writer of this letter is. I will therefore introduce myself before I begin with anything else. My maiden name is Basya Epstein, daughter of R' Yaakov and Lifsha Epstein, ztz"l. My grandfather was Rabbi Shmuel Tzvi Shachor, ztz"l, the brother of your father Reb Dovid, ztz"l. As a girl I lived in Otvock, Poland with my dear parents, z"l. A few months before the outbreak of war I married a talmid of Yeshivas Mir.*

*We arrived in New York at the outset of the war. B"H, we are settled here. … I feel guilty that I have not put myself together to write a few words. We are always busy and rushing and, in those first years, after the war, when we found out what happened to our closest and most beloved family members, among them my holy parents, we did not have the courage to write. That is how another few years went by. But my conscience is bothering me, and I feel I must write a few words to find out how everyone is.*

*When HaRav HaTzaddik Uncle Dovid ztz"l passed away a few years ago, there were hespedim in New York. Since then, I have wanted to write and find out about Aunt Chyene, tichya, and as far as I remember you had two sisters in Minsk, Sheindel and Teibel. Where are they? Do they have families? What about your family? Do*

---

3. Translated and condensed.

*you remember me? I was a young child when I used to come visit you in Minsk.*

*We are sending you a small gift, a food parcel that can be picked up when you receive the certificate we are sending …*

*Best regards from my husband and children, sheyichyu.*

*Respectfully,*
*Basya Bender*

Rebbetzin Bender's warm words and accompanying gift opened a new relationship between the Benders and the Shachors. Transatlantic phone calls were prohibitively expensive and letters were time consuming. Therefore, they corresponded only occasionally, but they thought fondly of each other, and remained grateful for the warm bond of family.

LIKE HIS WIFE, REB DOVID NEVER DISCOUNTED THE VALUE OF FAMILY. HIS father's brother, Reb Yisroel, had moved to Eretz Yisroel in 1933 with his wife, his daughter, and his son, Reb Yehudah Yitzchok, who was already married with a son of his own. Reb Yehudah Yitzchok's oldest son, Rabbi Shloimke Berman, was a child prodigy. He slept in the Chazon Ish's home as a youngster, where the Chazon Ish trained him to repeat an original Torah thought nightly before retiring. This training bore fruit. Reb Shloimke became one of the leading lights in Yeshivas Ponevezh and, when he married the daughter of the Steipler Gaon, the Benders in New York rejoiced.

Throughout his years in America, Reb Avrohom corresponded with his family in Eretz Yisroel, inquiring after their well-being and helping out when he could. When he moved to Eretz Yisroel, he remained close with his family there, and in the many letters that passed back and forth, Reb Dovid heard all about the Bermans of B'nei Brak. As his father had always done, Reb Dovid kept up with the cousins he had never met. They exchanged warm wishes at the beginning of a new year and remained interested in one another's lives.

RABBI DOVID AND REBBETZIN BASHA BENDER'S LOVE AND APPRECIA-tion of family was an extension of their love and appreciation for all of *Klal Yisroel*. This genuine feeling for others expressed itself in many forms, including Rebbetzin Bender's dedication to making *shidduchim* for the many older boys and orphan girls.

She arranged the *shidduch* between her good friend from Bais Yaakov of Crakow, Chava Weinberg, and her husband's friend Rabbi Avrohom Pincus. She arranged the *shidduch* between Zelda Zehnwirth, another Crakow graduate, and Rabbi Pinchas Litmanowitz. She did the same for Rabbi Feivel Hollander, another Mirrer *talmid*, and Faiga Sontag, a student of hers from Bais Yaakov of Williamsburg.

## Rabbi Yisroel Berman, older brother of Rabbi Avrohom Bender

*Rabbi Yisroel Berman*

*Rabbi Yisroel Berman with his son Reb Yehudah Yitzchok*

**Rabbi Yisroel Berman** *(1863-1953) learned in Novarodok. As a young man he established chadorim in various towns in Russia. After World War I, he settled in Smolowitz where he opened a yeshivah together with Rabbi Elchonon Wasserman. In 1933 he and his family moved to Eretz Yisroel where Reb Yisroel devoted himself to learning Torah.*

**Rabbi Yehudah Yitzchok Berman** *(1902-1965) learned in Radin under Rabbi Naftoli Tropp and then in Telshe. His years in Telshe made an indelible impression on him, particularly his close relationship with Rabbi Mottel Progamansky. He moved to Eretz Yisroel with his father and spent his life learning Torah.*

As word got out that Rebbetzin Bender had made many successful *shidduchim*, her students in Bais Yaakov eagerly sought her in the hallways of the school. *Maybe today she will have a shidduch for me*, was a constant thought.[4] They felt how much she cared about them, and so they allowed themselves the luxury of that hope.

One story, famous in the annals of Bender family history, involved a girl named Esther. Esther was a lovely American girl, with a big heart and a desire for a pure Torah home. She gravitated to the Bender home and stopped by there often. Rebbetzin Bender enlisted her aid in one of her big *chessed* projects. Every Friday morning, Esther picked up bread and cakes that Rebbetzin Bender purchased (with donated money, at cost price) from R' Shloima Weiss, and distributed them to needy *talmidei chachamim*. In the beginning, Esther lugged the bulky bags by train. Later she delivered them by car. She faithfully carried out this *chessed* project for many months.

Rebbetzin Bender was impressed with Esther's warmth, sincerity, and eagerness to do *chessed*. They had many long conversations about the

---

4. Mrs. D. Pichey.

home and husband that she yearned for, but Rebbetzin Bender was at a loss. The perfect match eluded her.

One day, Rebbetzin Bender had an idea. There was a Mirrer *bochur* who also frequented the Bender home. He was a budding *talmid chacham* with fine character traits and *yiras Shamayim*; in short, everything Esther was looking for. There was only one problem, and Rebbetzin Bender decided to let Esther decide.

"I have thought of a *bochur* for you. He is everything you have been looking for, everything you have described. There is only one problem: he stutters. He has gone out with several girls, but they all turned him down. I do not want to set him up for another disappointment. Listen to what we can do. I will arrange for you to be in the house one evening when he is here. While he speaks to my husband in learning, you will serve the tea. You will listen to him talk. If his stutter does not bother you, then I will arrange for you to meet him."

That is exactly what they did. Esther served the tea, listened as he spoke, and decided that the stutter did not matter to

*Rabbi Avrohom Yeshaya Karelitz (1878- 1953) was known as the Chazon Ish, after his famous series of sefarim. Born in Lithuania, his true greatness remained hidden until he arrived in Eretz Yisroel in 1933. In his concern for Torah in the new yishuv in Eretz Yisroel, he assumed the responsibility of leadership. His Torah scholarship, compassion, and practical wisdom inspired his generation. The Chazon Ish was considered the final halachic authority of his time.*

her. She asked that Rebbetzin Bender set up a date, and a short while later, they were engaged. This was another one of the many times that Rebbetzin Bender's thoughtfulness, wisdom, and love built a Jewish home.

SOME OF THE GREATEST LESSONS THE BENDER CHILDREN LEARNED from their parents were absorbed by simply observing them. Without any pomp or fanfare, Reb Dovid and his rebbetzin radiated love and concern for *Klal Yisroel*. This was not something the Benders preached; it was who they were.

The Bender children observed their father, whether he was raising money for a poor family or speaking patiently on the telephone with a parent. They observed how their mother stayed up late at night and, between whispered snatches of conversation, they knew that she was trying to help another orphan find her match, another newlywed cope with the intricacies of marriage, or another peaceful resolution to some sort of strife. They heard, they observed, and they absorbed. They sought to copy the pattern.

*Rabbi Mordechai Shlomo Berman (1930-2004) grew up in the home of the Chazon Ish who treated him as his own child. He later became a nephew of the Chazon Ish when he married the daughter of the Steipler Gaon, the Chazon Ish's brother-in-law. Reb Shloimke was a disciple of Ponevezh, and a close talmid of Rabbi Shmuel Rozovsky and Rav Shach. He became a Rosh Yeshiva in Ponevezh but, due to a prolonged illness and suffering, was unable to lead to lead the yeshiva in his later years.*

*"… Her chessed was what educated her children … The children were in the habit of being moser nefesh for other people … with all one's capabilities… you stay up at night to try to help… you give up for Klal Yisroel … The young children were exposed to that ahavas Yisroel and mesiras nefesh. Perhaps the children did not have as much time to spend with their mother, but what could be a greater lesson in the chinuch habanim than her mesiras nefesh for Klal Yisroel …"[5]*

---

5. Rabbi Mordechai Shapiro in his *hesped* for Rebbetzin Bender.

# Chapter Forty-Four

# Parents as Teachers

"DID TATTY EVER TELL YOU ABOUT THE FIRST TIME HE MET Rabbi Aharon Kotler?" Rebbetzin Bender asked with a twinkle in her eye as she ladled out soup. The children waited patiently for her to continue. "He was traveling from Otvock to the Mir. In the same train car, there was a man with a short beard looking into a *Chayei Adam*. Tatty was so excited to see a *heimishe Yid* among all the *Poilisher goyim*; he went right over to him to give him *Shalom Aleichem*. The man responded warmly and asked him where he was heading. Tatty told him that he was on his way to the Mir. 'Very good!' he responded happily. 'I have a letter for Reb Chatzkel. You can be my messenger.' At this point, the stranger had still not divulged his name. 'Here,' he said, handing Tatty the envelope, 'tell him that it is from Kletzk.' Tatty already suspected that that was the case, but he said nothing and the two continued speaking. As they were about to part, Tatty remarked, 'I will give the letter to Reb Chatzkel, and I will tell him the Kletzker Rosh Yeshivah sent it.' Rabbi Aharon Kotler laughed and nodded."

"But Mommy, why did they not introduce themselves to each other right away? Why did Reb Aharon keep his identity a secret?"

Rebbetzin Bender paused as she considered the question and served the supper. "Perhaps Reb Aharon felt he might be given too much *kavod*. Our *gedolim* have always run away from honor. Perhaps Reb Aharon was enjoying a lighter conversation, something that might have ended had his identity been known. Perhaps he enjoyed remaining anonymous, even for a short time. Whatever the case, when Reb Aharon realized that the secret was out, he and your father had a good laugh."

This was everyday conversation in the Bender home. Motherhood provided Rebbetzin Bender with endless teaching opportunities, and she looked for and cultivated these opportunities. Rebbetzin Bender told her children stories of *gedolim*, inserting a personal note here and there, if she had met that particular *gadol* or witnessed the incident. She spoke with awe and reverence, marveling over how privileged they were to belong to a nation with such giants. It did not matter if the story had a specific lesson or not; she wanted her children to feel a connection to greatness. They should revere our *gedolim*, not as vague individuals, but as real people. One day she mentioned Rabbi Aharon Kotler, another day the Brisker Rav, and another day she spoke about Reb Boruch Ber and Reb Chaim Ozer. Each anecdote settled these *gedolim* more firmly into the Bender home.

When the Benders lived on Hooper Street, their apartment was directly across from that of Rabbi Yonason Steif. "Come, *kinderlach*, look!" was Rebbetzin Bender's common cry as she excitedly summoned her children to the window. Every morning, at precisely 7:20, a car pulled up in front of their building and waited to take Rabbi Yonason Steif to davening. The Viener Dayan liked to arrive in shul for the 8 o'clock *minyan* before his *kehillah*. He did not want to walk into a roomful of people who would be obligated to stand up for him. He preferred to leave early, at precisely 7:20.[6] If the Benders were on the alert, they could catch him entering the car. "Look, *kinderlach*," Rebbetzin Bender said softly, gazing out the window, "you can see the face of a *tzaddik*. Look at the face of a *tzaddik*!"

The children looked and learned. They looked at the face of the *tzaddik* and they learned that their mother's reverence for *gedolim* was not confined to the gedolim of the past; she revered the *gedolim* of the present as well.

NEITHER REB DOVID NOR HIS REBBETZIN ASSUMED THAT THEIR CHILdren would naturally absorb proper values and *hashkafos*. They were on the alert for opportunities to guide their children, to clarify behaviors, and veer them in the proper direction. The baseball card incident is a typical example:

"COME EVERYBODY, LOOK WHAT I HAVE!" BLUMIE WAS SHLEPPING A BIG garbage bag into the house. "It's a package from Cousin Mary. I wonder what's inside."

---

6. "Once, the car stalled and he walked into the shul at 7:40 a.m. He saw the way the congregation lifted themselves slightly from their seats, and he was disturbed that they did not rise properly. After davening, he called together his *kehillah* and explained, 'I have an obligation to teach you what it says in the *Shulchan Aruch*.' The Viener Dayan took out a *Shulchan Aruch* and leafed through the pages until he found what he was looking for. He then proceeded to teach the chapter with the laws of how to treat a *talmid chacham*" (Rabbi Paltiel Bender).

They passed items of clothing from one to the other. Yankel let out a whoop of excitement, and all the children joined him on the floor as they went through the cigar box full of baseball cards.

"I can't believe it! Look, a Mickey Mantle!"

"Here's a Joe DiMaggio …!"

"And imagine, we didn't have to pay for any of it!"

"We're rich! Rich!"

The Bender children knew that their father did not like baseball cards, but this was different. This was a whole box of baseball cards for free. There had to be more than a hundred cards, and some were really valuable. Surely, Tatty would understand that this was different. The children were so engrossed in their find that they did not notice their father standing in the doorway. Reb Dovid watched in silence. Suddenly, Blumie looked up and caught his eye. Sheepishly, she dropped the cards on the floor. The other children turned to see what happened and they, too, caught sight of their father. All activity stopped.

"Tatty," little Michoel innocently piped up, "look what we found! So many cards!"

Reb Dovid did not answer. Blumie shifted nervously on the floor.

Reb Dovid squatted down beside the children and took a handful of baseball cards. "*Kinderlach*, let me tell you what we are going to do with these cards," he said as he handed them out. "Each of you is going to take your cards and rip them in half, one by one. Here, let me show you how." Reb Dovid proceeded to rip one card and then another. "Now, it is your turn," he said. Slowly, the children complied. One card after another, until the entire treasure was a mound of worthless paper scraps.

Reb Dovid noticed a few toy guns on the floor, leftovers from the same package. He called the children over and together they put the toy guns and the baseball cards into the incinerator.

"These are things that do not belong in a Jewish home," he stated simply.

And with that, the subject was closed.

BASEBALL CARDS WERE THE RAGE OF THE 1940'S AND 1950'S, AND NO normal child could escape that. The children saw them in school, in the park, and at their friends' homes. They still knew which ones were valuable, which were worthless, and when the newest ones came out. One of the children managed to hide a whole collection at his friend's house. At the same time, they understood what their father was trying to teach them. Baseball as a mode of physical fitness was one thing. When it became something glorified and admired to the point of being an obsession, it was something else. These cards represented an infatuation with American culture that had no place in a Jewish home.

Guns were taboo for a different reason. Killing was not a game, and guns should not be toys in a Jewish home.

Reb Dovid was a strict father, but he was also very devoted to his children, and they knew it. Reb Dovid spent much time learning with his boys and they were always well prepared for their classes.[7] Nonetheless, he never underestimated the effort and time that others devoted to his children. Reb Dovid showed profound appreciation to his sons' rebbeim. He went out of his way to tell them how much his children benefited from their *shiurim* and how much they were growing due to their efforts.[8]

Each of the Bender children, at one time or another, enjoyed playing principal or teacher. Even though sometimes they had to tolerate more strictures than their friends, they believed in their parents' love and wisdom. They wanted to emulate them.


SHMUEL SHOLOM KICKED THE DRY AUTUMN LEAVES BUNCHED AT HIS feet. The nip in the air indicated that winter was fast approaching. He hugged his jacket a bit tighter around himself as he walked home from Torah Vodaath.

Business was slow, and Mr. Spector[9] was standing and watching the passersby in front of his pharmacy at the corner of Hewes Street and Marcy Avenue. As Shmuel Sholom passed, he heard a voice call out, "Hey, kid!"

Shmuel Sholom turned around. Mr. Spector motioned him to come over.

"You go to yeshivah?"

"Yes," the little boy answered.

"You learned about Esau and Jacob?"

Shmuel Sholom looked back blankly; he had no idea what Mr. Spector was talking about.

"You know," the older man said, growing impatient. "The twins, Esau and Jacob, one was a hunter …"

By now, Shmuel Sholom knew what he meant and was nodding.

"Well, let me ask you a question. What happened when Esau came back from the field dying from hunger? He asked his brother for some

---

7. "One of the Bender boys was in my *shiur*. I had heard that the previous year, he had come to *shiur* very well prepared and proceeded to take over the class. I was not going to allow that to happen. So, on the very first day, as I saw his hand waving in the air, I told him that if the question had to do with the Gemara he should approach me after *shiur*. He was then forced to hear what I had to say first. It gave him time to rethink his questions and come to me privately if they remained. His being prepared for class then turned into an advantage" (Rabbi Reuven Scheiner).

8. "Rabbi Bender was one of the most gracious parents I ever met. In addition to the regular words of encouragement, he presented me with a beautiful *esrog* before Succos" (Rabbi Yisroel Belsky).

9. Not his real name.

food, right? And what does Jacob do? He tricks Esau into selling him his birthright. Tell me, was that nice? He sees his older brother, back from an exhausting day in the field, starved and tired, and he does not want to give him a little food. It's not as if Jacob was grilling steaks, he was cooking beans! Is it nice to tell your brother, starve or sell me your birthright? What kind of business was that?"

Shmuel Sholom did not know what to answer. Spector had a point, didn't he? The 8-year-old shrugged his shoulders and continued home, confused.

"Hi, Ma, I'm home!" he called.

Rebbetzin Bender cheerfully returned his greeting. Shmuel Sholom put away his jacket and schoolbag. He pulled out a chair and sat pensively at the kitchen table.

"*Nu*? How is everything?" His mother smiled as she stirred the soup for supper.

"Ma, you know what happened today? Spector, from the drugstore, stopped me and asked me a *gevaldige kasha*."

Rebbetzin Bender raised an eyebrow. Spector asked an unbelievable question? Shmuel Sholom repeated the entire conversation. Rebbetzin Bender stopped what she was doing and sat down at the table to face him.

"First of all, I don't want you to ever speak to this man again," she began. "As to his question, I'll answer it with a *mashal*. You're running for president against another fellow. This fellow is a very charming guy, everybody loves him." The image of newly elected John F. Kennedy flashed through Shmuel Sholom's mind.

Rebbetzin Bender went on, "But you know him very well. And you know that he is selfish and arrogant. All that he wants is to become famous. You know, without a shadow of a doubt, that as soon as he becomes president he's going to push the button and it's going to be World War III. He'll do all this just to take center stage and make history. You know this as a fact. Everyone else is blinded by his charisma and personality. Only you see the truth. Only you know that if he becomes president, it means the destruction of the world."

Shmuel Sholom sat riveted to his mother's voice, but how was this story going to answer his question? "Somehow," Rebbetzin Bender continued, "you get him into a corner. With some kind of trick, you can force him to drop out of the race. What should you do? Should you trick him, which is not so nice, or should you not trick him? Can you allow him to run and possibly win, and thus endanger the entire world? Which is the 'nicer' thing to do?"

Shmuel Sholom smiled, and let out a sigh of relief. He knew that Yaakov was the *tzaddik* and Esav the *rasha*. There had to be a good answer to the question. His mother's explanation removed all doubts.

This was Rebbetzin Bender. She had the uncanny ability to understand people and relate to them on their level. The *mashal* she gave to Shmuel Sholom was spontaneous. Doubtless, in her modesty, she would say that choosing the appropriate words was simply *siyata d'Shmaya* — help from Heaven — but Rebbetzin Bender seemed to have this *siyata d'Shmaya* more often than most people.

*Chapter Forty-Five*

# Rebbetzin Bender:
# A Mother Who Taught

**B**AIS YAAKOV HAD BECOME A WELL-ESTABLISHED INSTITU-
tion. Its enrollment soared from eight girls assembled around a
dining-room table in 1937 to a full high school with parallel
classes and a dormitory with more than 20 girls. Bais Yaakov was expanding rapidly, and Rebbetzin Bender had been a part of that growth from her
first days in America.

Rebbetzin Bender's teaching style reflected the profound influence of
her mentor Sara Schenirer. She entered the classroom slowly, a warm smile
on her lips, and a glow in her soft brown eyes. She sat at the teacher's desk
and surveyed her students, taking note of who was present and who was
not. She opened her notebook and began her lesson, in the calm, even tone
that was to become her trademark. Rebbetzin Bender did not pace around
the classroom in excitement, hoping to excite her students. She did not talk
loudly or quickly to keep the attention of the class. She spoke carefully and
softly, thoughts and words that emanated from her heart.

"*Maidelach*" — Rebbetzen Bender paused to momentarily digress from
the *pasuk* in her *Chumash* lesson — "the most important thing to remember is that the *fishelach* (little fish) you see today are the same *fishelach* that
*HaKadosh Baruch Hu* created by *Ma'asei Bereishis*. The *faygelach* (little birds)
you see today are the same *faygelach* that *HaKadosh Baruch Hu* created by
*Ma'asei Bereishis*. In those six days, He created this world, this very same
world that you and I are a part of."[10]

---

10. Rebbetzin B. Ribner.

THESE DIGRESSIONS BOTH PEP-pered her classes and encapsulated what Bais Yaakov stood for. For Rebbetzin Bender, Bais Yaakov stood for *Mesorah*, tradition. A Bais Yaakov teacher should be a guardian of *Mesorah*, fierce in his or her presentation of Torah so that *Mesorah* would never be distorted. Rebbetzin Bender and her colleagues, in their lessons, in class discussions, and in guiding their students, upheld this precious principle.

Rebbetzin Bender was neither ignorant nor unaware of new trends and ideas. She was very well read and continued to keep up with current world events. She subtly used that knowledge in her classes. She had no need to mention that her presentation of *Ma'asei Bereishis* was refuting the scientific theories of the

*Bais Yaakov of Williamsburg*

time. A proper presentation of *Ma'asei Bereishis*, based on *Mesorah*, was in itself such a refutation.

Rebbetzin Bender saw her teaching as a holy responsibility and could not imagine coming to class unprepared. Yet, merely transmitting information was not her goal. As a teacher, Rebbetzin Bender sought to address the whole student. She wanted her students to be not merely knowledgeable individuals, but quality individuals at one with their knowledge. Rebbetzin Bender wanted her students to use their newly acquired knowledge as a catalyst for growth and change.

The growth and change that Rebbetzin Bender and her colleagues envisioned was all encompassing. In those years, Bais Yaakov teachers faced an uphill battle against deeply entrenched American social mentality. What these teachers saw as *Mesorah*, their students saw as radicalism. Of course a girl should aspire to be religious, but why should that contradict marrying a successful businessman? Why could Torah not be the center of one's life in a more discreet way?

SHIRLEY WAS SITTING AND DOODLING ON A SCRAP OF PAPER. HER friend Miriam walked in. "I'm engaged," Miriam said suddenly, and then clamped her mouth shut.

"What!" Shrieks and shouts of mazel tov filled the air and Miriam was pulled, hugged, and twirled around.

"What does he do?" one of the girls innocently asked.

Miriam mumbled something unintelligible.

"What did you say?" her friends prodded. Suddenly, all was quiet.

"He learns," Miriam blurted out, red with embarrassment.

Shirley understood what was happening and stood up. "Are you ashamed that he is learning? What is going on here? You should be proud!"

Miriam felt a wave of gratitude toward Shirley. Miriam *was* proud but she knew that her friends might look down at her for such a radical choice. She had dreaded their reactions, but now, with Shirley's protest, she felt more at ease.

*Rebbetzin Basya Bender*

"You are so lucky that you have a *chosson* who learns," Shirley continued. "Would you have wanted a doctor or a lawyer? You knew you wanted a *chosson* who is learning. Be proud!"

Rebbetzin Bender walked in just as Shirley was speaking. She beamed with pride, like a mother proud of her children.

This was America and these were her Bais Yaakov girls.[11]

FOR THESE YOUNG WOMEN, ALL OF 18 AND 19, IT WAS A DRASTIC DEPARTURE from conventional thinking to agree to marry men who were learning and planning to continue learning Torah, even after marriage. Yet after only two years of Bais Yaakov's existence, numerous girls were open to this idea.

This metamorphosis did not occur by accident. Bais Yaakov and its dedicated teachers deserve a large share of the credit. Bais Yaakov teachers were earnest in their presentation to their classes, solid in their knowledge

---

11. When Rebbetzin Bender heard that her former student Shirley Gross, the widow of Rabbi Sender Gross, principal of the Miami Beach Day School, was engaged to Rabbi Ralph Pelcowitz, Rav of the White Shul (Congregation Knesses Yisroel of Far Rockaway), she had her son Rabbi Yaakov Bender call up Rabbi Pelcowitz to relay this story. Rebbetzin Bender recalled how thrilled she was then about the *ruach* in the classroom when American girls were excited by a *bochur* who was learning.

that they were speaking the truth, and confident that they were passing on the *Mesorah* of their ancestors and teachers.

Bais Yaakov girls saw teachers who lived what they taught: Rebbetzins Kaplan, Bender, and Wachtfogel had all married American *b'nei Torah* who continued to learn after they married. Through observing the choices these special teachers had made, their students achieved a new reverence for Torah, for *lomdei Torah*, and for *Yiddishkeit*. They were forced to re-examine their American values.

REBBETZIN BENDER RELATED TO HER STUDENTS WITH APPRECIATION and respect, for she truly believed in the innate goodness of each pupil. With that in mind, it was easy to judge even the most drastic offender favorably. She dealt with her students the same way she dealt with her own children: with love, understanding, warmth, and discipline. On the rare occasion she had to punish, it was appropriately meted out and then forgotten. The pupil's self-esteem remained intact.

Moreover, by viewing each student as innately good, Rebbetzin Bender sought to understand the cause of misbehavior rather than being quick to punish. This approach was crucial in the 40's and 50's where difficult home situations abounded.

MALKY RAN DOWN THE STREETS HUFFING AND PUFFING. OH NO, LATE again! What will they think of her? She tried to run faster, her thoughts dashing along with her. *Another punishment … they think I'm lazy … but I'm not, I'm really not!* She took the front steps two at a time, glided down the hallway, and ended up in front of the classroom. Gingerly, she turned the knob and pushed the door, hoping to unobtrusively slide into her seat.

Mrs. K. was taking attendance and did not look up as the door opened. Malky softly closed the door and inched her way along the wall where the coats were hanging. She held her breath, only a few more steps until her seat … "Malky!" Mrs. K. glared at her. "This is the third time this week …" Malky stared stonily ahead. "I hope to see some improvement immediately!" Malky gave a slight nod of her head as she sat down. Mrs. K. went back to calling out the names on the attendance list.

Later on, in the teachers' room, a heated discussion ensued. "I can't get over it!" Mrs. K. fumed. "Time after time, she comes in late — we all know how disturbing it is when a student walks in late — and yet she is not contrite at all. She seems almost brazenly defiant. What chutzpah!"

Rebbetzin Bender listened as her colleagues debated the issue. Finally, she interjected. "My dear friends," she said softly, but firmly, "this is not the way. When a good girl is consistently late, we must ask why. Perhaps something is bothering her? Maybe there is trouble at home? Before we think about punishments, let us speak to the girl. There must be an explanation here." Rebbetzin Bender went to seek out the girl they were discussing.

Malky was sitting at her desk, gazing listlessly out the window. Around her, girls were jumping, laughing, and playing — enjoying their recess. Malky was steeped in her sorrows and oblivious to what was going on around her.

"Come, *mein kind*, I want to speak to you."

Malky turned around, startled. There stood Rebbetzin Bender, her sweet loving smile radiating warmth. Rebbetzin Bender led Malky into a small office and took a seat facing her.

"Malky, you are such a sweet girl, such a good girl, something must be going on. I am sure you want to be in school on time, no?"

Tears welled up in Malky's eyes. Suddenly, the whole story spilled out. "I don't have a father. My mother works very hard to provide for me and my brother. She leaves for work early in the morning and it's my job to get my brother out in the morning. I walk him all the way to Torah Vodaath before I come to school. But that is not why I'm late."

Malky's voice was cracking, but she continued, "My brother is very skinny and my mother worries about him. I gave her my word that we will not leave the house in the morning until he finishes his cup of milk." Malky began to cry. "And he doesn't like to drink it. He plays and sips and it takes so long for him to finish. I keep looking at the clock, but what should I do? Then I still have to walk him to school. I don't want to tell my mother because she has enough to worry about, but it is so hard. And then I'm late to school. Every day I'm late."

Rebbetzin Bender's heart went out to the young girl. She was suffering at both ends: at home as she shouldered the responsibilities of one much older, and at school where she was so terribly misunderstood. With discretion and tact, Rebbetzin Bender worked behind the scenes to ameliorate the situation.

Rebbetzin Bender never forgot the incident. She resolved never to berate a child who suddenly began acting out in class or routinely came late. She would first try to find out what was going on, and even if there was no excuse for the misbehavior, she would take the child aside and deal with her privately. The important thing was to judge a child favorably and to rebuke her in a way that would preserve her dignity.

BAIS YAAKOV OF THOSE YEARS ALSO BECAME A SCHOOL FOR GIRLS who had fled Europe after the war. These war survivors had to adjust to a new land, language, and culture. They had to endure the gibes and taunts of their new schoolmates who often found them strange and annoying. These girls, more often than not, came home to parents who were too worn out from their own adjustments to give their children the warmth and attention they so badly needed.

Many of these children of survivors, even if they had two parents, still carried scars of war. In some families, the mother never really recovered from her losses and could not cope with her children. Sometimes, it was the father who was moody and withdrawn. Often, these children grew up swallowing their pain to shield their parents who had already suffered so much. There were many orphans in Bais Yaakov. Poverty was also common.

And, together with all the girls from the difficult family situations, there were the regular all-American effervescent teenagers, who could not fathom the painful baggage some of their classmates carried. Bais Yaakov was where all these personalities and situations met.

THE L. FAMILY LIVED IN THE BRONX. THEY WERE DESPERATELY POOR. With true personal sacrifice, the parents shouldered the expense of sending their three daughters to Bais Yaakov. After paying minimal tuition and transportation, there was no money left to outfit the girls properly. They came to school wearing coats that were terribly worn and outdated (and probably were not very attractive even when they had been new). Rebbetzin Bender's heart pitied them. Wearing these coats was like carrying a sign saying, "We are poor." It pained Rebbetzin Bender to see these girls so obviously needy.

One day, she told her daughter Blumie to bring the girls home with her. Mystified, the girls complied. Rebbetzin Bender greeted them at the

*Rebbetzin Bender with her colleagues: Rebbetzin Chava Pincus, Rebbetzin Rochel Cisner, Rebbetzin Vichna Kaplan, Rebbetzin Basya Bender, unidentified, Rebbetzin Shifra Yudasin*

door with her usual warm smile. "Come in, girls," she said as she led them inside, "I have something to show you." She motioned to Blumie to leave the room; one of the girls was in Blumie's class and she did not want her to be embarrassed.

"I came across three beautiful coats and I was wondering if you would like to have them." She took out three coats, each one stylish, pretty, and warm. She urged them to try them on. The girls did not need much convincing. They shyly slipped their hands into the sleeves and zipped up the front, as Rebbetzin Bender continued with words of encouragement, telling them how beautiful they looked in the new coats and how well they fit.

"Leave your old ones here," she urged them. "I'm sure that your mother won't mind." The girls were thrilled. They left the Bender home with smiling faces and Rebbetzin Bender's warm words echoing in their ears. "Wear them in good health," Rebbetzin Bender called out. They nodded happily as they ran to catch their train back to the Bronx.

The L. girls had many classes and many teachers, but only Rebbetzin Bender took action. Rebbetzin Bender understood that for her girls to grow spiritually, their physical needs had to be met. If a girl felt ugly because her clothing was shabby, or she was embarrassed to come to school because she only owned one skirt, she would not be able to learn properly. Her mind would be focused on her misery. Rebbetzin Bender looked at her students with a mother's probing eye, and that was why she clearly saw what no one else did.

"*Mamme* Bender" she was called, at home and in school. It was the mother in her that attracted family and friends, neighbors and strangers, old and young, and people from all walks of life to turn to Rebbetzin Bender for advice and guidance. Girls from solid homes would come to Rebbetzin Bender to discuss issues they did not feel comfortable discussing with their mothers. They confided in her because they felt that she truly cared about them. They gravitated to her love and warmth, and her unusual ability to see the good in everyone. "*Mamme* Bender" was always available to step in where no one else wanted to tread.

Perhaps this was why Rabbi Boruch Kaplan and Rabbi Yonason Steif crowned Rebbetzin Bender as the leading *kallah* teacher, a role that had traditionally belonged to the Jewish mother.

IT BEGAN ONE ORDINARY SUMMER, WHEN RABBI BORUCH KAPLAN AND his family went up to the Catskill Mountains. A neighbor in the colony was marrying off a child, and everyone was excited about the festive event. Reb Boruch, with his keen intuition, realized that though preparations were at a peak, the most important preparations were probably being neglected. He approached the father of the bride and began a casual conversation about the upcoming *simchah*. He then zeroed in on the purpose of his visit. "Have you seen to it that your daughter is prepared to establish a Jewish home? Does she know what this entails?"

The father laughed. "This is America, all those old-fashioned things are not necessary here."

Reb Boruch did not give up. He spoke forcefully to the man until he agreed that his daughter would learn the proper way to begin a Jewish home. Reb Boruch scribbled a phone number onto a scrap of paper and instructed the man to call. He assured him that in the limited time left, this woman would thoroughly prepare his daughter for a Jewish marriage. Rebbetzin Bender would know exactly what to say and how to say it. His daughter would be in good hands.

Although there were only nine days left before the wedding, Rebbetzin Bender managed. The bride-to-be came to the Bender bungalow every night and in that short time, Rebbetzin Bender was able to pack in all the basic knowledge needed to set up a Jewish home. This was Rebbetzin Bender's first foray in teaching young *kallos*. She would soon be responsible for establishing hundreds of pure Jewish homes.

FOR CENTURIES, JEWISH MOTHERS PREPARED THEIR DAUGHTERS FOR marriage. They embraced this sacred role with responsibility and joy; they were sowing the seeds of another pure Jewish home. America, with its "melting pot" attitude and tolerance, had eroded the mother/daughter bond. Girls were not following in their parents' ways. Jewish marriage was another sacrifice on the altar of assimilation. Even mothers who successfully raised their children in a traditional manner found it difficult to speak to them about how they should run their married lives. Often the mothers did not even bother to broach the topic.

Then there were those who had no mothers. A young girl who had been separated from her mother at the beginning of World War II found her way to America. She was engaged to be married and approached Rabbi Boruch Kaplan. "The last words my mother said to me before we were separated were that I remember that I am a Jew, that I only marry a Jew, and that before I marry I speak to a Jewish rabbi about how to create a Jewish home. Tell me, Rabbi Kaplan, I am engaged to a fine Jewish man, and now I must know — what did my mother mean?" Reb Boruch sent the girl to Rebbetzin Bender.

This girl was lucky. Her mother's message rang in her ears and she sought guidance. Others were not as fortunate. Even among truly religious people, there was widespread ignorance regarding this subject. A member of the Viener *kehillah* asked Rebbetzin Bender to give a class and just review basic points to a small group of newly married young women.

Rebbetzin Bender was hesitant. Traditionally, such discussions were not held in a public forum. Yet, when she was told that the request came from the Viener Dayan, she reluctantly agreed. That Friday night, she spoke in the Viener shul, completely oblivious that, on the other side of the *mechitzah*, sat the revered Viener Dayan, Rabbi Yonason Steif. As she spoke, he nodded his head up and down. "*Ya*," he whispered, "*well said!*"

That *Motza'ei Shabbos*, Rabbi Yonason Steif called in Rebbetzin Bender for a meeting. He insisted she go public and speak to groups of women. These *ehrliche* young women would never approach anyone on their own for guidance, for they did not know what they were lacking. The only way to reach them was to create an awareness through popular *shiurim*. The *shiurim* would then be a springboard for discussion and consultation and, hopefully, the widespread ignorance would be rectified.

Rebbetzin Bender was abashed. Such a thing — a woman speaking to other women in a public forum about private matters — had never been done. How could she, one so conservative, so steeped in tradition, even think of taking such a progressive step? The Viener Dayan would not give up. "The *Eibeshter* commanded Sarah Imeinu to nurse her child in public so that everyone would know that Yitzchok was her son and not Hagar's. Sometimes, for the sake of *Kiddush Hashem*, you have to do something that you are not comfortable with." Knowing that the *kedushah* of *Klal Yisroel* was at stake, Rebbetzin Bender agreed.

With that, Rebbetzin Bender's career as the premier *kallah* teacher took off. She spoke regularly to married women on Friday evenings in the Viener shul, and she taught classes of *kallos* in the evenings in the Bais Yaakov High School. As her reputation grew, more and more women sought her guidance, not only for basic halachos, but also for practical advice on life issues.

"SURI," WHISPERED CHAYA, "I HAVE SOMETHING TO TELL YOU, BUT, please, don't tell anyone else."

Suri nodded solemnly, eyes frankly curious. Chaya's voice dropped a little lower. "I am adopted."

"What!" Suri exclaimed.

"Shhhh!" Chaya clamped her hand over Suri's mouth. "I told you to be quiet."

"But I don't understand," Suri whispered. "Your home seems so normal."

"Well, it is not," Chaya stated grimly. "All my other siblings are regular, but I am adopted. That is why they gave me the name Chaya — life. They were not going to name a foundling like me for a grandmother or anything like that."

"What is it like?" Suri asked, suddenly fascinated.

"What is what like?"

"Being adopted. What is it like? I mean, I have never met anyone who was adopted."

"It is horrible," Chaya declared, "absolutely horrible. I am the Cinderella of my house. Any chore no one wants to do, little Cinderella must take care of. When my 'mother' bakes a cake, who do you think gets the last slice? Sometimes there is nothing left for me at all. And my bed, you should see what kind of tiny, hard, uncomfortable bed I have ..."

Suri shook her head from side to side in sympathy with her friend's plight. How terrible it must be for Chaya! During the course of the next few weeks, Chaya continued to tell Suri of all the indignities she had to endure. Suri was horrified. How dare anyone treat a sweet Jewish girl this way? And to think that Chaya's "parents" put on such a misleading public image of being a warm and loving family, when in reality they were torturing an innocent young girl.

Suri was very disturbed. She could not sleep at night and finally she confided to her mother what Chaya had told her. Suri's mother was shocked. How could something like this happen in their community? Who could deal with such a drastic situation? She picked up the telephone and called her good friend, Rebbetzin Bender.

When the conversation was over, Rebbetzin Bender was shocked. She was shocked because she remembered when Chaya was born, and the child was definitely not adopted. Obviously, Chaya desperately needed attention, and this was her way of getting it. Yet, how could she spread such ghastly rumors about herself and her family, and who knew to how many girls she had "confided" this tale?

From then on, Rebbetzin Bender kept a close eye on Chaya. She began to see other things, clear indications that Chaya had a problem. Nonetheless, Chaya was a relatively popular girl with good grades, and it was hard to believe that there was something definitely wrong inside of her. Rebbetzin Bender watched patiently from the sidelines, hoping that Chaya would quietly outgrow her issues.

Chaya became engaged to a fine *bochur*, a young man with an excellent reputation. Like many other former students, Chaya began attending Rebbetzin Bender's *kallah* classes. Rebbetzin Bender cautiously observed her. So far, so good.

Soon after Chaya's marriage, her problems surfaced. Her attitudes and demands were illogical and her young husband was feeling bewildered and frustrated. Chaya's parents-in-law came to Rebbetzin Bender. After all, Rebbetzin Bender taught Chaya in high school and prepared her for marriage. Surely, she would have some insight as to what was happening.

Rebbetzin Bender listened to the concerned parents with a heavy heart. Yes, she had been afraid that Chaya was not ready for marriage, but she could not have anticipated this. She recommended the parents speak with Rabbi Yaakov Kamenetsky. Reb Yaakov discussed the situation with the parents and then with Rebbetzin Bender. He concluded that Rebbetzin Bender must do her utmost to save the marriage.

Rebbetzin Bender spoke with Chaya, her husband, and with medical professionals. She worked with everyone to get the marriage on a healthy footing. With time and patience, she succeeded.[12]

This was one of many occasions where Rebbetzin Bender's roles as a Bais Yaakov teacher and a *kallah* teacher intersected.

REBBETZIN BENDER SUFFERED FROM DIFFERENT AILMENTS THROUGH-out adulthood, and despite her suffering, she always pushed herself to accomplish with joy. Ever since the kidney infection she had when she had given birth to Paltiel, she had problems with her kidneys. One time, the pain was so bad that surgery was the only option. In 1963, Rebbetzin Bender entered the hospital thinking that they would only be removing a kidney stone. During surgery, the doctor discovered that there were many huge stones that had eaten away at the kidney. He had to remove the entire kidney.

For the first few days after the operation, she was not allowed to get out of the hospital bed or even use the bathroom. After her first trip to the bathroom, she washed her hands and then enunciated each word of *Asher Yatzar* softly and slowly. The words were all the more meaningful after the surgery she had just gone through.

There were three non-Jewish women in her hospital room. One of the women was very religious and intently observed Rebbetzin Bender recite *Asher Yatzar,* but she said nothing. One day, the woman finally asked, "Tell me, you seem like an intelligent woman, not one given to talking to herself. What is it that you say after every time you go to the bathroom?" Rebbetzin Bender explained the *berachah* of *Asher Yatzar* to her and how much more the prayer meant to her now. Rebbetzin Bender added how important it is for us not to take the well-being of our bodies for granted. She then trans-lated the entire *berachah* word for word.

The gentile woman marveled at the beauty of the *berachah* and Rebbetzin Bender's clear and moving explanation. For the duration of their stay in the hospital, she continued to engage Rebbetzin Bender in conversation. She took down Rebbetzin Bender's address and she wrote to her even after they left the hospital.

During Rebbetzin Bender's stay in the hospital, two students came to

---

12. "Chaya" went on to raise a beautiful family.

visit. Rebbetzin Bender, still emotional over her ordeal, addressed the girls, "*Maidelach*, since my surgery, I have come to a greater appreciation of the *tefillah* of *Asher Yatzar*. Please listen carefully …" And then she proceeded to explain the *berachah* word for word, in depth.

The girls were overcome with emotion when they left the hospital. They had come as a kindness to Rebbetzin Bender, in fulfillment of the mitzvah of visiting the sick, and they had left enriched by her.[13]

Even from her hospital bed, Rebbetzin Bender was always a teacher.

---

13. "I have been teaching for over 30 years," one of the visitors declared at the *shivah* of Rebbetzin Bender, "and, from that day, I have never failed to teach *Asher Yatzar* or to say it slowly myself."

## Chapter Forty-Six

# Rabbi Dovid Bender:
# Principal and Personality

*T WAS A PLEASANT AUTUMN DAY. RABBI HENOCH COHEN WAS in Williamsburg raising money for Chinuch Atzmai and, as he often did when he had a chance, he decided to stop by the Old Mesivta and have a chat with his rebbi, Rabbi Dovid Bender. Reb Dovid, while pausing to answer the ringing phone, greeted his talmid warmly and motioned to him to take a seat.*

*"Yes? Oh, Mrs. R., how are you? It is so nice to hear from you."*

*Reb Henoch recognized Mrs. R.'s last name; she was from a well-known Williamsburg family. She had 12 children; her boys were very active. One of the boys had come to school wearing jeans and Rabbi Bender sent him home with a note that jeans were unacceptable attire and that he should please change.*

*Mrs. R. was screaming hysterically into the phone. "How dare you!" she shrieked. "My boys are very, very active. They are always ripping their pants. I finally discovered this durable material and now you, the principal, dare to tell me how to dress my kids!"*

*"I am sorry that you are so upset," Reb Dovid said soothingly. "We are not trying to dictate to you how to dress your children. You may not be aware that jeans have a certain connotation; they are the fashion of a certain type of boy. We want more for your son. We want him to grow up to be a mentsch, a true ehrlicher Yid. In Torah Vodaath, we are building mentschen and it is not fitting for a boy like your son, one who is becoming a true mentsch, to wear jeans."*

*Reb Henoch felt as if he was back in his rebbi's shiur, listening to him molding and shaping his talmidim. Whether or not he had ever used those exact words in*

*Rabbi Dovid Bender*

*shiur was irrelevant. Reb Henoch realized that the message as a principal was the same message he had given as a maggid shiur. His goal was to reach the whole person and turn him into the ultimate mentsch — a true ben Torah.*

FROM THAT OLD GRAY MANSION ON BEDford Avenue, Rabbi Bender strove to create *mentschen*. As he leaned over his desk to write to a parent, or back in his chair as he spoke to a student, he was nurturing and molding generations of *mentschen*: boys who would leave Torah Vodaath and go on to make their mark on the evolving Jewish world.[14]

Torah Vodaath was a legendary institution. In the years following World War II, enrollment climbed. At its peak, there were over 2,000 pupils enrolled[15] with over 120 boys graduating from the elementary school.[16] Boys traveled from all over New York to attend Torah Vodaath. There were students from Williamsburg, Crown Heights, East New York, and Far Rockaway.[17] There were out-of-towners, and even some boys who came from abroad. For overseas parents who wanted to send their boys to a yeshivah, Torah Vodaath was an option.

The elementary school had two divisions. Reb Dovid's childhood friend, Rabbi Avrohom Pincus, was principal of first through sixth grades at 206 Wilson Avenue. Reb Dovid was principal for the seventh and eighth grades, plus the *aleph* track of the sixth grade, in the Old Mesivta building on Bedford Avenue.[18]

Though Torah Vodaath had several divisions, it was one institution, one family. When an elementary school rebbi was needed in a pinch, a member of the Torah Vodaath Kollel stepped in.[19] Rabbi Hershel Wasilski, beloved elementary school rebbi, gave night classes to older students

---

14. "Rabbi Dovid Bender was a larger-than-life figure. Almost every *marbitz Torah*, almost every *ben Torah* in America today (from that generation) attended Torah Vodaath elementary school under Reb Dovid's guidance" (Rabbi Elya Brudny).

15. As printed on Torah Vodaath pushkes for many years.

16. "My class had 128 graduates" (Rabbi Yaakov Bender).

17. The Glicks from Far Rockaway traveled an hour and a half in each direction every day.

18. The New Mesivta and Bais Medrash were on 141 South Third Street, and the dormitory, which housed mainly Mesivta and Bais Medrash *bochurim*, was back to back with the Mesivta on South Second Street, with a playground between them.

19. Rabbi Yosef Leviton took over for Rabbi Cogan when he was still in kollel and *ybdl"ch* Rabbi Yisroel Belsky took over for Rabbi Yosef Leviton when he was in kollel.

Reb Dovid often went to visit Reb Yaakov on *Leil Shabbos* after the *seudah* On one visit, Reb Yaakov told Reb Dovid, "I have a wonderful idea for a new *Mashgiach* for the yeshivah." Reb Dovid listened with interest. "Rabbi Moshe Wolfson," Reb Yaakov stated. Reb Dovid was surprised. Up to that time, Reb Moshe Wolfson had been teaching young children and assisting Rabbi Nesanel Quinn in the high school. Promoting him to *Mashgiach* of the yeshivah was a dramatic jump. Reb Yaakov went on to explain all the reasons why he felt that Reb Moshe was suitable. A few weeks later, to the surprise of many, Rabbi Moshe Wolfson became the new *Mashgiach* of Torah Vodaath. Reb Yaakov's uncanny perception became clear to all.

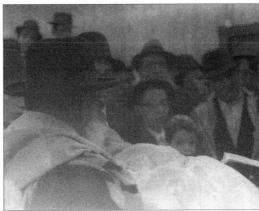

*Rabbi Yaakov Kamenetsky as sandek at his grandson's bris. The boy in the center is Paltiel Bender.*

*Rabbi Yaakov Kamenetsky (1891-1986) learned in Minsk and then became a student of the Alter of Slabodka. He served as Rav in several communities in Europe until his departure in 1937. Then he became Rav in Seattle, Washington and Toronto, Canada respectively. In 1945 he was appointed Rosh Yeshivah in Torah Vodaath where he shaped and inspired talmidim for nearly 30 years. Reb Yaakov was universally recognized as one of the gedolei hador. His involvement in Agudas Yisroel, Torah Umesorah, and Chinuch Atzmai were crucial.*

in the dormitory[20] while Luzer Margoshes learned in the Bais Medrash in the morning and taught secular studies to high school students in the afternoon. It was only natural that Reb Dovid, principal in the elementary school, be in regular contact with the Rosh Yeshivah of Torah Vodaath, Rabbi Yaakov Kamenetsky.

20. When Rabbi Moshe Rivlin, longtime dormitory supervisor, saw that he needed structure for the dormers at night, he established night classes and hired rebbeim to review lessons with the boys. Rabbi Chaim Brandstater and Rabbi Binyamin Steinfeld were among the rebbeim (Rabbi Avrohom Moshe Wasilski).

Reb Dovid was never too complacent to seek advice. Rabbi Yaakov Kamenetsky became his mentor and, in a school as complex as Torah Vodaath, Reb Dovid was relieved to have someone to turn to.

TORAH VODAATH OF THE 1940'S, 50'S, AND 60'S HAD A VERY VARIED student body. In the early years, there were no specifically *Chassidishe* schools, nor were there *Litvishe* or modern schools. There was either public school or yeshivah.[21] In any one classroom there could be a Satmar Chassid with a near-bald haircut and dangling *peiyos*, a *Litvishe* boy with his slight *tchup* and sideburns cut just to the end of the ear, a Hungarian boy who barely spoke English, a Mexican boy who was alone in a new country, and an all-American modern boy whose family barely observed Shabbos. The diversity was striking. The challenge of being principal to such a broad group of students was daunting.

Reb Dovid took on the challenge.

BORUCH GROSS[22] WAS HUDDLED IN A CORNER NEAR THE PRINCIPAL'S office trying to be invisible.

"Hello," a voice called softly. "How are you?" A hand cupped Boruch's chin and pulled his face upward. Reb Dovid saw the boy's tear-stained cheeks and knew something was wrong. "Tell me," he encouraged the boy while gently leading him into his office, "what happened?"

Boruch tried to speak, but the words just would not come. Then he tipped back his baseball cap and Reb Dovid understood. The Gross family were Skverer Chassidim *"fun der heim,"* but they were decidedly modern, and their boys sported fashionably long haircuts. As Boruch's bar mitzvah was approaching, Mr. Gross told his son he was taking him to the Rebbe to put on *tefillin* for the first time. But the Rebbe would only lay *tefillin* on a boy whose hair was cut in the traditional *Chassidishe* fashion. So, despite his son's protestations, Mr. Gross had Boruch's hair shorn so short that he was practically bald. Now that the *tefillin*-laying ceremony was over, Boruch had to return to school to face the taunts and teasing of his friends.

Reb Dovid looked down compassionately at the boy's miserable face. He leaned forward and slipped his own yarmulka off his head. "You see this?" he asked, bending lower so that the boy could easily see his bare head. "Bald. And my hair is not growing back." Boruch's lips twitched as he tried to suppress his smile. "Be happy. We might both be bald right now, but in a few weeks, you will have a full head of hair, while I …" By

---

21. Yeshivas Rabbi Shlomo Kluger, Rabbeinu Chaim Berlin, and Rabbeinu Yaakov Yosef all had the same kind of diverse student body as Torah Vodaath.

22. Not his real name.

now, Boruch was giggling aloud. Reb Dovid tweaked his cap, put his arm around his shoulder, and walked the boy back to class.

It might have taken weeks for his hair to grow back, but it only took a few seconds for Reb Dovid to make those weeks a bit more bearable.[23]

THE IDENTITY CRISIS THAT FACED RELIGIOUS JEWRY IN PRE-WORLD War II America continued long after the war was over. While asserting their "all-Americanism," many held on to small, symbolic, and/or traditional acts to prove their loyalty to *Yiddishkeit*. American values became so entrenched in the American Jewish character that many second- and third-generation parents forgot which values were American and which were Jewish.

One of Reb Dovid's goals was to uproot this Americanism. Through his weekly *shmuessen* given to each of the classes under his jurisdiction, Reb Dovid hammered away at many of these non-Torah ideas. He spoke about Sunday and how, for *Yidden*, Sunday is a day like any other weekday. We should never, G-d forbid, consider it otherwise. Mothers' Day and Fathers' Day — how can we set aside only one day to honor each one of our parents? Our parents deserve our acknowledgment and appreciation every day. Thanksgiving Day — a special day to give thanks to our Creator? We thank Him three times a day, but in reality, there can be no end to our thanking Him. His students remembered these words for decades.[24]

Many of the themes he spoke about as principal were those which he had taught his older *talmidim* when he had been a rebbi in the Mesivta, but now he brought these concepts down to the level of his younger students.

For example, when he wanted to explain a favorite concept from his rebbi, Rabbi Yeruchem Levovitz, he began with the basic idea, and then found a parable to make that idea more vivid.

"*CHESSED* IS ONE OF THE FOUNDATIONS OF THE WORLD," REB DOVID began, addressing a class of seventh graders. "*HaKadosh Baruch Hu* wants every person to do *chessed* and, if a person has the correct focus, he will find his day constantly occupied with *chessed*. Hashem created the world in such a way that we are constantly giving to and receiving from others.[25]

"For example, a typical storekeeper is doing constant *chessed* with his customers. Without the grocery store, from where would we have food to eat? Without the clothing store, from where would we have clothing to wear? On the other hand, the consumers are doing *chessed* with the storekeeper. Without customers, how would the storekeeper make a living?

---

23. Mr. Eli Kleinman.

24. "I remember some of these *shmuessen* now, 45 years later!" (Rabbi Elya Brudny).

25. *Da'as Chochmah U'Mussar — maamar* 56 (Rabbi Yeruchem Levovitz).

Even though both the storekeeper and the customer are themselves benefiting, it does not take away from the *chessed* that is being done.

"The key here is focus. If both the storekeeper and the customer are living lives of *chessed*, then when they are doing their jobs, they will each have the other person in mind. For example, the storekeeper will be thinking: *I really want to help this person buy a suit that will look good on him even though I would make more money on the other suit.* Meanwhile, the customer should be thinking: *It is so nice of the storekeeper to stock such a beautiful selection of suits. I must compliment him on his exceptional taste.* If both are focused on helping the other person, even if they are benefiting, they are still doing *chessed*.

"If someone lives his whole life this way — always thinking about the other person, always looking to be of help, always focusing on *chessed* — then his entire life will be a life of *chessed*."

By using a *mashal* that the boys could understand, Reb Dovid was bringing lofty concepts down to a seventh-grade level.

ONE OF REB DOVID'S FAVORITE TOPICS WAS ABOUT LEARNING TORAH. He would speak about cultivating a love of learning and would tell stories about *gedolim* and their *mesiras nefesh* for learning. Reb Dovid often repeated his famous train *mashal* to illustrate the value of learning without any interruptions or distractions:

"A person learning Torah is like a passenger on a train. Two people can board a train at the same time; one boards the D train and the other boards the Q train. The two passengers are heading for the exact same destination, going the same route, and they leave at the exact same time. Nonetheless, the Q train will arrive first. Why? The Q train is an express train because it makes very few stops and arrives at its destination with speed and efficiency. In contrast, the D train is a local. The D train does not make that many more stops, and each additional stop is only for a minute or two. Yet, each time the train stops, it slows down, stops, and then starts again. That break in the momentum slows everything down. That is how it is with learning. The actual interruption might be only a few seconds, but the break in the momentum, the stopping and restarting wastes valuable time."[26]

Reb Dovid's regular *shmuessen* brought him into the classroom on a regular basis and solidified his role. Reb Dovid was not some vague figure whose main purpose was to punish. He was a real part of their *chinuch*. The boys sensed that their principal understood them and was concerned about them.

Reb Dovid often used imagery the boys could relate to. "You *play* to win?" he would say. "You can also *learn* to win!" To these American-born

---

26. Many *talmidim* mentioned this *vort*, including Rabbi Yisroel Belsky and Rabbi Yaakov Fensterheim.

kids, ball playing was everything. Here he was telling them, I have no problem with you playing ball. Only, I want you to learn with the same excitement that you have when you play ball.

When Reb Dovid spoke about continued striving for greater spiritual heights, he also gave them concrete ideas as to how to accomplish their goals. For example, he introduced a biweekly night *seder* for elementary school boys, something unique in those years.

AS MUCH AS POSSIBLE, REB DOVID TRIED TO GIVE *MUSSAR* TO THE BOYS in ways that would encourage them to grow. He usually kept a bar of chocolate in his desk drawer, probably for an emergency snack. One day, he noticed that the chocolate was missing and assumed that one of the boys had stolen it. Reb Dovid went from classroom to classroom and spoke about the gravity of stealing and the importance of *teshuvah*. He reiterated that this had nothing to do with his personal honor or even with the missing chocolate. He wanted the errant boy to return the chocolate bar for his own benefit, to remove the stain of having stolen. "I am going to leave the building between 12 and 1 o'clock and my office door will be open. During that hour, the *bochur* who stole the chocolate will have an opportunity to return it. I will never know who he is and neither will anyone else, but he will be wiping his slate clean with true *teshuvah*."[27]

Whether or not the *bochur* actually returned the chocolate remains a secret, but the lesson was not wasted. In each classroom, 25 boys learned about the evils of stealing and the importance of *teshuvah*.

PINCHAS'S REBBI DIVIDED HIS CLASSES INTO ROWS. EVERY DAY A DIFferent row had to prepare part of the *parashah*, and the rebbi would ask them questions. One week, the rebbi was running behind schedule and Pinchas was certain that he would not get to his row … until the rebbi announced that he would definitely be getting to it later that day. Pinchas had not prepared the requisite *pesukim*. And so, he took his *Chumash* and placed it on his *Gemara*. As the rebbi was teaching *Gemara*, he was reviewing the *Chumash*.

Suddenly, the rebbi began walking toward him. Pinchas quickly slipped the *Chumash* down and put it on the shelf beneath the seat. The rebbi saw this maneuver and ordered Pinchas to Rabbi Bender's office.

"Well, Pinchas, what happened?" Rabbi Bender asked.

"Nothing," Pinchas protested. "The *Chumash* fell and I picked it up and returned it to the shelf. But, the rebbi thinks I took it out to study the *parashah* …"

Reb Dovid was quiet. The ticking clock suddenly sounded deafening.

"Are you saying the truth?" Rabbi Bender asked softly.

---

27. Rabbi Joshua Berkowitz in a letter, 1996.

*Rabbi Dovid Bender walking down the aisle at a wedding together with other illustrious rabbanim: Rabbi Yaakov Kamenetsky, Rabbi Mendel Zaks, Rabbi Abba Berman, Rabbi Moshe Feinstein, Rabbi Dovid Bender, Rabbi Nesanel Quinn, Rabbi Shmuel Brudny.*

Pinchas lowered his head in shame.

REB DOVID DID NOT HAVE TO RANT AND RAVE. WHEN HE SPOKE TO HIS students, they felt that he was speaking from his *neshamah* to theirs. He rarely raised his voice or lost his temper; his disappointment in them was the most effective reprimand. While there were rebbeim whom the boys feared, Reb Dovid's presence commanded respect, not fear.

Reb Dovid did not ignore misdemeanors. Discipline had to vary according to each situation. He knew how to be strict, but he also knew how to be flexible.

One of the rebbeim sent a student to the office for rebuke. The boy had just entered Torah Vodaath. He lived on the West Side of Manhattan where the community was decidedly more modern than in Brooklyn. The boy had a cowlick that caused the hair on his forehead to stand up. The rebbi wanted Reb Dovid to insist that the boy cut off his *tchup* and get a more conservative haircut. Reb Dovid waved the issue aside, understanding that certain things had to come with time.

Time was the panacea for some, but not all, problems. The yeshivah had major financial difficulties, and there were times the staff was not paid for months. Although this was not Reb Dovid's jurisdiction, he felt responsible for his teachers, and it pained him that his staff was not getting paid. Although he, too, was dependent on his salary, Reb Dovid still felt for his teachers.[28]

The yeshivah's precarious financial situation was one of the reasons why finding quality rebbeim was difficult. Another factor was image

---

28. The financial situation in Torah Vodaath was never good. The rebbeim were paid very little, and the yeshivah was often months behind in paying the salaries. One of the Bender children overheard his father and Rabbi Avrohom Pincus talking. The yeshivah had been six months behind in pay. They then gave out a year's worth of checks: six for the previous six months and six head checks. It was a very nice gesture but, typically, all of the checks bounced.

related. Unfortunately, the stereotypical village *melamed* was something of a *shlemazel* who, for lack of any other talent, taught children. Likewise, in America, being a rebbi was not regarded as an esteemed career.

Hence, some rebbeim were poorly qualified and let out their frustrations on their students. This was still the era where some rebbeim regularly hit their *talmidim*. Some truly believed in corporal punishment as a valuable teaching aide, while others hit for lack of any other way to deal with their incompetence. As principal, Reb Dovid had to defend his teachers, even when he really sided with the students. It was a tough balancing act.

SRULY WAS NERVOUS. HIS PARENTS HAD SENT HIM FROM COLOMBIA, South America to New York so that he could attend a real yeshivah. On his first day in Torah Vodaath, he felt lost and alone. He did not know the boys, he barely knew the language, and he was only 11 years old. The rebbi was not in the classroom and the boys were all over the place. In a rambunctious mood, they broke the classroom door. Just then, the rebbi walked in.

"Who broke the door?" The rebbi demanded an answer.

The boys were quiet. Then some wise guys pointed to Sruly. New and confused, with only a passable English, Sruly did not realize what was happening. In a fit of rage, the rebbi grabbed a hanger and pulled Sruly toward him. Sruly was well aware of what he was in for. The young boy grabbed the hand that held the hanger and pushed it firmly away, screaming in his *Chassidishe* Yiddish, "Only my father is allowed to hit me!"

The rebbi was outraged. This was in the days when the rebbi was boss, and a child did not dare open his mouth. The rebbi stormed into Reb Dovid's office. "*Ah chutzpah fun ah kind* (the nerve of the child)!" the rebbi roared. Patiently, Reb Dovid tried to calm the rebbi down. He finally succeeded, but only while agreeing to discipline the new pupil.

As usual, Reb Dovid was caught in the middle. He disagreed with the rebbeim who hit their students; but, as the principal, he had to defend them. He called Sruly into the office. The boy was shaking like a leaf. He was ready to go back to Colombia, pronto! Reb Dovid sat him down and closed the door.

"Listen," he said, "I'm in a tough spot. The rebbi is upset. I know you did nothing wrong. When the rebbi calms down, I'll speak to him. Everything will be fine." Reb Dovid did not say much — he didn't want it to seem that he was criticizing the rebbi — yet he made the boy feel safe and taken care of.

Sruly never found out exactly what Reb Dovid said to the rebbi but, after that incident, the rebbi treated him like a king. Sruly remained in Torah Vodaath for many years and, aside for that one incident, had only good memories.

*Rabbi Dovid Bender, in the halls of Torah Vodaath, 1960*
*with his colleague Rabbi Moshe Steinmetz*

Boys like Sruly felt Reb Dovid's love, his belief in them, and his desire to see them succeed. Whenever Reb Dovid visited the classrooms to test them and they knew the *Gemara*, his face lit up. They saw that their success was worth a million dollars to him. It was clear that he was not out to trap them with his test. He was looking for ways they could "show off" their knowledge.[29] When a boy was stumped, he would encourage him along, coaxing the answer from him.

Once, an exceptionally motivated sixth-grade class wanted to change the *Navi* curriculum. The existing *Navi* curriculum had the boys begin learning *Navi* in third grade, and by the middle of sixth grade, they finished *Melachim*. From the second half of sixth grade through eighth grade, they covered the whole cycle a second time. This class was unusually energetic, and they wanted to learn *Yirmiyahu* and *Yeshayahu*, rather than review what they had already learned. They relayed their request to Rabbi Bender.

Reb Dovid came to speak to the class. He smiled and leaned against the rebbi's desk, his arms folded.

"I just heard that you boys finished *Sefer Melachim*. Is that true?"

The boys sat up straighter in their seats, beaming as they nodded.

"I am very proud of you boys."

They appreciated their principal's endorsement, and they were proud of themselves as well.

"I hear that you want to go on to learn *Yeshayahu* and *Yirmiyahu*." Reb Dovid paused, taking in their eager faces. "Can I ask you a few questions?" Reb Dovid proceeded to ask them questions on the *Nach* they had learned and supposedly knew. Since they had not learned *Yehoshua* since third grade, it was not difficult to stump them. After a few relatively basic questions, the boys realized that they really did not know *Yehoshua* through *Melachim* and they agreed, without a challenge, to repeat the *Nach* cycle as the yeshivah always had.

---

29. Rabbi Leibel Katz.

The beauty of Reb Dovid's approach was that he was able to convince them without engaging in a battle of wills. The boys were proud of their accomplishments because he told them how proud he was of them. They felt good about making the request because he made them feel that, in theory, their request was valid. They felt comfortable backing down because they realized that he was right. [30]

LIKEWISE, ON A ONE-TO-ONE BASIS, REB DOVID TOOK TIME OUT TO speak to his students, to deliver a wise word at an appropriate time. One student presented the following situation: A child in a lower grade can be very smart and even if you put him in a higher grade, he will still be answering questions and outperforming others older than him. It does not seem fair. In whatever grade this child is in, he will be on top, while in whatever grade the weak child is in, he will be on the bottom. He might as well just skip every grade; the weaker child will never catch up with him.

Reb Dovid understood the boy's frustration and explained the illusion. True, the bright child will catch on quickly and seems to be ahead of the weaker, older child. But one must remember, knowledge is only one part of a child's development. Real growth comes through an accumulation of years, by actually going through the system. The younger child is far behind in experience and maturity. He might give a brilliant answer, one that the weaker child will never formulate, but that does not mean that he is well rounded as a student or even as a person. When the weaker child plugs away and attains a level of understanding, he is attaining much more than just knowledge. He is growing through the experience.

MOE WAITED IMPATIENTLY FOR THE TRAIN TO ARRIVE. HE WAS VERY nervous. It was his second day in a new school — a new principal, and new boys — and the train was delayed. He shifted from one foot to the other, but no amount of worrying would bring the train faster.

His tension mounted with each passing moment. How could he be late on his second day in a new school? Moe felt himself getting more and more anxious throughout the train ride.

He finally arrived at the yeshivah, entered the building, and went to the stairwell leading up to the classrooms. And who did he see at the top of the staircase? *Oy gevald!* He thought he would faint and his face must have shown it.

Rabbi Bender looked down imposingly from the top of the staircase. "Yes?" he asked.

---

30. "He was extraordinary in his dealings with *talmidim,* as this *Nach* story indicates. He was a role model for *menahalim* even though he was *menahel* at such a young age" (Rabbi Yisroel Belsky).

"I know that I am late," the boy stammered, "but the train was delayed … I am sorry … it won't happen again …"

Reb Dovid walked down the steps and put an arm around the boy. "In that case, you obviously missed breakfast as well." He took the boy to his office, sat him down with cornflakes and milk, and watched as he ate. Only after breakfast did he send him to class.[31]

EVEN IN HIS ROLE AS PRINCIPAL, REB DOVID WAS STILL A FATHER, PRImarily concerned with their well-being. On cold days, he would rise at 5 o'clock in the morning to go to the yeshivah to check that the steam was working properly.

He was keenly aware of the many "special" cases in his school. Just after World War II, there were many casualties of the war, and Reb Dovid treated them with extra care. He used a *mashal*: If you slap someone on his hand, it hurts. If you slap where he has a cut on his hand, it hurts even more. Every time you hurt an orphan, it is like slapping an already open wound. He thinks he is being hurt because he does not have a father to protect him.

Foreigners also had a special place in Reb Dovid's heart. He understood how difficult it was for them to adjust in a new country when they did not understand the language or culture. In the 1940's there were refugees from all parts of Europe, and in the 1950's the refugees were primarily from Hungary and South America. These refugees came from totally different cultural backgrounds than their American peers. Running a school with children from such varied backgrounds took sensitivity.

REB DOVID ENTERED A CLASS LOOKING FOR A VOLUNTEER. HANDS FLEW eagerly in the air, waiting to be chosen. Reb Dovid rested his eyes on Shmilu,[32] a new boy. Shmilu was part of the wave of Hungarian refugees who came after the Hungarian Revolution in 1956. Shmilu was still learning the language and trying to fit in. He could use a bit of extra attention.

Reb Dovid motioned to Shmilu. "Please take this letter across the street to the mailbox and mail it." He gave the child a pat on the shoulder and Shmilu eagerly ran out. Shmilu returned to the classroom a few minutes later, looking bewildered and with the letter still in hand. He could not find the mailbox. The rebbi sent another boy out with the letter and class resumed.

Suddenly, class was interrupted by the sound of sirens. Dozens of firemen headed for the hoses, others manned the ladders. A few bounded up

---

31. R' Moshe Marx. "R' Moshe told me that this episode was the single most significant story in his school life and had a profound impact upon him." (R' Yaakov Bender)

32. Not his real name.

the school steps and burst inside. "Where is the fire?" they demanded.

Hearing the commotion, Reb Dovid emerged from his office. "Good morning," he greeted the chief officer. "I think there must be a mistake. Thank G-d, there is no fire here."

The firemen looked upset. "See here," one of them said, "is this a prank? Someone definitely pulled the fire alarm box in front of this building. Which one of these kids is the jokester?"

Shmilu was staring ahead in fright. Suddenly, Reb Dovid understood. He walked over to the boy, put his hand on his shoulder, and looked down at him lovingly.

"Officer, I must beg your forgiveness, this has been a mistake, not a prank. Shmilu, here, is new in the country. When I asked him to mail a letter, he mistakenly pulled the fire alarm. We are really sorry to have troubled you."

The firemen grumbled as they filed out of the building with strict warnings that it not happen again. Reb Dovid kept his hand firmly on Shmilu's shoulder, reassuring him that he would not be punished for his mistake. After he herded all the boys back into class, he called on one student to take Shmilu outside and show him the difference between a mailbox and a fire alarm.[33]

EMPATHY WAS ONE OF RABBI BENDER'S TRADEMARKS. ONCE, WHEN Williamsburg was hit with a terrible snowstorm, Rabbi Bender awaited his students at the door, looking to see who was unduly wet and cold. At that time, it was a 15-minute walk from the dormitory to the Old Mesivta. The snow was knee high, and by the time some of the boys arrived at the Old Mesivta, they were wet and shivering.

"Sruly," Reb Dovid greeted a boy whose teeth were chattering from the cold, "come into my office." Sruly followed the principal, wondering what he planned to do. "Here," he said, "wrap this towel around yourself and put your pants on the radiator to dry. You cannot sit in class with cold, wet pants." Sruly was grateful to receive his principal's personal attention.

In January 1963 there was a devastating fire in Telshe Yeshivah. Two *bochurim* lost their lives and the building was destroyed. Reb Dovid understood that the morale in Telshe must be very low. He went to all the Torah Vodaath classrooms and spoke about the tragedy and our obligation to support our brothers in times of sorrow. He instructed each *bochur* to bring in one dollar, which would be sent to the Telshe Yeshivah with a letter conveying the pain and support of the *talmidim* of Torah Vodaath. It was a concrete action that instilled in the boys a sense of responsibility to *Klal Yisroel*.[34]

---

33. Rabbi Joshua Berkowitz in a letter, 1996.

34. "His talk that day had a tremendous impact on me" (Rabbi Dov Loketch).

*Rabbi Dovid Bender behind his desk at 505 Bedford Avenue*

RABBI BENDER TRIED TO KNOW each one of his boys. When Rabbi Nisson Wolpin became the dormitory supervisor, he went to speak to all the Torah Vodaath principals. Although most of the dorm boys were Mesivta and Beis Medrash students, there were a few from the elementary school. Reb Nisson went to all the elementary school principals — Rabbi Dr. Stern, Rabbi Bender, and Rabbi Pincus — to hear if there was anything specific that he should know about the dormers.

In the course of a friendly conversation, Rabbi Bender said, "Reb Shraga Feivel used to review the boys' names each night. By looking at each name, he was able to recall each boy, how he was doing, and where he was going. It's also a good idea for you to go over the names of the boys regularly." At that time, the dormitory had approximately 220 boys from all over the world. Getting to know everyone would be a challenge.

Reb Nisson appreciated the wise advice and realized that Rabbi Bender was recommending a method that he himself used. He, too, reviewed the names of the 200 to 300 students under his jurisdiction on a regular basis. That was how he was able to keep track of their progress and understand their personalities.[35]

"UM ... EXCUSE ME, MAY I COME IN?"

Reb Dovid peered closely at the *bochur* standing in the doorway. It was unusual for Reb Dovid not to recognize a *talmid*. Reb Dovid motioned him in.

"I am a student of the Mirrer Yeshivah, a *talmid* of Rabbi Shmuel Brudny."

Reb Dovid calculated that the boy was about 17 years old.

"My father is a working man and is not aware of the yeshivah system, but I see that my brother, who is finishing elementary school elsewhere, is not learning well. He just became bar mitzvah, but I do not feel that he is ready to enter the Mesivta. Would you admit him into a younger grade? I think he is much more capable than he seems."

Reb Dovid was impressed by this 17-year-old *bochur* and wanted to give

---

35. Rabbi Nisson Wolpin.

his brother a chance. He decided to put the bar mitzvah *bochur* in the weakest seventh-grade class.

"… and when you do well," Reb Dovid explained with a smile, "you will advance to a higher class."

Every week, Reb Dovid called the boy in for words of warmth and encouragement. Reb Dovid told him stories, parables, and minilessons to keep him motivated. Slowly, the boy progressed from one level to the next until he was finally ready for the Mesivta, where he developed into a true *masmid*.[36]

REB DOVID WORKED WITH HIS BOYS, HOPING THAT FROM TORAH Vodaath elementary school they would develop a lasting desire to learn. Nonetheless, he knew that his Torah Vodaath students were unfinished products when they graduated the eighth grade. Where they would go after Torah Vodaath would influence their future. This was especially true for boys from modern or irreligious homes. He knew that if they went to the Mesivta, they would probably remain religious; but if they went on to public school, their *Yiddishkeit* would be an inevitable casualty.

Public school was a real test for many. In those years, people believed that without a public high school education, their children would not be accepted to respectable colleges. For the modern or non-religious Jewish parent, having a son who was a doctor or lawyer was the fulfillment of the American dream. Such parents were convinced that Torah Vodaath elementary school had provided their children with sufficient Jewish background and there was no need for any further Jewish education. Dealing with these boys was very touchy.[37]

Even when the viable option was not public school, but a school with

---

36. Rabbi Aharon Zuckerman.

37. One year, the boy chosen to be English valedictorian was planning to go to public high school. His acceptance was contingent on a letter of recommendation from the English principal of Torah Vodaath. Some of his classmates were outraged. This boy was going to public high school with Torah Vodaath's stamp of approval. Furthermore, he was representing them as valedictorian. Since the English department was out of Reb Dovid's jurisdiction, they decided to appeal to Rabbi Yaakov Kamenetsky, then the Rosh Yeshivah of Torah Vodaath.

A delegation of students arrived at the Kamenetsky doorstep. The first thing that the Rosh Yeshivah did was call to his rebbetzin, "Bring out some Pepsi-Cola and seven-layer cake." Reb Yaakov sat the boys at the table and his rebbetzin brought in the refreshments.

Then the boys aired their complaints. Reb Yaakov agreed that a boy who was going to public high school should not be valedictorian, but the letter of recommendation should certainly be given. "Let me explain. This boy is going to go to public high school. With or without the letter of recommendation, his parents will find a way to have him accepted. He will enter public school and find out how horrible it is, and he is going to want to come back to Torah Vodaath. If we do not give him this letter of recommendation, he will become bitter about the yeshivah and will feel uncomfortable returning."

*A wise man is better than a prophet* (Bava Basra 12a). The boy received his letter of recommendation, went on to public school, and was back in Torah Vodaath a year later.

more modern leanings, Reb Dovid took a stand. The P. family sent their first two boys to Torah Vodaath elementary school and then onto a more modern high school. When their third son began the seventh grade, Rabbi Bender decided to skip a group of bright boys into the eighth grade. Mr. P. called Rabbi Bender, very upset. He demanded to know why his son was not among the boys skipped. Rabbi Bender explained that, certainly, his son was worthy of being skipped. But if he skipped, he would be entering the more modern high school a year earlier. If he remained in the seventh grade, the boy would have one more year in Torah Vodaath.

Mr. P. was outraged, and Reb Dovid offered a compromise. "Look," he said, "if you agree to send your son to the Mesivta for ninth grade, then I will allow him to skip. But if you insist on sending him to a more modern high school, than I refuse to deprive him of one more year in Torah Vodaath." The P. family refused to give the Mesivta a chance, and Rabbi Bender refused to skip their child. The boy remained in Torah Vodaath for seventh and eighth grade.

Rabbi Bender's goal was not just to fill the Mesivta classrooms. In fact, when he felt that a student would do well in a different yeshivah setting, he would guide him accordingly. His first consideration was always the spiritual growth of the student.

The newly formed Talmudical Yeshivah of Philadelphia was opening its first high school class.[38] Rabbi Bender knew the Rosh Yeshivah, Rabbi Shmuel Kamenetsky, and he was certain that the yeshivah had a bright future.

That year, he had a number of *talmidim* whom he considered exceptionally capable, but he felt that their strengths would be better developed in an out-of-town yeshivah, particularly a new yeshivah such as Philadelphia.

One day, Rabbi Yaakov Kamenetsky and his son Reb Shmuel visited the Old Mesivta building. Rabbi Bender singled out several boys: Yaakov Fensterheim,[39] Mendy Mendelowitz, Yossie Pruzansky, Larry Moskowitz, and Gershon Eisenberg. These were all bright boys, most of whom had been planning to go to the Mesivta. Reb Shmuel learned a piece of *Gemara* with them and then left the boys to decide for themselves. They all chose to go to Philadelphia, thereby forming the basis of its first high school class.[40]

---

38. The Beis Medrash was formed a year and a half earlier.

39. "We lived on 186 Hooper Street, two doors away from the Benders who lived at 168. I was close to the family, especially to Rabbi Bender. Rabbi Bender knew that I was interested in attending an out-of-town yeshivah and he guided me toward Philadelphia. He was a wonderful *menahel*, very warm and well liked" (Rabbi Yaakov Fensterheim).

40. They, and three local Philadelphia boys, made up the first Philadelphia Yeshivah high school class.

From the time Reb Dovid became principal, he sought to send boys to yeshivos where he felt they could build on their strengths, even if that meant steering good boys away from Torah Vodaath. Some of the Torah Vodaath *ba'alei battim* grumbled as they referred to Reb Dovid as *"Beis Din Chavlanis,"*[41] but Reb Dovid felt justified.

He had to do what he felt was best for his boys.

---

41 The literal meaning is "a Killer *Beis Din*," a *beis din* that sentences people to death too often (*Makkos* 7). The reference here is that Reb Dovid was "killing" Mesivta Torah Vodaath by sending some of the best boys to other yeshivos for high school.

### Chapter Forty-Seven

# Summers and Simchos:
# Opportunities for Growth

*W*E'RE ALMOST PASSING IT, EVERYONE LOOKING?" PALTIEL'S nose was pasted firmly on the window as he eagerly sought the familiar sights.

Every year on their way up to the Catskills, Reb Dovid would point out the interesting family landmarks, chief of which was the pier where he and his rebbetzin had docked that Erev Yom Kippur in September 1939. The children never tired of hearing the tale of their parents' arrival. Bender family lore connected them to something larger than their own simple existence. They were part of the Old World, where giants of Jewry had lived in storybook towns and villages. There, Mir was a real city with real people. There, the Chofetz Chaim existed outside his seforim, and Reb Boruch Ber relaxed in a hammock. "There" was no more, but the Torah and the scholars nurtured there were eternal.

This powerful connection to the past was not a wishful invention. Most of the Benders' friends and neighbors came from the same world, shared the same memories, and lived in the same present. Even on summer vacation, Rabbi Dovid and Rebbetzin Basha Bender sought to be with friends and acquaintances from a similar background and mentality. For many years, the Benders and other Bais Yaakov teachers and their families went to Camp Bais Yaakov. In 1954 they began spending summers in White Lake, New York, in a tiny bungalow colony called Wasserman's.

## Rabbis Lipa Eidelman, Mordechai Springer, and Yeshaya Wasserman — brothers-in-law and dear friends of the Benders with whom they shared many summers

*Rabbi Lipa Eidelman*      *Rabbi Mordechai Springer*      *Rabbi Yeshaya Wasserman*

*Rabbi Lipa Eidelman* (1906-1990) *was born in Brisk and studied in Lomza and Mir, but considered himself primarily a talmid of Rabbi Yeruchem Levovitz. He served as a maggid shiur in Mesivta Tiferes Yerushalayim and as Rav of the Netzach Yisroel Shul in the Bronx, New York.*

*Rabbi Mordechai Springer* (1905-1997) *learned in Mir and then Grodno. He married Rivka Eidelman, a sister of Rabbi Lipa Eidelman. Rebbetzin Springer was a popular teacher in Bais Yaakov of Williamsburg. Reb Mottel, as he was known, served as the Rav of the Toras Moshe Shul in the Bronx.*

*Rabbi Yeshaya Wasserman* (1912-1984) *learned in Baranovich and then in Eretz Yisroel, where he learned in Chevron and in Petach Tikva. He moved to America and married Shayna Eidelman, a sister of Rabbi Lipa Eidelman. He served as maggid shiur in Mesivta Tiferes Yerushalayim.*

---

Wasserman's had only eight bungalows: One belonged to the owners and the rest were rented out. There were the Benders, the Swiatyckis, the Posens, the Langes, the Eidelmans, the Springers, the Wassermans, and the Schreibers.[42] There were a few neighboring colonies of similar size and with the same type of fine *heimishe* Williamsburg families who were happy to enjoy the healthy mountain air among friends.

Just a few yards past Wasserman's was McCormick's, another small colony where the Pincus and Svei[43] families spent summers. Neither colony was big enough to have its own casino or *minyan*, so the McCormick crowd would come to Wasserman's where everyone davened in Rabbi Ezriel Lange's bungalow. After davening, the fathers shmoozed a bit before beginning their daily routines. The boys set off for another day of playing and adventuring in the woods.

---

42. Rabbi Chaim Swiatycki, Rabbi Peretz Posen, Rabbi Ezriel Lange, Rabbi Lipa Eidelman, Rabbi Mottel Springer, Rabbi Yeshaya Wasserman, and *ybdl'ch* R'Avrohom (Allan) Schreiber. See Biography Section.
43. Rabbi Avrohom Pincus and Rabbi Shmuel Leib Svei.

*Rabbi Chaim Swiatycki (1914-2004) was born in Kossov. He left Europe together with his uncle, the Chazon Ish, and moved to Eretz Yisroel. There he entered the Chevron Yeshivah. In 1938, he immigrated to the United States. He served as menahel and later maggid shiur in Mesivta Tiferes Jerusalem. He wrote the 15-volume series of seforim entitled Eitz Chaim on various mesechtos in Gemara.*

*Rabbi Chaim Swiatycki and Rabbi Moshe Feinstein in the Beis Medrash of Mesivta Tiferes Yerushalayim*

BEHIND ONE OF THE WASSERMAN BUNGALOWS, A QUIET SCHOLAR, Rabbi Chaim Swiatycki, sat at a wooden picnic table. His bent form was shaded by the trees. Open seforim were piled on his right and left as he wrote, line after line flowing from his wellspring of learning. Reb Chaim was a nephew of the Chazon Ish; his mother and the illustrious *gaon* were siblings. His quiet demeanor, personality, and way of life were reminiscent of his uncle. Reb Chaim rarely looked up from his work beneath the shady trees and did not take notice of what was going on around him. Yet one day, he emerged from his solitude to pursue a revolutionary idea.

Reb Chaim was troubled by the idleness of youth during the long summer months. In the 40's, 50's, and 60's, bungalow colonies were small, informal affairs, a few cottages here and there, without any day camps to provide structured times of learning and play. Part of the beauty of summer was the easygoing, unstructured atmosphere: hours of lying lazily in the sun, climbing up and down hills, or playing in the woods. Yet, too much free time was antithetical to Jewish values. Reb Chaim spoke to a few friends, including Rabbi Dovid Bender, about opening a "summer yeshivah" in the Catskills.

Reb Dovid was excited by the idea. He noticed that his oldest son Paltiel seemed to have nothing special to do with his time and was concerned about an entire summer of idleness. Reb Chaim wanted to organize a yeshivah in the Catskills that would service the many *heimishe* children vacationing in the various bungalow colonies.

That first summer, the yeshivah got started in the middle of the season. Reb Chaim made arrangements to use two rooms in a nearby shul. He convinced friends and acquaintances to enroll enough boys to warrant three separate groups with three rebbeim. Reb Dovid arranged for a bus to go from colony to colony and pick up the boys. And that was how the "summer yeshivah" began.

As time went on, the yeshivah grew. They needed more space for classes, and Reb Chaim went to the different colonies asking for space in their casinos and shuls. Reb Dovid would occasionally make appeals in various colonies asking people to support the summer yeshivah. The summer yeshivah remained in existence for a number of years.

LIKE HER HUSBAND, REBBETZIN BENDER REFUSED TO IDLE AWAY HER summer. Although she could easily have claimed to be busy with her children, Rebbetzin Bender always found time for yet another project. This time it was fund-raising for Beis HaTalmud.

Beis HaTalmud was founded by a group of Mirrer *talmidim* shortly after their arrival in America. Many of the Mirrer refugees came to America through Toronto, and Rabbi Peretz Posen[44] of Toronto developed lifelong relationships with them. When he moved to New York, he met his old Mirrer friends and decided to open a *yeshivah ketanah* division of the newly formed Beis HaTalmud. Among his many duties, Reb Peretz was in charge of keeping the *yeshivah ketanah* financially viable. As neighbors in Wasserman's, Reb Peretz would often speak to his good friend and colleague, Rabbi Dovid Bender. Naturally, they discussed the question of how to raise money for the *yeshivah ketanah*.

The two friends came up with the idea of making a *melaveh malkah* in the country. The vacationing families at Wasserman's already made a joint *melaveh malkah* every week. People were more relaxed in the summers and enjoyed getting together with friends. Certainly, if they could bring together friends and neighbors for the holy purpose of raising money for *tzedakah*, everyone would benefit.

That was how Rebbetzin Bender became one of the main organizers of the Beis HaTalmud *Melaveh Malkah*, which was always held either in their

---

44. See Biography Section.

colony or in a colony right next door. Rebbetzin Bender made the herring and coordinated the culinary contributions of the other women. The *yeshivah ketanah* closed down after a few years, but the summer *melaveh malkah* continued to support Beis HaTalmud.

BEIS HATALMUD WAS NOT THE ONLY YESHIVAH THAT BENEFITED FROM the Benders' summers in the country. For years, Rabbi Avrohom Bender had his "Catskill Route" — a string of towns up and down the New York mountain roads. The old *Yidden* in these towns knew him well and waited for his annual trip. They were eager to have a scholar in their midst, and they greeted him with reverence and respect. Reb Avrohom spoke on Shabbos and they, in turn, would fill him in on all the news of the previous year: who had been born, married, or died, and who had moved. In exchange for keeping alive the Jewish spark within them, the old folks were happy to donate to a yeshivah.

When Reb Avrohom moved to Eretz Yisroel, he was concerned about his Catskill Route. Although many of his old-timers had passed on to a better world, Reb Avrohom felt that abandoning his route would be a pity. Even though the youth did not view him with the reverence of their fathers, they still greeted him fondly and with nostalgia. His visit reminded them of their parents and grandparents and kept their connection to *Yiddishkeit* a little more alive. In addition, they were used to giving him money for yeshivos, which was a *zechus* for them and a boon to the yeshivos as well.

For the first few years after Reb Avrohom moved to Eretz Yisroel, he would return to America in the summers to do his rounds of the Catskills. As he got older, traveling became more difficult. Reb Avrohom voiced his concerns to his son and Reb Dovid took the bait. "I'll be happy to take over the route, Papa, just tell me where, when, and how."

Reb Avrohom patiently went over his list of towns, the people his son would meet, and the bus schedules from one place to the next. Then Reb Avrohom relaxed; now he could remain in Eretz Yisroel with a clear conscience.

Out of pure *kibud av*, Reb Dovid loyally took over the Catskill Route. Although he would certainly have preferred to spend his time learning, or just relaxing after a taxing winter, he knew that this was important to his father and he took the job seriously. He kept his father abreast about where he went, what happened, and how much money he collected. Reb Dovid initiated only one change: instead of collecting for Yeshivas Rabbeinu Yitzchok Elchonon, as his father had, he now collected for the Lakewood Yeshivah, Beis Medrash Govoha.

WASSERMAN'S HELD MANY FOND MEMORIES FOR THE BENDER FAMILY. Rabbi Dovid Bender reveled in getting a much-needed break in the country. He loved to swim, play handball, and spend time outdoors. At the same time, he was still very much the *mechanech*, with a natural affinity for people. *Leil Shabbos*, after *Kabbolas Shabbos*, he would gather all the boys and sing *"Ohr Zaru'a La'tzaddik,"* and then their joy would erupt in a spontaneous dance together to greet the Shabbos.[45]

The summer of 1959 was their last summer at Wasserman's. Then the Benders spent one summer in Camp Morris, and then they went to Nussbaum's. Wherever they went, the summer activities were the same: the summer yeshivah, the Beis HaTalmud *Melaveh Malkah*, and the Catskill Route. It was always important to Rabbi and Rebbetzin Bender that they spend their summers with people who had a similar Torah outlook. Bungalow colony life created a situation where everyone was living in one another's backyards, and the Benders were grateful to have neighbors with whom they enjoyed living and learning from.

Some of the Benders' friends from Wasserman's and McCormick's joined them at Nussbaum's: Rabbi Shaya Wasserman, Rabbi Mottel Springer, Rabbi Ezriel Lange, Rabbi Avrohom Pincus, and Rabbi Shmuel Leib Svei. Their new neighbors included some of the leading roshei yeshivos and *maggidei shiurim* of the era: Rabbi Shneur Kotler, Rabbi Zelig Epstein, Rabbi Simcha Sheps, Rabbi Elya Yurkansky, and Rabbi Aharon Kreiser. Other Torah scholars included Rabbi Yaakov Yaffen, Rabbi Yosef Myski, and Rabbi Elchonon Ozherchovitz.[46] Such an illustrious group provided many opportunities for spiritual growth, simply by observation.

"SH ... BE QUIET."

"What are you watching?"

One of the children giggled and pointed ahead. "I am telling you, he is going to bump. Just watch ..."

Three children huddled unobtrusively behind a tree, counting the seconds. "One, two, three ... now!" Sure enough, Rabbi Yaakov Yaffen walked right into the tree and the children ran away giggling.

Rabbi Yaakov Yaffen was always immersed in learning. His concentration was so intense that he did not notice people, places, or things. After bumping into a tree, he would jerk to attention and then continue walking.

One year at *Minchah* on Tishah B'Av, Reb Yaakov came into the shul. Young Heshy Kanarek,[47] then a *bochur*, had just finished putting on his *tefillin* and he left the bag and the empty boxes in the back of the shul.

---

45. Mrs. R. Grossman.

46. See Biography Section.

47. Now *menahel* of Yeshivas Ohr HaMeir of Peekskill, New York.

*Rabbi Yaakov Yaffen (circa 1916-2003) studied in Baranovich and then in Bialystok. In 1970 Reb Yaakov became Rosh Yeshivah of Bais Yosef, the Novarodok yeshivah in America, after the passing of his father, Rabbi Avrohom Yaffen. He was known to be a talmid chacham of unusual caliber.*

Meanwhile, Rabbi Yaffen, lost in thought, took his *tallis* out of its bag and slung it over his shoulder.

Then he began pacing back and forth, as he always did when he was preoccupied with his learning. Suddenly, he stopped pacing, as if he remembered something, and he put on his *tallis*. He continued to pace, back and forth, back and forth.

He stopped at the table in the back of the shul, picked up Heshy Kanarek's *tefillin* bag with the two empty boxes, took the empty box for the *shel yad* in his hand, "took out" the *shel yad*, and was putting it on his arm when he suddenly realized that there was nothing in his hand.

Startled, he "dropped" the nothingness and looked back at the table. There, sitting peacefully untouched, was his own *tefillin* bag ready to be opened. He grabbed his own *tefillin* and proceeded to put them on.

Although it was Tishah B'Av, the boys in attendance had a hard time keeping their laughter in check. Years later, they remembered the incident with awe, for it was clear to all that Rabbi Yaffen's total concentration in learning was extraordinary.

RABBI ELCHONON OZHERCHOVITZ, ANOTHER NUSSBAUM RESIDENT, was a *maggid shiur* in Mirrer Yeshivah. He had been a *bochur* in Kaminetz at the outbreak of World War II and was exiled to Siberia along with 85 *bochurim* from Kaminetz, of whom only 40 survived.

"I don't know," he once confided in young Yankel Bender,[48] "people say that those in Siberia were lucky. All I can say is that I was there for four years, and it was so bad I do not know how I survived. At times, the mosquitoes were so thick I don't think there was one space on my body without bites. I once fell into a ditch and had no strength to get out. I tried to scream but no sound came out. I said *Kri'as Shema*, expecting at

---

48. When both the Benders and the Ozherchovitzes moved on to Greenwald's Bungalow Colony, Reb Elchonon offered to learn with young Yankel Bender on a regular basis. It was during these learning sessions that Reb Elchonon occasionally allowed himself to reminisce about his rebbi and his experiences in the war. These musings were very infrequent since Reb Elchonon rarely digressed from learning.

any moment to greet the *Ribbono shel Olam*. Then a man — I am sure it was Eliyahu HaNavi — came, shlepped me out, and deposited me right at the doorway to my cabin. How did this stranger know where my cabin was? I am certain that he was Eliyahu HaNavi … I was sick all the time in Siberia. It was terrible."

Such personal confidences from Reb Elchonon were rare. Reb Elchonon was a true *masmid*, always learning. If he chanced to take a break, it was to impart some story or tidbit from his rebbi, Reb Boruch Ber.

"He *tzittered* (trembled) at the name of his rebbi, Reb Chaim Brisker, so great was his awe …" Reb Elchonon recalled wistfully. For a moment, Yankel felt himself transported away from the green surroundings, the worn wooden picnic table where they sat together, and the seforim opened before them.

Suddenly, Reb Elchonon stopped, aware that he had digressed from their learning. "*Nu,*" he demanded from his young *chavrusah*, "*lo'mir lernen!*" And their learning session would continue.

*Rabbi Elchonon Ozherchovitz (circa 1921-2001) was a talmid of Rabbi Boruch Ber Leibowitz of Kaminetz. He, along with 85 other students of Kaminetz, were exiled to Siberia. Only 40 of them survived the war. Reb Elchonon immigrated to America after the war. He taught in Yeshivas Toras Chaim of South Shore for two years and then in the Mirrer Yeshivah of Flatbush.*

RABBI EZRIEL LANGE, A LONGTIME FRIEND AND COLLEAGUE OF RABBI Dovid Bender, spent many summers with the Benders. Reb Ezriel met Reb Dovid back in Mir when they were still *bochurim*. Reb Dovid had been friendly with many of the *Yekkishe* boys in Mir but his relationship with Reb Ezriel blossomed in America. Reb Ezriel was an eighth-grade rebbi in Torah Vodaath[49] and the two men saw each other on a regular basis. Rebbetzin Lange had much in common with Rebbetzin Bender as well.

---

49. Rabbi Ezriel Lange's main message was to be a thorough *ben Torah* inside and out, and his students related to his sincerity. Once, Reb Ezriel called a talkative student over and said, "I will make a deal with you. If you keep quiet from 9 until 11 o'clock, I will give you $5." Five dollars was a lot of money and was a powerful incentive. The student kept quiet in class and earned his prize. "See," Reb Ezriel declared triumphantly, "you did it. That means you can control yourself even without a $5 incentive." The student was encouraged by Reb Ezriel's confidence in him and made up his mind to control himself further (Rabbi Mordechai Lerner).

**Rabbi Ezriel Lange often told *talmidim* how a *Yekkishe* boy like him ended up in the Mir, despite his parents' opposition. Rabbi Yechiel Michel Schlesinger (1898-1949), later founder of Yeshivas Kol Torah in Eretz Yisroel, was a *dayan* in Frankfurt. Rabbi Shlesinger suggested that Ezriel attend a yeshivah in Poland, patiently enumerating all that he would gain. Young Ezriel listened, but did not seem convinced. Finally Rabbi Shlesinger dismissed him in frustration, "You want to be a simpleton? Be a simpleton!" Taken aback at the *dayan's* vehement reaction, Ezriel went to Mir to learn.**

*Rabbi Ezriel Lange (1915-1996) was raised in Frankfurt, Germany. Reb Ezriel went with the Mir through Shanghai to America. He was a beloved eighth-grade rebbi first in Elizabeth, New Jersey and then in Yeshivas Torah Vodaath. His Torah lectures, entitled Ikvei Erev, were published by his student, Rabbi Mordechai Lerner.*

She, too, had been a student in Bais Yaakov of Crakow and, like Rebbetzin Bender, she was devoted to educating Jewish children.[50]

A typical morning would find Rabbi Ezriel Lange up at 4:30 in the morning, sitting at a table on the porch of his bungalow, learning and writing. Self-motivated and disciplined, Rabbi Ezriel Lange rarely deviated from his predawn schedule. When some of the neighboring children slunk back to their bungalows at the wee hours of the morning after visiting their friends in nearby Camp Morris, Reb Ezriel would shake his head. It grated on his *Yekkishe* sensibilities. Yet Reb Ezriel knew how to relax and enjoy a good swim, and he was known for his warmth and ready smile.

The Langes had no children, but they often took in *talmidim* who were going through a difficult time. Reb Ezriel treated these *talmidim* with parental care and concern, while being careful not to undermine their real parents. The boys lived with the Langes not just during regular school days, but often Shabbos and Yom Tov and sometimes even summers.

Reb Ezriel would arrive at the bungalow colony and immediately help his rebbetzin unpack. Then he would find a free picnic table, shlep it into the nearby woods, and sit down and learn. His *talmidim* marveled at how

---

50. Rebbetzin Lange taught first grade for over 40 years. Her students remembered her teaching methods decades later. She had an uncanny sense of when a child was not herself, and she would search for the reason, often unearthing a family problem that was unsettling the child. Her students felt such a profound connection to her, they came back to visit with their children and, later in life, with their grandchildren! (Rabbi Mordechai Lerner).

*Yankel Bender with Rabbi Yisroel Chaim Kaplan at Yankel's bar mitzvah*

*Rabbi Yaakov Kamenetsky speaking at Yankel's bar mitzvah*

quickly he went for his sefer. From observing Reb Ezriel's obvious pleasure in learning Torah, they understood that a true *ben Torah* looks forward to his hours of learning, even after he has fulfilled his obligations in the classroom.

SUMMERS AND *SIMCHOS* PROVIDED OPPORTUNITIES FOR GROWTH. The Benders celebrated their oldest son Paltiel's bar mitzvah in Wasserman's. Thirteen years earlier, at Paltiel's birth, Rebbetzin Bender had battled her first major illness. It was a toss-up which miracle was bigger: that Paltiel was born in the seventh month and survived, or that after her son's birth, Rebbetzin Bender had recovered from a serious kidney infection without the proper medications.

Rebbetzin Svei phoned Rebbetzin Bender to find out when the *simchah* would take place. During the fateful summer of Paltiel's birth, she had been at a neighboring bungalow and had kept abreast of the situation throughout. "You should only know how many tears I cried over you," she would admonish Paltiel whenever she saw him. She wanted very much to attend the bar mitzvah of this boy who had inspired so many of her *tefillos*.

The Benders made a *kiddush* in Wasserman's on Shabbos morning. They were joined by friends from McCormick's and other nearby colonies. *Motza'ei Shabbos* they sponsored the colony's weekly *melaveh malkah*. The Rottenbergs, the Zupniks, and Cousin Mary and her family all drove in from other areas in the Catskills to be with the Benders for the *simchah*. The bar mitzvah was a small, no-fuss affair, with plenty of warmth, gratitude, and good wishes. A true *Yiddishe simchah*.

Yankel Bender's bar mitzvah was also a small affair: an *aliyah* on Shabbos in the Mirrer Minyan on Marcy Avenue and a small affair the Sunday before in Rabbi Pincus's shul on Rodney Street.

When Michoel's bar mitzvah came around, Rebbetzin Bender was flustered. The guest of honor, Michoel, contracted the measles and she was nervous that he would not be better in time. Dedicated Dr. Sternberg came to the house every day to check on his young patient and try something else to get rid of his raging fever.

Dr. Helmouth Sternberg was the Bender family doctor. A self-proclaimed atheist, Dr. Sternberg was nonetheless proud of his Jewish heritage and enjoyed spending time in the Bender home, sipping a cup of coffee and kibbitzing with the kids in Yiddish. His house calls always extended far beyond the allotted time.

Dr. Sternberg loved children[51] and truly cared for his patients. He knew that many of them struggled to make ends meet, and he felt reluctant to take money for his services. After years of association with the Benders, Dr. Sternberg felt very close to the family. He gave them his home phone number and urged them to call for any reason. While nursing Michoel through the measles, Dr. Sternberg acquired a further appreciation of the Bender family and asked that he be invited to Michoel's bar mitzvah. At the reception, Dr. Sternberg asked to speak.

"When I became a doctor," he began, "I didn't think that I was G-d's gift to mankind. I thought I was G-d." He paused. "I felt I had the tools to heal people. I could heal people through *my* care, *my* medicines, and *my* treatments. I was sure I could bring life to the dying.

"Over the years," Dr. Sternberg continued, "I have seen so much. I have seen people I thought would live, and they died. I have seen people who should never have lived, and they are alive and well today."

Overcome with emotion, he stopped. Illustrious rabbanim, Torah scholars of note, some of the elite of Williamsburg Jewry, waited for him to continue. "I finally came to the realization that there has to be a G-d on this world."

With that, Dr. Helmouth Sternberg, an avowed atheist, sat down. He had just given the Benders a priceless gift. Declaring his belief in G-d at the Bender bar mitzvah was his way of letting the Benders know how much he valued them.

"ARE YOU SITTING DOWN?" REB DOVID WAS SMILING INTO THE TELEphone receiver, picturing his friend on the other end. "I cannot even get the words out … I myself am shocked … I can hardly believe it … Esther is getting engaged."

---

51. An example of this love for children was his founding of Camp Sternberg.

*Raabi Dovid Bender with his father and sons at
the wedding of his oldest child Esther*
*Left to right, sitting: Shmuel Sholom, Rabbi Avro-
hom Bender, Rabbi Chaim Epstein*
*Left to right, standing: Michoel, Rabbi Dovid
Bender, Yankel, Paltiel*

*Front row, left to right: Shmuel Sholom and Yankel
Back row, left to right: Michoel, Rabbi Chaim
Epstein, and Rabbi Dovid Bender*

Rabbi Yitzchok Freedman almost dropped the telephone. Esther? But she was only a baby! "Reb Dovid, correct me if I am wrong but Esther is only …"

"Sixteen and a half!" Reb Dovid answered jubilantly. "Such a *chosson*, we could not wait for. *Nu*, they will have a long engagement; we will give her some time to grow up."[52]

Esther became engaged to Chaim Epstein, an esteemed student of the Lakewood Yeshivah. Reb Dovid was ecstatic. A *kiddush* was held in the Bender home. The rooms were packed, and Reb Dovid beamed at the crowd from the head table. Every time the *chosson* tried to speak, the crowd burst into song.[53]

Since the *kallah* was very young, it was decided to wait a year until the wedding. Reb Aaron Kotler *zt"l*, the *chosson's* rebbe told him that the *zman* of the engagement can be a special time for him. "*Chap arayn*," as he will not have the responsibility of a household and at the same time, he will not have to look for a *shidduch*. He will be able to learn without any *tirdos*.

Even after the joyous wedding held almost a year later, Reb Dovid often spoke of his awesome *zechus* to have such a *talmid chacham* as a son-in-law. Not only did he continue to feel the privilege but, year after year, his

---

52. R' Yehudah Freedman.

53. "I remember when Rabbi Bender took Rabbi Chaim Epstein as a son-in-law. What *simchah* that engagement brought to Williamsburg!" (Rabbi Elya Brudny).

appreciation of his son-in-law grew.

"May we merit to see Blumie also married to a *choshuve talmid chacham,"* Reb Dovid would comment to his rebbetzin. Rebbetzin Bender nodded in agreement. Blumie was only a year younger than Esther. Hopefully, they would soon see *nachas* from her as well.

# Part V:
# Changes
## 5725 (1965)

### Chapter Forty-Eight:
Coping with Crisis

### Chapter Forty-Nine:
Growing Pains

### Chapter Fifty:
Blackout

### Chapter Fifty-One:
Upheaval

### Chapter Fifty-Two:
Aftermath

### Chapter Fifty-Three:
Acceptance

---

Unless otherwise noted, the information in this section is from the Bender family. Most of the letters were written in Yiddish and have been translated and condensed. Excerpts from the *hespedim* were taken from taped recordings.

### Chapter Forty-Eight

# Coping with Crisis

*Mordy Krieger was waiting outside Rabbi Bender's office. He needed an admission slip from the principal to enter class. Old Rabbi Cogan[1] was relaxing opposite Rabbi Bender as the principal filled out the form. Mordy thanked his principal and headed toward class.*

*Ten minutes later the hallway erupted in chaos. Doors were slamming and boys were running up and down the hallways. The rebbeim opened the classroom doors to see what was going on.*

*Old Rabbi Cogan, while sitting in front of the eighth-grade class, was spitting up blood. The boys ran to call Rabbi Bender. By the time he reached their classroom, Rabbi Cogan was slumped over his desk, lifeless from a heart attack. The levayah was that day, and Rabbi Bender requested the entire junior high school division to attend.[2]*

FEW INCIDENTS IN RABBI BENDER'S CAREER AS PRINCIPAL were as traumatic as Rabbi Cogan's death.[3] The eighth graders had seen their rebbi die before their eyes and became distraught. They expressed their confusion in their classroom behavior. Every rebbi brought in to teach them quit after a few days and some never tried teaching again. Finally, Rabbi Bender took over the class. Slowly, he got them back to normal.

---

1. Old Torah Vodaath students referred to Rabbi Cogan as "Old Rabbi Cogan" in order to make a distinction between his son and him. His son, Rabbi Marcus Cogan, was the long-time English principal of Torah Vodaath.

2. R' Mordechai Krieger.

3. "I remember my father discussing this difficult time years after it happened" (Rabbi Yaakov Bender).

*Rabbi Tzvi Nochum Cogan (1882-1950) was born in Lupch, a small town in Russia. He learned by the Alter of Novarodok and received semichah from Rabbi Avrohom Yaffen. He immigrated to America in the early 1900's and became a rebbi in Torah Vodaath and Rav of the Ari shul in Williamsburg. He was the initiator and one of the main organizers of the Shabbos Marches in Williamsburg.*

A few weeks later, Rabbi Bender was ready to bring in another rebbi to teach this eighth-grade class. He convinced Rabbi Yosef Leviton to leave kollel and give the class a try.

In the beginning, Rabbi Bender stayed in class with Reb Yosef; the mere presence of the principal commanded respect. When he was confident that Reb Yosef was in control, Rabbi Bender stepped aside but still made special allowances for this class. Instead of the usual 15-minute recess, he allowed this class a half-hour. After a week of half-hour recesses, Rabbi Bender told the students how proud he was of them and how well they were doing. "Boys, I wonder if you can squeeze in all your recess activities into 25 minutes …." There were muffled whispers around the rooms. Then the boys agreed: 25 minutes of recess was sufficient. The next week, they went down to 20 minutes of recess, and the following week they were down to the standard 15. The class was functioning normally.[4]

RABBI YOSEF LEVITON WAS A TORAH VODAATH LEGEND. JUST BEFORE his bar mitzvah, he came to the yeshivah from public school. At that point, he knew nothing more than how to daven. Rabbi Dr. David Stern, the principal of Torah Vodaath at the time, kindly listened to the boy's request to be admitted.

"I am sorry," the principal responded, "but there is no room in the classrooms."

"In any classroom?" the boy asked. "I would not mind being in a first- or second-grade class. I'll go into any class where there's room."

Rabbi Stern took him to a classroom and showed him how all the desks were nailed to the floor without one empty place. The boy shrugged his shoulders and began to leave. Then he turned around and asked, "May I have a note?"

"A note?" Rabbi Stern was puzzled.

---

4. "This all indicates how he knew, understood, and related to a bunch of eighth graders. He encouraged them to conform without coercion or making them feel bad. He was always able to motivate and capture the boys' hearts" (Rabbi Yisroel Belsky).

"A note that says I wanted to come to yeshivah but was refused admission. When I get to Heaven, they might tell me that I had the potential to be a *talmid chacham*. I want a note testifying that it is not my fault I didn't become one. I wanted to learn, but the yeshivah wouldn't let me."

Taken aback, Dr. Stern relented. For the next few years, Yosef Leviton sat in the aisles of classrooms with boys five and six years younger.[5] His desire and determination to learn Torah reaped results. Yosef Leviton climbed from one grade to the next until he became one of Rabbi Shlomo Heiman's most illustrious students.

*Rabbi Dr. David Stern with Rabbi Dovid Bender and Rabbi Yaakov Kamenetsky*

Rabbi Yosef Leviton was famous for his intense *hasmadah* and his search for *emes* in learning. One night, he and his *chavrusa* were learning the *Perek* of *Chezkas HaBattim* in *Bava Basra*, when they came across a difficulty in the Gemara. They searched through various *meforshim*, but they could not find a solution. When they parted that night, Reb Yosef looked depressed and dejected. The next morning, Reb Yosef was grinning from ear to ear when he walked into Torah Vodaath. His *chavrusa* was curious to know why he was so happy.

"Last night, I was very troubled about the unresolved question we had in *Chezkas HaBattim*. It was late, so I went to sleep. Then Rebbi[6] came to me in a dream. He told me to get up — it was 3 o'clock in the morning — wash *negel vasser*, and open up the *Ri Migash* on *Bava Basra*. He told me the exact *daf*, 29b in *Bava Basra* to go to, and said that there I would find the answer to my question. I followed his instructions and found the answer to my question. How can I not smile?"[7]

Rabbi Yosef Leviton's enthusiasm for learning and his ability to explain lofty concepts in a clear, orderly fashion made him an exceptional

---

5. *Reb Shraga Feivel*, p. 209, and Rabbi Yonason Shapiro.

6. Rabbi Shlomo Heiman.

7. "Reb Yosef penciled into the margin of the *Ri Migash*, 'This is the answer I received in the dream, etc.' Torah Vodaath has a library they call Yikar Hametzius Library, a library of unique seforim. The Leviton family donated the *Ri Migash* to that library" (Rabbi Yaakov Bender, as heard in a *hesped* for Rabbi Yosef Leviton at his *shloshim* in Torah Vodaath).

rebbi. Rabbi Bender usually gave him the class that had the most out-of-towners. These were boys from weak backgrounds — some had not attended a yeshivah until seventh grade. Rabbi Bender trusted that Reb Yosef would turn them into yeshivah *bochurim*.

For 12 years, Reb Yosef molded Torah Vodaath students into *b'nei Torah*. He was a warm and enthusiastic rebbi who put all his strength into teaching his *talmidim*.[8]

Then, one day, Rabbi Yosef Leviton had a heart attack. A short while later, he had a second heart attack. At that point, the doctors insisted that he stop teaching. Reb Yosef was such an enthusiastic rebbi, they were afraid that too much excitement would cause another attack. Reb Yosef felt obligated to obey his doctors' orders, and Rabbi Bender looked for a rebbi to take his place. Six months later, Reb Yosef suddenly appeared in Rabbi Bender's office.

"What are you doing here?" Reb Dovid demanded.

"If I can't teach Torah, then what is it all worth?" Reb Yosef answered simply.

A shouting match ensued. Reb Dovid insisted that it was suicidal for Reb Yosef to return to teaching and Reb Yosef insisted, just as emphatically, that he was determined to take back his post.

With the same kind of unwavering resolve he had shown as a boy, Reb Yosef resumed teaching. Six months later, he suffered another heart attack, but this time it was fatal.[9] Torah Vodaath reeled in shock. Just a year and a half earlier, yet another Torah Vodaath superstar had passed away suddenly. Rabbi Moshe Leiberman was a popular eighth-grade rebbi. He had been a Torah Vodaath *talmid* who had shown unusual sincerity and *hasmadah* as a *bochur*. When he was in his early 20's, he was offered the position

---

8. "He was tremendously devoted to his *talmidim*. They kept in touch with him for years" (Rabbi Chaim Werner).

9. "When I was teaching the seventh grade, we were renting classroom space from the 'Y.' One day, I met Alfred Schnell pacing the floors outside my classroom. He told me that he was waiting for an appointment with Steve Kaplansky, the executive director of the 'Y.' I wished him a good day and went back into class. The boys were a little restless; I decided to tell them the famous story of Rabbi Yosef Leviton and how Rabbi Shlomo Heiman had appeared to him in a dream. They were moderately impressed. Meanwhile, Alfred Schnell was still walking the hallways. I invited him into my classroom.

"Did you know Rabbi Yosef Leviton?" I asked him.

"Sure," he answered.

"Let me tell everyone a *gevaldige* story."

I proceeded to tell over the story of Rabbi Yosef Leviton and my father. I had been in the office when it happened, and I could not get over Reb Yosef's determination to keep on teaching Torah. As I finished speaking, Alfred Schnell turned to me and said, "You think that's a story? I'll tell you a better story. I was his *chavrusa* in Torah Vodaath. One night we came to a very difficult question in *Bava Basra* ..." and he proceeded to tell over the first story that I had told the class, almost word for word! By then the boys were in awe" (Rabbi Yaakov Bender).

*Rabbi Yosef Leviton (1925-1964) was a famous student of Torah Vodaath who was beloved by all the rebbeim and roshei yeshivah. He became an exemplary rebbi who infused his students with a desire and enthusiasm for learning, causing many of them to choose a life of Torah.*

*Rabbi Moshe Leiberman (1921-1963) studied in Torah Vodaath where he became a close talmid of Rabbi Shlomo Heiman. He taught in Torah Vodaath for 20 years making his mark as a much-beloved rebbi. Reb Moshe was regarded as a self-effacing, humble person who toiled diligently in Torah.*

of teaching eighth grade, and for the next 20 years he was a devoted and beloved rebbi. At the age of 42, he suddenly passed away after a heart attack.[10]

Rabbi Leiberman and Rabbi Leviton had been Rabbi Bender's friends and colleagues. He had to hide his own pain in order to bolster his students as they absorbed these difficult losses. Although neither situation was as dramatic as Rabbi Cogan dying at his desk in the classroom, Rabbi Yosef Leviton's sudden *petirah*, so soon after Rabbi Moshe Leiberman had passed away, was unnerving for the boys. Rabbi Bender's calm presence in the halls and in the classrooms exuded stability and continuity.

Rabbi Bender needed to find an exceptional replacement, someone who would be able to handle the emotional state of the boys. Until he would find the suitable candidate, he needed a qualified substitute. He turned to Rabbi Yisroel Belsky, then learning in the Torah Vodaath kollel.

Although Rabbi Bender was well aware that Reb Yisroel was only substitute teaching, he still took the time to give him encouragement and advice. He did so with such tact that Reb Yisroel never felt that Rabbi Bender was intruding. He would just drop in, smile pleasantly, and make a few remarks.

---

10. This information was taken from a *Kuntrus* put out by the Leiberman family, *Moshe M'Bachurav.*

"Never test your will against theirs," Reb Dovid told Reb Yisroel. "If there are two or three minutes left until the bell will ring, don't say, 'If you do not settle down, I will not let you leave…' Bend toward them and smile, and you will win them over."

Once after one of Reb Yisroel's classes, Reb Dovid commented, "The response of the top of the class is no indication if you presented your lesson well; they will quickly grasp whatever you are teaching. The reaction of the weakest is no indication because they do not catch on right away anyway. You have to monitor yourself by keeping the attention of the middle of the class. Look and see how they are doing, and that will be your barometer.

"You have an obligation to teach the majority, those in the middle. The best are eager and motivated to learn; you really have to 'mess up' to turn them off. The weakest have trouble catching on. If you manage to get to one or two of them, that is a great success. Teach to the middle." As a principal, he put much time and effort into the weak students, finding innovative ways to convey the material so that they too could succeed.

Reb Yisroel was not a total novice, since he had taught for a number of years in camp. Yet Reb Yisroel was amazed by Rabbi Bender's original and refreshing pedagogical insights. In that short time as a substitute teacher, Reb Yisroel felt that he was given more guidance than many rebbeim receive in their entire career. Every day Rabbi Bender would come in and offer some astute suggestions that made the time that Reb Yisroel spent as a substitute rebbi a significant experience.[11]

THE EXODUS OF RELIGIOUS FAMILIES FROM WILLIAMSBURG TO CROWN Heights, and then to Flatbush and Boro Park, took Torah Vodaath from its peak enrollment of over 2,000 students to half that number by the early 60's.[12] In response to the population trend, Torah Vodaath opened a branch in Crown Heights with Rabbi Avrohom Pincus as principal.[13] They then merged the entire Williamsburg branch and moved it over to the Wilson Street building with Rabbi Dovid Bender as sole principal.

Rabbi Bender adjusted to the change, but he did not enjoy his new position nearly as much as the old one. He was much more comfortable dealing

---

11. "Many principals are not like this. They would rather sit in their office, undisturbed, and keep occupied with other things. Rabbi Bender took an active role: he was in the hallways, in the classrooms, patiently and carefully observing, inserting a comment here and there, but always in a way that encouraged both student and teacher to take his words seriously" (Rabbi Yisroel Belsky).

12. The establishment of other *Chassidishe chadorim* also took away from enrollment in Torah Vodaath. In earlier years, the staunchest Chassidim, *Litvaks*, *Yekkes*, and even children who were only marginally religious all attended Torah Vodaath. This began to change.

13. This branch eventually closed down as Boro Park and Flatbush eclipsed Crown Heights as religious settlements. Torah Vodaath was reestablished in Flatbush.

with seventh and eighth graders than with first and second graders. He had been in the Bedford Avenue building for so long that it seemed strange to walk by and not go in. At least the sounds of learning still rang in the streets since the building now housed the Viener *cheder*.

*Reb Dovid with his father in Eretz Yisroel*

ONE DAY REB DOVID ENTERED THE house, a blue airmail letter in hand. "Hello," he called out, *"Vos hert zach?"* He slit open the letter with his car keys (a relatively new acquisition bought a few months earlier) and sat down at the kitchen table as his wife greeted him with a snack.

Reb Dovid skimmed the letter and then let it drop to the table. He sat quietly, warming his hands on the cup of coffee his wife had set before him.

*"Nu?"* his rebbetzin urged with a smile. There was obviously something on her husband's mind.

"You know," he finally said, "maybe the children are right. Maybe I should make a trip to Eretz Yisroel."

Initially, Reb Dovid had balked at the thought. It was such an expensive trip. In the 17 years Reb Avrohom had lived there, the idea had never even been mentioned. But Reb Avrohom was getting older and his trips to America were less frequent. Perhaps a visit was in order.

Reb Dovid kept toying with the idea. To travel around the world to be with his father, to spend five glorious weeks in his presence, to serve him in ways he could not possibly serve him from so far away — it was exhilarating to just think of the possibilities. As he discussed the idea with his family, he grew more excited. Over and over again he remarked, "Imagine the *kibud av* I'll be able to do." The children were overjoyed that he was finally taking their idea seriously, and they continued to cheer him on.

And so, during the summer of 1965, Reb Dovid flew to Eretz Yisroel.

SPENDING 24 HOURS A DAY IN HIS FATHER'S PRESENCE WAS A TREAT Reb Dovid had not known for years. Together they journeyed to *kivrei tzaddikim*, to Yerushalayim, to the hills and valleys that spanned Eretz Yisroel. Just walking the streets of Bnei Brak was a joy, because they were doing it together.

They spent Shabbos with Rabbi Shloimke Berman[14] and his family. Ever

---

14. Reb Shloimke treated his uncle Rabbi Avrohom Bender with tremendous respect. When Reb Dovid came, he spent a lot of time with him, even going with them on a trip to *mekomos hakedoshim*, something unusual for Reb Shloimke.

*Rabbi Dovid Bender with Rabbi Shloimke Berman on a trip*

*Rabbi Dovid Bender with his brother-in-law Yosef Epstein*

the warm father, Reb Dovid took 4-year-old Chaim Peretz on his knee and sang him the same song he sang with his own children: "*L'koved Shabbos bim, L'koved Shabbos bum, L'koved Shabbos bim bum ...*" Chaim Peretz loved riding up and down on Reb Dovid's lap.[15]

Reb Dovid visited his brother-in-law, Yosef, and met Sarah and their children for the first time. He visited Rebbetzin Bender's cousin, Rabbi Elya Shachor, and his son-in-law, Rabbi Mordechai Rimer, and brought warm regards from the family.[16] He and his father spent time with Rabbi Shabsi Yogel, the Steipler, and other *talmidei chachamim*. In Yerushalayim, Reb Dovid joyfully met with many old friends from the Mir, including Rabbi Chaim Shmulevitz and Rabbi Nochum Partzovitz.

REB DOVID DID EVERYTHING TOGETHER WITH HIS FATHER, DAY IN and day out, for five weeks. Whether they were visiting with friends and family or spending time alone, he savored every moment.

When Reb Dovid returned to America, he could not stop telling his children, "Can you imagine the *kibud av*? Can you understand what a privilege?" He was exultant and for weeks could speak of little else.

ON THE SECOND DAY OF CHOL HAMOED SUCCOS, 5726 (1965), REBBETZIN Bender received a familiar blue airmail letter. She scanned the contents and paled. Luckily, the boys were not back from davening and neither

---

15. Thirty-eight years later, Rabbi Yaakov Bender was in Eretz Yisroel during the *shivah* of his cousin, Rabbi Avrohom Yeshaya Berman. When he went to be *menachem avel*, Rabbi Chaim Peretz Berman pointed to the chair he was sitting on. "Right here was where your father Reb Dovid sat when he visited us that summer. I remember today how he pulled me onto his lap and sang with me ..."

16. Rabbi Binyamin Rimer.

was her husband. Blumie was puttering around the kitchen, oblivious to the letter. Rebbetzin Bender quickly folded it up and tucked it away in her pocket. She would keep the news secret during the week of Yom Tov.

Right after Yom Tov, Rebbetzin Bender handed Reb Dovid the letter. He read its contents and sank into a chair. Tante Ettel, his stepmother, had passed away.

Tante Ettel had been a very important part of the Bender family. After Rebbetzin Pelta Bender passed away in 1945, Reb Avrohom had been lonely. Although he traveled often, coming home had meant returning to his wife and, while it was nice to return to his son and daughter-in-law and their children, it was not the same as returning to a spouse.

When the *shidduch* with Tante Ettel was suggested, there were certain con-

*Rabbi Avrohom Bender and Tante Ettel*

ditions. She owned an apartment in Tel Aviv and wanted to move there. Although this meant leaving his family, Reb Avrohom agreed. He had always wanted to live in Eretz Yisroel and the *shidduch* with Tante Ettel gave him a reason to go.

They married in 1948 and had 17 happy years together. Tante Ettel had given her new husband much more than a tidy house and tasty meals. Rabbi Avrohom Bender was a man who enjoyed and needed people and Tante Ettel had been a loyal and caring companion. Now Reb Avrohom was alone again. Reb Dovid was saddened by the news and grateful his rebbetzin had hid it until after Yom Tov. He would have found it difficult to maintain a proper *simchas Yom Tov* had he known.

Just thinking of his father sitting *shivah* alone was difficult for Reb Dovid. His only consolation was his recent trip. He knew that he had left his father happy and invigorated from his visit. He hoped that his father would draw strength from the memories during his period of mourning.

*Chapter Forty-Nine*

# Growing Pains

W HERE HAD THE YEARS GONE? ESTHER WAS MARRIED AND had two children. Blumie was working for her father as a secretary in Torah Vodaath. Paltiel was in learning in Wood-ridge, Michoel was in the Mesivta, and Shmuel Sholom was fast approaching his bar mitzvah. And Yankel? Yankel was at a crossroads.

For as long as he could remember, Yankel had attended Torah Vodaath. Most of those years, he had been happy there. That all changed when he turned 15.

Yankel had always been a bright boy and was two grades ahead of his age group in *limudei Kodesh*. That had worked out well when he was young. But as he and his classmates grew older, Yankel's height did not keep up with his accelerated academic class level. At 15, he was the youngest and the shortest *bochur* in the Torah Vodaath Beis Medrash. He became very self-conscious about his age and height; he felt that everyone was looking down on him — literally and figuratively.

After Succos, Reb Dovid decided to send Yankel to the Talmudical Yeshivah of Philadelphia. He and Yankel hoped that in a new yeshivah everything would be different. Perhaps they would even allow him to go down to 11th grade as opposed to being in first year *beis medrash*. Yankel optimistically went to Philadelphia.

As soon as he arrived, Yankel realized that things were not as simple as he had hoped. The Roshei Yeshivah, Rabbi Elya Svei and Rabbi Shmuel Kamenetsky, wanted him to give Rabbi Mendel Kaplan's *shiur* a chance. It was Reb Mendel's first year in the *beis medrash*, and they were certain

*Rabbi Elya Svei. To his left is ybdl"ch Rabbi Avrohom Golombeck, Mashgiach of the yeshivah*

*Rabbi Mendel Kaplan with ybdl"ch Rabbi Shmuel Kamenetsky*

that Yankel would enjoy his *shiur* and grow in learning. Yankel's face fell. Again, he would be with boys much older than himself. Again, he would feel small and insignificant.

Reb Dovid urged Yankel to try it out. This was Philadelphia, not Torah Vodaath. These were new boys who did not know Yankel. So what if he was a bit shorter? Why should he think they would judge him by his height? Yankel nodded as he blinked back his tears. He waved to his father as the car pulled away heading back to New York, leaving him in Philly, alone.

*Erev Shabbos Kodesh,*
*Parashas Bereishis*

*To my dear son Yaakov,*

*I got up quite early this morning for I can't sleep; I just think about you the whole time. I am therefore writing these words to you, and please reflect on their contents well.*

*All right, you do not want to be in Reb Mendel's shiur, the reason being the older boys there. We will not force you. We will take you out and I will speak to Reb Shmuel and Reb Elya and request that they put you with Rabbi Taub.[17] We have to wait a few days though, for a couple of reasons:*

*We have to wait a few days to confirm that you are satisfied with the yeshivah and that you will be able to get used to it. We cannot make a request, drive them crazy to put you into Rabbi Taub's class, and then you will not want that either.*

---

17. Rabbi Leib Taub was the twelfth-grade *maggid shiur* in the Philadelphia yeshivah.

*Rabbi Yisroel Mendel Kaplan (1913-1985) learned in Baranovich and Mir. Reb Mendel and his family spent the war years with the Mirrer Yeshivah. After the war they immigrated to America and settled in Chicago where Reb Mendel gave a shiur in the local high school. In 1965 he joined the staff of the Talmudical Yeshivah of Philadelphia. He was known as a master mechanech who molded hundreds of talmidim into true b'nei Torah.*

*After you have been in Philadelphia a few days, you will be considered their talmid ... If I request it right away, they may say, "Rabbi Bender, we told you that we can only accept students for Reb Mendel's shiur." However, once you are there for a few days, you will be considered their student and it will nullify that reason.*

*Think it over well. We are with you: your mother is pained, I am pained, the children are pained for we know how you feel and we want you to feel good and happy. Give yourself a chance. The bad feelings will eventually disappear and you will laugh at the whole thing.*

*In the meantime, learn well these few days, make friends with all the boys — young and old — live it up with them, become like one family. And you will be happy. Make sure to eat all three meals. Go out for sports, recess time, and with everybody, be heimish ... Learn, listen to the shiurim, ask questions during the shiur, do not be shy. Go over to bochurim. Talk in learning — "zol gein ah fire."[18]*

*Your father, wishing you all the best wholeheartedly,*
*Tatty*

Shabbos came and went, and Reb Dovid could not shake the image from his mind of his son's forlorn face. He was certain that Yankel cried himself to sleep that night and every night since. Yet, as a principal and a father, Reb Dovid did not feel that quitting was the answer. True, the move to Philly had not turned out as they had expected, but Yankel had known, before he left for the new yeshivah, that he might end up feeling he had made a mistake. Dealing with the situation he chose was part of growing up.

Yankel wanted to run back home. He wanted to take the next train out of Philadelphia and be back in Williamsburg as soon as possible. He missed his home and family and was not comfortable in the yeshivah. Shabbos was a disaster. He begged Paltiel to explain to their parents how important it was that they bring him home. He could not bear to stay there even one more hour.

---

18. Literally "it should burn a fire," meaning, the learning should have the excitement of a fire burning.

Reb Dovid listened. He felt deeply for his son but, at the same time, he knew that Yankel would be able to grow from the challenge he was facing. Moving away from home was a change that Yankel had wanted. Weathering the changes and challenges of life is what turns children into adults. Reb Dovid briskly took out a pen and paper. As a loving father, he could and would encourage, nurture, and support; but ultimately, Yankel would have to learn to adjust.

*Sunday,*
*Parashas Noach*

*… I hope this letter finds you in a better mood. As I came into the house Paltiel told me that you called at 10 o'clock. We are very pained that you are so distraught. We do feel that it is getting a bit better. You get into these moods and become "out of order," but we see that it has become easier for us to talk you out of it when you phone. That is also worth something.*

*Again, we promise, bli neder, not to force anything upon you. But you must give the yeshivah a proper chance. A proper chance means that you make a conscious decision that you are staying for the whole week and you are not thinking about going home every other minute and, only by chance, does it turn out that you stayed another day. That is not the way to do it.*

*The way to do it is to be firm about staying another week. As soon as you will be strong about the decision to stay a full week, and you realize that there is no way out, you will get over it. If, chas v'shalom, you don't, you will come home knowing that you did everything that you could.*

*Understand, Yaakov'le, this all comes from homesickness. Homesickness can make a person feel so out of sorts — terrible — it is however a passing blemish, it goes away, for some quicker and for some slower, but it does pass. It disappears as if it never was.*

*Do us a favor and, mainly, do yourself a favor. When the bad feelings take hold of you, go over to Rabbi Shmuel Kamenetsky, shlita. Do not be embarrassed. Talk your heart out, and feel better. Go over to your rebbi, Reb Mendel, shlita. Fight these feelings on every front. You will see how happy you will become.*

*Paltiel is getting ready to leave. Stay well, learn well, and may everything be with success.*

*Tatty*

YANKEL FELT THE WARMTH AND LOVE IN HIS FATHER'S WORDS. BUT was that enough? How often had he tried to fight these bad feelings? The truth was, he did not understand what was going on. He had always been a friendly, well-liked, outgoing fellow. Why did he feel so strange and awkward in this new place? He wanted to make things work, he wanted to succeed, but it was so hard.

The boy sighed. Did all his bad feelings stem from homesickness? If so, would this terrible pain, this dull ache that accompanied him day and night, ever go away? His father wanted him to "fight these feelings on every front." Why? Was it so bad to want to be home? Yankel rubbed away the tears that welled up in his eyes. He knew his parents wanted the best for him, and he did not want to disappoint them. He would try to push all his negative thoughts away and focus on getting used to life in Philadelphia.

Brow furrowed with determination, Yankel hunched over a clean sheet of paper and began to write.

*Sunday,*
*Parashas Noach*

*Dear Parents,*

*How are you? I feel, b"H, fine. I got your package and I could not understand how so many things fit into one small box …*

*I will tell you the truth; I still am homesick, but less than before. In the morning, I am a bit grouchy, but when I start davening with kavanah, it gets better. It happens during the day too, but I think to myself that I must learn and "that's all." I believe that in less than a week I will not be homesick at all. Of course, I am waiting for Shabbos Chanukah, but it is much less than before.*

*When I arrived, I saw a bochur bringing a meal for his rebbi or somebody else's. Five or six boys do it each meal. So, on Sunday or Monday I started giving Reb Mendel, shlita, and sometimes other rebbeim, the meal (shimush talmidei chachamim).*

*My morning chavrusa is Petrekovski, a Philadelphia boy. He told me that his father, a former maggid shiur, a lamdan, founded this yeshivah. He went to Reb Aharon (Kotler), ztz"l, to tell him that he wants to start a small yeshivah with 10 boys and take a Rosh Yeshivah from Lakewood. That is how Reb Shmuel, shlita, became the Rosh Yeshivah.*

*At night, I learn with Yeruchem Septimus, Mr. Louis Septimus's son. After Ma'ariv, I learn in the beis medrash until approximately 11 o'clock. Last night was the first night that I learned after Ma'ariv, and I learned until 11:10. The night mashgiach, Mordechai Young,[19] who substitutes for Rabbi Avrohom Golombeck, shlita, found me in the beis medrash at 11:10. I told him that in another five minutes I would go up. He let me. I went up at 11:15.*

*At 11:25, a boy asked me to get him a soda from the canteen. He is in the first shiur and he said that since I am in the fifth shiur, I am a privileged character and therefore I should get it for him. I was not yet undressed, so I agreed. The night*

---

19. Now a Rav in Philadelphia.

*mashgiach had already seen me in the hall at around 11:20 and he had already told me to go into my room to go to sleep. I hoped that I would not meet him going down to the canteen. I went down to the first floor to get the soda and, whom do you think I met there? The night mashgiach. I did not say anything. I just went into the bathroom, took some tissues and held it in my hand. He probably thought I came down to get paper …*

*I am not used to sleeping only 7½ hours, but it is getting easier. Soon we will change the clock, and then I will be getting more sleep …*

*My temporary roommate is Yehuda Bakst[20] from Detroit. His father learned in Mir in Shanghai.*

*Don't think that because I am writing such a long letter now, I always will. I have time to write now because I do it mostly during the English period. We are reviewing the end of Julius Caesar, but I don't understand the end because I wasn't here at the beginning. I am trying to learn it alone. I got someone to teach me the French that I missed. We do it on Fridays. The boy's name is Laibel Beck, from Boro Park. He is in my Yiddish class.*

*What's doing by Blumie? What do you hear from Zaida? What do you hear from Lakewood? How are Paltiel, Michoel, and Shmuel Sholom? Tell them to write me letters. Blumie, too …*

*Regards to all.*

*Your son,*
*Yaakov*

YANKEL READ AND REREAD THE LETTER. IT MADE IT SOUND AS IF HE was doing a lot better. And if the letter sounded more upbeat than he felt, that was all part of the fight. He was pushing away the negative thoughts and distracting himself with the mundane events of the day. Maybe, soon the homesickness would disappear altogether.

The next day a letter arrived from Blumie. It was full of warmth and concern. She truly wanted to know everything that was going on in his life. Sharing the little details with her was a welcome distraction. Yankel penned another letter home.

***Monday,***
***Parashas Noach, English period***

*To my dear Parents,*

*How are you doing? I am feeling fine, b"H. I got Blumie's letter today and I thank her very much for the quarter for the tissues. I am not guaranteeing I will use it for what it was intended. Thanks anyhow. Now, I will answer Blumie's questions.*

*I got a room. I share it with four other bochurim, and it is in the other building. The fact that five sleep in one room is not bad, because it is set up like three*

---

20. Present-day Rosh Yeshivah in Gedolah Ateres Mordechai of Detroit.

*separate rooms.*

*My roommates are:*
*an Australian boy (my halachah chavrusa) by the name of Bernath*
*a Philly boy (he became an orphan two months ago)*
*a boy named Strassfeld*
*a boy named Gross*

*Please ask Dr. Sternberg for a note excusing me from physical fitness. My back hurts a lot during exercise and I could be excused if I have a doctor's note. I am giving my laundry in today with another boy.*

*Now, about myself. I feel well, b"H. I still feel, though, that the boys in my shiur don't want to mix with me. Since Succos only one boy asked me something. I know I am still new, but it bothers me. For instance, today I saw a boy asking my night chavrusa (Septimus) something, and he is also a new boy. Maybe it is because I am not learning so well yet.*

*During shiur, I was thinking about the boys and how they do not mingle with me, and my learning is therefore poorer. The rebbi must have noticed my mind drifting. He said to me four or five times, "Nu, you're listening?" It makes me feel worse, because that makes the boys think less of me. I know that the rebbi wants to help me. He keeps asking me during shiur if I understand. I think that since he knew I had a bit of a problem he wants to be mekarev me. He always gives me priority in class, when he asks questions and we raise our hands. (If not always, then many times.) I do not know, myself, what exactly my problem is. I am really going to try to put myself into the learning as much as I can. Then maybe the boys will mingle with me more …*

*I am learning much better now, b"H, and the davening is not to compare. Yet, what I have written about still bothers me. Not so much, yet it still bothers me. It is no comparison to what I felt like a few days after my arrival. I don't have the urge to run home, like in the beginning.*

*The meals are not bad — not great, but not bad. I think I've written enough.*
*Regards to all.*

*Your son,*
*Yaakov*

ALTHOUGH HIS LETTER ENDED ON SOMETHING OF A DOWN NOTE, IT WAS a far cry from the anguish of the previous week. Yankel had stopped calling home every day and was able to discuss the situation in yeshivah more rationally. He was still uncomfortable in his *shiur*, but he was reluctant to continue pressing to be switched down to Rabbi Taub. He still wondered how he would fare next year when they all moved up. Would he ever feel comfortable with them? Would they ever become his friends? Would it not be better to be with boys his own age?

Reb Dovid had dismissed all these concerns. In truth, Reb Dovid was relieved. Yankel was talking much more calmly, less emotionally. He seemed to be adjusting. Yankel wrote home every day at his parents' request. He was used to writing. The years of writing letters to his grandfather in Eretz Yisroel had trained him to put pen to paper and share his life. He still yearned to call home more often. His homesickness was far from gone, and no letter could replace the voices of his parents. Yet he understood his father's position. Calling home too often was a crutch that could hold him back from adjusting. If he wanted to fully acclimate to yeshivah life, he would have to get used to being away from home. For now, he was limiting his phone calls to twice a week.

Yankel spoke with his mother more often than his father since she was usually home when he called, while his father was often out. Rebbetzin Bender also wrote to her son, but less regularly than her husband. She and Reb Dovid differed in style but their message was the same: we support you, we care about you, we believe in you.

*B"H Thursday evening,*
*Parashas Noach, 1965*

*My dear son Yaakov'le!*

*Last night at the wedding, we got your letter; you probably got the regards from us as well as the $5. Use it in good health.*

*Dear son, you do not know, you cannot even fathom how happy we are, b"H, with every word that you write. We will always have nachas from you, I"YH, ad meah v'esrim. When Shabbos comes I think about how good it is that you are now in a good environment. You have friends, you have a suitable minyan of young boys, you have whom to talk to in learning, and whom to just spend time with. You know what it was like here. May you be well and successful for many long years.*

*My son, please write often and about everything, every detail. Everything is, b"H, fine by us. Paltiel left for yeshivah. The other boys are in yeshivah and (with) Blumie (it is) the same as before. Esther called today. Itzele spoke to me a bit and Aharon Dov was whining as usual.*

*The teachers in school made a tumult today (only among themselves) because of the intercoms that were installed. Many schools are installing them now. Teachers do not like it. We, the older teachers, do not mind.*

*Have a good and happy Shabbos,*
*Everybody sends best regards.*

*Mother*

LIKE SOMEONE GRABBING FOR A LIFE PRESERVER, YANKEL HELD ON TO his father's letters. In one way, they were even more sustaining than the phone calls. He was able to read and reread the words many times, whenever he needed a dose of love and encouragement. There were so many little things that shook up his confidence. He still did not have a feeling of belonging.

He was in a yeshivah full of *bochurim*, but he felt as if he was in isolation. He walked among the boys in his *shiur* as if there was an invisible wall between him and them. They barely looked in his direction, much less spoke to him. He felt like crying out, "Look at me! I'm right here in front of you, and I am a person. Acknowledge that I exist by saying something to me. Why should it matter that I'm new and I'm younger than you?" But Yankel was too afraid to confront them, and he continued to suffer in silence.[21]

He tried to judge them favorably. They did not need a young new upstart in their *shiur*. They were fine before he came along. A part of him understood that. He knew that he was not being his most outgoing and jovial self. But that was because everything was so new and intimidating, and he felt that all he seemed to do was slip up. Now he waited for a letter from his father to give him another perspective.

*Thursday evening,*
*Parashas Lech Lecha*

*To my dear son Yaakov'le,*

*… I hope this letter finds you in a better mood. Listen, Yaakov'le, you have to get this business about the boys not liking you out of your head; it is totally untrue. One can talk oneself into anything. Esther also convinced herself of it and then got it out of her head. She now laughs at herself. Paltiel was the same. It is real nonsense; you are old enough, smart enough, and intelligent enough to make friends with everybody. Look at Bluma'le — her best friend was Esther Frankl, who is older than our Esther. When one reaches that age, these issues straighten out.*

*You are convinced that they are looking at you and do not want to be friends with you. All of it is not true. To have friends one has to go out and make them. As is written in Pirkei Avos: "Knei l'cha chaver,[22] one has to buy a friend." How does one buy a friend? You throw yourself into your learning. You must get up early, "like a lion" — this is the first din in Shulchan Aruch. Do not think into it: jump out of bed, get dressed, go daven, and daven well — a very warm davening. Your day will start off with a bren, and then you'll be able to "drive at 60 miles an hour." Nobody will come over to "talk in learning" with you, they do not know*

---

21. In rereading the letters of that time, Rabbi Yaakov Bender commented that he did not remember it being so bad. Obviously, his feelings then were heavily colored by homesickness and not an accurate reflection of the boys in the yeshivah.

22. *Pirkei Avos* 1:6.

*you yet and you have to be aware of that fact. Go over, talk to them in learning …*

*Additionally, you should know, all these thoughts come up again only as a result of your homesickness. Sunday's story made you feel bad and that is why you got homesick again, and that's what brought up all those thoughts again. Just as it went away the first time around, and was getting better slowly, it is bound to get better this time, too. Fight it, Yaakov'le, like a lion. A lion has no fear. You, too, must not fear anybody.*

*Try to call home as little as possible. Since you started phoning again, your homesickness came back. If you decide that you are not calling, you will be less homesick.*

*We got an upbeat letter from Zaida. He says that he is feeling much better.*

*No special news on the home front. I am mailing the letter now so that you get it before Shabbos.*

*Wishing you all the best.*

*Your father*

IN THE END, RABBI SHMUEL KAMENETSKY IN CONSULTATION WITH REB Dovid felt that it would be good for Yankel to go home for Shabbos.

Being home for Shabbos was heavenly. Yankel was back in the happy security of family who loved and appreciated him. He wanted it to go on forever. As the sun set and Shabbos ended, that feeling of impending doom returned. No, no, no! He did not want to go back. He would not go back. He looked at his suitcase and could not bring himself to finish packing. His father walked into the room and cheerfully offered to help him. Yankel stared back mutely.

"Come, Yankel," his father coaxed him, "we are almost finished. What else has to go in?"

Yankel could not answer. The words would not come out.

Reb Dovid tried to be patient. He kept talking and encouraging, but Yankel remained paralyzed by his fear. In frustration, Reb Dovid burst out, "If you are afraid, don't go!" He began pulling things out of the suitcase, unpacking that which had been packed. Yankel fled to the bathroom where he burst out crying. He emerged a while later, his face streaked with tears.

Stoically, he declared, "I am confident enough to go now." He quickly packed his suitcase. But, an hour later, and again the next morning, his fears returned. He wrote one letter then and there. He wrote another letter two nights later.

*Tuesday evening,*
*Parashas Vayeira*

*To my Dear Parents,*

*Rabbi Avrohom Golombeck (1937-2008) grew up on the Lower East Side. He attended Yeshivas Rabbeinu Yaakov Yosef and then Beth Medrash Govoha in Lakewood. Rabbi Aharon Kotler sent Reb Avrohom to Ponevezh where he became a close talmid of Rabbi Yecheskel Levenstein. As Mashgiach in Philadelphia for over forty years, Reb Avrohom guided his talmidim in Torah and yiras Shamayim.*

*How are you doing? I am in a grouchy mood. I am finding the fight very difficult. The first half of the day is hard labor. I have already spoken to Reb Shmuel (Kamenetsky), shlita, and I told him that I have to fight and he also told me that that is the best I can do. Reb Avrohom (Golombeck) spoke to me yesterday, for a good 20 minutes, and said the same. I told him that I do not miss home, but I am planning to go over today to tell him that maybe it is my room. Maybe in the big room I feel more out of place. I don't know. In any case, I am going to ask him to switch me to the beis medrash building. Maybe that will make me feel better.*

*I am controlling myself with all my strength not to make a phone call; I have been to the bathroom quite a few times to cry. In the morning I can't eat properly. This morning I went out after breakfast for some fresh air. Reb Avrohom met me and asked how I am. At that moment, I was feeling terrible. I had tears in my eyes and it was difficult for me to answer. He noticed, and as he was talking to me, I cried to myself quietly. He told me to fight it and all will be well. I nodded and said all right.*

*Reb Mendel was not here today, and I am a little bit anxious to hear a shiur. The learning is going pretty okay. But, when the mood starts, I go out, get the crying out of the system, and continue learning …*

*Do not take it to heart, because I am sure that it will go away soon. I got both of Tatty's letters, and (probably) you got mine. I think the salami was off, and I threw it out. The rest is very good. Thank you very much.*

*Regards to all.*

*Your son,*
*Yaakov*

REB DOVID CONTINUED TO CONSTANTLY WRITE LETTERS OF ENCOURagement to his son. Each time he focused on something else: Yankel's inherent strengths, his ability to be a fighter, ways to remedy the homesickness, the importance of pushing away negative thoughts, the need to keep busy, and the ability to forge ahead as if nothing is wrong for soon the problems will fade away.

To my dear son Yaakov'le,

I received your letter from Sunday night, today. Yaakov'le, it is obvious from your letter that you've already undertaken the battle and that you are not afraid anymore. Get busy doing something immediately, and you will be amazed at how quickly they (the feelings) will disappear.

The whole thing stems from the advice of the yetzer hara. The yetzer hara works overtime when he catches someone accomplishing in positive areas. You must show him who is boss, and he will just have to drop the whole issue. He is only fighting you because he recognizes your strength and determination.

Iy"H, once you've gotten over it, yeshivah will become a thousand times more pleasant, "l'fum tzaara agra[23] — more pains are more gains." True success will follow.

I gave the car in to "Motsi" today to winterize. It cost me less than $100. I bought two good snow tires, the ones that cost $64 (including tax) — they are best. I got a tune-up, new spark plugs, anti-freeze, and an oil change. Let us hope it will ride well and I will be able to visit you, even in the bitter cold and snowstorms. I even had the thermostat for the heating changed …

… Mother and the children send best regards.

Wishing you all the best.

Your father

---

23. *Pirkei Avos* 5:26.

*Chapter Fifty*

# Blackout

**November 10, 1965**[24]

*Dear Yaakov,*

$\mathscr{I}$ AM NOW SITTING BY A CANDLE WRITING YOU THIS LETTER. YOU *probably heard what happened at 5:30 this evening. Almost the entire New York State lost its electricity. I was sitting in yeshivah, when suddenly it got pitch dark. The whole yeshivah was in a panic. Little by little, everyone was dismissed by candlelight. You should have seen the streets at 6 o'clock when I was going home — crowds and crowds of people walking, shouting, each one looking for part of his family. It was dangerous to walk in the streets. All the electricity was off: no street lights, cars and people going at the same time, people stuck in subways underground, people stuck in elevators. Thousands of people are still walking home from their working places — three to four hours of walking.*

*In the house, there is no electricity and no steam. We are sitting and waiting. So far there are no results. Iy"H, there will soon be, I hope. There are many big disappointments — we know of a few weddings tonight. There are people stuck in so many places. Hannah Yoffe just called. They are all stuck in the dark Lakewood office[25] eating tomatoes — that's all the food they have. Imagine the disappointment the Wachtfogels are experiencing now. The Wachtfogel daughters left happily*

---

24. This letter was written in English.
25. Located in Brooklyn.

*to the airport at 4 o'clock. Miriam's baby is here now. Because of these electricity problems, the planes could not land in New York. Chava just called us from Canada that her plane landed there. Reb Nosson's plane landed in your good old Philadelphia. Meanwhile, the girls are all at the airport waiting for them. I hope Miriam calls soon so that I can tell her that Chava called here. She would be very happy to hear that they landed safely.*

*The news about us is all over the world. You cannot imagine how it is. The streets are so silent and dark. The moonlight is, b"H, fantastic. No lights, no steam, no radio, no refrigerator. It is interesting that Boro Park and Bensonhurst do have light. It will, iy"H, be good, gam zu l'tovah.[26] We were very happy to receive your letter. I must tell you it was a lovely letter. We were very proud of you that you were able to control yourself so well. Keep up your wonderful efforts and, iy"H, you will succeed …*

*Be well.*

*Love,*
*Blumie*

YANKEL RAN HIS FINGER OVER A PIECE OF DRIED WAX THAT CLUNG TO the letter. He folded the sheet over to read his mother's letter, which was stapled to Blumie's.

*To my dear son Yaakov'le, sheyichyeh,*

*It was worth it for you to travel to Philadelphia, just so that we get to read your beautiful letters. I tell you, my son, your letters are exceptional in content and in style. You cannot imagine how much I enjoy your writing.*

*You will see, my son, in no time, everything will iron out and you will not believe yourself how fast your moods will disappear. You will laugh and you won't believe that you ever had a hard time for a short while. In the end, my son, you will enjoy it more, iy"H, and you will be successful in your learning and gain satisfaction for many long years.*

*Bluma'le wrote to you what it is like by us: it is cold (because the heating needs electricity to run), dark, no clocks, and no refrigerator. People are afraid to drive their cars because there are no traffic lights. Tens of thousands of people are walking home from work over the bridge. It is now already after 10 o'clock and it has been this way since 5:30. And they don't know when they'll repair it. You can't get a taxi either.*

*Imagine, a girl we know is getting married tonight.*

*Yaakov'le, my son, I hope you are eating and drinking, and you will see how fast your homesickness will disappear. Spend your time with friends, not alone. You will think less, and you will not have what to think about. Immerse yourself in your learning and you will see how happy you will be, iy"H.*

---

26. *Taanis* 21a.

*You are, b"H, liked by all and appeal to everybody. You are talented and smart, and not haughty. You will, i"yH, be successful.*

*I will end now, for it is simply difficult to write by the candlelight.*

*Be well, my son,*

*Your mother*

*P.S. You will probably get regards from Zaida through Reb Nosson, shlita. He is on the way to your yeshivah.*

THE MAJOR BLACKOUT WAS BIG NEWS. FOR DAYS, IT WAS ALL THAT ANY-one spoke about. No one could recall a similar event in all of New York history and everyone had a blackout story to tell, one more dramatic than the next. For Yankel, the blackout should have provided the respite he needed. It was a break in schedule, a shocking event that would have normally been a welcome distraction, an excuse to exchange wild and interesting stories.

Yet, even the blackout could not shake Yankel from his melancholy mood. So there was no power for a few hours. People recovered from the ordeal and were walking around normally afterward. Only he was still stuck in this fog of pain from which he could not escape.

Yankel was crying again from what seemed like a bottomless well of tears. He desperately wanted to succeed in Philadelphia, and there were already things that he liked about the place. He already felt a warm connection to all the rebbeim. Shabbos in yeshivah was a really uplifting experience: over 100 *bochurim* ate together and sang in unity and harmony.

Yet the negative feelings kept hounding him. He was afraid and could not even say what he feared. It was a vague, murky feeling which filled him with so much dread that all he wanted to do was run home. Instead, he crouched over a clean sheet of paper once again.

***Tuesday night,***
***Parashas Chayei Sarah***

*Dear Parents,*

*How are you? By me, all is as usual. Maybe today it was a touch easier. In any case, all the little details are eating me up alive … The rebbi had told us to discuss a Ramban. I was left stuck without anybody. He noticed and sent a bochur over to me. I spoke with him in learning. But since everything still bothers me, I wasn't too lively. Then someone made a comment and I felt bad all over again. After all my fighting and trying so hard … it bothers me so much. Believe me, I am fighting, but the going is difficult.*

*I got three letters today. First, Tatty's — thank you so much for the dollar. Sec-*

*ond, Blumie's, and third, Esther's. I liked Itzikel's chochmah with the Sefer Torah very much; I would like it much better if I were happier. If something good happens, I don't get the whole feeling because I walk around with the bad feeling.*

*I daven with the greatest kavanah that my mishugasim should go away. I don't know why I am so punished ... I really want to learn and I am trying so hard ... I want to stay, and I want it to work out well. I hope and pray that it should pass.*

*I play ball and I try to mingle with everybody as much as I can. English is going quite well. I get up early and jump out of bed. Today I stayed in bed a bit longer, because I was very exhausted.*

*Reb Avrohom met me at the telephone booth right after Monday's conversation and took me for a walk. He was going to the hardware store, and he spoke to me quite a long time. And, what do you think Reb Avrohom said? Fight, fight, fight and fight. I do fight it, but it's not moving. I really am trying ...*

*Please write and give regards to all.*

*Your son,*
*Yaakov*

*When are you thinking about coming? It will probably be better for me to discuss all these issues in person ...*

### Chapter Fifty-One

# Upheaval

**Williamsburg: 21st of Cheshvan 5726**
**(November 16, 1965)**

HEN MORNING DAWNS, IT IS ALMOST IMPOSSIBLE TO
know the significance of the new day. Will it be a day that
just passes like any other, or will it be a day that is engraved
forever in one's memory? Tuesday the 21st of Cheshvan was a day whose
every moment the Bender family would remember.

"Hi, Shmuel Sholom," Blumie greeted her brother cheerfully, "what's
up?"

"Nothing much," Shmuel Sholom answered, his face a picture of gloom.
"I feel lousy."

Ever the efficient school secretary, Blumie whipped out a thermometer
and placed it under his tongue. A few minutes later, she took it out and
held it up to read. "One hundred and one," she declared. "You are going
home." She wrote a note to give to his rebbi and sent him home. "*Refuah
sheleimah*!" she called after him. Then she dialed her mother to let her know
that Shmuel Sholom was on his way home.

REB DOVID STRODE PURPOSEFULLY THROUGH THE HALLS OF TORAH
Vodaath. He had already spoken in two classes and was entering a third.
He glanced around at the boys' faces and cleared his throat.

"… Let me tell you about the greatness of our *gedolim*," Reb Dovid began. "When the Ksav Sofer was 6 years old, he became very ill. The doctors gave up all hope that he would recover. The *chevra kaddisha* was waiting in the next room. The Chasam Sofer refused to accept the grim prognosis. He closeted himself in a separate room and poured out his heart to the *Eibeshter*. Hours passed, and the Chasam Sofer was still davening. Finally, he emerged, a smile of relief on his face. '*Oisgepoilt noch a yoivel yor,*'[27] he declared."

Reb Dovid paused.

"Boys, the Ksav Sofer was *niftar* when he was 56 years old. Through the *tefillos* of the Chasam Sofer, his son received 50 years of life, and we received a Ksav Sofer."[28]

That day, the story about the Chasam Sofer was the highlight of Reb Dovid's *shmuessen* in three classes. When he returned to his office, he was ready for his lunch.

*Rabbi Avrohom Shmuel Binyamin Sofer (1815-1871), known as the Ksav Sofer, was the oldest son of the Chasam Sofer. Rabbi Ephraim Fishel Sofer was his private tutor until he reached the age to enter his father's yeshivah. When the Ksav Sofer was 25 years old, his father was niftar and the Ksav Sofer succeeded him as Rav and Rosh Yeshivah. Like his father, he served the Pressburg community with diligence and piety for 33 years.*

"Any news?" he asked Blumie as he passed her desk.

"Nothing special," she answered, "except that Shmuel Sholom has fever, and so I sent him home." Reb Dovid registered the information and walked over to his desk. A few minutes later, Blumie came in with his lunch.

So far, the day had been more or less routine. At 3 o'clock, Reb Dovid left school and headed to Kerem Shlomo for his regular afternoon seder. His seder at Kerem Shlomo was one of the highlights of his day; he would see his good friends and talk with them in learning. Perhaps he would even share with them the *vort* he had told his good friend Rabbi Feivel Hollander that morning in the Mirrer Minyan.[29]

Reb Feivel had enjoyed the *vort*. He, Reb Dovid, and most of the others in the Mirrer Minyan and in Kerem Shlomo were in their late 40's and

---

27. Literally: Accomplished another 50 years.

28. Rabbi Shmuel Sholom Bender as told to him by a *talmid*.

29. "… In *Selichos*, we ask *HaKadosh Baruch Hu*, '*Al tashlicheinu l'eiss ziknah* — do not forsake us in our old age.' '*Tashlicheinu*' also means to throw out or discard. We ask *HaKadosh Baruch Hu*, do not throw us into old age. Even when a person is young, sometimes he feels worn out, old, and weak, as if he has been suddenly 'thrown into' old age. We daven that we should not feel old when we are still young."

early 50's. They considered themselves young in mind, heart, and spirit, but little aches and pains here and there reminded them that they were not as young as they used to be.

LATER THAT AFTERNOON, REB DOVID RETURNED HOME FOR SUPPER. HE asked his children about their day and they shmoozed over steaming hot meatballs. Then he and his rebbetzin drove down to Crown Heights to be *menachem avel* the Nussbaum family, owners of the bungalow colony they summered in. While in Crown Heights, they decided to visit the two young widows, Mrs. Leviton and Mrs. Leiberman. Then they headed back to Williamsburg where Reb Dovid dropped his rebbetzin off at home and proceeded to the Mesivta of Torah Vodaath.

"… RAV EXPLAINS, 'SHEHAYU OSIM SHUROS SHUROS SAVIV HA'AVEL *l'nachamo b'shuvam min hakever*[30] — and they make two lines surrounding the mourner to comfort him when he comes back from the *kever*.' Now look at the *Tiferes Yisroel* — *Sheha'avel over beineihem v'omrim lo HaMakom y'nachamecha*[31] — so that the mourner passes between them, and they say to him, 'The Almighty should comfort you …' Can you visualize this? After the burial, the *aveilim* and all those accompanying them walk toward the end of the cemetery. There, the people form two parallel lines for the mourners to walk through. This is called a *shurah*. As the *aveilim* walk through the *shurah*, the people surrounding them call out '*HaMakom yenachamecha* — May the Almighty comfort you.' " Reb Dovid paused, his finger still on the page.

Reuvain Rosenberg waited for his rebbi to continue. Their learning time was almost over and *Ma'ariv* was about to begin. Did he notice?

Reb Dovid slid his finger down the page, closed the *Mishnayos*, and said, "I think that we will stop over here." He smiled at his *talmid*.

Reuvain nodded. He and Reb Dovid went to get *siddurim* for *Ma'ariv*.[32]

"Have a good night," Reb Dovid called.

"You too, Rebbi," the *bochur* responded.[33] Berel Schwartz, a Mesivta *bochur,* had shnorred a ride home with Reb Dovid. They parted on Hewes Street.

AT 11 O'CLOCK, REB DOVID ENTERED HIS QUIET HOUSE AND THEN turned around and locked the door behind him. Blumie was sitting on the

---

30. *Berachos* 3:2.

31. *Tiferes Yisroel* 10.

32. R' Reuvain Rosenberg.

33. R' Berel Schwartz.

couch. She smiled when he walked in and offered to make her father a cup of tea.

Reb Dovid thought for a moment. "Yes," he said, "I would enjoy a cup of tea." Father and daughter entered the kitchen and chatted amicably as he sipped the hot drink.

"Would you like another one?" Blumie asked.

"No. Thank you," Reb Dovid answered, walking upstairs.

Blumie followed. It was late and she might as well go to sleep. She went into her room to prepare for bed. She heard the murmur of her parents' voices and understood that they were doing the same. A few minutes later she went to their room and knocked lightly on the door.

"I just wanted to say good night," she told her mother as she gave her a kiss.

"Good night, Blumale." Rebbetzin Bender affectionately kissed her forehead.

Blumie glanced over at her father. He was already in bed and she did not want to disturb him. She walked softly out of the room and into her own. She climbed into bed and closed her eyes. The house was quiet.

Then, a terrified shriek ripped through the silence.

### Chapter Fifty-Two

# Aftermath

**Philadelphia:**
**22nd of Cheshvan 5726 (November 17, 1965)**

*Y*ANKEL OPENED HIS EYES. SOMETHING WAS WRONG. THE morning rays of sun were blocked by Rabbi Shmuel Kamenetsky, standing over his bed.

"My father is dead," Yankel stated.

Reb Shmuel was taken aback. "Your father is not well," he responded evasively. "Come. Get dressed and we will go daven. Then we will go to New York."

Yankel pulled himself wearily out of bed. His head felt heavy, thick, and confused. He was too tired to think. He got dressed and went to the *beis medrash* to daven. After davening, Rabbi Elya Svei and Rabbi Shmuel Kamenetsky accompanied Yankel to the train station and boarded the train with him.

*It does not make sense*, Yankel realized. *Why are they both taking me to New York? Because my father is sick?* Since the alternative was too terrible to contemplate, Yankel closed his eyes and tried to block out any thoughts. From 30th Street Station in Philadelphia to 34th Street in Manhattan, they traveled in silence. They alighted in Manhattan and boarded the A train heading to West Fourth Street. At West Fourth Street, they had to change for the D train. As Yankel and the Roshei Yeshivah crossed the platform to meet the D train, they saw swarms of people, *frum yeshivaleit*, waiting for the train. Yankel recognized this one from Lakewood, and that one … was that his cousin, Boruch Ber Yoffe? Yankel caught his eye and then he knew for sure.

Yankel began to cry.

PALTIEL WATCHED THE HOUSES AND TREES WHIZ BY. THE TRAIN PASSED another hospital. He craned his neck to see if he spotted his mother or their car, but there was no sign of either. The whole thing was strange. Rabbi Pincus had called him in yeshivah early that morning and told him that his father was not well and he should come home. But why did Rabbi Pincus call? Why not his mother or Blumie?

He got off the train and walked home. Down Hewes Street, past Broadway, Harrison, and Marcy. There was his house, right between Marcy and Lee Avenues. He knocked lightly on the door and heard someone running to come. It was his mother. "Paltiel," she blurted out, "Have no *ta'aynos*. It is Hashem's will."

Paltiel took in his mother's pale face and red-rimmed eyes. Blumie, Michoel, and Shmuel Sholom were standing around, dazed.

Suddenly, he understood.

YANKEL WALKED INTO THE HOUSE AT TEN MINUTES TO 1, THE LAST of the Bender children to arrive home. They were waiting for him. Rebbetzin Bender and her children proceeded to the chapel at K'hal Adas Yereim where the *niftar* had already been prepared for burial. The family tore *kriah*, and amid tears of anguish, the *hespedim* began. Rabbi Mottel Weinberg, a talmid and cousin of Reb Dovid, and Rabbi Avrohom Pincus spoke at the chapel.

From there, the *aron* was driven by hearse through the streets of Williamsburg, followed by hundreds of people, until they reached 206 Wilson Street, the elementary school division of the Yeshivah of Torah Vodaath. It was a large *levayah*.[34] Thousands of people attended. The *beis medrash* was so packed with people that it was difficult to move. Everyone had come to pay their last respects to their rebbi, their principal, and their friend. Straining to hear the heartfelt *hespedim*,[35] *bochurim* stood on tables and chairs.

" '*Dodi yorad ligano la'arugos habosem ... v'lilkot shoshanim*[36] — *The Almighty descended to his garden, to the fragrant flowerbed ... to pluck roses.' Hashem descends to this world to visit His 'garden of human beings,' to choose from the 'cream of the crop,' to fetch a rose — a tzaddik, to take along with Him for His garden in Heaven ... a friend ... a dear friend.*

"*... We learned from his deeds, from his uprightness, from his beauty. He was*

---

34. The description of the *levayah* is based on an account written by Rabbi Yaakov Bender shortly after his father's *petirah*. It was estimated then that over 5,000 people attended, an exceptionally large crowd considering the suddenness of the news and the size of the Jewish community.

35. The *maspidim* were: Rabbi Dovid Lifshitz, Rabbi Moshe Feinstein, Rabbi Yaakov Kamenetsky, Rabbi Shneur Kotler, Rabbi Shmuel Brudny, Rabbi Yosef Shapiro, Rabbi Yosef Dovid Epstein, and Rabbi Mendel Kravitz.

36. *Shir HaShirim* 6:2.

*a marbitz Torah, a disseminator of Torah and a pillar of Torah in Yeshivas Torah Vodaath, the Rosh Yeshivah, the principal for many years …*

*"Reb Dovid, a modest and humble soul, did not have to flee from honor, for he did not know what honor was. He did not have to guard his tongue from evil, for he did not comprehend evil. Reb Dovid was a man of truth … of purity … of shalom …*

*"We were in Mirrer Yeshivah together, 'ashrei ayin ra'asah kol eileh — how lucky were those who saw all of it!' … Torah that brings yiras Shamayim, Torah that brings faith, Torah that brings out the middos of Hashem. The spirit of Torah, that is what the Mirrer Yeshivah was about! Lucky are you, Reb Dovid, for having acquired the essential qualities of Yeshivas Mir! Lucky are you that the praise given at your eulogy is that you are a true Mirrer talmid. Not a former student, no! You preserved the light to your last day. For 25 years you retained the sanctity and splendor of a Mirrer talmid!"*[37]

LOUD WAILING AND CRYING ACCOMPANIED THE HEARTFELT *HESPEDIM*. Rabbi Ezriel Lange delivered the *hazkorah*. From the *beis medrash* on 206 Wilson Street, they accompanied the *aron* until they arrived at the Old Mesivta on Bedford Avenue. Hundreds of people on foot, and over 40 cars, came to a halt in front of the building where Reb Dovid had guided and nurtured thousands of *talmidim*. They recited two chapters of *Tehillim* and continued.

ESTHER WAS DAZED, EXHAUSTED, AND DRAINED. MECHANICALLY, SHE walked where she was told to walk, and rode where she was told to ride. Suddenly, they stopped.

*What now?* she thought. She turned to the woman beside her, confused. "Why are we here? Why are we stopping?" Her voice sounded a bit shrill, even to her own ears. "Don't you see?" Mrs. Deutch pointed toward a famous apartment. "The Satmar Rebbe asked that the *aron* pass his house so that he could be *melaveh* the *aron*."

An unusual honor for an unusual person.[38]

THEY FINALLY ARRIVED AT THE OLD MONTEFIORE CEMETERY ON Springfield Boulevard. The sun shone through the nippy fall weather, as if it were oblivious to their sorrow. The boys said *Kaddish* and Rabbi Elazar Tarshish recited the *hazkorah* again.

---

37. Excerpted from the *hesped* said by Rabbi Zelig Epstein at the *shloshim*.

38. Many years later people still recall the great honor that the Satmar Rebbe asked that the *aron* pass his home so that he could be *melaveh*. Several people who were interviewed mentioned this.

"... 'SHEHAYU OSIM SHUROS SHUROS SAVIV HA'AVEL L'NACHAMO b'shuvam min hakever — ... and they make two lines surrounding the mourner to comfort him when he comes back from the kever.' 'Sheha'avel oveir beineihem v'omrim lo HaMakom y'nachamecha — so that the mourner passes between them, and they say to him, the Almighty should comfort you ...' "

Barely 15 hours earlier, Reb Dovid had quoted that very halachah. It was the last piece of Torah that he learned before greeting his Maker. Hours later, his family was following those very laws.

BLUMIE STILL COULD NOT BELIEVE IT. THE SCREAMS AND CRIES OF THE night before echoed in her ears. When she closed her eyes, she saw her father lying on the floor as Reb Eliezer Shmuel Noe, their third floor tenant, frantically tried to administer CPR. He lay over her father, his hands on his chest, and tried once again, and again. Her mother was crying ... she was crying ... the world was crying.

SHMUEL SHOLOM LAY IN BED THAT NIGHT WITH IMAGES OF THE LAST 24 hours filling his mind. The paramedics had arrived within minutes, lights flashing and sirens blaring. They rushed with a ready stretcher and trooped out, the stretcher still empty. They would not be taking anyone to the hospital; there was nothing to be done. A woman's grief-laden wail pierced the silent darkness of the night, *"Ober, vos vet zein mit di kinder?* (What will be with the children?)"

*What will be with us?* thought Shmuel Sholom.

THE WEEK OF *SHIVAH* PASSED IN A BLUR. CONSTANT PEOPLE, CONSTANT conversation. R' Yud'l Gordon burst into the house crying hysterically. He had not heard about the *levayah* until it was all over.[39] He was numb with grief and could not stop crying. Though the Bender children knew that their father had many friends, they were moved by how many people were truly broken by their father's passing.

People told of Reb Dovid's great deeds, hidden and revealed. They spoke of his love of learning, his powerful *shmuessen*, his dedication to his *talmidim*, his many acts of *chessed*, his love of mitzvos, and on and on. Sometimes, to create a time frame, someone would mention a particular event, like the infamous blackout. "Blackout?" Rebbetzin Bender shook her head sadly. "That was a blackout? That was not a blackout. This is a blackout."

---

39. Many people came to the *shivah* saying they had not heard about the *levayah* since Reb Dovid had been *niftar* in the middle of the night and the *levayah* was early afternoon — unusually quick.

So many visitors came, a constant stream of faces.[40] Two faces stood out. Mrs. Leiberman and Mrs. Leviton sat opposite Rebbetzin Bender and their tears flowed. Who would have thought that a mere few hours after visiting these two widows, Rebbetzin Bender would join their ranks? "I am sure," one of the women said, "that he came to us that evening to take back regards to our husbands." Rebbetzin Bender nodded. Certainly, the *neshamah* must have known.

"HOW IS YOUR FATHER-IN-LAW TAKING IT?" WAS A CONSTANT REFRAIN.

"We have not told him," Rebbetzin Bender always replied. "If we can keep it from him until after *shloshim*, he will not have to sit *shivah*. It is difficult enough for us, but for him … an older person … to sit *shivah* alone … and he just finished sitting *shivah* for Tante Ettel … now to sit *shivah* for an only child …" More words were unnecessary.

THE FIRST SHABBOS AFTER *SHIVAH*, ESTHER (BENDER) EPSTEIN AND HER family stayed in Brooklyn. *Leil Shabbos*, Esther heard a whistle as she lay in bed. *I'm sure it's nothing,* she told herself. Yet she whispered to her husband, "Chaim, I heard something strange. Maybe you should go downstairs and check." Reb Chaim met Paltiel on the landing. Paltiel felt cold and he wanted to go downstairs to see if any of the windows had been left open. He was grateful for Reb Chaim's presence. The two went downstairs together.

Esther had been right and wrong. She had heard a whistle, but it was not "nothing." One thief had been signaling to his partner as they made their escape. The entire dining room was turned over. Every sefer was taken out and opened, as if someone had looked through each one to see if it contained any money. In the coat closet, every garment had been searched and every pocket had been turned inside out.

The pushkes and plates that were in the house during the *shivah* were taken. Before Shabbos, Rebbetzin Bender had sent the $150 that had been collected for Keren HaYeled to Rabbi Godlevsky[41] who lived on the next block. This was the only collection that was not stolen. Everything else — money, jewelry, almost anything moveable — was taken. Many things taken had sentimental value, but little monetary value. Blumie's watch was taken. The watch Reb Dovid had bought for his wife in honor of their 25th anniversary was taken. Even Reb Dovid's Indian Head penny collection, a

---

40. Among those who came daily was Dr. Naftoli Hertz Burstyn. His mother lived in the building next door to the Old Mesivta. One day, while Reb Dovid was in his office, he noticed a fire next door. He jumped from his chair, ran next door, forced open the door, and ran upstairs to get old Mrs. Burstyn. Dr. Burstyn was so grateful to Reb Dovid that he came to the house every day of *shivah*, just to see how Rebbetzin Bender was doing. The *shivah* house was never empty.

41. See Biography Section.

childhood hobby, was taken.[42]

Rebbetzin Bender looked at the disarray and sorrowfully remarked, "When Tatty was alive, this never happened. It was in his *zechus*. Now ..."

Now, life would be very different.

---

42. The next day, Blumie and her mother went to the police station to file a report. The police came to the house, saw what had happened, and said it had taken at least three people three hours to do such a job. Rebbetzin Bender was not terribly upset about the monetary loss; the loss of the *tzedakah* money and the feeling of vulnerability bothered her.

*Chapter Fifty-Three*

# Acceptance

**Eretz Yisroel:
29th of Cheshvan 5726 (November 24, 1965)**

RABBI AVROHOM BENDER WAS WORRIED. A WEEK HAD PASSED and he had not received a letter from Dovid. Most weeks he received at least three letters, if not four. This week, none. He met Shimshy and Avner Pincus[43] in B'nei Brak on Shabbos and asked them if they had heard any news from America. They did not tell him anything special. His nephew, Reb Shloimke,[44] made little of his concern, as did Reb Eli Ber.[45]

Another few days passed and now Reb Avrohom was really nervous. He traveled to Yerushalayim, ostensibly to visit friends but actually to pump them for information. There too, he left clueless. Either nothing was wrong, or there was a conspiracy to keep something from him.

He decided to call America. He did not own a phone and a trans-Atlantic phone call was prohibitively expensive. So Reb Avrohom went to B'nei Brak to call from Reb Shloimke's house.

---

43. Rabbi Shimshon Pincus (see Biography Section) and *ybdl"ch* Rabbi Avner Pincus were good friends of the family.

44. Rabbi Shloimke Berman had consulted his father-in-law, the Steipler, as to how to deal with the situation. Reb Avrohom was 83 years old and had recently lost his second wife. His family was afraid that news of his only son's death would give him a heart attack. The Steipler agreed that they should try to keep the news from Reb Avrohom until after the *shloshim* so that he would not have to sit *shivah*.

45. Rabbi Eli Ber Wachtfogel.

"Basha?"

"Papa," Rebbetzin Bender answered, "how good of you to call."

"Basha, what is happening? I have not had a letter from Dovid in days. Is he feeling well?"

Rebbetzin Bender chose her words carefully. "There has been a bit of a problem … Dovid has not been well …"

"What is wrong? Tell me!"

Rebbetzin Bender was determined to keep herself composed. She would not allow herself to slip and say something to alarm her father-in-law, no matter how broken she was feeling. "It is his heart. Don't worry, Papa, he is under good care. *B'ezras Hashem*, everything will be for the good."

They spoke for a few minutes and then hung up. Rebbetzin Bender breathed a sigh of relief. The first phone call had gone reasonably well. She hoped that her father-in-law was reassured. How much longer could they put off telling him?

"Basha?"

"Yes, Papa. How are you?" Rebbetzin Bender was thinking frantically. What would she say this time? He had been calling every day, sometimes several times a day, and she was having a difficult time answering his questions. It was taking almost superhuman effort to put up a good front. The *shloshim* would be over in two days, if she could only keep it from him until then.

"Basha? Basha? I can't hear you. Tell me, how is Dovid doing?"

"Dovid is still not feeling well."

"Let me speak to him. I need to speak to him."

"He is very weak …"

"Basha, I want to speak to him."

"He is not here …"

"Where is he?"

"We called the ambulance to take him to the hospital …"

"He should call me from the hospital. Tell him that I want to speak to him."

"I don't think that that will be possible."

"I am coming to America right now. I am getting the next available flight. Tell him that I am coming."

"But Papa," Rebbetzin Bender said, fighting her tears, "you won't even be able to see him …"

"I don't care if I will have to stand across the street and gaze at the window of his room. I am coming."

"But Papa …"

"Please understand, Basha. I want to be near my son. Even in a building across the street from the hospital, I will still be nearer to him there than I am here."

Rebbetzin Bender composed herself. "I understand, Papa, I understand."

She hung up the telephone, shaking from emotion. They would have to break it to him now, before he traveled halfway across the world to see a son who was no longer here. It would have to be done in person, by someone on hand to give him comfort. She would speak to Reb Shloimke when her father-in-law was not around. He would know what to do.[46]

REB AVROHOM STARED AHEAD, SPEECHLESS WITH SHOCK. REB Shloimke was there, as well as other family members. He looked from one face to the next and realized they had known all along.

The room was silent. Reb Avrohom took off his shoes and sat down on the floor. Then he motioned to everyone in the room. "Gather around me," he said softly. "I have something to tell you."

Everyone in the room inched a bit closer. "Fifty years ago, almost exactly, my Dovid'l was very sick. He was 3 years old … he was so sick, he almost died. And then *HaKadosh Baruch Hu*, in His infinite mercy, saved him. He gave me a present … *HaKadosh Baruch Hu* gave me the most precious, undeserved present. He gave me back my Dovid'l for 50 years, 50 wonderful precious years. Do you have any idea how much *nachas* I have had from my Dovid? Do you have any idea how much *nachas* I have had from his beautiful children, my precious grandchildren? I must thank the *Ribbono shel Olam* for the tremendous good He has given me, the tremendous *berachos* He has showered upon me …"[47] Reb Avrohom continued on and on, for half an hour, without shedding a tear.

Then he stopped. "I think that I have expressed my *hakaras hatov* to the *Eibeshter*. I think that you can now appreciate what I have lost. Now I can cry."[48]

And then he broke down and cried.

FOR THE NEXT WEEK, REB AVROHOM SAT *SHIVAH*, ALONE. TO ALL THOSE who came to comfort him, he repeated his thanks to the *Ribbono shel Olam*. Over and over, he repeated how grateful he was for those precious 50 years. Had his son not recovered from his illness when he was 3, all those

---

46. Reb Shloimke told Rabbi Yaakov Bender that he had summoned all the family and close friends in Eretz Yisroel and a nurse to be present when they told Reb Avrohom the news.

47. Although he could not have known it, his words echoed the last *shmuess* Reb Dovid had given his *talmidim*. There, Reb Dovid had spoken about the Ksav Sofer, focusing not on his untimely death, but on the gift of 50 years of life.

48. Rabbi Yaakov Bender, in his *hesped* on his grandfather, repeated what he heard from Rabbi Shloimke Berman.

years would have been lost. Rather than cry and complain over why his son was taken from him at such a young age, Reb Avrohom only reiterated how special a gift he had merited for 50 years.

He thanked Reb Eli Ber for keeping the news from him. When he had finally heard the truth, it was not a shock. By then, he was ready to accept Hashem's will with love.

WHEN *SHIVAH* ENDED IT WAS TIME TO ASSESS THE SITUATION. LETTERS flew back and forth between Eretz Yisroel and America. Reb Avrohom wanted to be near his grandchildren, so they would not have to grow up without a father figure. He wanted to help replace what they had lost.

Six months later, Rabbi Avrohom Bender was on a plane to America.

# Book III

# Part I:
# **Going Forward**
## 5725-5735 / 1965-1975

Unless otherwise noted, the Bender family provided most of the information in this section. Letters have been translated and condensed. Excerpts from the *hespedim* were taken from tape recordings.

*Chapter Fifty-Four*

# Mourning

> *"… She was at her best when she had Reb Dovid, ztz"l. She was his eizer k'negdo. She helped him in his learning and in his avodas hakodesh. This is the legacy that she passed on to her students, and it is her greatest merit."*[1]

ITH ALL REBBETZIN BENDER'S ACCOMPLISHMENTS, THE crown she most proudly wore was that of wife and mother. She would always feel that something was missing without her husband at her side. Tears formed in her eyes every Shabbos and every Yom Tov. The children once thought that singing their father's favorite song *"Ah Succaleh"* would cheer her up. The song produced the opposite effect and they never again sang it in their mother's presence.

After that fateful night, Rebbetzin Bender could not sleep in her bedroom — the room where her husband had passed away. Right after *shivah*, the children dismantled his bed and she moved into the boys' room. The huge boys' room looked empty with four beds, a closet, and a desk. Yankel moved back home and attended the Mirrer Yeshivah, but Paltiel returned to Woodridge. There was still plenty of room for another person.

Since the Bender children were afraid to keep windows open at night after the robbery, they bought their mother a Fedder's air conditioner. When Rebbetzin Bender saw the gift, she cried bitter tears. "When Tatty was alive, we had no air conditioner. Now I should have one?" There were so many things to keep his memory fresh. Reb Dovid had kept

---

1. Rabbi Zelig Epstein in his *hesped* for Rebbetzin Bender.

meticulous records on little scraps of paper tucked in his billfold: $10 for a widow to pay her son's tuition, $20 for a struggling Torah scholar who needed a loan, $50 for *hachnosas kallah*. Rebbetzin Bender went through the many pledges and saw to it that all of her husband's commitments were met.

There were more *hespedim* on the *shloshim*.[2] Rebbetzin Wachtfogel came over the day after *shivah* to take her to school. For weeks, Rabbi Zelig Epstein stopped in every day to see how she was doing. Rabbi Ezriel Lange and Rabbi Aharon Kreiser were frequent visitors, as were the Litmanowitzes, the Rottenbergs, and others.

Although many kind people tried to comfort her, it seemed as if Rebbetzin Bender's tears would never dry up.

" 'Yofeh at babayis — how beautiful you are in your home!' Anyone who walked through the door of his home was witness to the beauty of his bearing and regal manner of conduct with his family. Chazal tell us that the walls and possessions will testify at the final judgment in the 'Days to Come.' The walls of Reb Dovid's home and all his possessions bear witness to his sanctity and holiness, his love and his fear, all of which his home has absorbed.

" 'Yofeh at basadeh — how beautiful you are in the field!' And so was Reb Dovid when he stepped out of the confines of his home. His bein adam l'chaveiro, the way he honored others, his friendliness, the way he loved everyone, the way he dealt with another's money, his honesty, can never be fully appreciated.

" 'Yofeh at l'Olam Hazeh — how beautiful you are in this world!' Even in our world of falsehood, of false ethics and values, Reb Dovid's personality stood out. Anyone who saw him recognized his true caliber. How much more so in the World of Truth.

" 'Yofeh at l'Olam Haba — how beautiful you are in the World to Come!' "[3]

RABBI ZELIG EPSTEIN'S CRIES CEASED ABRUPTLY. YANKEL PUSHED AWAY the tape recorder on the chair beside his bed, flipped onto his back, and stared at the ceiling. Would the pain ever go away? Did he want the pain to go away? Would letting go of the pain mean losing the already fading memories he still had of his father? Every picture, every scrap of his handwriting, every tribute written to his father's memory was precious.

He pulled over the scrapbook that he had made, slowly leafing through its pages. First were his own impressions of his father: his father's roots,

---

2. Rabbi Nosson Horowitz, Rabbi Yisroel Chaim Kaplan, Rabbi Shmuel Brudny, and Rabbi Avrohom Pincus spoke in Rabbi Nosson Horowitz's shul. Rabbi Yaakov Kamenetsky, Rabbi Yosef Dovid Epstein, and Rabbi Zelig Epstein spoke in Torah Vodaath.

3. Rabbi Zelig Epstein paraphrasing the *Midrash Shir HaShirim* in his *hesped* at the *shloshim* of Rabbi Dovid Bender.

There was his father as a young man ...

... as young newlyweds ...

... joyous on Purim ...

... at the head table of the Torah Vodaath melaveh malkah hosted in his honor ...

*Reb Dovid holding a grandchild*

*middos*, diligence in learning, *kibud av*, *gemilas chessed*, and ultimately, his *levayah*. Then he had the cover pages of the different publications dedicated to his father's memory: *The Scroll* — Torah Vodaath's eighth-grade yearbook; *Torah Ohr* — the Mesivta journal of *chiddushei Torah*; *HaPardes*;[4] and the Bais Yaakov Seminary weekly newsletter. Yankel included the first statement sent out by the yeshivah to the parents and the flier hung by the Mirrer Minyan announcing *hespedim*. He collected photos. There was his father as a young man, as a *chosson* posing with his *kallah*, as a young father with his children, joyous on Purim, at the wedding of his daughter, at the head table of the Torah Vodaath *melaveh malkah* hosted in his honor ...

Yankel's eyes were moist as he stared at the next picture. His father was holding his first grandchild. How clearly Yankel remembered his father's joy when Yitzchok Isaac was born. It was as if he had received a gift of inestimable value. When Esther asked her father what to name her child, his first thought was of his own father, and how thrilled Reb Avrohom

---

4. A Torah journal edited by Rabbi Simcha Elberg.

would be to have a grandson named for his father. Hence the name given was Yitzchok Isaac, after Reb Dovid's paternal grandfather.

Overcome by emotion, Yankel closed the scrapbook and stared out into space. Was there any part of his life that did not, in some way, include his father? Was it possible for life to go on without his father?

*Chapter Fifty-Five*

# Zaida Comes to America

### Williamsburg: 5726 (1966)

OME, WE HAVE TO GET MOVING. ZAIDA'S FLIGHT WILL BE arriving in another hour."

Six months had passed since Reb Dovid's *petirah*. Now Reb Avrohom was coming to be with his grandchildren and try to partially fill the terrible void created by his son's passing. For the first time in months, happy anticipation filled the air of the Bender home. Zaida was coming.

"Shmuel Sholom, stop tossing your hat up and down. It will be a *shmatta* by the time we reach the airport. Michoel, you can take the sefer with you. Let's just get moving." Paltiel was impatient. He had come from Woodridge for the occasion and was itching to go.

As the Benders piled into the car, Rebbetzin Bender's eyes misted over as she remembered her most recent trip to the airport. She had gone to greet her husband when he returned from his visit in Eretz Yisroel with his father. Reb Dovid had gone to honor his father; now his father was coming to support her over the loss of his son. She needed that support, especially now that Shmuel Sholom's bar mitzvah was only a few weeks away.

She looked back and could not fathom how she had survived all the painful months since her husband's death. Daily, she stoically faced the challenge of a new day without him. The smile on her face was a shadow of her former smile. Nonetheless, it was a smile, and she did it for him, for their children, and for *kavod Shamayim*. The year of *aveilus*, though not halachically imposed, allowed her to be anonymous, slightly removed from society. She could sit out a *simchah* and save herself the emotional energy of putting on a happy front. Her friends were understanding and sympathetic; they recognized her need for time to adjust.

That was fine until Shmuel Sholom's bar mitzvah. Suddenly, there was nowhere to hide. She had not known what to do. The children were *aveilim*. Should she make Shmuel Sholom a small quiet affair or something larger? She asked Rabbi Yaakov Kamenetsky. "It is enough that he does not have a father," Reb Yaakov advised. "Make him a nice bar mitzvah."

Rebbetzin Bender was conscious of the struggle to get herself moving. *Come foot, lift up, one foot, two feet, forward march. Shmuel Sholom needs a hat. Yes, I know, we already bought him a hat, Tatty and I, together, last year just before … but it was stolen in that awful robbery. Come hand, lift the receiver, call the caterer, we need to make a seudah. Yes, I know, Tatty and I were planning this last year together, building castles in the air, and now it is only me, alone …* Every step was an effort; every move brought back memories.

Most painful of all was imagining the *seudah* itself. For whom would she be dressing up? How would she feel standing alone to greet family and friends? She pictured her youngest son sitting at the head table without his father by his side. She was grateful that her father-in-law was coming in time for the bar mitzvah.

The bar mitzvah *seudah* was held in the Kaminetzer Yeshivah in Woodridge, New York.[5] The conspicuous absence of Reb Dovid made the *seudah* especially poignant. Rabbi Shneur Kotler spoke, as did Rabbi Avrohom Bender and the bar mitzvah *bochur*. Rabbi Zelig Epstein and Rabbi Levi Krupenia sat up front while family and friends crowded the dining room. All that Blumie could remember was the concentration she exerted to avoid looking at the head table, where her little brother sat without her father.

On Shabbos, Rebbetzin Bender made a *kiddush* in Greenwald's bungalow colony, where the family was spending the summer. Many residents were longtime friends of the Benders, and the whole colony attended. The *simchah* was bittersweet. Yet Rebbetzin Bender was determined to make it a joyous affair, and she succeeded. It was not a mindless or frenetic event, but rather a calm and tranquil joy that softly whispered, "Life must go on."

TIME PASSED. THEIR ZAIDA'S PRESENCE WAS TRULY A COMFORT TO

---

5. The Kaminetzer Yeshivah was originally in Boro Park. A wealthy man donated his hotel in the Catskills to the yeshivah, and the yeshivah moved part of its staff and students over to Woodridge. For a short time, the hotel was used both for the yeshivah and for summer guests. Paltiel Bender attended the yeshivah, and later Michoel and Shmuel Sholom did as well. One summer the Benders patronized the hotel as summer guests. Eventually, the yeshivah closed down the Woodridge branch, for it was too expensive to maintain two locations.

Shmuel Sholom's bar mitz-
vah. The bar mitzvah bochur
is flanked by his grandfather
on one side and Rabbi Shneur
Kotler on the other side. When
tragedy befell the Bender home,
the Lakewood Rosh Yeshivah
was at the family's side, first
as one of the maspidim at Reb
Dovid's levayah and then as a
comforting presence at Shmuel
Sholom's bar mitzvah.

*Rabbi Shneur Kotler (1918-1982) learned in Kletzk and Kaminetz
and then in Eretz Yisroel under his grandfather, Rabbi Isser Zalman
Meltzer. He succeeded his father, Rabbi Aharon Kotler, as Rosh
Yeshivah of Bais Medrash Govoha of Lakewood. Under Reb Shneur's
leadership the yeshivah grew almost tenfold.*

the Bender Family. Zaida was over 80 years old and had already sat *shivah*
for many family members. Yet he stood tall and proud, unwilling to allow
tragedy to break him. He never spoke about his own pain over losing his
precious son; he was there to comfort, not to be comforted. The Bender
children saw in their grandfather a man who pushed himself to do whatever he felt the *Ribbono shel Olam* wanted from him.

In all the years he lived with his grandchildren, they never saw him
sad or depressed. He strode through life vigorously, always motivated,
always accomplishing, even as his strength waned. In the summers
when he joined his grandchildren in the mountains, he went back to his
"Catskill Route," collecting money for yeshivos, and then contributing
the percentage he earned to worthy causes. On Tishah B'Av, he asked his
grandson-in-law, Rabbi Chaim Epstein, to bring him some rocks to put
under his head at night as is brought down in *Shulchan Aruch*.[6] Although
this is a practice few people follow, Zaida lived his life by his own exact-

---

6. *Orach Chaim* 555:2.

Friends of Rabbi Dovid Bender at his son's bar
mitzvah:
Rabbi Ezriel Lange, Rabbi Avrohom Aharon Sere-
browsky, Rabbi Pinchas Litmanowitz, Rabbi Spitz

Rabbi Avrohom Bender with his grandchildren at
Shmuel Sholom's bar mitzvah

ing standards.

Zaida was always thinking about others by anticipating their needs, reactions, and feelings. One day Zaida asked Paltiel to sit beside him with a pen and paper. "Come," he said, "let's make a list of all the people who came to greet me when I arrived from Eretz Yisroel this summer. Truthfully, these things mean very little to me. What difference does it make how many people came? But you have to understand, every person who came thought about me, an elderly man who had just lost his only child. They wanted to show how much they cared. They wanted to alleviate my pain. I barely noticed the crowd. But they deserve recognition for their efforts and when the opportunity arises, I want to be able to thank each and every one individually."

Zaida never allowed himself to become hostage to his feelings and emotions, but when it came to others, he empathized entirely. An acquaintance of his was in the hospital, in tremendous pain, and Zaida went to visit. Indeed, the man was suffering. Zaida sat beside his bed and cried along with him, tears pouring down his cheeks, as if he were suffering the same pain. This was just what his friend needed: true, heartfelt empathy.

Most amazing was how Zaida allowed himself to cry uncontrollably over his sick friend's pain during a hospital visit, but when the *shivah* for his beloved son was over, he never again publicly shed another tear over his loss. Crying over his son would have been crying over himself, which was something he would not do. Crying over his friend's pain was fulfill-

*Rabbi Avrohom Bender, rejoicing at his grandson Yankel's wedding*

ing the Will of his Creator.

Many times Zaida was up late, going through his papers, making calculations, and learning. Suddenly, the children would hear him call out from his room, "*Ribbono shel Olam*, thank you for all the many *berachos* you shower upon me. You gave me a wonderful son, beautiful grandchildren, even great-grandchildren. You give me *parnassah*, opportunities for *chessed* and *harbotzas haTorah*. Your kindness to me is endless."

These declarations of happiness and heartfelt gratitude might be puzzling to anyone who was aware of the many severe challenges that Reb Avrohom faced during his life. To begin with, he was orphaned young and poverty dominated his childhood. Then he was sent off to learn and fend for himself when he was only 12 years old. As a *bochur*, he was ill and could not learn for a period of time. He was happily married but lost a 10-month-old daughter. He and his wife finally had a son after 11 years of marriage. When was life easy? How was he able to see only the blessings?

Zaida understood that living according to the Will of Hashem meant that his emotions would not rule him. That was why he became such a powerful fixture in the Bender home. If he did not question or doubt, how could they? If he did not allow his emotions to overcome him, how could they? If he could remain strong, so would they.

*Chapter Fifty-Six*

# A Trip to Eretz Yisroel

**Fallsburg: 5727 (1967)**

*Shmuel Sholom stood at the side of the road and watched the cars whiz
by. He lifted his sleeve to mop the sweat dripping from his brow. "I'll be
burnt to a crisp before I get a hitch," he thought. Then a car of frum people
approached, and Shmuel Sholom flagged it down. Three-quarters of a mile
later, they deposited him again on the side of the road; his hitch was going in
a different direction. To top off his misfortune, he tore his plastic bag as he
was getting out of the car, and his socks, underwear, and pajamas spilled out
along the side of Fallsburg Road. Shmuel Sholom took a deep breath and collected his belongings. He bunched them together in his bathrobe, slung the
makeshift sack over his shoulder, and began the two-mile hike to the bungalow colony. "Boy, I hope Mommy and Blumie are having a better time than
I am," he thought to himself.[7]*

AT PRECISELY THAT MOMENT, A THOUSAND MILES AWAY,
Rebbetzin Bender and Blumie were ushering in Shabbos. It
was their fourth week in Eretz Yisroel and Rebbetzin Bender
still could not believe that she was there.

A YEAR AFTER HER HUSBAND'S PASSING, REBBETZIN BENDER WAS STILL
preoccupied with her grieving, and her children were concerned. Although
she put up a good front, her family knew better. They decided to cheer her
up.

---

7. Adapted from a letter Rabbi Shmuel Sholom Bender wrote to his mother.

They waited until summer vacation, when their mother was relaxing in the country. Then, one day, the children surprised her with a brand-new suitcase and a round-trip ticket to Eretz Yisroel. Rebbetzin Bender was aghast. She protested at the expense and trouble and besides, she was sure that her passport expired. Her children laughed, for they had expected her reaction. Yankel and Michoel hastily threw some things into the suitcase, coaxed her into the car, and kept up a lively chatter as they drove to the city. After a short stop at the passport office, they went to Williamsburg to pack. This is how she felt herself whisked off to Eretz Yisroel with her daughter Blumie to keep her company.

This trip would be Rebbetzin Bender's first flying experience, but that was not what was on her mind as she buckled her seatbelt. She had not seen her brother Yosef in 33 years. In a few hours they would meet.

YOSEF EPSTEIN KEPT CHECKING HIS WATCH; HIS SISTER AND HER daughter would be landing any minute. He paced back and forth in the waiting room. His children noticed his excitement and were concerned. Yosef had a heart condition and they were afraid that seeing his sister after all this time might be a strain. Yosef paused, lost in thought. *So many years have passed. Will we recognize each other?* He checked his watch again.

"THANK YOU FOR FLYING WITH US AND HAVE A NICE VISIT." THE STEW-ardesses nodded and smiled to each one of the passengers as they deplaned. "Watch your step," cautioned the co-pilot. Rebbetzin Bender barely noticed the pleasantries. How many more minutes until she would see him? A gush of hot air struck her full in the face as she went cautiously down the steps. Whew, it was sticky. The Tel Aviv humidity was a stark contrast to the air-conditioned airplane. She continued her descent, another step, and then another until her feet were finally touching the holy soil of Eretz Yisroel.

YOSEF CRANED HIS NECK. AS PASSENGER AFTER PASSENGER EMERGED, Yosef wondered if perhaps he had the wrong flight information and she was not on this flight after all.

And then suddenly, there she was.

For that moment, it was as if nothing else existed, just the two of them at the center of the whole world. They did not hear the cries of joy as family members greeted one another, they were oblivious to the hugs and kisses exchanged around them, they were blind to the traffic of people coming and going. They saw only each other and that was enough. For several minutes they just stood there, the tears running down their cheeks.

"Yosef," Rebbetzin Bender whispered.

"Basha," Yosef replied shakily.

There would be time for everything else later.

AT THE PLAIN WOODEN TABLE IN THE SMALL KITCHEN ON 6 PETERSON Street in Tel Aviv, brother and sister whiled away hours in pleasant companionship. There was so much to catch up on. Their regular letters back and forth had kept them in touch, but the written word could never replace the pleasure of being together. Rebbetzin Bender was content to sit in her brother's home and relax in his company.

Yosef was eager to show his sister around. "Come," he urged, "come visit Reb Shloimke and his family. They are waiting to see you. From there, we can go to Rabbi Shabsi Yogel, and ..."

"Wait," Rebbetzin Bender laughed, "do they all know I am here?"

"Of course! I have posted signs on the streets and ads in the newspapers," he teased. "What do you think I have been doing from the moment I heard that you were coming?"

Rebbetzin Bender laughed again. She had not laughed like this in a very long time.

REBBETZIN BENDER FOUND NEW LIFE AND ENERGY IN HER WEEKS IN Eretz Yisroel. There were so many people who she wanted to visit, places she wanted to see. Her base was her cousins, the Bermans of B'nei Brak. Rebbetzin Bender was grateful that Yosef understood she would be more comfortable staying in B'nei Brak than in Tel Aviv.

Rabbi Shloimke Berman and his rebbetzin welcomed the Benders warmly and accompanied them to their sleeping quarters at Rabbi Chaim Berman's apartment. Reb Shloimke had a houseful of children and he felt that Rebbetzin Bender and Blumie would be more comfortable staying by his brother. He encouraged them to return to his home for meals and conversation.

REBBETZIN BENDER AND BLUMIE ENJOYED WALKING THROUGH THE streets of B'nei Brak. How fortunate they were to be in this city of scholars! They knocked at the door of Rav Shach's house.

"Oh, look who's here," Rav Shach called out. He led Rebbetzin Bender into a room where Rebbetzin Shach sat in bed. "Guttel, look!"

Rebbetzin Shach was bedridden since her leg had been amputated, and she could not rise to greet her guests. But her eyes lit up in pleasure at seeing her old friend. Decades had passed since their days in Minsk when Guttel Gilomovsky had been a favored boarder in the Epstein home.[8] Guttel had married Rav Shach and accompanied him to Kletzk and eventually to Eretz Yisroel. Little Basha had moved to Otvock, attended Bais Yaakov,

---

8. See page 109.

married Rabbi Dovid Bender, followed him to Mir, and then moved
to America.

In an emotional meeting in that
small apartment, life came full circle.
Rebbetzin Bender and Rebbetzin
Shach had trekked across continents
and ended up on opposite ends of the
world, making their marks in their
respective countries. Forty years had
passed since their days together in
Minsk, and now the two friends were
meeting again.

Rebbetzin Bender took Blumie
with her to meet Rabbi Chatzkel Levenstein, the *Mashgiach* of Ponevezh
Yeshivah whom she had met in Mir
and again in America. Reb Chatzkel's

*Rav Shach*

daughter, Rebbetzin Ginsburg, brought out refreshments, and Reb Chatzkel
spent close to an hour speaking with Rebbetzin Bender about how she was
managing. When she was ready to leave, he walked her to the door. Rebbetzin Bender was overcome by the warmth and honor he showed her.

Rebbetzin Bender went back and forth from B'nei Brak and the Bermans
to her brother and his family in Tel Aviv. On one of her trips to Tel Aviv, she
visited Rabbi Michel Feinstein, a son-in-law of the Brisker Rav. The Brisker
Rav considered the Epsteins family and his children upheld this tradition.
Blumie marveled at the lavish *fleishige* meal that Rebbetzin Lifsha Feinstein
prepared for her guests.

AT EVERY PHASE OF HER TRIP, THE BERMANS WERE ON HAND TO HELP.
Rebbetzin Ahuva Berman took them to her parents' house to meet her
father, the Steipler Gaon. When Rebbetzin Bender wanted to spend some
time in Yerushalayim, Reb Shloimke helped her plan an itinerary. He also
arranged their stay with his brother-in-law and sister, Rabbi Rephael and
Bluma Wexelbaum, of Bayit Vegan.

The streets, the sounds, and the sights of Yerushalayim were so different
than those of B'nei Brak. In the summer of 1967, the streets of Yerushalayim
were still littered with leftover tanks. Although more than a month had
passed, people continued to marvel at the miraculous victory of the Six Day
War and the recapture of neighborhoods of Yerushalayim. The excitement
refused to dissipate. Rebbetzin Bender and Blumie joined the thousands of
*Yidden* who made their way to the Kosel in the summer of 1967. People

Left to right: Rabbi Shaul Barzam, Rav Shach, the Ponevezher Rav, the chosson Rabbi Rephael Wexelbaum, behind the chosson is Rabbi Avrohom Bender, partially blocked is Rabbi Dovid Povarsky

Rabbi Rephael Wexelbaum (1933-1996) was born in Germany. His family immigrated to Eretz Yisroel in the wake of Kristallnacht. Reb Rephael studied in the yeshivos of Be'er Yaakov, Kol Torah, and Ponevezh. He was a Rosh Yeshivah in Itri Yeshivah Ketanah and then in Yeshivas Beis Yosef in France.

were euphoric to reclaim the privilege of touching its sacred stones.

The Wexelbaums treated Rebbetzin Bender and Blumie royally during their stay in Yerushalayim. Rebbetzin Bender rented a car and Rabbi Rephael Wexelbaum graciously offered to be their guide.

For the next few days, the Benders and the Wexelbaums traveled the length and breadth of Eretz Yisroel. They went to *Me'aras HaMachpeilah*, *Kever Rochel*, and *Kever Yosef HaTzaddik*. The Arabs encountered along the way were still reeling from their recent defeat, and they kept a respectful distance. Reb Rephael drove up to Tzefas, and continued on to the reputed mountains of *Har Gerizim* and *Har Eivel*. Blumie held tightly to her seat as the rickety car pulled up the steep mountains. There was no real road, only a narrow path uphill with no guardrails on either side. Reb Rephael kept up a cheerful monologue while urging the little car upward; Blumie held her hand over her mouth, barely suppressing her frightened screams. They returned from their trip exhausted but content. They still had many visits to make before returning to B'nei Brak.

REBBETZIN BENDER MET WITH HER FRIENDS FROM BAIS YAAKOV OF Crakow, Rebbetzins Tzila Sorotzkin and Batsheva Hutner,[9] and they reminisced about what had happened since they had last learned together in their beloved school. She visited her friends from Mir, the Finkels and the Shmulevitzes. She made the rounds of her relatives, the Brisker family.

---

9. See page 249.

Rebbetzin Bender arrived at the house of Rabbi Yankel Schiff, the Brisker Rav's son-in-law, and knocked at the door. There sat Reb Yankel, his *Gemara* open in front of him, completely engrossed in his learning, with two of his children on his lap. He swayed back and forth in learning, his hands encircling the children, oblivious to everything. The children sat silently on his lap, lulled by the soothing sounds of their father's chant. Rebbetzin Bender stood there silently. So this is how a *talmid chacham* "babysits" his children.

"Basha! You are here already. I am sorry. I had to run out for a moment." Rivka Schiff greeted her cousin warmly. "Come, come inside."

Rebbetzin Bender followed her in, and the two women sat down together. Rebbetzin Bender was still so moved by the scene that she kept speaking about it. "This kind of *hasmadah* is not from today. I remember when your husband was in my husband's *shiur*…"[10] Rebbetzin Schiff smiled, bemused. She was accustomed to the sight that so impressed her cousin. She appreciated that Rebbetzin Bender's awe stemmed from a profound appreciation of *talmidei chachamim*.

REBBETZIN BENDER'S LAST STOP IN YERUSHALAYIM WAS WITH RABBI Berel Soloveitchik, the Brisker Rav's son. Reb Berel remembered her and her family well. They had a long visit, reminiscing about Otvock, recalling her *sheva berachos* and the story of the flowerpot,[11] and remembering family and friends who were no longer alive. It was finally time to leave.

"Family is not *yoitzeh* with just one visit," Reb Berel remarked.

Rebbetzin Bender smiled. "Thank you, but I am staying in B'nei Brak. It is difficult for me to return to Yerushalayim."

Reb Berel shook his head. "I am not saying good-bye."

Rebbetzin Bender left in a quandary. What should she do? She had already said good-bye to the Wexelbaums and would hate to impose upon them again, but she wanted Reb Berel's good wishes. After thinking it over, she decided to stay with the Wexelbaums one more night.

In the morning, she visited Reb Berel once again and then returned to B'nei Brak.

THROUGHOUT HER MONTH-LONG STAY, REBBETZIN BENDER WAS IN constant contact with her brother, Yosef. She stayed with him part of the time, and he took her to visit relatives in other parts of the country. When she had a kidney stone attack, he accompanied her to Dr. Poupko, their old friend and relative.[12] Dr. Poupko was happy to see her and even happier that he was able to relieve her pain.

---

10. See page 283.

11. See page 182.

12. See page 183.

*Rabbi Yosef Dov Soloveitchik (1915-1981), fondly known as Reb Berel, was the eldest son of Rabbi Yitzchok Zev, the Brisker Rav. He served as the Rosh Yeshivah in Yeshivas Brisk in Yerushalayim. He disseminated the legacy of the Brisker Rav by teaching his Kodshim shiurim and spreading his philosophy of yiras Shamayim and adherence to mitzvos. He produced many students who went on to become Torah leaders.*

SHORTLY BEFORE IT WAS TIME TO LEAVE, Reb Shloimke presented a box to Rebbetzin Bender. "Uncle left this here when he moved back to America. I think that you will enjoy it." Rebbetzin Bender opened the box. A sad smile played on her lips. It was a box of photographs. Over the years, they had taken photographs of the children and sent them to Eretz Yisroel for Zaida to enjoy.

The last 20 years of her life, in a box.

"May I see?" Blumie asked.

Rebbetzin Bender handed her the box. Blumie opened the cover. Right on top was a photo she never thought that she would ever see.

*FIVE-YEAR-OLD BLUMIE WAS SITTING cross-legged on the floor, an open box of photos in front of her. Flipping through the photos, she saw one of Esther, sitting on the stoop in Prospect Park. She remembered how her mother had hired Mr. Fish, the photographer, to come along because she thought the park setting would be picturesque. There was Paltiel, also on the stoop, smiling away. But where was she, Blumie?*

*Blumie took out some photos and spread them out on the floor: Esther on the swing, Paltiel on the swing, but ... where was Blumie? As she looked at photo after photo, little Blumie grew more and more agitated. Where were all the photos of her, especially the cute ones from Prospect Park? She remembered the photographer snapping her photo too. What did her parents do with all those photos?*

*Maybe they were at the bottom of the box. She dug deeper and pulled out more baby photos: Esther at 3 months in a cute little stretchy, Esther at 6 months with a bow in her hair, Esther at a year, smiling at the camera, Esther, Esther, Esther! Blumie felt a tantrum brewing. Where were her photos? Didn't her parents think that she was also cute? In frustration, she began ripping the photos one by one. Just then Rebbetzin Bender walked into the room.*

*"Blumie! Vos tust du (what are you doing)?" Rebbetzin Bender looked horrified at the torn photos on the floor. These photos were expensive and irreplaceable. Why was she doing this?*

*Blumie looked guilty but remained silent. She knew exactly why she was doing this. She was jealous of the other children. But how could she say that? Rebbetzin*

*Bender saw that Blumie was embarrassed. She did not want to push her against the wall and force her to answer, and yet something had to be done. Rebbetzin Bender did not deliberate long. She picked up Blumie, gave her a few swift petch, and took away the box of photos.*

NOW, 15 YEARS LATER, THE MYSTERY OF BLUMIE'S MISSING BABY PHOTOS was solved. In this worn cardboard box, right on top, were the photos that Blumie had frantically searched for when she was a 5-year-old child. Tatty must have thought her photos were exceptionally cute, and he had taken them from the family collection and sent them to Zaida. Blumie was stunned by the realization. Only vaguely did she hear her mother and Rebbetzin Berman[13] chatting in the background.

*How wise Mommy was,* Blumie reflected. *She never demanded an explanation for my behavior. Even then, I knew I deserved to be punished but I would have found it terribly humiliating to admit my jealousy. She punished me while still leaving my self-esteem intact.* Blumie's estimation of her mother's good judgment rose one notch higher.

During that month-long trip to Eretz Yisroel, Blumie had learned a lot about her mother. She saw firsthand the tremendous *kavod* with which *gedolim* — Rabbi Chatzkel Levenstein, Rav Shach, the Steipler, Rabbi Berel Soloveitchik — greeted her mother. She understood that not every woman is accorded such honor. She saw how her mother conducted herself with dignity regardless of where she was or with whom she was.

As impressed as Blumie was with the reception given her mother in Eretz Yisroel, she was even more impressed by a deeper aspect of her mother's character, which the story of the box of photos revealed. Her mother had respected her dignity, even when she was a young child who misbehaved. Blumie realized that her mother treated everyone with dignity: children, adults, the grocer, the baker, the mailman, and the janitor. Simple people did not receive the reverence that she reserved for *talmidei chachamim*, but they were still treated with respect. She never ordered workers around, nor did she tear down a child with rebuke. People were created in the image of their Creator and deserved to be treated with honor.

Perhaps the honor accorded her by the giants of the generation was due to the honor that she gave others.

---

13. Rebbetzin Bender enjoyed spending time with this wise woman. As the years passed and Rebbetzin Bender heard of the unusual *emunah* and *bitachon* Rebbetzin Berman maintained throughout the difficult twists and turns in her life, her esteem for Rebbetzin Berman continued to rise. She encouraged her children to keep a connection with their cousins in Eretz Yisroel. Rabbi Yaakov Bender happened to be in Eretz Yisroel when Rebbetzin Berman was sitting *shivah* for a son, and he went to be *menachem avel*. "What is there to say?" Reb Yaakov asked with a sigh. Rebbetzin Berman replied with spirit, "What the Creator does is good and what He will do is also good!"

### Chapter Fifty-Seven

# Everyday Events

### Sunday, Parashas Vaeschanan

*Dear Yosef and Sarah,*

*I write this letter to thank you for your warm welcome of my daughter-in-law and einikel. Tell me about the visit. I would love to hear about your beloved guests. What do you have to say about them? You owe us a thank-you for letting them go, while we sit here and long for their return. B"H, next week we will have them back with us. But Yosef, I do not want you to rely on the regards Basya and Blumie will bring with them. Write your own letter. I would love to hear how much you enjoyed them.*

*Shalom,*
*Avrohom*

REBBETZIN BENDER RETURNED HAPPY AND INVIGORATED from her trip to Eretz Yisroel. She and Blumie recalled all the details of the trip over coffee and cake with her family and all her friends from the bungalow colony. The photos and slides of her trip were a hit as everyone was enthralled at seeing the *Kosel, Kever Rochel, Me'aras HaMachpeilah*, and other sites and scenes of the Holy Land.

When the "public viewing" was over, Rebbetzin Bender sat with the children and Zaida and rehashed the stories about all the people that she had seen. Paltiel, Yankel, Michoel, and Shmuel Sholom had read most of the stories in letters, but they were happy to hear them firsthand. Zaida beamed when he saw her old sparkle was back.

Rebbetzin Bender unpacked souvenirs from her trip, commenting on where, when, and why she bought each particular item. "This is something else, special for you, Yankel," she said as she handed him a manila envelope with all the letters he had sent to her folded neatly inside. Thirty-seven letters, one for each day that she was gone (plus one), composing a chronicle of his life for the past month.

"Thank you, Yankel, I enjoyed every last one." Rebbetzin Bender continued, "Everyone sent beautiful letters ... The entire trip was beautiful. Some sights and experiences are so difficult to describe. The warmth with which everyone greeted us, the *berachos* they showered upon us, especially on Blumie ..." Her voice trailed off. They all hoped that the many *berachos* Blumie had received for a good *shidduch* would materialize quickly.

"What can I say?" Rebbetzin Bender explained, "Life there is so different. I would not say that everyone is poor, but everyone lives simply. While sitting on the chairs in Uncle Yosef's house, I realized that the material covering the cushions came from a dress that I sent Aunt Sarah 20 years ago!" She shook her head in disbelief. "They make do with whatever they have, and nothing goes to waste — even regular people, not only *talmidei chachamim.*"

Rebbetzin Bender relived her trip long after she returned. Even though she went right back to her regular routine, snippets from the trip peppered her daily conversation. The Bender children were pleased to observe how the month in Eretz Yisroel had revived their mother.

*Old friends sit together in the bungalow colony. Clockwise from the head of the table: Rabbi Pinchas Litmanowitz, Rabbi Ezriel Lange, Rabbi Yeshaya Wasserman, Rabbi Avrohom Pincus*

*Rabbi Avrohom Pincus and Rabbi Pinchas Litmanowitz*

*Rabbi Hershel (Tzvi Yosef) Wasilski — a beloved rebbi*

"YES, ONE MINUTE PLEASE." BLUMIE balanced the receiver between her ear and her shoulder as she took a pen and paper from the desk. "What is the message? Moishie should come straight home today? What grade did you say? Fifth? Fine, I'll tell him. No problem."

As soon as Blumie hung up the phone, it rang again. "Yeshivah. Yes, I'll put you through." She transferred the call to the principal's office.

"Excuse me …" a kind voice ventured. Rabbi Wasilski, an old family friend and Torah Vodaath's beloved first-grade rebbi, was waiting in the doorway.

"There is a Shapiro family in Pittsburgh … I seem to recall that you are related …?"

"Yes …"

"Is there a boy there of age?"

Blumie was startled. How did he know? Just last night they had received a call from the Shapiros. They were ready to proceed with the *shidduch*.

"Is there?" Rabbi Wasilski pressed gently.

"Yes …"

"I do not mean to upset you, but I felt that I had to tell you about the strange dream that I had last night. Your father came to me and he seemed very agitated. He explained that he is trying very hard to get the youngest boy of the Shapiro family of Pittsburgh. He was getting frustrated because he was finding it very difficult to get to him. It looked like your father was locked up, as if behind prison bars, while he was trying to get this boy. Suddenly, the bars were gone and he was free. Then he smiled and said, 'I'm not worried anymore — I got him.' " Rabbi Wasilski paused.

Blumie did not know how to answer. Luckily, Rabbi Wasilski did not expect a response. With a twinkle in his eyes, he bade her, "*Hatzlochah u'berachah.*"

The rest of the day Blumie had a hard time concentrating on her job. What would her mother say to this unusual dream?

"It is a good sign, Blumie, a good sign. Rabbi Wasilski is a *choshuver Yid*. It is a good sign."

A few weeks later, just before Shavuos, Blumie was engaged to Moshe Shimon Shapiro.

BLUMIE DREAMED OF MARRYING A TRUE *TALMID CHACHAM*, ONE WHOSE only desire in life was to learn Torah. Reb Moshe Shimon was exactly the combination of *talmid chacham* and *masmid* that Blumie had been looking for. The next few weeks were frenetic as Blumie and her mother shopped, cooked, baked, and prepared. The excitement over Blumie's upcoming wedding suffused the house.

That summer they went to Hereshevsky's bungalow colony. Once again they were surrounded by the many familiar faces of their bungalow colony friends. The Langes, Pincuses, and Wassermans were together again. Now the Litmanowitzes joined as well. Rabbi Chaim Levovitz, a Rav from Detroit who had been with the Benders in other colonies, was also in Hereshevsky's. His presence prompted a visit by his revered cousin, Rabbi Moshe Feinstein.

"Did you hear?"

"Hear what?"

"Reb Moshe is coming!"

"Reb Moshe Feinstein? Coming here?"

"Yes! Yes! Reb Moshe is coming here! He is coming to visit Rabbi Chaim Levovitz. Look, all the men are by the Levovitz bungalow waiting. He must be coming soon …"

Rabbi Moshe Feinstein was related to Rabbi Chaim Levovitz and they had both grown up in Luban, Russia. Reb Chaim was an unusual *masmid* and *talmid chacham*. As a young man, he suffered from a stroke and he remained an invalid for the rest of his life. Reb Chaim lived in Detroit and it was not often that he and his relative, Reb Moshe, had occasion to see each other. Every summer, Reb Moshe made at least one visit to Reb Chaim, usually on a Friday afternoon.

A car entered the colony grounds and all heads turned to peer at it. The men who had been standing by the Levovitz bungalow walked slowly toward the approaching vehicle; the children scampered to catch up.

The car came to a stop. All watched as the door opened slowly and the *gadol hador* emerged. His face glowed as he greeted Reb Chaim who had just emerged by wheelchair from his bungalow.

The men pulled up chairs to form a circle in front of the Levovitz bungalow. In the background the children were flitting here and there, trying to find a good angle to snap a picture without getting in the way of the adults.

"*Genug schoen mit di bilder*! (Enough with the pictures!)," one of the men exclaimed, motioning them away. The constant clicking of cameras, the maneuvering in between people, the flashes over and over again, were getting annoying. But not all the children managed to get a shot, and some

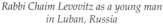
*Rabbi Chaim Levovitz as a young man
in Luban, Russia*

*Rabbi Chaim Levovitz (1908/10-1983) learned in the yeshivah in Slutzk which moved to Kletzk when the Communists took hold of Russia. Reb Chaim went on to the yeshivos of Mir, Grodno, and Radin. As a bochur, he wrote a sefer, entitled Toras Chaim. The sefer included letters of approbation from Rabbi Chaim Ozer Grodzenski, Rabbi Shimon Shkop, and Rabbi Menachem Ziemba. In the United States he served as a Rav in Detroit.*

looked disappointed at being told to stop. Reb Moshe realized that something was amiss.

"What is wrong?" he asked Reb Chaim. "What do the children want? A picture?"

Reb Moshe motioned to the children to come in front of him. He sat up straight in his seat, fixed his tie and closed his *kapole*. "*Nu,* take a picture!" Absolutely delighted, the children snapped away until they ran out of film. Then they dispersed and the adults resumed their conversation.

It was a Friday morning and time was passing. Reb Moshe rose to leave and everyone rose to accompany him. He shook hands with each of the men on his way to the car. The women were standing at the gate of the colony, taking a break from their Erev Shabbos preparations to join in the excitement. As Reb Moshe passed the gate to leave, he wished each of them, individually, "*Ah gut Shabbos.*"

And all of Hereshevsky's — men, women, and children — had this sweet experience to carry them into Shabbos, and remain in their memories.

RABBI AHARON KREISER ALSO CAME TO VISIT RABBI CHAIM LEVOVITZ at Hereshevsky's. Ever since Rabbi Dovid Bender's *petirah*, Rabbi Aharon Kreiser popped into the Bender home regularly to say "hello" and see how everyone was doing. As he passed by Blumie on the grass in front of her bungalow, he stopped.

"And this is the *kallah*," Reb Aharon remarked jovially. "When are you getting married?"

"There is still some time," Blumie answered shyly. "We are getting married *daled Shevat*."

"Listen very closely. I have an interesting story to tell you. My friend was with the Chofetz Chaim when there was a knock at the door. A young woman came in — a *kallah*, who desired a *berachah* from the *gadol hador* before her wedding. We can assume that she expected the standard response that she be worthy of building a faithful Jewish home."

Blumie was intrigued and Rabbi Aharon Kreiser continued, "The Chofetz Chaim told her that the biggest *berachah* a *kallah* could have is to collect for needy *kallos* on the day of her *chasunah*."

Surprised but moved, Blumie took these words to heart and, on the day of her *chasunah,* set out to collect for needy *kallos*. Shy to embark on her mission alone, she enlisted the aide of her close friend and neighbor, Mrs. Henchie Deutch.

The Deutches had been the tenants of the Benders ever since they had moved to Hewes Street. Mrs. Deutch and her husband Reb Yaakov Koppel were concentration camp survivors who lost their entire families in the war and, with courage and hope, built a new family in America. Despite their terrible suffering, the Deutches remained giving people. Mrs. Deutch traveled regularly to Chronic Disease Hospital to cheer up the Jewish patients and bring them nourishing foods. Every Friday afternoon, she sent a freshly baked challah to the Benders for she always baked large quantities and wanted to share with her neighbors.

Blumie was drawn to Mrs. Deutch's unaffected goodness and they shared a warm relationship. Now she turned to the older woman and asked that she help her acquire the *berachah* of the Chofetz Chaim. On the day of her *chasunah*, Blumie and Mrs. Deutch walked down Hewes Street, asking people to give money to benefit needy *kallos*. They chose Hewes Street as opposed to busy Lee Avenue so as not to attract attention.

WITH BLUMIE MARRIED AND OUT OF THE HOUSE, A NEW QUESTION arose. Was there a problem of *yichud* with Rabbi Avrohom Bender and Rebbetzin Bender in the same house? By day, they kept the door open, but what about at night? Zaida was agitated. He wanted an answer from the Steipler himself. He spoke to his nephew, Reb Shloimke, and asked him to please approach his father-in-law, the Steipler Gaon. He described the apartment in detail and would not rest until the Steipler gave him a clear *p'sak*.

*Left to right – the Steipler, Rabbi Avrohom Bender, Rabbi Chaim Berman*

*Rabbi Yaakov Yisroel Kanievsky (1899-1985) was known as the Steipler Gaon, after his birthplace, Hornsteipel. He learned in the yeshiva of Novarodok and, after his marriage to the sister of the Chazon Ish, served as rosh yeshiva in the Novarodok yeshivos of Semiatitiz and Pinsk. In 1934 he immigrated to Eretz Yisroel where he taught in the Novarodok yeshiva in Bnei Brak. The Steipler became the unofficial successor of the Chazon Ish after the latter's passing. His multi-volume work, Kehilas Yaakov, has become a classic.*

Zaida remained a mainstay of the Bender home. Rebbetzin Bender was both appreciative of his presence and solicitous of his needs. When he seemed to miss Eretz Yisroel and Rebbetzin Bender felt he needed a change of pace, she encouraged him to travel, using a family bar mitzvah as a legitimate excuse. Rebbetzin Bender stayed in touch with her father-in-law in their frequent letters back and forth.

### Monday, 8 Kislev

*Dear Father, shlita,*

*We do not understand why you are bankrupting us. We have not received a letter from you all of last week, neither did we receive one today. Two letters came the first week after you left and that was it. I hope everything is okay, b'ezras Hashem.*

*I was in Lakewood for Shabbos. B"H, everything is fine. We miss you and would love to see you, but perhaps it is better for you to stay longer, once you're there already …*

*We had a miracle last week. The stone pillars from our stoop suddenly came crashing down, five at a time. It is right above our entrance, and I had a class in the house when it happened. It was a true miracle that no one passed by at that moment …*

*Now I have a request. I have $17 for Binyamin Rimer's parents on the occasion of their son's bar mitzvah. He is also a grandson of Rabbi Elya Shachor, shlita. I'll*

*Rabbi Avrohom Bender making a berachah at the wedding of his grandson Paltiel*
*Left to right: Rabbi Paltiel Bender, Rabbi Eliyahu Shain, Rabbi Boruch Ber Yoffe, Rabbi Avrohom Bender, Rabbi Yisroel Chaim Kaplan*

*be very grateful if you can get it to them. I don't remember their address, but you can give it to the grandfather ...[14]*

*So, you most likely went to visit the holy sites and great people already. May all the tefillos and berachos be answered for good. Please get a berachah from Ahuva's great father, shlita, for all our children. You know, I'm a woman (Yidinne), and I believe in these things.*

*Regards to our family from all of us.*

*Shalom!*

*Basya*

WITHIN A FEW YEARS OF REB DOVID'S PASSING, MUCH HAD CHANGED in the Bender home. Paltiel married Miriam Shain, the daughter of Rabbi Elya Shain, and they moved to Woodridge. Esther and Blumie lived in Lakewood. With Michoel and Shmuel Sholom away in yeshivah, only Yankel and Zaida remained home.

The Bender home was no longer a lively house of children. Yes, there were the hectic times — when the boys came home for Shabbos, or when the grandchildren were around — but on a daily basis, the house was quiet.

Rebbetzin Bender extended her hours in Bais Yaakov and became more involved in her teaching. There was rarely a night when Yankel returned

---

14. Ever since the letter that Rebbetzin Bender wrote in 1950, where she introduced herself to Rabbi Elya Shachor, the families kept in contact. Rabbi Binyamin Rimer, who later married a daughter of Rabbi Elyashiv, looked up the Benders when he came to learn in Lakewood. He joined them for Shabbos several times. Reb Binyamin remembers being in the house and thinking that even though she lived in America so many years, she still ran a *Litvishe Yeshivishe* house. "America did not stick to her," he observed.

home from yeshivah and did not have to sneak up to his room to avoid the class of young women assembled in his living room.

Rebbetzin Bender's devotion to charity became greater. She expanded old projects and took on new ones. Her old partner, Mrs. Mehler, continued to help her in her endeavors and together they took on new commitments.

They continued their used-clothing distribution network. The Mehlers had moved from Crown Heights to the West Side of Manhattan, fertile ground for collecting high-quality used clothing. Mrs. Mehler routinely loaded boxes of clothing into a taxi or van, and sent it to Williamsburg. Rebbetzin Bender spent hours sorting the clothing and deciding what to pass on and what to discard. When Yankel received his driver's license, he often drove his mother to Mrs. Mehler's house and Rebbetzin Bender did the sorting there, rather than in her own home. Yankel loaded up the car with neatly labeled bags, ready to be shipped to this family in Williamsburg or that family in Lakewood. In the late 1960's, Rebbetzin Bender discovered a store on Lee Avenue that shipped packages to Eretz Yisroel. She began to send clothing there as well.

Rebbetzin Bender's *chessed* partnership with Mrs. Mehler blossomed. Together, they raised money to distribute to needy families for Yom Tov. They also raised money to pay the tuition for needy children. With tact and discretion, Rebetzin Bender made sure that the recipients never knew where the money came from.

Procuring bridal gowns was another Bender/Mehler project. Years before *gemachs* for wedding dresses had been established, Rebbetzin Bender and Mrs. Mehler lent out wedding dresses to save families the expense of purchasing a gown.

They created their famous Camp Fund. Rebbetzin Bender was alert for special cases of children who truly needed a camp experience but whose parents could not afford the expense. She and Mrs. Mehler collected money to send these children to camp. Rebbetzin Bender's breakfront had envelopes stuffed with money: one labeled Camp Bnos, another Camp Agudah, another Camp Bais Yaakov.[15]

REBBETZIN BENDER'S EXPANDED *CHESSED* ACTIVITIES DID NOT EXCLUsively define her. She led a multifaceted life for she was a multifaceted woman. The same woman who bathed her grandchildren, made potato kugel Erev Shabbos, and shmoozed with her daughters on the phone raised thousands of dollars in *tzedakah*, taught brides and married women, and spoke with *talmidei chachamim* and roshei yeshivos about weighty issues.

In her eyes, each act was precious.

---

15. The details about Rebbetzin Bender's activities with Mrs. Mehler came from Miss Brocha Mehler. After Mrs. Mehler passed away, the Mehler family continued many of her projects.

# Chapter Fifty-Eight

# Moving On

**Williamsburg continued to grow and change.**

O NE DAY,[16] AS YANKEL WAS ABOUT TO JOIN A *MINYAN* FOR *Minchah* in Torah Vodaath, he noticed a stranger walk in. Something about the man seemed familiar, and he tried to place him without staring impolitely. Then it dawned on him. Yankel rushed over to greet the Ponevezher Rav.

"*Shalom Aleichem.* My name is Yankel Bender, and I am a cousin of Rabbi Shloimke Berman. May I be of help to the Rav?"

The Rav smiled. "Perhaps you can. I have a *chiyuv* today and I need the *amud,*" he answered simply.

Yankel needed no urging. He went over to the *amud*, to the 80-year-old Torah Vodaath old-timer who seemed to be in charge. Torah Vodaath was still the unofficial community center of Williamsburg. The Mirrer *minyanim* and the *Chassidishe shtieblach* were smaller institutions whose members often popped into Torah Vodaath to "*chap ah Minchah.*" The Torah Vodaath regulars were American old-timers who were fine and *frum*, but not particularly up to date on the "*yeshivishe*" world. They gruffly shared their *beis medrash* but were protective of their turf. Yankel cleared his throat.

"The Ponevezher Rav is here. He needs to *daven* for the *amud* ..."

"I don't care who he is! He will wait for his turn like everyone else,"

---

16. This story occurred in 1966.

*Rabbi Yosef Shlomo Kahaneman (1886-1969), popularly known as the Ponevezher Rav, learned in Telshe, Novarodok, and Radin, though he considered the Chofetz Chaim his primary rebbi. In 1919 he was appointed successor of Rabbi Yitzchok Yaakov Rabinowitz, known as Reb Itzele Ponevezher. After escaping the Nazis, the Ponevezher Rav worked relentlessly to build Torah in Eretz Yisroel, hiring the most promising scholars to serve in his yeshivah without taking a position for himself.*

answered the octogenarian as he motioned to one of his friends to begin *Ashrei.*

"But he's the Ponevezher ..."

"I don't care who he is!" interrupted the original self-appointed *gabbai.* "We do not have to hand over the *amud* to every stranger who walks in."

"But he's the Ponevezher Rav!"

"Wait," one of the other old-timers interjected, "even I heard of the Ponevezher Rav. Sol, give him the *amud.*"

Sol reluctantly gave in.

After davening, Yankel approached the Ponevezher Rav again and asked if he could be of assistance. The Ponevezher Rav was grateful for the offer. "I am going to an engagement party in the home of the Satmar Rav.[17] Would you be able to find someone who can drive me over?"

Yankel ran outside and spotted Moishe Ackerman[18] standing near his car. "Moishe, the Ponevezher Rav needs a ride. Could you take him over to the Satmar Rav's house?"

"The what?!"

"The Ponevezher Rav ..."

"I heard, I heard. Go bring him over."

Yankel went back in and reported back, "I found the Rav a ride."

"*Nu,*" the Ponevezher Rav smiled broadly, "let's go."

Yankel led the Rav outside, opened the car door for him, and then slipped inside as well. There was a crowd of Chassidim milling around the entrance of the Satmar Rav's house, waiting for someone. As the car pulled up, they peered inside, and seeing the Ponevezher Rav, they immediately ushered him into the house. Yankel remained close at his heels.

The Chassidim brought the Ponevezher Rav to the head table, to the vacant chair next to the Satmar Rav. Yankel slipped in behind him.

---

17. The *chosson* was Barry Weiss from California, a *talmid* of Torah Vodaath.

18. R' Moishe Ackerman was a brother of R' Pinchas Ackerman of the Mirrer Minyan. He was an exceptionally good-natured fellow who used to stock local shuls with siddurim stamped "Never the Property of (shul)." He welcomed everyone to daven from these siddurim, and wanted the merit of providing them.

The Satmar Rav greeted the Ponevezher Rav warmly. They exchanged mazel tovs, spoke about the beautiful *simchah*, and as old acquaintances, volleyed quips back and forth.

"*Nu*, my dear friend, what is this business with these young marriages? The *chassanim* and *kallos* are mere children …" The Ponevezher Rav chided his friend, making a veiled reference to the spate of divorces that had shocked the neighborhood.

"What do you want from me?" the Satmar Rav countered good-naturedly. "There is a halachah in the *Shulchan Aruch: shemoneh esrei l'chupah.*"[19]

The Ponevezher Rav kibbitzed with a twinkle in his eye, "But when one says *Shemoneh Esrei* too fast, sometimes he has to daven again."

The Satmar Rav began laughing.

The *Litvishe* Rosh Yeshivah and the *Chassidishe* Rebbe shook hands and wished each other well; they remained respectful of each other's opinions, but each one stayed firm in his own perspective. The Ponevezher Rav wished the families mazel tov and excused himself as he left for another appointment in Boro Park.[20]

This encounter was a reflection of Williamsburg of the 1960's. Besides the old guard who were set in their ways, there was the *Litvishe* crowd who, with their own leaders and value system, were slowly changing Orthodox Jewry in America. And then there were the Chassidim, creating a society uniquely their own that, despite its insularity, would have a profound effect on Orthodox Jewry at large.

All these came together in that little corner of New York called Williamsburg.

YET WILLIAMSBURG WAS CHANGING. BY THE END OF THE 1960'S, THE exodus of the *Litvishe* crowd from Williamsburg had gained momentum. Torah Vodaath opened a branch in Flatbush, and Bais Yaakov opened a branch in Boro Park. Rebbetzin Bender divided her teaching time between Williamsburg and Boro Park.

YANKEL WAS APPROACHING *SHIDDUCHIM* AGE AND HE WAS NERvous. He was the only Bender child home on a regular basis. Zaida was spending much of the year in Woodridge with Paltiel; the climate there was better than smoggy New York for his asthma. Reb Chaim and Esther and Reb Moshe Shimon and Blumie were in Lakewood. Michoel and

---

19. One should marry at 18 (*Even HaEzer* 1:3).

20. "I will always remember the exceptional warmth displayed by the Ponevezher Rav in this brief encounter. I knew that my mother would value a *berachah* tremendously. When we parted, I requested a *berachah* for us. He hugged me and kissed me and blessed us with all the *berachos* I could imagine" (Rabbi Yaakov Bender).

*Yankel Bender with his mother and grandfather at his wedding*

*Yankel Bender with his mesader kedushin, Rabbi Yaakov Kamenetsky*

Shmuel Sholom were learning in Woodridge. When Yankel would marry, his mother would be alone.

There was talk of Rabbi Chaim Epstein accepting the position as Rosh Yeshivah of Zichron Melech in Brooklyn. As the talk grew more serious, Yankel grew hopeful. Bais Yaakov of Boro Park was growing. Rebbetzin Bender could sell the house in Williamsburg and purchase a two-family house in Boro Park which she could share with Reb Chaim and Esther. Rather than commuting between Boro Park and Williamsburg, Rebbetzin Bender could easily transfer all her teaching hours to Boro Park.

Within a few months, everything fell into place. Reb Chaim accepted the position in Zichron Melech, Rebbetzin Bender sold her house in Williamsburg and bought a house in Boro Park. And Yankel became engaged to Bryna Minna Diskind.[21]

AFTER THE WEDDING, REBBETZIN BENDER ENCOURAGED THE NEW couple to journey to Eretz Yisroel to visit family and friends and meet the

---

21. In the early years, Bais Yaakov of Williamsburg/Boro Park was something of a fraternity, a club to which either you belonged or did not. Other girls' schools had cropped up, but Bais Yaakov remained the undisputed torchbearer of Sara Schenirer. Although never an elitist, Rebbetzin Bender always assumed that her sons would only marry graduates of Bais Yaakov. Yet, Rebbetzin Bender was too open-minded to make such sweeping categorizations. When Rebbetzin Bruria David suggested Bryna Minna Diskind, a student from Esther Schonfeld Seminary, as a *shidduch* for her son, Rebbetzin Bender listened and a match was made. Bryna Minna is a daughter of Rabbi Yehudah Elchonon and Toby Diskind. Toby (Zimmerman) Diskind was the daughter of Rabbi Yaakov Moshe Zimmerman, who was the son of the Cremenshuker Rav, and a niece of Rabbi Boruch Ber Leibowitz. The Diskind home revolved around Torah learning.

giants of the generation. Zaida was also pleased with the idea. That summer, Reb Yankel and Bryna Minna set off with everyone's blessings.

Reb Yankel made it a point to visit the *Mashgiach*, Rabbi Chatzkel Levenstein. He knew that when he returned from Eretz Yisroel, his mother would ask if he had received a *berachah* from him. He was a bit fearful since he had heard many scary stories about the *Mashgiach* and his *berachos*. Reb Yankel

*Reb Chatzkel in Yeshivas Ponevezh*

mustered his courage as he approached the *Mashgiach's* room. Who knew what he would say?

The young couple went in. The *Mashgiach* was alone at the table in the home of his son-in-law, Rabbi Reuvain Ginsburg, with an open sefer in front of him. He looked up.

"Who are you? Why are you here?" The *Mashgiach* minced no words.

"I am Yaakov, the son of Rabbi Dovid Bender." Reb Yankel stammered as he tried to get the words out. "We got married not long ago in America and have come to Eretz Yisroel for a visit. We were hoping that the *Mashgiach* would give us a *berachah* for children."

"Learn *mussar*," he answered curtly.

"*B'ezras Hashem*," Reb Yankel ventured timidly, "but what about a *berachah* for children … *Yiddishe doiros*?"

"Why do you need a *berachah*? You are just married. Why are you asking for a *berachah* now?"

"I do not come to Eretz Yisroel often. I am here now."

The *Mashgiach* went back to his learning. Reb Yankel began to panic. For some reason, the *Mashgiach* did not want to give him a *berachah* for children. He tried again, a bit desperately, "But what harm would it do to give a *berachah*?"

The *Mashgiach* shook his head. "To give a *berachah* at an inappropriate time can do harm."

By then, Reb Yankel was at his wit's end. *What should I do, the Mashgiach does not want to give me a berachah. Should I leave?* The *Mashgiach* was immersed in his sefer, as if the young couple was not even in the room. Dispirited, Reb Yankel rose to leave.

Then he thought of one more thing. He would simply tell the *Mashgiach* the truth. "Okay," he said, "but when I come back to America, my mother is going to ask me if I went to the *Mashgiach* for a *berachah*. I will have to tell her that the *Mashgiach* did not want to *bentch* us. She will feel very bad."

The *Mashgiach* looked up. "If that is the case, then the *Ribbono shel Oilam* should bless you with children, *Yiddishe doiros, mazel, berachah, hatzlachah* …"

Profoundly relieved as he left the *Mashgiach*, Reb Yankel whispered, "*Heilige Mamme,* you saved me again."

*Chapter Fifty-Nine*

# An Unusual Grandfather

**Motza'ei Shabbos Chazon**

*Dear and beloved Yaakov and Bryna Minna,*
*Welcome to Eretz Yisroel! Yankel, you cannot read my Yiddish and Bryna Minna, I assume, neither can you,[22] so I write to you partly in English. We were all happy with your telephone call that was such a pleasant surprise. Mama told Blumie about it and Blumie wrote to me; it made me a freiliche Shabbos … I can imagine what kind of welcome you had from Uncle Yosef, from Reb Shloimke, and from everyone else. I can imagine your joy at being in Eretz Yisroel and seeing everything there.*
*Spend your time well. May we all merit meeting there with Mashiach. Be well.*

*Shalom,*
*Your Zaida*

THAT WAS ZAIDA, ALWAYS IN TOUCH AND ALWAYS INVOLVED. Even as his grandchildren married and established homes of their own, Zaida kept tabs on what was going on in their lives.

To the Bender children, he was "Zaida," and to the rest of the family, he was "Uncle." He was "Uncle" to the Bermans of Eretz Yisroel: Reb Shloimke, Reb Noach, Reb Chaim, Bluma Wexelbaum, and their families.[23] He was "Uncle" to the Bermans of America: Hannah, Mary, Mike, Abe,

---

22. He was referring to his difficult handwriting, not the language. Yiddish was the language his grandchildren used when they wrote to him.

23. Reb Avrohom took a great interest in the family; he corresponded with them regularly and tried to help out in many ways. In his will, he left money for his oldest nieces to be used for their dowries.

*The Berman family at the wedding of R' Moshe and Bluma (Yoffe) Davis*

*Front row, left to right: Chosson, Rabbi Mordechai Yoffe, Rabbi Yosef Shapiro, Rabbi Dovid Bender*

*Second row, left to right: Teddy Berman, Rabbi Henoch Berman, Abe Berman, Yankel Bender, Michoel Bender, Yechiel Seide, Paltiel Bender, R' Mordechai Dickstein*

*Third row, left to right: Rabbi Mottel Weinberg, Rabbi Elazar Tarshish, Rabbi Meir Shapiro, Rabbi Moshe Shimon Shapiro (partially blocked)*

*Top row, left to right: Mike Berman, Shloime Yoffe, Abba Yoffe, Rabbi Chaim Epstein, Rabbi Boruch Ber Yoffe, Rabbi Berel Peker*

Bluma,[24] Meyer, Jules, Teddy, and Esther.[25] He kept up with them, inquired about their health and well-being, and tried to help out. He was the family patriarch, a position he earned more through his warmth and feeling of responsibility for everyone than simply because of his elderly standing. From his example, his grandchildren learned that family is precious, responsibility is noble, and love is boundless.

ZAIDA WAS GETTING ON IN YEARS, AND HIS STRENGTH WAS WANING. Whereas once he seemed to be in perpetual motion, now he found it hard to get around. He curtailed his fund-raising activities and spent most of his time at home learning. In his last years, he found it difficult to concentrate on *Gemara*, and felt it frustrating to sit at an open sefer when he was unable to understand. Reluctantly, he switched to *Mishnayos* and spent many hours a day completing *mesechta* after *mesechta* of *Mishnayos*.

Once, Yankel noticed his grandfather crying. He was shocked. Zaida crying? What happened to Mr. Cheerful?

"Zaida, what's wrong?"

---

24. These were his brother Archik's children. Hannah married Rabbi Mordechai Yoffe (see Book II, Part I, Chapter 4). Mary married Abe Reiss, one of the pillars of the Empire Shtiebel in Crown Heights. Mike continued to run his father's suit business: the only factory producing non-*shatnez* suits at the time. Abe remained a traditional Jew. Bluma married Rabbi Yosef Shapiro of Pittsburgh. (See Book II, Part I, Chapter 2.)

25. Rabbi Avrohom Berman had a brother Reb Meyer, who passed away in 1933 when his son Henoch was 26. Reb Henoch married Sarah Hamburg and they had two children, Meyer and Jules. In 1936, Reb Henoch went to America on papers sent to him by his uncle, Rabbi Avrohom Bender. He sent for his wife and children in 1940. They settled in Conneccticut where Reb Henoch was a *shochet*. The Bermans had two more children, Teddy and Esther. Meyer and Jules attended Torah Vodaath and spent much time in the Bender home. The house was always full of cousins. Jules ate at the Benders every Shabbos for five years (Rabbi Julius Berman).

*Rabbi Avrohom Bender with grandchildren and great-grandchildren*

Zaida just shook his head and waved his grandson away.

"Please, Zaida, perhaps I can help."

Zaida sighed. "I wish you could help. I wish anyone could help. What can I say? I am an old man. I am finding even *Mishnayos* difficult to learn. *Oy vey, oy vey* ... what is life without Torah?" [26]

Yankel stared at his grandfather, so uncharacteristically morose, and it occurred to him, *I have never seen him shed a tear over his beloved son, but for not being able to learn, Zaida cries.*

Zaida's love of Torah was outstanding. He often sadly repeated the incident with the medication he was given in Radin and how it affected his concentration; the *bitul Torah* pained him terribly. He was elated when he watched others learn, especially his grandchildren. When the boys wanted to come from their out-of-town yeshivos to daven at their father's grave on

---

26. "We visited Reb Avrohom often. We were like family. He always greeted me with such warmth, as if I were a daughter. Reb Avrohom had always been a big *doer*, running from one activity to another. I went to visit him when he was old and weak, unable to run around. He was sitting at a table, a sefer opened before him. He smiled when he saw me, then he gave a *krechtz*, and motioned to the sefer. 'I used to be able to do so many things. I used to be able to sit and learn a *shtickel Gemara* with *geshmak*. Now everything is so hard for me. It is hard for me to concentrate. *Nu*, so I learn *Mishnayos*.' He felt very bad that he could not learn as before" (Rebbetzin Rivka [Yogel] Markowitz).

his *yahrtzeit* Zaida did not approve. "Keep to your regular schedule. Stay in yeshivah and learn," he urged them.

ZAIDA HAD COME TO AMERICA TO BE NEAR HIS GRANDCHILDREN. NOW most of them were married with families of their own. One morning, he made an announcement to no one in particular. "It is time to go back," he said simply.

As with all his other decisions in life, once his mind was made up, Zaida did not waste time. He booked a ticket, found out about an assisted living facility where he felt that he would be comfortable, and was soon on a plane returning to his beloved Eretz Yisroel.

***Thursday Parashas Nitzavim Vayelech,***
***Yerushalayim***

*Dear Yaakov and Bryna Minna,*
*Mazel Tov! Mazel Tov!*
*May he grow up to be a giant in Torah, a pride and honor to his family and all of Klal Yisroel, Amen v'Amen. I received the telegram just after the baby was born. How was it? I hope it went easy and everyone feels well.*

*When Esther's Yaakov'l was born, Michoel wrote to me that I am a great-grandfather to nine great-grandchildren, b"H. Now I am a great-grandfather to an entire minyan, may they all be well. I hope to live to see two minyanim of great-grandchildren. When my father was niftar he left over 140 children and grandchildren.*

*May you merit to raise him together.*

*Your grandfather,*
*Avrohom*

ALTHOUGH HE HAD MOVED TO ERETZ YISROEL, ZAIDA DID NOT GIVE UP his strong loving relationship with his grandchildren. Despite his frailty and the fact that his handwriting was growing progressively more illegible,[27] he still faithfully corresponded with them and wanted to be a part of their lives.

His grandchildren felt the same way about him. Reb Yankel hired a photographer to come to the house when little Dovid'l was 6 weeks old to take photographs of the baby. The proud parents dressed the infant up. They posed him with the cap, without the cap, lying on his back, then on his side, and then in a different outfit. Six weeks later, the photos came back. Reb Yankel picked out the best one and inscribed the back of the photo to

---

27. Reb Avrohom had a card printed apologizing for his poor handwriting, and he routinely inserted this card into letters he sent.

his grandfather, letting him know that he was sending him the first photos he had of his son.

"*Chochmas adam ta'ir panav* — a man's wisdom lights up his face,"[28] Zaida wrote back to Reb Yankel, clearly happy with the photos. The birth of a new "Dovid Bender" infused Zaida with joy.

FROM HIS LETTERS, ZAIDA SEEMED TO BE ADJUSTING WELL AND IN GOOD spirits. His neighbor Rabbi Chaim Scheinberg was inspired by the sight of Zaida standing in front of his building, waiting for a taxi on his way to get to a *minyan*. If a man was determined to attend a *minyan* when he was over 90 years old and only walked with difficulty, how could a younger man not do the same?[29]

Then came Rabbi Yona Michel Yoffe's[30] phone call. Zaida had contracted pneumonia and had been admitted to the hospital. Rebbetzin Bender immediately went into action. Since Reb Paltiel did not have a passport, Reb Yankel would have to be the one to go.

While Reb Yankel was preparing to leave on his trip, Zaida's health was deteriorating. His nephew, Rabbi Chaim Berman, came to visit and found his uncle hooked up to oxygen and connected to an IV drip. Reb Yona Michel was at his side learning aloud from a *Gemara* while Zaida tried to listen to the words. Reb Chaim marveled at the sight: an elderly man, sick and frail, yet still thirsty to learn.[31]

Just as Reb Yankel was about to leave for Eretz Yisroel, his infant son developed a fever of 105 degrees. Reb Yankel was in a quandary about whether or not to leave his family at such a time. In the end, he decided to push off his ticket for one day.

The next morning they received the dreaded telephone call. Zaida had passed away in his sleep. His dream of living to see two *minyanim* of great-grandchildren would never be realized.

*January 8, 1974*
*(15th of Teves 5734)*

The *levayah* set out from Yeshivas Torah Ohr in Yerushalayim.

" '*Margulis tovah haysah teluyah b'tzavaro shel Avrohom Avinu* — a precious

---

28. *Koheles* 8:1.

29. Rabbi Chaim Scheinberg in his *hesped* of Rabbi Avrohom Bender.

30. Rabbi Yona Michel Yoffe was Rabbi Mordechai and Hannah Yoffe's son, a great-nephew of Rabbi Avrohom Bender. He was living in Mattersdorf at the time, and he cared for his great-uncle with devotion.

31. Written by Rabbi Chaim Berman in a letter.

gem hung on the neck of Avrohom Avinu.'[32] Does that mean that he owned jewelry and wore a necklace? Of course not! The simple explanation is that his exemplary virtues shone, they were obvious to all, and one did not have to search for them. So, too, it was with Reb Avrohom: 'he wore a precious stone on his neck.' His excellence in yiras Shamayim and his specialty of chessed were outstanding. He was quick to do a favor, 'vayashkeim Avrohom baboker'[33] — he got up early, if he could only help a fellow Jew ...[34]

*Rabbi Avrohom Bender*

"... He had no private life. In the 60 years that he lived in America, he was always traveling. He visited many cities and towns. According to the Gemara, 'V'ahavta es Hashem Elokecha — you shall love Hashem your G-d,' means: 'sheyihei shem Shamayim misahev al yodcha[35] — His Name should become beloved through your actions.'

"Uncle (Reb Avrohom) had many connections, and with the many thousands of people he had contact with, he always fulfilled this mitzvah. He raised money for yeshivos. He was involved in helping many Torah institutions and convinced many people to do teshuvah. He accomplished much in the areas of kashrus and tefillin. People wanted to come to him again and again. He certainly made Hashem's Name beloved by many!

"... 'V'Yosef hayah b'Mitzrayim[36] — and Yosef was in Egypt.' Do we not already know that Yosef was in Egypt? Rashi explains: Yosef was his father's shepherd and he lived in Egypt, meaning (despite living in Egypt), he was unwavering in his righteousness. The same can be told of Uncle. He met many people, visited many places, and accomplished so much. And wherever he was, he was his Father's shepherd. When Yiddishkeit was being destroyed in America, he was unchanged. He was Uncle all the same."[37]

---

32. *Bava Basra* 16b.

33. *Bereishis* 22:3 This phrase is borrowed from the description of Avrohom Avinu getting up early to do the Will of Hashem and sacrifice his only son.

34. "I am talking from experience, and I saw it with my own eyes ..." Rabbi Peretz Yogel declared in his *hesped*.

35. *Yoma* 86a.

36. *Shemos* 1:5.

37. Rabbi Mordechai Yoffe in his *hesped*. There was no one to sit *shivah* for Rabbi Avrohom Bender; he outlived all his siblings and his only son. During the week of *shivah*, the family organized *hespedim* in the Boyaner Kloiz. These excerpts were taken from those *hespedim*.

WITH RABBI AVROHOM BENDER'S PASSING, THE BENDERS LOST A beloved grandfather, and one of their strongest links to their own father. Nonetheless, under Rebbetzin Bender's dedicated care, the Bender home continued to grow and flourish. Certainly, father and son were smiling from up high.

### Chapter Sixty

# Life Continues

**Boro Park, 1975**

> *"… When hard times came, she took upon herself the role of father and mother combined … I remember coming into the house, a home of little orphans … And she was father and mother to them, an immovable fortress in the face of wind and storms … and she built a home l'shem u'l'tiferes …"*[38]

REBBETZIN BENDER PAUSED IN A RARE MOMENT OF CONTEMplation. Ten years had gone by since her husband's passing. In those 10 years, much had happened. Her home was no longer a house of orphans. She was filled with gratitude to the *Ribbono shel Olam* for the wisdom and strength to raise 6 wonderful children and the merit to see them all married.

Michoel married Faiga Dina Schustal, the daughter of the esteemed Rabbi Simcha Schustal, Rosh Yeshivah of Yeshivas Bais Binyamin of Stamford, Connecticut. Shmuel Sholom married Naomi Weissman, the daughter of Rabbi Simcha Weissman, an old friend of Rebbetzin Bender's husband.

Her home was filled with life and laughter as grandchildren ran around the living room and then settled in the kitchen for a piece of fresh hot potato kugel or a slice of cake. Her parents had not merited to see any of

---

38. Excerpted from Rabbi Binyamin Zeilberger's *hesped* for Rebbetzin Bender.

At Michoel's vort:

Left to right: Rabbi Paltiel Bender, Rabbi Chaim Epstein, Michoel Bender, Yitzchok Isaac Epstein, Shmuel Sholom Bender, Rabbi Moshe Shimon Shapiro, Rabbi Yaakov Bender

Front: Aron Dov Epstein and Shloime Epstein

At Shmuel Sholom's wedding:
Shmuel Sholom dancing with his brothers-in-law, Rabbis Chaim Epstein and Moshe Shimon Shapiro

their grandchildren, and her husband had only seen two … and oh, how she still wished she could share her joy with them!

What would they say to the 1970's? A world where man walks on the moon and where air travel is commonplace, where the *Kosel* is in Jewish hands, where an entire planeload of people could be kidnapped and still returned to safety,[39] and where one president is assassinated and another one is almost impeached within a few years of each other.[40]

*Life in this new world is so different than when I grew up*, Rebbetzin Bender mused. Then she finished her cup of coffee, swept up the cake crumbs that had fallen on the table, made a *berachah acharonah*, and strode right back into the new world that she was a part of.

---

39. Reference to the famous 1970 hijacking, when Rabbi Yitzchok Hutner and other *talmidei chachomim* were held hostage for three weeks. During those three weeks, Rebbetzin Bender found it difficult to go about life as usual. Her thoughts and *tefillos* were constantly with the hostages.

40. References to the assassination of President Kennedy and the resignation of President Nixon, events that she blamed on the *hefkeirus* of America. Lawlessness and the lack of reverence for authority were things that she associated particularly with life in America.

# Part II:
# Rebbetzin Bender: Always an Inspiration
## 5735-5755 / 1975-1995

### Chapter Sixty-One:
Her Mission: Guardian of the Jewish Home

### Chapter Sixty-Two:
Her Crown: Beloved Teacher

### Chapter Sixty-Three:
Her Essence: Ah Yiddishe Mamme

### Chapter Sixty-Four:
Her Adornment: Loyal Friendship

### Chapter Sixty-Five:
Her Gift: To Expand Her "Self"

### Chapter Sixty-Six:
Her Joy: To Give

### Chapter Sixty-Seven:
Her Desire: To Honor Others

### Chapter Sixty-Eight:
Her Longing: To Serve Him

### Chapter Sixty-Nine:
Uniquely Hers

---

A pamphlet of memories, compiled by one of Rebbetzin Bender's grand-sons the summer after her *petirah*, served as the blueprint for this section. Additional information was provided by the Bender Family. Excerpts from the *hespedim* were taken from taped recordings as was the excerpt from Rebbetzin Bender's speech at the Bais Yaakov luncheon. Other sources are documented.

---

*Chapter Sixty-One*

# Her Mission:
# Guardian of the Jewish Home

> *"... She set thousands on the right path ... She was a 'chacham leiv yikach mitzvos,'[1] a 'v'lokei'ach nifashos chacham'[2] — through her teaching, she acquired souls. She taught generations of Jewish girls, thus enabling her students' influence to continue on in their homes and in those of their students. Her light spread to thousands upon thousands."[3]*

OR OVER 50 YEARS REBBETZIN BENDER TAUGHT YOUNG women how to create a proper Jewish home. Her innovative curriculum was built on the premise that marriage is the vehicle to bring *kedushah* into the home. Halachos are *kedushah*, *tznius* is *kedushah*, *ahavah* brings *kedushah*, *shalom* brings *kedushah*. Cleaning one's home, cooking for a family, dressing children and putting them to sleep — everything is *kedushah*. When a woman devotes herself to creating a home where peace and happiness reign, it is a home of *kedushah*.

Rebbetzin Bender preferred to teach girls privately, and toward the end of her life that was what she did. In the 1950's and 1960's, private teaching was not an option since there were so many girls and so few teachers. The

---

1. *Mishlei* 10:8: "A wise woman who acquires mitzvos."
2. Ibid. 11:30: "A woman with the wisdom of acquiring souls."
3. Rabbi Zelig Epstein in his *hesped* for Rebbetzin Bender.

*Rebbetzin Bender — 1985*

only way that she could possibly meet the demand was to teach girls in classes.

Nonetheless, she recognized that girls from different backgrounds and communities should be addressed differently. She scheduled classes for each specific group: one night was Pupa, one night was Satmar, one night was *Litvishe* Bais Yaakov girls, and one night was the girls from Central High School. The system worked. She was able to speak to each group of students with their particular upbringing, mentality, and focus in mind.

Rebbetzin Bender took a special interest in the young women she taught. If she was aware of particular financial problems, she would take it upon herself to help. At times, she used her *shiur* as a forum to collect money for a worthy cause. This was also part of the *chinuch*; she was teaching her girls that a Jewish woman should seek ways to do *chessed*. A diaper company going out of business had diapers to give away. Rebbetzin Bender wanted to send boxes of diapers to Eretz Yisroel. She appealed to her class of *kallos* and they volunteered to help pack the diapers and take them to the post office.

"IN THIS WEEK'S *PARASHAH*," REBBETZIN BENDER BEGAN, "WE LEARN about the construction of the Menorah. This vessel was so unique; it had to be made by a single piece of gold: not several pieces welded together, but one solid piece. Betzalel was puzzled as to how to make it. Moshe Rabbeinu could not make it. The Menorah was made by *HaKadosh Baruch Hu* Himself. The question remains: Why had Betzalel or Moshe Rabbeinu not been allowed to make the Menorah from several pieces of gold? Had they been able to, they probably would have been able to fashion it themselves. Why did the Menorah have such unique specifications?"

Rebbetzin Bender paused. "The Menorah symbolizes Torah. Torah is one piece. It is not an unrelated jumble of laws and halachos. It is one piece, coming from one Source. A person cannot look at Torah and decide, 'I will keep this halachah, but not that halachah.' We have to recognize that Torah is a solid mass. Keeping Torah means keeping everything, not picking and choosing."[4]

This was how Rebbetzin Bender opened her classes for married women. Here too, Rebbetzin Bender was a pioneer.

---

4. Mrs. R. Pollack.

In the 1950's and 1960's, there was a dearth of knowledge, even among married women, about the proper establishment of a Jewish home. Rabbi Moshe Leiber[5] worked with rabbanim to write the first English pamphlet on the subject. Rabbi Yona Zev "Billy" Herskowitz helped publish these pamphlets. Progress was being made but the problem was not yet solved.

R' Hershel Weber and R' Ephraim Pollack, brothers-in-law with tremendous idealism, asked Rebbetzin Leah Herskowitz for advice on how to deal with the widespread ignorance regarding Jewish family living. They came up with the idea of public classes for married women, and they asked Rebbetzin Bender to speak.

*Rabbi Moshe Leiber: a Williamsburg visionary*

For the first rally, they rented an auditorium and posted signs in shuls and local grocery stores announcing the event. To everyone's surprise, Rebbetzin Bender arrived to a packed auditorium. Jewish women of all ages and from all segments of Williamsburg society came to hear her class.

Success highlighted the need for more classes. Rebbetzin Bender designed a three-part series and by the time the first series finished, there were already requests from other communities. She traveled to Boro Park, the Lower East Side, Forest Hills, and Crown Heights. She returned to each neighborhood on consecutive Mondays, covering three sessions in three weeks. Soon she had requests for her classes in Lakewood and Monsey, and she began traveling there as well.

At the end of every session, Rebbetzin Bender allotted time for questions and answers. Many women preferred not to ask their questions in a public forum. They would write their questions on small pieces of paper, often with no identifying information. Rebbetzin Bender would go through these questions at home. From the basic questions women were asking, Rebbetzin Bender sadly concluded that there was gross ignorance. This realization caused her tremendous heartache.

In the following sessions, she would bring up questions the women had raised. Sometimes she would announce that questions she did not answer should be taken to a Rav. If questions were particularly problem-

---

5. See page 327.

| Rebbetzin Bender was in regular contact with the leading *poskim* of the time, among them Rav Gustman. |
| --- |

*Rabbi Yisroel Ze'ev Gustman (1908-91) learned in Remmailes Yeshivah in Vilna. Rabbi Chaim Ozer Grodzenski appointed him as a member of his beis din and then as maggid shiur in the yeshivah when he was still a very young man. Through miracle after miracle, Rabbi Gustman survived the war and, after many wanderings, reached Brooklyn, where he founded Netzach Yisroel-Remmailes. In 1961 Rabbi Gustman moved to Eretz Yisroel and transferred his yeshivah to the Rechaviah section of Yerushalayim.*

atic and the answers were not appropriate for a public forum, Rebbetzin Bender would call the women directly provided they had included their phone numbers. If no number was included, then she would make an announcement, "Would the woman who asked a question regarding 'such and such,' please call me?" Usually, that declaration elicited the desired response.

Over the years, Rebbetzin Bender regularly discussed *shaylos* with the leading *poskim* of the generation such as Rabbi Moshe Feinstein, Rabbi Yaakov Kamenetsky, and Rabbi Yisroel Gustman. At the same time, local rabbanim knew when she had spoken in their neighborhood, since her classes inevitably prompted a slew of telephone calls as women sought to clarify whether their actions fell within the boundaries of halachah or not.

After every class, Rebbetzin Bender's telephone began to ring with calls from women who attended her classes and preferred to remain anonymous. She became a wise, non-threatening mentor to many women. Family strife carried with it a stigma, and most women preferred to swallow their pain rather than admit that anything was wrong. Suddenly, with the advent of Rebbetzin Bender's classes, these women had a warm *heimishe* mentor to speak to, and they could do so under the cloak of anonymity.

Rebbetzin Bender discovered that many issues could be resolved if each side worked on their *middos*. She found it disturbing that time and again, she had to convince a spouse to overlook his or her mate's faults, to give the benefit of the doubt, and to recognize the inherent goodness of the other person. She encouraged her listeners to develop healthy marriages, and used many stories to illustrate her points. One of her favorite stories involved Reb Meir Simchah of Dvinsk.

A COUPLE CAME TO REB MEIR SIM-chah requesting a divorce. Reb Meir Simchah listened to their arguments. As they aired their respective points of view, their anger and resentment rose to a fever pitch. Their differences seemed truly irreconcilable.

"*Nu*," Reb Meir Simchah agreed with a heavy heart, "let us make a date." As they discussed the date, Reb Meir Simchah remembered something. "You have a child, yes?" They answered affirmatively. "I want you both to come here with the child on the day we are scheduled for the *get*."

The day came and the couple arrived with their child. Reb Meir Simchah put the child on his lap and began to croon and hug him. "Oh my dear child, what will be with you? You will be *ah leibedige yasom*[6]…"

*Rabbi Meir Simchah Cohen (1843-1926) joined the Perushim Kollel of Aishishok when he was 14 years old. After his marriage, he learned in Bialystok for 18 years and worked on his seforim, Meshech Chochmah and Ohr Sameach. He then became Rav of Dvinsk, Latvia and was involved in the Jewish affairs of the time. Reb Meir Simchah did not run his own yeshivah but he learned with bochurim who dormed at his home. He was offered the position of Rav of Yerushalayim, but his community refused to let him go.*

The child began to cry. The mother began to cry. The father began to cry. "I don't want my parents to have a *get* …" the child whimpered. "I also do not want a *get*," his mother sobbed. "Neither do I," the father echoed softly.

"*Nu*," Reb Meir Simchah declared, "there will not be a *get*! Come, let us make a *l'chaim*." They drank a *l'chaim*, and Reb Meir Simchah began to dance with the family.

REBBETZIN BENDER USED THIS STORY TO EXPLAIN HOW SO MANY THINGS can be resolved if each side is willing to rethink a situation. We are often stuck seeing things only one way. By pointing out where we are stuck, a wise person can help change our perspective.

In time, Rebbetzin Bender learned to recognize when a woman needed a listening ear and when she would benefit more from a sharp rebuke. She learned to accept that some problems were beyond her scope of expertise and her job was to recommend professional help. Even in these cases she maintained contact, letting people know that she cared.

---

6. A Yiddish expression literally meaning a living orphan, referring to a child who has parents but is nonetheless like an orphan.

With wisdom, patience, and perseverance, Rebbetzin Bender helped save many marriages. Yet, if there was no point in salvaging a marriage, she dealt with that as well. One of Rebbetzin Bender's friends married into a very illustrious and influential family. Only after the wedding did the young bride find out that her husband was not well. She soon realized that a peaceful marriage would be impossible. Yet her husband refused to give her a divorce and she did not have the strength to stand up to the family on her own. Rebbetzin Bender took on the entire dynasty and did not rest until the woman was free.[7]

REBBETZIN BENDER THREW OUT A QUESTION TO HER AUDIENCE. "WHAT is the most important *middah* for a wife to have?" The women offered many suggestions: being an *eizer k'negdo*, cheerfulness, tranquility, etc. Rebbetzin Bender listened to all these very valid points and waited for quiet.

Then she gave her answer. "The most important *middah* for a woman to perfect is patience. How does a woman merit *Olam Haba*? She earns her reward by waiting for her children to come home from *cheder* and waiting for her husband to return from yeshivah. Waiting requires patience. Running a home requires patience. Raising children requires patience. *Nachas* also comes with patience."

"*OLAM CHESSED YIBANEH*[8] — THE WORLD WILL BE CREATED WITH KINDNESS," she explained in her classes. "After the *Eibeshter* created *Adam HaRishon*, He looked at His world and saw that it was almost perfect. One thing was missing. There was no one with whom *Adam HaRishon* could do *chessed*. *I will make an eizer k'negdo,* another person with whom he can do *chessed* every day, many times a day. Marriage is the fulfillment of His desire to have a world that is a continuous cycle of *chessed*. People were put in this world to help others. Marriage provides endless opportunities."

Rebbetzin Bender's *shiurim* went beyond halachos and encompassed an entire approach to marriage and life. Perhaps that explains a conversation that Rabbi Paltiel Bender once had with Rebbetzin Feinstein. Reb Paltiel had traveled from Woodridge, New York to the Lower East Side to ask Rabbi Moshe Feinstein a *shayla*. When Rebbetzin Feinstein realized that he had come from far away, she insisted that he sit down and she served him refreshments.

"I feel very bad," she commented as she poured a glass of juice. "Your mother spoke in our neighborhood last week and I could not go to hear her. I am sorry that I missed her *shiur*."

7 Rebbetzin R. Brudny reminded the Bender daughters of this story during the *shivah*. While she told the story, there was a phone call from Eretz Yisroel; it was this woman calling to be *menachem aveilim*.

8. *Tehillim* 89:3.

Reb Paltiel stammered, "Rebbetzin, you know that her speeches are not really meant for you …"

Rebbetzin Feinstein shook her head emphatically. "No, no. Your mother's *derashos* are inspiring for anyone. I would have liked to attend and I am sorry that I missed it."

*Chapter Sixty-Two*

# Her Crown: Beloved Teacher

*"... Sixty years of chinuch habanos — girls' education ... She began (through) Sara Schenirer, who sent her students to different towns to educate the girls. Sara Schenirer, a"h, ignited the spark within her, as well as in all of her talmidos, and that very fire continued to blaze. From there they had the capacity to accomplish, for the sake of Heaven ..."[9]*

REBBETZIN BENDER WOULD LAUGHINGLY REMINISCE HOW, for many years, she was earning so little in Bais Yaakov, her salary did not even cover the cost of a babysitter. Yet, to stop teaching was never an option. Teaching out of conviction and idealism, Rebbetzin Bender saw Bais Yaakov as a holy mission that perpetuated the legacy of her own great teachers. An anecdote that occurred in 1960 illustrates the awe that she and her colleagues had of their Bais Yaakov of Crakow teachers.

IT WAS 1960. FRAU DOCTOR WAS COMING TO AMERICA! REBBETZIN Bender and her fellow Bais Yaakov of Crakow classmates were dizzy with happiness. They were light-years away from the grassy hilltops of the Carpathian Mountains where they had been transfixed by the eloquence of carefully prepared lessons in *hashkafah* and *mussar*. They had left their homes and lost their families. They had escaped and were now the rebuilders of *Yiddishkeit* in America.

---

9. Excerpted from Rabbi Chaim Epstein's *hesped* for Rebbetzin Bender.

*Rebbetzin Kaplan, Rebbetzin Grunfeld, Rebbetzin Bender*

In all the turbulent years that had passed, they had not seen any of their beloved teachers. Now they relished returning to their vanished youth and becoming adoring pupils once again.

The day dawned and Rebbetzins Kaplan, Wachtfogel, Rottenberg, and Bender were standing in front of the seminary in Williamsburg. The taxi they had called to take them to the airport was due to arrive in another few minutes. Esther Bender was standing there as well, and Rebbetzin Kaplan called her over.

"Come, Esther, let's go to Lasker's Flower Shop to buy a dozen red roses for Rebbetzin Grunfeld. By the time we come back, the car will be here."

Esther followed Rebbetzin Kaplan into the flower shop. Mr. Lasker looked up from his flower arranging and greeted his customers. "Yes, may I help you?"

Suddenly, Rebbetzin Kaplan began to giggle. She was so overcome with emotion about Rebbetzin Grunfeld's arrival that she could not get the words out. Esther was astounded. Rebbetzin Kaplan giggling? She was reserved, regal, warm, soft-spoken, and controlled — *not a giggler.*

When the moment finally arrived and these respected rebbetzins were reunited with their beloved teacher, they stood around her smiling, their faces shining with love and happiness, silent with emotion that could not be put into words. Frau Doctor had come to visit.[10]

---

10. "And one final point, talking about *hakaras hatov*, the biggest lesson that I have ever seen and received in that sphere was about a decade ago as I watched Rebbetzins Bender, Kaplan, Wachtfogel, and others greeting my mother with such love. I have seen many pupils greet their teachers, but I have never seen anything like that. It was really touching" (Rebbetzin Grunfeld's daughter, Naomi, at the Bais Yaakov Spring Tea, in reference to one of her mother's trips to America).

Rebbetzin Bender and her colleagues were founders of the burgeoning Bais Yaakov movement in America. They had already created a new generation of Jewish women in America. They were visionaries with ambition. Yet they viewed themselves merely as humble students of lofty teachers. That was their strength. Their students felt connected to something much bigger. They had confidence that they were a part of a larger picture. Their teachers were the bridge — a much-needed bridge — between the past and the future.

Sometimes, having teachers as a bridge was not enough. For Sandy,[11] a gaping chasm existed between her and her teachers. As an out-of-towner, Sandy did not understand the more subtle nuances of *Yiddishkeit*. No matter how hard she tried, she did not succeed in Bais Yaakov: not in her studies, not in her social life, and not in becoming a mainstream Bais Yaakov girl. The only teacher she felt close to was Rebbetzin Bender.

After graduation, Sandy disappeared. Rebbetzin Bender did not meet up with Sandy again until many years later. One day their paths crossed, and Rebbetzin Bender greeted her former student happily.

"Rebbetzin Bender, it is so good to see you!" Sandy exclaimed. "I must tell you that I owe you a tremendous debt. I was so frustrated during my years in Bais Yaakov. I was ready to throw everything I had learned out the window. Then I remembered how much you cared about me, and I couldn't let you down. Where I lived, no one wore a *sheitel*. I only had the courage to do so because of the warmth you showed me. Even though I knew we might never see each other again, I couldn't betray your trust in me."

REBBETZIN BENDER'S ABILITY TO INFLUENCE HER STUDENTS STEMMED from her boundless love for them. She loved them all, just as a mother loves all her children. She saw their faults and still loved them. This was her trademark. Bais Yaakov had many teachers, and each teacher had a special contribution to make because of her own unique personality. The girls left Rebbetzin Bender's class feeling loved.

CHANIE WALKED INTO SEMINARY WITH TREPIDATION. WHAT WOULD her friends say? She slipped into class just as the bell rang. A folded paper found its way onto her desk. Chanie snatched it and unfolded it in her lap. Five words were scrawled on the scrap of paper: *What's with the boy's haircut?*

Chanie's cheeks burned in embarrassment. O.K., her haircut was too short. It was a mistake. How many more snide comments would she have to suffer through that day?

---

11. Name has been changed.

Sure enough, between every period, Chanie had to put up with her classmates' wisecracks. Then Rebbetzin Bender walked in. She noticed Chanie's cropped hair, red face, and sullen expression. Rebbetzin Bender understood everything. She went right over to her and, in her firm, but loving way, she said, "Chanie, you look very nice. When your hair grows in, you will look even nicer." Chanie's face lit up. It was the first affectionate but honest comment that she had heard all day. She would always be grateful.[12]

REBBETZIN BENDER WAS ATTUNED TO THE NEEDS OF HER STUDENTS. When there was a class trip or a Shabbaton and Rebbetzin Bender heard that a girl was not going, she made sure to find out if money was the issue. If it was, she arranged for payment in an honorable manner.

A terrible fire destroyed the home of one of the girls in the seminary. Everything was lost and the family had to rebuild their lives from scratch. Everyone knew about the family's plight, and many well-meaning people sent over packages of clothing to help outfit the children. Rebbetzin Bender went one step further. She called the seminary girl out of class and handed her an envelope with money.

"What's this?" the girl asked in astonishment.

"I know you lost everything in the fire," Rebbetzin Bender explained. "You're a *kallah maidel*. You should have nice clothing. Take this and buy yourself whatever you need." The girl was speechless. In all the packages her parents received, very little was suitable for a girl of marriageable age. The clothing was outdated and worn and she was ashamed to be seen dressed in such shabby clothes. Only Rebbetzin Bender understood.

IN ADDITION TO THE MOTHERLY CONCERN SHE FELT FOR HER STUdents, Rebbetzin Bender took seriously her responsibility to stimulate their intellects. She, herself, was very educated and knowledgeable, and she bemoaned the ignorance of her students, particularly when it came to Jewish history.

"A person who does not know his own history is like someone who has lost his memory," she used to say.[13] Rebbetzin Bender designed her course to cure this amnesia. She did not focus on endless details that often make history classes boring. She infused the girls with pride in their past. They should want to know the trials and tribulations that *Klal Yisroel* has faced, and how they have endured them. The names of the *gedolim* should be as familiar to them as the names of their grandparents, sisters, and brothers.

---

12. Said at Rebbetzin Bender's *shivah*.

13. Rabbi Chaim Epstein.

*Rabbi Avigdor Miller (1908-2001) attended Yeshivas Rabbeinu Yitzchok Elchonon, and then journeyed to Europe to learn in Slabodka. He returned to America where he became a rabbi in Chelsea, Massachusetts. In 1944 he became Mashgiach in Mesivta Rabbeinu Chaim Berlin, and later assumed the position of Rav in the Young Israel of Rugbi in East Flatbush. When Rabbi Miller moved his shul to Flatbush, his shiurim attracted crowds of listeners. He inspired his generation through his tapes, books, and speeches.*

When she initially prepared for her Jewish History class, she searched for "kosher" materials. She used the notes Reb Dovid had saved from Rabbi Shraga Feivel Mendelowitz's classes in Torah Vodaath. One summer, she stayed in the hot city to research a topic rather than go up to the country to relax.

Rebbetzin Bender viewed teaching as an enormous responsibility and, even if she had been teaching the material for 25 years, she would always review her notes the night before.

When she taught, she was careful to quote *b'sheim omro,* citing the name of the source. Occasionally she forgot, and it bothered her that she might not have given her source the proper credit. One Erev Yom Kippur she saw Rabbi Avigdor Miller in her neighborhood coming to wish Mrs. Renee Hirshberg[14] "*ah gut yohr.*" Rebbetzin Bender approached him and explained how she had heard some of his lectures, and it was possible that she told bits and pieces to her students without mentioning his name. Would he forgive her for such an oversight?

Rabbi Avigdor Miller smiled and made a dismissive motion. "*Hagonev min haganev pattur,*"[15] he declared. Rebbetzin Bender enjoyed his answer for its astute observation and the humorous way it confirmed her innocence.

REBBTZIN BENDER USED MANY TRUE STORIES AND *MASHALIM,* PARABLES, to enliven her teaching and illustrate her points. When she spoke about the value of a husband who spent his life learning, she became animated. "Girls, imagine if your husband was given an hour to collect all the gold that he could from the king's treasure house. Would you disturb him for anything? When your husband is learning, he is digging for gold. With

---

14. Mrs. Hirshberg was a legendary *ba'alas chessed,* founder of N'shei Ahavas Chesed.

15. *Bava Kamma* 62b. Literally, "One who steals from a thief is absolved of guilt." This is a paraphrase of a general halachic principle. Rabbi Avigdor Miller, while poking fun at himself, was giving her permission. He was saying, "Where do you think I came up with this from? Do you think I thought it up myself? I probably also heard it from someone else and have forgotten from whom. Therefore, taking my *vort* is merely stealing from a thief and is therefore permissible."

every second of every minute, more gold is being acquired. Would you want him to take even a small break?"

However, she reminded her girls that a man is a human being and not a machine. She once challenged a class, "What would you do if you walked into your house in the middle of the day and found your husband sitting in the kitchen and reading a newspaper?" The class erupted in a vigorous debate. One girl said she would cry and when her husband would see her disappointment, he would surely stop. Another girl said that she would ignore him and go about preparing lunch; eventually he would get the hint. For several minutes, ideas were bandied about.

Finally, everyone was quiet. "Do you want to know what I would do?" Rebbetzin Bender asked, with her usual serene smile. "I would stand behind him and read along with him."[16] The ultimate role of a wife is to be supportive and understanding. Her message was, "Do not doubt your husband. Stand behind him."

Rebbetzin Bender was finely tuned to the changing times. Establishing the premise that a girl should embrace a life of Torah had become easier, and her students of the 1960's and 70's needed little convincing. However, sometimes zealousness replaced common sense, and Rebbetzin Bender addressed this as well.

"Girls," she said one day during *Mishlei* class, "why does Esti run to daven *Minchah* just when her husband walks into the house, after a long day in kollel or at work? Why does it happen every day? And what do you think of that?"[17]

The girls could see that something was obviously wrong. A woman should try to daven *Minchah*, but she has missed the point if she runs for her siddur as her husband walks through the door. A wise Jewish woman combines piety with sensitivity, and she knows when even pious actions may be inappropriate.

She often mentioned that in Bais Yaakov in Europe they did not learn nearly as much as the Bais Yaakov girls learn today. She explained that there are many reasons why today's programs are more thorough and require more homework and projects. The times change, and what might be necessary for one generation might be obsolete for another. She supported the decisions of the new generation of educators and expressed her appreciation for their ability to respond to the times.[18]

---

16. Rebbetzin C. Ginsburg.

17. Mrs. Y. Linchner.

18. However, when she heard from her granddaughters that girls have many tests before Pesach, she became very upset. How could girls be required to study when they needed to help their mothers in the house Erev Pesach? She immediately called up the principal of the school to discuss the issue. Although she was open to new ideas, when she saw a flaw in an innovation, she was quick to protest.

Sensitive issues were Rebbetzin Bender's forte. In the classroom, she could make any topic teachable. Out of the classroom, she felt that every person was reachable. Rabbi Boruch Kaplan had tremendous respect for Rebbetzin Bender, and he often sought her assistance in smoothing over delicate situations. When there were differences in opinion between the administration and a teacher, between a teacher and a parent, or between a parent and the administration, Rebbetzin Bender was often called in to mediate. When the school wanted to expel a girl, Rebbetzin Bender was at the front lines, looking for a way to keep the girl in Bais Yaakov. When a disgruntled teacher wanted to leave, Rebbetzin Bender was there, trying to make peace.

Perhaps her success had to do with her uncanny ability to understand others. She was a people person: she enjoyed people, cared about people, and understood people. When she was mediating a disagreement, each side was certain that she was working for them, and indeed she was. Her goal was always peace and she was convinced that peace could be achieved, if enough effort and *ahavah* were expended.

ROSIE[19] WAS NOT BY NATURE A LEADER, NOR WAS SHE EVEN AN ENERgetic follower. When she married and her husband's job took them to an obscure, out-of-town community, Rosie was faced with a dilemma. The nearest *mikveh* was very far away. How could a Jewish community not have its own *mikveh*? Yet, she shied away from initiating such an ambitious enterprise.

*You?* she thought to herself. *You are going to spearhead a project to build a mikveh?* Then she remembered the words of her teacher, Rebbetzin Bender, *Whatever you want to do, do it with ahavah. With ahavah, you will succeed.* Rosie took a deep breath. "Okay, I guess I will try — with *ahavah*!" With *ahavah*, Rosie succeeded.[20]

REBBETZIN BENDER'S POSITIVE OUTLOOK[21] WAS A NATURAL RESULT OF her conviction that life should be lived with *ahavah*. In her home and in the classroom, love permeated her thoughts and actions. "With *ahavah*, any-

---

19. Not her real name.

20. "This woman came to be *menachem avel* when we sat *shivah* for my mother. She attributed her success in having that *mikveh* built to my mother" (Rebbetzin F. Epstein in an interview with R' Yonason Rosenblum).

21. The Bender children rarely heard their mother complain. When the Benders came to New York, they lived with Reb Dovid's parents for five years. The apartment was small and it would have been understandable for mother-in-law and daughter-in-law to get on each other's nerves. Yet, the Bender children never heard their mother say anything less than positive about that time. She always spoke about what a wonderful mother-in-law she had and how much she respected her. Only many years later, when they were adults with their own married children, did they marvel at this greatness. At the time, their mother always made it seem so natural.

thing can be accomplished," was her constant refrain.

When Rebbetzin Bender saw students who needed extra attention or a little more warmth than the rest of the class, she invited them over to the house on a Friday night or during the week. She listened to their concerns and guided their decisions.[22] She spoke to her students in a way that made them feel that she loved them especially.

After one of the girls gave a model lesson, her supervisor enumerated all the problems with the lesson. As soon as the supervisor finished, Rebbetzin Bender ran over to the girl to point out all the good things she noticed about her lesson.

In keeping with her policy of positive reinforcement, Rebbetzin Bender always gave the girls marks a little higher than they deserved. She rarely gave a student a low mark. "It won't help to give her a 'D' when she cannot do better. She will not gain from the 'D'; the 'D' will just break her. *Ess iz nit ken mitzvah tzu shluggen ah kind* (it is no mitzvah to strike a child)."

Her students sought her out, instinctively, to share with her what they could not share with other people in their lives. When Gitty[23] discovered that she was adopted, she was overcome with confusion. She was plagued by nightmares; perhaps she was not even Jewish. Yet since she saw how uncomfortable they were with the situation, she did not want to discuss the issue with her adoptive parents. She followed her intuition and turned to Rebbetzin Bender.

Sorala was only 17 when she started seminary, but she was worried because most of her friends had found jobs and she was still jobless. She thought that no one noticed her moodiness. Then Rebbetzin Bender called her over. "Sorala, I see that you're down. What's wrong?" Sorala explained her predicament. "Is that all?" Rebbetzin Bender's face showed her relief. "What is the problem? Do you have a family to support? Is anyone depending on you for *parnassah*? You're young. You want a job? You'll find a job." Sorala perked up immediately. In this new perspective, her worries seemed trivial, and her bad mood simply disappeared.[24]

During the seminary entrance-exams she proctored, Rebbetzin Bender would suddenly ask all the girls to take a break. Then she would hand out cookies and juice so that everyone would feel at ease. One girl taking the exam was amazed. She had come from a school where tests were viewed with intense anxiety. In contrast, here was Rebbetzin Bender ordering a break and dispensing *nosh*. After everyone had something to eat, it was

---

22. A student related, "When I was in 11th grade, Rebbetzin Bender invited me to come over Friday nights. I still remember her warm smile and how she cared for me. She guided me in choosing which seminary to go to and I realized, years later, how right she was" (written in a letter to Rabbi Yaakov Bender in 2004).

23. Not her real name.

24. Mrs. S. Maiza.

back to business. No one took undue advantage of the change in atmosphere. Rebbetzin Bender proved that girls could learn even better with regular doses of love.[25]

MINNA GLANCED AT HER WATCH AND WAS APPALLED. IT WAS 3 o' clock in the morning and the girls were still carrying on as if it were 2 o'clock in the afternoon. Minna groaned and covered her head with a pillow to drown out the noise, but to no avail. Suddenly, she sat up in bed. *One minute,* she thought, *if I am unable to sleep because of the racket, what about Rebbetzin Bender and Rebbetzin Wachtfogel? They also have rooms on this floor.* She had felt guilty asking the girls to quiet down for her sake, even though having a 2-month-old baby was a legitimate reason to do so, but now she had an even better excuse.

She put on a robe and headed toward the lobby. *Ridiculous,* she fumed as she walked down the hall, *keeping me up is one thing, but disturbing Rebbetzin Bender and Rebbetzin Wachtfogel … what chutzpah!*

As she entered the lobby, her eyes widened. There, sitting on the couch, surrounded by girls — some right next to her, some leaning on the armrest, some sitting on the windowsill — was Rebbetzin Bender!

"Rebbetzin Bender …" Minna stammered.

"Yes?" Rebbetzin Bender inquired softly, her face wreathed in smiles. She had gotten dressed and had even put on a *sheitel* — at 3 o'clock in the morning.

"Aren't you tired? Don't you want to go to sleep? I can tell the girls to quiet down …"

"Quiet them down?" Rebbetzin Bender interjected. "No, no! *Loz zei hoben ah* 'good time.' They just want some fun. Leave them alone. You are worried about my sleep? I can sleep some other time."

"Are you sure?" Minna inquired uncertainly.

"Yes!" answered Rebbetzin Bender firmly.

Minna turned back toward her room, but not before she listened to a bit of the conversation Rebbetzin Bender was having with her students. She was telling them stories about Europe, about Bais Yaakov of Crakow, and about her childhood. Her audience was hanging on to her every word. They looked ready to stay there for as long as Rebbetzin Bender would continue speaking.[26]

Typical Rebbetzin Bender. Rather than quash her students' enthusiasm, she joined them. She truly enjoyed being with her students.

---

25. Mrs. K. Fruchthandler.

26. Rebbetzin M. Steinharter.

*Chapter Sixty-Three*

# Her Essence:
# Ah Yiddishe Mamme

*"... She was a mother who was involved with many other people, but still she was a mother ... [She was an example of] how someone can elevate her everyday life to be something very special ... and [she did it in such a way that] the people around her did not feel uncomfortable with her specialness ... People spoke and conversed with her and felt as if they were around a regular person ... This was her greatest strength ...*

*"... She was a regular mother. She made potato kugel every Friday ... and all the children would come Friday afternoon to her house and pick up their potato kugel from her. She was a regular mother. She was more than a regular mother ... she was an extraordinary mother, a very, very special mother; in every action she did there was greatness! ... There was greatness in every single day ...*

*"... The way she spoke to me was such a pleasure. Such an honor! ... It was a relationship of a mother to a child, but so much more than that ... the way she handled us, the way she worried about us ... Here we were marrying off children, and we were still her little kids ... A week did not pass that she did not say to me two or three times, "You are working too hard." Me, I am working too hard? She was on the phone in the middle of the night, a sick woman ... (And she was worried that I was working too hard?) ... But that was because she was a regular mother ... always a mother ..."*[27]

---

27. Rabbi Yaakov Bender in his *hesped* at Rebbetzin Bender's *shloshim*.

ANY PEOPLE SAY THAT A WOMAN CAN NEVER BE both: either she is a mother or a career woman. A dedicated mother cannot have a career, and a woman involved in her career cannot be a good mother. Rebbetzin Bender was able to do it all — with *ahavah*.

She was called "Mamme Bender," and later in life, "Bubby Bender," even in school, because those appellations described her essence and her strength. She wore her title with pride; in her eyes, there was no greater role for a woman than that of mother. For years, she taught only at night so that during the day she could be home with the little ones. When the children grew up, she was able to spend more hours teaching. The roles were complementary; as a mother, she taught and as a teacher, she mothered.

Her children grew up oblivious to the concept of *tza'ar gidul bannim* — the burden of raising children; even though, in retrospect, raising her children must have been a lot tougher for her than it is today. She had no mother, mother-in-law, or siblings to help her. Most of her friends were in the same situation, without any extra hands to go around. She was widowed at a young age with only one child married. Yet none of her children ever sensed tension or hardship. They always felt that they were her greatest joy and pleasure, the greatest gift that *HaKadosh Baruch Hu* could have given her.

" … [she] faced many difficulties, and she was not well off. She could not necessarily give us things of monetary value, but never did the love stop — that sort of wealth we always received. Let us imagine a couple who has difficulty having children and finally merit giving birth to a son. One can imagine that the first time the baby gets up in middle of the night, the parents are joyful. B"H, mir hoben derlebt — we lived to see the day! It's not the hardships but the feeling of love that stays in the foreground. 'Mayim rabim lo yuchlu l'chabos es ha'ahavah — many waters could not extinguish that feeling of love …' "[28]

THIS WAS HOW REBBETZIN BENDER FELT ABOUT EACH OF HER CHILDREN. She appreciated each child as if he or she had been born after 30 years of anxious anticipation.

"How much we have to thank the *Ribbono shel Olam* for our children!" Rebbetzin Bender would say. "Without children, a family is empty." When her children would call her about a problem they were having with a child, she would always remind them, "Think about how many people would love to be in your position." When her daughters threw their hands up in frustration at the constant mess in the house, she chuckled in Yiddish,

---

28. Rabbi Michoel Bender in his *hesped* for Rebbetzin Bender.

"Every Jewish home should be a mess," and then she would add, "We have to always thank the *Ribbono shel Olam* that we have what to cook and for whom to cook."

Love, respect, responsibility, and concern characterized Rebbetzin Bender's relationship with her children. Every child called her every day. And even though she knew what was happening in every household, she would never intrude or mix in.

Rebbetzin Bender was careful never to take advantage of her role as a parent. Although it was her right to ask her children for help or request a favor, she never took their good will for granted and she was careful to ask of them in a non-demanding manner. "*Ich heis dir nisht* (I am not commanding you)," she would say, "but perhaps I can ask you to ..." Then she would again clarify, "But I am not telling you to do it ..." She was afraid that if she gave a direct order and for some reason her child found it difficult to obey, he would be transgressing the mitzvah of *kibud av va'eim*. She did not want to be a stumbling block for her children.

Her children never heard her scream. If Rebbetzin Bender was upset by something a child had done and wanted him to rectify his actions, she would state in a soft tone of voice, "Don't do that ..." Being a mother did not give her license to lose her temper. Everyone was treated with love, respect, and deference.

Rebbetzin Bender never wanted to lean on her children, or be a burden to them. She insisted on paying back even small sums of money, even when a grandchild just picked up a small item from the local grocery store. If she did not have enough change in the house, she would write it down and pay a lump sum later on. If she failed to pay the balance at the end of the month, she would call up apologetically, "I owe you 63 cents. *Bli neder*, I will pay you back shortly." She was scrupulous about paying them back, despite the fact that the Epstein children often went downstairs to their grandmother's refrigerator or pantry to take food that they needed because the stores were closed and Bubby's house was conveniently stocked. There was an unspoken understanding that such food "borrowed" was not meant to be returned. But Rebbetzin Bender never used the food she gave to cancel out the money her grandchildren laid out for her.

This was not a matter of pride; it was a matter of perspective. She was the mother, and a mother gives to her children.

AS HER FAMILY GREW, REBBETZIN BENDER DELIGHTED IN EACH NEW addition. The way she welcomed a new son or daughter-in-law into her family circle was a lesson in sensitivity. She understood the delicate balance of in-law relationships and went out of her way to treat her children-in-law as royalty. She wanted them to feel at least as equally valued as her children.

*Bnei banim harei heim k'banim*[29] (grandchildren are like children) was her motto. If a grandchild brought her a robe to hem, even if it was brought to her on a Thursday night, she would call up on Friday morning, happiness in her voice, to tell her granddaughter that the robe was ready to be picked up.

She often went shopping with her granddaughters. On one such trip, they stopped at a pay phone to call home to find out if another granddaughter had been successful in her run for a student government position. In the phone call, they heard the news that the granddaughter had lost. Rebbetzin Bender turned to her shopping partner. "I would like to buy her something." They returned home from the trip with a pretty sweater, and the girl's spirits lifted.

Her love was laced with a sense of responsibility to teach her grandchildren in subtle ways. On *Leil* Shabbos, after the women had *bentched licht* and the men were still in shul, the grandchildren would gather around her and she would tell them a *mashal* and ask them to guess the *nimshol*. It was a stimulating, not preachy way to convey a message. If she had a *chessed* to do and she felt that it was beneficial for a grandchild to participate, she would approach the child with, "Come, let us do a *chessed*." She would be sure to make the child aware that he was not just doing her a favor; he was earning a share in a mitzvah.

The immature behavior of her grandchildren did not frustrate her. Amazingly enough, they all behaved in her presence. She had over 40 grandchildren and each one felt, "Bubby really loves me!"

When Rebbetzin Bender needed to correct her grandchildren, she did so in a soft, uncritical manner. The girls were playing Elimination in the bungalow colony. As they played, they shouted "Kill Chanie! Kill Malkie!" Rebbetzin Bender called over her grandchild and gently said, "Please, tell them not to say kill. Tell them to say hit."

However, if she heard that the child's father, be it a son or son-in-law, made allowances for behavior that she disapproved of, she kept quiet. "Who am I?" she would say. "*Ich bin ah poshuteh frau* (I am a simple woman)." Her respect for *talmidei chachamim* was such that she made her knowledge subservient to theirs, even though she remembered them as youngsters.

AFTER A VISIT, WHEN THE CHILDREN WOULD GO BACK TO FAR ROCKaway or Lakewood, Rebbetzin Bender would stand outside and watch as the car pulled away, saying: "*Yevarechicha Hashem v'yishmerecha, ya'eir Hashem panav eilecha v'chunecka, yisa Hashem panav eilecha v'yaseim l'cha*

---

29. *Yevamos* 62b.

*shalom.*"[30] Rebbetzin Bender learned this from her mother. A half a century earlier in Otvock, when Rebbetzin Bender would leave home to teach in the Bais Yaakov, her mother would accompany her out the door. Then her mother would run back into the house, up to the second-story porch, and with the *tefillah* of *Yevarechicha* on her lips, she would watch her daughter until she was out of sight.

Sixty years later, on a different continent and in a vastly different world, Rebbetzin Bender still carried that image of her beloved mother standing on the porch, following her with her eyes, radiating love and concern, and saying *Yevarechicha*, a prayer that *HaKadosh Baruch Hu* watch over her precious child.

---

30. *Bamidbar* 6:24-26: "May Hashem bless you and safeguard you. May Hashem illuminate His countenance for you and be gracious to you. May Hashem lift His countenance to you and establish peace for you."

*Chapter Sixty-Four*

# Her Adornment:
# Loyal Friendship

*The station wagon pulled up in front of 1608 46th Street. Rebbetzin Bender slid into the front seat with her small suitcase, exchanged pleasantries with everyone in the car, and settled down for the ride to the Catskills.*

*"Chavale," Rebbetzin Bender called to her friend Rebbetzin Wachtfogel in the back seat, "I made some kugel. You should have something warm and good to eat." She handed back a foil-wrapped package that was still warm.*

*"Bashale, I also made something for you. Take. It's a vegetable; it's healthy." Rebbetzin Wachtfogel extended a bag of peeled carrots to her friend.*

*The two women enjoyed the treats they had brought for each other. Their car mates had received a profound lesson in friendship.*[31]

W HILE FAMILY OCCUPIED A SPECIAL PLACE IN REBBETZIN Bender's heart, so too did her friends. Friendships were invaluable and she dedicated thought, time, and energy into maintaining those relationships.

Before Rosh Hashanah she sat with her telephone book calling her friends to wish them *"ah gut yohr."* She wanted to communicate her good wishes and she was certain that her friend at the other end wanted to do

---

31. Rebbetzin M. Steinharter.

**Rebbetzin Bender and Rebbetzin Wachtfogel**

*Shown here at a very special simcha for the two of them. The wedding of the grandson of Rebbetzin Bender to the grandaughter of Rebbetzin Wachtfogel.*

the same. It never occurred to her to think, "Why should I call her, she never calls me?" or "Since I am older, she should be calling me." She just picked up the telephone and called. "I have not heard from you for a while. How are you doing?"

RABBI EZRIEL AND REBBETZIN RAIZEL LANGE WERE CLOSE FRIENDS with the Benders for many years. After Reb Dovid passed away, they became even closer with his rebbetzin. Reb Ezriel was an exceptionally warmhearted person who was devastated by his friend's death and sought to help fill that void by stopping by regularly to see how he could be of help. The Langes were on hand from the beginning to end of every Bender *simchah*, rejoicing as if the *simchah* were their own.

Since the Langes did not have children, they rarely had an occasion to host their own *simchah*. When such an occasion did arise, Rebbetzin Bender was at their side, helping, hosting, and sharing along with them. And if she felt that the honor accorded them was insufficient, she stepped in, even if it embarrassed her.

Moshe, a Russian 12-year-old in a bad situation, moved into the Lange home and was treated as their son. They saw to all his needs, both physical and spiritual. Without pressure, they gently encouraged him to become a *ben Torah*.

About a year after his arrival, Moshe was ready for a *bris*. The Langes made the occasion a double event, a *bris* and a *pidyon haben*. They prepared with the same excitement as if he were their own child. They invited friends and relatives. Rebbetzin Lange cooked a lavish meal. There was singing and speeches, and all the trappings of a joyous family *simchah*.

Toward the end of the evening, Rebbetzin Bender turned to the women around her and cleared her voice. "Let us all remember," she began, "this is Reb Ezriel and Rebbetzin Lange's special *simchah* …" Then she launched into a speech about the Langes' complete dedication to whatever they set out to do.[32] As unconcerned as she was in receiving honor, that was how concerned she was about her friends' honor.

When Reb Ezriel became weak from old age and illness, Rebbetzin Bender sent a grandchild over with fresh potato kugel every Erev Shabbos. Rebbetzin Bender was suffering from her own ailments and weak from age and ill health, but she was still attuned to others, especially her friends.

FAIGA[33] WAS A FRIEND WHO, IN MANY WAYS, HAD STRAYED FAR FROM the life she had known in Europe. Faiga had survived the war, immigrated to America, and married Charles Freedman. He was a sweet man who had never had much of a Jewish education, but kept a somewhat traditional home. Freedman opened a shoe factory in Harrisburg, Pennsylvania and became a very successful and wealthy businessman. They had no children and all of Faiga's family had been killed in the war. They kept the rudiments of kashrus and Shabbos, but not much else.

Rebbetzin Bender wrote to Faiga regularly, letting Faiga know that someone was thinking about her. She had kosher for Pesach food shipped to Harrisburg, even though she knew that their standards in kashrus were well below hers. A friend was a friend, and Rebbetzin Bender kept in touch out of loyalty and genuine affection.

REBBETZIN BENDER HAD MANY CLOSE FRIENDS, YET ONE DID NOT have to be a close friend to enjoy her attention and affection. Esther was a neighbor in the country, and although she was much younger than Rebbetzin Bender, they were quite friendly. The summer that Esther was expecting her 10th child, she was told that she had to fast on Tishah B'Av. She was nervous about fasting, and Rebbetzin Bender advised her to spend the day in bed. Esther obediently parked herself in bed to wait out the day. Early in the afternoon, there was a knock at the door. It was Rebbetzin Bender.

"Rebbetzin Bender, what …?"

"I came to keep you company," said Rebbetzin Bender while pulling over a chair. Esther was astounded and somewhat embarrassed. The bun-

---

32. Rabbi Mordechai Lerner.

33. Names have been changed.

galow was a wreck for one does not straighten up the house on Tishah B'Av and she was confined to her bed.

Oblivious to the chaos and to her own health issues that made fasting difficult, there was Rebbetzin Bender, ready to spend the afternoon entertaining and helping a much younger woman. For hours, Rebbetzin Bender regaled her with conversation, stories, and advice until the sun set. Esther was amazed at how swiftly the time had passed, and she was doubtful that she would have had the patience to lie in bed alone and bored for the entire day.[34]

AS REBBETZIN BENDER GREW OLDER, HER STAFF OF COLLEAGUES IN Bais Yaakov grew younger. Yet she never felt the distance, was never too old to relate, never too jaded from life's experiences to care about their concerns that might be so different from hers. No matter how young the teacher in the teachers' room, she was still a colleague and friend.

One day in 1991, Rebbetzin Bender was in the teachers' room when one of the teachers took off her rings to wash for *HaMotzei*. The teacher gasped in horror as her rings fell down the drain. Everyone gathered around, murmuring words of sympathy. Each had a different suggestion or idea about how to rescue the rings. Then the bell rang and the teachers had to return to their classrooms.

Rebbetzin Bender also went to class, but her mind was still on her friend's lost rings. Before starting class, she called one of the girls. "Chavie, please run around the corner to Rebbetzin Helfand's house and ask her if I can borrow a telephone book."

Chavie did as she was told and returned to class a few minutes later with the phonebook in hand. Rebbetzin Bender took the phonebook and left the classroom. She returned a few minutes later and gave the phonebook back to Chavie to return.

"One of the teachers dropped her rings down the drain," Rebbetzin Bender explained. "I just called a plumber to come to school and try to retrieve them."[35]

While her friend was in distress over her lost rings, Rebbetzin Bender could not go back into class and teach as if nothing had happened. Only after she did something to help could she bring herself to begin the class.

"Who possessed a heart as big as hers …?" an old friend declared in wonder.

---

34. Rebbetzin E. Kops.
35. Mrs. C. Savitz.

### Chapter Sixty-Five

# Her Gift: To Expand Her "Self"

*... She thought nothing of herself, yet [she] extended [her "self"] to so many people. She had the ability to feel people's joy and pain — she worried about them and counseled them. The telephone calls began as soon as she came home from teaching ... People were constantly calling. Many problems found their way to her doorstep, and she accepted them all with equanimity, recognizing their innate value. Strangers felt comfortable discussing their issues with her for they merged into her "self" and became a part of her being ...*[36]

REBBETZIN BENDER NEVER LIVED A FAIRY-TALE LIFE. SHE remembered the terror she had felt when she and her family fled from Russia to Poland. She did not marry young, and she waited several years for her first child to be born. She lost her parents and much of the world she knew when she was a young woman. She was a hard-working adult juggling myriad responsibilities, rarely taking a well-earned vacation. She lost a vibrant husband and remained a widow for

---

36. In his *hesped* on Rebbetzin Bender, Rabbi Chaim Epstein paraphrased the words of Rabbi Shimon Shkop in the introduction to his sefer *Sha'arei Yosher*: "... Hashem implanted self-love into every human being and the Torah makes no demands of us to uproot that love; it is not expected of us. Rather the idea of *chessed* is benevolence through which we spread the 'Ani' — our selfness. There are people who extend their existence of self to their family. Others expand to include friends, neighbors ... and there are those individuals who have the ability to expand to all of *Klal Yisroel*, and some even to all of creation. The concept is the inclusion of more people in our 'selfness.' It brings giving to the level that another entity is perceived as an expansion of oneself."

more years than she was married. She suffered from several serious medical conditions that caused her much pain and suffering over the years. Her doctors called her "a living miracle."

Yet not only was Rebbetzin Bender *b'simchah*, she was always trying to alleviate other people's distress and improve the quality of their lives. Life was a gift from *HaKadosh Baruch Hu*, a gift for which she had endless appreciation. Those whose troubles blind them to the glory of this gift are truly unfortunate. For those people she worried, sympathized, and sought ways to help.

REBBETZIN BENDER WAS AN EXCEPTIONAL LISTENER. SHE CONCENtrated on every word, intent on understanding what she was hearing and what was left unsaid. She absorbed it all into her very being, allowing the other person's concerns and problems to become a part of her, an extension of her "self."

Once the other person became a part of her, how could she not try to help? What sane person does not help himself? Then she asked herself, *How can I help?* More often than not, the greatest help she could give was to listen with genuine interest.

Rebbetzin Bender rarely lost patience, no matter how much anyone moaned and groaned, no matter how many situations she considered self-made, no matter how often people did not listen to her advice and then came to complain about the same issue all over again. Just as a mother thinks nothing of getting up several times a night to take care of her child, Rebbetzin Bender thought nothing of giving of herself to any member of *Klal Yisroel* over and over again. They were all her children, all her family.

*"… Every Jewish life was of interest to her. She loved to hear women's stories, to see how Hashem's great compassion was woven into the tapestry of each life. She rejoiced in her friends' good fortune and in the gifts that they received. Her words flowed with praise and gratitude for the miracles of Jewish existence …"*[37]

REBBETZIN BENDER EARNED A REPUTATION AS ONE WHO LISTENED, understood, and gave wise advice. Russians, Sephardim, modern Americans, Chassidim, and *Litvaks* all sought her counsel. Rebbetzin Bender knew how to speak so that her words would be accepted. She was sharp and intelligent, with a soft unassuming manner. She noticed the nuances of each culture and used these subtleties to make her audience more comfortable.

Sometimes she would even change her *Litvishe Yiddishe* dialect to a *Gali-*

---

37. Quoted from the essay *Reflections at Rebbetzin Bender's Levayah* by Rebbetzin Sara E. Freifeld, Dean of Touro College Women's Division.

*cianer* dialect. One of her sons caught her at it and assumed that because Williamsburg was becoming more *Chassidish*, she felt that she had to change. "Not at all," Rebbetzin Bender replied. "It is easier for them. If they are more comfortable, I feel more comfortable. What is the difference how I speak as long as we understand each other?" It would not dawn on her to stick to her own dialect on principle. "Whatever is easier for the other person" was her motto.

At the end of a busy day Rebbetzin Bender would take the phone off the hook and tell her daughter some of the interesting things that had happened.[38] They would laugh, cry, and say that these stories were for a book, but it would make a ridiculous book because the stories were so farfetched!

*"ACHEINU KOL BEIS YISROEL,"* SHE WOULD SAY, "THEY ARE ALL FAMILY to me." Family members are available to one another during times of hardship and happiness. Family members accept one another non-judgmentally. Family members love one another, overlooking one another's faults, rejoicing in one another's triumphs.

*Acheinu kol beis Yisroel.* This statement was not mere lip service. She felt a real connection to all of *Klal Yisroel:* the smart and the silly, the pretty and the plain, the happy and the hopeless. They were all an extension of her "self."

A GRANDCHILD ONCE ENTERED HER HOUSE AND SAW THAT SHE WAS unusually happy.

"There is a new *chosson* and *kallah*," Rebbetzin Bender announced joyfully.

He asked the *kallah's* name. It was unfamiliar. "What is the great *simchah*?" he asked. "Is she family?"

She shook her head, still smiling.

"Is she from a family that has some kind of *tzarah* that makes this *simchah* so much greater?"

Again, she shook her head.

"Then why all the excitement?"

"You don't understand," she answered. "I saw a different world: a world of beautiful families, a world of beautiful *Yiddishe kinder*. This beautiful world was almost totally destroyed. So whenever I am worthy of seeing another generation of *Yidden* being built, it is the greatest *simchah* for me. For me, every *chosson*, every *kallah*, every child who is born is another *simchah* — my *simchah*."

*Acheinu kol beis Yisroel*, we are all family.

---

38. Without names.

# *Chapter Sixty-Six*

# Her Joy: To Give

*"... From the world she took nothing; she needed nothing. She was too inspired and excited with living and transmitting Torah to be detained by the details of material concerns ..."*[39]

REBBETZIN BENDER NEVER WANTED TO TAKE, SHE ONLY wanted to give and then give some more. Every day she sat beside the telephone with lists of names of people for whom she wanted to do *chessed*. When she was young and energetic, she went by foot, by bus, or by train. She went to counsel a friend who was going through a difficult time. She entered in the guise of a social call, but her real purpose was to encourage and uplift. She would stop by another friend to pick up a check for a needy *kallah*, a check that would only materialize if she picked it up personally.

As she grew older and found it difficult to get around, the telephone became her lifeline. From her modest apartment at 1608 46th Street, she collected for needy causes, counseled couples with marital problems, answered questions about complex *chinuch* issues, mediated business conflicts, made peace when strife arose, and made numerous friendly phone calls just to let people know that she cared about them. Even when she

---

39. Quoted from the essay *Reflections at Rebbetzin Bender's Levayah* by Rebbetzin Sara E. Freifeld, Dean of Touro College Women's Division.

humbly felt that she did not have an answer, she was there to lend an ear and a shoulder. She was busy from early morning until late at night.

She always had her "projects": a needy bride, a family of orphans, a disabled Torah scholar, and many more. Her breakfront was full of envelopes of money earmarked for different causes. She did not go from house to house collecting, nor did she organize big fund-raisers or make rounds of appeals. Almost all her fund-raising was done from her modest living room, with her old rotary black Bell telephone in hand and a ledger on the table next to her trusty telephone book. In her quiet, unassuming way, she helped hundreds of needy people.

Whenever she went upstairs to the Epsteins, she quickly returned to her apartment downstairs because someone might be calling on the telephone. Only when her grandchildren bought her a cordless telephone was she able to relax as she visited the Epsteins. Even then she rarely spent extended time simply enjoying her family. She went upstairs to see how everyone was doing, to help out, or to give some advice, and then she would head downstairs to deal with what still needed to be accomplished.

Wherever she went, Rebbetzin Bender looked for new opportunities to do *chessed*. One Tishah B'Av when she was up in the country, she asked a grandson in Camp Toras Chessed to collect money for a needy family in Eretz Yisroel. When she was visiting her daughter in Lakewood and she heard about a school for disabled children that was struggling to stay afloat despite crushing financial burdens, she immediately began to collect for the school. She had no personal connection with the children in the school or their families. After a while, she even forgot the name of the principal but the school remained on her agenda, and she continued to collect for it.

YAEL[40] PULLED UP IN FRONT OF 321 HICKSVILLE ROAD AND WAITED. Soon Rabbi Yaakov Bender emerged carrying a suitcase. At his side was an elderly woman.

*She must be his mother,* Yael thought.

Reb Yaakov opened the front door of the car. "Thank you, Mrs. Brander. We much appreciate you giving my mother a ride to Boro Park."

Yael smiled and waved her hand. "It's nothing. I am going anyway."

Rebbetzin Bender settled comfortably into the front passenger seat and Yael began driving. *Actually,* Yael thought to herself, *it is a big deal that I agreed to take a passenger. I have so much on my head; I could have used the ride just to think. Now I will have to make small talk …*

"So," Yael began politely, "how are you?"

---

40. Not her real name.

"*Baruch Hashem*, fine, thank you." Rebbetzin Bender paused. "How are you?"

*She should only know!* Yael thought sadly.

Rebbetzin Bender waited for an answer. Gently, she asked again, prodding the young woman at her side to reveal what was bothering her. Suddenly, it all came out. Yael was going through a very difficult time in her personal life, and it was cathartic for her to talk to someone who so obviously cared. They spoke all the way to Boro Park. Rebbetzin Bender insisted that Yael come inside. She took homemade cake out of the freezer and boiled water for tea. As Yael sat in the cozy kitchen, warming her hands around a mug of hot tea, she felt cared for and comforted.

EVEN IN TRANSIT REBBETZIN BENDER DID *CHESSED*. WHENEVER SHE had a ride — from Boro Park to Lakewood, from Boro Park to the country, or from Boro Park to Far Rockaway — she would never sit idle and silent. She would ask the people in the car about their family, their health, their livelihood, and their needs. When she saw she could help, she did not forget the conversation, but filed it away in her memory bank, and then acted.

Often, her travel mates were amazed to receive a telephone call from Rebbetzin Bender a short while later, suggesting a *shidduch* for a daughter they had spoken about, or a position for the family member seeking a job. To Rebbetzin Bender, no conversation was so trivial as to be forgotten. Even when no action was warranted, her travel mates came away uplifted.

Rebbetzin Bender gave of herself naturally. As she walked down the block, she greeted friends and acquaintances warmly, always remembering something kind to say. Guests were treated royally and, as they left her house, she would insist that they take with them a piece of cake or a bit of kugel wrapped in foil. No one left her house empty-handed.[41]

*"… Her own needs were insignificant. The need to ease someone else's burden was compelling …"*[42]

---

41. Rabbi Mordechai Lerner.

42. Excerpted from the *hesped* by Rabbi Chaim Epstein for Rebbetzin Bender.

### Chapter Sixty-Seven

# Her Desire: To Honor Others

*"Hello, Rebbetzin Spiegel? This is Basya Bender."*

*Rebbetzin Spiegel was so surprised that she almost dropped the phone. "Rebbetzin Bender, I am that little student you taught not so long ago. You call me 'Rebbetzin' and yourself ...?"*

*"Others you must honor," Rebbetzin Bender maintained firmly. "With yourself, you may do what you want."*[43]

**E**VERY HUMAN BEING WAS CREATED *B'TZELEM ELOKIM* AND WAS worthy of Rebbetzin Bender's respect. When the cleaning agency sent immigrant women to clean her house, Rebbetzin Bender sat them down at the table and insisted that they have something to drink. Often, this led to long conversations where they would pour their hearts out, grateful for a listening ear. When they left she paid them for the full amount of time they were in her house, regardless of how much time was spent talking.

The plight of the Russian immigrants especially tugged at her heart. They came to America for a better life, but "better" was a relative term. In many cases, they were better off financially and had more civil liberties, but they were forced into menial jobs that would have been beneath them in Russia. Rebbetzin Bender engaged the Russian cab driver or fruit-store owner in conversation, showing them genuine interest.

---

43. Rebbetzin C. Spiegel at the *shloshim* for Rebbetzin Bender.

Rebbetzin Bender was once on a bus during a trip "down South" on business for Bais Yaakov. She wondered why all the black people made their way to the back of the bus while the front section of the bus where she sat was virtually empty. As the ride continued, the black people stood packed together in the back. She was shocked to realize that no matter how crowded they were, the blacks were only allowed in the back of the bus. How dare human beings treat others in this way! Where is the simple respect that a person deserves? She never forgot the incident and spoke of it often. It was natural for Rebbetzin Bender to recognize and respect the humanity in every individual.

When Rebbetzin Bender arrived in America she went to Eastern District High School to learn proper English pronunciation. To teach the foreigners how to pronounce the "th" sound, a sound that does not exist in many languages, the teacher instructed the class to stick out their tongues. Rebbetzin Bender was shocked at this unrefined practice. She never forgot that she was an aristocrat, a daughter of *HaKadosh Baruch Hu*.

If one of her former students became a teacher, even if she was only 25 years old, Rebbetzin Bender addressed her as "Rebbetzin," and was mindful of her colleague's honor. She shied away from her own title.

Many a *tzedakah* organization asked for her endorsement, something she readily gave. "How can I say no?" she sighed to her Blumie over the phone. "If the *tzedakah* will make more money because my name is on the envelope, or because I signed the letter, I should say no?" Yet, when the envelope made its way into her house, she crossed out the "Rebbetzin" written in front of her name. It irked her terribly.[44]

Her humility was genuine. She honestly believed that there was something to respect in every person, young and old alike. She listened intently to what her little grandchildren learned in school or thought of on their own. And if it was something novel to her, she thought nothing of quoting a child. Every time she returned from a *shiur*, a *derashah*, or a *kinnus*, she came back animated, with something significant to say over. She never thought herself too accomplished to learn from others.

As the years went on, different organizations sought to honor her and, for the good of the Torah or *chessed* that would emerge, she agreed. She came home from these events with plaques or tributes that she promptly squirreled away under her bed, out of sight. No matter how many times she was asked to speak at a function or accept an honor, she still reacted with amazement that she was the one they approached.

---

44. Once there were many leftover envelopes from a fund-raiser. The envelopes were blank except for the return address: "Rebbetzin Basya Bender." Since the *tzedakah* organization had no use for these envelopes, they gave them to Rebbetzin Bender. Not one to waste something good, she used the envelopes, but she crossed out the "Rebbetzin."

One day, she came across a *vort* from Rabbi Moshe Feinstein that provided her with a satisfactory explanation for the honor coming her way.

In *Bircas Krias Shema*, we say, "*lilmod u'l'lamed.*" We ask *HaKadosh Baruch Hu* for help in learning and teaching Torah. Yet, what should be the thoughts of a simple person in saying these words? He is not a *talmid chacham* who learns or teaches. How does this plea apply to him?

Reb Moshe answered: Every person is a teacher. He teaches his friend, his neighbor, his taxi driver, the stranger in the street. How? In every action that a person does, someone else can learn from him. A friend can observe another friend and learn something beneficial, or observe a different friend and learn something detrimental. Lessons can be gleaned from large actions and from small actions. Everyone goes through life as a teacher. The question is: What are people learning from you?

After hearing this *vort*, Rebbetzin Bender found it easier to accept the honor people wanted to give her. While she never viewed her contribution to the world of Bais Yaakov as pivotal (there were many others she felt deserved more credit than her), and while she did not consider herself a pioneer in teaching classes in Family Living, she did view herself as an *ehrlicher* person trying to do the Will of her Creator. This *vort* gave her encouragement because it meant that even a simple *Yiddene,* as she viewed herself, was always affecting the lives of others.

Nonetheless, when her friends and colleagues in Bais Yaakov approached her with the idea of honoring her for 50 years of teaching at the Bais Yaakov Spring Tea, she was speechless. After the initial shock, she was moved. Her love for Bais Yaakov was so strong that no matter how convinced she was that the honor was unwarranted and unnecessary, she would accept this honor out of love.

An outstanding example of Rebbetzin Bender's disregard for her own honor was the speech she delivered at the Spring Tea. The speech was witty and warm, peppered with *divrei Torah* and nostalgia. But it was the way that she effortlessly diverted the attention from herself and cast others in the limelight that was vintage Rebbetzin Bender:[45]

*"I do have a bit of stage fright, eimasa d'tzibbura (awe of the public). One of our very beloved teachers in Crakow used to say, 'If you do not have stage fright, something is missing in you.'*

*"… I come from Poland, not a rich country, [but a country where] schools looked like something. If one littered on school property, one had to pay a fine. Then, I came to Keap Street and Marcy Avenue, on top of an old shul, an old*

---

45. The following is excerpted and translated from Rebbetzin Bender's speech. She brought in more *divrei Torah* lauding Rabbi Boruch and Rebbetzin Kaplan and other members of the Bais Yaakov staff.

*dilapidated structure — maybe some of you have visited that place. Pieces of plaster hung from the ceilings, and the whole place was really neglected, not what I was used to calling a school.*

*"There were two rooms: one room had 17 girls and one room had 14 girls. Rebbetzin Kaplan could not introduce me at the time, so I introduced myself. What should I tell you? Something attracted me to those girls. With open eyes and ears, they listened to every letter and every word that emerged from my mouth. They immediately asked me questions — not if I have electricity in my house, which was the first question everyone else asked me — they asked about Sara Schenirer, a"h, and the Bais Yaakov movement. And I tried my best.*

*"When I see you all here today, I must call out the pasuk that Yeshayah Hanavi says: 'Mi yalad li es eilah … v'eilah mi gidel.'[46] I see this crowd and the transformation is not to be believed! … And when I think about those two classes of 14 and 17 girls who had no proper education until then …*

*"… Hashem commanded Moshe to build the Mishkan and Moshe asks, 'Is it possible for the Jewish nation to do so in the desert?' And Hashem answers, 'Even one member of the Jewish nation (alone) can build the Mishkan if, in his heart, he wants to with emes.' Only with emes.*

*"Bais Yaakov was built with emes. Rebbetzin Kaplan did not know that Hashem chose her to be the Kohen Gadol: to ignite the light, to illuminate all the dark corners, not only in America. Everywhere she was, people were privileged to take from her light. She was unaware, but she had an iron will. And someone else had that will. That was, and still is, Rabbi Boruch Kaplan. Which husband wants his wife to be away for days on end? Which husband gives up his personal comfort so his wife can give her head, her time, her energy, and her efforts for Bais Yaakov, for the continuation of the work of Sara Schenirer, a"h? And Rabbi and Rebbetzin Kaplan worked tirelessly for Bais Yaakov.*

*"I must say this because Rebbetzin Kaplan used to say: 'How can I take the credit? It is him!' Without him, she would not have been able to do it. She came from Europe: no family, no knowledge of the language, nothing familiar. She lived in a small apartment on South Ninth Street. Reb Boruch took upon himself the burden not only of the finances, but of every decision that involved Bais Yaakov. He never gave in to any heteirim, no compromises on the standard of Yiddishkeit. Many times he turned down donations that might have imposed lower religious standards on the school. Now is not the time to recount countless episodes when we lost tens of thousands of dollars because we did not want to have the opinions of certain types of people … And baruch Hashem, Bais Yaakov grew and grew, without any leniencies or compromises …*

*"… How many times, at teachers' meetings, as my fellow teachers can attest, did Rebbetzin Kaplan ask, 'Is this what Sara Schenirer would think? Is this what Sara Schenirer would do? Would she be happy with what we are doing?' What her*

---

46. *Yeshayah 49:21: Who bore me these? … And who raised these?*

*mentor Sara Schenirer would think was constantly on her mind …*

*"Once, Rebbetzin Kaplan confided in me that she had a peculiar thought. She was expecting and she wondered if she would be able to have the same love for her older children once the baby was born. To a newborn, you give so much attention. Will this minimize the attention given to the older ones? After the baby was born, she commented to me that she regretted her silly question. She loves her newborn, and as for the older ones, she loves them even more!*

*"This was the kind of love she had for students as well. The school grew larger, many more girls, many more problems, many more hardships, and much more love. Endless love, like from a bottomless well, more and more love. More girls, more problems, more hardships, and more love! So many hundreds of girls and each one, individually, from the youngest to the oldest, occupied the same place in her heart. How strong she was, yet so soft, so friendly, and so motherly. However much I talk about her greatness, it will not be enough…*

*"Before I leave the stage, I would like to thank the audience. I hope you were not disappointed. This speech was very difficult for me … I did not know where to start, how to start … but, thank you!*

*"In addition, I would like to thank the staff for the honor, which I definitely do not deserve. Rebbetzin Wachtfogel reminded me that Rebbetzin Kotler was once honored and she found the honor embarrassing. Rabbi Aharon Kotler, ztz"l, said to her, 'For Torah, one must embarrass oneself.' All I can say is, too much Torah I have not learned, but if one has gained a bit of chizuk from my words, I accept the embarrassment with love. Thank you, ladies."*[47]

BAIS YAAKOV PRESENTED REBBETZIN BENDER WITH A GOLD PENDANT. Embossed on one side was the Bais Yaakov logo, and on the other side was a large number 50, commemorating her 50 years of teaching. This was the only commemorative gift that she did not hide. She wore the charm with pride, proud of her years as a Bais Yaakov teacher.

---

47. Although this is only a short excerpt from a much longer speech, most of the speech continued along the same lines: more *divrei Torah* pointing to the greatness of others, more about Bais Yaakov, and more about the Kaplans. She spoke almost nothing about herself, her family, her history, or her background.

*Chapter Sixty-Eight*

# Her Longing: To Serve Him

*"… [She was one of the cherished ones of Klal Yisroel, as the pasuk says] 'Haben yakir li Ephraim — Is Ephraim not my precious child?'[48] … The Midrash says 'yakir' (precious) is derived from the word 'mikreh' (chance). The chances of Hashem coming across a 'ben yakir' are slim. 'Adam echad mei'elef matzasi.' These beloved children are a minority, proportionately one to a thousand … 'v'ishah b'kol eileh lo matzasi'[49] — seldom, in all those chance encounters, does Hashem come across a woman of that stature. However, if there should be a woman who turns out to be that 'one of a thousand,' such a woman is truly cherished by Hashem.*

*"… Men have the means of obtaining that 'yakrus,' that preciousness through their Torah learning. But an 'ishah mikol eileh lo matzasi,' seldom is such a woman found (because they do not have the same mitzvah of learning Torah). Therefore, a woman who attains 'yakrus' is indeed very precious."[50]*

ORDECHAI,[51] *AH GUTEN* EREV SHABBOS. HOW WONderful to see you ..."

The young *avreich* peered closely at his grandmother. "*Ah guten* Erev Shabbos, Bubby, and how are you feeling?" She looked

---

48. *Yirmiyah* 31:19.

49. *Koheles* 7:28.

50. Excerpted from the *hesped* by Rabbi Elya Svei for Rebbetzin Bender.

51. This is a generic name for any one of Rebbetzin Bender's grandchildren. All were devoted to their grandmother and though only some were contacted for interviews, many had similar stories to relate.

weak and her greeting was more low key than usual.

"*Baruch Hashem, ah dank tzum Eibeshter* ..."

Rebbetzin Bender walked ahead of him toward the kitchen and sank onto a chair. "How are you?" she asked perfunctorily. "How are the children?" Her mind was not on the questions, nor did she seem terribly interested in the answers. Mordechai was puzzled. His grandmother had not been well, and perhaps that was why she seemed so distracted, and yet ... He glanced around the room. The house was neat and orderly, as usual, yet something was wrong.

"Bubby, the floor, I hope you are not planning to mop it. The doctors said that you must take it easy."

"I know, I know," she sighed, "but *l'kavod Shabbos kodesh*, not to have the floor mopped ...?"

Mordechai stood up and headed toward the broom closet. "Where is the mop? Let me mop the floors ..."

"Oh, no!" Rebbetzin Bender protested. "This is not befitting work for one who learns Torah."

"Never mind." Mordechai had already found the mop and was looking for the soap. "It will take me just a few minutes."

"But a *talmid chacham* should not do menial work ..."

Mordechai continued mixing the soap with water in a pail.

"Please, Mordechai, put away the mop. So the floor will not be mopped for Shabbos. I will manage." Distraught, Rebbetzin Bender had pulled herself out of her chair and was standing beside him at the sink.

Mordechai put the pail on the floor and the mop beside it. Then he took her by the arm and steered her toward a chair outside the kitchen. "Don't worry," he reassured her, "I am not really mopping the floor. I am just cleaning the spots that are dirty. The type of job that I am doing is not called 'mopping a floor.' " That said, he turned to the job at hand, careful to finish quickly so that his grandmother would have a clean floor with minimal heartache.

"See, Bubby? Already finished." Mordechai called out from the kitchen as he rinsed out the mop. Rebbetzin Bender sighed. "Thank you," she said simply. It was clear that she was relieved to have a clean floor, but she was nonetheless pained that a *kollel yungerman* was the one to do it.

RABBI ELYA SVEI DESCRIBED REBBETZIN BENDER AS AN "*ISHAH GE-dolah*," a great woman who attained "*yakrus.*" Her reverence for Torah was certainly one aspect of her "*yakrus.*" She had tremendous clarity about the supremacy of Torah and the need to honor those who studied it, whether it was an accomplished scholar or a young yeshivah student.

In the almost 25 years Rebbetzin Bender lived in the same house as her daughter Esther, inevitably, two people would be using the stairs at the same time. If the other person on the staircase was a *yeshivah bochur*, no matter how young, she would insist that he go before her. "I go slowly," she would say in her quiet way. The implication was that she had all the time in the world, while every minute of a *yeshivah bochur* was precious.

"In what merit did I earn two sons-in-law who are *talmidei chachamim?*" she would reflect. "Perhaps it is because of my *mesiras nefesh* for my husband's learning. When we first came to America, I knew no one. It would have been normal for me to ask him to spend at least part of the evening at home. After all, I was so alone. My parents and friends were trapped in Europe, I was struggling with the language, and everything was new and strange. Yet, I allowed him to learn late into the night. Perhaps in the merit of this self-sacrifice, I was deemed worthy of two such sons-in-law."

When the Epstein house was a beehive of youth and energy, Rebbetzin Bender came upstairs regularly, but not too often, happily offering to shop, sew, cook, clean, or help with the grandchildren. She understood, without being told, that if a child had to be taken to the doctor, then someone had to be home for the other children returning from school. Her daughter Esther could not be in two places at once and, inevitably, she would have to ask Reb Chaim to step in. For Rebbetzin Bender, any time taken away from her son-in-law's learning was a tragic waste. In her subtle, non-intrusive manner, she stepped in, offering to help.

*Rabbi Shloimke Berman visiting the Bender home*

Her entire life she strove to help her children and grandchildren, physically and financially, so that they could continue to learn and teach Torah with a bit more ease. Many times she commented that her bank account was empty, and then she would add, "How can I have money sitting in the bank when my children are learning Torah and find it difficult to make ends meet?"

Her reverence for *talmidei chachamim* was such that she always referred to her sons-in-law as Reb Chaim and Reb Moshe Shimon, nothing more familiar. Her joy at seing a *talmid chacham*, even a relative, was boundless. When her cousin Rabbi Shloimke Berman came to America for medical reasons, Rebbetzin Bender looked forward to the visit with both eagerness and awe. He was one of the leading scholars of the generation and she felt honored that he and his rebbetzin were coming for a visit.

Rebbetzin Bender had an active appreciation of Torah. Wherever she was — in camp, at a *simchah*, or at the Shabbos table of one of her children — Rebbetzin Bender loved to hear *divrei Torah*. She listened intently, and when it was appropriate, she would ask a question to clarify a thought.

The Epsteins spent their summers in Camp Toras Chessed and Rebbetzin Bender joined them. Their first summer there, Rebbetzin Bender noticed that at the beautiful Shabbos *seudah* they prepared for the *bochurim*, food was plentiful and spirited singing created a Shabbos atmosphere, but no one stood up to give a *d'var Torah*. She could not believe that a roomful of *b'nei Torah* could eat together on Shabbos and not say *divrei Torah*. She approached the camp management and aired her complaint, and from then on there was always a *d'var Torah* delivered at the Shabbos meal in Camp Toras Chessed. As for the women, they gained a regular speaker; Rebbetzin Bender spoke to the women every Shabbos and once or twice a week in the evenings.

"MORDECHAI, YOU ARE HERE." REBBETZIN BENDER BEAMED HAPPILY. "*Nu*, let us begin." She went into the kitchen and washed her hands. Then she took out her Pesach *machzor* and carefully reviewed the halachos aloud, pausing to concentrate, asking a question here and there, as if this was the first time she was doing this mitzvah. She closed the *machzor*, her eyes bright in anticipation. They were embarking on an exciting mission: they were searching for *chametz*.

Rebbetzin Bender followed her grandson's lead. At her age, it was difficult for her to bend and stretch, and most of the actual work was delegated to Mordechai. Nonetheless, she was at his side, eager for a share in the mitzvah. When they completed their search, Rebbetzin Bender headed back to her *machzor*.

"*Kol chamira …*" she read solemnly, and then she added her own blessing, "*Nu*, the *Eibeshter* should help me that I should merit to live another year *gezunterheit* and again fulfill this mitzvah."

The mitzvos of Yom Tov were precious to her, and she never looked for easy ways out of mitzvos. Pesach, she had her own stringencies that she did with happiness. Though this was not her practice throughout the year, before Pesach she made the trip to Lamm's butcher shop on Lee Avenue to watch as he *kashered* all the chicken and the meat that she would use for Pesach. It was a full-day affair between traveling to Williamsburg, watching the *kashering*, and then shlepping the meat and chicken back to Boro Park. She returned home exhausted but happy.

Her Pesach preparations included making all kinds of *Pesachdike* treats — kugels, cakes, candies — so that when the grandchildren would come to visit, she would have something to give them "*l'kovod Yom Tov*."

Any mention of *chametz* on Pesach was sacrilegious. The entire week she would not say the words "*chametz*," "*challah*," or "*bread*." If it was absolutely necessary in the conversation, she would say "*ches*," referring to *chametz*. The grandchildren loved to have fun with what they considered "*Bubby's chumrah*," and they would try to get her into a conversation that required mentioning bread just to hear her say "*ches*" instead. The only time she said the word "*chametz*" on Pesach was when she read the Haggadah.

On Succos, she beamed as she shook the *lulav* and *esrog*. On Yom Kippur, she cried if she was not permitted to fast. On Chanukah, as her children and grandchildren sang and danced in front of the lights, Rebbetzin Bender let tears of emotion roll down her cheeks.

She could feel *simchas Yom Tov*, despite the fact that Yom Tov had a bittersweet aspect. Usually at the first Yom Tov *Kiddush*, a cloud would pass over her face as she remembered her husband and when the family was whole. Then she would compose herself and embrace her *simchas Tom Tov* once again.

She would begin her Shabbos preparations early Friday morning and always finish early Friday afternoon. She would *bentch licht* 10 minutes before *bentching* time, just as her mother used to. It did not have to be exactly 10 minutes before, a little earlier was also fine. She gently encouraged her children to adopt this practice. "It is not so hard," she would say, "you get used to it." She could not understand how people were still preparing for Shabbos until a minute before *shekiah*.

"WHERE IS REB CHAIM? I HAVE TO ASK HIM A *SHE'EILAS CHACHAM* (question to a wise man)." How many times a week did Rebbetzin Bender troop up to the Epstein house to ask her son-in-law a *she'eilas chacham*? She never relied on something she once heard or the generally accepted "people say." If she had a question in halachah she wanted to hear the answer directly from the Rav. She wanted to make sure that the question was asked properly and she understood the answer.

This careful approach did not turn her into a nervous person, constantly trembling that she might make a mistake. On the contrary, Rebbetzin Bender was known for her equanimity and her gentle manner. But she was never complacent. She came from a home saturated with Torah and *yiras Shamayim*. She could have felt that she already knew how to be "*ah finer Yid*," a good Jew, and that any new practices that she did not remember from home were needless stringencies. Not Rebbetzin Bender. When she learned that a halachah might not be as she saw it practiced at home, or she heard of a *chumrah* that even *gedolim* of her generation had not insisted upon, she never discarded it saying, "Am I not *frum* enough?" She embraced her newfound knowledge and sought to see how and if it should be incorporated into her life.

For years Rebbetzin Bender used to daven outdoors, in Camp Toras Chessed. She enjoyed the open spaces and fresh air. Once, her son-in-law saw her davening outside. Reb Chaim commented that according to halachah, one should daven *Shemoneh Esrei* indoors. She immediately changed her practice.

At the same time, she did not take everything people said at face value. While she was in the country, she heard the fast-growing rumor that Rabbi Moshe Feinstein said that Tropicana orange juice was no longer kosher. Suddenly, no one was drinking Tropicana orange juice although no one knew for sure that Reb Moshe had ever made such a statement.

"This is silly," Rebbetzin Bender protested. "Let's call Reb Moshe and find out what the story is."

Within minutes, she had Reb Moshe on the phone. "Excuse me for bothering the Rosh Yeshivah, but I was wondering about something. People here are saying that the Rosh Yeshivah believes there is a problem with Tropicana orange juice. Is this true?"

Reb Moshe laughed. "Do you want to know what happened? I was at a *bris*. Someone offered me Tropicana orange juice. I don't drink orange juice so I told him that I don't drink that. Someone must have taken this to mean that I hold that it's not kosher. I never said anything of the sort." To create a *chumrah* based on a rumor was not her definition of *yiras Shamayim*.[52]

---

52. Rebbetzin Bender often called Rabbi Moshe Feinstein with halachic questions. One day, she noticed that she could no longer remove her rings for *netilas yadayim*. She promptly called Reb Moshe to ask him what to do. Reb Moshe immediately asked if there was blood circulation in the finger and if she was certain that she did not have to see a doctor. After she reassured him that blood circulation was not a problem, he reviewed the question and gave an answer. Rebbetzin Bender often repeated this story as an illustration of how a *gadol b'Yisroel* cares about *Klal Yisroel*.

IN DAVENING, REBBETZIN BENDER did not raise her voice or do anything outwardly different. She sat and simply spoke to her Creator, enunciating the words softly, slowly, and clearly. It was the davening of one who was fully aware that every word was being heard.

She often engaged her children and grandchildren in discussions about the meaning of certain *tefillos*, the significance of a word here and there. She always wanted to make sure that she understood what she was saying and that she was having the proper intentions as she said the words.

As she got older, it bothered her that when she was physically weak, her mind wandered when she davened. One day, she heard that the Manchester Rosh Yeshivah, Rabbi Yehudah Zev Segal, was staying with his son R' Getzel who lived on her block. The whole neighborhood was visiting him and receiving his *berachos*.

*Rabbi Yehudah Zev Segal (1910-1993) learned in Yeshivas Eitz Chaim of London. He went to learn in Mir when he was 20 years old. In 1940, when German bombers attacked Gateshead, he and his family moved to Manchester. He became maggid shiur and later Rosh Yeshivah in the Manchester Yeshivah where he was known for his diligence in learning. The Manchester Rosh Yeshivah championed the awareness of shmiras halashon.*

"Let's go, Ma," suggested Blumie, who was visiting then. "Why not?"

Rebbetzin Bender paused thoughtfully. "I would not just go in for a visit. The Rosh Yeshivah has a right to his privacy. But I do have this question …" Rebbetzin Bender was distressed by the way her mind sometimes wandered as she davened.

The Manchester Rosh Yeshivah listened intently to Rebbetzin Bender's question. "Let me tell you what I do. I make sure to look into a siddur, I keep my finger on the place, and I try to concentrate only on the literal meaning of the words. Try this, and I think that you will find an improvement."

Rebbetzin Bender davened this way for the rest of her life and was always grateful for the Manchester Rosh Yeshivah's advice.

No matter how many things Rebbetzin Bender had on her agenda that day, when it was time to daven, she would interrupt what she was doing and pick up her siddur. "You never know," she would say, "something might come up as a distraction, and one might even forget to daven. Better to daven as soon as possible." Then she davened slowly and carefully, with sincerity and concentration. She was a daughter speaking to her Father, a subject speaking to her King. What could be more precious than their time together?

### Chapter Sixty-Nine

# Uniquely Hers

*"… She lived **in** today's day and age but not **by** today's day and age … There are great people within every generation and there are those who serve as bridges between one generation and the other; continuity is a necessity, a pipeline. Rebbetzin Bender was one such bridge, bridging the gap between the previous generation and ours … She imbued the generation, her family, and students with the strength and the energy of the bygone generation …"*[53]

REBBETZIN BENDER HAD MANY QUALITIES THAT WERE uniquely hers. She had lived among giants of the previous generation. She absorbed what she saw and what she had been taught, and incorporated those teachings into her own life. She strode into a new era, the training of her past an intrinsic part of her. She transmitted her perspective on all aspects of life to the new generation of which she had become a part. Her perspective was often enlightening, exacting, encouraging, and unique.

"EVERY MEMBER OF *KLAL YISROEL* HAS *KOCHOS,* STRENGTHS," SHE USED to say. "We have limited time in this world, and people should use their strengths to accomplish. We were all put in this world to accomplish." It bothered her when she saw people with *kochos* not doing what they could

---

53. Excerpted from the *hesped* by Rabbi Chaim Epstein for Rebbetzin Bender.

with the gifts Hashem gave them. It bothered her to see people sitting idle.

Shabbos was the rare occasion when Rebbetzin Bender would relax with a book or a Yiddish newspaper. The paper once had pictures of women dressed immodestly. The publisher was a religious Jew, and she even knew who he was and where he lived. She was very upset. Immediately after Shabbos, she looked up his telephone number and called him to discuss the matter. "*Shehayah b'yado limchos v'lo michah* (one who is in the position of being able to protest but does not protest) …"[54] she remarked with satisfaction as she hung up the phone.

Her drive to accomplish was that much more astounding in light of her precarious health. She suffered a life-threatening kidney infection as a young woman, which eventually resulted in her kidney being removed about 15 years later. She continued to suffer from kidney stones, and then gallstones. She constantly felt nauseated. As she got older, she had difficulty walking more than a few steps without stopping to rest, but her attitude was always positive: "*Baruch Hashem*, I can still teach, I can still walk, I can still accomplish."

Rebbetzin Bender admired people who used their strengths and talents in service to *HaKadosh Baruch Hu*. Rebbetzin Chana Feigenbaum had been a student of Rebbetzin Bender and remained a devoted supporter of Bais Yaakov ever since. She raised money for Bais Yaakov, and she had a hand in almost every one of their campaigns and programs. Rebbetzin Bender used to marvel: Here was a woman who chose to spend most of her time strengthening and building Bais Yaakov. She was a prime example of a person who was using her *kochos* properly.[55]

DURING THE YEAR OF *AVEILUS* FOR HER FATHER, BLUMIE WAS WORKING as a secretary in Torah Vodaath. She learned that one boy, an eighth grader, was being expelled from the dormitory because he had been hiding inappropriate reading material under his mattress. The boy's mother came to the yeshivah crying hysterically. They lived too far from the yeshivah for the child to commute daily. If the yeshivah did not allow him to stay in the dorm, what would happen to him?

Blumie returned home very upset and repeated the story to her mother. Only a few weeks had passed since her husband's sudden *petirah*, and Rebbetzin Bender was still struggling with her own pain. Yet she never looked

---

54. *Sanhedrin* 103a. There it states about Tzidkiyahu HaMelech that "he did badly in the eyes of Hashem" because he was in the position of being able to protest, and yet he did not protest.

55. Rebbetzin Feigenbaum is the widow of Reb Yisroel Feigenbaum. This unusual couple devoted much of their time to *Klal Yisroel*. Through her constant involvement in Bais Yaakov, Rebbetzin Feigenbaum became a good friend of Rebbetzin Bender and, during the last year of Rebbetzin Bender's life, she came to the hospital daily to visit.

for excuses. For the rest of the year, the boy stayed in the Bender home, and Rebbetzin Bender also found a respectable yeshivah for him to attend the next year. The boy went on to become an influential member of his community and a generous supporter of Torah. All this was made possible because Rebbetzin Bender recognized her *kochos* and used them for *Klal Yisroel*.

REBBETZIN BENDER OFTEN LOOKED BACK ON HER CHILDHOOD AND wondered how such a shy child as herself could grow up and one day speak in front of hundreds of people. Since she had literally transformed her nature from shy and introverted to someone who could inspire and uplift *Klal Yisroel*, she was aware that others could do the same if they only use their will and determination.

When Rabbi Eliezer Litmanowitz, son of Rabbi Pinchas Litmanowitz, was killed in a tragic car accident during the summer, Rebbetzin Bender was asked to speak at a *kinnus* for women being held in honor of the *shloshim*. She was a natural choice since the Benders and the Litmanowitzes had been close friends for many years.

Just before the *kinnus* began, one of the organizers walked over to Blumie Shapiro to ask her if she would open the evening with a few *kapitlach Tehillim*.

"Me?" Blumie was astonished. She thought it obvious that she was too shy to stand up before hundreds of women and lead them in saying *Tehillim*. "I … I can't. I would faint."

The organizer nodded and walked away. The *kinnus* proceeded. Rebbetzin Bender spoke, Rabbi Kalman Krohn spoke, and then the attendees solemnly filed out. Blumie and Rebbetzin Bender proceeded up the hill toward Blumie's bungalow.

Rebbetzin Bender wondered aloud, "Hundreds of women together, and no one stood up to lead the crowd in saying *Tehillim*? How can this be?"

"Actually," Blumie began slowly, "they requested that I open the evening with *Tehillim* …" She saw the disappointment in her mother's eyes. "But you know me, Ma, I am so shy. I just could not do it …"

Rebbetzin Bender sighed. "Because you were embarrassed, there was no *Tehillim* at the *kinnus*."

Blumie was shaken by her mother's softly spoken words.

"Do you think that everything I do is so easy for me?" Rebbetzin Bender continued. "When I do something, I do it because it is the right thing to do, not because it gives me enjoyment." In her gentle way, Rebbetzin Bender was counseling her daughter to use her *kochos* even when it is unpleasant. One must use his *kochos* in order to accomplish for *Klal Yisroel*.

EXTRAORDINARY *HAKARAS HATOV* WAS ANOTHER *MIDDAH* OF REB-betzin Bender that was uniquely hers. She was inordinately grateful for any small favor done for her, and she remembered the favor for many years afterward.

Rebbetzin Bender related a story that happened shortly after her marriage, when she was not yet used to *shtetl* life in Mir. One day there was a fire, and since most of the houses were made of wood, the entire city was in danger.

One of the Zupnik brothers saw her confusion and distress. "Listen," he told her patiently, "go bring a large sheet. Then bring your real valu-ables. We will tie them into the sheet and you will take them out of the house, away from the approaching fire." His composure helped her to calm down. She quickly got a sheet and assembled her valuables on it. The young *bochur* helped her tie it up. She slung the sack over her shoulder and walked away to wait out the danger from a distance.

Rebbetzin Bender never forgot the *chessed* that *bochur* had done for her while Reb Dovid was in yeshivah. Just a mere mention of the name "Zup-nik" launched her into a rendition of the story, complete with a declaration of her gratitude. The fervor with which she told over this story did not diminish even 50 years later.

When one of the Bender boys was once ill, Rebbetzin Bender called Ha-tzolah and R' Ephraim Pollack came to the house. Rebbetzin Bender was so appreciative of his help that years later, he was one of the first people Reb-betzin Bender called to invite to the *vort* when this son became engaged.[56]

Rabbi Shloima Feldman,[57] proprietor of a seforim store on 18th Ave-nue, was well known for his acts of *chessed*. He called Rebbetzin Bender before every Yom Tov to wish her "*ah gut Yom Tov*," and he would also call her throughout the year if he had an opportunity to give her *nachas*. Reb Shloima had established an extracurricular learning program called Tiferes Yonah. He arranged learning groups for boys between the ages of 7 and bar mitzvah on Shabbos afternoon, Chol HaMoed, and other occasions where children had too much free time. Occasionally, Rebbetzin Bender's sons spoke at a Tiferes Yonah event. When this was the case, Reb Shloima would send her a flyer announcing the event and would call to tell her how well that particular son spoke. Rebbetzen Bender was effusive in her gratitude toward him. Whoever was in the house when he called was treated to a minispeech enumerating R' Shloima's unique qualities and acts of *chessed*.

A favorite story of hers illustrates the importance of *hakaras hatov*. The Satmar Rav went to Eretz Yisroel for a visit. His Chassidim were driving him around in a private car, and he asked them to make a slight detour.

---

56. Rabbi Yona Zev Herskowitz in an interview by R' Yonason Rosenblum.

57. See Biography Section.

The Rav asked them to stop the car and wait while he went inside. He knocked on the door. A very old woman answered. The Satmar Rav spoke to her for a few minutes and returned to the car. "When I was a little baby, this woman cared for me. She rocked me in my cradle to soothe me. I heard that she settled in Eretz Yisroel and I wanted to come see her and thank her for the care she gave me then."

Rebbetzin Bender repeated this story often. The Satmar Rav had no real memory of this woman; he was a mere baby when she cared for him. Yet, decades later the Satmar Rav went out of his way to show his appreciation.

"AND THIS IS FOR THE RABBANIT." THE EARNEST SEPHARDI COOK beamed with pride as he placed a platter of food in front of Rebbetzin Bender on Shabbos morning.

"Oh, thank you. It's so kind of you to prepare this for me. I look around and see hundreds of people enjoying your delicious food, and I marvel at the way you still manage to cook separate food for me." Rebbetzin Bender praised the man warmly, "May *HaKadosh Baruch Hu* bless you for your efforts."

The hard-working cook nodded happily and left the "Rabbanit" to enjoy her food. Rebbetzin Bender sighed as she picked up her fork. Maybe, this time …? She nibbled a little bit of chicken, a bite of kugel, a taste of string beans, and then she put her fork down. It was the same as usual. The food had too much salt and spices.

The bungalows in Camp Toras Chessed did not have cooking facilities and all the families ate food, prepared by the cook, in the camp dining room. Rebbetzin Bender had many dietary restrictions, and the spicy, salty food that the cook prepared for the rest of the camp was off limits. Rebbetzin Bender asked him if he could prepare special food for her, without salt and spices, and she would pay him for the effort. The cook was happy to comply and, for many years, he pleasantly and faithfully made separate food for Rebbetzin Bender. Nonetheless, his "no salt" foods still had more salt than Rebbetzin Bender was accustomed to eating and, many times, she could not even eat them.

"But, Ma," protested Rebbetzin Epstein, "say something to him. Maybe next time he will really leave out all the salt and spices."

"Never mind," Rebbetzin Bender said, shaking her head. "He probably feels that I can't possibly enjoy food without any salt and spices, and he can't bear to present me with such bland food. He is such a nice man, and he tries so hard …"

"But you pay him, praise him, thank him, and still go hungry …"

"Sh …" Rebbetzin Bender admonished her daughter, as she reached for another piece of challah.

SUCH WAS REBBETZIN BENDER'S UNUSUAL THOUGHTFULNESS. SHE HAD the uncanny ability of seeing the other person's viewpoint and responding with an acute sensitivity. She understood that the kind Sephardi cook was trying his best, and she was afraid that she would hurt his feelings if she told him to stop preparing separate food for her.

To whomever she met — an elderly woman, a young girl, the grocery store owner, the teller at the bank — she had something appropriate to say, be it a piece of advice, an opinion, or a comment, something that would make the other person feel understood and valued. Just walking with her down the block could take a half-hour as people stopped to speak with her and benefit from her words of wisdom and encouragement.

Rabbi Yaakov Bender would bring his children to visit his mother every Erev Shabbos. One particular Erev Shabbos, after the usual routine of playing, eating kugel, and talking, Reb Yaakov rose to leave. Rebbetzin Bender walked over to him and whispered, "Please take the children out quietly, without too much fuss." Reb Yaakov was surprised, but he obediently herded the children out of the house. "But Tatty, we didn't kiss Bubby," piped up one of the younger ones, plaintively. "Sh …" Reb Yaakov hushed the child and steered him out the door.

Later on, Rebbetzin Bender called her son at home. "Do you know why I didn't let the children kiss me goodbye, and why I shooed them out so quickly? Rebbetzin Lange was visiting. She has no children. I did not want her to see how the children kiss me goodbye. It might make her feel sad."

Similarly, if Rebbetzin Bender was in her daughter Esther's apartment and her son-in-law Reb Chaim came in, Rebbetzin Bender quickly left the room. She understood that her daughter might want some private time with her husband, but would never say anything to make her mother feel unwanted. It was best that she preempt an uncomfortable situation.

In Camp Toras Chessed there were always a few *bochurim* who helped out in the kitchen. Often these were Russian or Iranian boys who were away from home much longer than just the summer. Rebbetzin Bender always sympathized with these boys who were separated from their families. She would make it her business to speak to them: about how they were managing, about their families, about their homelands. Especially on Shabbos, she sought them out to wish them *"ah gut Shabbos,"* and see how they were doing.


HENNIE LEFT HER CIRCLE OF FRIENDS AND WALKED OVER TO THE two little boys on the side. Her son was sitting on a bike, a stubborn, petulant frown on his face. His friend was pulling at the handlebars. "Please, can't I have one ride. Just one …" he whined. Hennie turned to her son and said, "Oh, come on, why can't you share? Would it hurt you to give him one little ride?" The child shoved the bike at his friend. Hennie walked triumphantly back to her circle of friends.

Rebbetzin Bender was sitting nearby. She looked at Hennie and commented quietly, "And do you share your car so easily? His bike, to him, is like your car is to you. How would you like to be told to share your car?"

Hennie stopped in her tracks. Rebbetzin Bender was pointing out something that should have been obvious. How often do we try to see things from the perspective of the child? How often are our demands unrealistic and unfair? How was it that Rebbetzin Bender was able to see through accepted "*chinuch*" and see something was lacking?[58]

She had extraordinary clarity. When she looked at a situation, she could see beyond preconceived notions, popular psychology, and politically correct opinions. With a pithy saying or an "offhand" comment, Rebbetzin Bender could shed new light on her subject or bring something vague into sharp focus.

"Never comment or criticize something done or said by a daughter-in-law," Rebbetzin Bender would say. "It is normal for any daughter-in-law to be extra sensitive about what her mother-in-law says."

Thoughtful little things also showed her concern for others. "Chairs should always be pulled out a little — not so close to the table — more welcoming," Rebbetzin Bender would tell her children.

Back in the 1960's, Dina,[59] a former student, suddenly became a widow when her 44-year-old husband suffered a massive heart attack. She had attended Bais Yaakov many years earlier and had not kept up with her teachers. Nonetheless, on Friday afternoon, Rebbetzins Kaplan and Bender were *menachem avel*.

Rebbetzin Bender addressed Dina with compassion. "You should know that this Friday night is going to be the hardest time. You are going to sit at the table and you are going to see your husband's empty chair — I know, I have been through it; it is so hard. I want you to take your *leichter* and put them at your husband's place. That way, every time you look at his seat, you will see your *licht* and its flames rising to *HaKadosh Baruch Hu* … You will be comforted."

And so it was. That Friday night, Dina positioned her *leichter* at her husband's place. Throughout the meal, as she gazed at the flames across the table, she was filled with an inner peace and the certainty that her connection to her husband remained.

How did Rebbetzin Bender find exactly the right words to say? She could see a situation and break it down to its essentials. What exactly is

---

58. Mrs. H. Mandelbaum.

59. Not her real name.

troubling the other person right now? How can that problem be alleviated? When an issue was pared down to its essentials, clarity emerged.

ONE SUMMER EVENING, REBBETZIN ESTHER EPSTEIN WAS GOING TO A *chasunah*. She was concerned that she was leaving her mother alone for so many hours, and she asked some of her friends in Camp Toras Chessed to come around and keep her mother company. The women happily obliged and formed a small circle around the older woman. The conversation drifted to mundane matters, and one of the women commented self-consciously that their banter must sound so trivial to someone like Rebbetzin Bender.

"Don't you think that I am a regular human being? I have likes and desires just like everyone else. I remember the beautiful trousseau my mother prepared for me: the linens, the tablecloths, the dishes …" She paused wistfully. "When it came time to leave Europe, I felt so bad having to pick and choose and leave so much behind. Then, even what I took was lost. I felt terrible. And then I felt even worse knowing that this was what was bothering me when a war was breaking out. But I was a young *kallah*, I was human." In that short speech, Rebbetzin Bender gave over the message that we are all human, and there is nothing wrong with that.[60]

ONE YEAR, THE HONOREE AT THE BAIS YAAKOV SPRING TEA WAS MRS. Miriam Lubling, a dear acquaintance of Rebbetzin Bender. Rebbetzin Bender turned to this special woman, famous for her tireless efforts in medical referrals, and declared, "I give my good friend Mrs. Lubling a *berachah* that *Hakadosh Baruch Hu* should put her out of business!"

This emphatic statement, steeped with affection, was uniquely hers.

---

60. Mrs. H. Mandelbaum.

# Part III:
# **Rebbetzin Bender —**
# **Her Strength Wanes**
## 5749-5756 / 1989-1996

*Chapter Seventy:*
### Her Last Years

*Chapter Seventy-One:*
### Her Last Days

*Chapter Seventy-Two:*
### Her Passing

*Chapter Seventy-Three:*
### Her Legacy

*Chapter Seventy-Four:*
### Epilogue

Unless otherwise noted, the information in this section has been provided by the Bender family.

*Chapter Seventy*

# Her Last Years

**Brooklyn: Av 5749 (August 1989)**

ANKEL? I WANT TO GO HOME. TELL THEM TO LET ME GO home," Rebbetzin Bender pleaded.

"I don't know, Ma, Dr. Brickman is in charge."

"Please, Yankel, please, please, please … I want to go home."

Reb Yaakov was torn. His mother sounded so upset. "Let me speak to Dr. Brickman and I will get back to you."

As she hung up the telephone, Rebbetzin Bender blinked back the tears. She hated being cooped up in the hospital. When she was admitted on Tuesday, they told her that they were confident that she would be home for Shabbos. Now, Friday morning, they would not let her leave.

*But I feel better*, she told herself. Not that she remembered what it was like to ever feel perfect. She was accustomed to living with pain and discomfort. Kidney stones, gall stones, bursitis, high blood pressure, sleep apnea, and spinal stenosis[1] — she could qualify for a medical degree after listening to all her doctors describe her health issues. She rarely had a normal night's sleep. She rarely had a painless day. Yet, she would rather have her sleepless nights and painful days in her own home.

The bedside telephone rang. It was Reb Yaakov.

"I spoke to Dr. Brickman, Ma. There is something that he still wants to check out …" Reb Yaakov knew how disappointed his mother would be.

---

1. Spinal stenosis is a slow disintegrative spinal condition that can be very painful.

He did not want to worry his mother, but Dr. Brickman had seen something on the cardiogram that concerned him. He was ordering more tests, and Reb Yaakov was anxious. "He wants you to stay over Shabbos. I am sorry, Ma, please have patience. I will come back from the mountains on Monday and will come to see you."

Rebbetzin Bender sighed and replaced the receiver on the cradle. She felt so helpless, at the mercy of everyone telling her what to do. She wanted so much to go home. Her thoughts wandered on … Her children were so good. Someone was always with her to keep her company in the hospital and see if she needed anything. That was comforting. But nothing was as good as her own home and her own bed.

"Hello, Ma," Reb Yaakov greeted his mother cheerfully on Monday evening. "*Vos hertzach*? (What's doing?)"

Rebbetzin Bender smiled wanly and got straight to the point. "It is good to see you, Yankel. When am I going home?"

"Patience, patience. All in good time." Reb Yaakov made some more small talk and began to settle in for the night. At 1 a.m., Reb Yaakov left the room to say *Krias Shema*. When he returned, his mother was reading a book. She was nodding as she read, and Reb Yaakov assumed that she would soon fall asleep. He began to get comfortable, glancing over occasionally to check up on his mother. At about 1:45 a.m., he noticed that she began rolling off the bed. Immediately, Reb Yaakov leaned forward to cushion her fall, but he was too late. She was already on the floor, and he saw that she had stopped breathing.

"Help!" he screamed. "Doctor … nurse … somebody help me!"

A resident appeared at his side and together they rolled her over.

"She's okay," the resident assured Reb Yaakov, "she's okay."

It did not look that way to Reb Yaakov. His mother was foaming at the mouth, and she had stopped breathing.

"Doctor, she's dead!" he screamed in a panic. "She's dead! She's dead!"

The resident looked closely at the patient. "Maybe you're right," he muttered as he punched in Code Blue and immediately began CPR.[2]

Code Blue. Code Blue. Code Blue. The signal resounded throughout the hospital. The door to Rebbetzin Bender's room flung open as doctors and nurses streamed in.

"Electric shocks," one doctor called.

A nurse readied the equipment, and the doctors hooked her up.

"One, two, three …" Everyone watched to see if the shock treatment had taken effect.

"Again … one, two three …" All eyes were on the machine.

_____
2. At that point, being on the hard floor was an advantage since CPR has to be administered on a hard surface.

Minutes later, Rebbetzin Bender's heart resumed beating.

"Okay, we got her back. Let's wheel her into Intensive Care."

Reb Yaakov was sweating. Everything until now was child's play. Suddenly, his mother's condition was serious. They had almost lost her, and now she was in a coma.

TWO DAYS LATER, REB YAAKOV WAS DOZING IN THE INTENSIVE CARE Unit waiting room. The family was taking turns around the clock to be with Rebbetzin Bender, and once again it was his shift. The Intensive Care Unit was set up with partitions separating the different "rooms." Besides the waiting area just outside, there was not really room for family members to sit comfortably.

Suddenly, he noticed a flurry of activity as doctors and nurses rushed into the Intensive Care Unit. His heart skipped a beat. *Wait, Yankel*, he told himself, *don't jump to conclusions*. Minutes later the doors flung open again and those same doctors and nurses filed out, much calmer than before. Reb Yaakov cornered one of the staff.

"What happened?" he asked.

"It was a cardiac arrest," one of the doctors answered. "We had to do CPR. It's okay now, we got her back."

"Room 5?" Reb Yaakov asked, his heart pounding.

"Yeah …" The doctor looked at him curiously. "How did you know?"

Reb Yaakov shrugged his shoulders. "A lucky guess," he answered as he turned into the Intensive Care Unit and headed for Room 5. His mother seemed to be resting peacefully, but Reb Yaakov knew that looks were deceiving. A second cardiac arrest, especially at her age and with her precarious health, was not good. The doctors had hooked his mother up to a respirator and, although she looked peaceful, he realized that her situation had just gone from bad to very bad.

A WEEK PASSED WITH VERY LITTLE PROGRESS. WHAT WAS WORSE, Rebbetzin Bender had developed pneumonia. The Benders called in a top specialist, the biggest pulmonary expert in the New York area, to assess the situation. His prognosis was grim: The respirator was eating away at her lungs. If she remained on the respirator, her lungs would quickly deteriorate. If they took her off the respirator, she would not be able to breathe. He left no room for hope.

Reb Yaakov was desperate for an idea. He and his brother, Reb Paltiel, were at their mother's bedside feeling incredibly helpless. She was alive, and yet on the brink of death. They could not bear the thought of losing her.

"Wait," Reb Paltiel said. "The Gerrer Rebbe."

Reb Yaakov waited for his older brother to explain.

*Rabbi Avrohom Mordechai Alter (1866-1948) was known as the Imrei Emes. He was the son of the Sfas Emes, Rabbi Yehudah Aryeh Leib Alter, and the great-grandson of the Chidushei Harim, Rabbi Yitzchok Meir Alter. In 1904, with the passing of his father, he became the leader of the Gerrer Chassidic court with thousands of followers. Typical of the Kotzker Derech, he was a great masmid and his every word was measured.*

"Ger has so much gratitude to Mommy. Certainly, the Gerrer Rebbe will daven for her ..."

Then Reb Yaakov remembered the story about his mother and Ger.

*After the 1932 school year began, a letter arrived at the offices of Bais Yaakov of Crakow. Normally a request of this type would have been unequivocally ignored. But this was a letter from the Imrei Emes, Rabbi Avrohom Mordechai Alter of Ger, the leader of the largest Chassidus in Poland, a revered tzaddik and talmid chacham. The letter could not be ignored.*

*A girl, a member of a prominent Gerrer family, had been swept up by the winds of modernity so prevalent at the time. The girl had gone very far astray, but the Rebbe was still hopeful that perhaps Bais Yaakov could bring her back.*

*The administration was at a loss. This was not the purpose of the seminary. The seminary had the formidable job of training teachers, and therefore they accepted only girls with solid hashkafos into the program. Each graduate would go on to teach hundreds of others. Bais Yaakov did not have the framework to deal with this unfortunate soul. Yet, a request from the Gerrer Rebbe was not to be taken lightly.*

*The Bais Yaakov administration came up with a plan. They would accept the girl, and they would pick a student to be her shadow. They would choose someone whose personality and sterling character would convey the beauty of religious life and draw the Gerrer girl back to her roots. Out of the several hundred girls in Bais Yaakov of Crakow, the administration chose Basya Epstein.*

*While only a young girl herself, Rebbetzin Bender brought this girl back to Yiddishkeit. The Imrei Emes wrote Rebbetzin Bender a beautiful letter of gratitude and wished her many long productive years of life.*[3]

REB YAAKOV WAS CERTAIN THAT THOSE YEARS HAD NOT YET COME TO an end. Reb Paltiel ran to the home of the Gerrer Rosh Kollel, Rabbi Elya Fisher. Breathlessly, he repeated the story as he had heard it from his mother. Reb Elya immediately gave Paltiel a private number of the Rebbe of Ger in Eretz Yisroel, the Lev Simcha, Rabbi Simcha Bunim Alter. Reb

---

3. Rebbetzin Bender treasured this letter and mourned its loss when it was left with the rest of her luggage on the pier when they sailed to America (see page 215).

Paltiel rushed back to the hospital with the number.

"Here," he told his brother, Reb Yaakov, "you call."

Reb Yaakov dialed the number. The Gerrer Rebbetzin answered. Reb Yaakov repeated the entire story as they knew it. The Rebbetzin even seemed somewhat familiar with the incident. She assured him that she would see to it that a *minyan* of *bochurim* would go out to the *kever* of the Imrei Emes[4] and daven for Rebbetzin Bender's recovery.

Reb Yaakov hung up the telephone and looked silently at Reb Paltiel. Their mother had many *zechusim*. They just had to hope and pray that one of those many merits would save her.

TWO DAYS LATER, BLUMIE SHAPIRO was sitting by her mother's side saying *Tehillim* and checking on her mother every so often. The doctors were making their rounds, and they stopped at Rebbetzin Bender's bed to check her progress.

*Rabbi Simcha Bunim Alter (1898- 1992) known as the Lev Simcha, was a son of the Imrei Emes. In 1927 his father sent him to Eretz Yisroel where he established the Gerrer yeshivah in Tel Aviv. In 1939 he returned to Poland to persuade his father to immigrate to Eretz Yisroel. During that time, World War II broke out and the family was miraculously saved. In 1976 he took over the mantle of leadership after his brother, the Bais Yisroel, was niftar and, for over two decades, was the leader of thousands of Chassidim.*

"Unbelievable ... Here," he told his colleague, "take a look."

The second doctor let out a low whistle. "Unreal," he said, shaking his head.

"Excuse me," Blumie interjected, "but what is going on?"

"I must call my superior to confirm this, but it seems that the lungs are healing themselves. It's really hard to believe."

The doctor scurried off. Then the senior doctor arrived and was also amazed. "In my entire career, I have never seen this happen. I have never even read of such a possibility in medical literature."

Then the doctor became very businesslike. "O.K. Now is the crucial moment. We must take her off the respirator before the respirator harms her healing lungs. Normally, we do this gradually, and the lungs gradually 'remember' to breathe. By the time the respirator is shut off completely, the

---

4.The Imrei Emes is buried on Rechov Yosef Ben Mattisyahu 26 (Mekor Baruch), Jerusalem, in back of the Gerrer *beis medrash*.

patient is breathing on her own. We cannot do that here. We must take her off immediately so her lungs will continue to heal. The time on the respirator has caused her lungs to 'forget' how to function. We have to take her off the respirator and, at the same time, wake her up to 'remind' her lungs to breathe."

"You are Mrs …?"

"Shapiro," Blumie answered meekly.

"You have a crucial job here. People wake up better when they hear a familiar voice in a familiar language. As soon as we unhook the respirator, you will scream and shout in whatever language your mother is most familiar. You will continue to call to her and beg her to wake up until she regains consciousness. You'll see her face turn blue, and it's not a pretty sight. Ignore it and keep on going. Your mother's life is at stake here."

So began the most difficult 20 minutes of Blumie's life. As they shut off the machine, she began to call out in Yiddish, "*Mamme, Mamme*, wake up. Please, Mommy, we need you. Do you hear me? It's time to wake up …"

As the doctors predicted, Rebbetzin Bender's complexion turned blue, and Blumie had to keep herself from becoming hysterical.

"Continue," the doctor commanded. "Don't give up. Keep on going."

"*Mamme*," she screamed, "please, Mommy, we need you. Come back to us. Wake up, Mommy, wake up …"

Over and over, Blumie screamed and called. Five minutes passed. Ten minutes passed. Blumie was not sure how much longer she could go on.

And then, suddenly, Rebbetzin Bender opened her eyes. "*Vu bin ich*? (Where am I?)," she asked weakly. Blumie collapsed into a chair. She could think only one thought.

*Baruch Hashem*, her mother was alive.


ALTHOUGH REBBETZIN BENDER HAD HAD MANY PREVIOUS HEALTH issues, the double cardiac arrest signaled a slow waning of Rebbetzin Bender's strength. After she returned from the hospital, she began spending extended periods of time in her daughter Esther's house. Her cordless phone was still faithfully at her side, but it rang less frequently.

She continued to teach in Bais Yaakov, and she still had *kallos* come privately to the house for lessons. She did not fall back on her ill health as an excuse to neglect serving her Maker, not in matters of *bein adam lachaveiro* nor in matters *bein adam laMakom*.


"A WALKING PHARMACY," SHE DECLARED RUEFULLY ONE EREV PESACH, "that is what I am. Come, Mordechai, let's sit down and figure out which medications I can take on Pesach, and which are better not to take." She pulled out many little pill bottles and assembled them on the dining-room table.

Mordechai sat beside her obediently, bracing himself for what he knew was coming.

"Let us check this one. Any *ch'shash ta'aruvos chametz?*"

Mordechai picked up the small bottle and caught his breath. This medication kept her blood pressure steady. Even if it had a *ta'aruvos chametz,* there was no question that she would have to take it. It was not even a *shayla* for a Rav. Yet, she was asking a question: Does it have *ta'aruvos chametz* or not? How should he answer? If there was any *ch'shash ta'aruvos chametz,* she would be pained to have to take the medicine on Pesach.

"Uh, Bubby, let's go to the next one …"

This one is fine. This one is a problem, but she could skip it for a week. This one is a problem, but she had to take it anyway. She cried bitter tears over every medicine she had to take if its Pesach status was questionable. She never viewed herself as a sick person for whom allowances should be made. She wanted to serve Hashem as she always had.

"YANKEL, DID YOU SEND OVER THE *MISHLOACH MANOS* YET?" IT WAS the third time Rebbetzin Bender was calling to ask him the same question, on a typically hectic Purim day.

"Yes, Mommy, I sent it."

"Did you make sure to say that it was not from you, but from me?"

"I sent two," he was pleased to announce, "and I told Chaim Ozer to say, very clearly, that one is from his parents and the other is from his Bubby in Boro Park."

"Thank you, Yankel, thank you very much."

REBBETZIN BENDER SENT *MISHLOACH MANOS* TO ALL THE RELIGIOUS doctors who attended her regularly. If a religious doctor made a house call, for any reason, she would insist on giving him a piece of homemade cake or kugel. She was extremely grateful to her doctors.[5]

Her sense of gratitude was extraordinary. Almost a year after her double cardiac arrest, Rebbetzin Bender was in Far Rockaway for Shavuos. She was not feeling well and Reb Yaakov arranged for a local nurse to come

---

5. "She was always *makir tovah,* and she never forgot favors people did for her. I would like to mention all those who helped her with *mesiras nefesh,* days and nights, and above all, Dr. Brickman. The level of his unbelievable devotion is not fathomable, and we are forever grateful for his being a faithful messenger of Hashem, with dignity, *derech eretz,* and honor; Hashem keeps the records, but it is incumbent upon us to mention and be grateful" (Rabbi Chaim Epstein in his *hesped* on Rebbetzin Bender). Her main doctors were Dr. Yitzchok Brickman (general doctor), Dr. Gerald Hollander (cardiologist), Dr. Michael Bashevkin (oncologist), and Dr. Marshall Keilson (neurologist).

to the house to see her. Mrs. Esther Feigenbaum, the nurse, was able to calm her down and Rebbetzin Bender felt better after she left. Every time she returned to Far Rockaway for a visit, Rebbetzin Bender asked her son, "And how is Esther Feigenbaum doing? I so appreciate the kindness she did for me that Shavuos ... "

**5754 (1994)**

Rebbetzin Bender was diagnosed with lung cancer. The Bender family rallied around their mother and grandmother, offering help, support, and love.

Every Tuesday, Reb Yaakov drove in from Far Rockaway to take his mother for chemotherapy. After a treatment she was weak but, up until the last year of her life, she mustered her strength and went to teach. Her only concession to her condition was that her night classes now came to her house.

She refused to see herself as sick and frail, and she never wanted others to treat her as an invalid. Once, Blumie called a cab to take her mother home after a round of radiation treatments in Methodist Hospital. A cab with bold letters proclaiming "Medical" on the side pulled up in front of Methodist Hospital.

"Come, Ma, this car is for us." Blumie took her mother by the arm.

"What?" Rebbetzin Bender protested. "This car is for sick people. Blumie, no, I don't want to go. Can't we find a different taxi?"

"But Ma, you're so weak. It's still a bit of a ride until we get home. Please, it will be so much more comfortable for you …"

It took Blumie a few minutes to convince her mother to take the cab. Since this cab was already there, and no one knew how long they would have to wait for another one, Rebbetzin Bender sadly gave in.

SHE WAS GROWING PROGRESSIVELY WEAKER. OFFICIALLY, SHE WAS STILL teaching, but she could not manage the trip to school. Her substitute teacher called her regularly, and they discussed the curriculum and their students' progress. She yearned to return to the classroom.

Her grandson Mordechai came to visit her. He wanted to lift her spirits by reminding her of the *zechusim* that she had for a speedy recovery.

"Bubby," he said, "you slept on the hard floor for weeks so that the Chofetz Chaim could have a bed. Don't you agree that this *zechus* will now stand you in good stead?"

She smiled weakly and answered, "And do you think that the Chofetz Chaim never gave away a night of his for another *Yid*? He gave away many nights for *Klal Yisroel*. What is the greatness of what I gave to him?"

It was not that she denied her accomplishments. She just refused to believe that everything she had done and everything she had become entitled her to preferential treatment: not from people and certainly not from the *Ribbono shel Olam*.

DESPITE ALL THE PAIN AND SUFFERING THAT REBBETZIN BENDER endured from her illness, the first time she cried was after Succos, the last year of her life. Her students had come to her house to hear classes from her several times, and she saw that, even from her own home, she did not have the strength to teach. Then she began to cry. "If I cannot do for others, if I cannot teach, then what purpose do I have in this world?"

WHEN ONE IS YOUNG AND STRONG, HE CAN MASK HIS FAULTS AND present the world with a facade of goodness. Weakness strips away that facade and reveals the truth. During those years of illness, the truth of Rebbetzin Bender's greatness emerged:

*In her weakness*, Rebbetzin Bender was still doing *chessed*. A loyal family friend, childless and alone, suffered a number of debilitating ministrokes. From her sickbed, Rebbetzin Bender raised money to pay for the expenses of his illness.

*In her weakness*, Rebbetzin Bender was still careful with another person's honor. As she lay on her hospital bed, she had barely enough strength to converse. When a child or grandchild entered and began to speak in Yiddish, she stopped him or her. She whispered, "Speak English. The nurse might think that we are speaking about her … she will feel bad …" Occasionally, she would doze off in the middle of a conversation. She would then awake with a start. "I am so sorry," she would apologize, "such a lack of *derech eretz* …" Even in her weakness, she was concerned about having slighted someone's honor.

*In her weakness*, she was still careful how she spoke. During her long illness, Rebbetzin Bender's daughters and daughters-in-law regularly sent food to tempt Rebbetzin Bender to eat. Reb Michoel was visiting his mother, and she was eating some soup that her daughter-in-law, Bryna Minna, had prepared. "Oh! How tasty this is," she commented. Then she quickly added, "But your wife makes delicious food, too." She made sure to include her son's wife in the compliment.

*In her weakness*, she still recoiled from letting others serve her. Reb Michoel, who was staying with his mother in the hospital, saw her feeling around for the button to call the nurse. He jumped up to help her. She did not need the button then, but she felt secure knowing where it was in case she would need it. "No, no," she protested. "Sit, I will find it myself." She insisted that he remain seated so as not to inconvenience him. She lay back on the pillows, ostensibly calm even though she did not know where the button was. Five minutes later, she turned to Reb Michoel. "Please show me where the button is," she requested. She responded to his silent question, "I just realized that I might need the button while you are sleeping. Then I might have to wake you. I would rather ask you to show me where the button is now than wake you later."

*In her weakness*, she was still attuned to the needs and feelings of other people. The last summer of her life, she stayed with her son Reb Yaakov. Reb Yaakov's son Dovid was learning in Eretz Yisroel. During the year, Reb Yaakov was very busy and did not have time to write as often as he would like. In the summer he had more time, and he began sending eight-page faxes, mainly transcripts of his *shmuessen*, to his son's apartment in Yerushalayim.

Rebbetzin Bender grew alarmed. "Yankel, what if the other boys sharing the apartment do not receive long letters from their fathers? What if one of the boys does not have a father? Every time the fax churns out a letter, these boys feel bad."

Reb Yaakov was astounded. The thought had never occurred to him. "But Ma, I am sure that they do not mind."

"What makes you so sure? I think that you should call Dovid and ask him. Let him ask his friends. You must make sure that the attention that you are giving your son is not at someone else's expense." And only after a call to Eretz Yisroel clarified the matter did Rebbetzin Bender back down.

*In her weakness*, Rebbetzin Bender still yearned to accomplish. As the cancer ate away at her body, Rebbetzin Bender needed a full-time attendant in her house. Anna, a sweet Russian woman, filled that position. Rebbetzin Bender discovered that Anna's 10-year-old son had not had a *bris* and refused to have one. Daily, Rebbetzin Bender spoke to Anna about giving her son a *bris* until finally she agreed, if Rebbetzin Bender could persuade her son as well. Rebbetzin Bender asked Anna to bring her son over to the house. With utmost patience she spoke with him. She saw that he really did not want to go through a *bris*. What he did want was a bike.

"O.K.," Rebbetzin Bender told him, "you agree to a *bris*, and I will make sure that you get that bike." Phone in hand, Rebbetzin Bender collected the money needed to purchase the bike. By then, the boy changed his mind and asked for something else. "Anything," Rebbetzin Bender said. "I will buy you anything that you want, if you agree to have a *bris*." And yes, the boy had a *bris*.[6]

---

6. "I called up one day to wish her *mazel tov* on a family *simchah*," a grandson recalled. "She answered the telephone joyfully. 'There are two *mazel tovs* today,' she said. I was surprised since I had only heard of one. 'My dear friend Anna's son had a *bris*. For me, this is a wonderful *simchah*, no less than the *simchah* in our family.' "

*In her weakness*, she still yearned to serve her Maker. Every morning, even after a sleepless night, even when racked with pain, she sat, siddur in hand, finger on the place, as the Manchester Rosh Yeshivah had advised, softly enunciating each and every word, as if in actual conversation with her Creator.

*In her weakness*, her mind wandered. Sometimes she even dozed off in the middle of davening. This upset her terribly. "What should I do? Did I say *Baruch She'amar* or not? Am I allowed to repeat it?" She did not want the answer to be, "It's O.K., you're sick." She wanted to daven, she wanted to serve Hashem, and she wanted to do both in the best way possible.

*In her weakness*, she never looked for excuses. One Erev Shabbos she was so weak, she could barely hold a candle. Yet she still made sure that she was wearing something special for Shabbos as her grandchild helped her light.

She spent one Yom Kippur in the hospital, so ill that she did not have the strength to hold a siddur or read the words. She was so agitated that she could not relax.

"Ma, I will help you," her son Reb Yaakov comforted her. "I will be the *chazzan* and you will listen. Say *Amen*, join in when you feel that you can, I will be *motzei* you." That Yom Kippur Reb Yaakov stood by his mother's bed, and davened all the *tefillos* aloud. She listened, she answered, she said what she had the strength to say, and she was relaxed in knowing that she had tried her best to serve her Maker.

### Chapter Seventy-One

# Her Last Days

**Shevat 5756 (February 1996)**

HE WAS SLIPPING AWAY RIGHT BEFORE THEIR EYES; THEY were losing her. She barely spoke. She slept most of the time.

The doctors prescribed medication to give her some strength. One side effect often made a person talkative. One day, as her children Esther and Reb Yaakov were in the room with her, Rebbetzin Bender suddenly opened her eyes and was wide awake.

She turned toward her daughter. "Esther, I want you to know that you should remember all your life that the most important thing is *shalom*, peace. There should always be peace in our family. Peace among all my children and grandchildren …" She continued on in the same vein, her voice suddenly stronger than it had been in months. Then she stopped and lapsed into silence.

Esther was alarmed and burst out crying. It sounded as if her mother was giving them a last request. Reb Yaakov felt tears forming at the corners of his eyes. Was his mother trying to say goodbye?

Two weeks later, Dr. Brickman came to the house to check on Rebbetzin Bender. "I think that we should take her to the hospital," he said softly. He went to call an ambulance.

As they carried her out of her house on a stretcher, Rebbetzin Bender began to cry. As she walked alongside her mother, Esther said, "Ma, you

will come home *gezunterheit*, healthy and well. We are waiting for you ..."
Her voice cracked, and she could not hold back the tears.

Rebbetzin Bender shook her head. She knew she would not be coming back home.

FOR SEVERAL WEEKS, REBBETZIN BENDER DRIFTED IN AND OUT OF CON-
sciousness. Her condition was stable, but she remained in a semicomatose state. Reb Yaakov had come to Brooklyn to bake matzos and planned to visit his mother afterward. When he overheard the plans, little Chaim Ozer piped up, "I want to go, too."

Reb Yaakov resisted. "*Tattele*, I think that it would be better for you not to go. Bubby is not well. She will not even be able to speak with you."

"But Tatty, I have not seen her in so long. Please, can't I just see her?" The child was so innocently earnest. Reb Yaakov decided to give in.

As they walked through the corridors of Maimonides Hospital, Reb Yaakov was having second thoughts. Would this visit be a mistake? As they entered his mother's room, Reb Yaakov's heart sank. It was as bad as he remembered. Rebbetzin Bender was lying still, the beeps of the machines and her heavy breathing the only sound in the dreary hospital room.

Reb Yaakov cleared his throat. "Mommy, look who I brought. Chaim Ozer is here."

Chaim Ozer moved close to the bed and peered eagerly at his grand-mother's face. Suddenly, with her eyes still closed, Rebbetzin Bender began making kissing motions with her mouth. "Chaim Ozer, look!" Reb Yaakov called out in astonishment. "Bubby is blowing you kisses!"

Chaim Ozer nodded happily. The entire exchange lasted a few seconds. Then Rebbetzin Bender's mouth closed, and she once again drifted out of consciousness.

As Reb Yaakov left the hospital, he marveled to himself, *Heilige Mamme, I will never cease to be amazed by you. Your love shines through, even now.*[7]

BUT HER LOVE FOR HER CHILDREN, HER LOVE FOR *KLAL YISROEL*, AND her love for *HaKadosh Baruch Hu* were still not powerful enough to rescind the Heavenly decree. Her time in this world was nearly over. Reb Yaakov wandered aimlessly into the Bikur Cholim coffee room. He was physically and emotionally exhausted. Rebbetzin Bender had been in and out of a

---

7. "Toward the end of her life, when Rebbetzin Bender was drifting in and out of consciousness, I was in the hospital visiting Rabbi Ezriel Lange. It seemed strangely appropriate that they were in the same hospital on the same floor at the end of their lives. I stopped in to visit Rebbetzin Bender. She knew me well since I had spent so much time at the Langes, and the families were unusually close. 'Mordechai is here,' I said. I received no response. I tried again. 'I have come to say goodbye,' I said. Suddenly, Rebbetzin Bender gave a huge million-dollar smile. I was overcome with the warmth and the effort" (Rabbi Mordechai Lerner).

coma for nearly four weeks. If only there would be some kind of improvement, some glimmer of hope.

"Reb Yankel!" A diminutive woman jumped up from her seat in the corner and came toward him. It was Rebbetzin Berenbaum, wife of Rabbi Shmuel Berenbaum, Reb Yaakov's Rosh Yeshivah in the Mir. Reb Yaakov had just heard about the massive heart attack the Rosh Yeshivah had suffered the night before.[8] He had known that the Rosh Yeshivah was also in Maimonides Hospital but he had not expected to meet the Rebbetzin here.

"Rebbetzin, how is the Rosh Yeshivah feeling?"

"Reb Yankel, you must hear this story. It happened now, just now!"

*After suffering a massive heart attack, Rabbi Shmuel Berenbaum lapsed into a coma. Suddenly, the next evening, he opened his eyes. His rebbetzin was in the room, as was his son Reb Osher.*

*"Osher," Reb Shmuel whispered weakly, "bring me a Gemara."*

*Rabbi Osher Berenbaum could not believe what he was hearing. His father was so weak. Learning was out of the question. "Papa, you are not allowed to learn."*

*"Osher, bring me a Gemara."*

*"But, Papa," Reb Osher protested.*

*"A Gemara!" Reb Shmuel insisted.*

*Reb Osher went to the Maimonides chapel and brought back a Gemara Gittin.*

*"Nu," Reb Shmuel said, "learn a piece of Gemara."*

*Reb Osher opened the Gemara and began learning aloud. Reb Shmuel listened, murmuring along with him. After several minutes, Reb Shmuel motioned him to stop.*

*"Close the Gemara," Reb Shmuel said.*

*Reb Osher obeyed.*

*"Put it on my chest."*

*Reb Osher did as he was told.*

*"Now, put my right hand on the left side, and the left hand on the right side."*

*Reb Osher continued to follow instructions. His father lay on his hospital bed, his eyes closed, a Gemara on his chest, and his arms hugging the Gemara.*

*"Osher, sing 'Ki Heim Chayeinu.'"*

*Reb Osher was startled. His father was not usually a singer but if this was what he wanted …*

---

8. Rabbi Shmuel Berenbaum had gone to be *menachem avel* Rabbi Zeidel Leshinsky. Reb Shmuel suddenly keeled over, unconscious, in the living room. Someone began screaming for Hatzolah. *Hashgachah* had it that Mutti Hellman, son of longtime *Menahel* of Bais Yaakov High School, Rabbi Uri Hellman, had come to his brother-in-law's house across the street from Reb Zeidel. As Mutti Hellman was pulling his car out of the driveway, he heard the shouts coming from the *beis avel*. Again, *hashgachah* had it that Mutti had just completed a course in CPR. He jumped out of his car, into the house, and performed CPR on Reb Shmuel until Hatzolah came and took over. Hatzolah arranged to have Ocean Parkway closed down so that they could get Reb Shmuel to the hospital as soon as possible.

" 'Ki heim chayeinu v'orech yameinu u'vahem nehgeh yomam valaylah ... (For they [the commandments] are our life and the length of our days and about them we will meditate day and night),' " Reb Osher began singing softly. " 'Ki heim chayeinu v'orech yameinu u'vahem nehgeh yomam valaylah ...' "

Rebbetzin Berenbaum watched as her husband, just awakening from a debilitating heart attack, lay in bed, his eyes closed, embracing a Gemara, listening as their son sang that Torah is life.

REB YAAKOV LISTENED, MESMERIZED. HE HAD ALWAYS REVERED HIS Rosh Yeshivah, but this story was exceptional. He walked back to his mother's room in a contemplative mood. Perhaps *HaKadosh Baruch Hu* wanted to lift his spirits, to remind him that there is righteousness in this world, and to encourage him through this very difficult time.

*Rabbi Shmuel Berenbaum with his talmid Rabbi Yaakov Bender*

*Rabbi Shmuel Berenbaum (1921-2008) learned in Baranovich and Mir. During the war, he escaped with the Mirrer Yeshivah to Shanghai and from there, he went on to America. He married the daughter of Rabbi Avrohom Kalmanowitz and became a maggid shiur and later Rosh Yeshivah in the Mirrer Yeshivah in Brooklyn. Reb Shmuel was known for his legendary hasmadah, his unusual power of chiddush, and for molding hundreds of talmidim.*

*Chapter Seventy-Two*

# Her Passing

EB YANKEL, LISTEN CAREFULLY," DR. BRICKMAN SAID ON the phone. "Your mother's kidneys have stopped working, and the hospital is requesting that you sign a DNR.[9] You do not have to do anything you do not want to do, but I must relay the message."

Reb Yaakov raced to the hospital. Signing a DNR was out of the question, but he still wanted to be there to see how she was doing. He entered her room. She seemed to be resting peacefully. He went to speak to the doctors. Sadly, they told him that it was only a matter of time.

During the next few days, Rebbetzin Bender hovered between life and death. Dr. Brickman called Reb Yaakov aside. "Look, you must go somewhere to get some sleep. Only, don't go far. We will call you if there is any change." Reb Shmuel Sholom stayed the night shift, and Reb Yaakov went to his mother's house.

**11th** *of Iyar, 5756*
*(April 30, 1996)*

The ringing telephone startled Reb Yaakov. It was Dr. Keilson. "Reb Yankel, if you want to see your mother alive, come immediately." Reb Yaakov

---

9. DNR stands for "Do Not Resuscitate," which means that if the patient's vital organs begin to fail, do not hook them up to life-support machines. Later Reb Yaakov commented, "People say that the respirator just prolongs life and suffering. But let me tell you, from what I saw in the hospital, the people who were left without a respirator were in much more agony during the last weeks of their lives than those on life support."

slammed down the phone and glanced at the clock. It was 8 a.m. If he did not put *tefillin* on now, for the first time in his adult life he would probably not be able to put them on that day. He quickly donned his *tefillin*, said *Shema*, and ran to his car.

*Come on, come on*, Reb Yaakov muttered as he stood stuck in traffic. He really wished he could join the cacophony of beeping going on around him. *This is ridiculous. Nothing is moving.* Overcome with frustration, he leaned his head against the steering wheel.

It took 20 minutes for Reb Yaakov to drive from 16th Avenue and 48th street to the hospital on 10th and 49th. Reb Yaakov arrived at the hospital at 8:30 a.m. Reb Shmuel Sholom, his face white, was pacing the hallway. "They are inside … trying CPR …" A few minutes later, the doctors emerged from the room.

It was all over.

IT MAY HAVE BEEN THE LACK OF SLEEP OR THE UNCERTAINTY OF THE situation that had made him feel as if he were in a fog during the days before his mother's passing. Now the fog lifted, and Reb Yaakov knew what had to be done. The family had to decide immediately on when and where the *levayah* would take place.

He drove to his mother's house to confer with his brother-in-law Rabbi Chaim Epstein. They faced a dilemma. On the one hand, it was early morning and they could easily arrange the *levayah* for that day. However, the *levayah* would probably have to be scheduled for late afternoon, which might make it difficult for many people, especially out-of-towners, to come. Was it proper to push off the *levayah* until the next day? There was definitely room to argue that the *levayah* should be held as soon as possible.

Reb Chaim decided that this was a question he could not take upon himself to answer. He and Reb Yaakov hastened to Rabbi Zelig Epstein's home.

Reb Zelig did not deliberate long. "Tomorrow. Make the *levayah* tomorrow. Your mother has the *din* of an *adam gadol,* and it is appropriate to schedule the *levayah* in a way that will allow more people to come."

THAT HECTIC WEDNESDAY PASSED IN A BLUR. DOWNSTAIRS, IN REBBE-tzin Bender's apartment, her daughters-in-law and grandchildren were busy cleaning up. They needed to set up a room for the men, a room for the women, and sleeping space for the children who would be sleeping over during the week.

In all the bedrooms there were Bubby's "*pecklach,*" bags of used clothing that, until the end of her life, she used to collect and distribute. It took hours to clear out the rooms so that there would be maximum space for the *aveilim* and for those coming to comfort them.

Upstairs, Rebbetzin Esther Epstein sat with one of her children, her mother's personal phone book open before them. It seemed strange to be going through that worn little notebook, so closely identified with her mother. She felt almost like an intruder.

"O.K.," her son began, "let's begin. Mrs. S., does she have to be called?"

"Oh, yes," Rebbetzin Epstein answered. "Most definitely. Mommy would have wanted that."

Her son went to the next name on the list. "Ma, who is Mrs. P.? I never even heard her name mentioned."

"Mrs. P …" Rebbetzin Epstein furrowed her brow. "Yes, yes, I remember Mrs. P. She is a widow who was going through a difficult time at one point. Mommy collected money to help get her on her feet. That was years ago. But Mommy always kept in touch with her, and in the end, they became close friends."

"And Rabbi and Mrs. H.?"

"Oh, what Mommy did not do for them! They had a daughter who had a health issue, and no one wanted to touch a *shidduch* with her. Mommy not only found her a *shidduch*, she collected money to support the young couple comfortably in order to make the *shidduch* more attractive."

They went from name to name, a chronicle of the last 50 years of Rebbetzin Bender's life: the people she was close with, the people she helped, the people she loved.

*Chapter Seventy-Three*

# Her Legacy

**12th of Iyar, 5756 (May 1, 1996)**

*"… The great Chazon Ish, ztz"l, says, in his beautiful poetic way, that it seems from mathematical science that one plus one equals two and that half of two is one. No! Says the Chazon Ish, one plus one is far more than two. It is strength. It is a force. It is unity. Half of two is far, far less than two. It is divisiveness, fragmentation.*

*"There were many who came to the shores of America who had learned in the great yeshivos of yesteryear. Yet, America then was not what it is today. There was a 'one' — the ben Torah — but the plus one, the powerful mate, was missing … the great nifteres created the 'plus one'— the bas Yisroel who would be a fitting mate for a ben Torah …*

*"… The great nifteres gave of her wisdom, gave of her soul, gave of her warmth, with love and, mi yodei'a (who knows) what she did for the thousands of talmidos who are the 'plus one.' The changing of the face of the letzte stanza (last station) for Torah until the coming of Mashiach is not only the result of the wisdom of the mind of the great nifteres, but [also of] the warmth and wisdom of the heart …"[10]*

 PARADE OF ILLUSTRIOUS PERSONALITIES MADE THEIR WAY to the front of the Bais Yaakov auditorium to eulogize this special woman.[11] They spoke of her strength of character, her

---

10. Excerpted from the *hesped* said by Rabbi Mordechai Shapiro.

11. Rabbi Zelig Epstein, Rabbi Elya Svei, Rabbi Binyomin Zeilberger, Rabbi Shraga Moshe Kalmanowitz, Rabbi Aharon Zuckerman, Rabbi Chaim Epstein, Rabbi Simcha Schustal, Rabbi Aryeh Malkiel Kotler, Rabbi Mordechai Shapiro, Rabbi Avrohom Kaplan, Rabbi Yosef Dovid Epstein, and Rebbetzin Bender's four sons.

role in Bais Yaakov, her work to ensure the *kedushah* of *Klal Yisroel*, her unusual *chessed*, and her caring heart. For three hours they spoke, extolling her greatness and exhorting the new generation of Jewish women to continue down the path she had charted.

Inside Bais Yaakov High School, the auditorium was overflowing. It was hot and stuffy as hundreds of men sat in seats that had been set up in orderly formation that morning. Those who could not find a seat but wanted to be inside stood in the back, in the aisles, and anywhere they could find a space to stand. Uniform-clad high-school girls sat in their classrooms and listened to the *levayah* over the intercom system. Their mothers, grandmothers, and great-grandmothers sat outside.

*"… We sat in the street on white folding chairs, in the bright sunlight, between the old Bais Yaakov building and the still unfinished new one. The image of the two buildings evoked the metaphor of education of the Jewish woman in America; the old and new blending together …*

*"Time stood still; there was barely a breeze in the air. The leaves on the trees didn't move. Only the traffic signals continued to mark the passage of time. Utter silence in Boro Park … Beautiful phrases of Yiddish and Hebrew floated above the crowd … In quiet contemplation, in deep prayer … we felt the transmission of Torah inspiration from one generation to another …*

*"Rebbetzin Bender connected us. She was the bridge, the woman of history. She taught us to value our past, to see life as a testament to courage and faith because she had lived her life in that exalted tenor …"* [12]

AFTER THE *HESPEDIM*, A HUGE CROWD ESCORTED THE *ARON* FROM BAIS Yaakov to the Bender home, a block away. From there, they went to the cemetery.

During the week of *shivah*, lines extended out the door and circled the house. People waited for their turn to come in. So many people had something to say, a comment, a story, or an impression. She had touched so many people in so many different ways. Even in death, Rebbetzin Bender wielded her influence.

Anna, the Russian aide whose son had agreed to a *bris milah*, called Rebbetzin Epstein on the day of her mother's *shloshim*.

"I have decided to do it!" she declared triumphantly. "Your mother so much wanted me to have a Jewish wedding — a *chuppah* she called it. I kept pushing her off. After all, I am married. So what if a rabbi did not officiate? No one can say that I am not married. But ever since your mother passed away, I keep thinking about it. Why not be married by a rabbi?

---

12. Quoted from the essay *Reflections at Rebbetzin Bender's Levayah* by Rebbetzin Sara E. Freifeld, Dean of Touro College Women's Division.

What am I afraid of? So I decided that I am going to do it, and I would like you and your family to help me do it right."

Even near the end of her life, when she was so weak, Rebbetzin Bender still tried to convince her aide to have a proper Jewish wedding. This time she had not lived to see the fruits of her efforts.

How was she able to care so deeply for others, even as she was being consumed by pain and suffering? Her son Reb Yaakov summed it up at her *shloshim*: She lived and breathed *"ki l'kach notzarta* — because for this you were created."

*Ki l'kach notzarta* — to do His Will, to study His words, to help His people.

*Ki l'kach notzarta* — to serve Him through health and illness, through triumphs and trials.

*Ki l'kach notzarta* — to accomplish and to give honor to His Holy Name.

This was Rebbetzin Bender's legacy.

## Chapter Seventy-Four

# Epilogue

T WAS CLOSE TO REBBETZIN BENDER'S FIRST *YAHRTZEIT*.

*She appeared very old and weak, the way she looked at the very end.*

*"I have to go …" she said faintly. "I have to get up … I have to go … but I cannot … I am too weak … how can I go …?"*

*Rebbetzin Zoberman and I were encouraging her. "Come," we said, "we will help you … you can go … you can do it …"*

*She looked so sad and helpless. "No," she said. "I cannot … I really cannot." She sighed. "I should be singing, but I cannot do that either."*

*"Come, we will help you walk." I helped her get up. Rebbetzin Zoberman took one hand and I took the other.*

*"Really, I should be singing," she said tearfully, "but I am too weak … Oh, I really should be singing …"*

*"Don't worry, Mommy, don't worry … it doesn't matter."*

*I tried to comfort her, but she was so sad. We walked past one building and then another. Then we came to a gate, a big beautiful elaborate gate, with a door that opened upward, like a garage door.*

*"Here, we have to stop," she said abruptly. We stood before the gate and watched as the door lifted, revealing what seemed to be the inside of an elevator, a brightly lit elevator, glowing from within. There was singing in the background, beautiful singing, faint, but beautiful.*

*Suddenly, she dropped our hands and walked energetically inside. Then she turned to face us. A warm smile lit up her face, she looked so happy. It was as if, in those few seconds, she had acquired a new life. Her face was shining. She looked beautiful, healthy, and full of life. She was no longer a sick and weak old woman.*

*Happy and radiant, she called out to us, "Yetzt darf ich zingen viell zei zingen far mir — now I have to sing, because they are singing for me." She just stood there, looking so happy.*

*The door closed.*

And Blumie woke up.

# Biographical Sketches

**Ackerman, R' Pinchas** (1916-1985) was American born and bred. As a *bochur*, he learned in Yeshivah Chofetz Chaim. He davened regularly in Kollel Kerem Shlomo and enjoyed being in the company of *talmidei chachamim*.

**Barnetsky, Rabbi Avrohom** (1916-2006) was born in the United States where he learned in Yeshivah Rabbeinu Chaim Berlin Elementary School, and continued on in Torah Vodaath as a *talmid* of Rabbi Shlomo Heiman. He traveled to Otvock where he learned for a year until the outbreak of World War II. Reb Avrohom taught in Yeshivah Tomchei Temimim for over 50 years and in Talmud Torah Chaim Yosef. He was known for his unusual warmth toward his *talmidim* and his exemplary davening.

**Belsky, Rabbi Berel** (1913-2003) was born on the Lower East Side. His family moved to Williamsburg in 1918 and he attended Yeshivah Torah Vodaath. At 18, "Barney" Belsky left for the European yeshivos of Baranovich and Radin, respectively. He merited to daven with the Chofetz Chaim daily for the final two years of the Chofetz Chaim's life. He married the daughter of Rabbi Binyamin Wilhelm, founder of Yeshivah Torah Vodaath, and raised his family in Williamsburg,

**Bernstein, Rabbi Binyamin** (1911-1975) was sent by Rabbi Yaakov Yosef Herman (of *All for the Boss*) to learn in Kaminetz. After seven years in Kaminetz, he returned to the United States where he married. Then he returned to Europe where he learned in the Mir. At the onset of World War II, he fled Europe to the United States. He was a rebbi in Yeshivas Rabbeinu Yaakov Yosef for many years. After his retirement he moved to Eretz Yisroel.

**Berliner, Rabbi Pinchas (Phillip)** (1916-1959) was born in London to Polish immigrant parents. He learned in Eitz Chaim Yeshivah in London, in Gateshead Yeshivah, and then in the Mir. At the outbreak of World War II, he fled to Riga and from there to Telshe. In 1940 he was evacuated from Lithuania together with other British nationals and headed toward Australia. Phillip married the daughter of Rabbi Yitzchak Yaakov Super, Rav of Melbourne. Rabbi Berliner served the Melbourne community as *shochet*, *chazzan*, teacher, and general disseminator of Torah until he passed away at 43.

**Blau, Rabbi Chaim Moshe Yehuda HaKohen** (1912-2003) was born in Hamburg, Germany. He learned in Yeshivas Mir where he became a *talmid* of Rabbi Yeruchem Levovitz. He spent the war years in Shanghai, arriving in America in 1947. Reb Moshe Yehuda was instrumental in bringing traveling *sofrim* to many communities promoting the examination of *mezuzos* and *tefillin*. With great sacrifice he unearthed manuscripts of over 40 Rishonim, among them, the *Chidushei HaRitva* on *Bava Basra*, *Nimukei Yosef* on certain *Mesechtos*, *Sefer Habatim*, and *Rabbeinu Avrohom Min Hahar* on *Nedarim*.

**Bloch, Rabbi Shmuel** (1918-2005) hailed from England and journeyed to study in Yeshivas Mir, Poland. With the outbreak of World War II he fled to Australia and from there made his way to America. He joined the staff at the yeshivah in Boston, founded by Rabbi Michel Feinstein. At the war's end, he returned to England and spent a number of years learning in the Gateshead Kollel. Even after joining the business world, he still remained a regular in the kollel.

**Blum, Rabbi Refael** (1908-2005), the **Kashover Rav**, was born and raised in Kashau, Slovakia. His Rebbe was Rabbi Shaul Brach, and he acquired much from the Stropkover Rav, the Shinever Rebbe, and Rabbi Shmuel Engel. He married and founded a yeshivah in Michlowicz. In 1943 he was asked to serve as Rosh Yeshivah of the refugees in Pest. Though he lost his family and community in World War II, as soon as he was liberated he traveled around, encouraging his brethren to rebuild. In 1948, he arrived in Williamsburg where he set up a *kehillah* and was appointed Rosh Yeshivah of the Tzelemer Yeshivah. He yearned to establish a community without exposure to modernism and, in 1988, settled in Bedford Hills, New York. His two published works are *Tal Shamayim* and *Birkas Shamayim*.

**Borenstein, Rabbi Yitzchok Noach** (1909-1983) learned in the yeshivos of Lomza and Mir, and later in Brisk where he became a distinguished *talmid*. After World War II he was a rebbi in Mesivta Tiferes Yerushalayim, followed by a position in Yeshivah Rabbeinu Chaim Berlin, and then Yeshivas Rabbeinu Yitzchok Elchonon where he taught until his retirement.

**Chill, Rabbi Akiva** (1919-1997) grew up in Williamsburg, New York. He learned in Torah Vodaath and then went on to the Mir in Poland. He served as Rav in several different communities, including the Bronx, Manhattan, and Miami Beach, Florida.

**Chill, Rabbi Shlomo** (1916-1990) grew up in Williamsburg, New York. He learned in Torah Vodaath and then went to the Mir in Poland. Upon returning to America, he rejoined Yeshivah Torah Vodaath. He served as Rav in several different communities, including Kingsway Jewish Center in Brooklyn, and Long Beach, New York. He lived the last five years of his life in Yerushalayim where he learned daily in the Mir.

**Chinn, Rabbi Yisroel Yehoshua** (1918-1994) was raised in Liverpool, England and learned in the Gateshead Yeshivah. From there he went on to the yeshivos of Mir and Telshe. He escaped to Australia during the war and from there to America. He joined the newly formed Telshe Yeshivah of Cleveland as one of their first *talmidim*. He served as a *shochet*, and later in life retired to Eretz Yisroel.

**Cohn, Rabbi Moses J.** (1912-1994) was born in Hamburg, Germany. He studied in Mir, Poland and escaped Europe with the yeshivah. He settled in Boston, Massachusetts where he was the principal of Maimonides Day School for 31 years.

**Cyperstein, Rabbi Avigdor** (1903-1975) was a student of Slabodka and then learned by the Brisker Rav. After his marriage, he served as Rav in Lida. During World War II, he made his way from Bialystok to Shanghai where he learned with Rabbi Chaim Shmulevitz. After his arrival in America he gave a *semichah shiur* in Yeshivas Rabbeinu Yitzchok Elchonon, and founded Sridei HaCherev Kollel. Additionally, he served as Rav in Buenos Aires, Argentina, commuting for three to four months a year, where he supervised the *shechitah* there. His work was published as *Sefer Imrei Avigdor*.

**Ederman, R' Yaakov** (1921-2006) came from Loitzk where his father was Rav. He went to learn in Mir, Poland, and fled with the yeshivah to Vilna. He deserves credit for arranging "Polish passports" for hundreds of Mirrer *talmidim*, enabling them to travel out of Europe and on to Japan. After the war, he settled in Queens, New York where he became a *chazzan*.

**Ehrlanger, R' Elchonon (Heiry)** (1915-2004) was born in Lucerne, Switzerland. He went to Poland to learn in Baranovich, followed by three years in Yeshivas Mir under the guidance of Rabbi Yeruchem Levovitz. Rabbi Hersh Feldman was R' Elchonon's private rebbi in Mir, and the relationship they developed lasted a lifetime. With the outbreak of World War II, he escaped to Switzerland where he became a supporter of Yeshivas Lucerne for the subsequent 50 years of his life.

**Ehrlanger, R' Sholom** (1917-1974) was raised in Lucerne, together with his older brother R' Elchonon Ehrlanger. His private home rebbi, Rabbi Michoel Posen, brother of the Shoproner Rav, sent him to learn in Hungarian yeshivos where he studied for three years. He then followed his brother to Yeshivas Mir in Poland. He was a staunch supporter of Yeshivas Lucerne.

**Ehrlanger, R' Yaakov** (1883-1963) lived in Switzerland where he ran a successful business. He had the foresight to hire a rebbi, Rabbi Michoel Posen, to teach his sons Torah. Reb Michoel encouraged R' Yaakov to send his sons to learn in the yeshivos of Eastern Europe, a move practically unheard of in Switzerland at that time. During the war, he and his sons were involved in sending funds to people trapped in war-torn countries.

**Fajveshewitz, Rabbi Shmuel** (1913-1996) was born in Drevneh, Poland. When he was 11 he joined the yeshivah in Baranovich, and at 16 he left for Yeshivas Mir. After World War II he arrived in America and held the position of *maggid shiur* in Yeshivas Rabbeinu Yitzchok Elchonon. For the final 20 years of his life, he retired and returned to full-time learning in Yeshivah Bais HaTalmud.

**Feinstein, Rabbi Yechiel Michel** (1906–2003) learned by his grandfather Rabbi Dovid Feinstein, Rav of Uzda and then Starobin, and found additional guidance from his uncle Rabbi Moshe Feinstein. Afterward he learned in Slutzk, Mir, and Brisk. He rejoined the Mirrer Yeshiva in leaving Europe, but received a visa to America while in Japan. Reb Michel lived in America until 1946, and then went to Eretz Yisroel where he married the daughter of the Brisker Rav. He went back to America in 1948 where he was a *maggid shiur* in Mesivta Tiferes Yerushalayim. Four years later he returned to Eretz Yisroel where he opened Kollel Bais Yehudah, a *Beis Medrash* where illustrious *talmidei chachamim* learned.

**Feldman, Rabbi Shloima** (1948-1995) was orphaned at a young age. He was brought up by Rabbi Yonah Forst of Nitra. After Reb Yonah passed away, Reb Shloima began Tiferes Yonah, a learning program for young boys, in his memory. Reb Shloima was well known for his many acts of *chessed* and his devotion to *tinokos shel bais rabban*.

**Flamm, Rabbi Sholom** (1929-2003) was born in Montreal, Canada. His father, Reb Dovid, was known as the Olesker Rebbe. He left for New York when he was 11 to study in Yeshivah Torah Vodaath. Ten years later, he was one of the chosen few to join Bais Medrash Elyon in Monsey. After his marriage, he moved to Detroit where he was a rebbi in Beis Yehuda of Detroit. Reb Sholom later moved to New York and established the Strettiner Shul of Ocean Parkway.

**Foxman, Rabbi Ben Zion** (1913-1994) was from Slonim. After learning in Slonim, he went to the Mir and continued with the yeshivah on its travels during the war. When he first came to America, he taught classes to refugee youths in Torah Vodaath and then in Rabbi Ephraim Oshry's *cheder* in the Bronx. Even after he left *chinuch*, he continued to learn regularly, giving a Daf Yomi *shiur* for many years.

**Frankel, Rabbi Shabsi** (1909-2001) was known for his work in reprinting the Rambam's *Mishneh Torah* with references, additions, and corrections. *The Frankel Rambam* has become popular among scholars and laymen alike.

**Freidin, Rabbi Dov Nochum** (d. 1998) was the son of the Polisah Rav of Poland. Reb Berel, as he was known, studied in Yeshivas Mir, Poland. He was one of the closest *talmidim* of Rabbi Yecheskel Levenstein and, through the trials of World War II, never left his rebbi's side. He traveled with him to New York, later to Yerushalayim, and finally to Bnei Brak. He occasionally gave *mussar shiurim* in the Yeshivah Ketanah of Ponevezh and was known for his exceptional piety and intense devotion to serving his Maker.

**Friedenson, Rabbi Eliezer Gershon** from Lodz, Poland, was a leader of both Agudas Yisroel and the Bais Yaakov educational network, and was editor of the Bais Yaakov magazine. He was killed during World War II.

**Genauer, Rabbi Tzvi** (1915-1953) was born in Seattle, Washington. As a young *bochur*, he went to learn in Kelm, Lithuania. At the outset of World War II, he returned to America where he married and joined

Rabbi Mordechai Yoffe as a founder of the White Plains Kollel. Reb Hershel moved to Eretz Yisroel, where he studied in the Mirrer Yeshivah in Yerushalayim and developed a close relationship with many *gedolim*. Tragically, he was killed by an Arab in the prime of his life, while learning in his own home.

**Ginsburg, Rabbi Reuvain** (1915-1985) learned in the Mir in Poland. He married the daughter of Rabbi Yecheskel Levenstein while spending the war years in Shanghai. Reb Reuvain accompanied his in-laws to New York and then Eretz Yisroel. He succeeded his father-in-law as *Mashgiach* in Ponevezh and was widely respected for his scholarship and piety.

**Godlevsky, Rabbi Yehoshua** (1917-1995) was born in Posen, Germany. He learned with Rabbi Yechiel Michel Shlesinger in Frankfurt and later traveled to Lithuania to learn in Telshe. He joined with the Mirrer Yeshivah on their travels to Japan and Shanghai. In Shanghai, he and Rabbi Elchonon Hertzman founded a Bais Yaakov and a home for refugee girls. Upon arriving in the United States after the war, he became a renowned teacher in Bais Yaakov of Williamsburg and founder of Keren HaYeled, an organization to benefit orphans in Eretz Yisroel. In 1974 he moved to Eretz Yisroel where he established Keren HaYeled Orphanage.

**Gordon, Rabbi Yehudah** (1914-1968), known as Yud'l, was an American-born boy who went to Europe to learn in the great yeshivos of Mir and Kaminetz. Later, he served as Rav in Denver, Colorado and Hartford, Connecticut. Even after entering the business world, he retained a connection to his friends from Mir, and considered those years in Europe the most significant years of his life.

**Greenhaus, Rabbi Mordechai** (circa 1906-84), known as Markel, was born in Lebedov, Poland. He learned in the yeshivos of Radin, Remmailes, Mir, and Kaminetz. At the onset of the war he came to Vilna and rejoined the Mir contingent, escaping with them as well. He was widely esteemed for his scholarship and *yiras Shamayim*. Over his three decades in America, he held various positions in the world of Torah and *chinuch*.

**Grozovsky, Rabbi Chaim** (1926-1999) was the son of Rabbi Reuvain Grozovsky. He learned in Torah Vodaath, continued on in Bais Medrash Elyon of Monsey, and later became a longtime *talmid* of Rabbi Aharon Kotler. Reb Chaim was the *menahel* of the Kaminetz High School, ran a kollel, and was a Rav in Boro Park. He diligently served Rabbi Shlomo Heiman, who was their neighbor, during Rabbi Heiman's last years.

**Gryngras, Rabbi Chaim Yankel** (1914-2004) was born in Rodzelov, Poland. As a youngster he learned in the Lomza Yeshivah and then went on to Yeshivas Mir. He was well respected for his learning and exemplary character. He ran the American office for Yeshivas Kaminetz of Eretz Yisroel. His office was situated across the street from Mesivta Tiferes Yerushalayim where he learned with Rabbi Michoel Berenbaum every afternoon for 50 years.

**Gutwirth, R' Nosson** (1916-1999) was born in Antwerp and raised in Holland. As a *bochur*, he went to learn in Yeshivas Telshe, Europe. During World War II, he traveled with Yeshivas Mir to America via Shanghai. R' Nosson is credited for the idea of the Curacao visas which enabled hundreds of *b'nei Torah* to escape Europe. He lived in America for 12 years and then moved to Antwerp.

**Herman, Rabbi Nochum Dovid** (1910-1985) was the son of Rabbi Yaakov Yosef Herman, a pioneer of *Yiddishkeit* in America. He attended the New Haven Yeshivah in Connecticut and then the Slabodka Yeshivah in Eretz Yisroel. He was one of the first American boys to travel overseas to study in a yeshivah. After returning to America, he married and went to learn in Mir, Poland. He later served as Rav in various communities, such as Burlington, Vermont, the Bronx, and Williamsburg, New York.

**Herzog, Rabbi Yitzchok Isaac HaLevi** (1889-1959) was born in Poland. When his father, Reb Yoel, left for England, he remained to study under the famed Ridvaz of Lithuania, who ordained him with *semichah*. He later served as Rav in Belfast, Ireland and then in Dublin, eventually becoming Chief Rabbi of Ireland. He served as the second Chief Rabbi of Palestine/Israel. He used his power and never-ending love for his fellow Jew to procure many certificates of entry to Palestine from the British.

**Herzog, Rabbi Yoel Leib** (1865-1933) was a student of Slabodka and a member of the kollel in Aishishok founded by the Chofetz Chaim. In 1907 he left Lomza, Poland to lead the community in Leeds, England. In 1913, he was called upon to become Rav of the Orthodox Eastern European community in Pletzel, the Jewish quarter in Paris, France, where he served until his passing.

**Horowitz, Rabbi Tzvi Hersh (Harry)** (circa 1913-1997) was raised in Pittsburgh, Pennsylvania. He learned in Baranovich and Mir. Upon returning to America, Harry became the Rav in the Fur Trade Center Synagogue in downtown New York and later served as a rebbi in Yeshivah Torah

Vodaath. Eventually, he went into business but remained forever connected to the yeshivah world. He was instrumental in helping the Mirrer Yeshivah of Brooklyn acquire their building in Flatbush and davened regularly in the Mirrer Minyan in Boro Park.

**Horowitz, Rabbi Yosef Shlomo** (d. 1962) was a *talmid* of the Chofetz Chaim and *menahel* of the Yeshivah Ketanah of Mir, Poland. At the beginning of World War II, he traveled to Vilna with the Mirrer Yeshivah but was subsequently exiled to Siberia. His family perished during the war. He immigrated to Eretz Yisroel and was taken in by the Ponevezher Rav and spent the rest of his life learning in the yeshivah. He became a legend in the yeshivah, as an example of achievement through toil.

**Jung, Rabbi Leo** (1892-1987) attended the Hildesheimer Rabbinical Seminary in Berlin. In 1920 Rabbi Jung undertook his first American pulpit at the Knesset Israel Congregation, Cleveland. He was involved in raising standards of Jewish observance in America and in other countries. As such, he supported the Bais Yaakov movement. He was on the Executive Committee of the Rabbi Samson Raphael Hirsch Society, whose goal was to translate works by German Orthodox thinkers into English.

**Kalisch, Rabbi Yitzchok** (circa 1914-1991) was the **Amshinover Rebbe** of America. Having lost his father as a young man, Reb Yitzchok spent his time in Otvock with his uncle, Rabbi Shimon Shalom Kalisch. On the advice of his uncle, he escaped the Nazis through Vilna, Japan, and Shanghai. Reb Yitzchok settled in Brooklyn and toiled to maintain the Vorka-Amshinov traditions, including the upkeep of the shul in Tel Aviv.

**Kaplan, Rabbi Boruch** (1909-1995), in his youth, learned in Mesivta Tiferes Yerushalayim and the New Haven Yeshivah. He went to Eretz Yisroel to learn in Slabodka/Chevron but returned to the United States after miraculously surviving the Chevron massacre of 1929. He then traveled to the yeshivos of Mir and Kaminetz. Reb Boruch married Vichna Eisen, an illustrious pupil of Sara Schenirer. They moved to America where he became a *maggid shiur* in Mesivta Torah Vodaath until, with the urging of Rabbi Aharon Kotler, he joined his rebbetzin in building Bais Yaakov in America.

**Kaplan, Rabbi Moshe** (1915-1982) was a student of the Mirrer Yeshivah, where he was known as Moshe Minsker. He learned under Rabbi Shimon Shkop in Grodno, as well. Rabbi Yaakov Kamenetsky invited him to join the faculty of Yeshivah Eitz Chaim in Toronto, where he took the position of ninth-grade rebbi. Rabbi Elya Svei, Rosh Yeshivah of the Talmudical Yeshivah of Philadelphia, commented that he could spot a student of Rabbi Moshe Kaplan by his proficiency in learning.

**Kashover Rav,** see **Blum.**

**Kranzler, Rabbi Dr. David** (1928-2007) was born in Germany and raised in Williamsburg, New York where he studied in Torah Vodaath. He was a noted professor in CUNY College and wrote many books about the Holocaust.

**Kravitz, Rabbi Mendel** (1907-1991) was born in Vilna. He learned in Slutzk and then in Kletzk and remained a close *talmid* of Rabbi Aharon Kotler for the rest of his life. He studied with the Brisker Rav for two years. During the war, he became engaged to the daughter of Rabbi Aharon Berek, secretary of the Vaad HaYeshivos. He joined the Mirrer Yeshivah on their escape route via Shanghai. In America he became Rosh Yeshivah of Yeshivas Rabbeinu Yaakov Yosef.

**Kreiser, Rabbi Aharon** (1919-1998) learned in Baranovich as a young *bochur* and went on to Yeshivas Mir, Poland where he was known for his unusual diligence in learning. Having survived World War II, he settled in America where as a devoted disseminator of Torah, he influenced hundreds of *talmidim.*

**Krupenia, Rabbi Levi** (circa 1913-1998) was raised in Slonim and left to learn in Yeshivas Mir at a very young age. He journeyed with the Mir to Shanghai and eventually America. In the United States, he married the daughter of Rabbi Reuvain Grozovsky. Reb Levi was one of the early founders of Yeshivah Bais HaTalmud and later served as Rosh Yeshivah of Yeshivas Kaminetz in Woodridge. When Kaminetz closed its doors in Woodridge, he took the position of Rosh Yeshivah of Kaminetz in Brooklyn.

**Lebor, Rabbi Yeshaya** (1918-1996) was born and raised in England and went to study in Yeshivas Mir, Poland. Early into World War II, he immigrated to America and eventually became Rav of the Young Israel of Woodmere. In 1980, with the desire to spend his time learning as he had done back in the Mir, he moved to Eretz Yisroel. The subsequent 16 years of his life were spent immersed in Torah.

**Leibowitz, Rabbi Alter Chanoch Henoch** (1918 -2008) learned under his father Rabbi Dovid Leibowitz, Rosh Yeshivah of Torah Vodaath and later of Yeshivas Chofetz Chaim. After Reb Dovid was niftar in 1941, at the young age of 23, Reb Henoch took over the Yeshivas Chofetz Chaim. He led the yeshivah for over sixty years, molding hundreds of *talmidim* and showering them with personal paternal love. Though he had no children, hundreds of *talmidim* considered him their father. His gave analytical *shiurim* with tremendous fervor, and deep *mussar shmuessen*, continuing in the *derech* of the Alter of Slabodka.

**Leschinsky, Rabbi Dovid** (1898-1986) learned in Grodno and then in Yeshivas Mir. After his marriage, he lived in Mir where he continued to learn. He and his family traveled with the Mirrer Yeshivah during World War II. Reb Dovid was widely respected for his scholarship and piety. He often gave *shiurim* in Torah Vodaath in the evenings in an unofficial capacity, and was a rebbi in Lubavitch for a number of years.

**Lesman, Rabbi Nochum** (1917-1969) was one of the most illustrious younger *bochur*im in Yeshivas Mir, Poland. He settled in Bnei Brak where he became the son-in-law of Rabbi Mattisyahu Shteigler, one of the founders of Bnei Brak. Reb Nochum served as a *maggid shiur* in Yeshivah Beis Yosef Novarodok, followed by his position as Rosh Yeshivah of Yeshivas Magdiel, and later of Yeshivas Tifrach. He was recognized as an extraordinary *talmid chacham* who spent his every moment learning.

**Lieber, Rabbi Moshe** (circa 1896-1953) was born in Galicia and studied under the guidance of the *Baal Be'er Shmuel*, the Unsdorfer Rosh Yeshivah. He immigrated to the United States when he was 44 years old, settling in Williamsburg, Brooklyn. Reb Moshe gave daily *shiurim* in the Bostoner Shtiebel and in the Agudas Yisroel of Williamsburg. Shabbos evening, after the meal, he gave a *shiur* in *Chumash* in his house as well. By day he worked in the diamond industry and founded Lieber's Kosher Chocolate Co. He was very active in community affairs, most notably taking a pivotal role in the establishment of Bais Yaakov of Williamsburg elementary school.

**Litmanowitz, Rabbi Pinchas Shlomo** (1916-2004) was born in Lodz, Poland and went to learn in Yeshivas Mir. During World War II he escaped with the yeshivah through Vilna, Russia, Japan, and Shanghai. He arrived in the United States where he married and taught in Yeshivah Torah Vodaath. Toward the end of his life he joined some of his children in Eretz Yisroel.

**Mallin, Rabbi Aryeh Leib** (1906-1962) was born in Bialystok and learned in Grodno where he was famous as the star pupil of Rabbi Shimon Shkop. Later, in Mir, he became the right-hand man of Rabbi Yeruchem Levovitz, whose teachings in *Daas Chochmah U'Mussar* were gleaned from Reb Leib's notes. He also studied under the Brisker Rav for two years. During World War II, he and his colleague Rabbi Chaim Wisokere conceived and implemented the brilliant idea of the yeshivah leaving Vilna for Japan. Once on American shores he founded Bais HaTalmud with Rabbi Chaim Wisokere. His *sefer, Chidushei Reb Aryeh Leib*, is highly regarded by serious scholars.

**Mashinsky, Rabbi Hershel** (1925-2005) grew up in New York. He learned in Torah Vodaath and Bais Medrash Elyon. Reb Hershel married and raised a family in Monsey, where he joined the faculty of Yeshivah of Spring Valley as a seventh-grade rebbi. In his 50 years of educating the young generation he became famous as a teacher par excellence. Reb Hershel's love for a fellow Jew expressed itself in his work for the public in the worthy organization of Kupath Ezra of Monsey.

**Meisels, Rabbi Nosson Yosef** (1927-2006) was *menahel* of the UTA (United Talmudical Academy of Satmar) and then Rosh Yeshivah of Satmar. In 1980, he became Rav of the Satmar community in Stamford Hills, London. Ten years later he returned to America and moved to Monsey where he became known as *Admor M'Avnei Shlomo*.

**Moore, R' Menachem Mannis (Monty)** (1920-1999) left his hometown in England to learn in Yeshivas Mir in Poland. When World War II broke out, he fled to Riga with many of the other foreign citizens of the yeshivah. He went on to Telshe where he learned for a number of months. Afraid of being drafted into the army in England, he waited for an opportunity to travel to America. Once he reached America, he learned in the White Plains Kollel and later in Lakewood. After the war, he moved back to England.

**Myski, Rabbi Tzvi Yosef** (1909-1986) was from Slonim where his family were Slonimer Chassidim. His father sent him to learn in Baranovich where he acquired the *Litvishe* method of learning. Rabbi Myski survived the war and moved to Williamsburg where he became very close to the Skulener Rebbe, Rabbi Eliezer Zusia Portugal, and eventually married one of the Rebbe's adopted daughters. He taught Halachah in Bais Yaakov of Williamsburg for many years and wrote the six-volume *Sha'arei Halachah* on the *Orach Chaim* section of the *Shulchan Aruch*.

**Neuschloss, Rabbi Moshe** (1911-1997) learned in the yeshivah of Rabbi Akiva Sofer and became famous as an elite student. Reb Moshe married and studied under Rabbi Asher Anshel Katz of Serdahel. Despite his tremendous suffering during World War II, he set up a yeshivah for survivors in Serdahel. With the rise of Communism, Reb Moshe and his yeshivah left for Paris where they awaited their visas to America. In Williamsburg, he forged a relationship with the Skverer Rebbe and later served as a dedicated Rav in New Square.

**Newhouse, Rabbi Avrohom** (d. 1972) studied in the yeshivos of Mir and Telshe. He arrived in America during the war. Following a brief stint assisting the rebuilding of Telshe in the Midwest, he founded Bais Yaakov of Williamsburg elementary school. Reb Avrohom also purchased and developed Camp Bais Yaakov in Ferndale. He laid the groundwork for a united network of Bais Yaakov schools by creating workshops, seminars, and conventions.

**Partzovitz, Rabbi Nochum** (1923-1986) was a son of the Rav in Truyi, a grandson of the *Cheshek Shlomo*. He studied in the yeshivos of Remmailes, Baranovich, Kaminetz, and Mir. He escaped to Shanghai and then immigrated to the United States. In 1949 he joined the Mirrer Yeshivah in Yerushalayim, where he married the daughter of Rabbi Chaim Shmulevitz. He suffered tremendously the last 15 years of his life from a debilitating disease and it was during those years that his love of Torah was so readily apparent as he toiled to give *shiurim* despite his weakness. His *shiurim* were known for their penetrating *lomdus*.

**Pincus, Rabbi Shimshon** (1944-2001) learned in the yeshivos of Bais HaTalmud, Ponevezh, and Brisk. He became a Rav in Ofakim in Eretz Yisroel and through his warmth and wisdom brought about a religious revolution in that city. He helped establish Shalheves, an organization to strengthen *Yiddishkeit* and spiritually uplift his fellow Jews. He was killed in a tragic car accident when he was 57. Many of his *shmuessen* have been printed and remain popular among scholars and laymen.

**Posen, Rabbi Peretz** (1921-2002) learned in Gateshead until the outbreak of World War II. The Posens were then exiled to an internment camp in Canada with other German nationals. Reb Peretz was impressed with the devotion to Torah of the many refugees of the Mirrer Yeshivah who passed through Canada on their way into the United States, and he relocated to New York to be in their proximity. There he founded an elementary school, a branch of Bais HaTalmud. Reb Peretz's affiliation with Bais HaTalmud continued even after the school's closing. He learned the first *seder* in Bais HaTalmud for 45 years.

**Quinn, Rabbi Nesanel** (1910-2005) was born in Williamsburg. He studied in Yeshivas Rabbeinu Yaakov Yosef for a short while and then joined Yeshivah Torah Vodaath as assistant to Rabbi Shraga Feivel Mendelowitz. He later became his successor. He worked at establishing Ohr Shraga, Torah Vodaath's learning camp, and oversaw its subsequent daily functioning. Reb Nesanel was devoted to disseminating Torah in Torah Vodaath for over 40 years.

**Schneersohn, Rabbi Yosef Yitzchok** (1880-1950) was the son of Rabbi Sholom Dov Ber, whom he succeeded as the leader of the Chabad Chassidic movement in 1920. With World War I and the ensuing Communist Revolution yielding a state of perpetual chaos, the Rebbe worked fearlessly at reconstructing Jewish life. In 1927 he was arrested and with continued intercession his release was secured. Following his release he continued strengthening *Yiddishkeit* from Riga, Latvia. Eventually he moved to Poland, where it was easier to conduct his activities. With the outbreak of World War II, he escaped to the United States and rebuilt the Chabad *Chassidus* there.

**Schneider, Rabbi Gedaliah** (1912-2007) was the son of Rabbi Moshe Schneider, founder of a yeshivah in Memel which moved to Frankfurt and eventually to London. Reb Gedaliah learned with his father and then in Mir and Kaminetz. He spent his life studying, teaching and supporting Torah. He was known for the unusual light that suffused his face when greeting another *Yid*. In the latter part of his life, he moved to Eretz Yisroel where he continued his lofty ways.

**Serebrowski, Rabbi Avrohom Aharon** (1921-2002) learned in Slonim and joined Yeshivas Mir as a young *bochur*. During the last summer before World War II broke out, he was a *ben bayis* by Rabbi Yecheskel Levenstein. After the war, in America, he set out to make a living. When he found an opening in *chinuch* he returned to learning, even though it meant a drastic cut in salary. He was a rebbi in Yeshivah Chasam Sofer for many years.

**Shachor, Rabbi Leibel** (1913-1953) was a student of Kobrin, Kaminetz, Radin, and Mir. Additionally, he learned by the Brisker Rav. He was of the elite of the Mirrer *lamdanim* and for the rest of his life considered himself "a Mirrer." He married the daughter of Rabbi Yeruchem Leiner, the Radziner Rebbe. Reb Leibel was one of the founders of Yeshivah Bais HaTalmud and worked on a compilation of commentaries that was published at the back of the *Schulsinger Yoreh Deah* and the *Minchas Chinuch*.

**Shapiro, Rabbi Mordechai** (1929-1997) learned in Torah Vodaath and then in Lakewood under Rabbi Aharon Kotler. He was a very effective and beloved Rav in several places, including Bridgeport, Connecticut; Scranton, Pennsylvania; and Miami Beach, Florida.

**Sheps, Rabbi Simcha Avrohom HaKohen** (circa 1911-1998) learned in Baranovich and Mir and then under the Brisker Rav. He traveled with the Mir to Vilna and Japan. He received a visa in Japan in 1941, enabling him to immigrate to New York. After Rabbi Shlomo Heiman's passing, Rav Sheps became one of the leading *maggidei shiur* in Torah Vodaath.

**Shereshevsky, Rabbi Chaim** (1905-1988) was born in Slonim. As a *bochur*, he learned in Mir, Poland. Rabbi Shereshevsky escaped from Europe shortly after World War II began and immigrated to America. He held many different positions in *chinuch,* most notably, *Mashgiach* in Yeshivah Rabbeinu Chaim Berlin and a longtime teacher in Bais Yaakov of Williamsburg.

**Shreibman, Rabbi Mordechai** (1914-1985) learned in Baranovich and had a very close relationship with Rabbi Elchonon Wasserman. He then joined Yeshivas Mir and, during World War II, traveled with the yeshivah to Shanghai and eventually to the United States. After the war he took a position as a *shochet* in Chicago.

**Silver, Rabbi Chaim Dov** (1912-1996) was born in Liverpool, England to *Litvishe* parents. His parents sent him to learn in Telshe, Lithuania and from there he continued on to Kelm where he married into the prestigious Udvin family of Kelm. He and his family fled to Australia soon after the outbreak of the war. He remained in Australia for 10 years and was a force in building Torah. In 1950 he moved to Eretz Yisroel where he became Secretary of the Vaad HaYeshivos, a position he held till the end of his life.

**Soltan, Rabbi Ella** (1910-1994) was born in Nesbitz. He was orphaned from both parents before his bar mitzvah and was raised by his brother Reb Alter, the Rosh Yeshivah in the Yeshivah Ketanah of Mir. During World II Reb Ella escaped with the Mirrer Yeshivah to Shanghai. In the United States he served as Rav in a shul in East New York. When he relocated to Flatbush he opened a store on Kings Highway and kept up his connection with the Mirrer Yeshivah in Flatbush, davening and learning there daily for many years.

**Steinberg, Rabbi Yosef** (1908-2000) was born in Brisk and studied in the Imrei Moshe Yeshivah of Brisk. When he was 17, he left for Yeshivas Mir. He traveled with the Mir to America and, along the way, married Nechama Zuchovicki, a student of Bais Yaakov of Crakow. In America he became a rebbi in Yeshivah of Spring Valley and Rav in Kehillas Yisroel of Spring Valley. In his later years he retired to Eretz Yisroel.

**Steinfeld, Rabbi Binyamin** (1915-2003) came from Vienna, Austria, where his father was a city leader. He learned in Yeshivas Mir and traveled with the yeshivah in its exile during World War II. In the United States, he took on the position as a rebbi in Toras Emes of Kaminetz. Throughout his life, he learned with tremendous diligence, keeping up a regular second *seder* in Yeshivah Shaarei Yosher of Boro Park.

**Stern, Rabbi Dr. David** (1893-1969) attended Yeshivas Rabbeinu Yitzchok Elchonon and was very active in the establishment of Young Israel. He was the first rabbi of the Young Israel Movement and wrote sermons for all other branches of Young Israel. Though he lived in Williamsburg, he walked regularly from Williamsburg to the Lower East Side of Manhattan on Shabbos to speak for his congregants. He was principal in Torah Vodaath Elementary School for many years. He later moved to Eretz Yisroel where he spent his time learning until his passing.

**Sternbuch, Rabbi Yitzchok and Mrs. Recha** — Reb Yitzchok Sternbuch came from a *Chassidishe* family that moved to Switzerland where they founded the first Chassidic *shtiebel* in Basel. Recha was the daughter of Rabbi Mordechai Rottenberg, Chief Rabbi of Antwerp. The couple was known for their kindness and hospitality. In 1938 they opened their home to the countless refugees pouring in from Nazi-occupied countries. In a whirlwind of rescue activities that entailed great risks, Mrs. Recha Sternbuch fought desperately for every Jewish life. She was instrumental in saving thousands of Jews from war-torn Europe. At the war's end she undertook the task of taking Jewish children out of convents, homes, and farms.

**Svei, Rabbi Shmuel Leib** (1890-1983) learned in Slabodka and was one of the early members of the famous Slabodka Kollel. Reb Shmuel Leib came to America to raise money for the kollel and subsequently stayed. He spent much of his time learning and continued to collect money for yeshivos.

**Tarshish, Rabbi Elazar** (1911-86) was born in New York where he learned first in Torah Vodaath and then in Yeshivah Rabbeinu Chaim Berlin. He went to learn in Mir, Poland in 1936. He returned to America before the outbreak of the war and became Rav and a *shochet* in Hunter, New York. After a number of years there, he returned to New York and settled in Bensonhurst.

**Taub, Rabbi Yehoshua Yecheskel** (1913-1952) was the son of the Modzhitzer Rebbe, Rabbi Shaul Yedidya Taub. He contracted rheumatic fever at 18 and remained sickly thereafter. Known for his wisdom and *yiras Shamayim*, he passed away at the young age of 39. His son, Rabbi Yisroel Dovid Taub, is the Modzhitzer Rebbe of Flatbush.

**Taub, Rabbi Yitzchok** (1918-2005) was the son of the Modzhitzer Rebbe, Rabbi Shaul Yedidya Taub. He survived the war with his father and eventually settled in Crown Heights.

**Tennenbaum, Rabbi Bezalel** (1906-1966) was born in Kobrin. He studied under Rabbi Pesach Pruskin and went on to Yeshivas Mir where he was regarded as one of its great *lamdanim*. He traveled with the Mir to America and was part of the group of Mirrer *talmidim* who founded Bais HaTalmud. In 1950 he became a *maggid shiur* in Yeshivas Karlin where he taught until his passing.

**Tress, R' Elimelech Gavriel (Mike)** (1909-1967) was born in New York City to a young immigrant couple from the Ukraine. Six months after joining Zeirei Agudath Israel he was elected its president. In the 1930's he dedicated much of his time to creating Pirchei and recruiting youth from Camp Agudah and Yeshivah Torah Vodaath, and saving countless prominent Torah leaders and their families. Later, he visited and assisted Jews in the DP camps. Mike also oversaw rescue efforts during the Hungarian Revolution. He developed a close relationship with many *gedolim* who accorded him great esteem.

**Unger, R' Michel** (1917-1985) was born in Vienna. He went to Poland to learn in Mir and escaped with the yeshivah to Japan. There he received an American visa, procured through an aunt, and he arrived in America in 1941. Throughout his life, he maintained a connection with his friends from the Mir, most notably as a member of the Mirrer Minyan in Williamsburg. He was the *ba'al Shacharis* there and is remembered for his unusually heartfelt davening.

**Wasilski, Rabbi (Tzvi Yosef) Hershel** (1922-1981) went to learn in Baranovich under Rabbi Elchonon Wasserman. There, young Hershel joined up with some of the best *bochurim* of the yeshivah who also happened to be Breslover Chassidim, and he became a Breslover Chassid. He went to Mir for a short time and then went back to Baranovich. After surviving the war in Siberia, Reb Hershel immigrated to America where he became a rebbi in Torah Vodaath. In over 35 years of teaching, he acquired a reputation as an unusually effective educator.

**Weinberg, Rabbi Mordechai** (1929-1992) was born in New York and attended Torah Vodaath elementary and Mesivta. Reb Mottel went on to the Telshe Yeshivah in Cleveland and from there to Yeshivah Rabbeinu Chaim Berlin in New York. He was later chosen to be a *maggid shiur* and *menahel* of Yeshivah Rabbeinu Chaim Berlin, followed by his taking a position as Rosh Yeshivah of the Yeshivah of Eastern Parkway. In 1972 he moved to Montreal, Canada, where he was a Rosh Yeshivah until his sudden passing.

**Weisfogel, Rabbi Alex** (1917-2007) came from England to learn in Mir, Poland. He escaped to America in the early years of the war and became the secretary of Rabbi Avrohom Kalmanowitz for his Holocaust rescue activities. He served as a rabbi in several congregations and was active in strengthening American Jewry.

**Weiss, R' Shloima** (1907-1998) hailed from Vienna where he learned his trade in his father's popular bakery in the Schiffschul community. In his youth, it was his responsibility to distribute bread and charity to the needy, while he devoted his time to Torah study and leadership in Zeirei Agudath Israel. R' Shloima arrived in the United States before World War II as a member of a group of Austrian refugees, who joined the Zeirei in Williamsburg. He later joined the new *kehillos* of the Tzelemer Rav and eventually the Satmar Rebbe. He was recognized as a learned man and an *ehrliche Yid* who ran his bakery in Williamsburg to support his family and feed the poor, and was uncompromising in kashrus and Torah values.

**Weissman, Rabbi Simcha** (1917-2005) was born in America. He learned in Torah Vodaath and Yeshivah Chofetz Chaim. Upon the urging of Rabbi Chaim Pinchas Scheinberg, he traveled to Europe to learn in Mir. He returned to America shortly before the war and married. He was a Rav in Brighton Beach for over 40 years and brought many people closer to Torah and mitzvos.

**Wiskowsky, Rabbi Avrohom** (1910-1981) was the son-in-law of the Modzhitzer Rebbe, Rabbi Shaul Yedidya Taub; he was married to the

Rebbe's daughter Malka. Rebbetzin Malka perished during the Holocaust, while Reb Avrohom survived the war with his son Chatzkel. He opened a Modzhitzer *shtiebel* in the Bronx and, though he ran a business, he spent much of his days learning.

**Wohlgelanter, Rabbi Max J.** (1910-1994) was born in Stacja Miechow, Poland and emigrated from Poland to Toronto, Canada and then to Detroit, Michigan. In Detroit, he was Rav of the Taylor Street Shul and, as such, generated much energy toward building religious Jewish life in Detroit. He helped found a day school and served as its president. He moved to Israel in 1954 and continued to be active in Jewish affairs.

**Wolbe, Rabbi Shlomo** (1914-2005) learned in Mir, Poland. With the outbreak of World War II, as a German national, Rabbi Wolbe fled to Sweden. There, he and Rabbi Wolf Yaakovson became contacts for Vaad Hatzalah and created a seminary for young girls who survived. After the war, he moved to Petach Tikva, Eretz Yisroel, where he married the daughter of Rabbi Avrohom Grodzinsky, *Mashgiach* of Slabodka. Rabbi Wolbe served as *Mashgiach* in Yeshivah Be'er Yaakov, Bais Medrash Govoha d'America b'Eretz Yisroel, and Yeshivah Givat Shaul. Rabbi Wolbe gave *mussar shmuessen*, created *Bais HaMussar,* and published the very popular *Alei Shur* on varied *mussar* topics.

**Yaakovson, Rabbi Binyamin Zev** (1895-1973) was known as Reb Wolf. He was very active in prewar Agudas Yisroel and developed a connection with great personalities, such as Rabbi Chaim Ozer Grodzenski, Rabbi Meir Don Plotzky and the Chortkover Rebbe. He became Rav in Copenhagen, Sweden. During World War II, he founded and operated Camp Lidingo, a camp for refugee women and girls. He moved to Eretz Yisroel where he continued as an Agudah activist and served as Rav in the Pagi neighborhood of Yerushalayim.

**Yaffen, Rabbi Avrohom** (1886-1971) studied in Slutzk, Kobrin, and under Rabbi Zalman Sender of Krinki and then Novarodok. In 1912 he married the daughter of the Alter of Novarodok. When World War I broke out, Reb Avrohom joined the yeshivah in exile in Homel, and succeeded the Alter after his passing. After much suffering under the Bolsheviks, the yeshivah escaped to Poland where Reb Avrohom established many branches of the yeshivah. During World War II he escaped to America through Japan. There he reestablished the yeshivah and served *Klal Yisroel* as an active member of the Vaad Hatzalah and Agudath Israel. In the last years of his life he established the yeshivah in Yerushalayim.

**Yurkansky, Rabbi Eliyahu** (1908/9-2005) came from Minsk. Shortly after World War I ended, Reb Elya's parents encouraged their son to flee Communist Russia and head for Poland where he could learn in a regular *cheder* and later in yeshivah. Reb Elya always marveled at the *mesiras nefesh* of his parents who sent him away knowing that they would never see him again. Reb Elya spent many years in Baranovich, eventually learning *b'chavrusah* with Reb Elchonon after which he went to the Mir. He traveled with the Mir to America. There he became a *maggid shiur* in the reestablished Mirrer Yeshivah, saying *shiurim* until he was 95.

**Zelcer, R' Abba** (1910-1981) was a Kletzker *talmid* who joined the Mirrer Yeshivah in Vilna at the outbreak of the war. He immigrated to America and settled in the Bronx.

**Zuchovicki, Rabbi Feivel** (1913-1962) learned in the yeshivos of Baranovich and Mir. Upon his arrival in America, he moved to Baltimore, and took the family name **Zakkai**. Reb Feivel took a position as *maggid shiur* in Rabbi Mordechai Yoffe's yeshivah in Kansas City. Later he returned to Baltimore and served as a *mashgiach* of kashrus.

# Index of Personalities

## A

## B

# H

# Y

# Z